Pablo Ruiz
PICASSO

Pablo Ruiz
PICASSO

A Biography

PATRICK O'BRIAN

W. W. Norton & Company
New York • London

Coadjutorici amoenissimae Mariae do dedico

First published in 1976 by William Collins Sons & Co. Ltd.

First published as a Norton paperback 1994
by arrangement with the author

ISBN 0-393-31107-4

W.W. Norton & Company, Inc.
500 Fifth Avenue, New York, N.Y. 10010
W.W. Norton & Company Ltd.
10 Coptic Street, London WC1A 1PU

Printed in the United States of America

1 2 3 4 5 6 7 8 9 0

Preface

Since this life of Picasso was written several other books have appeared, some on particular aspects of his work, some on the artist as a man; but none has raised such an outcry as Arianna Stassinopoulos Huffington's *Picasso, Creator and Destroyer* (Weidenfeld and Nicolson 1988), nor has any been more strongly condemned since Françoise Gilot published her *Life with Picasso* in 1964.

For my part I felt the general indignation very strongly and I had hoped that the timely re-issue of this book would allow me to utter a counterblast to Huffington in the form of a preface. I wrote one with some care, and Tom Phillips, who felt even more indignant if possible, very kindly said that I might use his much-admired review in *The Independent*, a strongly-worded criticism in which he, as a painter, dealt with some points far better than I could. Altogether it was, I thought, a good foreword, a thorough-going, heartfelt counterblast. But as a matter of routine my publishers showed it to their lawyer for a libel-report and to our astonishment he said it was actionable.

It was actionable because I too had written a book on Picasso and therefore I could be looked upon as Huffington's trade-rival, a rival actuated not by honestly-held beliefs but by sordid malice. If I had produced a book on white mice it would have been actionable if I had said that another book on white mice was ill-informed, ill-written and ill-natured. And in this case, believe it or not, it was also dangerous to quote from Tom Phillips' review, thus giving it a more lasting form than it had in a newspaper.

That, according to the company's expert, is the state of the English law; and since Coke defines law as the perfection of reason, one can but bow with all the respect due to perfection, whatever shape it may assume.

Patrick O'Brian
1989

Preface

THIS BOOK is an attempt at presenting Picasso whole, the man as well as his art; and its title is designed to emphasize the importance of those years of his life when he was Pablo Ruiz, his childhood in Málaga and La Coruña, and above all his adolescence in Barcelona. They shaped him forever; and since the enormous body of his work cannot be fully appreciated without a knowledge of its Spanish, and even more of its Catalan foundations, the early chapters go deep into his family background and his formative years, drawing on the immense collections of early works and documents that he presented to the Museo Picasso in Barcelona in 1970 and on many Catalan texts.

Art-historians have sometimes divided Picasso the painter, sculptor, draughtsman, lithographer, engraver, and potter from Picasso the man, and for their purpose no doubt the method answers; other writers have spoken of Picasso as though he were only incidentally an artist, concentrating upon the man as he was to be seen away from his easel. The present book aims at striking the mean between these two extremes and at showing a man who, though wholly devoted to his art, spending the most significant and perhaps even the greatest part of his life in his studio, nevertheless lived intensely outside it: yet it does not stray far into the field of criticism, analysis, or interpretation.

There are several reasons for this, and the first is that Braque was surely right in saying that the only important thing in art is that which cannot be explained. Then, while detailed analysis and technical description certainly have their value, they would be out of place in a book that is intended for the intelligent but unspecialized reader. And as for interpretation, that source of so many books about Picasso, it seems to me of value only when the author is a man as interesting as his subject. In the course of my reading I have necessarily waded through thick clouds of interpretative Teutonic metaphysics and a great deal of homespun psychology; but few of the writers came anywhere near this standard and little of what they wrote shed much light on Picasso. What I have done, therefore, when I come to an important picture, is to describe it as accurately as I can, without obtruding any attempt at explanation on the reader, still less telling him what he ought to think. Then I say something about its impact on me; and when, as it sometimes happens, this differs from the generally accepted view, I give that view as well: it is only for the very early or the very late work, where there is as yet no consensus, that I offer my own opinion and little more.

Since this is not a book for specialists I have not encumbered it with notes and references, nor with a bibliography. Indeed, the formal bibliography, referring the reader to books long out of print and to articles published in obscure journals fifty years ago, seems a show of erudition of little use to the general reader when it is genuine and ridiculous when it is false: many that I have seen give what they call the first newspaper criticism, an article by Rodríguez Codolá entitled *Exposición Ruiz Picasso* and published in *La Vanguardia* of Barcelona in 1897. But as Juan Antonio Gaya Nuño has shown in his *Bibliografía crítica y antológica* the article does not exist: nor did the exhibition.

Apart from the many learned and sometimes illuminating monographs on various aspects of his art, there are of course valuable works among the great number that have been written about Picasso; and no one interested in him can fail to find instruction in Barr or delight in Sabartés, Brassaï, Penrose, Fernande Olivier, Geneviève Laporte, and some others. Yet it seems to me more useful to speak of them in some detail in the course of the book rather than giving a bald list of all the authors I have read.

But although I give no bibliography, it would be the basest ingratitude if I were not to acknowledge the great kindness and help I have received from Monsieur and Madame Pierre de Saint-Prix, and from many of the friends I have had the honor of sharing with Picasso. Most are mentioned in the text, but there are others whom I must beg to accept my thanks in this place, particularly Madame Marguerite Matisse-Duthuit, the Comte and Comtesse de Lazerme, Señor Maurizio Torra-Balari, and Monsieur Jean Hugo. And I should like to express my gratitude to Señorita María Teresa Ocaña of the Museo Picasso in Barcelona, to the kind people at the Museum of Modern Art in New York, the Barnes Foundation at Merion, Pennsylvania, the Pushkin Museum in Moscow, the Louvre, the Bibliothèque nationale, and the Musée national d'Art moderne, who have been so very helpful and cooperative.

Chapter I

Picasso was born on October 25, 1881, in Málaga, the first, the only son of Doña María Picasso y Lopez and her husband, Don José Ruiz y Blasco, a painter, a teacher in the city's art school, and the curator of the local museum. The statement is true: it is to be found in all the reference-books. But perhaps it does not convey a great deal of information except to those Spaniards who can as easily visualize the Málaga of Alphonso XII's time as English-speaking readers can the St. Louis of President Arthur's or the Southampton of Queen Victoria's—to those who know the economic, cultural, and social position of a middle-class family in that town and the pattern of life in nineteenth-century Andalucía as a whole. For even the strongest individual is indelibly marked by the culture in which he is brought up; even the loneliest man is not an island; and even Picasso carried his cradle with him to the grave. "A man belongs to his own country forever," he said.

Picasso's Málaga, then, was an ancient city in the far south of Spain, an essentially Mediterranean city, and after Barcelona the country's most important seaport on that coast: it had been a great port for centuries before Barcelona was heard of, having a natural harbor as opposed to Barcelona's open beach; but long before Picasso's time the silting up of this harbor and the activity of the Catalans in building moles had reversed the position, and whereas in 1881 ships had to lie off Málaga and discharge their cargoes into lighters, in Barcelona they could tie up in their hundreds alongside the busy quays. Yet Málaga still had a great deal of shipping; its great bay provided shelter, and the smaller vessels could still use the harbor at the bottom of that bay, where the white town lies along the shore with the hills of Axarquía rising behind it, while the Gibralfaro rears up five hundred feet and more in the city itself, with a huge Moorish castle standing upon its top.

Compared with the booming town of the present day, the Málaga of 1881 belonged to a different world, a world innocent of concrete and in many ways much nearer to the middle ages than to the twentieth century: tourism has changed it almost beyond recognition. When Picasso was born Málaga still relied upon its ancient industries, shipping, cotton-spinning, sugar-refining, the working of iron, and the production of wine, almonds and raisins, and other fruit: the fertile, irrigated, subtropical plain to the west of the town supplied the cotton and the sugar-cane (the Arabs brought them to Spain) as well as oranges, lemons, custard-apples, and bananas, while the slopes behind produced almonds, the grapes for the heavy, potent wine and for the raisins; and iron-ore came from the mountains. The city of that time had only about 120,000 inhabitants as opposed to the present 375,000 (a number enormously increased by holiday-makers from all over Europe in the summer), and they lived in a much smaller space: there was little development north of the hills or beyond the river, and what is now land on the seaward side was then part of the shallow harbor. This made for a crowded, somewhat squalid city, particularly as there was little notion of drains and the water-supply was inadequate; a real city, however, with its twenty-seven churches and chapels, its four important monasteries (the survivors of a great many more before the massive suppressions, expropriations, and expulsions of 1835), its bull-ring for ten thousand, its still-unfinished cathedral on the site of a former mosque, its splendid market in what was once the Moorish arsenal, its garrison, its brothels, its theaters, its immensely ancient tradition, and its strong sense of corporate being. Then, as now, it had the finest climate in Europe, with only forty clouded days in the year; but in 1881 traveling in Spain was an uncommon adventure and virtually no tourists came to enjoy the astonishing light, the brilliant air, and the tepid sea. Only a few wealthy invalids, consumptives for the most part, took lodgings at the Caleta or the Limonar, far from the medieval filth and smells of the inner town. They hardly made the least impression upon Málaga itself, which, apart from a scattering of foreign merchants, was left to the Malagueños.

Their town had been an important Phoenician stronghold until the Punic wars; then a Roman municipium; then a Visigothic city, the seat of a bishop; and then, for seven hundred and seventy-seven years, a great Arab town, one in which large numbers of Jews and Christians lived under Moslem rule. The Moslems were delighted with their conquest: they allotted it to the Khund al Jordan, the tribes from the east of the sacred river, who looked upon it as an earthly paradise. Many Arabic travelers spoke of its splendor, Ibn Batuta going so far as to compare it with an opened bottle of musk. Málaga was a Moslem city far longer than it has subsequently been Christian, and the Arabs left their mark: even now one is continually aware of their presence, not only because of the remains of the Alcazaba, a fortified Moorish palace high over the port, and of the still higher Gibralfaro, from which the mountains in Africa can be distinguished on the clear horizon, but also because of the faces in the streets and markets and above all because of the flamenco that is to be heard, sometimes from an open window, sometimes from a solitary peasant following an ass so loaded with sugar-cane that only its hoofs show twinkling below.

The Spaniards who reconquered Andalucía came from many different regions, each with its own way of speaking; and partly because of this and partly because of the large numbers of Arabic-speaking people, Christian, Jew, and Moslem, they evolved a fresh dialect of their own, a Spanish in which the *s* is often lost and the *h* often sounded, a brogue as distinct as that of Munster: one that perplexes the foreigner and that makes the Castilian laugh. In time the Moors and the Jews were more or less efficiently expelled or forcibly converted, and eventually many of the descendants of these converts, the "new Christians," were also driven from the country; but they left their genes behind, and many of their ways—their attitude towards women, for example. Then again there is a fierce democratic independence combined with an ability to live under a despotic regime that is reminiscent of the egalitarianism of Islam: no one could call the Spaniards as a whole a deferential nation, but this characteristic grows even more marked as one travels south, to reach its height in Andalucía. And as one travels south, so the physical evidence of these genes becomes more apparent; the Arab, the Berber, and the Jew peep out, to say nothing of the Phoenician; and the Castilian or the Catalan is apt to lump the Andalou in with the Gypsies, a great many of whom live in those parts. For the solid bourgeois of Madrid or Barcelona the Andalou is something of an outsider; he is held in low esteem, as being wanting in gravity, assiduity, and respect for the establishment. Málaga itself had a solid reputation for being against the government, for being impatient of authority: it was a contentious city, in spite of its conforming bourgeoisie. In the very square in which Picasso was born there is a monument to a general and forty-nine of his companions, including a Mr. Robert Boyd, who rose in favor of the Constitution and who were all shot in Málaga in 1831 and buried in the square; it also commemorates the hero of another rising, Riego, after whom the square was officially named, although it has now reverted to its traditional name of the Plaza de la Merced, from the church of Nuestra Señora de la Merced, which used to stand in its north-east corner. There were many other risings, insurrections, and pronunciamientos in Málaga during the nineteenth century, including one against Espartero in 1843, another against Queen Isabella II in 1868 (this, of course, was part of the greater turmoil of the Revolution), and another in favor of a republic only eight years before Picasso's birth. But although many of these risings, both in Málaga and the rest of Spain, had a strongly anticlerical element, with churches and monasteries going up in flames and monks, nuns, friars, and even hermits being expelled and dispossessed, the Spaniards remained profoundly Catholic, and the Malagueños continued to live their traditional religious life, celebrating the major feasts of the Church with splendid bull-fights, making pilgrimages to local shrines, forming great processions in Holy Week, hating what few heretics they ever saw (until 1830 Protestants had to be buried on the foreshore, where heavy seas sometimes disinterred them), and of course baptizing their children. It would have been unthinkable for Picasso not to have been christened, and sixteen days after his birth he was taken to the parish church of Santiago el Mayor (whose tower was once a minaret), where the priest of La Merced gave him the names Pablo, Diego, José, Francisco de Paula, Juan Nepomuceno, María de los Remedios, and Cipriano de la Santísima Trinidad, together with some salt to expel the devil.

In most countries this array of names would imply an exalted origin: but not in Andalucía. The Ruiz family belonged to that traditionally almost non-existent body, the Spanish middle class. José Ruiz y Blasco, Picasso's father, was the son of Diego Ruiz y de Almoguera, a glover and by all accounts an amiable and gifted man with artistic tastes, a great talker; but in that subtropical climate there was no fortune in gloves, and Don Diego also played the double-bass in the orchestra of the municipal theater. This Diego Ruiz was born in Córdoba in 1799, well before Goya painted the "Tres de Mayo," and he remembered the French occupation of Málaga very well indeed (his father, José Ruiz y de Fuentes had removed there during the Peninsular War), for not only did the French sack the city in 1810, but they also beat the young Diego for throwing stones at them. It is said that they beat him almost to death, for it was during a general's parade that he threw his stones: however that may be, he recovered sufficiently to set up shop in due time, to marry María de la Paz Blasco y Echevarria, and to have eleven children by her. It is the Spanish custom to use two surnames on formal occasions, one's father's and one's mother's, often connected with a y, but to hand down only the paternal half: thus Diego's son José was called Ruiz y Blasco, both the Almoguera and the Echevarria disappearing. Echevarria, by the way, is a name that has a Basque sound about it, and this may account for the often-repeated statement that Picasso's father was of Basque origin. Then again a Spanish woman retains her patronymic on marrying and adds to it her husband's, preceded by de, so that Diego's wife was known as Señora Blasco de Ruiz.

As for origins, it has been attempted to be shown that the Ruiz family descended from one Juan de León, a hidalgo of immemorial nobility who had estates at Cogolludo in the kingdom of León and who was killed in 1487 during the war for the reconquest of Granada: his grandson settled at Villafranca de Córdoba; and he is said to be the ancestor of the Ruizes. It may be so; but the sudden and irregular appearance of the name Ruiz is not particularly convincing, even taking into account the strange anarchy of Spanish family names at that period. In any event this remote Leonese origin is scarcely relevant: for although, as Gibbon says, "we wish to discover our ancestors, but we wish to discover them possessed of ample fortunes, and holding an eminent rank in the class of hereditary nobles," and although we sometimes succeed, the practical effect of the more or less mythical Don Juan on the Ruizes cannot have been very great four centuries and eleven generations later; nor can that of the Venerable Juan de Almoguera, Archbishop of Lima, Viceroy and Captain-General of Peru in the seventeenth century, who is stated to have been a collateral.

In more recent and verifiable times, however, there was another Juan de Almoguera, a Córdoban and a notary, who died in deeply embarrassed circumstances at Almodóvar del Río, leaving a widow and eleven children, the eldest of whom, María Josefa, married José Ruiz y de Fuentes, Picasso's great-grandfather, while the tenth, Pedro Dionisio, became a hermit. He joined the Venerable Congregación de Ermitaños de Nuestra Señora de Belén in the mountains of Córdoba in 1792 and became their superior some twenty years later; his health was always poor and he could not always remain in his hermitage; nevertheless he nursed the sick most devotedly during the cholera epidemic of 1834. And when his community was suppressed, expropriated, and expelled at the time of the anticlerical outburst of 1835 he managed to retain a little of their land, a spot from which he could look out over the mountains. He died in 1856, at the age of eighty-one, and he left a vividly living memory: his great-grand-nephew Pablo often spoke of "Tío Perico, who led an exemplary life as a hermit in the Sierra de Córdoba."*

The most diligent research has discovered little reliable information about Picasso's maternal ancestors: they seem to have been obscure burgesses of Málaga for some generations; but Picasso's maternal grandmother at least was tolerably well provided for, since she owned vine-

*Family trees are always difficult to follow in a narrative: these are shown diagrammatically in Appendixes 1 and 2.

yards outside the town that supported her and her daughters until the phylloxera destroyed them. Her husband, Francisco Picasso y Guardeño, went to school in England, returned to his native Málaga, married Inés Lopez y Robles, had four daughters by her, and went off to Cuba: there he became a customs-officer and eventually died of the yellow fever, in 1883, the news taking some fifteen years to reach his family. The origin of the name Picasso, which is most unusual in Spain (the double *s* does not occur in Castilian), has resisted all inquiries: some writers have pointed to Italy and particularly to the Genoese painter Mateo Picasso, a nineteenth-century portraitist, and Pablo Picasso himself went so far as to buy one of his pictures. On the other hand, Jaime Sabartés, one of Picasso's oldest friends, his biographer, secretary, and factotum, discovered a Moorish prince called Picaço, who came to Spain with eight thousand horsemen and who was defeated and slain in battle by the Grand Master of Alcántara on Tuesday, October 28, 1339. And there have been assertions of a Jewish, Balearic, or Catalan origin. These are not of the least consequence, however; the real significance of this unusual, striking name is that it had at least some influence in setting its owner slightly apart, of making him feel that he was not quite the same as other people—a feeling that was to be reinforced by several other factors quite apart from that isolating genius which soon made it almost impossible for him to find any equals.

To return to Diego Ruiz, the glover, Picasso's paternal grandfather: in spite of his beating at the hands of the French soldiers, in spite of the near anarchy that prevailed in Spain almost without a pause from 1800 to 1874 (to speak only of the nineteenth century), in spite of the risings for or against the various constitutions, of the Carlist wars, the pronunciamientos, the continual (and often bloody) struggles between the conservatives, the moderados, and the liberals, in spite of the mutinous political generals, the loss of the South American possessions, the stagnation of trade, and the tottering national finances, Diego Ruiz, like so many of his relatives in Málaga, had an enormous family, four boys and seven girls.

The second of these boys, Pablo, had a vocation that must have rejoiced all his relatives: he entered the Church and did remarkably well, becoming a doctor of theology and eventually, although he had no gift for preaching, a canon of Málaga cathedral and his family's main prop and stay.

The profession chosen by Salvador, the youngest boy, cannot have caused anything like the same satisfaction: he decided to study medicine at Granada, and at that time neither medicine nor medical men were much esteemed in Spain. Richard Ford, writing only a few years before Don

Salvador began his studies, speaks of the "base bloody and brutal San-grados," observing that in all Sevilla only one doctor was admitted into good company, "and every stranger was informed apologetically that the MD was *de casa conocida*, or born of good family." In Granada Don Salvador met a young woman, Concepción Marin, the daughter of a sculptor; and being unwilling to part from her he took a post at the hospi-tal when he was qualified, at a salary of 750 pesetas a year. But although Spain was then a relatively cheap country he found that this sum, which at that time represented about $112, or £28, did not allow him to put by enough to marry and set up house; he returned to Málaga, practiced (the Reverend Dr. Pablo was useful to him and his patients included the French Assumptionist nuns and their schoolgirls as well as the convent of Franciscans, whom he did not charge), prospered, and in 1876, seven years after he had qualified, he married Concepción, who gave him two daughters, Picasso's cousins Concha and María. Later Don Salvador be-came the medical officer of the port and he also founded the Málaga Vac-cination Institute. He was a kind man and a brave one (in the anticlerical troubles he protected the nuns at the risk of his life), and from the finan-cial point of view he did better than any Ruiz in Andalucía: it was as a successful, cigar-smoking physician that he attended Picasso's birth, re-animating his limp and apparently stillborn nephew with a blast of smoke into his infant lungs. Later he also contributed to the support of young Pa-blo in Madrid and to the buying of his exemption when the time came for his military service.

But if Don Salvador's choice of a calling met with certain reserves at first, his brother José's can have caused nothing but dismay. Having some skill in drawing, a knack for illustration, he determined to become an art-ist, a painter; and for some years he persisted in this course. He acquired a fair academic technique; he had a craftsman's talent and an ability to use his tools; but he had nothing whatsoever to say in terms of paint, or at least he never said it. He produced a large number of painstaking decora-tive pictures of dead game, flowers (particularly lilacs), and above all of live pigeons, a few of which he sold; and he painted fans. He lived with his elder brother, the Canon, who also supported his surviving unmarried sisters, Josefa and Matilde.

It is the sad fate of towns that have once been capital cities (and at one time Málaga was the seat of an independent Moorish king) that when they lose this status they become more provincial than those which never emerged from obscurity. Málaga was deeply provincial. Yet it did pos-sess a struggling art-school, the Escuela de Artes y Oficios de San Telmo, which had been founded in 1849; and in 1868 the quite well known Valencian artist Bernardo Ferrándiz became its professor of painting and composition. He was followed by Antonio Muñoz Degrain, another Valencian (they had come to Málaga to decorate the Teatro Cervantes); and the presence of these two painters of more than local fame, more than common talent, coincided with a revival of interest in the arts—a small and temporary revival, perhaps, but enough to induce the municipality to set up a museum of fine arts on the second floor of the expropriated Augustinian monastery which they used as the town hall. José Ruiz succeeded his friend Muñoz Degrain at San Telmo and he was also appointed the first curator of the museum. His duties included the restoring of the damaged pictures, a task for which his meticulous craftsmanship and attention to detail suited him admirably: what is more, he had a room set aside for this work, and as the museum followed the ancient Spanish provincial tradition of being almost always shut, he did his own painting there as well.

It was a fairly agreeable life; he had a small but apparently assured income, and any paintings that he sold added jam to his bread and butter; he had many friends of a mildly bohemian character, some of them painters; and he delighted in the bull-fights, better conducted, better understood in Andalucía than anywhere else in the world: at all events it was the happiest life he ever knew.

But his youth was passing—indeed, it had passed: he was nearly forty—and his family urged him to marry. None of his brothers or sisters had yet produced a son, and the family name was in danger of extinction. They arranged a suitable marriage for him, and although he could not be brought to like the young woman of their choice he did make an offer to her cousin María—María Picasso y Lopez. Yet before the marriage could take place the Canon died: this was in 1878, and he was only forty-seven. His loss was felt most severely; and either because of this or because Don José felt little real enthusiasm for marriage, the wedding was not celebrated until 1880.

José Ruiz took a flat in the Plaza de la Merced, on the third floor of a double terrace recently built by a wealthy man, Don Antonio Campos Garvin, Marqués de Ignato, on the site of a former convent. Don José was now responsible for a wife, two unmarried sisters, a mother-in-law and, after 1881, a son. Then, in 1884, during a violent earthquake, a daughter appeared: three years later another: at some point María de Ruiz's unmarried sisters Eladia and Heliodora, whose vineyards had been ravaged by the phylloxera, moved in. And in the meantime the municipality decided to abolish not the museum, but the curator: or at least the curator's salary. Don José offered to serve in an honorary capacity; and as he had hoped a newly-elected council eventually gave him back his pay.

But these continual difficulties, the daily worry, overcame a man quite unsuited to cope with them: there was little that he could do, apart from offering to pay his rent with pictures, giving private lessons, and selling an occasional canvas. Fortunately his landlord was a lover of the arts, as they were understood in Málaga in the 1880s; or at least he liked the company of artists, and he accepted a large number of José Ruiz's paintings. Several were found in his descendants' possession some years ago; but it was thought kinder not to exhibit them.

Don José's worries were real enough in all their sad banality, and many, many people can sympathize with them from experience; but there was also a factor that perhaps only another artist can fully appreciate in its full force. He was a painter; he was entirely committed to painting; and he was losing his faith in his talent—a few years later he gave up altogether. Whether he realized that his original vocation had been false, whether he found at the age of forty and more that he had been no more than one of the innumerable young people with "artistic tastes" and a certain facility who fling themselves into painting only to find that they have no real creative power, or whether he found that what he might have had inside him had now been crushed by domesticity, the artist sucked dry and rendered sterile by women, children, routine, teaching, the result was the same. In his son's portraits we see a weary man, tired through and through, deeply disappointed, often very near despair. Again and again there is this sad head leaning on his hand, with an expression of profound, incurable boredom, the taste for life all gone; and having seen this José Ruiz one finds it hard to imagine any other. Yet he must once have been young: by all accounts he was a gay bachelor, a haunter of cafés, a witty young man, well liked. His son saw none of this.

The relationship between the father and son is obviously of the first importance for an understanding of Picasso's character; but like everything else to do with him it is immensely complex and full of apparent contradictions. On the one hand Picasso dropped his father's name, a most unusual step in Spain (the only other example that comes readily to mind is, curiously enough, Velásquez), and although Sabartés and others say that Picasso's Catalan friends to some degree forced the change upon him, and although Ruiz is comparatively commonplace in Spain and difficult for the French to pronounce, these reasons and the rest sound very much like *post hoc* rationalization. On the other, all through his life Picasso quoted his father's dictums on painting, finding wisdom in such gnomic utterances as "In hands you see the hand" and speaking of him with great affection and respect. Talking to Brassaï in the thirties he spoke of his bearded father as the very type of man. "Every time I draw a man, automatically I think of my father. . . . As far as I am concerned *the man* is Don José, and that will be so as long as I live. . . . He had a beard. . . . I see all the men I draw with his features, more or less." Don José was a good teacher, with a considerable share of technical knowledge; and later, when he found that he could teach him no more he ceremonially handed his brushes over to the boy and never painted again. Could any castrating son ask more? He did all he could to further Pablo's career; he stretched his canvases; he gave him an independent studio at the age of fifteen; he parted with all his money except for the loose change in his pocket to enable the nineteen-year-old to go to Paris; yet when he died in 1913 his son did not come to his funeral although Picasso was then at Céret, only about a hundred miles away, and although he was not then particularly short of money. Picasso did not bury his father; and late in his life, when he was eighty-seven indeed, he executed a series of etchings in which Don José appears, sometimes as a watcher of bawdy scenes, sometimes as a participant.

But these complications did not exist—or at least did not exist on the surface—in those early days in Málaga. Don José was the Man: tall, bearded, ageless, dignified, bony, with pale eyes and a grizzling sandy beard (his friends called him el Inglés), quite unlike his busy, plump, entirely human, black-haired wife, and so far removed from his son in every conceivable way that no one could possibly have guessed the relationship. He was the only man in a household full of women; and although it would be wrong and indeed absurd to say that every Spaniard regards women, apart from the sacred mother, as a race to be exploited either as sex-objects or as domestic animals, the notion is common enough in the Mediterranean world, both Moslem and Christian: a century ago it was commoner still, and in Spain it increased the farther south one went. Neither José Ruiz nor his son was likely to be wholly unaffected by it; and this was the atmosphere in which Pablo spent his early years, the only boy of his generation, cosseted by a host of subservient aunts and female cousins, many of whom accepted the doctrine of their inferiority, thus communicating the deepest and most lasting conviction to the young Picasso. His mother, however, stood quite apart: the relationship between them was uncomplicated love on either side, with some mixture of adoration on hers; and it is perhaps worth while recalling Freud's words on Goethe, with whom Picasso has often been compared: "Sons who succeed in life have been the favorite children of good mothers."

These early years were cheerful enough for a child who knew little or nothing about the struggle for existence and to whom the overcrowded, somewhat squalid flat was as natural as the brilliant and almost perpetual sunshine in the square. His father's increasing gloom was no more than the normal attribute of the Man, and in any case Pablo did not see much of Don José, who went off regularly to teach and to work at the museum in a room "just like any other, with nothing special about it," as Picasso told Sabartés, "perhaps a little dirtier than the one he had at home; but at least he had peace when he was there." Besides, the final gloom, the total withdrawal, of Don José did not take place until he left Málaga: at this time he still visited his friends, particularly the admired Antonio Muñoz Degrain, and he still went to see every single bull-fight, taking Pablo with him as soon as the child was no longer a nuisance.

This man about whom the household revolved, the only source of power, money, and prestige, the women's raison d'être, had as his symbol a paintbrush. Although he did not work at home, it was Don José's custom to bring his brushes back to be cleaned; and from his earliest age Pablo regarded them with an awful respect, soon to be mingled with ambition. At no time did he ever have the least doubt of the paramount importance of painting.

José Ruiz could not very well work in his flat: it was full of women (to say nothing of the tame pigeons, Don José's models, and every year the paschal lamb, a pet for a week or so and then the Easter dinner); and two of these women, the penniless aunts Eladia and Heliodora, spent their days making braid for the caps and uniforms of railway employees. What contribution their sweated labor made to the common purse history does not relate; it cannot have been very much, but even a few reales would have been useful in that secret, hidden bourgeois poverty. Only a woman of great good sense, accustomed to frugality, to managing with very little, and to wasting nothing, could have run such an economy: happily for her family Doña María, in addition to a great many more amiable qualities, possessed all these. Nothing was thrown away: the flat may not have been particularly clean, but appearances were kept up: and one of Picasso's earliest memories was that of his grandmother telling him to say nothing to anyone, ever.

Many children have been told to avoid waste without hoarding great piles and heaps of their possessions, trunks, cardboard boxes, crates overflowing and filling house after house, leaving no room to live, nothing ever thrown away: many have been told to be discreet without growing secretive, if not hermetic, in later life: but these precepts sank deep into Picasso's unfolding mind. As for the secrecy, which Françoise Gilot speaks of as so marked a characteristic in both Picasso and Sabartés, it is not altogether fanciful to invoke the Holy Office: with short breaks from the thirteenth century right up until 1834 Spain had suffered under the Inquisition, hundreds of years during which Spaniards learned to keep a close watch over their tongues. A relapsed Jew and a Quaker were publicly tortured as late as 1826, and in the Carlist wars (vividly present in his parents' memory) the supporters of absolute monarchy hoped to bring the inquisitors back with their king. Then again, in some crypto-Jewish families (and there were a great many in Spain) the habit of secrecy was passed on even longer than the faith: by this I do not mean to imply that either the Ruizes or the Picassos had Jewish ancestors, though it is by no means impossible, but only to suggest one more reason for the country's traditional discretion, since the tradition necessarily affected Picasso.

The household was poor, but with a poverty that did not exclude the presence of some agreeable things, such as a set of Chippendale chairs that had presumably reached Spain by way of Gibraltar and that eventually came down to Picasso, and some pleasant Italian pieces of furniture; and Aunt Josefa, at least, owned a gold watch and chain. Nor, in the Spain of that time, did poverty mean the absence of servants, any more than it did in Micawber's England: there is, indeed, something a little Micawberish about Don José, if Micawber can be conceived without gaiety and without a bowl of punch. Don José too was a hopeless man of business; he too hoped for something to turn up; he too had a wife who never deserted him, although a flat in which the cooking had to be done over charcoal in little raised holes, the water and slops to be carried up and down some fifty stairs, and oil lamps to be cleaned, filled, and lighted every day must have been a trial to her constancy, servants or no servants.

The flat is still there, and since 1962 (the year of a great Velásquez commemoration) the house has borne a plaque recording Picasso's birth; it is now numbered fifteen, and it makes the corner, being the most westward of the range of buildings erected by Señor Campos, two matching terraces that fill the whole northern side of the square. They were not built at the happiest period of Spanish architecture, and they do not compare well with the two or three remaining eighteenth-century houses on the west side, but they have a restrained, somewhat heavy dignity and they are at least conceived as a whole: the balconied façades are uniform and the proportions make sober good sense. Each number has its own door that opens on to a hall paved with white marble. Modest double flights of marble stairs lead up to the first floor, where they give way to tiles, growing shabbier as they wind up round the wells in the middle of the building; but all the way up, on each landing, there are fine doors, each with a bright brass judas. Lifts have been installed in some of the houses, spoiling the staircases; electricity-meters by the dozen line the halls; and no doubt the water-supply and drainage have been improved; but otherwise there has been little change, and the pigeons still fly up to the balconies in greedy, amorous flocks.

Little change in the square itself, either. Many of the plane-trees under which young Pablo and his sisters played are still there; so are the massive stone benches, calculated to resist the successive generations of children who have haunted the gardens since they were first laid out; so are the little plump lions on pillars that guard the side entrances, though their tails have suffered since Picasso's day. Ninety years ago the paths were sanded: now they are covered with asphalt. The sand made it more convenient for the children to play one of their immemorial games, the tracing of arabesques, those calligraphic patterns with which the Moors (to whom images were forbidden) decorated anything they could lay their hands upon—buildings, carpets, manuscripts, astrolabes: part of the game was to begin the arabesque anywhere and to come back to the starting-place, finishing the whole in one sinuous stroke, never taking one's finger from the ground. The sand has gone, but there is still plenty of dusty earth under the municipal plants, and the children of Málaga still play this game; and they still cry *Ojalá*, which may be rendered O may Allah will it.

It is certain that some of the very earliest Picassos were drawn in the dirt of the Plaza de la Merced; and as he had no inhibitions about the living form it is probable that they were not sterile abstractions. He very soon acquired a mastery of this technique, and it stayed with him. As a very old man in years he would still start a drawing anywhere at all, just as he had done when he was a little boy, amazing his cousins Concha and María by beginning a dog or a cock at any point they chose to name—the claws, the tail—or by cutting the forms out of paper with his aunt's embroidery scissors on the same terms. Curiously enough this calligraphy never overflowed into his writing: except for some early labored inscriptions he always wrote like a cat.

Behind the respectable houses lining the east side of the Plaza de la Merced began the slums of the Mundo Nuevo and the Coracha, the gap between the hill of the Alcazaba and that of the higher Gibralfaro; a place full of ruins, with swarms of Gypsies and desperately poor Spaniards living among them. In those days the slums continued round the Gibralfaro; under the Alcazaba they still remain, a most desolate spectacle even in the sun—ruin, filth, makeshift hovels, excrement. The district was called Chupa y Tira (which Penrose happily renders "Suck and Chuck"), from its inhabitants' way of eating nothing but shellfish soup, shellfish being free and abundant in the more polluted parts of the harbor, and of chucking the shells out of the window once they were sucked clean. This whole

23]

area provided the needier housewives of Málaga with an inexhaustible supply of servants, rough no doubt and illiterate certainly, but undemanding. Perhaps the great point of servants is not that they move dust, which does no great harm where it is, but that they bring children of the bourgeoisie into contact with earthy good sense, with real life, its virtues, values, and miseries comparatively undisguised. Picasso may have learned more from Carmen Mendoza, the powerful, strong-voiced, mustachioed woman who took him to school than he did sitting there at his desk (he was an exceptionally dull scholar); and his unrivaled capacity for making a slum of any house in which he lived, however elegant, may perhaps have been based upon his early experience of the Gypsies of the Alcazaba, many of whose values he shared. And it was certainly from them that he derived his taste for the only music that ever really touched him, the *cante hondo*. Its strange, un-European cadences, its passionate outcry above the sound of a guitar, could be heard—can still be heard—from those miserable booths huddled together out of odd planks and surrounded by filth. *Canta la rana, y no tiene pelo ni lana*, say the Spaniards: the frog sings, though she has neither fur nor wool.

Picasso had a prodigious memory, both for forms and for events. He could remember learning to walk with the help of a biscuit-tin, and he could remember his sister's birth when he was three. The circumstances of his sister's birth were striking enough, to be sure. Don José was gossiping with friends in the back room of an apothecary's shop one evening in December, 1884, when the bottles shot from their shelves with a crash. Earthquakes are common enough in those fiery regions for no one to sit pondering when they begin. Everyone darted into the open, and Don José ran home, up the stairs, seized his heavily-pregnant wife, his cloak, his son, and ran down into the square. Pablo was wrapped in the folds of the cloak, but his face peered out, and he saw that his mother had a kerchief over her head, a sight hitherto unknown, and deeply memorable. They hurried along the Calle de la Victoria (it commemorates the Christians' perhaps illusory victory over the Moors), right along to the far end, skirting the Gibralfaro, to Muñoz Degrain's little one-storied house, built solidly into the rock. Degrain was visiting Rome at the time, but they settled in, and here Picasso's sister María de los Dolores—Lola—was born. (This earthquake killed over a thousand, devastating the whole region, and the cholera epidemic of the following year killed at least another hundred thousand more.)

But even with this astonishing power of recall he could not remember when he began to draw. He had in fact been drawing even before he could talk, and his first recorded words (recorded by his mother) were "piz,

piz''—all that he could manage of *lápiz*, a pencil. He drew in season and out, particularly at school. His parents sent him first to the parochial school and then, when he was declared a "delicate child" after some illness that was supposed to have affected his kidneys, to a private establishment dedicated to St. Raphael: at neither did he learn anything in the scholastic line, neither reading nor writing nor arithmetic. Somehow the rudiments of these arts seeped into him quite early, but they did not do so in the classroom: to the end of his life he was not at home with the alphabet, and although in later years he was as keen as a hawk where the calculation of merchants' commissions was concerned, his spelling remained highly personal. The one thing he did learn at school was that other people were willing to admit that he was an exceptional being, not subject to the common law.

Even in a very easy-going establishment a child who sat, not minding his book but drawing bulls or the live pigeon he had brought in his bosom, and who got up without leave to gape out the window, would have been sharply rebuked at the least and more probably flogged; but not Picasso. He would often arrive late when his father rather than Carmen brought him (the school was on the way to the museum) and he would sit there staring at the clock, waiting anxiously for the moment when he would be released, sometimes nursing the walking-stick, pigeon, or paintbrush that he had wrung from Don José as a hostage for his return. It does not appear that he was a wicked, turbulent, or dissipated pupil, but rather that he belonged on another plane: the master and even more surprisingly the other boys accepted this and they neither complained nor imitated his example when he stood up and walked out of the room altogether, looking for the headmaster's wife, to whom he was much attached. "I used to follow her about like a puppy," he said.

Counting came hard: so did telling the time. Once when he was gazing from the classroom window he saw his uncle Antonio, Aunt Eloisa's husband, who had a post in the town hall over the way. Pablo called out, begging his uncle to come and fetch him away—he was always very much afraid that they would forget him—and in reply to the question "When are you let out?" he replied "At one," supposing that since one was the first of the numbers it would also be the nearest hour.

Don José does not seem to have troubled much about his son's lack of progress in the subjects taught at school, but he did teach Pablo a great deal about drawing and later about painting. He was the heir of the tradition of Spanish realism, but of a tradition sadly diminished and watered-down over the generations by academic doctrine, and most of what he taught was of course purely academic, a photographic realism, very slightly touched with fantasy; but he did have some ideas of his own. For example, he would cut his pigeons out in paper and move them about on the canvas in search of a satisfactory composition: he also handled cardboard and glue with great dexterity. In other hands and in another atmosphere these ideas might have borne earlier fruit. However, he provided his son with a solid, firmly-disciplined basis, and never can a man have had an apter, more eager pupil.

This may well have been the time of their happiest relationship. The father knew a great deal about the craftsmanship of his calling; at that age the son can hardly have distinguished between technique and the purpose of technique; and Don José, less glum in those years, less battered by life, was vested with the nimbus of the omniscient initiator. Long, long after, Picasso recalled one particular picture of pigeons. He remembered it as an enormous canvas. "Imagine a cage with hundreds of doves in it," he said to Sabartés. "Thousands of doves. Thousands. Millions. They were perched in rows, as though they were in a dovecote, a prodigious great dovecote. The picture was in the museum at Málaga: I have never seen it since." Sabartés found it: the physically present birds amounted to nine: the canvas was quite small.

Picasso never threw anything away if he could possibly avoid doing so, and some of the drawings and paintings of those days in Málaga have survived, together with many more from the following years at La Coruña and hundreds from his adolescence in Barcelona. Of these Málaga pictures, that which is usually called the earliest and which is dated 1890/91 is a little painting of a picador: it is oil upon wood (the smooth cedar tops of cigar-boxes were useful to a child rarely indulged with canvases) and it shows a burly man in yellow seated upon a little miserable bony blindfolded old horse up against the pink barrier of a bull-ring. The spectators, two men (one in a bowler, one in a Cordovan hat) and an opulent woman, are so large that they make the horse look even more wretchedly small. The horse is unpadded—the eight- or nine-year-old Pablo had already seen some dozens disemboweled in the arena—and the picador with his armored leg sits right down in the deep Spanish saddle. The two are remarkably well observed; and my impression is that they are observed quite objectively: but I may be mistaken; there may be compassion for the horse.

The picador has a little of that wonderful quality which is often to be seen in children's paintings, but not a great deal. And some of this quality may be owing to the holes that take the place of the people's eyes, holes that do away with the surface and give their expressions an impassive fixity. These holes, however, were supplied by Lola, Picasso's sister, when she was busy with a nail.

Upon the whole, these early pictures from Málaga and La Coruña that have survived rarely show anything of that almost impersonal genius which inhabits some children until the age of about seven or eight, then leaves them forever. Picasso's beginnings were sometimes childish, but they were the beginnings of a child who from the start was moving towards an adult expression: and perhaps because of this the drawings are often dull. It may be that his astonishingly precocious academic skill did not so much stifle the childish genius as overlay it for the time so that it remained dormant, to come to life again after his adolescence and to live on for the rest of his career—an almost unique case of survival. Certainly, during many of his later periods he produced pictures that might well have been painted by a possessed child—a child whose "innocent," fresh, unhistoric, wholly individual genius had never died and that could now express itself through a hand capable of the most fantastic virtuosity.

The routine of those days in Málaga must have seemed everlasting to a child: the flat full of people, school when he could not get out of it, perpetual drawing, mass on Sundays, the slow parade up and down the Alameda, families in their best clothes, bands of ornamented youths all together, bands of swarthy tittering girls, grave adults, innumerable relatives, connections, friends, and always the splendid sun—eternal, natural, and taken for granted. All this, with the sea at hand and the pervading warmth, formed the basis of Picasso's life, the matrix from which he developed. A great deal of it remained with him forever: this Mediterranean world, his wholly real world, was the object of his nostalgia, the only place where he could really feel at home. All his life he loved the sun, the sea, a great deal of company; yet of these early influences one seems to have bitten much less deeply. He was brought up in a deeply Catholic atmosphere, with several unusually devout relations and a religious family tradition (quite apart from his uncle and namesake the Canon and Tío Perico, one of his cousins was destined for the priesthood), and although in some of its aspects the Church in Málaga may have been rather more a processional than a profoundly spiritual body, it is still surprising that Picasso should have been apparently so little marked. There are many contributory factors that can be brought forward for what they are worth: Andalucía, with its large population of crypto-Muslims and crypto-Jews surviving into the eighteenth and even the nineteenth century and its ancestral memory of the Inquisition's way of dealing with them, was never the most fervent province in Spain; then again the extreme contrast between the slums of Chupa y Tira and the wealth of the Alameda on the one hand and the elementary teachings of the faith on the other may have had its effect in time; while the growing clericalism, not to say religiosity, of the Establishment, the renewed identification of the Church with power, wealth, and authority during Alphonso XIII's minority cannot but have caused a reaction in an already strongly unconformist and anti-bourgeois mind. "My joining the Communist Party is the logical consequence of my whole life, of the whole body of my work," he said in 1944; and later in the same interview, "So I became a member of the Communist Party without the least hesitation, since fundamentally I had been on their side forever."

Yet no effort of will, no social consciousness, can undo the past nor give a man born and bred a Catholic the same foundation as a child brought up in another faith.

In those days when the Church still knew its own mind, when it spoke Latin, and when a personal Devil ruled over a blazing Hell filled with the hopelessly damned, damned for ever and ever, many a Catholic child was uneasy about dying. The inward eye more readily forms an image of Hell than of Paradise—in Last Judgments the damned and the terribly power-ful, terribly eager fiends that carry them shrieking away are infinitely more convincing than the blessed: the torments can be felt, whereas the ill-defined happiness of a perpetual Sunday cannot—and the descent into the one, or at least into Purgatory for a thousand years, is so much more likely than admission to the other. Absolution is not the magic sponge that some Protestants suppose: it is conditional upon true and whole confession, contrition, reparation, and many other factors. To an anxious mind (and the young Picasso was an anxious child) it is difficult to be quite certain that what seems to be contrition is not mere remorse of con-science, sterile and invalid: it is difficult to be sure that what one has con-fessed is all that should have been confessed: and perhaps it is even hard-er for a Spanish child. Spanish Catholicism has always dwelt heavily upon the last things; the skull is a very frequent symbol, and Picasso was less unaffected than he seemed.

He rebelled against the Church, as he rebelled against everything else, but he retained a deep religious sense: deep, but also obscure, Manicha-ean, and in many ways far from anything that could possibly be called Christian. I am not referring only or even mainly to his fear of the end, although it reached such a pitch that the slightest illness made him un-easy, while as for death itself, he avoided all mention of it as much as ever he could, except silently in his art, and he often took refuge in anger: as he lay sick in the last weeks of his life an intimate friend, a Catalan, urged him to make a will. "Doing things like that draws death," he cried furiously, and shortly afterwards turned his friend out of the room—he left no will, only a huge shapeless fortune to be wrangled over: no testament about anything at all except the eventual destination of "Guernica." Nor am I speaking of such remnants of orthodox belief or perhaps of orthodox magic that led him to make Françoise Gilot promise him eternal love in a church, with the benefit of holy water, or to observe to Matisse that in times of trouble it was pleasant to have God on one's side—did not Matisse too say his prayers when life was hard? What I mean is his sympathy with such mystics as El Greco and St. John of the Cross and his sense of unseen worlds just at hand, filled with forces good and evil, a sense so strong that he said it was nonsense to speak of religious pictures—how could you possibly paint a religious picture one day and another kind the next? How vividly present the immaterial world was to his mind can be seen from his conversation with André Malraux, which I quote later and in which he spoke of the spiritual essence of African carvings; and nothing shows his sense of the sacred more clearly than his telling Hélène Parmelin that a really good painting was good because it had been touched by the hand of God (whose existence of course he denied from time to time).

As for the traditional Catholicism in which he was brought up, a most significant aspect of Picasso's relationship to it is his silence. Apart from such set-pieces of his boyhood as "The First Communion" and "The Old Woman Receiving Holy Oil from a Choirboy," some adolescent Biblical scenes (including a fine "Flight into Egypt") and a few imprecise hagiographical pictures, he produced almost nothing with an evident religious bearing until the Crucifixion drawings of 1927, his strange Calvary of 1930, and the 1932 drawing based on the Isenheim altarpiece. Then silence again until the Christ-figures in the bull-fight engravings of 1959, although many other painters, atheist, agnostic, Jewish, vaguely Christian, or ardently Catholic, were working for the Church. Some authorities see no religious significance whatsoever in the "Calvary" and some find it blasphemous; this surprises me, since Picasso's statement on the Crucifixion strikes me as valid, moving, a furious cry of protest, the expression of a strong emotion that certainly lies within the wide limits of Catholicism. Although this is no more than a tentative hypothesis, it seems to me that Picasso, however desperately lapsed, did retain a certain residual Catholicism at some level of his being, an affectionate or perhaps a cautious respect for the old Church that showed itself in this silence and in the nature of these occasional outbursts. Apart from anything else, he looked upon his sacramental marriage as something different in kind from his other connections; and it is perhaps significant that as he came into the world with the rites of the Church, so he left it with at least some of them.

In 1891, in Málaga, the ten-year-old Picasso was more concerned with the ritual of the bull-ring than with any other sacrifice, and he recorded it diligently: but the days of his ordered, natural life were coming to an end. He now had a second sister, Concepción, born in 1887, and the flat was by so much the smaller; his father was growing even more withdrawn; and then, in a decision that caused great unhappiness, the municipality finally closed the museum. There had never been any margin for living in the Ruiz family, and this blow was disastrous.

In his distress Don José found a post at La Coruña: he was to teach drawing and decoration in the Escuela Provincial de Bellas Artes. La Coruña is in Galicia, on the Atlantic coast of Spain, a great way off in the north, and obviously the whole family would have to live there. All at once Don José became aware that his son was if not wholly illiterate then something very like it. Illiteracy and a total inability to add two and two would for the time being have mattered little in his native city, where friends and connections would naturally stand by the boy; but in a remote and savage province like Galicia the rules would have to be obeyed, at least by strangers, and to get into any school Pablo would have either to pass an entrance examination or present a certificate of competence. There was no possibility of his passing an examination in any subject but drawing, no possibility at all, so Don José went to see a friend who had the power of granting certificates. "Very well," said the friend, "but in common decency the child should at least appear to be examined."

The child appeared, and after some fruitless questions of a general nature, the child remaining mute, the examiner presented him with a sum, three plus one plus forty plus sixty-six plus thirty-eight, telling him kindly how to write it down and begging him not to be nervous. The first attempt was not wholly successful and the sum had to be written again: this time, when he showed it up, Pablo noticed that the examiner had made the addition himself on a scrap of paper, left obviously in sight. He memorized the figure, returned to his desk, wrote down the answer, drew a line beneath it with some complacency, and received his certificate.

This valuable paper was packed, together with all the family's portable possessions, and the home in the Plaza de la Merced fell to pieces. Dr. Salvador helped his brother to a passage by boat, and at the end of that summer of 1891 Picasso first took to the sea, at the beginning of his long voyage.

Chapter II

La Coruña: a leaden sea and a weeping sky. Don José had looked forward with misgiving to this remote little town in a backward province, but he could never have imagined the cold, sodden reality: on seeing it, he withdrew into his humid lodgings, appalled. Until a southerner has had the living experience of it, he cannot possibly conceive the difference between the Mediterranean civilization, lived largely out of doors, and that of the north, where people huddle in unsociable family groups, each in its own house, to keep out of the cold and the rain.

The voyage had been arduous in the extreme, and rather than face the equinoctial gales off Finisterre and the full horror of the Bay of Biscay the family left the ship at Vigo, although this meant taking the train to Santiago de Compostela and then the diligence on to La Coruña—eight hours of a crowded, lumbering horse-drawn vehicle, something between a coach and a covered wagon, in the pouring rain with two small children and a baby: the road in a chronic state of disrepair.

Their arrival was inauspicious; they had left Málaga with the grapes ripening in the sun and the sugar-cane standing tall, perhaps the most delightful season of the year, and they reached La Coruña in time for the onset of the prodigious autumn storms. All this ironbound north and northeastern coast of Spain is exposed to the great winds that tear in over three thousand miles of Atlantic ocean, sweeping low cloud and vast sheets of rain before them; and the north-east corner is even more exposed than the rest. Galicia's rainfall is the highest in the Peninsula, five and a half feet a year falling upon every square inch of Santiago, as opposed to London's twenty-three and a half inches and New York's forty-two. When it is neither blowing nor raining it is often foggy, as though the elements were hopelessly entangled; and this fog resolves itself into a cold, penetrating drizzle that streams upon the granite cliffs and the wet granite houses. There are pleasant days in the course of the year, when the sun peers through, lighting the pure sandy beaches, and when the deep fjords take on a certain charm; but then the warmth acts upon the piles of rotting kelp that the gales and furious tides (unknown in the Mediterranean) drive up to the high-water mark, and they breed swarms of noisome flies. In any case the Ruizes saw none of these fine days for the first months of their stay: autumn, winter, and spring had to pass slowly by before there was any hope of sun, as they understood the term.

These horrors impressed the young Picasso deeply, as well they might; but perhaps even more than by the incessant rain, the wind, the coal fires, the smoke-laden fog and the cold, he was shocked by the fact that in the streets the people spoke a different language. This was his first experience of being a foreigner, cut off; and for many small children the experience of hearing another language all round them, so that they are outsiders, debarred from the incessant, involuntary communication of the crowd and surrounded with secret, incomprehensible words, is deeply disturbing. The language spoken in La Coruña and the rest of Galicia is Gallego, a somewhat archaic variety of Portuguese, and although it is of course a Romance language other Spaniards do not understand it at all. The people can speak Castilian too, but among themselves it is Gallego: even now, with generations of military service and compulsory education in Castilian, a great many of them communicate in their own tongue, and in 1891 it was still more general. Figures for the turn of the century show 1,800,000 Gallegan-speakers out of a total population of just under two million.

The contrast between Málaga and La Coruña was very great indeed, but it could have been equaled in other parts of Spain, a country separated by its geography and its history into such markedly distinct regions that some of the early rulers took the title of emperor of the Spains, dwelling upon the plural. Navarra, Aragón, Castilla, León, and Catalonia were once sovereign states, so were Asturias, Estremadura, Jaén, Córdoba, Sevilla, and several others; and Galicia was one of them, a geographic, economic, and linguistic entity far closer in habits and culture to Portugal than to León or Castilla, and inhabited by a race with the reputation of being hardy, honest, industrious, stupid, and unpolished: indeed, the word Gallego had a certain currency in the rest of Spain as a term of reproach, meaning boor. Traditionally, in such cities as Madrid, it was the Galician who brought the water, coal, and wood, carrying it up innumerable flights of stairs.

This damp former kingdom, then, retained its individuality (and its diet) over the centuries, and the uprooted child Picasso was confronted not only with a strange language but also with strange forms and faces that to an Andalou scarcely seemed Spanish at all. The Moors did reach

Galicia; but although they came from bitterly inhospitable regions, most being Berbers, they withdrew after no more than five years, unable to bear the climate. It is true that they were also encouraged to withdraw by the plague and the army of King Alphonso of Asturias, but the great point is that they went away without having bred there. No trace of the Moor remains in blood, customs, or architecture: these are the descendants of the native Iberians, the Suevi and the Visigoths, with perhaps the slightest touch of Roman.

Faced with this different civilization, the Ruizes retired into their second-floor flat in the Calle Payo Gómez and watched the rain beating against the windows. They discussed the weather interminably—there was a great deal of it to discuss—and Don José at least felt the cold reach to his heart. His wife had a new home to set up, three children to look after, and the strangeness of Galician shopping to cope with—the makings of a *gazpacho* were hardly to be found, far less a bottle of generous wine. This left her little time for introspection, and in any case hers was a much happier temperament. For Pablo and his sisters too the initial horror faded; there was, after all, a new town to be seen, a town built on a peninsula with a harbor on one side, a beach on the other, and cliffs at the far end. It was not much of a town compared with Málaga—about a third of the size—and its solitary delight, apart from the port and the bull-ring, was a Roman tower on the howling eminence at the end of the peninsula, an erection called the Torre de Hercules by the inhabitants and the caramel tower by Don José. With its later additions it soared up four hundred feet, still serving as a lighthouse; and when the great Atlantic rollers drove in to break with a measured thunder at the foot of the cliff and sent their spray up to the tower it had a splendor of its own.

The port was busy enough, but even when it was visible it was not to be compared with Málaga. The exports were hogs, horse-beans and roots (mostly for Cuba, then still a Spanish possession), and the imports mainly coal, arriving in dirty tramp-steamers from England and South Wales. The bull-ring was closed when they arrived, but even when it opened it was a disappointment. There is little comprehension of the corrida outside Andalucía, little grasp of those fine points that distinguish it from mere bull-baiting (or at the worst a vile butchery) and so raise it to the level of a savage, dangerous, poetic sacrifice. When the bullfighters are aware that the congregation does not know what the mystery is about, they will only perform, not officiate; and after a while, the season having come round at last, Don José was so disgusted that he gave up attending.

Picasso drew the tower, as he drew everything else in La Coruña. The early drawings are still childish, or rather boyish, many of them being illustrations to jokes about the weather; others, particularly those in the margins and blank pages of his schoolbooks, show the kind of battle that most schoolboys draw—Romans, savages, people with spears, swordsmen slashing away at one another. There are also some capital bulls. The school-books which Picasso preserved are in the museum at Barcelona: they resemble almost all school-books in being dog-eared, battered, and tedious, but they are of a considerably higher standard than might have been expected. One, which has selections from the classics and which Picasso adorned with a pen-and-ink Moor's head and some pigeons far livelier than his father's, has quite advanced Latin verse and passages from Cicero. How much Pablo made of it is another matter, but at least he had got into the school and he did well enough not to be sent away; furthermore at this time he wrote, or was compelled to write, a far more elegant, legible hand than he had ever used before or was ever to use again. The school in question was the Instituto da Guarda, and Picasso was admitted to the *primer curso*, the first year of the secondary cycle: the next year, in 1892, he also matriculated at the Escuela de Bellas Artes, where his father was teaching, while at the same time he carried on with his studies at the Instituto.

At no time of his life was Picasso a willing writer of letters. In La Coruña he invented a way of communicating with his relatives in Málaga that called for little effort in the literary way: this was a small news-sheet "published every Sunday," called sometimes *Asul y Blanco* and sometimes *La Coruña*, in which he drew local people, dogs, pigeons (one of his small advertisements reads "Pedigree pigeons purchased: apply second floor, 14 Calle Payo Gómez"), the "caramel tower" on a tray, and wrote short dispatches such as "The wind has started, and it will go on blowing until there is no La Coruña left," or "The rain has begun already. It will not stop before summer," or "At the time of going to press this publication had received no telegrams of any kind." Then there were more jokes, some illustrated and most of this general nature: During an arithmetic examination: *Master, "If you are given five melons and you eat four, what have you left?" Pupil, "One." Master, "Are you sure that is all?" Pupil, "And a belly-ache."* Most of the people are struggling with the wind or the rain or both (La Coruña's main industry seems to have been the manufacture and repair of umbrellas); and to show Málaga the extreme wild remoteness of these parts there is a drawing of the Galician bagpipes.

These too are still entirely boyish productions, with little hint of what was so soon to appear; and it is worth pointing out that the spelling *entonses*, for example, or *asul*, rather than the orthodox *entonces* and *azul*, shows that Picasso had retained his Andalusian way of speaking (the Castilian pronounces *z* and soft *c* as *th*, whereas the southerner makes no attempt at any such thing—nor do many South Americans, Andalusian in origin). These mistakes, together with others that have nothing to do with phonetics, also show that Picasso remained impervious to printed shape: which is strange, when one considers his astonishingly accurate recall of other forms, even then. And what is more curious still is his mirror-version of the final question-mark: this might have been influenced by the Spanish convention of starting a question with another question-mark, upside-down, but later he sometimes inverted the esses of his signature, and when he took to etching and engraving he could not or would not grasp that the printing of the plate necessarily reversed the legend. It is as though there were some confusion in the mental process that separates right from left.

These childish things were soon to be left behind, however, and although the facetious illustrative sketch reappeared at intervals, the young Picasso suddenly moved on to an extraordinary degree of maturity, to serious and as it were *total* painting. He might perhaps have done so a little earlier if his father had set about his education as a painter more seriously; but the separation from his friends, his native climate, his whole way of life, coming on top of his other reasons for unhappiness, quite crushed Don José's spirit: he hardly ever went out, but stood at the window, watching the rain. When he did leave the house, it was to go to the art-school, just over the way, or to Mass: the then unchanging Mass was one of the few remaining links with his former life—that and the pigeons, which he still kept, and which he still painted from time to time, although with little enthusiasm, and that little diminishing fast. This is the Don José that his son painted, a man so deeply sad that it is painful to look at some of the portraits. Yet at this time he was still capable of making friends—his final withdrawal came later—and one of them was Dr. Raimundo Pérez Costales, an interesting man who had been minister of labor and of the fine arts under the short-lived and anarchical First Republic of Pi y Margall in 1873: according to Sabartés he was so much attached to Don José that when the Ruizes left La Coruña, Dr. Costales settled at Málaga in the hope that his friend would eventually return to his native town.

However, in time José Ruiz did turn his mind to a thorough-going artistic education for his son. He taught Pablo the techniques of pen-and-ink, charcoal, pastel, and crayon; later he promoted him to painting in oil and watercolor, though at the same time he insisted upon a great deal of drawing, of exact and conscientious drawing. As a teacher Don José was a strict disciplinarian, obeying the law to the letter and requiring both obedience and hard work; it was a rigorously academic training, of course, for even if Don José's tastes had not lain in that direction, the school was under the Royal Academy of San Fernando in Madrid, a deeply conservative body. Picasso accepted the discipline happily, and in the antique classes he made drawings of casts that astonish the beholder not only with their accomplishment but even more with their power of giving the faded model's back their life, a life that had been there when the statues were first carved and that his pleasure in the act of drawing restored to their degraded plaster shadows. What for most people is a hopelessly arid exercise was a delight to Picasso, and his art-school studies glow with pleasure: controlled, disciplined, and almost anonymous, but certainly pleasure.

Picasso told Brassaï, when he and the photographer were talking about children's painting and infant phenomenons (they never last, said Picasso), that the precision of these academic drawings frightened him; and certainly there is something a little monstrous about their easy virtuosity when they are compared with the decorations that he was drawing at the same time in his school-books, a time when he was in fact no more than a little jug-eared boy of twelve or thirteen. Perhaps it was at this period that Picasso was first inhabited by his particular demon: not the more or less impersonal spirit that comes to children in their nonage, incapable of sin, but the fully adult creature that Sartre calls the vampire and that certainly, in the case of some writers, lives upon their blood. Except for Friar Bacon's squat black dog, the demon has never, I believe, been isolated and identified, but it is a real presence, and those who have known this possession report the experience as both extraordinarily exalting—mind aglow, senses concentrated, hand flying, body, heat and cold forgotten— and as something with an element of dread.

Outside the school his work was much more free: among the surviving oils there are some little tentative pictures dating from 1892 and 1893, then a more assured cottage, probably of late '93, technically far more competent and painted on a properly stretched canvas; and then suddenly, with no apparent transition, the extraordinarily accomplished head of a man that Cirlot, an authority on these early years, places in circa 1894, that is to say when Picasso was twelve or at the most thirteen. It is a small picture (thirteen and a half inches by eleven and a half), though it looks much larger; the head and shoulders of a man, bald-fronted, tanned, with a short grizzled beard: he is shown almost in profile, looking slightly upwards and to the right, and he does not have the least air of sitting for his portrait. The background of a very light gray sets off this ruddy brown head and browner neck, but it does not cover the fine-grained canvas entirely; and the whitish shirt below the neck is only suggested. Picasso certainly meant to leave the picture in this state, for in the little portrait of his uncle Baldomero Chiara, which is firmly dated July 3, 1894, the paint shades off into the virgin paper, and in that of Dr. Costales (a fine old gentleman with mutton-chop whiskers and a deep fur collar) which he painted in 1895, the top of the canvas is quite bare. The picture is full of light, full of life, and the finely proportioned head—finely proportioned to the limits of the canvas—is quite wonderfully striking. An eminently Spanish picture, with the best of Spanish naturalism, absolutely nothing childish about it at all: it has little or nothing of the nineteenth century, nothing in the least sentimental, and Velásquez would have admired it, whether he knew the painter's age or not. Indeed, it has a certain kinship with the head of the elderly man in Velásquez' "Los Borrachos" at the Prado, which the young Picasso had never seen.

The next year, when Picasso was still thirteen, he painted many more pictures, several of which have come down to us. There is not much point in describing them in detail, but they show many different lines of approach, many different techniques, always more assured. Among them is his dog Klipper, one of the earliest in the long series of Picasso's animals—cats, mice, apes, pigeons, an incontinent goat, turtle-doves, owls, and always dogs. Klipper is a brownish-yellow creature, a basic dog of medium size, more smooth than rough: an intelligent head with a large, knowing eye.

The picture has all the marks of a good portrait; and it is painted without the least trace of sentimentality. Picasso's relations with his animals were very close: he had an extraordinary gift for entering into direct contact with them: could handle a wild bird or walk up to a furious dog when most people would have provoked an ugly scene: and the tired old cliché about the power of the human eye finds its justification in Picasso. He had in fact a most luminous and striking eye, a singular, penetrating gaze, always the first thing that people noticed. But these relations were quite unlike those which are usual in Anglo-Saxon countries. A child brought up on the spectacle of slaughtered bulls does not have the same reactions as one brought up on flopsy bunnies or the products of Walt Disney's muse: Picasso did not shift his animals to a semi-human plane—he met them on their own. He loved cats, not the sleek castrated fat domesticated creatures, not pussies, but the rangy feral cats of the southern gutter, who will fly in your face at the drop of a hat. His animals lived according to their own codes, more or less, with no undue notions of right or wrong, nor of cleanliness, imposed from above.

Then there are more remarkable heads of poor, elderly men, masterly pieces of strong, sober Spanish realism, brown pictures. There is nothing of the picturesque peasant to be seen in these worn, stupid, hopeless people; even the torn shirt has no hint of the theatrical rags so common at the time. Yet only a very little earlier Picasso was drawing highly picturesque and rather feeble Moors and Moorish palaces: the development was extraordinarily rapid, and only months lie between the schoolboy doodling and the unbelievably accomplished throw-away pen and ink sketch of a Pantheon with a minute Velásquez, a pair of doves in flight, and some truly delightful putti, apparently bringing him a color-box.

To all these pictures Picasso preferred his "Barefoot Girl" and his "Beggar," both painted in 1895; and these he kept with him all his life.

I will not describe "The Beggar," which is a most able, confident study in the idiom of several others of that time, but the subtly different "Girl" must have a few lines. She sits on an uncomfortable straight-backed chair against a broken dark-green background, dressed in a long russet frock with a white cloth over her shoulders, her hands folded in her lap and one large chilblained foot dangling. She is a sad child, deep dismay struggling with sullenness in her face at repose: dismay not at her present situation, but at the world into which she has been pitched. She is of about the same age as the painter, and she sits there patiently; her immense, lustrous, asymmetric eyes gaze forward, a little down, at nothing. Here the technique is surer still, the brush-stroke firm and decisive on the dress, gentle and flowing on the face; and here there is much more personal involvement. Picasso did not spare her big hands, thick ankles, and coarse great feet; he was not in the least degree concerned with prettiness; but it is evident, not merely from her eyes and the pure oval of her face, that he was entirely with her.

Both these canvases were rather large for Pablo at that time, about two foot six by one foot eight, and it is said that the model for the second and perhaps the canvas too were given him as a present for his good behavior during the Christmas holidays.

Once Picasso had begun his true ascent, acquiring at the same time a mastery of his tools, Don José let him help with the details of the decorative pictures he still produced. He would, for example, cut off a dead pigeon's pink legs and claws, pin them to a board, and tell Pablo to paint them in. In the course of a few months it became evident to both that even on the technical plane the boy's painting was far beyond the man's. José Ruiz could no more have painted that beggar's head or the barefoot girl than he could have confronted a bull in the arena. He acknowledged it; solemnly handed over his brushes to his son, and never painted again.

It was perhaps an unfortunate impulse. The truth must in time have become even more obvious, but this gesture crystallized the situation and by so doing altered it, making it far more extreme. The young are often cruel; and there are circumstances in which they can be devoid of pity, especially towards those whose role it is to be strong and who are weak. Even now a father who abdicates, who declines the absurd role of the omniscient, omnipotent, infallible monarch of the glen, is liable to arouse a confused but strong resentment; and the status, thankfully laid aside, can never be convincingly resumed when at a later date it may become necessary: at that time, and in that place, such an action was more exceptional by far.

One of Picasso's outstanding characteristics as a man was his kindness, and this was evident in his face, in his habitual expression; but he was no more all of a piece throughout than any other—indeed he had more contradictions in him than most—and he could be very hard. There are also discreet, muffled, imprecise rumors of marital discord at this period: José Ruiz, aging fast, cannot have been a very lively companion. It is not surprising that Pablo's affection should have shifted almost entirely to his mother in such an event; nor that the *Picasso,* which had been absent from the signatures of most of these early paintings, should now reappear. The bold *P. Ruiz* is replaced by *P. Ruiz Picasso* after 1895, and with few exceptions the *Ruiz* vanishes altogether after about 1901. And most of his portraits of Don José are not signed at all, whereas those of his mother are.

Yet this does not mean any decided, lasting, definitive, and evident animosity between José and Pablo Ruiz: the portraits alone prove that, and there is a great deal of evidence for an enduring, though tempered, affection on both sides. Then again at this point the family was struck by a cruel blow that certainly brought its members together. Concepción, Pablo's youngest sister, fell ill with diphtheria, and in spite of Dr. Costales' devoted care she died: at that time the disease could kill in three or four days, and in Spain it did kill about half of those it attacked. Don José felt the loss most bitterly: she was the only one of his children who resembled him in the least, a fair-haired child, tall for her age, and slim.

But in any case the La Coruña days, with their dreary, oppressive atmosphere, the shut-in life so conducive of secret domestic war, were in their turn coming to an end. A former assistant of Don José's, Ramón Navarro García, who taught figure-drawing at the famous art-school of the Llotja at Barcelona, wished to return to his native Galicia. When he proposed the exchange there could be no hesitation on José Ruiz's part. Not only would they get away from the sad house, so very much sadder now, but Barcelona meant the Mediterranean once more, an escape from the gloom and rain of La Coruña; furthermore, the Llotja post carried a better salary: three thousand pesetas a year, almost exactly £100, or $482. At the end of the term the family packed their bags. They were to spend the summer holidays of 1895 in Málaga, taking the train, which would carry them there by way of Madrid. Picasso's luggage included a great many pictures: he had tried to sell some in a little exhibition at an umbrella-maker's shop (in the doorway, says Gómez de La Serna), but that had not been markedly successful; and he had given a few to Dr. Costales. The drawings and paintings that remained might be grouped in the following categories: juvenilia (though even among these there is the occasional prophetic pure, unhesitating line, especially in the bulls), boyish "histori-cal" scenes, the interiors and other paintings that show the influence of his father's friends Ferrándiz and Muñoz Degrain, sketch-books of great interest to the art-historian, drawings of hands (all his life he was preoc-cupied with hands, singly and in pairs), and these strong, firmly-painted canvases of his twelfth and thirteenth years. There were also two little things that could be lumped in with the juvenilia if they did not seem to have a particular significance for the later years—they are little cut-outs, a dog and a dove, that only need to be stuck to a canvas to be the first of all collages. And these small paper silhouettes are perhaps the only examples of his father's direct influence in the whole collection.

A couple of days or so in Madrid, after the prolonged horror of a creep-ing Spanish train—more than thirty hours to cover the five hundred miles of line winding about the mountains, with four changes and innumerable stops—a Madrid at the height of its blazing summer, cannot have been very gratifying; nor can the travelers have been at their most receptive. However, Don José and his son did visit the Prado, and there for the first time in his life Picasso saw Velásquez, El Greco, Zurbarán, Ribera, Goya, to say nothing of Valdes Léal, Murillo, and the host of illustrious foreigners.

Whether the immense indigestible wealth, the heat, his fatigue, and the lighting that made it almost impossible to see "Las Meninas" whole, op-pressed him or not, he had recovered his spirits by the time they reached Málaga, four hundred miles farther on. They were welcomed, feasted, made much of. Their native air, their native speech and food, revived the returning exiles, and Pablo, still the only boy the Ruiz brothers had be-tween them, was particularly caressed. He was always in his element at a party—conviviality was meat and drink to the abstemious Picasso all his life—and this may well have been the happiest holiday that he spent in Málaga. He was so taken up with having fun that his work, even his sketching, shows a falling-off in quantity. However, he did paint a picture of the kitchen, and he did make a very delicate pencil drawing of their old servant Carmen, with her sleeves rolled up as once she had rolled them up to lead him to school by force; and perhaps influenced by the familiar atmosphere recovered, he signed it P. Ruiz, as he had done in former days.

His relations were proud of him. Painting was now no longer the desperate career that it had been when Don José made his choice, and they may even have distinguished between the canvases he brought back from La Coruña and his father's work. In any case, despite the shaky condition of the peseta, twenty years of peace had led the richer sort to buy paintings more frequently, and Muñoz Degrain, Moreno Carbonero, and other men they knew were doing well in Madrid, so well that the State bought their pictures for the Museum of Modern Art in the capital itself. Pablo's manifest destiny was accepted without question: Dr. Salvador, who had grown more prosperous still, hired an aged seafaring man as model and gave his nephew a duro a day to paint him, five pesetas, a sum at least twice as much as a laborer could earn.

Towards the end of the summer they took to the sea once more, coasting along northwards past Almería, Cartagena, Alicante, and Valencia; and the September sea was so kind that during the voyage Picasso could paint, not hurried sketches of the shore, but oil upon canvas, and that of a considerable size. After three days of sailing, Barcelona came in sight, an immensely busy port with the vast city spreading wide on either hand, the sinister Montjuich to the left, Tibidabo rising behind, and mountains beyond: to the right, factory chimneys, gasworks, palm-trees, industrial suburbs.

As soon as he set foot on the quay, Picasso found that once again he was surrounded by a different language. All around him the people spoke Catalan, as incomprehensible as Gallego or even more so; and many of them were dressed in the fashion of their country—a red bonnet like a Phrygian cap, curiously plaited rope-soled cloth shoes, a broad red sash, a little waistcoat.

And as the Ruizes walked along to the lodging that a friend had found for them in the Calle Cristina, not far from their landing-place, this impression of being *abroad* grew stronger. For the Barcelona of 1895 was a wholly European city, something they had never known before; a huge, busy, and intensely Catalan city, with half a million people in it, all talking their own language and all living according to customs and values that were foreign not only to Málaga but to Madrid and the whole of the rest of the Peninsula. The thirteen-year-old Pablo could not have felt more a stranger if he had landed in Marseilles or Genoa: once again he was entirely uprooted.

Chapter III

THIS is not the place for a detailed history of Catalonia and its capital: but the culture into which Picasso was plunged was determined by that history, and since he passed his most formative years in Barcelona, becoming integrated with the Catalan community, speaking their language, and making his earliest and most lasting friends among them, some modest outline is essential to an understanding of the forces that worked upon the vital years of his adolescence and early manhood.

In the middle ages Catalonia was an independent country, lying on both sides of the eastern Pyrenees, but with most of its territory in the Peninsula. The Moors had held it for a while, but Charlemagne soon thrust them out, and in the ninth century Wilfred the Shaggy cut himself free from all foreign allegiance and ruled without contest as a sovereign chief of state.

His country was poor in natural resources, but rich in an active, enterprising population. ("From a stone the Catalan will draw bread" says the Spanish proverb.) After the turmoil of the Moorish wars those who lived upon the coast early returned to commerce, carrying on the Roman tradition; and in spite of their indifferent harbors they soon became one of the most important trading nations in the Mediterranean. Barcelona rivaled Venice and Genoa; Catalan ships sailed to the North Sea and the Baltic, to Alexandria and points beyond; Catalan maritime law and marine insurance were accepted as standard far and wide; and while the other states of Spain were shut off from the rest of Europe, preoccupied with centuries of war against the Moors or with fratricidal struggles for power, Catalonia flourished, with a splendid literature of its own, a highly distinctive architecture, a school of painting which bears comparison with that of Lombardy, a renowned university, and a general culture that had long been wide open to influences from France, Provence, Italy, Byzantium, and the learned Moors and Jews of southern and central Spain.

This was the golden age to which Picasso's Catalan friends looked back with a resentful nostalgia—the age when the Counts of Barcelona, who by marriage had become kings of Aragón, carried the Catalan tongue far beyond its original limits, conquering the Balearic islands, Sicily, Naples, Corsica, Sardinia, the Moorish Valencia, and all the Moslem country down to Murcia, an age whose architectural glories still filled their city.

Even in the early seventeenth century Cervantes could speak of Barcelona as "the seat of courtesy, the haven of strangers, the refuge of the distressed, the mother of the valiant, the champion of the wronged, the abode of true friendship, unique both in beauty and situation," but although the splendid buildings were still there, the glory was already gone. That unhappy marriage with the heiress of Aragón was followed in the course of time by the union of Aragón and Castilla in the persons of Ferdinand and Isabella. Their heir, the Habsburg Charles V, inherited a united Spain from which the last Moorish rulers had been expelled, together with vast possessions in America; and already Catalonia was an oppressed country, cut off from all commerce with the New World, the great fresh source of wealth. For centuries the Castilians had disliked their industrious neighbors, and the Emperor Charles, who knew little of Spain when he came to the throne, sided with the Castilians; and so it continued, generation after generation, with what the Catalans looked upon as one piece of oppression after another, and with bloody risings from time to time, until the end of the Habsburg line in Spain.

In the bitter wars that followed—Marlborough's wars—the Catalans supported the Austrian pretender: his successful rival, the French Bourbon who ruled Spain as Philip V, took Barcelona by storm and turned upon the Catalans with great severity. He suppressed Catalan as the official language, imposing Castilian in its place, abolished their ancient privileges, the *Cortes* and the *fueros*, closed the university of Barcelona, and built a citadel and a much-hated ring of walls to enclose and overawe the city.

The policy of repression and assimilation continued with even greater force; local laws and customs were done away with; the language was discouraged. In the eighteenth and early nineteenth centuries this policy had some success; it certainly came close to destroying Catalan literature, although it was unable to kill the language itself—a language closely related to the Provencal in which many of the earlier poets wrote; a harsher language to the unaccustomed ear, but one capable of the utmost subtlety in the hands of such writers as Ramon Llull (Caxton published him in translation) or Ausiàs March; and, with its comparative absence of vowel endings, perhaps the most masculine of Romance dialects.

But there was always a resistance, both political and cultural; and with the coming of romanticism the Catalan poets began their Renaixença, a movement designed not only to revive the country's literary culture but to express the nation's wish for at least some measure of independence. The Renaixença was strongly supported, often by people with little concern with poetry or the arts: in 1841 the university was restored, and some years later the hated walls went down but still the Catalan was not master in his own house.

The Barcelona that Picasso explored in 1895 presented some analogies with Joyce's Dublin: there was the same nationalist revival, the same passionate resentment of a foreign government, the same memory of a glorious past now overshadowed, the same tradition of deep opposition to central authority, the same conviction of a higher culture oppressed by a lower; and historically there had been the same readiness to call in foreign aid to get rid of the oppressors. But the religious element was lacking; and whereas Joyce's Dublin was desperately poor, Barcelona had been growing steadily richer ever since the restoration of the monarchy in 1874. The port was now handling eight thousand ships a year; the manufactures had increased enormously; the city had spread far beyond its ancient limits; and Barcelona's taxes, though grudgingly paid, provided a great part of the government's income.

Yet these were the days of unrestrained capitalism, and Barcelona also possessed a huge urban proletariat. Picasso had been acquainted with squalor ever since he was born, but the misery of a great industrial city was something far beyond his experience; so was the reaction to this misery. For whereas the victims of the chronic agricultural depression in Spain suffered in silence, or at least without rioting, the intolerable conditions in Barcelona led to strong left-wing movements, to frequent strikes, and to anarchism. Anarchism was preached all over Europe and America at that time, but nowhere did it take such a hold as in Barcelona; and there it added a still more eruptive element to the general anti-government atmosphere. An anarchist had set off a bomb in the crowded Liceo theater shortly before Picasso's arrival, on the grounds that "there could be no innocent bourgeois"; and the Ruizes had hardly settled down before another bomb was lobbed right into the great Corpus Christi procession. The Establishment called the bombs "infernal machines": it had no sympathy whatsoever for those who thought that the existing order had to be destroyed to bring a decent society into being, and very little for those who proposed a less radical reform. But Picasso never belonged to the Establishment at any time, and protest, both moderate and extremely violent, appeared early in his work.

It did not appear at first, however. As a boy he was no part of the community: although he had no difficulty in making himself understood, the city being bilingual, he had only to open his mouth to make it clear that he was a stranger and a stranger of no great consequence, for an Andalou was instantly labeled idle, Gypsyish, mercurial, and above all *not serious*, a very grave charge in hard-headed Catalonia. And since he had no gift for languages this was his status throughout his early adolescence. It was as an outsider that he discovered Barcelona, and perhaps for that very reason he saw the squalor and injustice more clearly than the natives.

Little of this was visible in the new districts outside the walls, with their broad streets crossing at right-angles, but the heart of Barcelona lay in the old town, and that was where the Ruizes lived. The flat in the Calle Cristina soon proved too dark and inconvenient and after a short stay in the nearby Calle Llauder they removed to number three in the Calle de la Merced, a tall, five-storied house with a battered coat of arms over its gloomy entrance, facing equally tall houses on the other side of a street some four yards wide: a dank street into which the sun could hardly penetrate except at midday and the kind of house that Don José would naturally have chosen. It was only a hundred yards or so from the art-school and he stayed there for the rest of his life.

Immediately northwards stood the still older Barrio Gótico, with its medieval houses and palaces by the cathedral, which itself was no distance at all from the Ramblas, the main artery of the old city, a broad, tree-filled avenue running right down to the port, with a fine shaded promenade in the middle, always crowded with people and enlivened by a flower-market, a bird-market, cafés—a continual flow of life. And on the far side of the Ramblas lay the densely-populated Barrio Chino, a rabbit-warren of deep, winding lanes, full of whores and sailors: picturesque slums, with their dark wine-shops lined with enormous barrels, seamen's bars full of music, purple characters walking about, and the Mediterranean sun blazing down on the innumerable lines of colored washing hanging from the high façades, but slums nevertheless.

It was a dirty city, upon the whole, with the middle ages lingering on in many parts of it, and the streets packed with horses, mules, and asses, carrying paniers or pulling carts, drays, wagons, carriages, omnibuses, cabs; a city smelling not only of horse and humanity but of the port, the fish-markets, hot olive oil, and the countless factory-chimneys.

But it was an immensely living one, with nothing of that air of decrepitude and death so familiar in the rest of Spain, and it was inhabited by a race with the reputation of working extremely hard, of worshiping money and success, an unpolished, hard-headed nation. The removal of the court had long since changed the nature of Cervantes' "seat of courtesy," and Picasso's Barcelona was emphatically a commercial city, one that according to Jean Cassou "had never heard of good taste": which, when one considers the castrating effect of good taste, was just as well for Picasso. Yet the prevailing materialism was tempered by a strong sense of religion, by a natural gaiety, and (whatever Cassou may say) by a certain feeling for the arts.

It was Catalan businessmen who had launched Gaudí some twenty years before Picasso's arrival; it was they who supported the thriving opera-house, the concerts, and the many choirs that sang Catalan songs both for pleasure and as a means of nationalist assertion. Their sensitivity to painting was less than it had been in the fifteenth century, when the municipality commissioned masterpieces from Huguet and Dalmáu; and one gallery alone, the Saló Parés (together with temporary exhibitions in the hall of the *Vanguardia* newspaper), was all that Barcelona could support in the way of living artists. Yet even at this time, when in every country but France painting was at its lowest, most dreary ebb, they did patronize their favorite Fortuny, they did possess an artistic club, dedicated to St. Luke, and it was their sons and even daughters who filled the busy art-school.

This school was in the Exchange, a fine late-eighteenth-century building that incorporated the great Catalan-Gothic hall of its fourteenth-century counterpart built during the reign of Peter the Ceremonious. It was down by the harbor, its function being to accommodate merchants, ship-owners, and marine insurers in their dealings, and the Catalans called it the Llotja, just as they called Peter En Pere. The official, Castilian, name was La Lonja, while En Pere came out as Pedro; and this dual system, which is to be found at every turn, makes it difficult for a writer to be consistent. The Catalans themselves often waver; Jaume Sabartés, a Barcelonan born and bred, signed his invaluable books on Picasso with the Castilian Jaime, and many a Catalan Joan uses the more familiar Spanish Juan outside his own country.

This was the school that José Ruiz wished his son to attend. The elementary classes would have been an insult to his talent, but for entry to the higher schools of life, antique and painting two examinations were required, both of them of an adult standard, the minimum age being twenty.

These examinations he had to undergo, for although Don José's colleagues might be persuaded to accept that a short boy of thirteen was "apparently about twenty years of age" if in fact he really could draw as well as a mature art-student, they did not choose to make public fools of themselves by admitting a beginner, and they set him the tests in all their rigor.

At this level they had nothing to do with ordinary school subjects, which perhaps was just as well: his first task was to draw a school model draped in a sheet; the second was a standing nude.

A certain amount of legend has gathered about these examinations, and while some writers say that although a month was allowed, Picasso did the work in a single day; others prefer one hour instead of the permitted twenty-four.

In fact the two surviving drawings are dated September 25 and 30, 1895, but even so there is no doubt that he produced them in a surprisingly short time. They ignored the art-school convention that would have turned the first model into a toga'd Roman and the second into a reasonably noble figure: Picasso drew exactly what he saw, a school model draped in a sheet and a stocky, ill-proportioned little man, very naked in the hard north light. But he did so with such extraordinary academic ability that there could be no question of the result; he was at once put down on the list of those admitted to the higher school for the academic year 1895–96. There were a hundred and twenty-eight of them, in alphabetical order, and he was the hundred-and-eighth, his second surname being spelled Picano.

Most of the other names were typically Catalan—Puigvert, Bosch, Batlle, Campmany, Creus—and none achieved any wide notoriety. But number eighty-six was Manuel Pallarès Grau, who happened to be Picasso's neighbor in his first anatomy class. Pallarès was a powerful rustic youth of rising twenty, an art-student of some standing, and of course he was much bigger than Pablo; but in spite of these differences they made friends at once. Indeed, the whole school accepted him, his personality and his obviously outstanding gifts doing away with the chasm between thirteen and twenty, a time when each year counts for ten. Here again it was taken for granted that Picasso was an extraordinary being, to whom common laws did not apply. Neither extreme youth nor extreme age ever mattered to Picasso where human relationships were concerned; all his life he met people he liked on the direct plane of immediate contact, unobscured by the accidental differences of birth, age, or nationality; and he and Pallarès, his earliest and certainly his most valuable friend in Barcelona, remained deeply attached as long as they lived.

These first two years in Barcelona were comparatively quiet, industrious, and dutiful. It seems absurd to speak of any exceptional industry and sense of duty in a man who never stopped working all his life, whose output has been estimated at over fifteen thousand paintings to say nothing of his sculpture, engravings, and countless drawings, and whose sense of what was due to his art led him again and again to throw away success, critical and financial, when he was poor and needed both; but his later morality was his own alone, and here the words are used as they are understood by bourgeois families who want their son to "get on." He lived at home, of course, and he attended the school regularly: he had put himself down for several courses, including History of Art and Aesthetics, and although in time he took to cutting these lectures, he was assiduous in all classes where there was a model. What is more, he perpetually walked about Barcelona with Pallarès, drawing with scarcely a pause, filling albums and sketch-books with street-scenes, horses, cats, dogs, whores, bawds, anarchist meetings, scores and scores of hands, paired and single, beggars, soldiers leaving for the unpopular Cuban campaign, soon to end in war with the United States. And he was busy at home, drawing and painting his family—a pastel of his mother, at least three portraits of his father, many drawings and paintings of the patient Lola—and preparing a big canvas for the spring exhibition of Fine Arts and Artistic Industries. It is a strictly academic picture, somewhat in the manner of the respected Mas y Fontdevila, and certainly painted under Don José's supervision: it shows Lola in the white dress and veil of a girl at her first communion, kneeling before an altar with her father standing beside her. There is more Industry in it than one usually associates with Picasso, but within its limits it is an accomplished piece of work, and when it was shown (with the wild price-tag of 1500 pesetas—fifty pounds at the then rate of exchange) it met with a certain amount of mild praise.

This was also the time when Picasso produced a sudden little output of religious pictures, including the charming "Rest on the Flight to Egypt" that he kept with him all his life: they amount to a dozen or more, and it is as though the fourteen-year-old Pablo were making a determined effort to be a "good boy." At about this period, however, he also rid himself of his virginity: he and Pallarès went to all manner of places, and Picasso's drawings show an early, exact knowledge of the female form, although the models at the school were all men. Picasso himself, when asked when he had first made love to a girl, held his hand a little more than a yard from the ground. One of these bawdy-houses was nearby, in the Calle d'Avinyó (Avinyó is the Catalan for Avignon, and to be consistent I should also put the Catalan *carrer* rather than *calle;* but *calle* is what the pilgrim will find written up on the wall), the very street to which the Llotja has recently been removed.

With so much work to do—and the list should include the great number of careful studies from the school's collection of plaster casts, one a prophetic charcoal drawing of a man carrying a lamb—and with such a close companionship with Pallarès, Picasso had not much leisure for the other students. He did make friends among them, particularly with Josep Cardona Furró, a sculptor, and with Joan Cardona Lladós, a draughtsman; but upon the whole they seem to have been rather a dull lot, and there is no record of the animated discussions of the new worlds of painting and philosophy that were to come a little later, when Picasso frequented the Quatre Gats, with its much maturer, far more aware and living company.

Yet even if these students knew little or nothing of Impressionism and still less of the Neo-Impressionists and Symbolists, they must all have been conscious of the Art Nouveau that was sweeping southwards from France, Germany, England, and the north in general, and that in its Spanish form took on the name of Modernismo. Santiago Rusiñol, one of the most advanced of the earlier generation of painters and a poet (and one of the first men to buy Picassos), had organized several well-publicized Fiestas Modernistas at the nearby Sitges; and during the celebrations of 1895 two of his recently-acquired paintings by the then neglected El Greco were carried in procession. The sillier, more mawkish manifestations of later Art Nouveau make any association with El Greco seem strange, but the connection was more evident in 1895; and whether Picasso was at Sitges or not (most probably he was not) El Greco certainly had great influence on him when in time he reached Madrid.

Before seeing the Prado again, however, he was to spend another year at the Llotja and two summer holidays in Málaga. The first holiday, in 1896, was a period of the most surprising activity. Of the many drawings, pictures, and portraits that he produced in those months, two stand out as being quite exceptional; and neither shows the least trace of Barcelona. Although Picasso respected the professor of painting at the Llotja, Antonio Caba, the director of the school (an awful figure) and an able portraitist, in later life he said he did not like the pictures he painted when he was a boy in Barcelona: he preferred those of La Coruña. Now, back in his native town, he seems to have returned to that earlier state of spirit, with a greater power of expression and more to express.

The portrait of his aunt Josefa (a difficult old lady, pious and contradictory, his father's eldest surviving sister) has been called by Juan-Eduardo Cirlot "without doubt one of the greatest in the whole history of Spanish painting." Other authorities might not go so far, but the statement is not downright ludicrous: as it hangs there amidst the juvenilia the picture is immensely striking. Against a dark background the little old woman's strong-featured yellowish face with its big, lustrous eyes, as dark as her nephew's, peers out under a black cap, completely dominating the room: the brushwork is bold and assured; the picture is eminently successful.

Yet Picasso never painted like this again: he never again used the same Rembrandtesque chiaroscuro nor the same Expressionist approach.

In its way the second picture is more surprising still. In the first place, it is a landscape, a rare thing in Picasso's work, and then it is painted in a manner unlike anything he had done before or was ever to do again: looking at this picture of the red Málaga earth sloping up to the light blue sky and partly covered with prickly-pear cactuses, some living, some dead (they grow wild there) one thinks of the Fauves and, more strongly by far, of van Gogh. The first did not yet exist; the second he cannot have heard of: yet there is the fierce color, and there is the powerful, living brushwork of the earth, a heavy dry impasto laid on as with a palette-knife, contrasting wonderfully with the thinly-painted sky. A second glance shows that the picture is entirely his own, entirely individual; a second thought makes it clear that these influences were utterly impossible; and one wonders how any professor can have had the confidence to teach this fourteen-year-old boy anything but the mere technique of his media.

The confidence was not lacking, however, and back in Barcelona that autumn the men at the Llotja continued to show him how to draw, while his father stretched him two big canvases for pictures that were designed to continue the modest success of the "First Communion" and lead on to sales, commissions, and a steady income. Don José went further than buying the raw materials and giving advice on their use; he even hired a studio for Pablo, in which the paint could be laid on. This first independent studio was in the Calle de la Plata, which runs down into the Calle de la Merced: the word studio, applied to those Picasso knew in Barcelona, does not mean a fine high airy place with a north light but simply a bare room, often very small and ill-lit, where he could work—where the mess would not matter; and here the word independent was strictly relative too, since the garret was only just round the corner from the family flat, within easy reach of parents.

One of these pictures, a bayonet charge (probably connected with the fighting in Cuba), has vanished: the other, which Don José planned and which he named "Science and Charity," shows a medical man taking the pulse of a sick woman, while a nun, holding a fair-sized baby, stands on the far side of the bed, proffering a drink (soup, says Sabartés). The doctor was Don José; the nun's habit was lent by a Sister of Charity from Málaga who now lived in Barcelona; and the genuine baby had been hired from a beggar-woman. Picasso made several drawings and studies in watercolor and oil for this picture; he worked hard on it, and the result pleased his family. "Science and Charity" was sent to the National Exhibition in Madrid, where it received a *mención honorífica* from the jury and a dart of facetious criticism from a journalist who thought the sick woman's lead-blue hand looked like a glove (which it does), and to the Provincial Exhibition at Málaga, where not unnaturally it was given a medal, nominally made of gold. The kindest thing that can be said about the picture is that technically it is most accomplished, that there were a great many far worse in the same tradition, and that it gave and still gives pleasure to those who like craftsmanship, anecdote, and realistic description. In any case it was the last work of this kind that he ever painted. It was his farewell to the academic tradition in which he had been brought up and which his world accepted; but the fact that he painted no more Science and Charities does not mean that he was yet the full Picasso, the anarchist whose aim was to destroy the false and flabby world of illustration by violence and to bring another, infinitely more meaningful, into existence, a painting that should purge by pity and terror in its own language and according to its own logic rather than provide ornament, prettiness, or transposed literature. At this time his revolt was still latent: he was still in many ways a boy, and protest, aesthetic or social, was still no more than protest within the context of the world in which he lived. But it was also a time at which he covered sheets of paper with all possible variants of his signature, including the *zz* for *ss* which is sometimes to be seen in his early pictures; and although it is perhaps going too far to say that this "anxious search" shows a doubt of his own identity, it may well be the sign of an underlying uneasiness soon to rise to the surface.

The rest of his stay at the Llotja was taken up with school studies and with his own drawing: his sketch-books are filled with much the same scenes as before, some of them frankly picturesque, though now the touch is even more confident and the variety of approaches greater, ranging from the purely traditional to a number of experiments in which the geometrical simplification of the essential forms is already apparent. Yet although the beginning of several possible points of departure from tradition can be made out in the drawings and pictures, the evolution, the progression, is not that of an iconoclast but of an extraordinarily gifted student who does not doubt the nature of his world—of Pablo rather than of Picasso.

And it was still as Pablo, the wonderful boy, that he packed his canvases and drawings for the summer holiday of 1897. It was not nearly so happy as those of former years, and although he was seen to take a lively interest in his cousin Carmen, and although his talents were celebrated at a feast attended by local artists, who had the effrontery to baptize him painter in champagne, he did comparatively little work.

His uncle Salvador had grown even more prosperous; he had recently married the forty-year-old niece of the Marqués of Casa-Loring, a great social advancement; he had a fine house on the Alameda itself, and he was looked upon as the head of the Ruiz family, some members of which he either helped or supported entirely. As such he disapproved of Pablo's way of signing his pictures Picasso, or P. R. Picasso, or at the best P. Ruiz Picasso. Don Salvador liked the pictures (he hung "Science and Charity" in a place of honor) but there were sides of his nephew's character that he did not care for at all. It may be that in imposing his authority as the protector and in making Pablo aware that he was a poor relation he overplayed his part, and it is certain that although Don Salvador himself suggested that Pablo should be sent to Madrid, to the Royal Academy of San Fernando, where his friends Moreno Carbonero and Muñoz Degrain were now influential professors, he nevertheless calculated the sum necessary for his nephew's support with all the sensible, contriving economy that the rich so often exercise on the poor's behalf. The Málaga medal turned out to be made of brass, only very, very thinly plated with gold. The sum was to be advanced by the Doctor, by Don Baldomero Chiara, María Picasso's brother-in-law, perhaps by some other relatives, and by Don José: it was to pay for his journey, his keep, his fees, and his materials.

"It must have been a small fortune," said Sabartés.

"I'll tell you what it was," replied Picasso.. "A mere vile pittance, that's what it was. A few pesetas. Barely enough to keep from starving to death: no more than that."

In the autumn of 1897 (the same year that an anarchist killed Canovas, the prime minister), the pittance carried him to Madrid, that expensive capital, where he found himself a room in the slummy Calle San Pedro Martir, in the heart of the town; and there he celebrated his sixteenth birthday. He had never been away from home before; he had never had to manage his own affairs or handle anything but pocket-money; and although the Ruizes had always been poor in the sense of having little or no superfluity, Pablo had no intimate, personal experience of true poverty; he had never lacked for food or warmth. This essential lesson was soon to come, but first he had to put his name down for the Academy—once called the Academia de Nobles Artes and familiar to Goya: much decayed since then, but still filled with his works—and to undergo the severe entrance examination.

He described himself on the form as a "pupil of Muñoz Degrain." He may have thought this a politic stroke or he may have wished to set himself off from his father. He cannot have meant it as a statement of fact.

But pupil of José Ruiz or of Muñoz Degrain, he passed the examination with stupefying ease, just as he had done at the Llotja; and the same amount of legend surrounds the feat.

Having been admitted with acclaim, he attended a few of the classes, found that they were as bad as the Llotja or worse, and then neglected the Academy entirely, except for its splendid collection of Goyas. There was no family routine to oblige him to go, and in any case he had all the wealth of the Prado just at hand, with time to absorb, copy, and enjoy El Greco, Velásquez, and Goya, who with van Gogh and Cézanne were the most important masters he ever knew.

A less obvious reason for his neglect was the presence of Muñoz Degrain and Moreno Carbonero at the Academy. They were both shockingly bad painters, and although Muñoz Degrain had some notion of light and although Carbonero was a good draughtsman, their canvases were the epitome of official art at its nadir. (There is some connection between size and worth in the official mind, and their pictures were often huge.) And they were not even competent: one vast Muñoz Degrain, preserved at Málaga, is the illustration of an anecdote about a man serenading a woman on a balcony; a cloaked rival, now slinking off, has shot him with a blunderbuss; and the woman's face has turned a startling green, as well it might, for her lover is *weltering in his gore.* It is so eminently, ludicrously, bad that at this distance of time one feels a glow of affection for the painter; but in 1897 this cannot have been the case with Picasso. As a small boy he had liked Muñoz Degrain: since then he had developed enormously, and although he had not yet made the decisive move to Modernismo, he was now surrounded by the greatest paintings that Spain had yet produced, and the contrast must have been painfully striking. At no period of his life was Picasso easily embarrassed, but meeting Muñoz Degrain just then must have been painful; and as for Moreno Carbonero, Picasso simply despised his teaching. He despised all Spanish teaching: "If I had a son who wanted to be a painter," he wrote to a friend at this time, "I should not keep him in Spain for a moment, and do not imagine I should send him to Paris (where I should gladly be myself) but to Munik (I do not know if it is spelt like that), as it is a city where painting is studied seriously without regard to set theories of any kind, such as pointillisme and all the rest. . . ."

In Madrid he found a class-mate from his first year at the Llotja, Francisco Bernareggi, an Argentinian; and when Picasso was not walking about the streets of the city, drawing indefatigably, they went to the Prado together and copied the pictures they admired. It is significant of Picasso's continuing respect for his father's judgment that they both sent their copies back to Don José in Barcelona. Velásquez, Goya, and Titian he approved of, but when they sent him their versions of El Greco he wrote, "You are taking the wrong path." Among Picasso's was a late Velásquez portrait of Philip IV, from which it is clear that the student had either not yet acquired the master's touch or that in his poverty he could not afford the master's materials, particularly his famous brushes. There is also a version of one of Goya's "Caprichos," the bawd and the whore who were to reappear so often in much later years, and a careful, affectionate drawing from an early nineteenth-century print of José Delgado, otherwise Pepe Illo, the illustrious Andalusian bullfighter and the author of *La Tauromaquia o Arte de Torear*, which Picasso was to illustrate sixty years later. He had something of Picasso, and of the Gypsy, in his amused, knowing, proud old face—he was close on fifty (ancient for a torero) when a bull killed him at last, in 1801. Bulls: all these years, from early Málaga to Madrid, Picasso had loved to see them live and die. The drawings and paintings that he made have not always been mentioned in their place, often being more by way of personal memoranda, but they run through his life, a constant presence.

The sketch-books are filled with his usual street-scenes, including some wonderfully drawn horses; and here again we see his preoccupation with his name. On one page Ruiz is written in careful capitals, each letter beneath the other: next to it P. Ruiz, ringed about with the kind of halo-line that he was using then, and not far off the initials P.R. several times repeated. And in some places we see the Picazzo that he had tried out before. This was at a time when his father had shown particular love and generosity.

The most striking of the drawings and paintings, however, are those which show his first steps towards Modernismo and indeed towards a world far beyond it. Two landscapes of the Buen Retiro, painted in misty fin-de-siècle colors, clearly point in that direction; and in a drawing labeled "Rechs the Pre-Raphaelite," with its symbolic oil-lamp, the connection is obvious. (The Pre-Raphaelite movement, though at its last tepid gasp, formed one of the heterogeneous ingredients of Modernismo.) And of course he was aware of the movement: in a letter written at this time he said, "I am going to make a drawing for you to take to the *Barcelona Cómica* to see if they will buy it. . . . Modernist it must be . . ." But there is also a group of gaunt chimneys rising above a wall that foreshadows an art from which anecdote and the picturesque are entirely banished, while unnamed forms, new or archaic, assume a vital significance; and an enigmatic window with an iron balcony, a subject to which he was to return again and again in later life.

Another friend he met in Madrid was Hortensi Güell, a young Catalan writer and painter from Reus, whose portrait he drew later in Barcelona, a few months before Güell killed himself. This was the first of Picasso's friends to commit suicide.

Young people are surprisingly frail, in spite of their ebullient spirits and elasticity, and there are times when misfortune or unkindness will destroy them: Picasso was working hard in Madrid, but he was never to be seen at the Academy. News of this reached Málaga. Rich Don Salvador saw it as another proof of Pablo's indiscipline, want of purpose, and defiance of established authority: he and the Málaga relations cut off their supplies. Don José, on the other hand, took Pablo's side; he maintained his contribution and even increased it as much as he could; but his £100 a year did not allow him to do much, and the pittance dwindled to subsistence-level or below. One of Picasso's many self-portraits, drawn considerably later, shows a thin adolescent, wan and pitifully young. Had he drawn it at the time, the face would have been more pinched by far. This cutting-off of his allowance came at a time when he was growing fast, and although he would probably never have reached his father's six foot however much he had been fed, a reasonable diet at this point might have added those few inches that make all the difference between a small man and one of average size. As it was, he remained short; and it is a matter of common observation that in men of a determined character, combativeness is in inverse proportion to height. Perhaps it was just as well: if Picasso had been as tall as Braque, would he ever have painted the "Demoiselles d'Avignon" or "Guernica"? At all events (and this is another instance of the peculiar and unpredictable sweetness that made part of his extremely complex and often contradictory character) he bore no grudge for this or many other affronts: when Don Salvador lay dying in 1908, Picasso wrote to his cousins Concha and María most tenderly, with obviously sincere anxiety and pain. Though to be sure since 1897 Don Salvador had paid for his nephew's exemption from military service.

The days passed, and winter came on: it comes early in Madrid, a city of extremes, perched on a bare steppe two thousand feet up, with icy blasts from the Sierra de Guadarrama, and it can be most bitterly cold even for a native, let alone a Mediterranean sun-worshiper like Picasso. Furthermore, the air is so desperately unhealthy even in a dead calm that it will, as the local proverb says, "kill a man, although it will not blow out a candle."

Between bouts of painting, Picasso moved house several times, following his harassed landlords as they fled from the bailiffs, always keeping to the same kind of street—San Pedro Martir, Jesús y María, Lavapiés—

never far from the great rag-fair of the Rastro. It was in the last of his garrets that the Madrid air and the effects of privation caught up with him. He fell ill with a violent fever, his throat was excoriated, his flayed tongue assumed the appearance of a strawberry, he came out in vermilion spots all over, the spots rapidly coalesced, and he presented the classic aspect of a patient suffering from scarlet fever.

The illness could be mortal then, but Picasso was tough. After some weeks of bed, losing his old skin and growing a new one, he was able to creep out for the *verbena* of San Antonio de la Florida, on June 12. These *verbenas* take place on the eve of the saint's day, and although no doubt they were pious in their origin, for centuries they have been little more than fairs, with a great deal of singing, dancing, drinking, and fornication of a secular, if not pagan, character: Picasso was not going to miss a moment of it.

Then he took the weary train to Barcelona, where home cooking, kindness, and his natural resilience restored his strength and spirits so quickly that a week or so later when Pallarès invited him to convalesce in the country air, at Horta, he accepted at once.

Horta, where Pallarès was born and where his parents lived, was a village of some two or three thousand people; or perhaps one should say a very small town, since it possessed a mayor, a doctor, and a *sereno*, a watchman who called the hours and the weather throughout the night and who represented the law: he also buried the dead. It stands on a steep small hill in the middle of a plain surrounded by mountains, and it lies in the high limestone country known as the Terra Alta, on the far limits of Cataluña, within sight of Aragón: it was then called plain Horta, or Horta de Ebro (though it is miles from the river), and now it is Horta de Sant Joan, a mayor of some sixty years ago having had a particular devotion to that saint.

Even now it is at the back of beyond: in 1898 it was more so. They took the train to Tortosa, where Pallarès' brother was waiting for them with a mule. They piled their easels, canvases, color-boxes, and baggage on to the mule and walked, first up the fertile valley of the Ebro, with its orange-groves still in flower and its rice-paddies, then they struck southward across the mountains for its tributary, the Canaleta. Sometimes one or another would perch himself on the baggage and ride for a while, but most of the time they walked, rising continually into a new air and a new vegetation—arbutus, rosemary, lentiscus, rock-rose, thyme—the highland country with vast stretches of bare mountain, forests of Aleppo pine, and wastes: only a few primitive villages in the fertile parts and an occasional isolated dwelling, a saw-mill where there was running water, a charcoal-burner's or a lonely shepherd's hut. The road dwindled as they went, and in fifteen miles or so it was no more than a mule-track. In a deep and sunless gorge, haunted by vultures, it wound about on either side of the rapid stream, crossing it by fords in the less dangerous places; but by the time they reached the end they had traveled close on twenty miles, and there were only two hours to go—only three or four more great mountains to cross and they would be home.

For one who had never been outside a town and who had never walked five and twenty miles in his life, even with the help of a mule, this was a striking introduction to a new world—a world in which it was natural to step out briskly in the falling dusk, because of wolves.

A new world for Picasso: an ancient world for its inhabitants. The Pallarès and their neighbors had lived in this remote village since the night of time, living off the land as people had always lived, long before ships plied from Barcelona. The ancient ways, language, skills, and values came naturally to them: Manuel Pallarès himself could carry a two-hundredweight sack on his shoulders, plough a field, saddle a mule, or milk a cow without having to think about it. His father owned land in the plain surrounding the village, and an olive-mill, renowned for the purity of its oil; and the family, together with their animals, lived in a big, rambling house built round a courtyard. It made a corner with the lane now called Calle Pintor Ruiz Picasso and the village square, a finely-conceived, dignified little plaza with the church on one side and deep, massively-pillared arcades, on the top of Horta's hill, the only flat place in it.

In these parts the peasants do not live out among their fields, but warned by Moorish raids, brigands, civil wars, and insurrections, they huddle together in little more or less fortified towns or villages. Horta is happy in its site, an abrupt, easily-defended mound, and the houses are tight-packed from top to bottom, a fascinating mass of lines, angles, and volumes; it is also happy in its local stone, and the church is a handsome building, ancient, but done up in the seventeenth century, at about the same time as Pallarès' house; while the smaller houses, which often bridge the lanes, are substantial, made to last for generation after generation: and they are mostly washed with blue.

In the evening the steep narrow streets (often rising in steps and always carefully ridged for hooves) are crowded with animals coming home: mules, asses, cows, goats, sheep, and a great many busy dogs. They live in byres and stables on the ground floor, among the domestic hens and rabbits, filling the town with a pleasant farmyard smell and warming their owners on the floor above; and early in the morning, woken by countless household cocks, they go out into the plain, a great saucer rimmed with mountains. It looks flat from a distance but in fact it undulates, and the less fertile higher ground is covered with almond-trees and olives; there are figs and vineyards too, but this is near the limit for grapes. All round the rim dry-stone terraces carry more olive-groves as high as they will go: an enormous investment over the centuries, not of money but of time and labor (they being unmarketable in that economy), for a minute return. The lower part of the plain is taken up with arable and pasture, in strips; but there is not a great deal of fertile land, and the people of Horta have to work very hard indeed to wring a living from it. This is not the misery of central and southern Spain, where absentee landlords own huge estates and where the landless peasants are hired by the day in a buyer's market, but it is a harsh life, and the possibility of disaster is always present. Apart from all the natural calamities of farming—cattle diseases, swine-fever, chicken-pest—the crops can often fail: moisture does not lie on limestone ground, and Horta is no great way from those parts of Aragón where wine is exchanged for water, in times of drought.

In 1897 their works and days had scarcely changed since Hesiod's time: the acceleration of history (in which Picasso was to play his outstanding part) had not touched the Terra Alta. On the contrary, with the chronic agricultural depression it had slowed down since the spurt of the seventeenth century, which had seen the rebuilding of Horta's church and the square. Theirs was still essentially subsistence-farming; a bad year, a drought, could bring death from starvation, and they knew it. There was little cash in Horta's economy and that little was guarded with extraordinary pains—heavy iron bars to the windows, deep peasant suspicion—an odd contrast with their overflowing hospitality. They practiced the ancient virtues of thrift and hard work; their ordinary diet was sparing, their feasts enormous, with measureless wine; they were intensely pious and correspondingly blasphemous, the commonest oath being "My shit in the face of God."

This may seem an unlikely background for a Llotja student, but Manuel Pallarès had early shown a gift for drawing, and although his father was of course the absolute ruler of the family, his patriarchal authority acknowledged by one and all, he was no more capable than another man of withstanding his wife's steady, unremitting pressure. He would have preferred to keep Manuel on the land, but he had three other sons, and in any case the gross materialism of the petty bourgeois is no part of the Catalan peasant's tradition. With tolerably good grace he resigned himself to parting with a capital farm-hand and with a considerable sum of money; and in time Manuel reached the Llotja, by way of Tortosa and a private art-school.

Manuel Pallarès had a typical Catalan head, round, male, far from beautiful, a good deal of space between his nose and his mouth, with shrewd good sense shining from it. He fitted into his place the moment he came home, helping with the innumerable chores of a farm—no airs or graces at all. There was little about the land he did not understand, from building a stack to gelding lambs; and since he was a passionate hunter he also knew a great deal about the mountains and the game that lived in them.

"Everything I know I learnt in Pallarès' village," said Picasso in later years: and "everything" included not only the use of the curry-comb and the scythe; an intimate acquaintance with the making of wine and oil; the harvesting of hay, corn, grapes, and olives; the shearing of sheep; the killing of a pig; and the milking of a cow; but also the ability to speak Catalan with total fluency as well as a deep understanding of essentials that no townsman can ever know directly.

But he and his friend were also there to paint, and to do this they retired to a cave, miles and miles away in the mountains, in an uninhabited, deeply-wooded region called the Ports del Maestrat, almost in Aragón. The cave was inadequate, uncomfortable, and shallow as well as being inaccessible, but they had the curious idea of painting two large compositions there. Picasso's father sent the canvas, the village carpenter made the stretchers, and they set off with a mule, provisions, a dog, a small boy, and Pallarès' younger brother, Salvador. They went as far as the mule could go, made a fire, and camped for the night in the open air. The next day, carrying their easels and color-boxes, Picasso and Pallarès climbed up through the forest and eventually found their cave. Here they stayed for weeks and weeks, painting, drawing, walking about, bathing in the nearby stream, collecting firewood and sometimes fossils. They slept on a deep bed of scented grass and leaves, and just outside the cave they kept a great fire burning until late at night: every few days Salvador brought them food—bread, wine, rice, beans, potatoes, stockfish, salt pork, oil—and among other things Picasso learned to cook. He had a knife that served to split kindling, peel potatoes, slice the fat bacon, and feed him at table: he kept it forever, and Josep Palau i Fabre, the Catalan poet to whom this account is due, he having had it from the mouth of Pallarès himself, saw it at Notre-Dame-de-Vie some sixty or seventy years later.

As the days grew shorter and the summer waned, thunder gathered in the mountains, and one night rain, driving right into the shallow cave, soaked them and all their belongings. A few days later a prodigious wind blew all night: at dawn they hurried to the place where they had been working, and they found that their pictures had been hurled far and wide, the stretchers broken. (Picasso had been busy with an Idyll and Pallarès with a Woodcutter.) They detached the canvases, lit the fire with the stretchers, and decided that this was enough. Salvador brought the mule, they loaded their battered pictures on to it, and returned to Horta.

In the village they found men back from Cuba, in a dismal state. The war with the United States was over; the island was nominally independent; Spain had suffered a most humiliating defeat. Yet this could have little effect upon a community that had never felt itself bound to Madrid by anything but taxes and conscription; the village welcomed the returning soldiers and then turned straight to its immediate, necessary tasks. Harvest would wait for no man, nor would the gathering of the grapes. The gutters ran purple with the washing of the lees, the presses creaked, and for weeks the lanes smelled of fermenting wine. Then came Saint Martin's day, and Horta echoed with the shrieks of dying swine: *their* blood did not run down the streets, however; it was carefully preserved for that local treat—the *butifarra,* a bloated, black-mottled sausage. And as the olives ripened, turning color as the winter advanced, they had to be beaten down or picked, and the great millstone began to turn, grinding out their oil.

Picasso helped wherever he could, but even saddling a mule or wielding a pitchfork has a knack to it: when the great dunghill in the central court was to be cleared away and taken to the fields he set to with the best will in the world, but presently his fork had to be taken away from him for his own protection, and he was put to carrying the dung in baskets and loading them into the paniers of the ass. He was well liked in the family and in the village, and when he went to the mill the people there would give him their particular delicacy, a great round of dark country bread, toasted, set to swim in the virgin oil, fished out when it began to sink, rubbed with garlic, sprinkled with salt, and eaten on the spot.

At other times, apart from making a great many drawings, he worked at a painting called "Aragonese Customs." It has not survived, but if a caricature in *Blanco y Negro* is to be believed, it was strictly representational—a woodcutter with an ax: a woman kneeling in the background. And he had the opportunity of painting what might have been an outstanding example of Spanish realism. The winter storms are furious in those parts, and during one of them an old woman and her grand-daughter were struck by lightning. In such cases an autopsy had to be carried out: the medical man invited Picasso and Pallarès, imagining that it would please them. His colleague should have come from Gandesa to help, but as it was raining he did not do so, and the doctor asked the *sereno* to proceed without him. All this took place in a dark night in a hut by the grave-yard. The *sereno* took the saw kept for the purpose, lifted the child from her coffin, placed her on a table, and sawed her head in two down the middle to satisfy the doctor as to the cause of death. He was smoking at the time, and as he worked, his hands and his cigar became deeply spat-tered. Then came the old woman's turn, but Picasso declined to stay for the second operation. Indeed, he did not even make a drawing of the first; yet might not this vertical division have had some effect upon his own treatment of the human head in later days?

Life in Horta during the autumn and winter of 1898 was not all work, however: far from it. Picasso and Pallarès often went for walks—one took them to Gandesa. twenty miles for trousers to replace those worn out in their cavé—and they often went to the village café. But these mild joys were nothing in comparison to the traditional feasts. Apart from All Hal-lows, with its chestnuts and new wine, and Christmas, there was St. An-thony's day in January, a most important festival at which horses, mules, asses, and sometimes oxen, beautifully groomed, adorned with plaits and ribbons, their hooves blacked and polished, are blessed outside the church, and at which the popular religious ballads called *goigs* are handed about, together with those prints, the remote ancestors of the strip-car-toon, which are called *auques* in Catalan and *aleluyas* in Spanish and which, in a series of charming woodcuts on a single sheet, show the chief events of a saint's life. Very often, in Catalan feasts, the people are un-able to wait for the day itself; and here too the main celebrations took place on St. Anthony's eve. They took the form of a kind of free-running play, with plenty of room for improvisation, in which the saint appeared, was tempted by as many demons and fair women as Horta and the sur-rounding hamlets could provide, and did resist. Picasso did not: at least he did not resist the prodigious quantity of wine drunk on these occasions, and was found fast asleep on the staircase of Pallarès' house.

This vitally important period of his life, in which he acquired new val-ues and a far wider understanding of the world, the best part of a year spent in completely new surroundings, produced no obvious, radical change in his drawing or his painting; and the volume of his work was un-derstandably less—for one thing, he lacked materials.

The drawing is even more assured, and there are some truly wonderful sheep and goats, studied essentially for their life and movement. The touch is more determined, and in some of the drawings he paid more at-tention to texture than before: in his intricate shading he used some meth-ods new to him, but his general approach was still the same, in spite of a greater interest in light and darkness and the use of a heavier outline for the figure. And still there is this preoccupation with his name: a peasant in wooden shoes, sitting on the ground in front of a broken pipkin, is surrounded by P. Picazzo Picasso Picaz P. Ruiz Picasso Picasso Picas.

In the paintings that have survived, much the same applies. Apart from the rural nature of the subjects, most of them might have been painted a year or so earlier; and there is one of a cart-shed which, with its strong light and deep brown shadow, harks back farther still.

Upon the whole the drawings are more obviously brilliant than the pictures. There is a timeless quality about very good drawing which is lacking in the fin-de-siècle colors he was sometimes using then; yet among the paintings there were some landscapes in which hindsight can see the seed of that Cubism which was to flower in Horta itself some ten years later and others which give the lie to the statement that Picasso took nothing from nature itself but saw the world only through other men's pictures, a statement made by those who had never seen this then invisible part of his work, and one upon which a great deal of theory has been founded.

However, of these pictures it was certainly "Aragonese Customs" that pleased Don José most. Before it vanished it won another honorable mention in Madrid, another piece of facetious criticism, and in Málaga another gold medal.

He finished this picture in February, 1899, waited for the paint to dry, rolled the canvas up, made his farewells, and returned to Barcelona. There could be no more convincing evidence of his amiability among those he esteemed than the fact that in spite of his having stayed with the Pallarès three quarters of a year, he was urgently pressed to come back again.

Chapter IV

Horta de Ebro had given Picasso a complete break, time and peace for reconsideration of everything that was important to him; it restored his health and strength to such a degree that he resisted the privation of the coming years; and even more important for the immediate future it provided him with the language of the country he lived in. He did know a little Catalan before going there, but he had not been obliged to use it: at Horta he swam in the language—not a word of Castilian around him for close on a year—and it had sunk in deeply. He now spoke it without effort, using the language, says Sabartés "exactly, and with no literary turns or affected phrases." Sabartés should have known, since he and Picasso went on speaking it together for the next sixty-nine years: but on the other hand, for Sabartés Picasso could do no wrong; and Cirici-Pellicer, a more objective witness, says that Picasso "usually employed a mixture of the two languages [Castilian and Catalan], which made his manner of expressing himself eminently picturesque." Certainly he wrote it incorrectly. He was no good at languages: in 1911, after years and years of Paris, a monoglot French mistress, and the perpetual company of French friends he could still begin a letter *"iyer de toute la journé je ne ai pas eu de letre de toi"*; and to the end of his life he never lost his very heavy Spanish accent nor his highly individual approach to the French language.

Picasso had a brilliant and original mind, but it did not do its important work in words; it was not primarily a verbal mind. It traveled into regions where words are either non-existent or irrelevant; he worked out no consistent verbal theory whatsoever, and his dicta on art can be made to say anything at all. He did utter some fine aphoristic flashes, some of which he undoubtedly meant; but what he really had to say he said in paint, sculpture, and line. He loathed art-criticism, analysis, and verbal aesthetics: his philosophy is to be seen on the wall, and rightly taken it is all of a piece.

[64

But as far as Catalan is concerned he was certainly fluent and perfectly comprehensible, and this meant that on returning to Barcelona he could form an integral part of the group of writers, painters, and poets who met at Els Quatre Gats, a café or tavern or beer-hall or cabaret modeled on Rudolphe Salis' Chat Noir and Aristide Briant's Mirliton in Montmartre. They were a mixed body of men, differing widely in tastes and abilities, but they were united in their love for Modernismo and for their own language: an habitué speaking only Spanish would have been an intruder. And since some were anarchists, believing that the new world would dawn when the last king was strangled with the guts of the last priest, and most were Catalan separatists, there might have been some danger in admitting an outsider to their intimacy. (Not that this should be exaggerated: the real, the hard-line anarchists who tried to put Bakunin's ideas into practice were almost exclusively working-men, whereas the conscientious bohemians of the Quatre Gats belonged to the middle class—their anarchism was theoretical, and their separatism did not go far beyond singing "Els Segadors," the nationalist song.) Picasso was well introduced, however; not only did he speak the language, but he already knew several of their members; and within a few weeks of his return he was perfectly at home there.

The Quatre Gats was founded in the summer of 1897 by a versatile character named Pere Romeu, who had taught gymnastics and run a puppet-show in Mexico; he had traveled a good deal, and at one time he worked at the Chat Noir. The name may have been chosen to avert ill-luck, since it means "nobody" or "almost nobody."

"Were there many people in the procession?"

"Four cats, no more."

Whether the charm was intended or not, it worked: the place was thronged with people, mostly of the kind to whom this announcement, printed in a kind of blackletter, was directed:

"To persons of good taste, to citizens on either side of the Ramblas, to those who require nourishment not only for their bodies but also for their minds.

"Pere Romeu informs them that from the twelfth day of the month of June, in the Calle Montesión, the second house on the left as one goes from the Plaza de Santa Ana, there will be opened an establishment designed to provide both enchantment for the eye and good things for the pleasure of the palate.

"This house is an eating-place for the epicure, a glowing hearth for those who long for the warmth of a home, a gallery for those who seek delights for the soul, a tavern for those who love the shade of the vine and the true essence of the grape, a Gothic beer-garden for lovers of the north, an Andalusian patio for those of the south; it is a house of healing for those who suffer from the sickness of our century, a refuge of friendship and harmony for those who shelter beneath its roof.

"They will not be sorry to have come, but on the other hand they will certainly regret having stayed away."

The Calle Montesión was an out-of-the-way little street on the then unfashionable northern edge of the old town: the house was the work of the young architect Puig y Cadafalch, to some extent a follower of Gaudí and a whole-hearted, unselective lover of Modernismo. Els Quatre Gats had a great many beams, a great deal of ironwork wrought into bulbous, vegetable, art-nouveau shapes, a fully arched brick entrance, and a general Teutonic air of phony medievalism in keeping with the atmosphere in the Barcelona avant-garde of the time, which was much influenced by Wagner and by the north in general, including England, as well as by France. At the back it had a large room for shadow-plays (like the Chat Noir) and puppet-shows; and this room was also used for exhibitions.

The ingredients that went to make up Modernismo ranged from Ruskin, the Pre-Raphaelites and beaten copper on the one hand to Bakunin, Nietzsche and El Greco on the other, with Hiroshige, Schopenhauer, Hegel, Kate Greenaway and a morass of cheap sentimentality in between. Naturally there were a great many contradictions in the Quatre Gats, a fair amount of silliness, and some of its customers were hangers-on of the arts who dressed up as decadents or anarchists and gave it to be understood that they were consumptives or syphilitics or both; but the senior members of the group were men of talent.

The most important of these were Santiago Rusiñol, Ramón Casas and Miguel Utrillo. Rusiñol was a painter and poet twenty years older than Picasso: he was one of the leading figures in the movement, and it was he who organized the Fiestas Modernistas at Sitges, where he built the neo-Gothic Cau Ferrat and saw to the erection of a monument to El Greco. During these fiestas he uttered fluent, cloudy, mystical, enthusiastic orations, in one of which he exhorted his hearers "to translate the eternal verities into wild paradox; to draw life from the abnormal, the extraordinary, the outrageous; to tell the horror of the reasoning mind as it gazes upon the chasm, the earthquake-crash of disaster, and the creeping dread of the imminent; to descry the unknown, to foretell fate," and thus to practice an art "at the same time resplendent and nebulous, sophisticated and barbaric, medieval and modernist." He did not tell them how to do it however, and the only book of his the writer has seen is innocuous, sentimental, and pretty. Yet he was a fairly good painter, infinitely beyond

Muñoz Degrain or Carbonero, and he did write articles in the *Vanguardia*, the great Barcelona daily and probably the best paper in the country, supporting the Impressionists and the Symbolists when they were virtually unknown in Spain, and he did love El Greco. Picasso did not need Rusiñol's example to do the same—writing from Madrid in 1897 he had spoken of "El Greco's magnificent heads"—but it may have strengthened his admiration: at all events in that same year of 1899 he painted an "El Greco figure," a dark and impressive, rather diabolical, long, bearded face with something of the Cretan's own technique. And the fact that there was something eminently sound in Rusiñol's ideas may have helped the rest of the oration down: Picasso did not hear it—he was in La Coruña at the time—but Rusiñol was a great one for speeches (J. M. de Sucre says that he gave Picasso a copy of these "Oraciones" illustrated by Miguel Utrillo and Suzanne Valadon) and like most orators he was given to repeating himself—in any case his views were shared by the rest of the group, and with variations they were to be heard daily at the Quatre Gats. Not the slightest relation of direct cause and effect is here suggested, but the absurd thing is that in the course of his life Picasso did in fact fulfill something closely resembling Rusiñol's excited program; although to be sure he was never nebulous or medieval and there is something to be said for the view that he was never modern either, but outside time: a painter modern for us only by the accident of contemporaneity.

Casas and Utrillo were also painters and writers, and between them they ran *Pèl i Ploma*, the Catalan literary and artistic review. Both were successful men, and both, like Rusiñol, had lived and studied in Paris, where Miguel Utrillo acted as the *Vanguardia*'s correspondent and where he met Suzanne Valadon, to whose son Maurice he gave his name. Utrillo was also one of the earliest and most percipient authorities on El Greco.

Generally speaking the other men Picasso met there were younger: far and away the most important was Nonell, whose painting he admired and even more his drawing; then there were Casagemas, Junyer, and Andreu, with whom he went to Paris; Manolo Hugué the sculptor, whom he helped until the end of his days; Sebastià Junyent, who went mad; Josep Xiro, who did the same; Joachim Mir (he and Picasso exchanged portraits); Brossa the anarchist; Zuloaga, who turned Fascist in Franco's time and denounced his former friend; Eugenio d'Ors, who wrote the well-known *Pablo Picasso* and other studies; Sabartés, who looked after his affairs for the last thirty-odd years of his life; the brothers Reventós and many, many others.

One of the reasons why he had time for making all these friends in spite of working as hard as usual—and the number of pictures and drawings from these years is very great—is that shortly after his return from Horta in February, 1899, he and his father disagreed.

Being a father is generally acknowledged to be an ungrateful trade; being a son is another—Zeus and Saturn found it an impossible relationship. Don José was then rising sixty, an age at which nine months count for very little; Pablo was seventeen, when less than that makes the difference between a boy and a man. He had just come back from a long period of total independence, with no one to speak to him in parental terms; and it would have been strange if they had not disagreed.

He left home and spent several weeks in a bawdy-house. He cannot possibly have been a guest who paid in cash, but he returned the girls' kindness by decorating the walls of the room in which they sheltered him. The location of the murals (covered over long since, no doubt) and the exact sequence of events has eluded the researches of even Josep Palau, yet it is probable that it was after the brothel had fulfilled its didactic purpose that he moved in with his friend Santiago Cardona, the brother of the sculptor he had known at the Llotja. Picasso had a small room where he worked and slept, and its window gave on to the Calle d'Escudellers Blancs, a narrow, densely-populated street leading from the Ramblas towards the cathedral: it was here that he was painting in April, 1899. The other rooms were devoted to the making of corsets, and at intervals of painting and drawing Picasso loved to operate the machine that made the holes for the necessary tapes; since the workmen liked him, as workmen always did, he could indulge himself as much as ever he chose.

The break with his family was neither violent nor lasting, however; there are kindly drawings of his father from this period, and his sister often came to see him. And it was here, too, in this little room, that later in the same year Sabartés first met Picasso, brought by a fellow sculpture-student, Mateo de Soto. "Science and Charity" was leaning up against a wall, together with "Aragonese Customs," and Picasso, among piles of drawings and sketchbooks, was busy at another painting for which Soto was the model. His piercing black gaze put his diffident visitor out of countenance; the pictures and the drawings quite overcame him; and when they said good-bye Sabartés bent in a kind of respectful bow. This was the beginning of what may be called a friendship, according to one's definition of the word, and of what must be called a domination that lasted, with one long interruption when Sabartés was in America, until his death in 1968.

For Dr. Johnson every conversation was a contest for superiority: this was also true of Picasso, and there were few relationships in which he did not quickly establish himself as the dominant partner. Later in his life, when he could bring world-wide notoriety and great wealth into play, victory was fatally easy; but even at this stage, when he was eighteen, penniless and unknown, he was accepted as a leading figure at the Quatre Gats, even by those who can have had little notion of his talent and even by those who disliked him.

It was not that he talked much at the Quatre Gats; in fact he was often silent, moody, withdrawn, absorbed or apparently bored, as well he might have been with some of the morphine creeps who frequented the place—he was always easily bored, and more easily as the years went by. But when he did speak he spoke well, often wittily, and always with the unconscious authority of a man who could already draw and paint better than any of the artists there except perhaps Isidro Nonell.

A man: in some ways certainly a man. Much of his painting had been fully mature these four or five years past. But he was not yet formed: he had read little, he had had virtually no formal education, and in the nature of things he had very little experience of adult life; what is more, the child Pablo still lived on in him then, as it was to live on for the rest of his life, with comic hats, false noses (and child-fresh painting) at the age of ninety.

At this time he was beginning to work out his own aesthetic, an aesthetic destined to destroy painting as it was then conceived and to thrust the boundaries of perception far beyond their known limits: one is tempted to say "to enlarge the idea of beauty" except for the fact that Picasso was primarily concerned with *being* rather than with what is ordinarily understood by that vague word beauty. "Beauty?" he said to Sarbatés, ". . . To me it is a word without sense because I do not know where its meaning comes from nor where it leads to."

It was an enormously ambitious project, and it was accompanied by self-doubt, periods of depression, and false starts: one does not shatter one's own matrix, eat one's own father, without some hesitation; yet in ten years from this time it was largely accomplished. Already the results of the process were evident in the prodigiously rapid development of his work in 1899 and 1900; but as a wholly conscious process it was only just beginning, and the milieu in which it began helps to explain at least some of the external forces acting upon it.

As I said earlier, Picasso has often been compared to Goethe, and certainly they had much in common, including the "virtue of lasting" and an extraordinary physical vitality; but whereas Goethe was an insider, solidly based in his social and national contexts, endowed with an elaborate education and with money, and supported on all sides by the culture of his time, Picasso was socially peripheral, his sense of national identity was at least troubled, his schooling had scarcely passed the elementary stage, and the culture of his time, such as it was, oppressed him on every hand. His eventual aim was to revolutionize a great part of this culture, and apart from his native genius all he had to help him in his intellectual formation for the task were his contacts in Barcelona and his early years in Paris: the Quatre Gats and Montparnasse were to be his Leipzig and Strassburg, his Greek, Latin, and philosophy.

As far as it was political at all, the general feeling at the Quatre Gats was of course left-wing. In this it was opposed to the Cercle Artístic de Sant Lluc, the respectable haven of the academic painters, good Catholics, patronized by Church, state, and big business. The two groups did resemble one another in being separatist and in the fact that at least some of the Sant Llucs were devoted to Modernismo—Gaudí himself was a member—but as far as religion was concerned they were poles apart. The Sant Llucs sympathized with the strong rise of right-wing Catholicism so evident in Spain during the long regency of the Habsburg Queen Christina: whereas at the Quatre Gats, although plenty of mysticism was to be found, it was mostly of the cloudy, imported kind, pantheistic, wooly, scarcely of the native growth at all; and since there was also a strong anarchist element, downright atheism was sometimes added to the left-wing anticlericalism—a striking contrast to a young man fresh from the age-old rural piety of Horta de Ebro.

The anarchism, in its more general implications, struck a responsive chord in him: Picasso was increasingly conscious of the misery caused by the system and its injustice—the evidence lay all about him in Barcelona—and his awareness was increased by Nonell. In 1896 Nonell, who was eight years older than Picasso and who had been drawn to Modernismo earlier, went to Caldas de Bohí, a village with hot springs right up in the mountains, under the Maladetta, and notorious for its goitrous idiots. He made a series of drawings of them which he exhibited in the hall of the *Vanguardia* and at the Quatre Gats. They are masterly, disturbing drawings, with a strong, fluid line enclosing the highly simplified figures. They may be said to belong to Art Noveau, but they injected a vital hardness into the milk-and-water lakes and fairies, chlorotic maidens stuff produced by Puvis de Chavannes, Maurice Denis, and so many others at the time, and they made a considerable sensation. Nonell's was a direct expression of true, unsentimental sympathy: when Picasso produced his hospital patients in the article of death and his raddled whores it is tempting to say that he went one better, for here the savagery is not only far more intense, but it is unjudging, a flat statement—empathy rather than sympathy. Yet, "one better" implies competition or at least influence, and it is dangerous to speak of influence where Picasso is concerned. So much was already implicit in his early work and he had preconceived so many tendencies before their public birth elsewhere that an apparent influence is often no more than another man's discovery of something that Picasso had already found out for himself—a discovery more fully developed, perhaps, by the kindred spirit (van Gogh comes to mind), but not radically new to Picasso. In this case the savagery, the guts, which both he and Nonell brought to Modernismo was perfectly evident in Picasso's childish work; and in this case as in so many others "reinforcement" is nearer the mark than "influence."

Anarchism too had formed part of his early outlook, and the talk at the Quatre Gats can have done little more than illustrate and encourage an existing hatred for authority and a determined rejection of rules imposed from without.

The most esteemed anarchist at the Quatre Gats was young Jaume Brossa: he had no great opinion of the artists he beheld there—"neurotic dilettanti, only concerned with being different from the philistines and the bourgeois"—but he did feel that there was promise for the art of the coming century, the anarchists' secular millennium. "Man, carried away by a just and iconoclastic pride, the result of the psychological atmosphere created in his intelligence, will no longer tolerate the slightest barrier to his free-ranging mind; and this exaltation of the individual means that not a single myth, not a single idol, not a single entity, human or divine, will remain to stand in the way of the total liberation of individuality. Some people may say that these theories imply a general dissolution; but as well as a negative they possess a positive spirit, one that renews and builds up lost powers and forces," he wrote. And referring once more to the cult of the individual, of the Me, Brossa said, "it leads to a turning in upon oneself . . . and in its turn this withdrawal leads to the discovery of a compensation for disgust with life, that is to say the wonderful image of the world that lies deep in the camera obscura of the Me." As Cirici-Pellicer observes, one could scarcely ask a fairer picture of Picasso's progress. Destruction, repeated destruction, withdrawal from apparent reality, synthesis, new worlds, new powers, new visions: everything is here, including, it is to be hoped, compensation for some degree of disgust with life.

There was a great deal in the political anarchists' creed that appealed to Picasso: Bakunin, for example, had said, "The passion for destruction is also a creative passion," and nothing could have harmonized better with his own views.

But although Brossa had clear notions of their ideology, he did not succeed in passing them on to Picasso, who was never a political animal. Nor did he succeed in passing on the anti-Semitism that infects some of Nietzsche's followers, for Picasso, although given to superstition, was far, far too strong a personality for that kind of self-inflating myth.

What Picasso did draw in was a generalized anarchism and a deep sympathy for Catalan independence: the people around him preached contempt for bourgeois art, which some of them produced, and hatred for intellectual snobbery, which most of them practiced, but the very young and ingenuous Picasso either did not notice their inconsistencies or did not find them shocking: whether he needed the encouragement of the Quatre Gats or not, he remained the very type of anti-bourgeois, antisnob all the rest of his days,

The disastrous war with America, the loss of Cuba, Puerto Rico, and the Philippines, had plunged Madrid into gloom, introspection, and pessimism: it had no such effect on Barcelona, where, in spite of labor troubles, agitation, bombs, and repression the mood was sanguine, forward-looking, interested in the outer world. At the Quatre Gats Picasso swam in an atmosphere of Ibsen, Tolstoy, Wagner—an Associación Wagneriana met there regularly from 1900—Schopenhauer, the Symbolists, Nietzsche, Maeterlinck, Verhaeren, all new and exciting names in Catalonia; and although he was no great reader he came by at least a second-hand notion of their ideas.

He was no great reader. In their love for him some of his friends have maintained that he was: they admit that they never saw him with a book in his hands, but they assert that he read in bed, by night, and they mention books that he owned—Verlaine, for example, at a time when Picasso could neither read, write, nor speak French. Yet Picasso was one of the hardest-working painters, sculptors, draughtsmen, etchers that ever lived: "Where do I get this power of creating and forming? I don't know. I have only one thought: work. I paint just as I breathe. When I work I relax; doing nothing or entertaining visitors makes me tired. It's still often three in the morning before I switch off my light," he said to Beyeler. He was also extremely convivial—loved a late gathering of friends; his days were full and sometimes his nights as well, since he loved working by artificial light. And as it made him uneasy to spend his idle nights alone he nearly always had a companion: not one of these companions has ever spoken of his reading in bed.

He illustrated books magnificently; he owned a considerable number, some of the greatest bibliographical interest; but he did not read a great many. This is not to say that he was not a keenly intelligent man, capable of profound understanding; yet his was an exceedingly quick and sometimes impatient mind, not very well suited for the slow accumulative absorption of prose. Verse was another matter: here the concentrated essence could be grasped almost as quickly as a picture or a carving; Picasso certainly read poetry and he certainly loved poets all his life— Max Jacob, Guillaume Apollinaire, Paul Eluard, to name but three. To be a poet was a passport to his kindness.

On the other hand he was always surrounded by men who did read enormously, some of them brilliant writers themselves; and his keen, retentive intelligence gathered more from their distillation than years in a library would have given him. As far as Barcelona was concerned, Nietzsche was available to him through the medium of Joan Maragall, one of the best of the Catalan poets and a great translator from the German. Picasso liked and admired Maragall, as well he might, for not only did Maragall destroy rhetorical convention and "risk his life on every line," but his *Excelsior* was a noble expression of faith in the future of art for those brave enough to launch far out into unknown seas. Then again Nietzsche's aphoristic manner was perfectly suited to Picasso: when the philosopher died in the summer of 1900, at the term of his long madness, the papers were filled with appreciations of him; and Picasso undoubtedly read papers. 1900 was also the year that saw the first performance of *Tristan* and *Siegfried* in Barcelona (well before Madrid, of course), and although no music other than his native *cante hondo* or the Catalan *sardana* ever meant much to Picasso, he was necessarily affected by the admiration for things of the North so general in Barcelona at the time.

The North was a capital place, seen from the shores of the Mediterranean: not only was it medieval—and the middle ages were golden to the Catalans—but it was modern too, with advanced ideas on sexual freedom. The area included Norway—Munch was already known in Barcelona, as well as Ibsen—and when the young Picasso was asked to illustrate a poem called *El Clam de les Verges* he produced a somewhat Expressionist young woman dreaming of a Man (his upper half floats in the middle distance of the night).

The poem and its illustration appeared on August 12, 1900, in *Joventut*, *Pèl i Ploma*'s rival, whose artistic editor was Alexandre de Riquer, a member of the Cercle de Sant Lluc; and some of it reads:

We are maidens, maidens
By the force of hateful laws that keep us enslaved.
Night and day we seek the wild delights that we dream of . . .

If the mind is not virgin must the body be so?
No, no, let us be free, let us take pleasure in love!
Tear our white virginal robe: it is a shroud,
A shroud, and a frail one, hiding a treasure within.

Obviously the poem was written by a man, Joan Oliva Bridgman, but it does express a modest hope of what might be, and it is typical of the climate of the time. So is another, also written by Oliva and illustrated by Picasso: the excited verse, which begins "To be or not to be," calls upon the reader to banish the dark smoke of base routine with the sacred light that pierces the shades of mystery—the reader is to *be* fully or not at all. There is no mention of the sea, favorable or otherwise, but Picasso, perhaps with Maragall in mind, drew a man guiding a boat through menacing waves towards the horizon.

The North also embraced England, Oscar Wilde and Aubrey Beardsley, and at one time Picasso had some faint notion of going there; this was less out of love for the Pre-Raphaelites than from an opinion he had formed of Englishwomen from an account of the intrepid Lady Hester Stanhope. Señora Romeu was said to be an Englishwoman, while Señora Maragall was certainly related to the British Dr. Noble who built a seamen's hospital in Málaga, and perhaps he found they did not quite answer his expectations; at all events London very soon yielded to Paris.

The North was the vague metaphysical goal; for most of the painters and literary men of the Quatre Gats Paris was the immediate and concrete aim. Quite apart from its being the center of artistic life and of everything that was new, it was accessible: all educated Catalans and a great many others spoke French, whereas few knew German and fewer still English—they were persuaded that Wilde was a poet. Many of the older men and some of the others had already been to Paris, bringing back a cloud of glory—Nonell had even exhibited in Parisian galleries. And it was Paris that provided the reviews, papers, and magazines that Picasso saw at the Quatre Gats.

There were many others, such as Casas' and Utrillo's *Pèl i Ploma*, Alexandre de Riquer's *Joventut, Catalunya Artística*, and the English *Studio*, but it was the French *Assiette au Beurre*, the *Gil Blas illustré*, the *Figaro*, and the famous *Revue Blanche* that introduced him to Théophile Steinlen, Jean Louis Forain, and above all to Henri de Toulouse-Lautrec.

These and the company of his many friends was his spiritual food. What he did for earthly nourishment it is difficult to say; and some of the self-portraits of these years show him looking wan and hungry. But he did sell a few drawings and pictures; Romeu commissioned advertisements and menu-cards; and Barcelona had many small shops up and down the Ramblas that specialized in *tapabocas*, little dishes to be eaten cheaply at any hour of the day or night: a shallow pipkin of sparrows stewed in their own juice was to be had for little more than a farthing, and although blackbirds or squids in their ink came dearer they were still very moderate, particularly as bread was thrown in; and bull's flesh was cheap after corridas.

At all events he ate well enough to go for long walks. Sabartés mentions their expeditions to Tibidabo, the mountain that stands some five or six miles behind Barcelona, giving a magnificent view of the whole spreading city, the harbor, the sea, and the remote sierras: a heartbreaking climb for which all but the most energetic of the penniless young take the funicular railway. And to do an immense amount of work: he had moved from the Calle d'Escudellers Blancs to a large, unfurnished, well-lit garret workshop on the top floor of number 17, Riera de Sant Joan, high in the old city, which he shared with his friend Carlos Casagemas, a strange-looking young man, well educated (he had been trained for the Spanish navy until the American war put an end to any hope of a career in it), the son of the United States consul-general in Barcelona. Since there was no furniture they painted it on the walls: tables, chairs, chests, a sofa, the necessary safe, together with servants, a maid and a boy, to look after it. And wherever the furniture left room there were pictures, pictures that overflowed on to the walls of the ladder-like staircase.

No doubt many of them were outrageous; he always had a strong earthy sense of fun—to the end of his days shocking people amused him—and it was even stronger then. For example, on the ground floor of the house there was a grocery that sold fresh eggs from Villafranca, and he was attached to the daughter of the shop, so much so that he produced an advertisement for the eggs. The great men of the Quatre Gats, Rusiñol, Casas, Utrillo, and the rest, appeared, each holding an egg: the point of the advertisement was a comparison of their testicles with the eggs, from which it appeared that the fresh eggs of Villafranca were larger.

But there were others too, and if only they had been preserved or even photographed we should have a fascinating account of his development at this crucial stage when an infinity of potentialities were opening in his mind and when he was making those deliberate elections that were to prove vital for him and for the art of the twentieth century. Yet although the camera was usual by then and although he was highly valued by those who knew him, nobody recorded them in any way. Would there have been a hint of the sharp angles and interlocking planes of Horta de Ebro, a longing for the clean straight line after the curving lilies and languors of Art Nouveau, a precursor of Cubism? A foretaste of the Blue Period, so soon to come?

They valued him highly; and a group of his friends, Pallarès, Sabartés, and Casagemas among them, urged him to give a show of his drawings at the Quatre Gats, a show that would in a way be a challenge to the able, accomplished, established, and fashionable draughtsman Casas. Several men had shown there: Casas himself, Rusiñol, Utrillo, Nonell, Pichot, Canals, Mir, and Opisso. Picasso liked the idea, and in the winter of 1899/1900 he set to work on a series of portrait-drawings of the Quatre Gats habitués. Most of his friends appeared in this gallery. Among them Sabartés, slim in those days, but even then myopic, even at nineteen wearing that expression of weak meek obstinacy, skepticism, and deep unshakable self-satisfaction that is more apparent in some of the portraits of later years—a born and willing victim. Nonell, a strong round Mediterranean head, secretly amused, not unlike Picasso himself. (Indeed, almost alone among all those self-conscious people, affected, bearded, pipe-smoking for the most part, Picasso and Nonell had the look of real men, fully alive, who had wandered onto a stage full of minor actors playing dull, unimportant roles forever and ever, stilted creatures, devoured by their self-chosen parts.) Lluisa Vidal, one of the few women of the group, a former pupil of Eugène Carrière in Paris and a great admirer of his. Carlos Casagemas, who had an exhibition at the Quatre Gats just after his room-mate, Picasso: an anxious, haunted face, narrow, all jutting nose and receding chin: he was impotent, but it was not generally known at the time. Manuel Hugué, another fully human being, an admirable sculptor, extremely idle and utterly unreliable, much loved by the friends upon whom he lived, though forever penniless and somewhat given to stealing their possessions: the bastard son of a Spanish general, perhaps, and ordinarily called Manolo. Manuel Pallarès, who was less often to be seen with Picasso these days because of a long-drawn-out and difficult love-affair, but who remained a firm friend. Ramon Pichot, a painter, one of a large family all devoted to the arts, who lived in wild disorder in the splendid Calle Montcada—splendid not in the modern sense, with light and tree-lined space, but in that of the middle ages: a dark and malodorous lane, yet one lined with Gothic, Renaissance, and baroque palaces opening onto secret inward patios; one of them, restored, is now the Picasso Museum. (The Catalan version of Pichot is Pitxot, just as Carlos Casagemas comes out as Carles Casagemes: here I use the forms they used themselves in France.) Opisso, a talented draughtsman and the son of the *Vanguardia*'s art-critic: although in after days he told Cirici-Pellicer that "because of Picasso's reserved character it was difficult to assert that they had ever really been friends." In the same passage Cirici-Pellicer speaks of a somewhat later studio belonging to Soto where Picasso came to work and which he so filled with his own things and his own powerful personality that even Soto took to calling it "Picasso's studio"; and he goes on to say, "This quite describes the overpowering, encroaching nature of the future creator of Cubism: those who knew him when he was young all agree that . . . one could only worship him or hate him. His worshipers have told us of his charm, his sound, quick, precise, clear-cut judgment, his immense gifts for improvisation and for perfect imitation [he could instantly produce a pastiche of any known artist, and this talent, indulged with unthinking freedom, brought the charge of plagiarism from the envious or the obtuse], his way of drawing a nude, starting with a toe and sweeping round with one sure, unfaltering line, and of his wonderful steadfast perseverance in his work. . . . On the other hand, his enemies have told us of his pig-headedness, his boundless self-confidence, his skill at seeing just where he could make a way for himself, and of his contempt for the work of those around him."

This is not wholly objective testimony: Cirici-Pellicer was out of sympathy with Picasso's later work; Opisso knew no fame comparable to Picasso's, but remained set in the late nineteenth century, when, he affirms, the work of the one could be mistaken for the work of the other: so much so that a collector once gave ten thousand pesetas for a charcoal drawing by Opisso, supposing it to be a Picasso. Yet it is worth recording because of the light it throws on the reactions of his friends to the eighteen-year-old Andalou, a small, commanding figure of no physical size at all but of a caliber hitherto unknown.

The drawings and a few other works were ready in February, 1900. Neither Picasso nor his friends could afford frames, so they were hung with drawing-pins, more or less at haphazard. The general effect was indifferent, and from the commercial point of view amateurish: nothing like the smooth efficiency of the Saló Parés, where the citizens of Barcelona were accustomed to buying their pictures.

Drawing has always been less generally valued than painting, and at that time, in spite of Casas' success, it was held in particularly low esteem. A contemporary artist has given the scale of values that obtained in Barcelona at the end of the nineteenth century: first the painter of religious subjects; he was a somebody, a señor. Second the portraitist: he was understood to possess a natural gift for catching a likeness and he was granted the respect due to a photographer. Third the landscape and genre painter, and he was little better than a halfwit. Last, and far below any classification by number, the draughtsman: he was scarcely an artist at all. And in this case the draughtsman was known to come from Andalucía, the home of idleness, levity, Gypsies, bullfighters, and wild extravagance, and to be absurdly young. He had no network of cousins, no local interest. Few people came, apart from the artist's friends; and of those few none bought.

In the end the unsold drawings passed to Pere Romeu; he gave some to their originals, and after his death his widow sold the rest, many to the Barcelona collector Graells.

But these amounted to only a small part of Picasso's work in 1899 and 1900. What can usefully be said of the countless drawings, the great number of paintings of these eighteen months? Only that they range from what academic realism ought to be to Modernismo and beyond, a range that includes a kind of proto-Fauvism and Expressionism, together with darts in many other directions, most of them enough to satisfy the most exigent, and some deliberate reminiscences of El Greco and Toulouse-Lautrec. Yet just as "influence" has little meaning as far as Picasso is concerned, so isms do not signify a great deal: they never really fit him and he never even fits his own, or rather those that theoreticians impose upon him; nor his "periods" either. Both isms and periods are mentioned in this book, since they do have a certain utility, but they are mentioned sparingly and with strong reserves: apart from such clearly-conceived theories as Divisionism most seem to be post hoc, approximate labels, fortuitous in origin and often misleading in application.

On the other hand, a repeated theme, a steady preoccupation, is something else again; and at this time Picasso was particularly concerned with windows, as he had been earlier and as he was to be again. The first of the present series is quite straightforward, a drawing of the window over the way from his in the Calle d'Escudellers, a window with a young woman in it, sewing: she is labeled Mercedes. The next is the same window, but closed and blind: a painting this time—the gray house, the iron bars of the balcony, the yellow curtain behind the glass, all strangely important. Then comes a painting of his own window, the lower part veiled with a piece of translucent cloth: just that and nothing more. The cloth is suffused with amber light; the dark brown crossbars and frame stand out against the pale, featureless day beyond. The picture belongs entirely to the twentieth century; it is devoid of literature and it is profoundly satisfying: it is the truth, or *a* truth and a significant one, about that window and that light. Nothing could be farther from Art Nouveau.

After that another window, closed but showing a suggestion of a land-scape beyond, green and white: the room is dark, the inner window-sill is draped with something so deeply gray as to be nearly black; and here again there is that feeling of great unspecified significance.

Still more windows appear, but not alone; they form part of sick-bed or death-bed scenes (his concession to the "decadence" of the time), and they are always closed. In later years Picasso's windows grew broader; they were often wide open to a world full of sun and color and doves. But in these Barcelona days only one swings back to let the glow of the tawny, sunlit town into the vague gloom of the room: Lola Ruiz stands in front of it, wearing a ghostly white dress. There is something white on the floor beside her, possibly paper with which she is about to light her brother's fire.

Another very striking picture indeed is that which he called "El Greco's Bride," one of the very few he gave a name. It is a masklike greenish egg-shaped face, bald, sexless; the highly formalized convex forehead and the arches above the blind eyes sweep down the long straight nose in a manner that he was to recognize six or seven years later, when he first saw African sculpture. Yet the mask itself, again like some carved in Africa, gives the impression of concavity as it hangs there upon its white, black-bordered cloth scattered with violets below, reminding one of the Holy Face of St. Veronica, with which the general idea may have originated—there were plenty to be seen in Spanish churches.

Then again he painted a plunging view of the Riera de Sant Joan from his studio: and he painted it as no one else would have done. The people far below, the little cart, take their urgently living form from two or three strong brush-strokes, and the heavy impasto swirls about to give an effect of aerial height. It has been said that in this period of extraordinarily rapid development Picasso passed through every stage except Impressionism; but surely this is his contribution?

Of course there are a great many other pictures, most of them still entirely representational, and innumerable drawings; among them a number concerned with poverty, illness, sick-beds and death; bars, café, theater and dance-hall scenes, such as a café-chantant on the Paralelo; a good many whores, including the Lautrec-ish La Chata, a tough one, smoking a cigarette; bull-fights too and bullfighters; studies for posters; nudes, sometimes treated geometrically; and some self-portraits. The Barcelona museum has a dozen and more, and they range from the boy who arrived in the city and the awkward youth of 1896 with large red ears and his hair all over the place to the self-possessed through rather desperate young man of later years. They are interesting not only because he was an interesting person with an interesting face but also because he never saw it twice in the same way. They are all unflattering, they all have that somewhat melancholy, unfocused look of a man gazing in a mirror; but the man in the glass cannot make himself out. Sometimes the face is young, sometimes old, sometimes angular, sometimes (as his friends saw it) round; but although one is labeled Me and although another carries the repeated inscription ''Yo el Rey'' the nature of each is different; there is no sure, total grasp of the subject, never the unfailing certainty of his portraits of Don José, for example.

In all this outpouring there is a great variety of approach and a great variety of achievement. An aesthetic so personal and so radically new as Picasso's necessarily had a long and painful gestation; and his anxiety, doubts, and hesitations are apparent in his work.

If a man has had premonitions of what in an entirely different context would be called the beatific vision, and if expressing it in his own language of paint entails the destruction of what he and his fathers have understood by painting, it is understandable that he should have periods of doubt about the validity of his revelation: particularly if he is surrounded by people who can have almost no notion of what he is about—by people who swim in the present and the recent past while he is well out into the future. A man reaching as far as Picasso was reaching even then is necessarily lonely: he cannot follow; he can only lead. But he can only lead when he is sure of himself and when he is on the top of his form, when mood, health, light, food, sleep, women, freedom from interruption are all in favorable conjunction.

It is no part of this book's aim to represent Picasso as a paragon of all virtues nor indeed of any; he was quite capable of turning out dull pictures and some that most people would call thoroughly bad. These horrid lapses, which would not matter in any of his contemporaries, were perhaps more the effect of gratitude, kindness, and hunger than conviction: when Romeu asked him to do advertisements and menu-cards for the Quatre Gats he produced things in the worst Art Nouveau manner, the thick treacly line, the vulgar, silly romanticism rendered with a sickening virtuosity. And there is a somewhat later portrait of his friend Sebastià Junyent, one of the few labored and technically inept pictures that Picasso ever painted, which can only be explained by tenderness for his model.

The general impression this period gives is that of eager restless search, of deep and sometimes very unhappy thought, yet with cheerfulness often breaking through. It is true that much later Picasso said, ''I do not seek: I find.'' But he was always much given to stunning his interlocutors, particularly the more earnest souls; he was extremely impatient of talk about art and he loved a pointed saying far more than what some would call the literal truth, plodding and often essentially false: He would speak according to his mood and according to his audience; he hated to be even very slightly manipulated—the oracle that can be made to work—and his collected sayings contain a mass of mutually exclusive statements. A writer with a point to make could prove any thesis he chose to advance by selecting those that support it. For instance, he also said, "I never do a painting as a work of art. All of them are researches. I search incessantly and there is a logical sequence in all this research."

This second remark certainly seems to fit the years 1899-1900 even more than it does the rest, for not only did he run in every direction, using his already formidable battery of techniques—pen, pencil, gouache, watercolor, pastel, tempera, oil—but he added etching and wood-engraving, his first essays in which date from 1899, and probably sculpture, though here the date is less certain.

The story of his first etching has often been told: his friend Canals showed him how to prepare the plate, how to draw the line through the protective coating with a needle so that the metal was exposed, and how to dip it into the acid so that the mordant should bite into the bared copper, thus giving a recess for the ink in the subsequent printing process. Picasso drew a massive picador, booted and spurred, holding his pike, with a fair-sized owl on the ground beside him; but he could not grasp the fact that printing would reverse the image, and the picador's pike came out on the wrong side of the picture. This did not puzzle him for a moment: he at once entitled the etching "El Zurdo," the left-handed picador.

The wood-engraving, a bullfighter holding his cloak, is less well known: here the technique is far more difficult, because the line has to be cut into the wood with a graver and no mistake can be corrected, but Picasso handled this new and unforgiving tool with almost the same ease as his pencil: the line is easy, fluent, unconstrained.

He learned a great deal in Barcelona: but he was outgrowing Modernismo whereas most of his friends at the Quatre Gats were still devoted to its somewhat faded innovations. His friend Junyent did say, "The nineteenth century has died with the consolation of seeing the splendor of a great art on the horizon of the infinite, a lofty art, strong, complex, earthy and spiritual," but he also observed that Dante Gabriel Rossetti, Holman Hunt, and John Everett Millais had reached the highest point ever achieved in painting.

The more Picasso heard of Paris, particularly in this year of 1900, the year of the Exposition Universelle, the talk of the western world, and the more he learned of France from the papers he saw, the more provincial Barcelona seemed. A great deal of its modest intellectual ferment was closely connected with nationalism, separatism, Catalan autonomy; and none of this, nor Catalan politics, affected him essentially: in spite of all their kindness for him and of his for them, he remained an outsider in Barcelona. Certainly it had given him a great deal, and certainly it was a tough city, as tough as Marseilles or Naples, with bombs, violence, strikes, repression, a sinister secret police, and the extremes of wealth and poverty: and the Quatre Gats were thorough-going in their amusements in spite of their pipes and their whimsy—morphine was readily available, and both cocaine and the more economical laudanum were to be had over the counter at the nearest chemist's shop. But Picasso was growing tired of their humorless Sturm und Drang: he had already poked fun at them with his picture of Sabartés, labeled *"Poeta Decadente,"* draped in a cloak, crowned with a wreath, holding an iris in his hand, and standing in the midst of flames in a dark graveyard. Picasso could be desperately unhappy and he could be moody to the point of getting up in the middle of a conversation and of walking out of the café without a word; but he was never dreary: nor was he reverent. For a being so overflowing with life, the sight of these people taking their decadence so seriously had begun to be wearisome now that it was no longer new.

Several of the Quatre Gats went to Paris that year, partly to see the exhibition; several were already more or less settled there; and Picasso, Pallarès, and Casagemas made plans to go too. These plans were complicated not only by the general lack of money but by the possibility that Pallarès might obtain a commission to decorate a chapel at Horta; but as the year wore on they grew more substantial.

By the autumn of 1900 Picasso had become reconciled with his family, and in October it was with his father's reluctant consent and his mother's active support that he set off for Paris with Casagemas. Pallarès had in fact received his commission and he could not be with them at the Estación de Francia, but he was to join them in a week or two.

"And the money for all this, where did it come from?" asked Sabartés.

"Pallarès, Casagemas and I were going to share. My father paid for the ticket. He and my mother came to the station with me. When they went home, all they had left was the loose change in his pocket. They had to wait until the end of the month before they could get straight. My mother told me long after."

By dawn Picasso had crossed the Pyrenees at last. They were well behind him and the train was tearing northwards through France at an exhilarating pace unknown to Spain, belching smoke. A thousand kilometers from the frontier it drew into Paris: they crept from their third-class carriage, deeply covered with smuts, loaded with easels, color-boxes, portfolios, baggage. For a moment it was still Spain, with Catalan and Spanish all around them, tourists for the exhibition, immigrant workers with shapeless bundles; then as the stream flowed off the platform into the open it was Paris. A Paris as dirty as Barcelona or even dirtier but infinitely more full of color: brilliant posters everywhere—Chéret, Bonnard, Steinlen, Forain, Toulouse-Lautrec; sandwichmen; women dressed in bright colors rather than the black of Spain; startling umbrellas. Everywhere the enormous roar of the iron tires of horse-buses, drays, carts, and wagons on the crowded stone-paved streets, littered deep with dung, speckled with the bills handed out by the sandwichmen and thrown away; and mingling with the accustomed omnipresent reek of horse-piss and dung, the new sharp smell of petrol fumes. (Picasso always had a very strong sense of smell.) A bewildering great city, vaster by far than Barcelona or Madrid, and immensely active—no leisurely Spanish pacing here: the French language all round them, a babel of signs, street-cries, directions, people talking, policemen, carters, cab-drivers bawling in their native tongue; and Picasso, the eternal outsider, did not possess a word of it.

But he did at least know one thing: artists in Paris lived in Montparnasse. Rooms and even regular studios were to be had cheaply in Montparnasse. Junyent was already living there, and they went to see him at once. Although this might only be a short stay, hotels were out of the question, and they must find a room, preferably with some furniture in it.

They had hit upon a place in the rue Campagne-Première, just off the boulevard Montparnasse, and Picasso was on the point of taking it when he ran into Nonell, who was on the wing for Barcelona, portfolio packed and ready to depart. He at once offered them his studio in the rue Gabrielle, far over on the other side of Paris, on the hill of Montmartre, close to the Sacré Coeur.

There was no refusing so handsome an offer, and when Pallarès arrived in a few days' time, too soon for them to have had his letter so that they could meet him at the station, he found them comfortably installed, quite at home, with two young women, Germaine and Odette.

It was clear that Picasso was quite pleased with Odette, in his cheerful way, although he could not communicate verbally with her at all: it was equally clear that Casagemas was very, very much more affected by Germaine. Presently Ramon Pichot came to see them and a third girl was produced, Germaine's sister Antoinette. (Pallarès was already deeply in love in Spain; and he was some ten years older than the rest.) How five of these shifting relationships developed is far from clear, but the sixth, Casagemas' longing for Germaine, grew steadily more obvious.

Picasso was much attached to Casagemas; they were intimate friends, and he knew about his impotence—in fact, he had introduced Casagemas to Rosita, one of his favorite Calle d'Avinyó girls, in an effort to help him. Exactly what he did to deal with this present situation has not been recorded except in his subsequent pictures, which are open to various interpretations. What is certain is that later he felt the outcome as deeply as it was possible for him to feel anything.

A hypothesis, based on his pictures and a few other circumstances, is this: he tried to detach Germaine from Casagemas—no very difficult task, perhaps, once the poor man's condition had become evident—and then possibly to transfer her to Pichot, whom in fact she eventually married. If he thought that by taking the girl away from Casagemas he would cure his friend's unhappy passion, he was wrong: he may have succeeded with Germaine, but Casagemas still went about with her, and his desperate love grew day by day.

In any case these days were filled to overflowing for Picasso, and he had little time to look after his friend. There was such a very great deal to be seen: the enormous wealth of the Louvre; the vast, spreading Exposition Universelle itself, which included exhibitions of art in the new-built Grand and Petit Palais and, in the Champ-de-Mars, a retrospective of French painting over the last century—acres of official pictures, but also David, Delacroix, Ingres, Daumier, Courbet, Corot, the Impressionists.

All this was exciting for the foreign artist, but less so for the native. The Paris of 1900 had grown used to Impressionism and although Monet, Sisley, and some others were still painting purely Impressionist pictures, the first impetus had long since died away. The group's last exhibition had taken place fourteen years before amidst a violent quarrel about who was Impressionist and who was not, and their successors had never had quite the same impact. Neo-Impressionism produced some wonderful pictures, but Seurat had died in 1891, and apart from Signac and perhaps Cross there were few painters whose divisionist or pointillist technique looked anything more than the application of another man's rules. There was much talk of Synthétisme, and the Nabis, with Sérusier, Maurice Denis, Vallotton, Vuillard, and Bonnard were carrying on with modern painting in their quiet, domestic way, sometimes galvanized by their connection with Gauguin; but the strong current had been broken, and although there was still a feeling of newness and discovery in the air, the younger artists had no clear rallying-point. The writers of the time, always ready with theory, tried with some success to persuade them that they were or should be Symbolists in the literary sense. They lived in an odd mixture of fin-de-siècle aestheticism and the slowly-crystalizing new outlook, between Mallarmé and Jarry as it were: much of the confused, eclectic Art Nouveau with which they were surrounded looked backwards, and so did the Rose-Croix of Joseph Péladan and his followers; yet many of the young men had seen something of van Gogh, Gauguin, and even Cézanne.

The Parisians of 1900 were not starved for painting. Every year the huge official Salon des Artistes français showed room after room of unbelievably debased academic pictures—slick portraits, illustrations of trifling, often sentimental anecdote, picturesque nooks, and very, very curious nudes—while the dissident Société nationale des Beaux-Arts did much the same, though in their Salon might be seen the now semiofficial watered Impressionism. Yet neither of these Salons was always and entirely devoid of worth: the young Matisse was happy to show at the Nationale, and the Beaux-Arts professor who taught him and for whom he retained a respectful affection all his life, the amiable Gustave Moreau, regularly sent his pictures to the Artistes français, where Rouault also exhibited. But it was at the third Salon, that of the Indépendants, that the new painting was really to be seen. The Société des Indépendants was founded by Seurat, Signac, Redon, and their friends in 1884, and at their second exhibition they hung four pictures by Henri Rousseau, commonly known as the Douanier, while in the years before 1900 they also showed Bonnard, Munch, Toulouse-Lautrec, the then virtually unknown and quite unsalable van Gogh, and many other splendid painters.

This was the atmosphere in which Picasso was to live, but for the moment it was not the pictures shown in any of the Salons nor yet the crowded Exposition that gave him his view of the living art of Paris. His most profitable days were spent walking about the streets. In the first place there were the posters everywhere, and then such shows as the *Revue Blanche*'s Seurat retrospective, and of course the commercial galleries. There were fewer than there are today, and most were concerned with old masters or established academics; but among those dealers who handled modern painting some rose far above the shop-keeper level. Durand-Ruel in the rue Laffitte encouraged many of the younger men, including Odilon Redon, Bonnard, the Nabis and the painters of the Rose-Croix, who were also to be seen at Le Barc de Bouteville's place; Bing's Galérie de l'Art nouveau showed Munch; Berheim-Jeune van Gogh; and Ambroise Vollard, also in the rue Laffitte, was devoted in a more than commercial sense to Cézanne, whom he had inherited from Tanguy. Although the State had refused to accept Caillebotte's Cézannes as a gift in 1894, Vollard bought no less than two hundred, holding important exhibitions in 1895 and again in 1899, while he also showed several of the new painters, including Picasso's friend Isidre Nonell, as well as publishing books such as Verlaine's *Parallèlement* with illustrations by Bonnard. And then there was the struggling Berthe Weill, who did her best for all the young; sooner or later almost every famous name in twentieth-century painting from Matisse to Modigliani passed through her shop, though with very little profit to herself—as late as 1909 she sold "a pretty little van Gogh" for sixty francs. In his wanderings Picasso saw a great deal in these shops and their windows: he made his first-hand acquaintance with Cézanne and Degas and Gauguin, for example, and it was now that he came to realize what a truly great painter Toulouse-Lautrec was.

There were other factors that kept him from keeping a close watch on Casagemas, and one was his conviviality. He had quantities of friends whom he saw every day, an abundance of animal spirits, and a great deal of energy. He may have been something of a foreigner in Barcelona, but here in Paris he was a thorough Catalan; and like those American expatriates who never move outside the American colony, he stayed almost entirely in his own well-populated Paris Catalonia. He did meet Steinlen, then at the height of his fame, but apart from that and the girls in Nonell's studio and a few other contacts he remained in the little world to which his ignorance of French confined him.

Yet he also longed to know Paris as a whole, and being a great walker he explored it thoroughly on foot, at least in a north and south direction. Muffled in a great-coat against the northern air and carrying his sketch-book, he would emerge into the rural Montmartre and hurry down the hill. Rural it was in those days, in spite of the growing night-life, a village with quiet, unpaved, tree-lined lanes, vineyards that still held out against the spreading town, and genuine, if motionless, windmills; there was even a sloping stretch of waste-land covered with bushes called the maquis, where people shot cats and called them rabbits; and Parisians used to take their summer holidays in Montmartre, for the benefit of the air. But Paris was building fast, and it was building in stone, much of it from the nearby quarries. His route soon led him to new and busy streets where houses were going up at a great pace and where a singular noise rose above the din of wheels and the clop of hooves—the masons sawing their blocks of stone. These great blocks, white, pure, and sharp-angled, rose up through rectangular wooden towers—Cubism for those who could see it—and these towers were also covered with brilliant posters, a form of art practically unknown to Barcelona. The masons sang as they worked, and the streets were filled with the cries of greengrocers pushing their barrows, the call of glaziers walking along with a frame of glass on their backs in the hope of broken windows, and that of coopers, offering to sell new barrels or to repair old ones: wandering dealers in old clothes, too, and the rhythmic howl of Savoyards, wheeling a boiler, with a tin tub and buckets to carry the hot water upstairs, in case anyone should choose to take a bath.

Still farther down and nearer the Seine with its bâteaux-mouches, river-buses, barges, and general shipping, his path brought him to fashionable quarters: a luxury unheard of in Barcelona and an even greater contrast between rich and poor—the familiar international rags on the one hand and then men in tall shining hats and morning-coats, women of an astonishing elegance, and a colored elegance. Color everywhere, above the filth, and perhaps the most brilliant of all the countless soldiers: France had half a million men under arms, waiting for the inevitable war against Germany; and most of them wore baggy crimson trousers, splendid Impressionistic dashes in a crowded street.

Then across the water and right up to Montparnasse, leaving the great exhibition and its innumerable tourists far behind. Here there were dozens of Catalans, many of whom he had known at the Quatre Gats—Casas, Utrillo, Fontbona, Isern, Pidelaserra, Junyent—and here were some of the most important contacts he was ever to make, contacts that he did not seek but found. How kind they were to him, particularly these older, established, French-speaking men who were in a position to give their kindness an evident form! They introduced him to their friends, in spite of his singular garments—loud checks, decadent ties, a vile "English" cloth cap—and in spite of a certain roughness of manner: for although in some areas he was the most sensitive man living, in others he could be strangely obtuse: no one ever succeeded in really civilizing Picasso. They introduced him to Steinlen; and among others he also met Josep Oller and Pere Manyac.

The first was a middle-aged Catalan who had lived in Paris since his childhood and who had done very well. He owned the Moulin Rouge, the Jardin de Paris, the Nouveautés theater and a race-course or so. He too liked the young Picasso, and he gave him a pass that admitted him to all the Oller establishments, to a night-life that he could never have afforded and one that provided him with an immense amount of raw material.

The second was also a Catalan, the son of a Barcelona manufacturing ironmonger in a large way of business. His name was sometimes spelled

Manyac, sometimes Manyach, and sometimes Mañac: Picasso spelled it Manach. Finding himself on bad terms with his father in the early nineties, he came to Paris; and there, having artistic leanings, he set up as a picture-dealer, acting as an intermediary between the Catalan painters and the Paris market. He was perfectly fluent in French and he knew a great many people, including Berthe Weill, "the good fairy of modern art." It was he who introduced Nonell, Sunyer, Canals, and Manolo to her, and on this occasion he produced Picasso, whose work impressed him deeply. Berthe Weill at once bought three pictures, an oil and two gouaches of bull-fights, for a hundred francs; and Pere Manyac, his opinion fortified by her approval—what more convincing than payment in cash?—offered to take Picasso under contract.

These contracts are perhaps somewhat less known in England and the United States, but they were and are common practice in France: they stipulate that the artist shall make over the entirety of his production to the merchant in exchange for a stated sum, usually to be paid by the month. In principle the whole of the artist's work becomes the merchant's exclusive property, although a clause often gives the artist the right to retain say a dozen pictures for himself. In this case there was no such clause; and the stated sum was a hundred and fifty francs a month, then about five pounds sixty or twenty-two dollars.

When one reflects that a good Picasso of this period, his "Moulin de la Galette" for example, would fetch at least fifty thousand times this amount, the contract seems a little hard, if not unconscionable, particularly as Picasso would produce two hundred pictures a year and sometimes many more, to say nothing of his drawings. But on the other hand Manyac could not tell how soon the public would share his taste nor whether they would ever do so at all: and he did not know, nor could he guess, Picasso's enormous dynamism and the consequent volume of work that the contract would cover. He was taking a risk; he was not at all rich, having no gallery of his own and living in a two-roomed flat; and although perhaps he was a keen dealer with an appetite for profit, he cannot be called a shark. Picasso's portrait of him, in Washington, shows a big man with uneven eyes, deeply puzzled.

It is difficult, perhaps impossible, to say what a hundred and fifty francs represents in our money: needs have changed so widely, and the pattern of life is no longer the same. As far as exchange-rates go, the franc was worth 9.4 old pence or a little over 19 cents in 1900: but here are some figures that may give a better notion of what money meant to the Parisians at the beginning of the century. (To be exact, they were compiled in 1903; but the cost of living was fairly stable in those years.) Of the

883,871 households in the city, 71.1%, classed as poor, had an average annual income of 1,070 fr (£43), and they paid 275 fr of this in rent; the 16.2% who were called comfortably off had 5,340 fr a year; the 5.4% of rich had 28,925 fr (£1,157); and the 1.3% of very rich 282,500 fr. In those days a workingman's average daily wage was four francs fifteen, a good cook earned sixty-five francs a month, and a judge of the court of appeal a thousand. A copious dinner with wine in a moderately good restaurant cost two francs fifty; a common eating-house would feed one for a franc, with bread and wine thrown in; and one could go from one end of Paris to the other on a bus for fifteen centimes. A hundred and fifty francs was not wealth nor anything like it, but a man could live with less: it meant a well-filled belly, wine, tobacco, and shelter.

Few unknown painters, just nineteen years old, who had never seen a hundred and fifty francs all in one golden mass, nor yet the promise of a year's independent carefree living, ever had such an offer; fewer still would not have been overjoyed, filled with an elastic excitement and delight renewed every waking day for weeks; and none would have refused to sign it. Picasso signed: but his joy was diminished if not done away with by the state of Casagemas. He perceived that the unhappy man was drinking himself sodden, and that he was getting worse day by day.

It is said that Picasso had promised to spend Christmas with his family in Barcelona. He may well have done so: in his unwillingness to give immediate pain he would very often make large promises for tomorrow, next week, next month, or another time, but he rarely felt bound where the future was concerned. Whether or no, as December wore on it became clear that Casagemas would have to be taken away: he was in great danger in Paris.

Between the train that had brought Picasso north and the train that was now taking him south again, only some sixty days had elapsed. They were sixty days into which he had crammed an enormous amount of experience: he had seen a very great number of pictures; he had seen the exhibition, the Grand Palais and the Petit Palais (with friezes colored at so much the yard by a host of needy painters, including Matisse and Marquet), the great telescope, the moving pavement, and the official pavilions of the various nations including that of Spain, in which there were pictures by Moreno Carbonero and other worthies known to Picasso, but only Zuloaga excited much favorable comment: the papers called him the new-born Goya. As for the attractions, he probably left them to one side; they were expensive and rather dreary for the most part: "One hoped to discover Sodom and Gomorrah," said one visitor. "All one found was the Dead Sea." He had seen a brilliant night-life very unlike the dives of

Barcelona; and although his had been no more than a foreigner's Paris he had seized some essential aspects, both within himself and in the form of several paintings and many, many drawings. And as well as his sick, distracted friend, he took with him a contract that meant his freedom, his living, and perhaps recognition.

Yet Casagemas was his main concern. After a few days at home in Barcelona, which did Casagemas no good, Picasso took him down to Málaga: the sun, the total change of air and scene, the New Year festivities with aunts, uncles and cousins would set him up.

But the sun of Málaga was cold, Picasso's family distant. The Ruiz affair and his conduct in Madrid were still rankling. They did not ask him or his unkempt and now unpresentable friend to stay and they had to take a room at a *fonda*: even there the woman of the house would not let them in until Picasso told her who his relations were. Málaga was no longer his home.

He felt it very deeply indeed. Presently the Ruiz and even the R vanished from his signature for ever. And after some days of going from café to wine-shop to brothel with Casagemas he saw that his effort had brought him not only a mortal affront—it had not only destroyed his Málaga forever—but it had also been useless. He could do nothing for Casagemas. The unhappy man kept himself steadily drunk and he sat there hour after hour in those dreary brothels; but all the brothels in the world would do no good to him.

Nevertheless Picasso went on trying. Málaga had failed to provide the affection, the family atmosphere, and the New Year cheerfulness that an affectionate heart would have expected, but at least it had Gypsies, the - *cante hondo* and the guitar, and Picasso knew where to find them. He took Casegemas there, and he drew the singers and their audience. But it was no use. Casegemas vanished, taking the train northwards.

There was no point at all in remaining in Málaga: Picasso fled from the unhappy place—he never saw it again—and went to Madrid. Why Madrid I cannot tell, unless he had already conceived the plan of collaborating with Soler, who appears in the next chapter: though a desire to avoid Casagemas may have had something to do with his decision.

Casagemas traveled on, reaching Paris early in 1901. He was in better physical shape now and on February 17 he wrote a large number of letters: Manolo came to see him in the boulevard de Clichy and Casagemas welcomed him kindly, promised him help, and asked him to dinner that same evening. On the way they posted the letters.

In the restaurant just at hand they were joined by Pallarès, the Catalan art-collector Alexandre Riera, Odette, and Germaine. It was a good din-

ner and they drank several bottles of wine. Casagemas seemed nervous
and on edge, and towards the end of the meal he stood up to make a
speech in French, which Manolo did not then understand. While he was
still speaking he darted his hand to his pocket: Germaine saw the pistol
coming and ducked; the bullet only grazed the back of her neck. Manolo
grappled with him, but Casagemas wrenched the gun up to his temple,
fired, and died within the hour.

Chapter V

It was in Madrid that Picasso heard of Casagemas' death. Apart from the immediate shock it did not seem to affect him a great deal at first: his painting showed no evident signs for several months.

He was extremely busy in the capital, for he and a friend of his who lived there had decided to found a literary and artistic review: it was to be called *Arte Joven*—*joven* being young—and it was to bring Catalan Modernismo to the Castilians, playing the part of *Pèl i Ploma* and *Joventut* in Barcelona, but in a more decided and more generally left-wing manner—not that it was to be in any way a political review, however.

This friend, Francesc d'Assís Soler, a Barcelona Catalan, had already published some pieces in the intellectual magazines, and he was to be the literary editor. He was also to provide the money: not that he had much, but he was the son and the Madrid representative of the manufacturer of a wonderful Electric Belt that would cure almost anything, especially impotence in men, and he did at least possess the few pesetas that would launch *Arte Joven* and keep it going until advertisements and increasing circulation should set it on its independent feet.

Soler already knew Madrid and many of its inhabitants, including several of the "generation of '98," then very much the avant-garde in Spanish letters, such as Pio Baroja and his brother the painter, Martinez Ruiz, who wrote under the name of Azorín, and Bargula, and when the first issue of *Arte Joven* came out, dated March 31, 1901, and priced at fifteen centimos, it contained not only Baroja's *Orgía macabra* but three noble sonnets by Miguel de Unamuno, no less. There was also a letter from Barcelona by Ramon Reventós and some translations from the Catalan. And just as Casas, the art-editor of *Pèl i Ploma*, filled the review with his own work, so Picasso did almost all the illustration of *Arte Joven;* and among his drawings, pastels, and decorations there blazed and sparkled the indispensable Belt, the only paying advertisement in the paper.

The other numbers had pieces in favor of Nietzsche by Pompeu Gener and in favor of anarchy and of killing the law by Azorín: but *Arte Joven*'s anarchism was of the armchair kind, and neither Azorín nor the editors were in much danger from his article, since all it recommended was abstention from voting in the elections. They also contained advertisements for the Quatre Gats, for the Belt of course, and for a book to be written by Soler and illustrated by Picasso. It was to be called *Madrid, Notas de Arte*, a pictorial and poetic discovery of the city on the lines of Verhaeren's *L'Espagne noire*, the Spanish translation of which had woodcuts by Dario de Regoyos, the friend of Gauguin. The advertisement shows the two authors side by side and it is the only example among the many self-portraits in which Picasso makes himself appear serious and respectable, intelligent, earnest, and sensitive: like Soler he is wearing a fine black silk stock, his hair is carefully arranged, and he has done away with the disastrous little bristly beard that made him look so like one of the four cats in an advertisement he did for Romeu. Several of his drawings for the book appeared in *Arte Joven*, together with portraits of his friends both in Madrid and Barcelona, bar and café interiors, women, ranging from a flowered Pre-Raphaelite yearning head (perhaps his very last bow in that direction) to a truly sinister stout middle-aged whore in a dark doorway numbered 69, and a good many "social" scenes of bourgeois and the like, remarkable for their direct cruelty.

But the book never came out, and after five issues *Arte Joven* appeared no more. Picasso had been living hard in Madrid. First he had stayed in a boarding-house, where they regaled him with fried eggs; but fried eggs, his figure for high luxury, were beyond his means and the regular hours irked him; presently he moved to a place of his own, and since he meant to stay in Madrid indefinitely he took a lease for a year. This lease he preserved, together with innumerable other papers long since out of date; it survived removal after removal, part of a steadily growing mass of mingled junk and precious drawings, all stuffed into worn cardboard boxes; and some forty years later Sabartés chanced upon it in one of the slums piled upon a piece of furniture in the dining-room of Picasso's house in Paris. The agreement, dated February 4, 1901, covered one room on the top floor of 28 Calle Zurbano.

"Handsome street," said Sabartés. "Fashionable district."

"Yes," said Picasso. "But I lived in a garret. No fire; no lighting. I was never so cold in my life."

All he could afford was a camp-bed with a straw mattress, a deal table, and one chair; and at night he worked by the light of a candle stuck in a bottle. He had lived hard before and he was to live hard again, working furiously all the time, and it never worried him unduly—it certainly never checked his flow. He put up with lack of water, drainage, and light as an ordinary part of a painter's life; as far as food was concerned he was naturally abstemious, and although he smoked continually he drank little wine and his apéritif was mineral water. But even his Spartan frame had its limits; the cold numbed his generous Mediterranean spirit; and here in Madrid there was the paper to look after too. He and Soler had to try to find subscribers and to sell advertising space; they did not know how to do it and they failed. It was not for want of effort: Picasso went to great lengths, even writing to one of his Málaga uncles, presumably not Salvador but the husband of an aunt, asking him to take the paper. "What are you thinking of?" replied the uncle. "And what kind of a man do you think I am? This is not what we had hoped for from you. Such notions! Such friends! If you go on this way . . ."

He also had to satisfy Manyac, who expected regular deliveries according to their contract, but who expected in vain: at no period of his life did time mean much to Picasso, still less puctuality; and writing a letter, finding an envelope, a postage stamp, were only a little less of a torment than doing up a packet and sending it away—the hand that could model the most satisfying statue of a goat known to man could only with the greatest reluctance be brought to make a parcel. And even then the resulting bundle, with its inadequate paper and odd bits of string, could scarcely confront the post.

Then again Modernismo was only now reaching Madrid, that un-European town. Picasso had already had years of it in Barcelona and a most concentrated dose in Paris, where a great deal of the enormous exhibition sagged and drooped in *Modern' style*. His own work had for some time been reaching far beyond this stage, and the prospect of living through it again, of promoting it in *Arte Joven*, cannot have been agreeable. Besides, although Art Nouveau was to live on for many years, growing steadily more debased, industrialized, and commonplace as the first genuine excitement died away, it had already given what little it had to offer. Yeats, looking back at the year 1900, said, "Everybody got down off his stilts . . . nobody drank absinthe in his black coffee; nobody went mad; nobody committed suicide; nobody joined the Catholic Church." Picasso was perfectly in tune with the Zeitgeist; he was already ahead of it in many ways and he was soon to be recognized as one of its chief formers: yet here he was in 1901, surrounded by amiable people who were just getting ready to mount on their stilts for the first time. If Barcelona had seemed provincial after Paris, Madrid, apart from the Prado, was a desert.

It has also been suggested that he fell out with Soler and there is nothing improbable in the suggestion: two men in an unsuccessful partnership are not likely to agree, and Picasso was at all times highly susceptible to any hint of an affront or an assumption of superiority. Furthermore Soler was tall, well dressed, and comparatively moneyed: Picasso was short, shabby, and poor. As a young man he was sensitive about clothes in a spasmodic way—something of a dandy when he could afford it—and here was another source of discontent. But far, far more important than these was the fact that the death of Casagemas was working in his mind.

Although he knew many interesting people in Madrid—he was popular among the literary men, who looked at him with some wonder as "the little Andalou who spoke with a Catalan accent"—although he had sold some pictures, and although the cruel Madrid winter was turning to a hope of that blazing sun in which he thrived, in May he abandoned his garret, his table, and chair and his dying *Arte Joven* and returned to Barcelona.

He brought with him a large number of pastels, a medium he was using a great deal at the time, though with a ferocity contrasting strangely with the gentle word, together with other works that may have included the "Dwarf Dancing-Girl." Phoebe Pool quotes "an old friend" who remembered Picasso coming into the Quatre Gats on his return from Madrid, showing a copy of part of "Las Meninas" that he had just made at the Prado and then next to it his own "Dancing-Girl." "Velásquez did this," he said, "Picasso did that." On the other hand the Picasso Museum dates the canvas "Autumn 1901," and certainly it looks as though Picasso's van Gogh tendency had been reinforced by his later and deeper study of the Dutchman's work: in any case it is a violent, savage picture, brilliant in its conception, coloring, and execution. The vulgar, strident, indefinably malformed girl amounts to the same basic statement that Velásquez made with his dwarf attendant, but in a completely different idiom; and although at first glance one recoils from the cruelty, presently one sees that the apparent harshness overlies a deep fellow-feeling, a wholly unsentimental sympathy. Just as Toulouse-Lautrec points no accusing finger at his grotesque poxed alcoholics, reserving his real venom for the bourgeois whoremasters on the spree, so Picasso's real kindness is apparent in his treatment of other outsiders; it is strikingly obvious too in his marvelous animal drawings. "In the end there is only love," he said to Tériade; and at another time he said that you could paint nothing you did not love—women should not paint pipes, for example—and perhaps in this context *love* would be a better word than *kindness*.

But, as the critics pointed out, neither love nor kindness was evident in the pastels he showed at the Saló Parés. This exhibition, the first real, full-blown exhibition of Picasso's career, was a gesture of reparation on the part of the senior members of the Quatre Gats; they had not done a great deal to help him gain a footing in Barcelona and *Pèl i Ploma* had published little of his work. Now his friends welcomed him back, and although this was only a flying visit, a stage on the journey to carry his promised, overdue pictures to Paris rather than send them, and to collect more, the review sponsored this show in the only worthwhile gallery the town possessed; it did so in style, and although since Ramon Casas also exhibited it was not a one-man show, the fact of sharing with so well-known a man was in itself a compliment.

Pèl i Ploma also published an appreciation of the artist, with his portrait drawn by Casas in Paris, with Montmartre, the Sacré Coeur, and the Moulin de la Galette in the background. The appreciation was written by Utrillo, a man whose opinion carried weight. After some disobliging remarks about the painters of Málaga, among whom Picasso would have accomplished nothing, and about official art in Barcelona, and after speaking of Picasso's recent history, he went on, "Picasso's is an exceedingly youthful art; it is the product of an observing eye that does not forgive the weaknesses of the people of our time, and it is one that reveals the beauty even of the hideous, a beauty recorded with the restraint and measure of one who draws because he sees, not merely because he can hit off a face from memory. The pastels shown here . . . are only one aspect of the talent of Picasso, an artist whose work will arouse a great deal of controversy but also the esteem of many who reject ready-made forms and who seek out art in all its manifestations . . . *Pèl i Ploma* bows low to the established artists of merit; it also does whatever it can to help the first flight of those who may become the great men of tomorrow." Then, having recalled that in Paris Picasso was called "the little Goya" because of his looks, Utrillo went on, "We hope that this physical resemblance will not be belied; and our heart tells us we shall prove right."

This was a kind reception for a nineteen-year-old foreigner in a clannish city where patronage was both scarce and jealously guarded, but Picasso was almost certainly not there to enjoy it. He rarely attended the opening of any of his shows: an understandable reaction, since an exhibiting painter has not only to expose his nakedness on the wall—a nakedness that is no longer under his control, that can no longer be altered, any more than a book that has passed its final proof—but he also has to stand there in his best suit with a dubious drink in his hand, while strangers ask him "what that is meant to represent" and while his friends, uneasily aware that they ought to buy something, conceal their determination not to do so by labored praise. And on this occasion he was short of time as well; as Sabartés observes, he darted through Barcelona like a meteor.

At all events, while the show was still on, and it lasted from June 1 to June 14, 1901, Picasso was in Paris. He had made the journey with Jaume Andreu, a Quatre Gats acquaintance: not a particularly interesting man, it seems, but Picasso needed company, and he rarely made any considerable journey alone.

Manyac was living in Montmartre on the top floor of 130 ter boulevard de Clichy, in the small flat Manuel Pallarès had occupied earlier in the year: he welcomed Picasso and the pictures he brought, invited him to stay and told him that he had already arranged an exhibition, not with Berthe Weill but at the larger, more important gallery run by Ambroise Vollard in the rue Laffitte.

Vollard was a remarkable figure among the Paris art-dealers: dingy, bearded, dusty, apparently bemused. He was one of the few who knew what painting, rather than the sale of pictures, was all about; and although he was not indifferent to profit he loved the living art of his time far more. Indeed he was so much ahead of the taste of his time that the commercial success of his gallery touches upon the miraculous, particularly as there was little of the salesman in his nature. Gertrude Stein had to struggle to buy a picture from him; and her description of his gallery is particularly convincing. "It was an incredible place. It did not look like a picture gallery. Inside there were a couple of canvases turned to the wall, in one corner was a small pile of big and little canvases thrown pell mell on top of one another, in the centre of the room stood a huge dark man glooming. This was Vollard cheerful. When he was really cheerless he put his huge frame against the glass door that led to the street, his arms above his head, his hands on each upper corner of the portal and gloomed darkly into the street. Nobody thought then of trying to come in."

He came from Réunion, far away in the Indian Ocean; he still had a strong Creole accent and the murk of Paris weighed upon his spirits; he was only thirty-three at this time, yet he looked middle-aged. Perhaps a nostalgia for the tropics was a factor in his love for painters with the sun in their belly, above all Cézanne. Since his great purchase he had not sold many of the pictures—with a few exceptions even the educated public remained indifferent or even hostile—but at least this did mean that there were plenty of Cézannes to be seen in the gallery when the young Picasso was introduced to its owner.

The show, which opened on June 24, 1901, was another shared exhibition, the second man in this case being the Basque Iturrino, a man in his thirties, much esteemed by Vollard; but there were seventy-five Picassos on the wall—bull-fights, nudes, flower-pieces, night-life and café scenes—as opposed to thirty-six Iturrinos, and the critics took more notice of the younger man. For although the Galérie Vollard may not have been as smooth as Durand-Ruel farther along the street or the fashionable Bernheim-Jeune, an exhibition there was taken seriously by the Paris press, and the critics appeared in numbers. Gustave Coquiot, one of the most influential, was enthusiastic about Picasso; so was the perspicacious Félicien Fagus, who wrote in the *Revue Blanche* itself. Although he indulged in the art-critic's favorite game of influences, detecting no less than nine—Delacroix, Manet, Monet, van Gogh, Pissarro, Toulouse-Lautrec, Degas, Forain, and Rops—and although he said that Picasso's enthusiasm had not left him time to work out a personal style of his own, the general tone of the review was strongly favorable: "prodigious skill—youthful, impetuous spontaneity. Picasso is a painter, wholly and beautifully a painter, and his exaltation of his subjects is enough to prove it. Like all absolute painters he worships color for its own sake, and each subject has its own. He is in love with every theme, and for him everything is a theme—the flowers hurling themselves out of the vase towards the light, the flight of the vase itself and even of the table beneath it, and the dancing light-filled air all around them. . . . The danger for Picasso lies in this very impetuosity, which may well carry him away, leading him to an easy virtuosity, an easier success."

There is no doubt about the critics' reception of the exhibition; but although some writers confidently state that all the pictures were sold, while others maintain that the show did fairly well, Vollard himself says that it was not a success. What the merchant considered a success is less plain, yet whether pictures were sold or not, it cannot have made much immediate material difference to Picasso, since most of the money, if not all of it, would have been divided between Manyac and Vollard.

What this exhibition certainly did bring him, apart from praise, was the friendship of Max Jacob, an exceptionally percipient, witty, poverty-stricken critic, poet, and writer who was deeply impressed by Picasso's work and who sought his acquaintance.

Picasso was living with Manyac in the boulevard de Clichy; he had the second, the larger room at the back; and he still moved about in his Spanish and Catalan world: Pichot, now firmly attached to Germaine; Paco Durio the sculptor, Gauguin's friend; Fontbona; and many others, including the resourceful Manolo—it is said that on being called up for his military service in Spain he found himself in a cavalry regiment on frontier duty, and that he at once rode his horse into France, sold it, pawned his uniform and weapons, and took the earliest train to Paris, disguised as a monk.

Max Jacob was then twenty-five, but he looked much more; he was an extremely gifted man, well-read, short, bald, charming, sharp-tongued, salacious, fantastic, painfully sensitive and vulnerable, terrified of women, and hopelessly impractical: the son of a Jewish tailor in Quimper. He left an appreciative note at the gallery and Manyac asked him to call on Picasso at the boulevard de Clichy. "He was surrounded by a swarm of poor Spanish painters, who sat on the floor eating and talking. He painted two or three pictures a day, wore a top hat just as I did and spent his evenings behind the scenes in the music-halls of those days, drawing portraits of the stars." They shook hands, smiled repeatedly, and then, being unable to communicate, shook hands again. Jacob examined the canvases—Picasso had already painted scores since his arrival—and more Spanish friends appeared. Presently formality died away; someone cooked a dish of beans and they sat about in the dust, eating them. Dinner being over, they all of them, except for Picasso, who had no gift in that direction, uttered sounds intended to represent an orchestra playing Beethoven. The next day Picasso and his friends returned the call, flooding into Jacob's little room on the Quai aux Fleurs: after a long, long time some of the Spaniards went away; Manyac, the interpreter, fell asleep; and Picasso and Jacob, left to themselves, gazed at the Daumiers, the Gavarnis, and the Dürer woodcut on the walls. In some way Picasso conveyed his wish to hear Jacob's poetry, and he listened to it for what was left of the night. At dawn they separated, and Jacob gave Picasso the Daumiers, the Gavarnis, and the Dürer.

They saw a great deal of one another after that, although Picasso was working at his usual steam-engine pace: sometimes they used Oller's pass to go to places such as the Moulin Rouge where Picasso not only enjoyed himself but also stored up material for one side of his painting. Yet this second Paris was not all success or the promise of success, not all this new friendship and wandering about the brilliant town by night. Among other things, Picasso's relationship with Manyac was turning sour. Few men can successfully mix business and friendship: and perhaps one has to be a creative artist to live in close proximity with another, if indeed it is possible at all, creative artists being so very often, and perhaps necessarily, the most selfish and exigent of men. Picasso's was a naturally dominant personality; his life was irregular even for a Spaniard; his habits squalid; the flat exceedingly small. *Envahissant* has often been used in connection with him, a word for which the English "encroaching" or "overwhelming" are inadequate approximations. For some years he used to summer with friends of the present writer in a town where many Spaniards lived, most of them Republican refugees: he would walk about in the afternoon, often meeting with old acquaintances or making fresh ones, and his hostess never knew whether there would be five for dinner or twenty-five, nor whether they would sit down at eight o'clock or eleven. However, she and her husband had a very great affection for Picasso, a deep respect for his painting, and they were perfectly happy to suit their ways to his. Manyac was made of less noble stuff, and presently he began to resent this influx of friends, the virtual annexation of his home.

But the merchant was of little importance compared with the shade of Casagemas. Picasso was living within a few paces of the café where his friend had killed himself (he painted its interior); the studio that Nonell had lent them was only just round the corner; Pichot and Germaine were always in view; and Picasso could scarcely go to a single place in the Paris he knew that was not haunted by the poor tortured suicide.

In the late, dead season of the year Sabartés arrived in Paris, solely with the idea of following Picasso. Many things astonished him—the lightless sun like an orange through the fog, the sight of Picasso waiting for him at the station although it was only ten in the morning, an unheard-of hour for him to get out of bed. But he was still more astonished when Picasso took him back to the boulevard de Clichy and showed him his recent painting.

It had changed entirely. There were, to be sure, pictures in what might be called his Toulouse-Lautrec manner, which had begun during his earlier visit—pictures such as the sumptuous ram-you-damn-you harlot in her high collar of jewels or the delightfully perverse "Jeune Femme" with auburn hair and a vast complicated hat—but others at first glance seemed to have no connection with the Picassos that Sabartés had known in Barcelona. There were several Maternities, grave, somber studies of the ancient theme, one at least of the most poignant beauty; there were the fierce, brilliantly-colored pictures that resulted from the fusion of Picasso's own vision, or rather one of his visions, with that of van Gogh, whom Picasso specifically named to Roland Penrose as the strongest influence on him in 1901, and it is most probable that the "Dwarf Dancing-Girl" was among them; portraits, such as those of Coquiot, as variegated as playing-cards; there were Harlequins already, those sad, lonely figures in the outsider's uniform that were to haunt his work, his private mythology, for so many, many years; there were paintings of Casagemas alive and dead, of mourners at an open coffin, and among the studies a limp, drooping nude that he afterwards used to place around one of his rare drawings of Christ crucified; there was an ambitious great picture some-times called the "Evocation" and sometimes the "Burial of Casagemas"; there was Casagemas himself, seen close to, in his coffin with a huge radiant "van Gogh" candle burning beside him; and then, as from another world entirely, an impressionistic boulevard de Clichy; a girl standing in a hip-bath in his room (it has a Toulouse-Lautrec poster on the wall, probably stolen from a hoarding while the paste was still wet) sponging herself in a flood of light; and a most satisfying still-life, as deeply satisfying as a Cézanne: but above all, Picasso's universe had been invaded by the color blue.

Blue was nothing new to Picasso: "Blue, so full of grace" was the color he loved best, although in early days he did not use it a great deal; and only recently, in Spain, he had turned to it more frequently. Indeed, it is likely that he had already painted his entrancing blue nude with long black hair and her hands open in offering before he came to Paris in 1901. But his friend had not particularly noticed the beginnings of the new trend, and now he was amazed to find that this blue, or rather a slightly colder blue, was drowning all the other colors: the earlier Casagemas of this year came from the brilliant, varied palette Picasso was using in the summer of 1901; the later head was drained of vividness; and with the "Burial" Picasso was fully into that stage soon to be called his Blue Period.

It is a strange picture, full of private symbolism, and it was the result of much thought: Picasso had already made the first studies for it before leaving Spain. It is composed in three tiers, connected by a rising helix: below, in the right-hand foreground, the door of a funeral-vault stands open; the corpse in its shroud and the mourners, all cold blue or touched with green, are grouped about it; they are deeply grieved and two stand locked in one another's arms (Picasso had studied this attitude closely during the last years in pictures with titles such as "The Embrace"). From the mourners one's eye rises to the middle plane, where a bowed figure from one of his Maternities, a blue-cloaked woman carrying a baby, walks on cloud, preceded by two running children: behind her and in a somewhat different focus, outside the rising spiral, stand two nudes, while before her and in much the same relation, three whores, naked but for their striped colored stockings, look up towards the highest plane, where a white horse carries a dark-clothed man up and up into whiter clouds. His arms are stretched out as stiffly as though he were nailed to a cross and a naked woman clings about his neck, pressing her head to his.

Analysts, iconographers, and art-historians have written a great deal about this picture, naming the various influences—El Greco, Redon,

Cézanne—that they detect, pointing out the religious, profane, and psychoanalytic symbols as they understand them, and trying to give a coherent literary interpretation of the whole: if industry and erudition could command success Picasso's statement would now be devoid of mystery. If he had given the picture a title their task would have been easier; but he hated doing any such thing. He hated mixing two entirely different kinds of language, and nearly all the titles given to his pictures were invented by merchants or critics or, as in the case of the "Demoiselles d'Avignon," by friends. And it is not impossible that this absence of titles may also in some degree be due to his reserve, his secrecy, and his dislike of being penetrated. However, the one point upon which all agree is that this picture and those which followed it show Picasso's deep concern with Casagemas; and it is worth pointing out that in his essay on Picasso Jung speaks of the blue and of the figures that peopled his world during this period as symbols of his "descent into Hades, into the unconscious, and of a farewell to the upper world."*

In a sense this may well be so. But superficially at least Picasso was capable of abrupt changes of mood and of great cheerfulness in company: life was not all inspissated blue.

"What do you think?" he asked, referring to all these new and disturbing pictures.

"I shall get used to them in time," replied Sabartés; and Picasso, quite unmoved, hurried out to find him a room in a nearby hotel—a double room, since Mateo de Soto had also arrived from Barcelona and had been staying with Picasso for the last few days, a visit that made Manyac uneasy.

It was not only the streams of poverty-stricken Spaniards that made Manyac low in his spirits: it was also this unpredictable change in Picasso's painting. The bull-fights and other "Spanish" pictures he had brought with him from Barcelona and the brightly-colored canvases he had painted during his first months in the boulevard de Clichy were marketable: at this rate Picasso might be a profitable investment. But nobody would buy these latest pictures: the merchant hated the Blue Period entirely. How rarely tradesmen know their own business! Not one would buy a single painting from van Gogh in his lifetime; and Manyac, with the wealth of the Indies in his hands, urged Picasso to keep to a sound commercial line. The wealth of the Indies, for the Blue Period contains some of the most generally accessible pictures he ever painted, and in time their prices soared to heights unknown for a living painter. Why this

*For the very curious essay itself, see the Appendix.

should be so has puzzled many observers, including Picasso. It is as though cultivated (and immensely wealthy) lovers of the arts, who would never think of requiring music to tell a story, still longed for a certain degree of literature in their pictures: as though, on being asked, "What is that meant to represent?" they wished to be able to give an answer. (In later days Picasso himself, when asked by a woman "what that represented," replied, "Madame, that represents twenty million francs.")

In most of the recollections of those early days in Paris, it is of the cheerful young Picasso, overflowing with an extraordinary vitality, that one reads, the leader of the *bande à Picasso,* fooling about all night, haunting low cafés, music-halls, the circus. Yet the other Picasso, the very lonely man, working for six and working in solitude, striking out into an unknown sea, never certain of his direction except when he was in the very act of painting, was there and his pictures prove it: but clearly a man who works alone is, as a worker, largely invisible.

The loneliness of the creative artist has often been described; but can it ever be emphasized enough? People may hinder him, but since by definition self-expression is not the expression of any other man, none can help him. It is as though the artist were walking a tightrope, with only room for one; and although an ordinary hack may stagger along in no great danger, six inches from the ground, the fall of an enormously gifted, enormously ambitious man with something important to say is a plunge into a measureless abyss. Picasso certainly had something very important to say, and although Toulouse-Lautrec, van Gogh, and above all Cézanne were of value to him in his preparation for saying it, the essence of the matter was his alone; he either succeeded or failed entirely by himself; and if he failed his life had no meaning. Death and creation have this in common, that a man is entirely alone in both.

Even in a time when a strong, living tradition carries an artist along, the amount that a man as exceptional as, say, Uccello, owes to it is surely very slight; in the young Picasso's day painting, as a corporate activity that he could respect, was dead, and he had to rediscover it for himself. For himself and by himself: even if he had been acquainted with them, the pleasant, comfortable Nabis, the avant-garde of the time, would have had no idea of what he was talking about; van Gogh had killed himself eleven years before; Gauguin was in Tahiti; Cézanne was equally inaccessible in Provence; Toulouse-Lautrec was in his grave. Picasso did not yet know Braque or Matisse, and although he moved about with a crowd of gay, amiable companions, as though he were afraid of being alone when he was not working, only one of them was a man of anything remotely like his size; only Max Jacob was a man with whom, if it had been his way, he could have talked about the deeper implications of his painting. It was not his way at that time, and although he did go profoundly into these matters with Braque and Derain in their Cubist days, it was not his way in later life either: he preferred producing the evidence of his views to talking about them, partly no doubt because words are essentially beside the point where painting is concerned, and also perhaps because his deep-seated reserve made him unwilling to expose his private springs—no one was so adept at evading a question on aesthetics as Picasso: to avoid being pried into and made to commit himself he would use mockery, bad faith, and self-contradiction with baffling skill. But even if he had chosen to take Max Jacob into his confidence, the barrier of language would have prevented it. By this time he had picked up a rudimentary sort of French, but it was totally inadequate for such purposes; and even if he had been as fluent as Bossuet no amount of words could have said so much, nor so accurately, as a single picture.

One of the most eloquent pictures of this period is the self-portrait that he painted late in his stay. It is a half-length of a man muffled in a dark greatcoat, standing against a background featureless except for a darker upright bar on the extreme left: from the somber coat and the almost black hair his pale face stands out with startling intensity, and from a distance you think it might be a van Gogh. Then you see that it is a Picasso, and with a shock you realize that it is the artist himself. He has a collar of beard, a ragged mustache, and his singular great eyes are sunken and diminished. They look somewhat down, focused on infinity, and they have something of that same loneliness which is to be seen in his famous blue portrait of Sabartés, painted in this same year: the picture that is often called "Le Bock." (It shows Sabartés waiting in front of a tall mug of beer, and like many of Picasso's portraits it was painted from memory.) But whereas the loneliness of Sabartés was due to his being alone in a foreign city and to his being so myopic that he was cut off even from that strange world, Picasso's was the loneliness of a man cut off by genius, one who is beginning to realize that on anything but the superficial plane he can communicate only in a language that will not be generally understood for years, if at all. Sabartés' could be cured by the eventual appearance of his friends in the café; Picasso's could only be alleviated, never completely removed.

The face in this self-portrait is no longer youthful: Picasso had been living hard, he had been ill, and he suffered much from the winter cold; but there is much more to it than that. This face is marked by a different kind of suffering altogether, by doubt and inner conflict and deep unhappiness.

"He believed that Art was the child of Sadness and Pain," says Sabartés. "He believed that unhappiness suited reflection, and that pain was the basis of life." It is easy to make fun of a pronouncement of this kind; but no candid observer, looking at this portrait and the other pictures he painted at the time, will deny that Picasso had a right to utter it, nor that he paid the full price for his opinions.

Yet this haggard face belonged to the same young man who racketed about Montmartre, the Latin Quarter, Montparnasse, and the music-halls. It was largely the music-halls that accounted for the top-hat mentioned by Max Jacob; and he mentioned the hat not because it was as rare and formal an object as it has since become—in 1901 the top-hat, though hard pressed by the bowler or derby, was still common even on the lower fringes of the middle class—but because it was unusual in a young painter, who would ordinarily have worn a beret or a felt or, in the case of Picasso, a broad-brimmed anarchistical sombrero. However, Picasso was an odd mixture of lavishness in some things and parsimony in others: equipping himself for Paris was important to him at the age of twenty and although his income scarcely allowed for any clothes at all he set about it so thoroughly that Vollard speaks of him as being "dressed with the most studied elegance." He bought a fine black coat, a white silk scarf, a gardenia on occasion, and this top-hat. He was proud of it, and he made an India-ink drawing of himself in his glory, looking a little self-conscious, with a background of bare-bosomed women.

This is a very different portrait from the big oil: yet both are genuine, both are aspects of the same being. But a very short study of the two shows which says more about the subject: the sadness was deeply engrained, the gaiety superficial and intermittent, though intense.

Where the hat was kept, Sabartés does not relate, although he gives a convincing description of the slum to which Picasso had reduced two-thirds of poor Manyac's flat—the "Burial of Casagemas" propped up against the wall to hide what even Picasso felt should not be seen, the little table covered with books and papers that were put on the floor when they wanted to eat, the newspaper table-cloth, the heaps (which were on no account to be mixed) never moving from the floor but gradually taking up more and more of the restricted space, the pictures accumulating along the walls—but at all events Picasso did not wear it for his ordinary evening's entertainment: a top-hat would have been somewhat out of place at the Zut.

This was a deeply squalid little establishment in what was then the Place Ravignan, itself a deeply squalid unpaved unlit stretch of mud high up in Montmartre, not far from the boulevard de Clichy and just round the corner from Picasso's first studio, the one Nonell had lent him; it was surrounded by mud walls and a few low houses, and by night it was haunted by the local apaches, who were said to scalp their victims. The Zut was run by a guitar-playing character called Frédé, who served little but beer, and that only when his credit with the brewers was good: the main room had a floor of beaten earth, some tables and benches, and it was usually filled with a mixed band of painters, sculptors, models, vague young women, and of course the neighborhood toughs. Picasso, Manolo (very much at home in this atmosphere), Pichot, Durio, and other Spaniards went there so regularly that Frédé gave them a small, filthy room to themselves. At this stage they were still shy of going into the main room, where all the people knew one another and where everybody spoke French, and this little den was better than the outer bar, the entrance, with its three barrels and nothing else: at any rate they had fun there, and although they were sometimes interrupted by differences of opinion next door (harsh words and the thumping of benches and tables always, knives and pistols on occasion), they grew so fond of the place that they decided to decorate it, and perhaps even to get rid of some of the vermin. Frédé whitewashed the walls and cleaned the lamp; Sabartés and Soto hung paper garlands, helped by a girl they picked up on the way (she also swept the floor), and Pichot and Picasso painted pictures. Picasso had brought all he needed—a little blue—and while Pichot did an Eiffel Tower and an airship in one corner, he dipped his brush and, says Sabartés, "with the tip he drew a group of nudes, all in one continuous line of blue. Then, in a space that he had left, a hermit." Someone cried out "The Temptation of Saint Anthony" and he stopped at once: but there was still the rest of the wall to cover. He turned back to his work, never lifting his brush except to take more blue. "He did not seem to hear us talking, nor even to realize that we were there. . . . Next to the group of nudes there appeared a half-length portrait of me, larger than life, in an oratorical pose, holding a paper in my hand."

Portraits: Picasso loved them, and he was immensely gifted for this strangely discredited form of art; many of his friends, merchants, critics, women, and children were his models, but until he saw old age gazing back at him from the looking-glass one day his most usual subject was himself. There was no vanity, no complaisance, in this, but a profound, objective, and probably always unsatisfied curiosity; yet whereas all his portraits of, for example, Sabartés are instantly recognizable as the same man, even under the utmost distortion, the Picassos still continued to vary so widely, particularly in the drawings, that sometimes experts differ as to their identity—they wonder whether it is Picasso at all.

He drew and painted a hundred different aspects of himself; but at least for this period there is one aspect, perhaps the most important of all, that is not represented. We have no self-portrait of the man whose iron determination to express himself as he thought fit could not be broken by any force whatsoever, certainly not by poverty, discouragement, success, or persuasion: none that shows his incorruptible strength of purpose.

Picasso was fond of money: he was eager to get it when he was young and all his life he preferred keeping it to spending it—above all he hated being parted from it against his will. His parsimony could reach a point where an enemy might call it sordid avarice, a trait connected with his dread of death, perhaps. For example, when Sabartés was his secretary, in Françoise Gilot's time, Picasso was a very wealthy man with several homes; yet according to her he kept his old friend on the equivalent of thirty pounds or $150 a month, barely enough for him and his wife to live, with strict economy, in a minute flat in a dreary part of Paris. Or there is the wholly reliable testimony of Brassaï, who, though very poor in 1943, could not induce Picasso to pay for proofs of the photographs he was taking for a book on Picasso's sculpture. And there are many other instances, early and late, which show that money was of great importance to Picasso: but when it was a question of changing his style for material gain, or even of keeping to a manner he had thought valid and satisfying only a few months earlier, there was nothing to be done—the money counted no more for him than it would have counted for Saint Francis. Again and again he threw away the prospect of fortune with unfeigned indifference.

If he had made a portrait of this quality, and if Manyac had understood it, the merchant would not have tried to stem the flood of blue. As it was, he wasted his breath and embittered their relationship to such a degree that at length Picasso, who had spent all his money, went to the extreme length of writing to Don José for the fare home.

Days went by: the money did not come. Picasso suspected Manyac, who knew what was afoot, and early one morning, when he and Sabartés had spent the night in Durio's studio, the three friends crept up the stairs of the house in the boulevard de Clichy, hoping to get there before the postman. They were too late, but the letter was there, pushed under the door; and Manyac was there too, lying face down on his bed, fully dressed, and moaning, "The letter, the letter . . ."

That was the end of Picasso's second Paris. The next time Sabartés saw him, in the spring of 1902, he was living at home and working in a studio belonging to Angel de Soto and the painter Rocarol. It was just off the Ramblas, in the Calle Conde de Asalto; and just across the way stood the

107]

remarkable house or palace that Gaudí had built for his patron Güell in 1885, a mass of labored stone, wrought iron, and bronze. Gaudí was one of the earliest exponents of what might be called the Catalan Gothic revival and by far the most gifted, by far the most interesting: yet even his highest flights left Picasso unmoved. Gaudí belonged to an earlier generation (he was some thirty years older than Picasso); he was a member of the Cercle de Sant Lluc, a practicing Catholic, and, in spite of his increasingly adventurous, highly individual architecture that went far beyond Modernismo towards a kind of surrealism, he was very much a part of the Establishment. As far as Picasso was concerned, Gaudí was old hat.

The studio was on the top floor (Picasso spent most of his young life up a great many stairs), and it was flooded with the light of the Mediterranean sun. The change from winter in Paris could hardly have been more pronounced, but his painting was still blue, indeed bluer than ever.

He stayed in Barcelona until the autumn, and he worked hard all the time, falling into a steady routine of getting up late, working all day, going to the Quatre Gats or some café on the Ramblas, and talking until the morning hours; then, when even the hardiest had gone home, he would walk about in the coolness of the night.

During these months his painting, for the most part, followed the line that was already evident in Paris and that was to develop even more strongly when he returned there: blue, of course, and with an increasing concentration upon the single figure. Ambitious compositions such as the "Burial of Casagemas" were no longer to be seen; the backgrounds lost their richness both in brushstroke and incident, while the simplification of his figures, often enclosed by a heavy outline in the Gauguin manner, grew more pronounced, detail giving way to unified masses; and the heavy impasto was replaced by a lightly-brushed, even surface. And increasingly, not only at this time but throughout the Blue Period, his subjects could be understood as social protest—beggars, very poor women with children, blind men, lunatics, outcasts. This has led to a charge of sentimentality. Yet there is a world of difference between true feeling and sentimentality, and it may be that those who bring this charge are using the smear-word as a form of defense, a denial of the facts. When Picasso spoke of the horror of extreme poverty, alienation, hunger, and loneliness he knew what he was talking about; then again he was living in close touch with the people in a city where working conditions were so intolerable that riots broke out in the very month of his return, and they were followed by a general strike in February. The authorities sent the notorious General Weyler to deal with the situation in Barcelona, and he did so with such an extreme brutality of repression that the government fell. However, it recovered a week later and carried on, leaving the working-class exactly where it had been before, apart from the disappearance of many of its members, some of whom "vanished," while others were shut up in Montjuich, that cruel fortress.

It is true that at the age of twenty, that is to say in 1901 and 1902, Picasso had not reached his purer and in a way more impersonal painting, utterly cut off from all literature; and it is true that at twenty he did not always avoid slickness, particularly in his drawing; but talk of the sentimentality of the Blue Period surely tells us more about the speaker than it does about Picasso. He was in fact a remarkably unsentimental being by Anglo-Saxon or even by Spanish standards; in the case of Casagemas, whose death he felt very deeply indeed—it haunted his painting for years, and already he was thinking of another important canvas based upon it—he had no objection to using the Burial as a screen, nor to returning to the studio in the Riera de Sant Joan that they had shared, nor to painting his friend with little wings, smoking a pipe, wearing a hat, and presenting himself to Saint Peter at the gates of Heaven.

Yet the blue of this time was not always sad by any means: it could be wonderfully tender, as it is in the child holding a dove in London or the little girl eating her soup in New York; or it could be the neutral medium for a statement, as it is in his night-painting of the roofs of Barcelona seen from his studio and other pictures. The period was not always blue, either: throughout his life Picasso confounded those who love neat labels by suddenly producing something anachronistic, either in a backward or a forward sense. During this stay he not only painted a cheerful nude in green stockings and a mother and child by the sea without a touch of blue about them, to say nothing of an advertisement for Lecitina Agell (guaranteed to cure lymphatism and weakness in the bones) and posters for a neighboring food-shop, but he also made several drawings which do not belong to this epoch at all, since they prefigure his work in the 1930s.

Another drawing shows a corner of his studio, the *"ingrato y sordido taller de la calle del Conde de Asalto"* as Eugenio d'Ors calls it. It is of no great importance in itself, being a kind of private note, perhaps to do with the interesting angles made by the easel, the canvas, and the chair, for Picasso drew to himself as some men talk to themselves, and he drew incessantly; but it is worth mentioning here because it also says something about his way of working. Although he used a palette as his symbol for the painter (he did so this year in a drawing of himself on the beach), he was never seen with one on his thumb: he asserted with some indignation that he *could* hold one, and no doubt as a boy he did hold his father's; but as a man he either left the palette on the floor or he used newspapers or a chair or a little table or the floor itself or a combination of some of these. And here in the drawing there is the chair with a piece of cardboard on it, a pot, and some brushes. He also had a highly personal way of approaching his canvas. Sabartés describes this in 1901: "I usually found him in the middle of the studio, near the stove, sitting on a rickety chair, rather a low one as I remember. The discomfort did not worry him in the least . . . he fixed the canvas on the lowest notch of the easel, which forced him to bend almost double as he painted. . . . If he had to look attentively at the palette (it was on the floor, a mass of white in the middle and the other colors, mostly blue, dotted round the edge) he still kept a sideways eye upon the canvas; his concentration never left either. Both were in his field of vision and he took in both at the same time." And again in 1940, when he had no easel in his refuge at Royan he bought a gimcrack object so small that he was obliged to paint crouching, with his belly between his knees. Nevertheless he strongly resisted Sabartés' attempts at making him buy another, just as he resisted all change in his habits or his physical surroundings: his bones were intensely Spanish, and Spaniards, on taking leave of one another, will often utter their ancient, traditional spell, *"Que no haya novedad,"* may no new thing arise: a curious wish for Picasso, but one that he accepted with perfect equanimity.

Any account of Picasso must be a tale of apparent contradictions: his work was of essential importance to him, of an importance that cannot be exaggerated, and he vehemently insisted upon quietness and solitude for it, yet he would use bad tools and perishable materials, so that many of his constructions are now little more than wrecks and some of his finest pictures are crumbling off the fibro-cement upon which he painted them; he was totally indifferent to comfort, yet he fussed about his health and he was easily terrified by a scratch or a cold. He was eager to get money, yet in France, where the law gives artists a royalty of 3% on the price of all their works sold by auction (and in his later years Picassos not only fetched enormous prices but also passed rapidly from one speculator to another), he refused to cash the large and frequent checks; he was intensely conservative in his habits, yet his painting was a continuous revolution, in perpetual flux. At this time he was particularly concerned with solitude—again and again the theme of the solitary recurs, often a woman, sitting hunched at a café table—yet he was himself gregarious.

One of the places where he sought company was of course the Quatre Gats, where he painted a capital portrait of Corina Romeu, produced some more advertisements, and designed the card announcing the birth of the Romeus' first son; another was the Guayaba, in the now-vanished Plaza de l'Oli. It began as a studio in which his friend Joan Vidal Ventosa worked as a restorer, a photographer, and a maker of poker-work decorations and it developed into a kind of club frequented mostly by the younger customers of the Quatre Gats: its name was a facetious corruption of Valhalla, for Barcelona was still at the height of its enthusiasm for Wagner and the North. Here he renewed many old acquaintances and made several new ones, some of which ripened into friendship. There was Eugenio d'Ors, then a young law student, and who early in that year of 1902 had published a much-discussed article on Nonell in *Pèl i Ploma*. He maintained that the object painted should be an active, not a passive, element in the painter's life, and that it should be an entity with a continuing existence of its own—a view that coincided with Picasso's and that might have strengthened it, if Picasso by this time had needed any outside support. But by now he had come out of his egg, as the Catalans say: agreement may have been agreeable; it cannot have been decisive.

Other friends were the Fontbonas, the sculptor Emili, whom he had known in Paris, and his brother Josep, a medical man. It was at Gracia, in the Fontbonas' house, that Picasso made his first sculpture (also of a woman, bowed down, sitting on the ground with her arms folded); and in his invaluable *Picasso i els seus amics catalans,* the fruit of years of patient, scrupulous research to which this book owes a great deal, Josep Palau i Fabre shows that he almost certainly did so in this same year of 1902. Picasso himself could not remember, and experts have wrangled over the date for years.

The Reventós brothers, Ramon the writer and Cinto the gynecologist, also came to the Guayaba: Picasso had known them long before, and he often went to see Cinto at his hospital, where he walked about the wards in an atmosphere of complicated misery, disease, loneliness, and death. He was also allowed into the place where the corpses lay, and to the end of his life he kept a woman's head that he painted there.

But although these meetings and these studies were absorbing, and although for a while he was passionately interested in a strip-tease girl called La Belle Chelita—so interested that one day Sabartés, calling at noon, found him still in bed, surrounded by his night's work, a great series of delicate, exquisite, explicit nudes that were never seen again—Barcelona was not Paris; and Picasso was not happy; he was not even superficially happy.

He wrote to Max Jacob: it was an illustrated letter, and the drawing on the back—a dead horse being dragged out of the bull-ring—is wonderfully fluent; the same cannot be said for his handwriting, which was now further embarrassed by attempting a foreign language. As far as the letter can be made out it runs:

> *Mon cher Max il fait lontaim que je ne vous ecrit pas—se pas que je ne me rapelle pas de toi mes je trabaille vocoup se pour ça que je ne te ecrit Je montre ça que je fait a mes amis les* artistes *de ici me ils trouven quil ia trot de amme me pas forme se tres drole tu sais coser avec de gen con ça mes ils ecriven de libres tres movesas et ils peingnen de tableaux imbeciles—se la vie—se ça*
>
> *Fontbona il trabaile vocoup mes il ne fait rien*
>
> *Je veux faire un tableaux de le desin que je te envoye yssi (les deux seurs) set' une tableaux que je fait—set' une putain de S. Lazare et une seur*
>
> *Envoys moi quelquechose crit de vous pour la "Pel & Ploma"—*
>
> *Adie mon ami crit moi*
>
> *ton ami*
>
> PICASSO
> *Rue de la Merced 3—Barcelona*
> *Espagne*

My dear Max it is long since I have written to you—it is not that I do not remember you but I am working a great deal that is why I do not write

I show what I do to the *artists* of this place but they think there is too much soul but no form it is very amusing you know talking to people like that but they write very bad books and they paint idiot pictures—that's life—that's what it is

Fontbona works a great deal but he achieves nothing

I want to make a picture of this drawing I am sending you with this (the two sisters) it is a picture I am doing of a St. Lazare whore and a nun

Send me something you have written for *Pèl i Ploma*

Good-bye my friend write to me

Your friend

PICASSO

On the front of the letter, surrounded by the text, there is a drawing of himself labeled "Picasso in Spain" and showing him in a broad-brimmed hat, with a Romanesque church and a bull-ring in the background. And the drawing which he enclosed did in fact turn into a grave, statuesque, and even hieratic painting, highly formalized and reminiscent of some Catalan Romanesque carving and fresco—in 1902 there was a great exhibition of medieval art in Barcelona, and Catalonia is extraordinarily rich in Romanesque. (The St. Lazare to which he refers was a hospital in Paris where venereal diseases were treated and to which still another medical friend admitted him as a visitor.)

In April of this year Manyac's remaining rights in Picasso enabled him to arrange a show with Berthe Weill, who now had a gallery of her own. Most of the thirty works she hung were painted before the full Blue Period: there were some of the "Spanish" pastels that he had brought to Paris, there was the hetaira with the collar of jewels, several of his cabaret or Toulouse-Lautrec phase, and some of those pictures which had shocked the newly-arrived Sabartés with their violent colors, but there were also blue pictures such as "Le Tub," and it may be that the exhibition seemed to be running in several directions at once. The well-known critic Adrien Farge wrote the preface to the catalog in the usual dithyrambic strain; but everyone knows that the writer of a preface is not on his oath, and although many of the kind things that he said were also true, the visitors remained, upon the whole, unconvinced. There is the usual uncertainty about just what was sold and how the proceeds were shared, although Berthe Weill does state that at about this time a collector bought the splendid "Moulin de la Galette," the first picture Picasso painted in his second visit to Paris, for two hundred and fifty francs, while the "Omnibus" fetched a hundred and sixty. But in any case the artist's gains were not enough to allow him to make his third journey north.

This had to wait until October of the year 1902, when he set off, full of hope, with a friend, the painter Sebastià Junyer-Vidal. Once more Picasso recorded this journey in an *auca*, a series of drawings that show the pair in their third-class carriage (unforgiving wood and iron in those days), with Picasso in the corner seat, smoking his pipe. It is clear that they are cold—they pace the platform at Montauban huddled in their greatcoats—and that they were colder still by the time they reached Paris some twenty-three hours later; but they stride away from the Gare d'Orsay—Junyer carrying the trunk—with every appearance of good spirits; while a last but alas purely hypothetical picture shows the famous art-dealer Durand-Ruel giving Junyer a great bag of money. Picasso might reasonably have had great expectations, for although his earlier visits had not made him much richer they had brought him valuable contacts and a far greater measure of success than usually falls to a very young man.

But this time everything was against him; nothing went right. First he took a room in the Hôtel des Ecoles, in the Latin Quarter, far from his old haunts in Montmartre and Montparnasse, far from his established friends; then he shared a still cheaper room under the roof of the primitive though picturesque Hôtel du Maroc in the rue de Seine with the sculptor Agero.

A vast bed under the sloping ceiling almost filled the room, so that the painter had to lie down if the sculptor wanted to move about; while a single round window, like a port-hole, provided all their working light. Nevertheless, Picasso managed to paint an admirable Maternity, a mother and child by the sea, in pastel; and he did a great deal of drawing. The rent was small, something in the nature of five francs a week for both, but even so it was beyond their means, and Max Jacob observed that "neither Picasso nor the sculptor used to eat." From time to time he brought them fried potatoes.

In 1902 Max Jacob was twenty-six; after a brilliant school career in his native Brittany he had attended the Ecole coloniale in Paris, with some idea of governing the French empire. This only lasted for about six weeks, however, and his art-studies at the Académie Jullian were equally brief, although he was in fact unusually gifted. By 1902 he had already been a lawyer's clerk, a barrister's secretary, a baby-sitter, a piano-teacher, and an art-critic, and now he was keeping body and soul together by coaching a small boy. Yet brighter days were coming: a wealthy relative called Gompel, who owned Paris-France, a shop in the boulevard Voltaire (and who later owned several Picassos) said that Max might come and work there as a warehouseman in the basement. Jacob took a fifth-floor room nearby, fair-sized but unheated, and although it had only one single bed in it he at once invited Picasso to come and stay. This was the timeliest invitation, for Picasso had recently had a most unpleasant experience with a group of Spaniards who also lived in the rue de Seine. Exactly what this experience was is not known: Picasso was unwilling to speak of it even to Sabartés, and Sabartés has passed on even less; but it evidently concerned money (these people were quite well off), selfishness, and contempt, and it filled him with a disgust for life, a disgust that he remembered with far more pain than the hunger and the piercing cold of that Paris winter. Clearly he had been wounded in his pride; and as Zervos says, he was the proudest man on earth.

Picasso was always fond of working by lamp or candle light, and this was just as well, since it allowed the two friends equal shares of the narrow bed; Picasso slept in it by day, while Jacob was at the shop, and Jacob slept in it while Picasso drew all through the night.

For a while life was kinder; they ate omelets, beans, and Brie. But Max Jacob was not quite suited to a fixed employment and he gave so little satisfaction at the shop that in spite of the tie of blood, of his evident distress, and indeed of his imminent starvation he was turned away.

In later years Picasso told the story of a sausage that they bought in their last extremity of destitution: it was, it seems, a great bargain, bought from a stall in the street; but on being brought home and warmed it swelled, swelled, and at last exploded, leaving nothing but its skin and the reek of putrid flesh: it cannot have been so amusing at the time, however, particularly as most of his valuable contacts were behaving in much the same way. Nobody would buy his pictures. It is true that some people did try to help him: Berthe Weill showed his work no less than three times during this year, for a fortnight in spring, a fortnight in summer, and now for a full month in the winter: they were mixed shows, and in two of them the almost unknown Matisse was of the company, though he and Picasso did not meet. Félicien Fagus, who had praised Picasso in 1901, praised him still, while Charles Morice at least took notice of him in the influential *Mercure de France.* Fagus' article in the *Revue Blanche* was less in connection with one of these exhibitions than with the Spanish painters in general, those "who had recently invaded Paris, bringing with them a freshness untainted by the least academicism, a painting neither weary nor exploited": but most surprisingly in one of his good sense he ended, "They do not yet have a great man, a conquistador who absorbs everything and renews everything, the originator of a fresh epoch, the creator of a boundless world." For his part Morice, writing in December, 1902, spoke of "the extraordinary, sterile sadness that weighs upon the whole of this very young man's work—a body of work that is already beyond counting. Picasso, who was painting before he learned to read, seems to have been given the mission of expressing everything that exists, and of expressing it with his brush. It might be said that he is a young god who wants to refashion the world. But a gloomy god. The hundreds of faces that he has painted all grimace. Never a single smile. One could no more live in his world than in his leprous, scaling houses. And his own painting is shut in. Hopelessly so? There is no telling. But undoubtedly it has power, ability, and talent."

As it became increasingly obvious that he would have to go home again he offered all the pictures that Berthe Weill had been unable to sell, to anyone who would give two hundred francs for the lot. This was in January, the cruelest month, and to warm them a little—warmth being a substitute for food as well as a blessing in itself—he burned his drawings and his watercolors, a great heap of them.

He remembered this as the hardest time he ever went through, not only because of the hunger and the cold but above all because of his disgust, deep discouragement, and near-despair. Yet it came to an end: Madame Bernard bought the "Maternity" alone for two hundred francs. On January 13, 1903, Picasso drew another of his *auques,* showing the story of Max Jacob—Max writing a book, taking it to a publisher—reading it aloud—leaving the publisher's office with his hat on one side, crying *Olé, olé!*—dining at Maxim's with women of the town—being given a crown of laurels and a ham by Fame—and almost immediately afterwards he took the train for Barcelona.

Before leaving he went to Montmartre and asked Pichot to keep his pictures for him: in the course of the next year or so Pichot mislaid them entirely, and if they had not eventually been found, stuffed away out of sight on the dusty top of a cupboard, "there would," said Picasso, "have been no Blue Period, because everything I had painted up until then was in that roll."

If Picasso was speaking seriously he must have had an idea of the Blue Period quite unlike that of the art-historians, since many of the finest Blue pictures were painted during the following eighteen months in Barcelona, and since the period does not come to an official end until 1904: but it is a thousand to one that he was doing nothing of the kind—he almost never spoke of the official periods at all, but said, "that was painted at the Bateau-Lavoir, that at Céret, that in the boulevard de Clichy," and so on. At all events his palette showed little change until he returned to Paris, met his first relatively permanent mistress, and exorcised the ghost of Casagemas.

For Casagemas was with him still: Picasso lived at home in the family flat, and, above all at first, he ate at home; but he worked in the very studio in the Riera de Sant Joan that he had shared with Casagemas, his friend Angel de Soto having taken it some time before. Here he was surrounded by the immediate presence of his friend; even the pictures, the furniture, and the servants they had painted together were still there; and presently he began a series of drawings that was to culminate in one of the most significant pictures of this period, that which some dealer or critic entitled "La Vie" and which, although its allegorical content is open to many interpretations, is certainly concerned with Casagemas' death and the part Picasso played in that tragedy.

But although the drawings began early, the picture itself was not painted until the end of 1903 or more probably in early 1904, and Picasso did a great deal before then. First he picked up the threads of his old life, going to see Pallarès, Sabartés, his friends at the Quatre Gats, and many, many others. And then, although he was never concerned with politics, the atmosphere of Barcelona in 1903 was enough to force itself upon a man with much less social awareness, much less human solidarity, than Picasso. Revolutionary agitation among the students was so great that the authorities closed the university altogether; there were seventy-three strikes in that one year alone, some accompanied by riots; the repression was exceptionally harsh and bloody; and the hunting down of anarchists and "subversive elements" went on with even greater zeal. Unemployment increased; the fate of the poorer working people and of the outcasts, the old, the blind, the crippled, grew more desperate still. This was reflected in Picasso's painting: 1903 was the year of the "Old Jew" (an ancient blind beggar with a little bright-eyed boy guarding him), the "Blind Man's Meal" (a thin figure, quite young, seated at a table, holding a piece of bread and feeling for the pitcher), and of the "Old Guitar-Player"; of many lonely whores, drinking without joy and waiting interminably, of "La Celestina," a dignified wall-eyed bawd (bawds are a great feature of the Spanish tradition: another Ruiz, the Reverend Juan, archpriest of Hita in the fourteenth century, wrote about one, and both the young and the old Picasso drew and painted dozens, though few men can have needed their services less), and of "The Embrace," a recurring theme, here exemplified by a naked pregnant woman clasped to a naked man, their bowed heads merged in great but motionless distress. Picasso was deeply concerned with poverty, with blindness (poverty's ultimate degree), and with solitude; and his means of communicating his concern at this period has been labeled mannerist because of a similarity between his treatment of emaciated limbs, angular postures, and elongated hands and that of El Greco or Morales. The label is useful, no doubt, and certainly Picasso had the greatest respect for El Greco; but perhaps it is even more to the point that he, like so many other Spanish painters who could really see, lived in a country where extreme poverty was endemic and where emaciated forms were common—a country, too, which was the first to receive the greater and the lesser pox, with its attendant blindness, from the New World, and where both were so very widely spread.

Hands: Picasso studied them from his earliest days to his last, and it is easy to pick striking examples of his use of those almost autonomous creatures to say widely different things. One is the "Guitar-Player" of 1903, whose tall, gaunt figure is cramped into the rectangle of the frame and whose raised left hand, stopping the strings at the top of the diagonal formed by foot, knee, the guitar, and the guitar's long neck, suddenly arrests the line with four pale transversal bars across the darkness, forming a point of tension that counterbalances the sharply-bowed blind head. Another is a somewhat later watercolor of a madman, whose gesticulating, reasoning fingers are far more lunatic than even his hairy face.

But not all the work of the Barcelona Blue Period is sad; far from it. Picasso often went to see his friends the Junyer-Vidal brothers, who had inherited a haberdashery, so that Sebastià now devoted more of his time to cotton thread and knitted drawers than to painting. Picasso spent many an evening behind the shop, and since he could not be easy without a pencil in his hand, he drew on the backs of their trade-cards and sometimes on their bills: the drawings were generally amusing and often bawdy, though many harked back tenderly to his peasant days with Pallarès at Horta; and the brothers kept them, forming a collection of scores or even hundreds.

Another friend was Benet Soler, a tailor who is said to have worked in Paris; he had a shop in the Plaza de Santa Ana, a few steps from the Quatre Gats, and he loved pictures, especially Picasso's. In exchange for clothes he accumulated one of the finest collections of the Blue Period ever gathered under one private roof, including a great many drawings and even some curious engravings done, as Soler's daughter told Josep Palau, with the point of a needle in the flat triangular chalks that tailors use for marking cloth. What is more, Picasso painted the tailor's portrait several times, just as he painted so many of his friends, particularly Sebastià Junyer-Vidal, Angel de Soto, and Sabartés; and this year he undertook a family piece, a calm, good-humored triptych showing the whole household and their dog.

There were many other portraits this year, among them perhaps that of Corina Romeu, though it is sometimes dated 1902. If it does belong to 1903 it may have been a farewell present, for in July the Quatre Gats closed its Gothic doors; when they opened again it was to admit only the members of the Cercle de Sant Lluc, the new masters of the place. This was a severe blow to Picasso and his friends: they had met so often at the Quatre Gats and it had been there for so many years of their youth that it had come to seem eternal. They were lost without it, for the more recent Guayaba was not the same thing at all; and Picasso, for one, was driven to even harder work. Then came a second blow. *Pèl i Ploma* died, to be succeeded by *Forma*, from which Picasso was excluded, although the leading figure in the new review was still Utrillo.

Picasso wrote to Max Jacob from the Riera de Sant Joan: as usual he put no date, but from his mentions of work and boredom he was probably writing after the death of the Quatre Gats. The letter is written on the official paper of Soto's father, an inspector-general of internal customs, and it is illustrated back and front with the view from the studio window—churches, roofs, a bell-tower.

> *Mon chere Max je te ecrite en face de ce que je t'ai desine premier-*
> *mente il y a beaucoup temps que je ne te ecrit pas et vrement ce pas*
> *pour ne penser pas à toi cet pasque je trabaille et cuant je ne trabail*

pas alors on se amuse ou on se enmerde. Je te ecri ici à l'atelier je ai
trabaiye toute la journe

 ¿Ce que on te donne de vacances dans Paris Sport o Paris France?
Si ce que on te donne alor tu dois venir à Barcelona me voir tu peux
pas penser con ça me feras plesir.

  Clocher à Barcelone
 Mon vieux Max je panse à la chambre de Buolevard Voltaire et à
l'omeletes les aricots et le fromage de Brie et les pommes frite me je
pense osi à les jours de misere et se bien triste, et je mant souviens de
les espagnols de la Rue de Seine avec degut je pens rester ici l'iver
prochain pour fer quelquchose

                    Je te anbrase ton vieux ami
                            PICASSO

       My dear Max I am writing to you looking out onto what I drew
for you first it is a long time since I wrote to you and really it is not because I do not think about you it is because I work and when I am not
working why then I have fun or I am bored black I am writing to you
here in the studio I have worked all day long

 Do *Paris Sport* or *Paris France* give you holidays? If they do you
must come to Barcelona to see me you cannot imagine how that would
please me

  A bell-tower in Barcelona

My dear old Max I remember the room in the boulevard Voltaire and
the omelets the beans and the Brie and the fried potatoes I also remember the wretched days of poverty and it is very sad, and I remember the
Spaniards of the rue de Seine with disgust I think I shall stay here next
winter to get something done

                    I embrace you your old friend
                            PICASSO

Picasso had contributed drawings up to the very last number of *Pèl i
Ploma:* why was he excluded from *Forma?* At this distance of time it is
impossible to say, but Josep Palau may well be right when he points out
that a formalist aesthetic was gaining favor in Barcelona and that Picasso
had been reproached for the want of that very quality and for "too much
soul." For some temperaments conflict of opinion is much the same as
personal antagonism—artists who care deeply about their work rarely remain friends for long—and in any case Picasso was never an easy man to
get along with.

 He and Soto, for example, disagreed about how their studio should be
used. The sharing should have been ideal, since Soto worked at the town

hall, leaving the daylight hours to Picasso; but Picasso was a night-bird, and all his life he found it hard to leave his bed: often he would only start to work in the afternoon, going on far into the darkness by artificial light. But by then Soto would be back, and often he brought friends. When Picasso had been working well for most of the day this did not matter and they would all have a splendid time, with a bucket on the end of a rope bringing wine and ready-cooked food from the shop below; but when he had not—when their noisy presence broke even his powers of concentration and obliged him to leave his holy work, then his fury spread general gloom, if it did not provoke ugly scenes.

Early in 1904 they parted, but without quarreling; and as Picasso had sold some pictures he was able to move to a place of his own in the Calle de Comercio, a dreary broad street near, but not too near, his parents' home and just by Nonell.

It was here that he painted the portrait of one Lluis Vilaró, a flour-merchant; and since he wrote *Al amigo, recuerdo de Picasso, 15 Mz 1904* on the back, it is likely that the canvas was a present from the poverty-stricken artist to the wealthy businessman. Picasso, like his father before him, had long known the shameless greed of buyers, their appetite for free pictures, their conviction that they are doing a favor by paying anything at all, and their profound if unacknowledged belief that "painting is really play, not work"; and although he never descended to the anxious baseness with which many painters approach potential customers, the portrait •was probably thrown in as a make-weight for some pieces that Vilaró actually bought. This early experience was one of the factors that made him so exceedingly unwilling to be manipulated in later life—to have pictures wheedled out of him. He could be stone deaf to a hint, although at the same time he could be wonderfully generous when the impulse came from within.

Yet neither the immortalized flour-merchant's hypothetical purchases nor other sales can have amounted to very much, for although Picasso could pay his rent he could not afford the more expensive materials (some people, in search of a simple explanation of this period, have suggested that it was all based on the cheapness of blue paint) and just then his father was busy stretching him an important canvas: perhaps the kind and it must be said long-suffering Don José still dreamed of another "Science and Charity."

These details we owe, as we owe so much, to Sabartés, who had himself taken a couple of rooms not far away, opposite the Llotja. They were at the very top of an ancient house, and a narrow spiral staircase led up to them. In theory one room was to be a studio, but Sabartés had long since ceased to believe in himself as a sculptor; he was a modest creature, and a visit to the Egyptian rooms in the Louvre had quenched his ambition forever. In fact he took the place as much for the stairs and its dilapidated charm as anything else. Picasso came to see him, and almost at once the bare whitewashed walls were covered with murals, blue murals: first appeared a great nude, and then over against it a half-naked Moor hanging by the neck from a tree, his phallus erect in his death-agony and his one remaining slipper about to drop on to a couple making violent love beneath the tree, without a stitch between them. Then, turning to the oval window in the partition between the rooms, Picasso made it into an enormous eye; and beneath the eye he wrote, "The hairs of my beard, though separated from me, are just as much gods as I am myself."

He painted these pictures at great speed, with the same total concentration that he had shown at the Zut, and, says Sabartés, as though the pure line were already there and his concentration allowed him to see it. Few people ever beheld them: the sculptors Fontbona and Gonzalez, Soto, the landlord, some prospective tenants, and the workmen who effaced them.

This does not apply to the important picture I have already mentioned, the big oil called "La Vie," one of the largest of the Blue Period, the outcome of the many drawings that he made in the Riera de Sant Joan but painted in the Calle de Comercio. A very great many people have seen it, and a very great many have explained its meaning. The explanations differ, but they do possess one thing in common—the assumption that the interpreter knows more about Picasso than ever Picasso knew. In the course of a wide reading on the subject I have been surprised to find how often writers will say "unconsciously Picasso was expressing . . .", "without being aware of it, Picasso absorbed . . .", or (speaking of the mourners and the figure on the white horse in the "Burial of Casagemas") "these were Picasso's subconscious symbols for himself."

For his part, the painter, speaking to Antonina Vallentin, said, "I was not the one who gave it that title, 'La Vie.' I certainly had no intention of painting symbols; I just painted the images that rose before my eyes. It is for other people to find hidden meanings in them. As far as I am concerned, a painting speaks for itself. What is the use of giving explanations, when all is said and done? A painter has only one language . . ."

The images that rose before him in this case were four figures and two of his own paintings: on the left of the picture there is a girl, naked, standing very close to Casagemas and leaning both arms on his shoulder; Casagemas is wearing a slip, and his hand, held low, points at an older woman on the other side of the picture, barefoot, dressed in a dark, "classical" robe and holding a baby in its folds; her head, seen in profile, looks fixedly at the pair. At shoulder-level in the background a picture shows two nude women sitting clasped in one another's arms, the younger perhaps comforting the older; below there is a larger picture of a woman sitting on the ground, her head bowed on her knees. The whole gives an impression of deep, static unhappiness.

It has been called a problem picture by those who are concerned with its literary content; and perhaps that is fair enough, in a way. At all events the preliminary studies are of unusual interest: they all show one or more pictures in the background, sometimes on an easel; most show the figure on the right, and in some cases it is not the severe woman with the child but an elderly man, who may in one instance be painting the pair on the left and in another holding out his hand for charity. In all the couple is to be seen, with little variation but the pointing hand; but whereas in the final version the man is the impotent Casagemas with his sex hidden by the slip, in the drawings he is Picasso himself, quite naked, unmistakably male. Yet neither in the studies nor the picture is the girl Germaine. Picasso could have painted her with perfect ease—a portrait without a model was nothing to him—particularly as she had already sat for him in 1902. He painted her again in 1905, and their curious relationship continued for at least another forty years, when he took Françoise Gilot to a little house in Montmartre where Germaine was living, a poor, sick, toothless old woman, confined to her bed. Picasso's aim was to give her money, which was obviously his practice, and to exhibit her to Françoise Gilot as a memento mori. "When she was young she made a painter friend of mine suffer so much that he committed suicide," he said.

"La Vie" was the result of a great deal of thought, perhaps too much for the spontaneity he so valued, for the figures are somewhat set, stiff, and over-organized; but to lay Casagemas' ghost to his own satisfaction, by processes known only to himself, he would surely make sacrifices on the plastic side. However that may be (and it is mere hypothesis) the picture was ready in his head when the big canvas, almost certainly the one Don José had prepared, reached the studio; and Sabartés describes him setting about it at once, "roughing out a group as briskly as though he were attacking an ordinary picture."

He also describes Picasso's extreme nervous tension at this time, his need for inner silence, his mental exhaustion, his need for another air to breathe, a fresh atmosphere that Barcelona could not give him. Sabartés was his constant companion; and one day when they were with friends in a café the conversation grew boring, at least for Picasso in the darkness of his mood. While the others were in full flow, he glanced at Sabartés, said, "Are you coming?" and got up and walked off.

He scarcely spoke on the way back to the Calle del Comercio, nothing but, "What God-damned fools. Don't you think them fools?" And Sabartés would have left him at the door if he had not pressed him to come in.

In the studio Picasso looked keenly at Sabartés, set a canvas on the easel, and said, "I'm going to do your portrait. All right?"

He needed a companion, a human presence, but a dumb one: he did not want to talk. Sabartés stood there, dutiful and mute, while Picasso worked in silent concentration. At last all that mattered was set down on the canvas, and putting away his brushes Picasso cried, "Well, why don't you say something, brother? Have you lost your tongue? Anyone would think you were in a bad temper."

He was happy again, voluble and gay. They went for a walk: the world was worth living in: people were no longer bores.

The next day he finished the portrait with a few strokes. It was a blue picture, certainly; but the sensual red of the lips, the brilliant gold of the tie-pin, were something new, the forerunners of a fresh approach.

Chapter VI

W<small>HAT</small> sales, what subsidies, what savings carried Picasso to Paris in what proved to be his definitive removal is not recorded, although Sabartés (and Sabartés alone) does speak of an exhibition of his work at the Galérie Serrurier in February of 1904, with the catalog prefaced by Charles Morice. At all events he set off in May or June of that year, again in the company of Sebastià Junyer-Vidal.

In Paris they found Paco Durio on the point of leaving his studio at 13, rue Ravignan for another place nearby where he could set up a kiln, since his sculpture was taking more and more the form of ceramics: and they took over from him at once. Junyer, who had renounced haberdashery, soon went off to paint in Majorca, leaving Picasso the sole tenant of the studio. Number 13 was a ramshackle building made mostly of wood, zinc, and dirty glass, with stove-pipes sticking up at haphazard; it stood on so steep a part of the Butte de Montmartre that while one spectator, standing where the rue Ravignan broadened into a muddy little square, would see it as a one-floored shack, another, looking up from its back-entrance in the rue Garaud, would gaze at an irregular mass, five stories of rickety studios towering up and holding together by some especial grace. A vast comfortless hutch with no lighting, the most primitive sanitation, and only one source of water for all the tenants; an oven in the summer, when the sun poured through the many skylights, and so cold in the winter, with its thin plank walls, that Picasso's tea, left overnight, would be frozen in the morning. At one time it had been called the Maison du Trappeur, because of the log-cabins in which fur-trappers dwell; but Max Jacob's poetic eye detected a likeness to one of those vessels moored in the Seine for laundresses to wash clothes in, and from that time onwards it was called the Bateau-Lavoir. Some laundresses did in fact live there, together with seamstresses, a large number of painters, sculptors, writers, itinerant greengrocers, and actors, all watched over from a distance by Madame Coudray, the good-natured concierge.

Picasso's studio was at the end of a long passage on the ground floor, counting from the rue Ravignan: a lofty, fair-sized place with vast beams and a small alcove at the far end that could be curtained off. There were no curtains however; and apart from an iron stove in the middle there was no furniture either. But Picasso was in touch with his Spanish and Catalan friends, and among them he found the sculptor Gargallo, who was packing up to return to Barcelona. Gargallo sold Picasso all his furniture for eight francs, to be paid in cash: a small folding bed, a mattress, a chair, a little table, and a bowl. But Gargallo's studio was in the rue Vercingetorix, right over on the other side of Paris, in Montparnasse: Picasso and Manolo hired a hand-cart, loaded it, and with the help of a hungry young Montparnasse Spaniard they wheeled it across the city, Manolo directing the operation rather than doing any actual work. At last they reached the studio, high on the Butte, and the young Spaniard collapsed. He may really have expected the five francs he had been promised; but when Picasso pointed out that if such a sum were paid it would be impossible for them all to eat, he submitted, agreeing that it should be pooled and converted into one great general meal.

Spaniards and Catalans formed the greater part of Picasso's acquaintance at this time. As well as the nomads there was a considerable settled colony, including Pichot; Rocarol, with whom he shared the Conde de Asalto studio; the then well-known Zuloaga; Canals, who had first shown him the technique of etching and who was now encouraging him to make another and a far more ambitious attempt; Durio; and of course Manolo, who, being left the use of one of Durio's studios while he was away, sold all the Gauguins on its walls to Vollard. He also stole Max Jacob's only pair of trousers, Max being then in bed, and brought them back only because no dealer would make him an offer.

The friendship between Manolo and Picasso was of long standing and it lasted all their life. Picasso admired Manolo's sculpture and Manolo admired Picasso's painting, but there was far more to it than that: Manolo was some ten years older than Picasso, a love-child who had been early turned out on the streets of Barcelona to pick up what living he could; he kept alive in the face of literally cut-throat competition, and in the course of this education he grew very sharp indeed, not to say piratical. Harsher words, such as bandit, thief, and pickpocket have been used; and the face that Picasso often drew is that of a lean and wary character, though curiously distinguished. But above all he was an outsider, a complete outsider, tough, self-reliant, and capable, and it was this that bound them together: piracy was a quality latent in Picasso too, and he esteemed the quality in his friend. What is more, Manolo was extremely witty and gay;

even his victims—that is to say almost his entire acquaintance—bore him no ill-will; and Picasso had more fun with him as a companion than ever he had had with the melancholy Sabartés, who had now gone off to the New World in search of a fortune. It was a true companionship: each respected the other (and, by the way, neither of them drank; they both retained their lucidity at all times). Maurice Raynal knew both intimately, and when he was telling Brassaï about Manolo he said, "I was very, very fond of that man, and Picasso was devoted to him . . . Manolo was the elder by ten years and for him the young Ruiz was always 'Little Pablo.' And Picasso took more notice of him than of anyone else . . . he was perhaps the only person from whom Picasso would take criticism, teasing, contradiction."

A fellow-tenant in the Bateau-Lavoir, a big, sleepy, beautiful young Frenchwoman named Fernande Olivier or Bellevallée, the detached wife of an insane sculptor, used to watch Picasso laughing with Manolo, talking all day long with his Spanish friends under the trees of the little square. Sometimes he also showed the local children how to draw chickens, hares, and what the cautious André Level terms *"ruminants"* in the dust. She wondered when he found time to work, and presently she found that it was in the quiet of the night, lit by an oil-lamp or sometimes by a candle.

At this point Picasso was twenty-two and Fernande about the same (some say older, some say younger): and although she did notice his small feet and hands she did not see anything particularly attractive about him at first—*rien de très séduisant.* She was not alone in this: a friend of Gertrude Stein's described him as a "good-looking bootblack." Nor could she place him socially; his days of purple and fine linen were over (there was no Soler in Paris and in any case Picasso's dandyism had only been for the fun, a kind of dressing-up) and now he usually wore a boiler-suit or the French workingman's blue cotton jacket, with the red Catalan sash, the *faixa,* under it. But like everybody else Fernande was struck by his extraordinary eyes—huge, dark, and piercing, generally kind, always compelling; and by the immense vitality that flowed from him. She did not think him particularly young at the time; but she does observe that he stayed the same fairly mature twenty-two for all the twelve years they lived together. For that matter, photographs taken when he was well past fifty still show an absurdly boyish face, with the same black forelock drooping over his forehead; and even in 1952, when I first met him and when by the calendar he was over seventy, there was nothing at all of the old man about him: he was trim, compact, well made, his round head burned brown in the sun—age was irrelevant.

All the people in the Bateau-Lavoir knew one another without formal introduction, because they met daily at the tap by the front door, carrying jugs, but some little time passed before Picasso and Fernande became more intimate. It was on a hot, oppressive, overcast day that she hurried into the house to escape the thunder-rain; Picasso was there, holding a kitten in his arms; he blocked her passage—they both laughed—he offered her the little cat and invited her to come and see his work: indeed, his etching.

Fernande had been used to studios since at least the age of seventeen, for not only had she married her sculptor, but she also had a thin, acid, shrill-voiced sister who was mistress to Othon Friesz; nevertheless this one astonished her, not only by its poverty in furniture (apart from Gargallo's sticks the only object was a little sad black trunk, used as a seat), not only by its exceptional squalor, accentuated by squashed tubes of paint all over the floor, jars of turpentine, and a pail of filth, but by the crowd of canvases that filled it. They were all blue. She had never seen anything like it. He was obviously working on several at once—some were unfinished—and although she thought them morbid she liked them, particularly one of a cripple leaning on a crutch and carrying a great long basket of flowers on his back: "tender, strange. . . . infinitely sad . . . a painful crying out to the pity of mankind." And then there was the etching, an emaciated couple sitting at a paper-covered table with a two-liter bottle of wine on it, an empty glass, an empty plate, and a hunk of bread: the starving man wears a bowler hat and a kind of ragged vest that does not cover his poor stringy neck; his head is turned from the woman (he is probably blind), but his arm is round her shoulders and his other hand presses her arm; the pair have reached their uttermost limit, but their elongated, bony hands form a marvelous intricate pattern holding their wretchedness together. This was, of course, the etching that became so famous in later years under the title of "Le Repas frugal," and Picasso made it on an old zinc plate (copper was too expensive) given him by Canals: his only tool was a common pin.

Picasso had not yet been long in Paris, but he had already done a great deal of work: and of course he had acquired an animal, as well as the vague cats that walked in and out. It was only a mouse; but it was a white mouse, and unusually tame. Its home was in the table drawer, safe from the cats. He was also beginning to acquire French or at least French-speaking friends: for the moment Max Jacob was away, visiting his family in Quimper, but others soon appeared—Apollinaire, Salmon, Reverdy, Raynal, the Steins, to name but a few. And sooner or later all these friends, as well as his merchants and mistresses, wrote books about him;

indeed almost everybody who ever met Picasso seems to have taken to print, and as early as 1966 Gaya Nuño's massive bibliography numbered one thousand five hundred and seventy items (though to be sure some of them are critical works) and today the total is even greater. With this mass of documentation the biographer's task should be straightforward, if laborious; and so it would be, if only the principal witnesses, the prime sources, the people who were actually there, had the least notion of accuracy. They have not: Fernande Olivier, for example, places her meeting with Picasso in a year when he was in Barcelona, and she has the long-dead Casagemas walking about the Place Ravignan; André Salmon repeats Fernande's error and long, long before they ever met he adds Matisse to those who frequented Picasso's studio; while Gertrude Stein makes so many wild statements that it is impossible to rely upon her. The chronology of Picasso's movements is difficult to establish; so is that of his early work. Later, when his foresight overcame his modesty and he realized that posterity would wish to follow his development—or rather the temporal sequence of his works, since he denied any evolution—he dated everything, even to the month and the day; but for the early periods there is no certainty. Even Picasso's astonishing memory could not encompass eighty years of ceaseless activity: he could not recall, for instance, just when he had made some of his undated sculptures.

It was some time before Fernande moved in with Picasso. The exact date is of course uncertain, but it must have been after his meeting with Apollinaire, since it was the poet's active mind that hit upon a way of cleaning the studio floor. Fernande had said she would pay Picasso a visit that evening, and as he gazed about it occurred to him that the place was not as inviting as he could wish; yet he could not tell what to do: even if he had possessed a broom, sweeping would not deal with the half-dried mounds of paint on the floor, the trodden, embedded tubes, and it would disturb the layers of dust, causing it to settle on the wet, unfinished canvases that stood in all parts of the room. Apollinaire had the answer: they would wash it with paraffin, that powerful solvent. This they did: the paraffin soaked into the wooden floor, spreading the dirt more evenly and turning the studio into the most dangerous fire-hazard in Montmartre (no company would ever insure it and in fact it burned down entirely a few years ago) as well as the smelliest. The smell was strongest when they had finished and when the greatest possible area of floor was exhaling its mortal fumes: clearly there was nothing to be done but to sprinkle the whole place with a large quantity of eau de Cologne.

In spite of the lingering stench Fernande did move in, threading her way through the precariously-balanced canvases and bringing with her curtains for the alcove in which they sometimes slept and where she took refuge from morning callers, an alcove which Picasso turned into a shrine to love, partly burlesque and partly serious: a hanging portrait, a white blouse, two blue vases with artificial flowers, a variety of symbols. Fundamentally serious, probably; for at about the time of Fernande's appearance the Blue Period and its deep unhappiness came to an end, giving way to the Rose: Picasso may have seen Fernande as little more than a splendid pink body—this obliquity of vision, this unfortunate inheritance, hampered all his relations with women—but at least it was a body that changed his view of the world and the whole current of his plastic approach to it.

Fernande was a curious being, not easily to be classed nor yet described. Picasso's pictures show a large, placid woman, with a beautiful complexion and great almond eyes, sleepily sensual: natural and at ease with no clothes on. She might have suited Renoir or Matisse far better than Picasso. She was remarkably idle, and she seems to have had nothing maternal about her at all; she would lie in bed watching Picasso do whatever housework was done, and although she records the efforts made by other women to help their artists (some shelled peas in the market, and the seamstress wives of Reverdy the poet and Agero the sculptor, who lived in the Bateau-Lavoir, worked late into the night to provide for them), she herself did nothing in Picasso's hardest times apart from charming a merchant into delivering coal on credit. Her people had been manufacturers of artificial flowers in a small way of business; it is said that she was trained as a schoolmistress; and foreigners at least thought her French so pure that at a later time she gave them lessons.

At all events she was no fool: she may have had little notion of what Picasso was at, although his prodigious, disinterested, and persevering industry did impress her, and no understanding of Cubism nor liking for it; she may have been so vague about Spain that when he took her there she was not sure of what part of the country she was in; but her book, *Picasso et ses amis*, has some brilliant portraits in it. Where ill-will distorts her judgment, as it does in the case of Juan Gris and Marie Laurencin, she talks nonsense; but where it does not, and where she writes about those she liked, such as Max Jacob or Salmon, or those she watched objectively, such as Apollinaire, her descriptions are sharp, concise, and finely shaded. It is a book that no mere odalisque could have produced; and whatever Gertrude Stein may say, Fernande was capable of a great deal more than talking interminably about hats, furs, and scent.

Picasso was proud of her; he was also intensely jealous. A true descendant of the Moors in this, he liked to keep her shut up indoors, and at least to begin with it was he who did the shopping, going out daily with a small string bag. It could not last, and presently Fernande took over, doing as well as she could on an allowance of one franc a day, or two at the most, and those handed over with reluctance. But their Spartan regime was more theoretical than real except in the hardest times, because they often ate out. There were small restaurants in Montmartre where one could eat cheaply and often on credit; Vernin, for example, or Azon, where dinner cost ninety centimes (and dear at the price, said some). Then there was the Lapin Agile, to which Frédé had moved from the Zut with his guitar, his ass, and his Burgundian wife (a famous cook) and where an excellent supper with unlimited wine cost two francs. Some purists said Lapin à Gill in memory of the caricaturist who painted the sign, a rabbit leaping out of a pot, when the cabaret no longer wished to be called Aux Assassins; but Agile won the day—there was already a Lapin Vengeur near enough for the force of analogy to come into play. It was an agreeable place, in spite of the remaining assassins, and the painters who went there now sound like a Hall of Fame or the pride of the Museum of Modern Art—Picasso, Braque, Derain, Utrillo, Vlaminck, sometimes even the grave Matisse, to say nothing of van Dongen and a host of minor lights. There were writers too, though none of a comparable magnitude; and one of them, Pierre Mac Orlan, married Frédé's daughter, that enigmatic girl whom Picasso painted with the Lapin's tame crow, her shoulders hunched over the bird in that typical Blue Period attitude and her long bony fingers fondling its feathers. Then there were the pimps of nearby Pigalle, whores and demi-whores, journalists, actors, riffraff, second and third murderers: but no tourists as yet. Both the gaiety and the squalor were still authentic, as authentic as the pictures that lined the walls and that ranged from a yellow and red "Toulouse-Lautrec" Picasso to the vilest daubs.

Most of his life, and even more at this time, Picasso could live at a high rate of tension, playing hard and working harder still. Well before he took Fernande into keeping, she had often been woken by the return of the *bande à Picasso* bawling speeches in the moonlit square or letting off pistols or shrieking, *"A bas Laforgue! Conspuez Laforgue!"*—it seems that they preferred Verlaine. This band, a loose shifting association, consisted at various times of such people as Max Jacob, Apollinaire, Manolo, Braque, Derain, and Vlaminck; and it is significant that although its members were often very considerable men—and in the case of the last three very big ones too, topping six feet—Picasso was always named as the leader.

Not that he was aggressive or dominating in those days: he never attempted to trample on Max Jacob as he trampled on Sabartés, for example. Many reasons could be brought forward in explanation, such as that Picasso's French, although improving, was still no more than an indifferent weapon; and that whereas in Barcelona many of his acquaintances had been no more than slightly disguised bourgeois, this did not apply in Paris, and in any case the people he met here were of a far greater intellectual quality. But surely, if explanations are required, they must take into consideration the fact that throughout all Picasso's inconsistencies there ran a deep kindness and a great capacity for affection. He felt it for Jacob—it would have been strange if he had not—and he felt it for Guillaume Apollinaire, in many ways a completely different being spiritually, physically, and sexually, mean where the other was generous, flamboyant rather than reserved, superficial and sometimes obtuse where Max Jacob was deeply-read and extremely sensitive. Guillaume was another lovechild, born in Rome to Angelica Kostrowicka or de Kostrowitzky, who is said to have been expelled from a convent for young ladies of good family on his account; she was the daughter of a Polish papal chamberlain and her lover was probably a former Neapolitan officer called d'Aspermont. He did not marry her, nor did he recognize the child; but two years later he was good enough to give her another son, and three years after that he left her. Guillaume was first registered, shortly after his birth in 1880, as Guglielmo Alberto Dulcigni; then his mother legally gave him him the name of Guillaume Albert Vladimir Alexandre Apollinaire de Kostrowitzky; but at home he was always called Wilhelm. He and his brother were brought up somewhat at haphazard, first at Monte Carlo, where d'Aspermont's brother was a Benedictine abbot and where Angelica could indulge her passionate love for gambling, then at Cannes and then at Nice, where he failed to pass the baccalauréat. Here his formal education came to an end, and for a while his life followed the movements of his increasingly formidable mother and her then "protector," a much younger Alsatian Jew whom Guillaume must have liked, for he was a convinced supporter of Dreyfus. He went to Aix-les-Bains, Lyons, the Ardennes; and from Paris a tutorial job took him to Germany and even as far as Prague. And all the while he wrote and fell unhappily in love with a variety of young women. By the time he met Picasso late in 1904 he had had almost as many jobs as Max Jacob; he had published some excellent verse, several short stories, and some anonymous pot-boiling erotic novelettes; and he and André Salmon had run a little magazine, *Le Festin d'Esope:* he knew a great deal about the literary life in Paris and a great deal more about poetry, but not much about the plastic arts; in fact it is said that his natural taste inclined rather to Bouguereau and straightforward representation. But Picasso filled him with enthusiasm, if not with instant knowledge; and since Apollinaire was an immensely active journalist as well as a poet and a novelist, he spread the fame of Picasso and the new painting abroad.

He and Picasso and many others of the band used to go to the Closerie des Lilas, far over on the Left Bank, particularly for the evenings of *Vers et Prose*, when poets spoke or tried to speak their verse in the vinous tumult. Paul Fort, the editor of the magazine, piped away with some success, but the great voice there was that of Jean Moréas, the founder of the Ecole romane, a group that was heartily tired of decadence, lilies, and languors, and that saw classical, Mediterranean purity as the one salvation. Moréas was himself a Greek, born Papadiamantopoulos; he was poor, quite old (nearly fifty), exceptionally dirty in his person, completely uncompromising in his verse, a magnificent talker, and a great leader of the young. He liked Picasso, referring to him as a "monsieur très bien." Whenever he appeared Moréas would boom out, mocking his Spanish accent in a kindly way, "Tell me, Picasso, did Velásquez have any talent?" There were scores of other poets there as well, all labeled: Symbolists, of course (no longer modern now), Romanists, Naturists, Instrumentists, and many, many more, for no French writer could rest happy without a label and a cause; and even Jacob and Apollinaire were united as Unanimists. Alfred Jarry might be there too, the father of Père Ubu, in whom many have seen an influence on Picasso: certainly they were kindred spirits in unreason, and certainly both were so strongly individual that they escaped all easy labels. Jarry too was fond of Picasso, and gave him a pistol, a little Browning that Picasso always carried in his pocket. If people spoke slightingly of Cézanne he would lay it on the table and say, "One word more and I fire."

Then there were the parties in other studios. The whole of the Bateau-Lavoir was soon known to Picasso, all its inhabitants from the concierge (his portrait of her, a charming little gouache, shows a kind face under a mob-cap, a face that would never dun for the rent), to the laundresses and a couple called Princet: Alice Princet was a handsome dissatisfied woman who eventually ran off with Derain, and Princet was a mathematician who is said to have explained Einstein's theory of relativity—the fourth dimension was in all the newspapers around 1905—to Picasso, thus precipitating Cubism: a likely tale. Some of these parties were devoted to merriment; Picasso drank a little in those days, and was occasionally disguised in wine. Others, in his own studio, were long calm nights of opium during which the chosen friends lay about the floor on mats, drinking cold tea and floating in a mild and infinitely wise benevolence: Picasso had his own seasoned bamboo pipe and his little lamp. Others were for the more direct purpose of eating. Apollinaire and Picasso's Spanish acquaintances would often arrive at meal-times—Jacob in his dark lair farther down the rue Ravignan was far more discreet, and he always waited for an invitation—and quite as often Picasso and Fernande would dine with other painters. With the Pichots, for example, or with Canals, Nonell's great friend and a companion from Picasso's early days in Barcelona, although he was some ten years older. By now Canals was reasonably well established; he had a contract with Durand-Ruel, supplying him with fairly easy "Spanish" pictures in exchange for an assured though frugal living, he also had a Roman wife, the lovely Benedetta Coletta, who had posed for Renoir and Degas and many another great man. She was a strong-minded wife and she kept her husband hard at work, allowing him only one cigarette at stated intervals; but she was a good-natured one, feeding him and Picasso and Fernande and often others too with mountains of spaghetti. Picasso's friendship for the pair can be gauged by his portrait of Benedetta, a big oil that he painted in 1905. This is one of the few studied pieces that can be called flattering in the ordinary sense of the term; his mother's is another. It is usually reckoned an admirable picture, and as a picture no doubt it is, though some may feel that here Picasso did not altogether resist the mortal danger of virtuosity; but as a portrait it seems to me to represent Benedetta Canals as she would have wished to see herself, proud, statuesque, and touch-me-not; and although neither money nor career nor ambition nor poverty could wring the least concession from Picasso, on some rare occasions affection could. Most of his women had pretty pictures at first; so did his children; and the drawings of Max Jacob are invariably very kind.

Then again there were the animals: the mouse, more cats, more dogs, eventually a little ape. A photograph of Fernande and Picasso—Picasso in a most horribly wrinkled suit, Fernande in a becoming head-scarf—shows a huge and stupid brute having its head scratched, while a very large vague white puppy swarms over Picasso's shoulder, its eyes closed in adoration: and Alice Toklas, visiting the studio for the first time, saw a massive bitch that Picasso moved about from one place to another exactly as if it had been a large piece of furniture. Later there was a sick fox-terrier that often had to be taken to the vet. But although Picasso certainly loved these creatures in his own way, demanding no semi-human intelligence, no fanatical cleanliness, and only a limited fidelity, he was no more tender to them than he was to himself; in hard times they were expected to find their own victuals; and one particularly enterprising cat, coming home with a length of sausage, unwittingly fed the entire household.

From animals to circuses is but a step; and at this time the circus was Picasso's great delight. The splendid traditional Médrano was just at hand, with its lion-tamers, elephants, broad white horses, trapeze-artists, jugglers, riding-girls, acrobats, clowns, and at least figuratively its harlequins: when they were in funds Picasso and his friends went there three and even four times a week. He loved the smell of the place, the artistic integrity, and the total professionalism of the people: it was an international world—Dutch clowns, Serbian tumblers, Indian elephants—making little use of any language, French or otherwise, a world apart, remote and often hungry, made up of outsiders whose contact with the public was confined to the performance of very highly skilled and often perilous motions, the fruit of endless practice. Furthermore, the circus was a link with his past: not that the glories of the Médrano had been familiar to him, but all over the Spain of his childhood hereditary troupes of tumblers were to be seen, sometimes leading apes or bears; and fire-eaters, sword-swallowers, and mountebanks were common at the fairs. They were essentially from the same world as the circus-people; and it is significant that most of the ''saltimbanque'' pictures that he painted in these years show not so much the circus proper as dusty vagrants, wandering through bare, indeterminate landscapes in the clothes they wear for their performance, just as they were to be seen on remote roads in Spain and southern France until some twenty years ago. And then there was boxing: Picasso loved the beauty of a fight; he looked like a boxer himself, with his well-made broad-shouldered body and little round head, and he loved to be taken for one; but he did not box.

All this sounds extravert and gay, a rosy, conventional Bohemia in which the hard times appear only for their picturesque effect, the Chelsea or Montparnasse of any painter's nostalgia; and above all it seems to leave no room for the immense amount of work that was actually done.

Yet we possess the physical evidence of this work in hundreds of canvases, drawings, etchings, and sculptures. The early years of the Bateau-Lavoir saw not only the whole of the late Blue Period, the harlequins, the saltimbanques, and the Rose Period, but the beginnings of Cubism too, together with many other works that do not fit into these categories.

It may seem obvious to say that the Blue Period was not only a large group of pictures but also a state of mind; and not only a state of mind but also a continual inquiry into the nature of volume and form, movement and immobility, the balance between sculpture and painting, and many other aesthetic problems whose partial solutions are more profitably expressed in paint than in words. They are problems to which there is of course no final answer, but the inquiry was essential to him: he carried it out in solitude, uneasiness, and doubt. Leonardo da Vinci said, "The painter who has no doubts makes little progress"; and although Picasso would not have it that there was progression in his art, he never for a moment denied his continual self-questioning and anxiety, an everlasting trial in which he was the judge, the jury, and the accused and in which only his verdict counted.

The process often led to unhappiness, particularly during those years when his painting was still deeply concerned with fairly direct, subjective statements about the human condition; and although it would be as absurd to speak of uniform sadness in the Blue Period as it would be to find general gaiety in the Rose, there are some pictures belonging to 1904 and 1905 that make one wonder how he reached the apparent detachment of Cubism without hanging himself. One of these is a big oil that shows Picasso and Germaine Pichot at the bar of the Lapin Agile with Frédé in his wooden shoes playing a guitar in the background: Germaine, wearing a tawdry hat and a pink dress, is sulking in front of her empty glass; Picasso, dressed as a harlequin—and the red lozenges clash subtly with her pink—is half turned from her and his greenish face has a look of profound disgust and weariness. In another, a watercolor of 1904, he is sitting by the side of a bed with a woman in it, a vaguely-drawn, generalized, stupid woman; she is fast asleep, peaceful and relaxed; he leans his chin on his hand and gazes forward into the void with an expression not far removed from despair. He and his half of the picture are blue; blue spills from his tea-cup: the woman is in a golden light with a rosy haze above her. Almost anything can be read into almost any picture; but surely, aesthetic considerations apart, this is a statement about the failure of communication if not its ultimate impossibility. At all events the picture conveys a sense of the man's utter loneliness. This solitude, weariness, and exhaustion is to be seen in so many of the Blue pictures, even very late in the period: for example there is the famous "Repasseuse," the young woman in a white shift pressing with both hands on her smoothing-iron in an atmosphere of blue that has invaded her hair and the deep hollow of her eyes; and however much Picasso's gregarious social life may have masked it, his work, his night-time work with Fernande sleeping close at hand yet removed from him by an immeasurable distance, very often bears its trace. What kind of a companion was she for a man like Picasso? Did he ever want a woman as a companion in anything but a Moorish sense? Apart from Dora Maar he never chose one who was anywhere near his own level. But in such a matter the springs of a man's conduct are so infinitely numerous and so deeply hidden that speculation is not only impertinent but useless: one can only look at the more obvious results, which seem generally to have been more unhappy than otherwise in Picasso's case. Yet most men, or at least most creative men, do expect their women to show an interest in their work, if not necessarily a deep understanding; and although it is unfair to tax Fernande with forgetting the year of their first meeting and the time of Picasso's journey to Holland (not all people have a biographer's passion for dates), it is surely a sign of stark insensibility that the "Demoiselles d'Avignon," one of the most important pictures of the century, should have made so little impression on her that her memoirs pass it over without a word. And then although Cubism was certainly difficult to accept at first—difficult, that is to say, for minds formed and set in the traditions of late European painting—it may be thought that affection would have led her through its shifting planes. She did know that he was rarely satisfied with his work and she speaks of him as a "perpetually uneasy, dogged seeker" for whom painting was never really going very well; but she does not appear to have tried to help him much, even materially. There seems to have been a certain complacency, a satisfaction with her own undoubted beauty, an assurance of her own worth, and a persuasion that as a witty Parisienne, speaking excellent French, she was at least the equal of any foreigner—"I never knew a foreigner less suited for life in Paris" she said of Picasso: a very severe reflection in the mouth of a Frenchwoman.

The material side of his life was precarious in the extreme. He no longer exhibited; he sent no pictures to the Salon des Indépendants nor yet to the new Salon d'Automne, far less to the salons of official art; and when it was suggested that he should contribute drawings to the comic *Assiette au Beurre* for a sum that might have attained eight hundred francs he refused. To be sure, he was in touch with some dealers: Vollard, of course, and Berthe Weill, and with Clovis Sagot, a former Médrano clown with a flair for painting who had set up shop in what had been a chemist's (he dosed his artists from the remaining stock, choosing among the pills by intuition alone), but except when he was unusually hard-pressed he preferred them to come to him, which they did but seldom. Another resource was the Père Soulié, who sold beds and bedding in the rue des Martyrs, just by the Cirque Médrano; he had been a wrestler and he too had a taste for painting, an eclectic taste that embraced the highest and the lowest. Outside his shop he exhibited a large variety of pictures, old and new; it is said that a Goya was found there, and a Renoir; and certainly Picasso discovered his first Henri Rousseau among the heaps of junk. Soulié paid very little—twenty francs for some ten Picasso drawings—but he would produce these minute sums at once, or at least after a pause in the nearest bar; and often his purchases meant the difference between dinner and no dinner.

Credit was still another; but credit is a perilous refuge, as Picasso found when his bill with the color-merchant reached the awful sum of nine hundred francs and the man cut off supplies. This, for a painter, was starvation in every possible sense. There seemed no hope of accumulating such a mass of money. Vollard was hanging off, and when Max Jacob took him a picture Vollard said, "The belfry is crooked. Your friend is mad. Go away." And Sagot, though full of good will, had very little capital: I say "full of good will" in spite of Fernande's hostile testimony, because Sagot, whose brother was a print-dealer farther along the rue Laffitte, marketed the first collection of Picasso's etchings, which included the "Repas frugal," the delicious "Salome" drypoint, and a number of circus-people and harlequins (this was the same collection, famous under the title of "Les Saltimbanques," that Vollard published in such large numbers in 1913, having steel-faced the plates, thus taking away from their delicacy); because contemporaries speak of *l'excellent Sagot;* and because Picasso liked him, painting a mildly Cubist portrait of his knowing, bearded, long-nosed face in 1909. But Fernande loathed the dealer. She tells of the penniless Picasso asking "the old, unscrupulous, and almost merciless fox" to come to the studio: Sagot appears, chooses three pictures, and offers seven hundred francs, Picasso refuses; days without food, without materials go by. Picasso returns to Sagot, who now offers five hundred, again refused; more hungry days, and eventually the cruel sum of three hundred francs is accepted. It may be true; it probably is true; but Picasso bore no grudge. He accepted many forms of sharp practice calmly: later, for example, when asked why he did not prosecute those who forged his work he laughed and said that if he were to do so all his Spanish friends would be in the dock.

This was a time when through shortage of materials he was obliged to produce a twenty-franc flower-piece for Soulié without the use of white, that fundamental pigment, and when he would paint one picture over another and then restretch the canvas and work on the back: the lovely "Fillette à la corbeille fleurie," for instance, has no less than three superimposed pictures behind, a portrait of a woman, two men in top-hats, and a composition of three figures.

As the summer of 1905 began to turn the studio into an oven rather than a refrigerator, temporary relief came in the form of an invitation to spend a month in Holland. He went with Tom Schilperoot, a Dutchman who was busily squandering his fortune; and in Holland Picasso beheld with dismay the schoolgirls built like dragoons, the fog, the stout young women who would set their fifteen stone upon his lap. He did paint some of them, since work was a necessity to him, but although in painting them he resolved some interesting new problems to do with the volume of flesh, these pictures are not among his happiest works, and it cannot be said that the Low Countries had any decisive effect upon his career.

When he returned to Paris he sold some of these pictures, very cheaply, to Sagot, and returned to his acrobats, his harlequins, and his "classical boys." These combine something of his long-past studies from the antique, his young tumblers, and the classic Mediterranean aspirations of Moréas and his other literary friends: Gauguin, Cézanne, and even Puvis de Chavannes may be added to the list of influences, Cézanne with very real justification, since the previous Salon d'Automne had honored him with a whole room to himself and since Picasso repeatedly stated that "he was my one and only master"—an influence that had started in 1901 and that was to grow steadily in strength: almost the only influence, apart from van Gogh, that Picasso ever directly acknowledged. His grave, short-haired boys resemble Greek *kouroi* (they are plumper than the acrobats), and like the *kouroi* these belong to no period and to all: "Youth has no age," he said. Sometimes they ride upon horses or lead them, and although Picasso's circus horses are miracles of grace, here for once his extreme virtuosity and his visual memory let him down: his lead horse, advancing towards the spectator, is a knock-kneed creature with a lamentable action. But he failed in good company, for the charger in van Dyck's great "Charles I" has much the same wretched bosom: and in any case Picasso's horse has the kindest face and a beautiful silvery coat, while the whole picture, with its pink boy outlined in darker rose and its even pinker sand, breathes a grave, quiet happiness, a sense of well-being.

This too was the year of the "Bateleurs," otherwise the "Family of Saltimbanques" (which also overlies two other paintings), a very large picture, physically (84 x 90 3/8 inches) and aesthetically, in which he summed up a great deal of what he had to say by means of his wanderers. In a bare, desolate landscape five people stand: a tall, lean harlequin talking to a massive elderly jester and holding a little girl by the hand; behind them two boys, an adolescent carrying a roll or kit-bag on his shoulders and a child wearing clothes far too big for him, both boys unsmiling, sunken-eyed. All these people wear their tired finery, their working clothes, as a matter of course; and these working clothes remove them from all contemporary allusion. Then in the foreground, in the right-hand corner of the picture, on another plane, entirely isolated from the rest, sits a young woman in a Majorcan hat. There is no explanation of her presence, no explanation of the ghostly water-jar that helps to set her so far apart, and none of the other figures: they simply exist there in their timeless world.

Throughout most of 1905 life was as hard as it had been in 1904, and neither Fernande's ratatouilles nor Benedetta Canals' pasta nor the restaurant meals at about a franc a head were really enough to sustain his prodigious output: an occasional sale, followed by wild extravagance, particularly in bottles of scent for Fernande, just kept him going, and he had the reserves of youth to draw upon; but total destitution and sickness were there, immediately at hand, in a world that had no Social Security and very little mercy on failures; and the ordinary climate of his life away from the easel was that of penury.

Yet better days were coming. The Blue-Rose and the full Rose periods were more generally accessible, even popular; and in November of that year Leo and Gertrude Stein, wandering along the rue Laffitte, saw two paintings in Sagot's shop that pleased them, the one by a young Spaniard whose name is not recorded, the other by Picasso. Stein bought the first and showed interest in the painter of the second, so Sagot sent him to Père Soulié. At the sight of these people in brown corduroy and sandals and at the sound of their French, Soulié perceived that they were Americans and therefore asked almost as much for his Picasso as Vollard asked for the Cézannes the Steins were then buying. They went back to Sagot, who laughed and said that in a few days he would have a big Picasso for them, presumably at a reasonable price. When they returned to the rue Laffitte the dealer showed them the "Fillette à la corbeille fleurie," a slim rebellious blackhaired child, worm-naked but for a little necklace and a hair-ribbon, looking sullenly at the painter as she stands on something tawny and holds an ornamental basket of red flowers, brilliant against the blue-green background. Gertrude Stein did not like the picture; she found the child's long legs and big feet repulsive. But in the ensuing contest she was defeated; the price of a hundred and fifty francs was paid, and Leo Stein carried the "Fillette" home to the rue de Fleurus to join the Cézannes, the Gauguins and Matisses.

Presently the Steins were taken to Picasso's studio by a French writer who knew him, and they bought eight hundred francs' worth of pictures straight away. This was a most important meeting for Picasso, not merely because of the sudden flood of money at a crucial moment, but because the Steins, though not rich by American standards, were steady, discriminating buyers: they owned a remarkable and rapidly-growing collection, which they hung in a studio attached to their house in the rue de Fleurus and which their many friends and acquaintances viewed with awe on Saturday evenings, and they helped to make Picasso's name known among those who could buy his works. The Steins and Picasso took to one another directly; they asked him and Fernande to dinner, and there Picasso sat at Gertrude's right hand. In the course of the meal she took up a piece of bread; he snatched it violently from her, crying, "This piece of bread is mine!" Although Toklas says that he "looked sheepish" on being reminded of his party manners the incident did away with formality. In any case, Picasso was genuinely fascinated by Gertrude Stein's appearance: his eye detected qualities in her massive person that were concealed from the world in general, for by ordinary standards her looks cannot have recommended her at any time; and very early he asked to paint her portrait. She sat for him eighty or ninety times; their intimacy increased and with it their mutual esteem, helped perhaps by their imperfect command of French; and they remained unusually close to one another for many years, long after Picasso had not the slightest need of buyers.

What is more, this meeting led to his friendship with Matisse; for friendship it must be called in spite of the odd currents of jealousy and rancor, mostly on Picasso's side; a friendship that lasted, increasing towards Matisse's death in 1954, and that was based on respect and a certain odd affection. Although Picasso and Matisse had exhibited together at Berthe Weill's in 1902 they had not met before; and the date of their present meeting is uncertain: it may have taken place in the autumn of 1906, but since it appears that Sergei Shchukine first bought Picassos before this, 1905 seems the more probable year. At all events it was the Steins who took Matisse and his daughter Marguerite to the Bateau-Lavoir, and more than fifty years later she still remembered the vast bulk of the bitch Frika, whom she judged to be a Saint Bernard. Fernande's extraordinary beauty, her amiability and her size also impressed the child deeply; so did her way of producing sugar for their coffee—she went to a cupboard, scooped up a handful, and emptied it onto a clear space on the filthy table. So did the meal they ate at the Lapin Agile, a beef-steak, then some ham on top of it, and crowning all a fried egg.

At this point Matisse, though still not generally recognized and still desperately poor, was an outstanding, controversial figure, the leader of the Fauves, whose savage, brilliantly-colored pictures had amazed the visitors to the Salon d'Automne of 1905, arousing the usual storm of protest.

In 1905 Matisse was an elderly thirty-five, and Picasso a boyish twenty-four: Matisse was a tall, fair-bearded, good-looking man, well-read, well-educated, well-mannered; a northern Frenchman of bourgeois origins, somewhat reserved, but at ease in society and particularly gifted for civil, intelligent conversation; and he delighted in the domestic joys—his wife and his daughter Marguerite were of the very first importance to Matisse. Apart from their common devotion to painting, no two men could well have been more unlike. Yet Matisse was the only painter to whose achievements Picasso reacted all his life long, the one standard by which he judged his own. Nothing could be more pointless than discussing which was the "better" painter; but two observations from these opposite and perhaps equal poles throw some light upon the men who created the aesthetic atmosphere in which we move. Matisse said, "A work of art must, both for the businessman and for the artist, be a mental tranquilizer, something in the nature of an armchair that gives him ease and comfort after bodily fatigue." (Admittedly he said this in 1908, when his armchair was not the most comfortable of objects.) Picasso said, "I am proud to say that I have never looked upon painting as an art intended for mere pleasure or amusement," and, "No: painting is not there just to decorate the walls of a flat. It is a means of waging offensive and defensive war against the enemy."

At the time of their meeting Picasso did not take a great deal of notice of the Fauves, although he knew some of them, particularly van Dongen: he was never much concerned with other people's trends, or at least not immediately. But Matisse liked him, and sometime later he proved his liking, his generosity, and his magnanimity by doing him the kindest service that one poor painter can do for another: he brought Sergei Shchukine, a middle-aged, sober, vegetarian cloth-merchant from Moscow, immensely wealthy. Fernande describes him as a little tallowy swine-faced man with a huge head and a terrible stutter; she also adds that he was a Jew: but Fernande saw Jews everywhere (she was said to be Jewish herself) and in fact Shchukine was an Old Believer. Plain or not, he was a sensitive, clear-sighted connoisseur, one of the most enlightened collectors of the age: his favorite occupation during his frequent visits to Paris was visiting the Egyptian galleries in the Louvre, where he, almost alone in his generation, saw the parallels between that ancient sculpture and Cézanne. At his first appearance in the rue Ravignan he bought two pictures, paying handsomely, and between that time and 1914 he bought at least fifty more—they are now in the Pushkin Museum in Moscow. He was followed by the gigantic sugar-millionaire Ivan Morosov, and by the outbreak of the war Russia possessed many splendid Picassos from the Blue Period to analytical Cubism; an inheritance that the lovers of socialist-realism have sometimes found embarrassing.

Matisse and Picasso understood the real worth of these wealthy amateurs: neither would for a moment have denied the value of money, but both knew that there was more to it than material gain. Recognition, acknowledgment, and intelligent praise are not only proofs of communication but also an immense stimulant. "The applause of even a single individual is of great moment," observed the dying Johnson; and speaking to Brassaï Picasso said, "But success is an important thing! It has often been said that an artist should work for himself, for the love of art, and scorn success. It's a false idea. An artist needs success. Not only in order to live, but primarily so that he can realize his work." No doubt some degree of success is necessary for every creative man to fulfill himself entirely; and for one like Picasso, half of whose mind was filled with doubt, moderate success was essential. Moderate success: for towards the end of his life, when fame, notoriety, wealth, and isolation from the common world had reached monstrous proportions, he said to David Duncan, "Of all—hunger, extreme poverty, the incomprehension of the public—fame is by far the worst. It is the castigation by God of the artist. It is sad. It is true."

Success was necessary, and it was coming, though with gradual and uneven steps that still left Picasso's livelihood in its usual state of total insecurity. Montmartre, that closed village of painters, writers, quiet citizens, and assorted toughs, had as yet no tourists; but it had plenty of visitors, most of them Parisians in search of fun. Yet some few were foreigners, Hungarians, Germans, Czechs, long pale Swedes, concerned with the arts and in quest of particular artists: some looked for Picasso, and some of those who found him asked him to explain his painting—what did it mean? All his life he loathed questions of this kind, and all his life he was plagued with them. "Everyone wants to understand art," he cried angrily. "Why not try to understand the song of a bird? Why does one love the night, flowers, everything around one, without trying to understand them? But in the case of painting people have to *understand* . . ." In later days he escaped by way of paradox or facetiousness or downright rudeness, but when he was young he set about it more briskly, with his pistol; and one night when he had been cruelly bored by an earnest band of Germans in the Lapin Agile he walked out, going towards the place du Tertre; with thick incomprehension they followed him, but on reaching the square he turned, whipped out his Browning, and fired a volley, a hint that even they could not ignore.

Yet not all the Germans were bores by any means: among them was a tall, formal young man with private means, Wilhelm Uhde. Whatever he may have read into Picasso's pictures, he concealed all unwelcome aesthetic philosophy and metaphysics, and became a collector and a friend.

In a book written much later he revealed his conviction that Picasso was the embodiment of the Gothic and the German soul, possibly because of his Basque origins, possibly because of the Spanish Visigoths, and even more probably because he was born under the sign of Uranus; but at the time of their close association he kept this to himself, displaying only his real love for the pictures. He began his career as a collector by finding a nude with tow-colored hair taking her bath in a blue room by an unknown young artist in Père Soulié's shop. (The famous "Blue Room," now in Washington and once offered to all comers by Berthe Weill, but in vain.) He bought it for ten francs, and then a few days later he walked into the Lapin Agile for the first time: "The low-ceilinged room was filled with young painters from the rue Gabrielle and the place Ravignan. Someone was reciting Verlaine. I sat at the big table in the middle and called for wine. In the course of the evening I learnt that the young man who had painted my picture was called Picasso and that he was sitting at my right."

Another who found his way to Picasso's door and knocked on it in the morning, obliging him to rise before twelve o'clock (not that he would do so unless the good concierge called out that this was a "serious visitor," meaning a merchant or a solvent amateur) was Olivier Saincère, a councilor of state, no less; and another, who kept more reasonable hours, was Paul Poiret, the eminent dressmaker.

These gentlemen brought money with them, and it was at about this time that Fernande scandalized the whole of Montmartre and even parts of Montparnasse by displaying a bottle of scent that had cost eighty francs: for now Picasso might have several hundred-franc notes at one given time. They came at irregular, unpredictable intervals, but they came, and he loved them: he could not bear, or he did not choose, to leave them at home, and he bought himself a wallet, which he fastened into his breast-pocket with a large safety-pin. One day he fancied that the pin was not quite as he had left it, and he stared round with a most suspicious and foreboding air. Fernande reports the fact; finds it amusing; and does not appear to feel that it throws an unusual light upon their relationship—a shaky relationship, by the way, for Gertrude Stein was accustomed to their partings; and if Toklas were a reliable witness (which she is not) one of the most dramatic of these came as soon as Picasso had enough money—by his code a man had to provide for a woman on leaving her.

Picasso liked to have money, there is no doubt about that, and he liked to keep it; but what sets him apart from most men in this respect is the fact that getting it did not fill him with elation. He found the whole business exhausting, particularly if it was accompanied by bargaining; but much more than that, he hated parting with his pictures. This was one of the very few things that stopped him working: the deep depression would not lift for days. He loved his pictures, and he loved painting them—could not conceive painting without love. Once, when he was very poor, Vollard passed on an order for a replica of "L'Enfant au pigeon"—"Picasso looked at me in surprise. 'But I should have no pleasure in copying my own work, and how do you suppose I could paint without enjoyment?' "

Gertrude Stein thought Vollard an amusing, unbusinesslike character; Fernande Olivier thought him deeply cunning, though agreeable: but a picture-dealer, if he is to survive, must possess flair and an acute sense of the shifting market; though he was far from infallible, Vollard had both, and a high degree of enterprise as well. He knew Shchukine, he knew the Steins; and although his interest in Picasso had hitherto been great enough for him to keep some Picassos in his mysterious cellars, to be shown only to the initiated, and to buy his small sculptures and have them cast in bronze, it now suddenly increased. He came to the Bateau-Lavoir and bought almost everything in the studio. His purchase included some thirty canvases; and he paid two thousand francs for the lot.

The sum of £2.64 may not seem a great deal for a big Picasso oil, but the total was a larger sum of money than Picasso had ever seen in his life. At Fernande's minimum rate of housekeeping the two thousand francs would have lasted three years, and even with what would have been prodigality for the abstemious Picasso it was a good twelve months' living. He decided that they should take a holiday; and the desolation of his empty studio may have helped his decision. He tore himself away from the sittings with Gertrude Stein, leaving her portrait unfinished (at the last session he painted out her face, in spite of all protests); he tore himself away from the Louvre, where a fascinating exhibition of ancient Iberian sculpture, unearthed in his native province, was being shown; and they took the train for Barcelona.

Fernande's presence neither surprised nor displeased the Ruizes; they liked her, regretted her irregular situation, and wondered that she did not marry Pablo: she did not mention the mad sculptor, still her legal spouse. She delighted his friends, Pallarès, the Sotos, and many others, some of whom she already knew from their Paris days; there is a surviving photograph of her, wearing a splendid hat, sitting in the Guayaba with Picasso and Ramon Reventós, and she and Picasso went to see his former haunts, including the studio in the Riera de Sant Joan, where his painted furniture still adorned the walls.

But this was only a pause in their voyage. A few days later they set off for Gósol, a remote mountain village at the far end of the province of Lérida, high in the Pyrenees and so close to the Andorran border that smuggling was an established way of life.

Why they chose it cannot be told with any certainty, but a connection between Picasso's friend the sculptor Casanovas and Gósol is the likeliest answer: their route is equally uncertain, for even recent maps show no road, only faint wandering tracks. However, their most probable way was to take the train to Ripoll, a diligence to Berga, and a wagon to Sant Llorens de Morunys: from that point onwards there was nothing for it but feet or a powerful mule. The track, a little wider now than it was in 1906 but still abominable, climbs over a series of improbable sierras by passes well over five thousand feet, through limestone mountains shattered and upheaved by ancient convulsions; sometimes the peaks are bare, with sheer ocher-colored precipices, and sometimes they are covered with pine-forest, where the trace of prodigious winds can be seen, the trunks lying like a heap of spillikins; but nowhere does there seem the least room for men. Eventually the path rises over one last barren pass, and there in the valley below lies Tuixent, a close-packed village on its own little hill, like Horta but in a far more savage landscape, far higher too and far more severe—gray stone houses, gray roofs, slightly relieved by the blue of shutters and embrasures. Now that Picasso has given one eyes to see it, the village is purely Cubist, and late Cubist at that, with intersecting or superimposed planes, shifting in sober color; and it seems to have no depth in the ordinary sense, for all perspective is confounded. Another day's ride, rising and falling through still more and still more spectacular mountains, with sheltered streams a great way down lined with tall poplar trees, would have brought them to the next inhabited place, Josa, a village the twin of Tuixent, though with an even finer Romanesque church crowning its hill: then climbing right out of the Josa valley through a deep forest and over still another watershed they would have reached the upper rim of a great smoothly-rounded cirque gouged out by some glacier long ago, and far below they would have beheld Gósol at last, a village somewhat like the other two, but richer, lying in a patchwork of bright green fields and sprawling wider from its hill—a hill topped by ancient ruined fortifications and an ancient ruined church. North of the village and hemming in the valley, the great bar of the Sierra del Cadi, rising eight thousand feet and more and shutting it off from Andorra: beyond, to the south and the east, a chaos of gray, green, and ocher mountains, with this small complex pattern of rectilinear walls and roofs providing order in the chaos.

Gósol is not a hundred miles from Barcelona in a straight line, but it was another world. Unlike Tuixent and Josa, which could only live by sheep and goats, some hardy cattle, and wood-cutting, Gósol was agricultural as well, and its life was very like that of Horta, a better watered, alpine Horta. Like Horta too it was well within the boundaries of the Catalan language and culture, so that Picasso felt perfectly at home—more at home than ever he was in Paris, says Fernande. They settled at the only inn, the Can Tempanada, a small house giving on to the vaguely triangular square, the heart of the village, where cattle drink at the perpetually flowing fountain and fill the air with their sweet breath: the house is still there, although it is no longer an inn, and in recent years a plaque has been set up on its outer wall, celebrating with some emphasis the stay of the *Spanish* painter Picasso.

Horta had left the deepest impression on him, and this was essentially the same unchanging, timeless life, with the additional pleasure of smuggling and the possibility of bears, boars, wild cats, the Pyrenean chamois, and even lynxes, as well as wolves. He understood the people, their work and play, their relationship to the land, and the rhythm of their days. His health, which had been much tried by the last years in Paris, was restored by the clean sharp air, the exercise, and the simple, copious food. What Fernande made of her mule, her journey, her surroundings, her diet, and her neighbors, and what they made of her cannot be deduced from her memoirs; she does not seem to have been quite sure where she was and she certainly could not communicate with anyone but Picasso; but so long as she could lie long abed she was content, and in her somnolent way she was quite pleased to see the improvement in her lover. His difficult manner disappeared; he made friends with the villagers, particularly with one ancient savage mountaineer, a smuggler by trade; and above all he worked. At intervals of roaming about the Sierra del Cadi and the lower valley with its astonishing geology of blood-red soil and green shattered rock with bands of native vermilion and coal, he turned out a great number of pictures and drawings; and these show some important new and apparently divergent approaches to the problems that concerned him so deeply. The order in which he produced them cannot now be followed with any certainty: years later Picasso himself put a wrong date on one of the most important, and even the devoted cataloguer Zervos assigns fourteen of them to 1905, when Picasso was in Paris. However, the following account, which is based on Barr, cannot be far out. When Picasso began working at Gósol he appears to have carried on with his classical manner, painting still, gently molded forms and using pink as he had once used blue, so that some of the canvases are monochromatic. There was a fairly straightforward portrait of Fernande, herself a statuesque figure by nature;

but a better example is a classical nude with both hands over her head (a pose that preoccupied him in the following years), arranging her hair in a glass held by another woman, this one clothed: both have Fernande's almond eyes and sleepy grace. Then came a certain hardening, the pink growing less rosy, the figures assuming a still more sculptural form and their faces an impassive, mask-like quality, as though the severe, archaic Iberians in the Louvre were showing through: the "Porteuse de pain," a big oil of a woman in a white kerchief carrying two huge flat rye loaves on a little white cushion on her head, shows this change, which became very much more marked when Picasso returned to Paris.

This steady progression is suddenly broken by a large and particularly important painting to which Picasso, no doubt badgered by some merchant or critic, gave the unmeaning title "Composition": it may have been actually painted when Picasso was back in Paris, but the conception and the preliminary drawings almost certainly belong to Gósol, as the bullocks do without a doubt—to Gósol and to the perfect, mild-eyed cattle of antiquity. Two barefoot peasants, carrying flowers, run beside a couple of bullocks: the man is immensely tall, his minute lemon-shaped head towers up, his forearms are enormous, he carries a great basket of flowers on his shoulders and their varied colors fill the top of the picture; the slim girl, half his size, has a simple bunch of them, held at her waist. They all run very close together, bullocks and people intermingled, and the canvas is alive with movement. In the flowers, the tall man, and the small girl there is a strong resemblance to the El Greco "Saint Joseph and the Child Jesus" at Toledo both in the arrangement and the physical distortion of the figures, a likeness still more apparent in a preliminary sketch before the bullocks were added; while the unification of the whole, both by means of this distortion (which Picasso had never carried so far before) and by the use of color in angular planes, looks back to El Greco and Cézanne and forward to Cubism.

Why the wild rushing delight? Why the bullocks? Far be it from me to offer an explanation ("In general those who try to explain pictures are entirely wrong," said Picasso to Juan Larrea) but I will mention a circumstance that may have some bearing on their presence: in mountain country the cattle usually stay out on the high pastures for the summer, and when the right season comes they are brought down, often with rejoicing and sometimes with wreaths of flowers about their horns.

These summer months of 1906 were an idyllic holiday; they produced a great deal of work; they restored Picasso's health and his immensely valuable contact with unchanging rural life, strengthened his body, mind, and spirit in isolation from all extraneous intellectual contacts; and they might have produced even more—they might have been prolonged far into the autumn—if a child at the inn had not fallen sick with what some describe as typhoid fever, others as typhus, the plague itself. Picasso was always terrified of illness, the precursor of death, the utter negation of all he stood for, and he insisted on instant flight, on leaving at once for France.

Fernande gives no details of how they crossed the entire range of the Pyrenees, but she does remember that they traveled from five in the morning until five at night before they reached a village from which they could take a diligence. This agrees with Josep Palau's statement that they rode from Gósol to Bellver on mules, there took a diligence to Puigcerda and another to Ax-les-Thermes in France, where the train carried them to Paris. (He also says that they first reached Gósol by taking the train as far as Guardiola, covering the last twenty miles by mule; but in 1906 it seems that the Guardiola line was open only for minerals, mostly coal.)

Back in Paris Picasso could refurnish his studio with the pictures brought from Gósol: almost the only canvas left from former times was the unfinished portrait of Gertrude Stein, with its face now a mere blur. Before ever he saw her again he painted it in from memory. The features that had so pleased her friends were replaced by a mask, immobile and intent, with severe, uneven, asymmetric eyes, the whole quite removed from the earlier hands and the careful drapery, thus acquiring a strange haunting value, another reality—surrealist before the letter. The friends were shocked; the sitter was delighted, as well she might have been, for it is a noble picture, a Gertrude Stein without self-consciousness, affectation, or complacency—and as for likeness, she came to resemble her portrait in time, as Picasso foretold.

This was followed by another, a portrait of the artist himself, holding his symbolic palette; and here the mask-like quality is even more accentuated. Then came two nudes, massive, stocky, sculptural women, coppery pink, archaic, ugly by conventional standards, devoid of sentiment. Only their color connects them, and that but tenuously, with the Rose Period: the whole feeling, the present climate of Picasso's mind, was entirely different.

His solitary meditations and countless other circumstances, including "primitive" art, were producing a radical change. He was perfectly open about the continuing influence of the Catalan Romanesque sculpture and frescoes he had known in his youth, just as considerably later he acknowledged the importance of Iberian art to his painting at this period, when he had not only been studying it at the Louvre but also possessed two small figures of the same epoch, acquired from Apollinaire's friend Géry Piéret.

But the influence of African carvings is another matter. Negro art was in the air, common property, much as Japanese prints had been for an earlier generation; nevertheless there was then and there has been ever since a great deal of talk about who first discovered it, as though African sculpture were all the same, and as though all these different aspects of reality or rather all these different approximations to truth from the angle of another culture were a trick that could be used to produce "modern" art, a gadget that could be invented, patented, and applied to the solution of contemporary problems. Claims to priority, foolish or disingenuous, accusations of plagiarism, flew about; and some of them so irritated Picasso that he uttered some equally foolish rejoinders, such as "Negro art? Never heard of it." And it may be that in time his continuing irritation led him to magnify the importance of the Iberians, as a counterweight to the Negroes: at all events, even the erudition of Alfred Barr cɹn find no reference to the Iberians in any book on Picasso nor in his own recorded conversations before 1939. Yet this "African controversy" did not arise until after 1907, and on the evidence it seems safe to say that in late 1906 and early 1907 Picasso was aware of African, Oceanic, and other "primitive" carvings, but not yet acutely aware of them.

He was also aware of the Fauves. There was much more talk of them in Paris than there had been before he went to Spain: they were by far the most exciting group since the Neo-Impressionists. He did not join their ranks, of course—he never joined anybody's ranks—but as soon as he called at the rue de Fleurus he saw the great "Joie de Vivre" that Matisse had exhibited at the Indépendants during his absence and that Leo Stein had purchased; and not only this picture but also his increasing acquaintance with Matisse, Vlaminck, Derain, and a little later Braque convinced him that although their answer was not his answer, they were men of such stature that a counterblast was in order, to restore the balance.

Then again Cézanne died in October of 1906, and the subsequent exhibitions brought him even more closely to Picasso's mind: he had always admired Cézanne, and the more he saw of his work the more he realized that Cézanne had been obsessed by the same problems that he was trying to answer himself. Whether he read the words "Deal with nature by the cylinder, the sphere and the cone, and put them all into perspective. . . . For us men nature exists more in depth than on the surface" when they were first published or not, he very soon heard them from Jacob or Apollinaire or Raynal or Salmon, and they brought an instant response, the agreement of a like-thinking mind. Furthermore he saw the version of Cézanne's "Trois baigneuses" that Matisse possessed: and here again that unfortunate word "influence," so freely bandied about, suggests itself. Sometimes it is used to mean the mere copying of a mannerism, direct theft, and sometimes it hovers ambiguously over a wide area; but there is a strong case for the assertion that no man can be influenced—influenced to the degree of producing a valid work of art and not a mere pastiche—by anything that is not at least latent in his mind.

With all this present to his spirit and with innumerable other stimuli, reflections, decisions for which his subsequent work is the only evidence, Picasso's mind was in a ferment during the autumn of 1906 and the spring of 1907. The outcome, after the pictures that have just been mentioned and a few more, was a long series of drawings and preliminary studies for a most ambitious composition in which he was to combine his pictural and sculptural concepts and a great deal more besides, ideas to do with space, volume, mass, color, surface, and line: the starting point in conventional reality was a brothel and its more or less naked women, a recollection of his younger days in the Calle d'Avinyó; and in an early sketch a sailor is sitting in the middle of them with fruit and flowers at his feet, while on the left a student appears, carrying a skull. As the studies progressed and as Picasso came to grapple with the real issues at stake (morality went by the board as soon as anecdote) the sailor vanished, leaving only his melon, grapes, pear, and peach; and when the final painting reached completion in the spring of 1907 only five whores remained. Their humanity had been abstracted, left behind, together with all trace of feeling: their pink or ocher bodies, almost devoid of modeling, are arranged in a low left to right diagonal anchored by a squatting figure on the lower right, a figure resembling one of Cézanne's bathers. The three women on the left have the mask-like faces of Gósol, but more so; one head in profile shows a full-face eye and two full-face heads show the nose in profile, as sharp as a wedge of cheese; the bodies are made up largely of straight lines and angular planes and they stand against a shallow background of varying blue, the only hint of depth being a brown curtain thrust by an upheld hand. But on the right the violence of distortion reaches a new pitch and a difference of kind: the face of the squatting figure, turned right round over her back, has its features savagely jumbled, and that of the woman above is a long ridge, a snout, strongly hatched to give it height, very like some Congo masks: neither of these heads is of the same nature as the other three, and in this half of the picture, the last half painted, all the angular planes—drapery, breasts, interstices—are much sharper, much more definite. At one point he thought of repainting the earlier, left-hand half; but then he reflected, ''No: people will understand what I am trying to do,'' and he left it alone.

When at last he stood away from the whole great incantatory picture he had produced the first direct statement of Cubism with its whole range of new potentialities and its new aesthetic; a frightening, revolutionary canvas, his anarchist bomb tossed into Western European painting. If he had meant to equal or even to surpass Matisse he had certainly done so.

He called some chosen friends to his studio, wishing to communicate this message from another world whose aesthetics were based not on conventional beauty, still less on anecdote, prettiness, or charm, but on some great force without a name. They could not grasp it at all: their only reactions were shock, alarm, regret, dismay, some nervous or indignant laughter. Even the percipient Shchukine shook his head and said, "What a loss to French art."

The bomb had not gone off. At least, it had not gone off when Picasso hoped it would: for the explosion came in time, if a long, gradually strengthening process can be described as an explosion, and the "Demoiselles d'Avignon" (it was André Salmon who gave it that arch and foolish title) proved one of the most dynamic, liberating pictures of our age.

Chapter VII

THE ordinary human side of Picasso was discouraged, hurt, and even dismayed by this reception: by Braque's "You want to make us eat tow and drink paraffin," by the anger of Matisse, by Leo Stein's "You have been trying to paint the fourth dimension; how amusing," accompanied by a braying laugh that Picasso could still imitate a generation later, and by Vollard's "It's the work of a madman." He put the picture by and about ten years later he even took the carefully prepared reinforced canvas off the stretcher, rolled it up, and laid it away in a corner. But the extraordinary side of the painter paid no attention to any judgment but his own. The idea was still strong in him; he had not fully worked it out, and he continued painting brilliant postscripts to the "Demoiselles" for months. It is true that Uhde and Kahnweiler liked the picture; but Uhde, though enthusiastic, was not the wisest of men, and Kahnweiler, a very young German Jew who, to Vollard's indignation, had recently opened a gallery, wanted to be Picasso's exclusive dealer. He did in fact buy all the preliminary sketches in time, but for years the wounded Picasso would not sell the picture itself, on the pretext that it was not finished; and in the end it was not Kahnweiler who bought it but Jacques Doucet, who added it to his collection in 1921. In the intervening period, however, while it stood about in his various studios it was seen by the countless painters and lovers of painting who called on him, and it worked on them powerfully, like a radio-active source whose effects are seen in the long term rather than in the moment of its creation.

The essential Picasso carried straight on into this new country, into what is labeled his Negro Period, although his other half, the ordinary, ambitious man, was perfectly aware of the probable consequences of his action. He had appeared in a most respectable light when he took to his unmarketable blue pictures in 1901 and 1902; but he was then little more than a boy and the material success he threw away did not amount to a great deal. But by 1907 he was on the threshold—beyond the threshold—

of a great career leading to fame and wealth; he had already tasted the delight of real money in his pocket, all the canvases, colors, and sable brushes he could want, a carefree, properly-nourished life; and his deliberate renunciation, which would mean a return to his old shifts, to Père Soulié and a most dubious future, perhaps to a short lifetime of poverty, was heroic. Yet he took the step without the least hesitation, as the most natural thing in the world: and if those people who still speak of Picasso as a charlatan, an impostor perpetually trying to scandalize the bourgeoisie, a professional publicity-seeking outrager, cannot be convinced by his painting (and obviously they cannot) then this gives them the lie direct.

On some occasions Picasso said that his painting was one continuous process of research; on others he said it was nothing of the kind. For the moment it is convenient to take the first dictum, since it allows one to say that the "Demoiselles" brought him to the verge of explicit Cubism, and that before he carried on in that direction his quest led him to those associated studies of form and volume that constitute his Negro Period.

The whole question of "who discovered the blacks first and who told whom" is hopelessly confused. Vlaminck had two Dahomey figures and four from the Ivory Coast in 1905, one of which, a white mask, he sold to Derain, in whose studio Picasso and Matisse beheld it with amazement: Matisse bought a Negro head at an antique shop in the rue de Rennes because of its affinity with Egyptian art and showed it to Picasso at the Steins: and there are many other accounts. Picasso's own version was that he happened to be in the Musée de Sculpture Comparée in the Trocadéro sometime after he had painted the "Demoiselles," that out of mere curiosity he walked through the door that led to the Musée d'Ethnographie, and that there African sculpture was first revealed to him.

Here the priority of dates is irrelevant; nor does it seem to me to matter whether Picasso saw Itumba masks before he painted the upper right-hand figure in the "Demoiselles" or not, though he almost certainly did. What does matter is the word *revealed*, because although Braque, Matisse, Vlaminck, and the whole advanced artistic world of Paris took to admiring and collecting what they called fetishes, they admired them as sculpture, whereas Picasso alone saw them for what they were.

In *La Tête d'Obsidienne* André Malraux relates a conversation that he had with Picasso in 1937, at the time he was painting "Guernica." Picasso said, "People are always talking about the influence of the blacks on me. What can one say? We all of us liked those fetishes. Van Gogh said, 'We all of us had Japanese art in common.' In our day it was the Negroes. Their forms did not influence me any more than they influenced Matisse. Or Derain. But as far as Matisse and Derain were concerned, the Negro masks were just so many other carvings, the same as the rest of sculpture. When Matisse showed me his first Negro head he talked about Egyptian art.

"When I went to the Trocadéro, it was revolting. Like a flea-market. The smell. I was all by myself. I wanted to get out. I didn't go: I stayed. It came to me that this was very important: something was happening to me, right?

"Those masks were not just pieces of sculpture like the rest. Not in the least. They were magic. And why weren't the Egyptians or Chaldees? We hadn't understood what it was really about: we had seen primitive *sculpture,* not magic. These Negroes were intercessors—that's a word I've known in French ever since then. Against everything: against unknown, threatening spirits. I kept on staring at these fetishes. Then it came to me—I too was against everything. I too felt that everything was unknown, hostile! Everything! Not just this and that but everything, women, children, animals, smoking, playing . . . Everything! I understood what their sculpture meant to the blacks, what it was really for. Why carve like that and not in any other way? After all, they were not Cubists. Because Cubism did not exist . . . all these fetishes were for the same thing. They were weapons. To help people not to be ruled by spirits anymore, to be independent. Tools. If you give spirits a shape, you break free from them. Spirits and the subconscious (in those days we weren't yet talking about the subconscious much) and emotion—they're all the same thing. I grasped why I was a painter. All alone in that museum, surrounded by masks, Red Indian dolls, dummies covered with dust. The 'Demoiselles' must have come that day: not at all because of their forms, no; but because it was my first exorcizing picture—that's the point.

"And that's why later on I also painted pictures like the ones I had painted earlier on—Olga's portrait, other portraits. You can't be a witch-doctor all day long! How could you live?

"That's another thing that cut me off from Braque. He liked the Negroes, but as I've said because they were good sculpture. He was never just a little afraid of them. He was just not interested in exorcism. Because he never felt what I've called Everything, or life, or what shall I say—the World? Everything around us, everything that is not us: he never thought it hostile. Nor even strange: can you imagine that? He was always at home. . . . Still is, even now . . . he hasn't the least notion of these things: he's not superstitious."

This is by far the most revealing piece of Picasso's conversation that I have ever heard or read. Whether the reference to the "Demoiselles" is literally, chronologically, true or not is insignificant compared with the statement of his attitude of mind. Admittedly the conversation is reported by a brilliant writer of fiction thirty-seven years after the event; admittedly Picasso was speaking to an author deeply concerned with aesthetics, and Picasso could play any man's game and often play it better; but even when all allowances are made it seems to me that this account of his reaction to Negro art is perfectly sincere, and what is much more important—indeed fundamental to an understanding of the man—that it is a truthful record of his spiritual state, the state of one who is not at home but who is surrounded by an inimical world: a true outsider.

I have rarely felt the inadequacy of translation so much as in trying to convey the feeling of this piece: I have done what I can, but the English does not and perhaps cannot bring Picasso's racy tone across, the slightly inaccurate though fluent French, the slightly incongruous foreigner's slang. But I hope the sincerity does come through, together with his strong sense of the immanent (immanent evil in this case, but immanent good in others) that constituted his largely but not wholly pagan religion and that explains so much of his outlook, including, among other things, his comparative unwillingness to touch traditional Christian subjects.

Picasso's Negro Period certainly had nothing remotely to do with Christianity nor with current Western tradition: to the learned eye the strange figures of 1907 and 1908 show a merging of ancient Iberia, of Romanesque Cataluñia, and of Africa in varying proportions, while to the unlearned they seem to be essentially Picasso, a Picasso thinking along new lines and in an idiom enriched by fresh acquisitions. There was still the old conflict between the pictural and the sculptural, between vivid decorative color and somber monochrome, movement and stillness; sometimes the one prevailed, as in the barbaric "Dancer," sometimes the other; and hindsight sees Picasso working back towards the Cubist solution he had already used, without perhaps realizing its full potentiality, in the "Demoiselles."

Among the fresh acquisitions of 1907 and 1908, Picasso's twenty-sixth year, were a deeper knowledge of Cézanne, the friendship of Braque, and the discovery of Rousseau. To these might be added a large number of Negro and Oceanic masks and the two Iberian figures of mysterious provenance, given him by Piéret.

The Salon d'Automne of 1907 had a retrospective exhibition of Cézanne's work, a far larger number of paintings than Picasso had ever seen before, and his admiration for the great man increased still more. In spite of his unshakable determination and his dominating personality, Picasso's was a lonely spirit, often tormented by doubt; and he found deep comfort, a source of strength, in the knowledge that another mind had moved in the same direction as his, grappling with the same problems and arriving at not dissimilar answers, answers improbable in the France of his day and misunderstood or ignored by most of his contemporaries. And however much he and Matisse and the other advanced painters of the early century might differ, they all agreed in this. "For us, Cézanne was like a mother who protects her children," he said to Kahnweiler; and to Brassaï, "He was my one and only master. . . . I've spent years studying his pictures . . . Cézanne! He was as you might say a father to us all. It was he who protected us." Yet influence (for want of a better word) was a process that took a long time to work on Picasso, and little that is obviously connected with Cézanne can be seen until the summer of 1908.

In the case of Braque and Picasso there was no question of influence: it was a matter rather of interaction, the exchange of ideas, of the most animated, stimulating conversation, often shared by Derain, in the fetid atmosphere of Azon's eating-house, and eventually of collaboration. Braque was a tall, burly Norman, a few months younger than Picasso. He came from a family of house-painters and decorators; he was himself apprenticed to the trade, and he had a professional's respect for technique and sound craftsmanship. Although he had gone to the lycée at a time when secondary education in France was reserved for the privileged few, he preferred an artisan's style of life: Fernande did not care for him—"a powerful head like a white Negro, a boxer's neck and shoulders, dark complexion, curly black hair, heavy . . . an often deliberately rough, churlish expression, a coarse way of speaking and acting. No kind of elegance, but free and easy in his ready-made clothes. By way of a tie, the loosely-knotted little black string that Norman peasants often wear. Rather carelessly dressed or wishing to appear so. Features deeply marked with a subtle intelligence: suiting himself very easily to others, suspicious, clever, cunning—in short, a typical Norman." It may be that the accordion-playing Braque offended her gentility, which would suddenly dart out at strange moments, or it may be that she was jealous of Picasso's incessant conversations with him on subjects that he rarely discussed with anyone. At all events she did not cherish Braque, and she accused him of secretly cribbing Picasso's Cubism: yet in the long run he and his wife, Marcelle, were better friends to Fernande than her former lover.

At this time Braque was a leading Fauve: he was doing well, and Kahnweiler had taken him under contract. At first, when Apollinaire brought him to see the "Demoiselles," he would have nothing to do with the picture nor with the concepts behind it; he argued with Picasso for weeks and went away unconvinced. But both Cézanne's and Picasso's words and example worked on him; he embarked upon a fresh series of plastic experiments, and by the end of 1907 he had painted his "Grand nu," of a definitely Cubist tendency; while during the summer of 1908, which he spent at Cézanne's old haunt of L'Estaque, near Marseilles, he carried them still farther in that direction.

1908 was also the year in which Picasso bought his first picture by Henri Rousseau: this was a very large canvas, the portrait of Yadwigha, a kind Polish schoolmistress. "It obsessed me from the moment I saw it," he told Florent Fels. "I was walking along the rue des Martyrs. A second-hand dealer had piles of canvases all along the front of his shop. A head stuck out, a woman's face with a hard look . . . French penetration, clarity, decision. A huge canvas. I asked the price. 'Five francs,' said the dealer, 'You can paint over it.' It is one of the most revealing French psychological portraits."

At this time Rousseau was sixty-four, a timid, gray-bearded man who blushed easily: a self-taught painter of wonderful oneiric pictures whose true worth was recognized by few people in his lifetime. Even now many writers adopt an insufferably condescending tone, calling him a "little man" (he was no smaller than Picasso), a naïf, and challenging his statement that he went to Mexico in the 1860's as a bandsman; and many of his contemporaries in that unspeakably vulgar Belle Epoque made open fun of him. Apollinaire called him the Douanier because he had been employed in the *octroi*, the internal customs, at the gates of Paris, and the nickname has stuck, losing its unkindness with the years; the initial hostility lasted, and even as late as 1912, when Uhde observed in the preface to the catalog of the Rousseau exhibition at Berheim-Jeune that his detractors were being defeated, a newspaper critic replied, "Defeated? Yes, it is true. It seems that Henri Rousseau is much prized in Germany and the Russias. That is quite possible. But most fortunately we are Frenchmen, and we are in France."

In our day the prophet is honored even in his own country: Rousseau is in the Louvre, and it is universally acknowledged that his painting is of a very high order indeed. It cannot be classified: to call it the best children's painting raised to the highest degree is to say something valid about its spontaneity, innocence, and directness of vision, but it is to ignore Rousseau's remarkable technique, his wholly personal and magic perspective, his masterly use of black (Renoir's touchstone for a very good painter), and many, many other factors. Certainly he was an unworldly man, as well as a lovable one; and his own words show his nature better than any description. There is his often-quoted remark to Picasso, "We are the two

greatest painters of our age, you in the Egyptian, I in the modern style,"
but this conversation with Vollard on the subject of ghosts tells us more
about him, and about Apollinaire:

Vollard: No, I don't believe in them.

Rousseau: Well, I do. I've seen some. There was one that persecuted
me for quite a while.

Vollard: Indeed? What did it look like?

Rousseau: Just an ordinary man. . . . He used to come and defy me
when I was on duty at the *octroi*. He knew I couldn't leave my post, so he
used to put out his tongue or make long noses at me and then let off a
great fart.

Vollard: But what makes you think he was a ghost?

Rousseau: Monsieur Apollinaire told me so.

Rousseau was not unknown, although Picasso had never heard of him.
He had exhibited for years at the Salon des Indépendants and the Salon
d'Automne; Jarry had reproduced one of his pictures in *L'Ymagier;* and
Uhde, a man of exquisite sensibility in spite of his foolish theories, was
buying his works. Yet his was a very modest reputation, overshadowed
by gross mockery; and Picasso, deeply impressed by his value, determined to do him honor—to offer a banquet to Henri Rousseau.

It was a perilous undertaking. Rousseau was as vulnerable as a child,
and few of the people to be invited had any real appreciation of his painting. Apollinaire, for example, put "Le Poète et sa muse" (a portrait of
himself and Marie Laurencin, a present from Rousseau) in his cellar, and
several of them were capable of treating the whole thing as a cruel hoax.
Fernande herself was so ignorant of Picasso's mind and so unaware of
Rousseau's merit even after she had lived with his work for years that she
could say that the group, the *bande à Picasso,* was "delighted to pull the
Douanier's leg"; while through the mouth of Alice Toklas, Gertrude
Stein says it was to be a "jokeful amusement." Furthermore, neither Pi-
casso nor Fernande had the least notion of how to give a banquet.

Still, they set about it: the studio was cleaned to a point that satisfied
Picasso; crockery, glasses, tin forks and spoons were borrowed from
Azon; Yadwigha was hung among the larger African carvings, with Chinese lanterns and colored garlands on the pillars and the beams, and a
great streamer, surrounded by flags, reading HONNEUR À ROUSSEAU.
Food was ordered from the caterer Félix Potin (an excellent move, if
either Picasso or Fernande had told Félix Potin the right day), Fernande
prepared a paella to eke it out, drink was laid in on an heroic scale, the
people were invited. Marie Laurencin and Apollinaire (he was to bring

the guest of honor), Leo and Gertrude Stein and Alice Toklas, Braque, Ramon Pichot and Germaine, Agero, Cremnitz, Raynal, and many more including a number of young women. Some say that Max Jacob was not asked, he having had one of his periodical quarrels with Picasso; but nevertheless his studio—for he now lived in the Bateau-Lavoir—was taken over as one of the cloakrooms.

There were about thirty guests in all, and several of them have left accounts of the banquet, accounts that differ widely, not only in detail but in their view of the nature of the feast, some seeing it as general fun, others as an elaborate practical joke, so that one reads them with a mounting anxiety for the good, ingenuous, unarmed old man, their potential victim. But it ended happily, and this I believe was due to Picasso's real determination to do him honor: Picasso was in his own studio, he had an ascendancy over most of those present, and with Braque's powerful help he was perfectly capable of dealing with anyone who grew out of hand.

It began badly. The guests assembled in a bar for apéritifs while the dinner was preparing; the wait was strangely prolonged, and a somber Dane passed out, while others poured drink into the pretty young Marie Laurencin (a new arrival in that world, and already hated by Fernande), so that on reaching the studio she plunged into a dish of tarts on the divan and then, covered with cream and jam, tried to embrace the company. Meanwhile, Potin's dinner not having appeared, Fernande and Alice Toklas scoured Paris to supplement the paella: with reasonable success.

In time everybody was seated at the long rickety trestle table: amidst cheers Apollinaire arrived with Rousseau, who gazed at the lanterns and whose shy face broke into a delighted smile. He was placed on a throne made of a chair on a little platform, and the banquet began. After the paella and some unrecorded dishes came poems, declamations: Apollinaire produced what he swore was impromptu verse—

> *Tu te souviens, Rousseau, du paysage aztèque,*
> *Des forêts où poussaient la mangue et l'ananas*
> *Des singes répandant tout le sang des pastèques*
> *Et du blond empereur qu'on fusilla là-bas.*

. . .

> *Nous sommes réunis pour célébrer ta gloire.*
> *Ces vins qu'en ton honneur nous verse Picasso*
> *Buvons-les donc puisque c'est l'heure de les boire*
> *En criant tous en choeur: "Vive! Vive Rousseau!"*

[You remember the Aztec landscape, Rousseau, the forest where the mangoes and the pineapples grow, the monkeys shedding the water-melon's blood, and the fair-haired emperor who was shot over there. We are gathered to celebrate your fame. And since now is the time for drinking let us drink this wine that Picasso pours out in your honor, crying all together "Long, long live Rousseau!"]

More poems, toasts; and Rousseau, who had drunk more than he was used to, dozed gently under his lantern, which dropped wax onto his head, though from so considerable a height that it did not hurt him, but formed an unnoticed mound.

The night wore on, and if anyone had gone to bed in the Bateau-Lavoir Salmon put an end to their sleep: all at once he sprang on to the table, pronounced a eulogy, drained his glass, and instantly became violent—he and Cremnitz had agreed to simulate an attack of delirium tremens with the help of soap for the froth, but it seems that Salmon's zeal, prompted by measureless wine, carried him away. In the ensuing battle the Negro figures were threatened; but Braque protected them, while Picasso dragged Salmon away and locked him in a cloakroom, where he went to sleep, having eaten Alice Toklas' new hat and a box of matches. Rousseau dozed throughout.

Then came songs, some by Marie Laurencin, some by Rousseau, who also played his fiddle. At times he dropped off again, waking to listen to his neighbors with particular civility and attention, and quietly telling them of his days in Mexico. At some point the tall, gaunt, bearded Pichot danced a Spanish mime of the Passion; and at some other point Frédé came in with his ass from the Lapin Agile; and again a horde of Montmartre acquaintances appeared, seizing upon the remains of the feast; but it is difficult to establish the sequence of events or to state how the evening came to an end for some of the guests. At about three in the morning the Steins went away, taking Rousseau with them in a cab; and it is certain that Picasso had achieved his aim—Rousseau had had the happiest time of his life; his candor had seen nothing but the good in the banquet; he felt that he had been deeply honored and he wrote Picasso a beautifully penned letter to tell him so.

Some of his contemporaries say that this marked the end of Picasso's most sociable period, and it is true that in 1908 and 1909 he was working even harder in the direction of explicit analytical Cubism. But during these last years at the Bateau-Lavoir he still saw a great deal of his friends: being gregarious by nature, he could not do without company after the intense solitude of work. And there was no lack of it. Quite apart from his old Catalan friends—and he lost few of them from sight—there were all the people of the crowded Bateau-Lavoir, where everybody visited everybody else and where he was now one of the senior residents. Max Jacob had deserted his somber lair farther down the street for what had been Mac Orlan's studio, and here he carried on with his new practice of palmistry, of reading cards and coffee-grouts, casting horoscopes, fabricating talismans, terrifying his friends, who in spite of all their rational doubts dared not abandon his charms: Picasso, for one, kept Jacob's reading of his hand with religious care to the very end of his life.* Presently André Salmon moved in too, and Modigliani and Freundlich made their appearance. Another arrival was a young German called Wiegels who came to Paris persuaded that Impressionism and *Modern' Style* were the very latest thing, discovered his error, and took to evil courses. Van Dongen was still there, with his Dutch wife and their little daughter, for whom Picasso made a sinister doll out of a black stocking; but van Dongen's days of extreme poverty, his diet of spinach alone, were almost at an end, for he had painted a fine erotic nude of Fernande (though its origin was never acknowledged) which excited a great deal of comment and launched him on his career as a fashionable "modern" portraitist.

When the nineteen-year-old and utterly destitute Gris arrived from Madrid, where he had studied under Carbonero, Picasso housed him, helped him to place his humorous drawings in *L'Assiette au Beurre* and *Le Charivari*, and Fernande fed him. She disliked young Gris however, and she says that "he studied what might be called the dodges of Cubism, made use of them with a sort of cleverness but without art, and contented himself with that."

Many of Fernande's other judgments were, if not grotesque, then certainly unkind: Marie Laurencin, for example, vexed her extremely, and she not only demolishes her painting but says that the tip of her nose was often red. It was Braque who first brought Marie Laurencin into the *bande à Picasso;* they were fellow-students at the Académie Humbert and one day he took her to Sagot's, where she met Picasso and Apollinaire. (Some say that Apollinaire was not there, but that Picasso introduced him to Marie Laurencin later, meaning to do him a kindness: all the sources of information for Picasso's earlier years, except perhaps Sabartés, are unreliable for detail, date, and often truth.) Hitherto Apollinaire had been uniformly unfortunate as a lover, but he and Marie Laurencin were happy for several years; and she moved on to a more ambitious painting. She continued to live a very proper, even a prim, bourgeois life with her mother,

*It is given in the Appendix.

being allowed out from time to time to plunge into tarts or hashish parties and to make love with Apollinaire in his armchair; for he carried neatness to such a pitch that he would not allow his smooth counterpane to be disturbed.

In Fernande Olivier's book more harsh words are reserved for Kahnweiler, a new and important factor in Picasso's life, in fact his dealer: she represents him as "Very young, operating very much on the German method, clever, tenacious, cunning, though not so cunning as Vollard, a real Jewish businessman, capable of taking a risk in order to make a profit. Daring, busy. He wanted to have Picassos, Matisses, van Dongens, Vlamincks, and he got them . . . bargaining for hours on end until at last the exhausted painter agreed to a lower price." By definition, a dealer cannot be wholly disinterested; but in addition to being a dealer Kahnweiler was also a highly cultivated man with a deep understanding and appreciation of art, and he remained Picasso's friend for the next sixty years and more: yet on the other hand even after all these years Picasso did not use the intimate *tu* when speaking to Kahnweiler. It is true that the adult Picasso always maintained a certain distance, yet it is surprising to see this formality so early in his career, and it may be significant of his views on the relationship between a painter and a dealer.

Then there were the visitors to the studio, continually increasing in number, for Picasso's radical change had not thrust him back into obscurity, as it might reasonably have been expected to do: Schchukine came, and although he could not accept the "Demoiselles" he still bought pictures; so did Uhde. Many were foreigners, Germans, Russians, Hungarians, even Chinese, but some, like André Level, were French. And there were the evenings at the Steins, meetings with Matisse, Dufy, and many more, Poiret's sensational parties, and above all Picasso's eager, searching conversations with Braque, one of the few to whom he talked for hours and hours without any other company, ("The things Picasso and I said to one another during those years will never be said again, and even if they were no one would understand them anymore. It was like being roped together on a mountain," said Braque) for in general he liked to move about with a group. Gertrude Stein has a fine picture of him looking like a small but dominating Napoleon, followed by his four enormous grenadiers Derain, Apollinaire, Braque, and Salmon. She also uses the figure of a "bullfighter followed by his squadron." And Fernande has another of Picasso with Max Jacob, Paul Fort, Princet the mathematician, Apollinaire, Marie Laurencin, and Salmon at Azon's, all eating hashish pills. The evening finished at the Bateau-Lavoir, in Princet's deserted room, his wife Alice having run off with Derain; their host wept, though not without a certain satisfaction; Jacob smiled quietly to himself; Apollinaire imagined that he was enjoying himself in a brothel (Marie Laurencin, totally unaffected, had gone home to her mother and Pussy Cat); but Picasso had a wretched trip—it came to him that he had invented photography, that he had nothing more to learn, and that worst of all he had come to a dead end, painting the same thing over and over again.

These experiments ceased abruptly as far as Picasso was concerned: not only was there the threat of entering the creative artist's hell forever, but one day the inhabitants of the Bateau-Lavoir found poor Wiegels dead, hanging by the neck from a beam in his studio: opium, said some, ether-drinking, hashish, said others.

Picasso was appalled, and one of the reasons for his decision to spend his summer in the uncongenial damp, fungus-smelling north French country was the crippling depression that came down on him after this suicide. Another was his health, a source of constant worry all his life. He smoked far too much, at first a pipe and then Gauloises for the rest of his days, and in the mornings he had a smoker's cough: he was persuaded that this was the onset of consumption, and when one night his coughing broke a small blood-vessel so that he spat red, the mortal disease became a certainty—he was near his end. He was seized with panic, and André Salmon ran for a doctor, a nearby friend. The medical man inspected his patient, laughed, and said, "He is as sound as a bell." Picasso did not believe him, and from that time onwards his diet grew more abstemious still and his apéritifs were replaced by mineral water, though he never abandoned either wine or tobacco.

He and Fernande found a primitive cottage or outbuilding belonging to a farm in the hamlet of La Rue-des-Bois; it was only about twenty-five miles from Paris, but it was surprisingly remote; and it stood on the edge of the forest of Halatte. They took it for the summer and moved in with the big bitch and a she-cat near her time. Friends came to stay, Max Jacob, Apollinaire, Derain; but not Braque, for he was away in the far south, painting at L'Estaque.

Picasso was just as busy at La Rue-des-Bois: it would have been strange if he had not painted with at least equal zeal, and it would have been strange if his mind and Braque's had not moved on roughly similar lines.

For some time now Picasso's painting has been tending more towards the sculptural and the static and away from the active figures of what had been called the barbaric part of his Negro Period. Many of the canvases are painted in varying shades of reddish-brown and in all the color is subdued, compared with the violence of the postscripts to the "Demoiselles." But La Rue-des-Bois was a green world: green filled the forest; and the fields, so unlike the sun-baked pastures of Horta, were an even stronger green; green reflected from innumerable surfaces into the damp northern air; it gave him a green colic, he said: and green suffused his canvases. Before the summer ended he had painted a large number of pictures—landscapes, portraits and still-lives. Most were landscapes, which were unusual in his work since Horta: but for Picasso a landscape was a particular form of statement; he was not concerned with making remarks about the weather nor about the light at that time of the day, not with the contingent aspects of what lay before him but rather with what he *knew* to be its essential bones. And these bones he arranged with the classical rigor of a Poussin, though without the earlier painter's convention of perspective to give his picture depth. Picasso was looking for what he conceived to be a truer relation between volumes, and this he achieved by a variety of methods, including the use of superimposed planes and naturally of a high degree of simplification, a stripping away of all accidentals. Here and there a deliberate array of leaves or a black, sinuous branch gives a hint of his admiration for Rousseau; but, leaving Picasso's overwhelming personality aside as far as such an abstraction is possible, it is Cézanne that comes to mind, especially in the deceptively simple still-lives, one of which actually used the tall billycock hat so familiar in Cézanne.

Towards the end of his stay he painted the farmer's wife, wearing a blue dress and sitting in a chair. It was a picture that Shchukine particularly admired, a powerful great motionless form built up of largely symmetrical angular planes, emphasized by shadow and standing away from a green and purple background. Superficially it is far removed from Cézanne's woman in a blue dress, "La Femme à la cafetière," but a second glance shows the kinship: the Cézanne is more accessible to the citizen's eye, but it would be interesting to know what Picasso's peasant made of her own picture. It is the portrait of a figure outside time, perhaps of one so unaffected by recent convention that she would have gone directly to its significance, just as Catalan peasants go straight to their fierce archaic black Virgins.

But before this he painted one of the most significant pictures of 1908, of what some historians prefer to call the Proto-Cubist rather than the Negro Period: a wooded landscape with figures—two great trees embracing a dell—in which the rocks, the sloping ground, and above all the recumbent figure in the foreground are treated according to the geometry of

Cézanne as interpreted and expanded by Picasso: the picture is fully Cubist in all but name.

The name itself was soon to come. Autumn brought the painters back to Paris, and Braque and Picasso found that their independent summer's work had converged. There was no remaining hint of Fauvism in the landscapes and still-lives Braque had painted at L'Estaque; on the contrary, the seven pictures he submitted to the Salon d'Automne of 1908 had entirely abandoned the unrestrained and lawless brilliance of his earlier phase; they were severely disciplined, "geometrical," subdued in color. Now, long after all passion and personal antagonisms have died away, it is said that Fauvism, with its disregard for perspective and modeling, its deliberate distortion, and its use of flat surfaces, was in some respects quite close to Cubism, particularly in Matisse's later work. Be that as it may, Matisse himself, a member of the committee, was shocked and displeased by the pictures Braque had sent; it is said that he made some disparaging remark about "little cubes." Five were rejected, and in his anger Braque withdrew all seven. In November of the same year Kahnweiler exhibited them at his gallery, together with twenty more, and Apollinaire wrote the preface to the catalog. Louis Vauxcelles, the same critic who had given the Fauves, the Wild Beasts, their label, said, "M. Braque is a very daring young man. The misleading example of Picasso and Derain has made him bolder still. And perhaps he is more obsessed than he ought to be by the style of Cézanne and by distant memories of the Egyptians' static art. He builds up distorted, metallic, shockingly simplified little figures. He despises form and reduces everything—views, places, people, houses—to geometrical diagrams, to cubes." The word caught on, particularly after the paintings Picasso brought back with him from his holiday at Horta in the summer of 1909, and presently Picasso and Braque, to say nothing of Gleizes, Herbin, Le Fauconnier, Léger, Metzinger, Picabia, and somewhat later Gris, Delaunay, and many more, were universally known as Cubists.

Chapter VIII

For Leo Stein Cubism was "Godalmighty rubbish"; for Vauxcelles it was "pretentious impotence and self-complacent ignorance"; for Apollinaire it was a polemic into which he flung himself on the side of his friends, soon getting out of his depth but keeping more or less afloat by means of rhetoric; for Gleizes and Metzinger it was an elaborate intellectual theory; and for many other writers it has been the subject of muddle-headed, vehement explanations in which the word "truth" continually recurs. It meant different things to the various painters and sculptors who practiced it, and no doubt some of the theories put forward do suit some of the artists; but what really matters for the purpose of this book is what Cubism meant to Picasso.

In the first place it had nothing whatsoever to do with any theory, nor with absolute truth. Although on many subjects his reliably quoted words are often contradictory, seeing that they depended on his mood and on the person he was talking to, yet his contempt for theory and for the verbal explanation of art remains constant from his earliest recorded remarks to the last. As for truth, he maintained that it did not exist; and that if it did exist, then at best a painting was only an approximation to a certain aspect of it, a symbolic reflection of a single facet; observing that if a painting could encompass the whole truth it would be impossible to paint a hundred canvases on the same theme. "Art is a lie that makes us realize the truth, at least the truth that it is given us to understand," he said; and after all, the doctrine of Nietzsche, so much admired at the Quatre Gats, was that "we have art in order not to perish from the truth."

For Picasso Cubism was a way of saying what he wanted to say in the language that he felt was right, a language neither better nor worse than others, but different. When Felipe Cossío del Pomar asked him what had been his aim when he launched into this new phase he replied, "To paint and nothing more. And to paint seeking a new expression, divested of useless realism, with a method linked only to my thought—without enslaving myself or associating myself with objective reality. Neither the good nor the true; neither the useful nor the useless. It is my will that takes form outside of all extrinsic schemes, without considering what the public or the critics will say."

To Marius de Zayas he said, "Many think that Cubism is an art of transition, an experiment which is to bring ulterior results. Those who think that way have not understood it. Cubism is neither a seed nor a foetus, but an art dealing primarily with forms, and when a form is realized it is there to live its own life. A mineral substance, having geometric formation, is not made so for transitory purposes, it is to remain what it is and will always have its own form. But if we are to apply the law of evolution and transformation to art, then we have to admit that all art is transitory. If Cubism is an art of transition I am sure that the only thing that will come out of it is another form of Cubism.

"Mathematics, trigonometry, chemistry, psychoanalysis, music, and whatnot have been related to Cubism to give it an easier interpretation. All this has been pure literature, not to say nonsense, which brought bad results, blinding people with theories." This does not sound in the least like the Picasso who talked to Malraux, and it is probable that Zayas, who carried on the conversation in Spanish and who afterwards translated it, having written it down from memory, gave Picasso's words a far more literary form in English than ever they had when they were first uttered; but I do not believe that he deformed their general sense, particularly as the same idea is repeated and amplified in Picasso's statement to Florent Fels, "Cubism has been explained by mathematics, geometry, psychoanalysis. All that is mere literature. The aims of Cubism are plastic. We only saw it as a means of expressing what we saw with our eyes and minds, expressing it with all the potentiality that drawing and color possess in their own right."

And to Zervos he said, "When we invented Cubism we had no intention whatsoever of inventing Cubism. We simply wanted to express what was in us. Not one of us drew up a plan of campaign; and our friends the poets followed our efforts attentively, but they never dictated to us."

"When we invented Cubism": and certainly what is called by that name is the child of Picasso and Braque. Yet Cubism was already implicit in Picasso's work as early as some of the harlequins, where the pattern of the traditional costume breaks Harlequin's body into angular planes: this is particularly evident in the "Mort d'Arlequin" of 1905/6, in which three isolated lozenges are of capital importance. And of course other men before him had approached the problems of volume, space, and the re-creation of a structure by means of geometrical forms: it may seem strange to speak of Uccello, who so delighted in that linear perspective which the Cubists rejected, as one of Picasso's precursors; but he too used broad schematic planes to build up his marvelous, dreamlike horses in the "Rout of San Romano"; and Picasso deeply admired his work. Like Uccello, Piero della Francesca was fascinated by the geometry of the *mazzochio*, the thirty-two sided hat worn by the Florentines—fascinated by it as a piece of pure form, form in itself; and he also used the cube and the cylinder for the fortified town in his "Invention of the True Cross." Georges de La Tour would have been lost without his great geometrical planes; and Poussin, whom Picasso esteemed so very highly, was at one with the Cubists (and with Leonardo da Vinci) in stating that painting was *cosa mentale*—that the painter's eye must see deep, and that it must *know* the essence of what it sees. He said, "You have to understand that there are two ways of seeing things, the one by just looking at them and the other by gazing at them with real attention. Just looking is merely the eye's natural reception of the shape and likeness of the thing seen. Gazing with real attention is not only that but also an intense study of the means of acquiring a thorough knowledge of the object. So it might be said that what I call just looking is a physical operation and what I call gazing is an operation of the mind."

This brings us straight to Picasso and to his unparalleled concentration of eye and spirit. It was a quality that he valued as highly as Poussin and for the same reasons; and it was one that he admired in others. Speaking to Sabartés he said, "People never concentrate enough. . . . The reason why Cézanne was Cézanne is that he *did* concentrate: when he was confronted with a tree he looked hard at what was there before his eyes; he looked at it as hard as a man with a gun aiming at his quarry. If he fixed his eye on a leaf, he never let it go. And since he had the leaf, he had the branch. And the tree could never get away. Even if he only had the leaf, that was worth while. Often enough painting is no more than that. . . . You have to put all your concentration into it. . . . Oh, if only everyone could do just that!"

And to Liberman he said, "Painting is a thing of intelligence. One can see the intelligence in each of Manet's brushstrokes, and the action of intelligence is made visible in the film on Matisse when one watches Matisse draw, hesitate, then begin to express his thought with a sure stroke."

This emphasis on intelligence may seem to imply an intellectualism, a theoretical approach, that Picasso utterly denied; but it was with a painter's intelligence that he and Poussin were concerned, an intelligence whose realm is neither scientific nor verbal but solely plastic.

The word beauty, like the word love, has been so bandied about that it now defies all definition; yet still it has a meaning, and although some of those who should know have asserted that Picasso never knew love, at least not for women, he had an immense awareness of beauty—of *a* beauty—an awareness so catholic that it embraced many things from which the common sensibility recoils. And for him beauty was not to be ranked: from the aesthetic point of view the blue of a Gauloise packet had the same value as the beauty of a girl. And he may not have been entirely joking when he proposed sticking dog's droppings on to a canvas and framing them.

This sense of the beauty and significance of an object in itself is said to be quite general among the very young; and there can be few who do not remember being entranced by wet pebbles on the strand, sea-worn glass, or oil on puddles.

In most people the vision dwindles or even perishes as the process of growing up, receiving accepted social, moral, and aesthetic notions grinds them down to size; but it certainly never did so in Picasso, who from his nature and from his status as an outsider was not to be ground down. In him it grew steadily more intense, and often he was able to persuade those who were still open to persuasion that other values, often very ancient, were still available to them. There is his magnificent, disreputable goat, for example, that defies all established, academic canons of beauty, and that has given innumerable beholders the joy of seeing the quintessence of the creature.

Others he never could persuade; his attempts to do so angered them, producing a flood of vituperation and acrimonious mockery. A witty Italian summed it up in a burlesque interview with Picasso, who is here supposed to be speaking: "In art, the mass of people no longer seek consolation and exaltation . . . but whatever is new, odd, original, extravagant, or scandalous. I myself, since Cubism and even before, have satisfied these masters and critics with whatever bizarre extravagances passed through my head, and the less they understood the more they admired me. By amusing myself with all these games, rebuses, and arabesques I became famous, famous very quickly. And for a painter fame means selling, making money, making a fortune, growing wealthy. So today, as you know, I am famous and I am rich. But when I am quite alone I have not the courage to think of myself as an artist in the ancient, splendid sense of the word. Giotto and Titian, Rembrandt and Goya, were true painters; I am only a public entertainer who has understood his times and to the utmost of his powers has exploited the silliness, the vanity, and the stupidity of his contemporaries. Mine is a bitter confession, more painful than it may seem; but it has the merit of being sincere." Picasso's enemies seized upon the alleged interview with delight and at once pronounced it to be genuine. It has been translated, with variations, into many languages, and it keeps reappearing, like the Protocols of the Elders of Zion: only the other day I was sent an English version from a parish magazine in which it illustrated the text "Be ye perfect."

Although the malevolence is surprising, a certain amount of initial incomprehension is not, since for the adult Picasso painting was not the imitation of some given body, house, or tree, but the creation of an object for itself—of a statement valid per se and at the same time valid in relation to the subject. In this conceptual re-presentation the original starting-point, "reality" in the common sense, was never lost to sight—indeed new aspects of it were revealed—but Picasso was using a difficult language: difficult, that is to say, for those of his contemporaries who still saw painting if not as anecdote, direct illustration, then at least as something with a literary and perhaps an ethical or a social content; or as something to do with light, if not with sweetness. And even now, when Cézanne's "For a painter light does not exist" has been well digested, and when sweetness has been banished to Disneyland, Picasso's language is still difficult for those who try to translate it into another idiom, to "understand" it in words.

Gómez de la Serna illustrates this with a dialogue between a critic and a sage:

Critic: It is true that these pictures do not displease my eye; but since I do not understand them, I cannot like them.

Sage: What did you have for lunch?

Critic: Oysters.

Sage: Do you like oysters?

Critic: Passionately.

Sage: Do you understand oysters?

A more open, or a less conditioned mind goes straight to the point without these detours: Picasso's Cubist portrait of Vollard was the object of a good deal of merriment among the dealer's friends—"What is it meant to represent? Which way up is it supposed to be?"—but a child, still young enough to speak imperfectly, looked at it and instantly observed, "That's Monsieur Voyard."

If Picasso's language was difficult in Paris and La Rue-des-Bois it became even more so in 1909, when he and Fernande traveled down to Barcelona in the early summer. There he spent some time with his family (as little as possible, says Fernande) and saw all his friends again, particularly Pallarès, who at once wrote off to his uncle to arrange for the couple's holiday at Horta. During these short pauses in Barcelona the pace of entertainment was usually too great for even Picasso to do any work, and this time he was exceptionally busy with arrangements for resuscitating *Arte Joven* (Soler had died in the intervening years); nevertheless he did make time to paint a magnificent portrait of his old friend. And in accordance with the painters' custom of exchanging pictures Pallarès gave him a landscape showing the mountain of Santa Barbara at Horta, which they had climbed together so many years before.

A little later Picasso saw the mountain with his own eyes. Fernande gives no account of their journey, merely observing that they were "somewhere in Aragón"; but as she traveled with a cooking stove it is probable that they went the longer way about, through Gandesa and Bot, by cart. In some ways she was a remarkably uncomplaining woman: there is a photograph of her, standing on the scorched grass, holding a little Pallarès by the hand, and looking placid; yet the rigors of Spanish roads and Spanish inns were even greater in her day than they are in ours. Nor, though she thought little of Cubism, did she make the least objection to her lover's filling the place with Cubist landscapes.

These pictures show what he had been aiming at: by now he had thoroughly worked out his problems, and the powerful but tentative experiments of the Negro Period and what might be called the Cézannian Cubism of La Rue-des-Bois and even of Pallarès' portrait were laid aside. He could see his way clearly at last, and the line ran straight from the "Demoiselles d'Avignon" on into full analytic Cubism. Immensely stimulated by this and by his surroundings, the countryside, the heat, and the smells he loved, happy to be among old friends for whom he was still En Pau, full of health and good food, he worked with even more than his usual energy.

He began with landscapes: the conical mountain of Santa Barbara, several views of the village, including the reservoir (it is now a swimming-pool, blue-tiled alas). One of the best known of all these Horta pictures is one in which a factory chimney, square in section, rises among palm-trees, their fronds bursting like rockets among the severe straight-edged planes: it has puzzled many plodding observers, including the present writer, because Horta is too high for palms and it possesses no factory. The answer is that Picasso invented the palms entirely, and that a small brick-kiln may have given him the idea for the valuable truncated pyramid, the towering chimney shape.

The colors are mostly the bleached ocher, silvery-gray, and tawny of Catalonia, and the already-Cubist village required little more than simplification to coincide with Picasso's mind; but in his wilder scenes the superficially amorphous rock is analysed, broken down into geometrical planes, often prismatic (in shape, not color), and so reconstructed, the tilted planes sometimes sliding over one another and sometimes meeting in a ridge: in some cases the geometrization is carried into the sky, whose faintly shimmering crystalline facets bind the whole into a rigorous composition with a depth that owes nothing to traditional perspective.

In the heads this analysis is far more evident, since the starting-point is naturally more obvious than an unknown mountain-side: in one of the long series Fernande's face is broken down into curved planes, while her forehead and the vase of flowers in what is just the background are strictly angular; in another (which was recently sold in London for £340,000, or $790,000) the entirety is made up of rectilinear forms; and in a bronze which he modeled as soon as he got back to Paris and González' studio, the two are combined in one of the most striking sculptures Picasso ever produced: that is to say they are combined as far as it is possible to combine a two-dimensional surface with a three-dimensional form.

It may seem trifling to speak of a somewhat vain young woman's reaction to Cubism, but Fernande was an important part of Picasso's life away from the easel: her reaction necessarily affected him, and she was intimately concerned with this particular phase. Her face was her fortune; and she could scarcely watch with philosophic detachment while it was carved into ridges, especially as the ridges and their corresponding hollows in the sculpture belonged to a woman of sixty or more. Braque once said something to this effect: "A portrait is a job in which there is always something wrong with the mouth. . . . Show a bourgeois the most advanced art you like, and he is delighted; but just you touch his mug and there's all Hell to pay." And as far as her physical appearance went Fernande was a true bourgeoise. Hitherto Picasso had been kind to her face and her person; there are some exquisite drawings and pictures, and the sculpture he did of her head in 1905 had a calm, smooth, classical beauty that any woman would be proud of. Now all this was changed. Fernande did not like Cubism, and although she fought like a tigress to defend Picasso as its only begetter he cannot have been unaware of her feelings. But nothing on earth could stop Picasso painting exactly as he chose to paint: neither the threat of poverty nor the possible loss of a valued and beautiful woman.

In the event poverty never returned at all, and Fernande and Picasso continued their life together for another two or three years: but among the many discontents that caused their parting it may well be that Cubism was not the least.

Poverty never returned. Perhaps that was a pity, for although it is difficult to imagine any outside force that could have changed the course of his work, a more modest financial success would surely have spared him the crowd of toad-eaters, the silly and pernicious adulation, that tended to cut him off from ordinary humanity and that certainly depressed his opinion of his fellow men, thus making him unhappier than he need have been. However, the Midas-touch was not to come for several years: in 1909 Picasso was not rich, although Kahnweiler had been doing well for him (and for Kahnweiler) and although his faithful Russians and some Germans introduced by Uhde were buying steadily. Kahnweiler was now Picasso's dealer; but he had either not chosen to drive the exclusive, permanent, and often leonine bargain under which some painters suffer all their lives or he had not been able to do so, and this year Vollard also exhibited Picassos, mostly the blue pictures that he had bought in 1906. Against all reasonable expectation and against almost all critical prediction, Cubism was gaining a wider audience; Picasso's reputation as one of the most important painters of the rising generation had spread far beyond Paris and Barcelona; foreign pilgrims came to his studio in ever-increasing numbers, and in Munich the Thannhauser Gallery put on a show of his work.

Foreigners also sought his acquaintance at the Steins', one of the few swept and dusted houses he frequented. On his return to Paris in the autumn Gertrude (though not Leo) Stein received his Horta pictures with enthusiasm, buying three and hanging them among the astonishing collection that was building up in the rue de Fleurus, the most useful place for any young painter's work to hang—a place where it would be seen by an endless stream of visitors, some of whom were rich, some appreciative, some both, and nearly all talkative and eager to be in the swing. Yet it would be unwarrantable to say that Picasso went there from interested motives. On the contrary, everything goes to show that he visited the Steins because he liked them, particularly Gertrude, whose portrait is a noble piece of work (Leo's is that of a comparatively dull man, painted without much distinction). He either let her have his pictures for very small sums or, as in the case of the portrait and his "Homaje a Gertrude" (angels, one of them blowing her own trumpet), for love.

And he continued to go to her evening parties although he was bored there and morose, although people badgered him to explain his painting, although the Steins varnished two of his pictures, a crime that altered their delicate values, and although there could never be any certainty that even Gertrude knew what he was at—"Gertrude Stein joyfully announced to me the other day that she had at last understood what my picture of the 'Three Musicians' was meant to be. It was a still-life!"

The Steins' must have been the strangest great room in Paris: the general aspect was that of a rich person's studio—good waxed furniture, art-istic knickknacks and rapiers carefully arranged, yet still retaining its painter's windows and its grim old working stove. But then, all round the walls, four or five deep, there were these amazing pictures. Some were by painters such as Manguin, Vallotton, Maurice Denis, and later Francis Rose, but there were also Cézannes, Matisses, and Picassos in such num-bers as to make one gasp. The numbers grew with the years until there was scarcely any wall to be seen; so did the crowds who came to see them on Saturday evenings, crowds that included foreigners visiting Bohemia, lovers of the arts, hangers-on of the arts, and sometimes the producers of the highest, most adventurous art the century had seen.

Matisse and Picasso often met there. A certain rivalry for the friendship of the Steins was one of the causes of friction between them; another was the fact that Derain, who had been particularly intimate with Matisse, staying with him at Collioure, was now far closer to Picasso—physically closer, too, since he had moved to Montmartre. But the animosity has been exaggerated by their followers: it was industriously put about that when the two painters exchanged pictures each chose a poor example of the other's work, a miserable ploy far beneath either of them; and André Salmon goes so far as to tell a story of the *bande à Picasso* throwing rub-ber-ended darts at Matisse's present, a portrait of his daughter, and crying "Bang! One in the eye for Marguerite!" The gang might have done so—there were some vulgar brutes in it—but I am very sure that Picasso was not there at the time. He valued the picture highly, keeping it all his life. He did not store it away, as he did in so many other cases, and it was so much part of his daily existence that fifty years later his children Claude and Paloma used to copy it to give him pleasure: when he showed it to John Richardson he said, "At the time people thought I had deliberately chosen a bad example of Matisse's work out of malice. That is quite un-true. I thought it a key picture then, and still do." He had a great respect for Matisse, and although he would sometimes let fly with a cruel gibe he would never allow anyone else to criticize him. There is a great deal of evidence to prove this, and of the many testimonies that come to mind one of the best is that of Christian Zervos. It is contained in a letter to Dore Ashton, the author of *Picasso on Art*, a valuable collection of his sayings, and it runs, "One afternoon we were at the Coupole with a num-ber of people, among them Matisse and Picasso. Matisse left for a min-ute. When someone asked what had become of him, Picasso answered that he was assuredly sitting on his crown of laurels. Most of those pres-ent, thinking they might please Picasso, began attacking Matisse. Then

Picasso became furious and cried out: 'I refuse to let you say anything against Matisse, he is our greatest painter.' "

Speaking of Salmon and a little girl brings me to another story that he relates: it is difficult to place chronologically, because although Salmon's general picture of literary and artistic Paris is entirely convincing, his dates are unreliable; but it certainly occurred in the days of the Bateau-Lavoir, which Salmon now inhabited—he was married there in the summer of 1909, and Apollinaire wrote an epithalamium. I have been able to supplement his account with the recollections of a friend who knew the Bateau-Lavoir well, and briefly the story is this: Fernande Olivier, unable to have a child herself, went to look at the orphanage in the nearby rue Caulaincourt. There she found a girl of about eight or ten: the child hated spinach, but was obliged to eat it. Fernande hated spinach too, and in her indignation she adopted the child out of hand, bringing it back to the Bateau-Lavoir. For some time the little girl was fed with sweetmeats, given dolls and toys: Picasso and everyone else in the Bateau-Lavoir was kind to her, particularly Max Jacob. Then Fernande suddenly grew tired of it: she decided that she had nothing maternal in her composition and asked Max Jacob to return the little girl to the home. This he did; but in the course of the formalities an official stated that once relinquished the child could never be taken back; at this she burst into tears, threw her arms about Jacob's neck, and begged him not to leave her. He could not bear it; he led her away, fed her at a restaurant, and took her home.

"I can't keep you," he observed.

"Why not?" said the little girl. "No one will want to take me away. I am only a waif."

"I too am a waif," said Max Jacob, weeping.

In the end he placed her with a local concierge. Picasso's share in all this, apart from general kindness and the provision of dolls, is not recorded.

Most biographers would like to sympathize with their heroes' vices and shortcomings even when their subject is a painter, whose excellence has nothing to do with any kind of moral quality whatsoever apart from artistic integrity; and it would be pleasant to think that during this wretched episode Picasso was absent or bemused or misled, or at least that it had some bearing on his decision to leave the Bateau-Lavoir.

The only certainty is that in 1909 he did leave, abandoning his squalor and his happiness for a flat in the boulevard de Clichy not far away, just by the place Pigalle. Abandoning his happiness is not mere rhetoric: many years and many women later, as he passed in front of the Bateau-

Lavoir with a friend he said, "That is the only place where I was ever happy." This relatively sumptuous new flat had a studio, naturally, but it also had a real bedroom, a dining-room, and a small sunny drawing-room that looked out onto the trees of the avenue Frochot: there was even room for a servant, and improbable as it may seem a maid appeared in time, a real maid with a long white apron. But before her advent Picasso and Fernande had to move in and furnish the place: first came the easels and the canvases from the Bateau-Lavoir studios (Picasso had taken a second for the increasing number of unfinished paintings—he liked to go from one to another and he hated finishing any—and to house the cardboard boxes in which objects and papers necessarily accumulated, since they could not be thrown away); then the few sticks among which they had lived all these years, consisting of one spring-mattress with no feet, one round table, one stained white-wood chest of drawers, several broken chairs; then the tin bath in which he kept his books (Sherlock Holmes, Nick Carter, Buffalo Bill, Verlaine, Rimbaud, Mallarmé); three cats, the huge furniture-like bitch Frika, and one small ape.

At first they could only furnish the maid's room, but presently Picasso filled the rest of the flat with more or less seventeenth-century oak, some mahogany, and a huge cherry-wood sideboard for the dining-room; and his parents sent him the Chippendale chairs he had known as a child, together with some other pieces. By the time the maid arrived there was plenty for her to dust, had she felt so inclined; but on the whole it must have been an easy place for her. Picasso and Fernande slept until eleven or twelve, and soon the maid took to doing much the same; the studio was never, never to be swept except once in every two or three months, when Picasso arranged it for the ordeal; and the cooking was pitifully simple. Picasso was now pushing Cubism farther and farther; the stress of doing so affected his digestion, and he could eat nothing but vegetables, fish, rice pudding, and grapes. He had even given up his wine. Fernande could not fail to see his diet; but just as she never noticed that he had painted the "Demoiselles d'Avignon" so now she had little idea of his inner tension.

He ate little; he drank mineral water: yet his new appetite for acquiring objects never flagged. He had started with reasonable purchases, such as the large brass bed, but now things bought primarily for delight began pouring into the flat. A great many pieces of moth-eaten tapestry; a vast nineteenth-century couch upholstered in worn violet velvet and sprinkled with bright yellow buttons; a pedal-organ that no one could play but that emitted a scent of incense on being pumped; guitars; mandolins; boxes; chests; popular colored prints in frames of plaited straw; countless African and Oceanic figures. A great many of these went into the studio, which soon took on the perilously overcrowded and slum-like appearance that best pleased his muse.

Yet the flat could be made respectable, and sometimes it was. Picasso and Fernande not only received all comers on Sundays but they also gave small dinner-parties—small, because the table took up so much space that there was little room for guests, particularly for guests as bulky as Apollinaire and Gertrude Stein. Sometimes Matisse came, and his natural dignity always acted as a restraint; but even when Max Jacob, van Dongen, Pichot, Salmon, or Braque were there it was no longer the same; and for Fernande at least the old comradeship of their poorer days was slowly dissolving. Devouring bread and sardines at a table covered with newspaper, with one napkin for everybody, in a studio smelling of turpentine and dominated by the "Demoiselles d'Avignon" was one thing: eating a regular number of courses in a proper dining-room, waited upon by a starched and silent maid, was another. Whether Fernande was right about its causes or not, the change was there; it was felt by them all, and it is apparent in a pair of photographs taken in the following year. In the one, taken by Pichot, Picasso is sitting on a sofa with a cat on his stomach, a Siamese, not an alley cat; his feet are on a rug, and a mandolin stands by him, propped against a respectable piece of Aubusson tapestry: he is still dressed in terribly wrinkled clothes and he still looks like a boy, but it is one of the few photographs in which he does not seem at ease: in the other, taken by Picasso, poor Pichot sits stiff and glum, wearing a collar and tie, with his boots shining and a strained, formal expression on his bearded Christ-like face. On the wall behind the couch can be seen roots of the past: Pallarès' "Muntanya de Santa Barbara," Matisse's portrait of Marguerite, Picasso's first Negro mask; and now they have something of the look of souvenirs.

But in the studio past and present came together, with the future rapidly taking shape. The man most often there with Picasso was Braque, the co-founder of the movement. Their temperaments were entirely different: Braque was sure of himself, Picasso was tormented by doubt; and as far as these national distinctions have any sense when they are applied to exceptional individuals, Braque was perfectly French in his sense of restraint and measure, whereas Picasso had been nourished on a tradition that loved monstrous excess and enormous gestures. Yet the two worked together in the most remarkable harmony, and in their hands—hands not easily to be distinguished in some cases—Cubism became steadily more and more analytic; modeling diminished and with it the sculptural quality of the figures, plane surfaces replaced volumes and these surfaces, more and more fragmented into luminous and often transparent facets, tended to fold back upon themselves so that another conception of volume returned; and whereas Cézanne's "passage" or the merging of one plane with another became more general, his evocative color, particularly his blues, gave way to pale ocher, gray, and green. At no point did Cubism ever abandon nature; the original object was always present, different aspects of it sometimes being seem simultaneously (hence the talk about the dimension of time in Cubism), always existing as the painter knew it to exist and possessing a reality beyond that of its immediately perceived appearance. To divorce the painting from the object, to turn the picture into abstract design, would have been to make nonsense of what Picasso was trying to do, since for him the whole strength and validity of his work resided in the vital link between the two realities, the initial reality of the object, the thing that "started the artist off, excited his ideas, and stirred his emotion," and the ultimate reality of the picture. The existence of the object in itself was essential to that of the picture in itself.

André Level proposes the analogy of a fugue on a known theme: as the fugue abbreviates, inverts, and transposes the air, eventually suggesting it only by a few notes, so the Cubist picture merely hints at the original object by a line or so, sometimes repeated, sometimes shown in depth. It is a useful comparison, although perhaps it does not convey the full value that Picasso attributed to his starting-point.

As Cubism progressed so its symbolic language grew less legible, the starting-point less evident; and this is apparent as early as the portrait of Braque that Picasso painted late in 1909, a picture in which the planes of the features slide, not into a chaos but into a new order, with a taut rhythm of its own yet into one whose systematic dislocation, transposition, and near-disintegration was to grow virtually hermetic as the years went by.

Braque's was accompanied by several other portraits. A much more accessible, almost naturalistic, Clovis Sagot, which may have been painted before Picasso went to Horta; and in the autumn of 1910 a somber Vollard, glooming out of his cubes and prisms, half asleep; an intricate, difficult Wilhelm Uhde, for which Picasso was given a little Corot; and a most interesting, complex Kahnweiler that is a compliment to that dealer's clarity of mind and his real comprehension of the new language. It was painted a full year after the Braque, and it shows a far higher degree of analysis as well as a hallucinatory shifting of the facets back and forth, so that the picture seems to possess not one surface but several. The "Jeune fille à la mandoline" is not a portrait in the strictest sense, seeing that the girl was a model hired to sit, but it has so much the character of a portrait that it belongs with the rest. It was probably painted earlier than the Kahnweiler and it retains a good deal of modeling, even an attenuated chiaroscuro; but it is wholly Cubist, and the girl's geometrized breasts and shoulders are dislocated with the happiest effect. Her head, reduced to a square with an immense eye in it, rises with singular grace above the dark pear-shaped mandolin, and the picture is among the most delightful that he ever painted. It has been said that in the "Jeune fille à la mando-line" Picasso was getting the best of several worlds, and certainly he makes use both of immediate and of remote symbols in what even the most sullen and dogged opponents of Cubism confess to be a masterpiece of its kind.

A striking thing about these portraits is that Picasso, who ordinarily never required a model but who drew upon his astonishing visual memory for any head, body, or scene, however complex, now made his sitters pose for long and repeated sessions.

Picasso and Cézanne had this in common: when they were working on a picture it was the most important thing in life—it was life itself. Then with the last stroke it would die. Sometimes Cézanne would abandon his pictures under olive-trees: and moved by the same impulse or rather creed Picasso said, "A finished work is a dead work, killed," and he was very unwilling to give the last mortal stroke. Yet in this as in everything else Picasso was full of apparent inconsistencies: the man who maintained that the "Demoiselles d'Avignon" was never finished and who spent months and months on Vollard's portrait would also dash off three pictures in a day; he did not leave a few dozen laboriously perfected paintings behind him but several thousand; and although he said that his work was of no interest to him once it was done he would fly into a pale rage if he saw one of his pictures, or Cézanne's, varnished, cleaned, or interfered with in any way. What is more, although the whole of his work was carried out in contemptuous defiance of the critics, he was exceedingly sensitive to approval: even in his eighties he would still show people his work, piling the canvases up in a tottering pyramid and watching intently for the reaction.

By early 1910 he was firmly settled at 11, boulevard de Clichy. Spring saw the congestion in his studio reach its customary pitch; musical instruments—more mandolins, guitars, violins—invaded his canvases and Braque's; and when summer came he and Fernande went to Spain once more, this time to Cadaqués, a Catalan fishing-village on what is now so widely known as the Costa Brava. It is a beautiful little place running down to a sheltered rocky bay on the sunny side of a cape reaching far out into the Mediterranean, and on calm evenings the aromatic scent of the mountains behind wafts down to the harbor. In those days never a tourist was to be seen, but the Pichot family had a house there, where they spent their holidays.

Picasso, Fernande, and the massive Frika traveled down with Ramon Pichot's married sister María, now a well-known singer, and several of her friends: apart from the pleasure of her company, and Picasso had known her since they were both adolescents, it was cheaper to travel in a group; and although he was now richer than he had ever been he was still far from wealthy—extravagance still alternated with something like the old penury, and on one occasion, hard pressed for money, he was obliged to sell almost all his sculptures (one was of Alice Derain) to Vollard, who, in his secretive way, had them cast in bronze and kept them out of sight for years. The Picassos did not stay with the Pichots, however, since the Derains were coming from Cagnes to join them, but they often went over to that hospitable, crowded house, full of painters, poets, and musicians.

Derain can hardly be said to have been a Cubist painter in the full sense, but he was much attached to Picasso, whose work he so admired; and although he could not go all the way with him—he was too much wedded to color, among other things—during this summer at Cadaqués he did paint some still-lives of a strongly Cubist character, paintings far more balanced and classical than those of his Fauve period. But Derain's Cubism was much nearer to Cézanne than to Picasso; he had not passed through the same severe process of self-doubt, trial, error, and discovery as his friend, and the difference between the two men is apparent when one compares Derain's "Pichets de Grès" with the "Nu" that Picasso painted at the same time: the one a delightful picture to have on the wall, warm, friendly, and eminently decorative, in no way disturbing; the other austere, cerebral, and ultimately far more rewarding.

Picasso painted hard at Cadaqués; but even for Picasso a holiday was not entirely work. He and his friends spent a good deal of time lying in the sun, bathing, playing about in the Pichots' boats, and placidly fishing for those dark purple sea-urchins which, being brought from the bottom with a split reed and cut in two, are so good with *aioli*, bread, and wine. Josep Palau has a pleasant account of Picasso, the Pichots, and the Derains setting out for more urchins in the larger boat, the *Nabucodonosor*, and of their getting no farther than the little islands called Es Cucurucú in the mouth of the bay, because Frika, left on shore, saw fit to prove her fidelity by swimming after them; and there can hardly have been room for a wet dog the size of a calf as well as all the baskets and the crew.

They also went to Figueras, the nearest place with a bull-ring; and here the infant Dalí, a native of the town, may have beheld them, Derain wearing a brilliant tie that he had bought in the market. And to Barcelona: Picasso's health and spirits always revived in Spain; so did his appetite. He gave up his unnatural abstinence from wine, and at one place down by the port, where very salt ham might be eaten in any quantity for the same stated sum, he and Derain drank so much that their women were obliged to lead them away.

In the autumn they went back to Paris, leaving the best part of the year behind them, the grape-harvest and the perfect autumn days; for although Picasso never showed his work at the Indépendants or the Salon d'Automne he was as delighted by these exhibitions—the crowd, the innumerable friends and acquaintances, the gossip, the occasional new ideas—as those who did.

Braque too returned, bringing with him his summer's pictures from L'Estaque, mostly still-lives and figures, including his own girl playing a mandolin, and a few landscapes: all very much on the same lines as Picasso's from Cadaqués. Some were painted on oval canvases, and for a while both he and Picasso thought this a good way of dealing with corners; for while the sharp angles of an ordinary frame might harmfully reduplicate the geometrical forms in some of their compositions, the curve emphasized their austerity.

This austerity increased throughout the coming year, and with it the analytic process: although the original object was always perfectly clear to Picasso, others found its presence still harder to detect. Yet in these lush days of the Belle Epoque, in a Paris filled with a hopelessly degenerate and commercialized *Modern' Style* and with the not dissimilar vulgarities of official art, many painters were fascinated by these rigorously-composed, uncompromising pictures; they saw them as a most radical and convincing break with the past, far greater than Neo-Impressionism in any of its various forms, and as a living hope for the future. Many became Cubists, at least according to their understanding of the form, and when the next Salon des Indépendants came round in the early summer of 1911 a whole room was given up to their pictures: and even that was not enough—Cubist works, including some of Archipenko's sculpture, were scattered through the rest of the exhibition. The critics were angry, of course: *Le Journal* spoke of "the pictures' novelty, which is a return to barbarism and primitive savagery, a repudiation and an utter abasement of all the beauties in life and nature," while even André Salmon said, "Let us just remind these 'innovating' young masters that Cubism was invented five years ago by a Spanish painter after long, rambling aesthetic discussions with philosophers, poets, and mathematicians. At first it seemed a harmless metaphysical caper. But Picasso laid the first stone, the first cube, of the temple; and it was not the most praiseworthy thing he ever did.'' Only Apollinaire in *L'Intransigeant* held out, though weakly: ''At the present moment we see an art taking shape, a spare and disciplined art whose still somewhat severe aspect will soon grow more human.''

As far as Picasso and Braque were concerned he was mistaken. In the course of 1911 and 1912 their painting, drawing, and engraving grew more ascetic still as they moved to high and then to higher Cubism; dun and pale ocher was their utmost indulgence in color; and *less being more* they limited their vocabulary, apart from figures and musical instruments, to a few common and apparently trivial objects such as pipes, goblets, pots, and bottles. And between 1908 and 1913 they either did not sign their pictures at all or signed them on the back, partly to avoid any interference with the taut rhythm of the composition and partly for the sake of impersonality. Theirs was an art primarily concerned with forms, as Picasso observed, with those forms in themselves and their rhythm, not with extraneous associations. The result was a language incomprehensible to those who used the wrong key, and when in 1911 the enterprising Alfred Stieglitz first introduced Picasso to the Americans with a collection of drawings and prints, one nude, admittedly a difficult, highly analysed work, was held to be a fire-escape.

But as far as Apollinaire's prediction applied to most of the latter-day Cubists it was right, if color and legibility are more human than a deliberately restrained palette and statements limited to forms for their own sake—if flamboyant Gothic is more human than pure Romanesque. This is not the place for a history of Cubism in general; but a life of Picasso must speak of his influence on the painting of his time: it must glance at the converts.

They can scarcely be called his followers, partly because Picasso had no notion of founding a school—he had no time for disciples, still less for explanations; and partly because some of them knew far more about Cubism than its inventors. Confronted with the earlier Cubist pictures they felt a strong aesthetic emotion, and very soon they produced theories to show why they felt it: as early as 1912 Gleizes and Metzinger published a book on the subject, and several others followed. The theories were ingenious but not much more convincing than Apollinaire's ''In the following year [1906] Derain and Picasso became friends, and the almost immediate result of this friendship was the birth of Cubism''; and they did not enable their authors to paint interesting pictures.

But there were also men of far greater value who were drawn to Cubism, men whose language was paint or sculpture: among them Léger, Picabia, Delaunay, La Fresnaye, Le Fauconnier, Dufy for a while and Friesz, Lhote, Kisling, Herbin of the Bateau-Lavoir, Survage, Marcoussis, Diego Rivera, Mondrian, Archipenko, Brancusi, Lipchitz, and perhaps the most important of them all, the three brothers Jacques Villon, Duchamp-Villon, and Marcel Duchamp. Several of these, together with Apollinaire and the American Walter Pach, formed the Groupe de Puteaux, which met at Jacques Villon's studio, where they worked out their several ideas of what Cubism was and what it should be. They differed from one another and they differed from Braque and Picasso: Delaunay, for example, was unorthodox from the beginning; he insisted upon the role of light and color, and presently he moved on, or off, to a painting that Apollinaire baptized Orphism: Léger's variations earned him the name of Tubist: Marcel Duchamp introduced movement: Jacques Villon described himself as an Impressionist-Cubist, and he refused to abandon his subtle shades: and in time many of the others relinquished the object entirely and with it all reference to reality, their pictures becoming wholly abstract. But all these differences were nothing compared to the difference between the Cubists' work and any painting that had been seen before: the Cubist revolution was fundamental; the "Demoiselles d'Avignon" had changed the very nature and concept of painting, and it could never be the same again.

Some of the Cubists were not wholly convinced; Marie Laurencin, for instance, had been drawn into the movement by her friendship for Apollinaire, Braque, Picasso, and the other painters of the Bateau-Lavoir and she soon returned to her own manner; and some few, excited by the prodigious outcry and publicity, may have jumped on to the band-wagon, for superficially a Cubist painting, like an abstract, seems an easy thing to fake. But for most it was a matter of the greatest importance, nothing less than the acceptance of this wholly new approach, with all that it implied of renunciation of former values, certainties, and comfort of mind, as well as comfort of living. And if martyrdom is a proof of religion, then the voluntary giving-up of a livelihood is a proof of artistic conviction. Marcoussis was a case in point: like so many of the Cubists he was an excellent draughtsman, and he made a good income by supplying *La Vie Parisienne* with drawings: his connection with Picasso not only deprived him of this resource but also, though this was less voluntary, of his mistress, who preferred his master. It was Marcoussis' conversion, by the way, that convinced the skeptical Salmon that Cubism was something more than a metaphysical prank.

But Picasso was not interested in proselytizing; nor did he ever attend the gatherings at Puteaux. He was too busy with his own work, which at this point included engravings to illustrate Max Jacob's *Saint Matorel,* - which Kahnweiler, following in Vollard's footsteps as a publisher, was to bring out in 1911, as he had earlier brought out Apollinaire's *L'Enchanteur pourrissant,* with wood-engravings by Derain. Jacob's book was one of the results of his religious conversion: Christ had appeared to him on the wall of his studio in September 1909, sometimes moving, sometimes still. Derain did not feel capable of illustrating it, but Picasso had no such hesitations and he produced four capital plates for his friend.

Friendship also determined the place for Picasso's summer holiday. This was Céret, a little town in French Catalonia, not far from Matisse's Collioure; it lies in the Pyrenean foothills, a remarkably green, well-watered spot, famous for its cherries; and it was here that Manolo had retired in 1908, with his wife Totote and a contract, arranged by Picasso, with the long-suffering Kahnweiler. Manolo, now an established sculptor, never made the least bow towards Cubism, preferring the ideas of his fellow-Catalan Maillol, who lived at the nearby Banyuls; but this had not the least effect upon Picasso's affection for him, an affection that also embraced Totote, a remarkable woman with a fascinating husky voice: she belonged to a good Breton family, but disagreeing with their values, she became a barmaid in Paris. Later she and Manolo adopted a daughter, Rosita, to whom Picasso was much attached.

Quite early in the year, probably in mid-May, Picasso set out; and this time he traveled without Fernande. It may be that she hesitated to make a journey of six hundred miles and more with Frika, the ape, and all the easels, canvases, and baggage: but she was to come on later, and in the meantime Picasso would have the company of Braque and several other friends from Paris and Barcelona.

Although Céret had been politically French since the time of Cardinal Richelieu, and although politically it had been Spanish before that time, it remained stubbornly Catalan, and both Picasso and Manolo were entirely at home there. They had the familiar language all around them; the bullring was a natural feature of the town; and on holidays the people danced the *sardana,* the only dance that Picasso approved of, to the sound of the harsh archaic oboes and the little drum.

One of the best-known paintings of that fruitful summer of 1911 is an echo of the dance: it is usually called "La Clarinette," but its real point of departure is, I believe, the outwardly similar instrument that the Catalans call a *tenora,* and the rhythms of the picture seem to me connected with the rhythm of the dance. An even better-known picture is "L'Accordéoniste," a shimmering great canvas alive with transparent planes, Picasso's last analysis of a man sitting in a chair with his accordion drawn out in a descending diagonal: but it is now housed in the New York Museum of Non-Objective Painting. Even then Picasso and Braque felt that for others the hermetic aspect of their Cubism might tend to do away with the vital tension between the original object and the resulting picture, since for the tension to have its full effect some hint at least of the starting-point must be sensed. They therefore began to scatter "realistic" clues, such as the trompe-l'oeil nail in Braque's "Violon et Palette" of 1910 and the large printed letters in Picasso's bottles.

At Céret Picasso returned to his Spanish ways, working all day and going to the café at night. The Grand Café where he met his friends is still there under the shade of its enormous planes, in whose upper branches the untiring scops owl utters its single note throughout the warm and tranquil night: the marble tables alas have long since been washed clean of Picasso's innumerable drawings, but a few of the paper napkins that he tore into wonderful shapes and patterns (a lifelong habit) have survived. Yet though he loved conviviality the Grand Café did not see him every night: sometimes his town-bred friends sat there without him; they were happiest with their feet on a pavement and for them a hillside was something to be viewed from a distance. But Picasso loved the country, and he was a tremendous walker: one evening he and Manolo, lost in talk, went on and on until they found themselves at Le Perthus, at the frontier itself. They could go no farther, for Manolo was liable to be taken up the moment he set foot in Spain, imprisoned and made to do his military service; but it was quite far enough, since even if they had gone through the vineyards it was at least twelve miles there and twelve miles back.

It is interesting to reflect upon the state of Picasso's studio, with a dog, an ape, and an intensely busy painter in it and no woman, not even such a moderate housekeeper as Fernande. For August had come, and she was still in Paris. Picasso wrote to her; and if a proof of the quality of his French after a seven-years cohabitation with a monoglot Frenchwoman and an even longer use of the language were wanting, the letter provides it.

8 AOUT 1911

MA CHERE FERNANDE
 Ier de toute la journé je ne ai pas eu de letre de toi et ce matin que je l'atandais non plus esperons que cete apres midi je serai plus eureux.

Dans une letre que jai reçu ce matin de Braque je vois que K. est
arrivé dejá a Paris allors je espere que dans tres peu de jours vous
serez ici
   Il fait ici un peu plus frais et le soir ont est bien de chaleur.
   Ne te preocupe trop pour l'argent ont le arrangera.
   Prenez le train que je ai pris il et le meilleur. Maintenant je crois
que tu vas venir bientott. Braque me dit que la semaine prochaine vous
arriverez ici
   Ma famille sont a Mahon depuis quelque temps deja.
   Tu ferais bien de porter ton ombrelle si tu veux sortir dans la journé.
   Le singe il et asez rigolo ont le a doné une couvercle de un boite en
fer blanc et il pase sa journé à se regarder il et tres inteligent
   Le trabail marche toutjour je trabail toutjour à les même choses.
                     Je te embrasse et t'aime
                  toutjours PABLO

[My dear Fernande
   All day yesterday I had no letter from you and none today though I
was expecting one let's hope I shall be luckier this afternoon.
   From a letter Braque gave me this morning I see that K. has already
reached Paris so I hope you will be here in a very few days
   It is rather cooler here and in the evening the warmth is pleasant.
   Don't worry too much about money it will be all right.
   Take the train I took it is the best. Now I really believe you will be
coming soon. Braque tells me you will be here next week
   My people have been at Mahon for some time now.
   You would be wise to bring your parasol if you mean to go out in the
daytime
   The monkey is really amusing he was given the lid of a tin and he
spends the day looking at himself in it he is very clever
   Work still goes well I am still working on the same things.
                  Love and kisses
                  always PABLO]

   Fernande came at last, and she brought with her the latest news from
the artistic world: the Salon d'Automne was setting aside a whole room
for the Cubists, and Marcel Duchamp, La Fresnaye, Gleizes, Kupka, Le
Fauconnier, Léger, Lhote, Metzinger, Picabia, and Jacques Villon were
going to exhibit; and the "Gioconda" had been stolen from the Louvre.
   She came, but it was to do little more than gasp in the heat for a few
days, pack up their belongings, and then take the train once more. They
were back in Paris early in September; and on the day of their arrival Pi-

casso ran into Apollinaire, but an Apollinaire whose pear-shaped face was haggard, terrified.

The wretched Iberian figures that Géry Piéret had produced in 1907 came from the Louvre: he had stolen them from the Louvre. Now the "Gioconda" had been stolen too. The connection was obvious. Apollinaire was a suspect: the police had already searched his flat: and Picasso was deeply implicated.

Chapter IX

Every book on Picasso speaks of these figures, but as far as I know no one has ever seen them since they were recovered by the Louvre. They are not exhibited, nor are they easily to be found: however, it appeared to me that in addition to their slightly morbid interest as stolen goods they might be of some value as evidence in the question of the relative importance of Negro and Iberian sculpture to Picasso, so I asked the authorities if I might be allowed to see them. The curator of Oriental antiquities could not have been kinder or more helpful, and eventually I was led across a muddy courtyard and into a vast dim barn: my guide turned on a light, and innumerable pots and stony objects sprang into view, some of them of enormous size and all packed close together, Baal nose-to-nose with Ashtaroth, cuneiform tablets, amphorae, lovely bowls, a whole regiment of Phoenician gods, carved perhaps by some Punic proto-Picasso (the Carthaginians colonized his part of Spain in the third century before Christ). There we wandered about the shelves, gazing up at Tanit, Moloch, Eshmun, and Melkarth, all deeply covered with dust; at last, high up, we found the right reference-numbers, and standing on tiptoe I edged the larger head forward until I could bring it down. It was only about a foot high, but it was surprisingly heavy, and as I blew off the dust I thought of Picasso trailing it about the quays of the Seine. It was a straightforward female head with an elaborate coiffure topped by a smooth kerchief, carved in a pale, compact freestone and apparently designed to be seen only from the front as it stood in a niche: I thought it an uninteresting piece of rather mechanical late Hellenistic work: its weight and its associations (it is labeled as having been "temporarily in the possession of M. Picasso") were the most impressive things about it. But the second head, far older as I understood, proved to be completely different: here was no run-of-the-mill example of the provincial stonemason's craft, but an object with another kind of life entirely, a rough, "primitive" carving in somewhat darker stone, with no facility or prettiness about it at all, a free-standing head on a long neck, a stronger sculpture by far. And as I tilted the ancient, battered face so that the light fell glancing from above, emphasizing what features time had left, I saw two great almond eyes that seemed to me akin to those of the woman on the left-hand side of the "Demoiselles d'Avignon," while the stony, masklike quality of the whole had a distinct relationship to Picasso's painting of 1907 and 1908.

The most probable recent history of the Iberian figures seems to be this: Géry Piéret stole them from the Louvre sometime after the exhibition in 1906; two of them passed either directly or through Apollinaire to Picasso; and at least one remained with Apollinaire. It is said that they came with a warning that they should not be freely shown; and that later Apollinaire told Picasso of their origin, suggesting that they should be returned by way of a newspaper, a course that would get rid of the statuettes and at the same time bring about favorable publicity. According to this account Picasso replied that he had broken them up to discover the secret of their making.

Fernande, who describes them as stone masks, says they were kept in the bottom of a cupboard, where with the passing of the years they were forgotten. During these years Piéret went to America, where he made a considerable amount of money: returning to Paris he lost it all at the races and turned for help to Apollinaire, who employed him as a secretary. In May of 1911 Piéret took another figure, which made Apollinaire uneasy: and then on August 21 the "Gioconda" was stolen. There was an enormous and universal uproar; and Piéret carried his latest statuette to Salmon's paper, *Paris-Journal,* which published an indignant, righteous article on security, the nation's heritage, and civic duty. Piéret was a featherbrained creature, and although at first he seems to have had some notion of taking advantage of the situation he now panicked and ran away. He traveled southwards, recovering his confidence as the distance grew; and presently he took to sending facetious letters to the authorities at every stop.

The first impulse of Picasso and Apollinaire was to imitate his example and fly; but Fernande, who remained wonderfully calm, persuaded them to do nothing of the kind. Their position was ludicrous; it was also extremely unpleasant. They were both foreigners in a somewhat xenophobic country: Apollinaire, like any other man brought up in France, knew that preventive detention might last for months and even years before a trial; Picasso had first-hand experience of the forces of order in action—the repression in Barcelona had been terrible. Neither could have been described as a man of the world, of the bourgeois world whose powerful machine might be preparing to crush them, and neither knew what to do.

Manolo would have been the most valuable counselor among their friends, but Manolo was far away, and the best thing they could think of was to destroy the evidence. They sat in a state of the most intense anxiety, waiting for the dead hour of the night when they could throw the figures into the Seine unseen. Midnight came, and they left, carrying them in a bag: early in the morning they returned, worn out and desperate, still carrying the incriminating evidence. The banks of the river had been lined with watchers; they had certainly been followed; Paris had been full of suspicious lurking forms.

The next day Apollinaire took the figures to *Paris-Journal*. The newspapermen were delighted and no doubt they promised to keep Apollinaire's name to themselves; but within twenty-four hours the police were at his door. A little later he was in a cell.

Picasso had no news of his friend; he was deeply anxious, but he dared not to go to Apollinaire's flat. Two days passed, and then his fears were realized: at seven in the morning a figure in plain clothes rang the bell, woke the household, showed his police-card, and desired Picasso to come with him to the investigating magistrate. Picasso huddled on his clothes, in such agitation that Fernande was obliged to help him with the buttons, and he was taken away.

At first Apollinaire had denied everything, but the French police were accustomed to dealing with far tougher characters than the poet, and the Apollinaire with whom Picasso was now confronted, a pale, terrified Apollinaire, his shirt and collar torn, had confessed to everything and more. Picasso did much the same. Neither meant to incriminate the other; there was no sort of treachery; yet each acknowledged, with tears, the truth of every accusation, however monstrous, however false. In Fernande's account Picasso is less than heroic: she may exaggerate, but it is generally acknowledged that he dreaded the law, the police, and any threat to his freedom—he always took great care to have his papers in order.

Once he was convinced that he had not caught the stealers of the "Gioconda," the magistrate was not unkind; and although he kept Apollinaire in jail he let Picasso go, only requiring him to be ready to appear when he was called for.

The interrogation had been shattering, but Picasso soon recovered, and with Max Jacob, Salmon, and a few others he began a campaign for Apollinaire's release, collecting signatures to a petition. But many of Apollinaire's friends kept studiously away from him until the whole sordid business came to an end early in 1912, when the charge was dismissed; and whether the statuettes had any influence on her or not, Marie

Laurencin took against him, so much so that in June she resolved to see him no more, and to his despair she kept her word.

The year 1912 did not begin well for Picasso either: the affair of the statuettes so preyed on his mind that he would not go out in the day-time—he was sure he was still being followed and he would change taxis to throw his pursuers off the scent. Then somewhat later in the year his long relationship with Fernande Olivier came to an end. Yet the first did not bring his painting to a halt, and the second, or rather its conse-quences, stimulated him to a fresh outburst of creative activity.

At the height of his anxiety about the Iberian figures he produced not only some of the purest examples of analytic Cubism, including the "Pi-geon au petits pois" and the "Homme à la mandoline," but a most sur-prising "Nature morte à la chaise cannée," in which he glued a piece of oilcloth that imitated chair-caning to an oval canvas; then over and around it he painted some ordinary café objects—a glass and a sliced lem-on, severely analysed, a newspaper with the first three letters of Journal large and plain, a trompe-l'oeil pipe-stem. The result, which he framed with rope, is a bewildering array of different realities at a variety of lev-els, fused into a whole by some magic peculiar to Picasso: it is also the very first of all the collages and the forerunner of what the theorists, though neither Picasso nor Braque, were to call synthetic Cubism.

As for his break with Fernande, all that can be said with any certainty is that it happened. What third person can give a true account of what is in its nature secret and often incommunicable, the essential causes of a di-vorce? At the most he can only record the visible effects.

Picasso's café was at this time the Ermitage in the boulevard Roche-chouart, just along the street from his studio; it was also the favorite haunt of the Futurists; and as the Ermitage and the Futurists were connected with the break it is proper to make some mention of them here.

The café was a large, noisy, cheerful place with an orchestra and a mixed clientele of bourgeois, painters, pimps and whores from the nearby Pigalle, and some boxers. The Futurists were an Italian group of writers and painters, who had launched their first manifesto, announcing a revo-lution in art, a complete break with the past, as early as 1909; this mani-festo was followed by thirty or forty more, some of which Picasso may have seen—the *Figaro* published the earliest almost as soon as it appeared in Milan. In any case, since Apollinaire was much taken up with the Paris Futurists and since Picasso was acquainted with several of them himself, he knew that their ideas differed from his: the Futurist painters were in fa-vor of a dynamic rather than a static art; for them a running horse should have not four but twenty feet, and the movement of those feet should be triangular; they also wished to express mood and even sound. None of this disturbed Picasso, who was always willing to let any man paint as he saw fit: besides, although the Futurists were very unkind to Cubism, accusing it of being academic, reactionary, and bourgeois, it is difficult to believe that Futurism would ever have come into existence without Picasso and Braque; and in any case a few of them, with or without the help of their theories, painted unusually interesting, living pictures.

Some of these Italians had been in Paris as long as Picasso; Ardengo Soffici, for example, had met him during his earliest days at the Louvre, where they had admired the Egyptian and Phoenician sculpture together; and when they brought their Futurist compatriots to see him he received them kindly, though some may have been a little tedious. Fernande speaks of being taken by Picasso and Apollinaire to see Emilio Marinetti, who talked throughout the night, never stopping until sunrise, ten hours without a pause: it is true that she says they were not bored, but not all the Futurists had Marinetti's talent, though many had an equal flow.

The main wave of Futurists reached Paris about 1912; and they frequented the Ermitage, wearing socks of one color on their right foot and of another on their left. Among them was the young, charming, intelligent Oppi, who knew Severini, an old Paris hand, and who begged for an introduction to Picasso. Severini took him to the Ermitage, where Picasso, Fernande, Marcoussis, and Marcelle Humbert, his companion, were spending the evening, just as they often went to the Cirque Médrano together, Fernande and Marcelle being great friends. "Fernande," says Severini, "was far from being a serious-minded woman. She fell in love with . . . Ubaldo Oppi."

Was this before Picasso fell in love with Marcelle? There is no telling. Gertrude Stein only gives the vague date of "the spring of 1912" when she says that shortly after Picasso, Fernande, Marcoussis, and Marcelle had been to see them at the rue de Fleurus, Picasso told her he was going to work at the Bateau-Lavoir again. She and Alice Toklas called on him there: he was out: she left her card. A few days later they called again, found him painting a picture with the words *"Ma Jolie"* in large letters above a musical score and in the lower corner an imitation of the visiting-card, Miss Gertrude Stein. She was a modest woman as far as her looks were concerned and it never occurred to her to connect the two: "Fernande is certainly not *Ma Jolie*," she said as they went away. "I wonder who it is?"

Fernande may have known, for according to Crespelle she now ran off with Oppi, her idea being to make Picasso jealous and thus to reclaim him from *Ma Jolie*. She had miscalculated, however; Picasso was relieved rather than jealous, and he at once left Paris with Marcelle, taking her to Avignon. Marcoussis was surprised, disturbed, displeased, but he neither cut his throat nor gave up Cubism; the height of his resentment was a drawing which shows Picasso loaded with chains while a free Marcoussis gambols happily, as though liberated from a wearisome companion, perhaps a shrew.

Yet Picasso never felt those fetters. He was deeply attached to Marcelle, and he called her Eva for the obvious reasons. And although he never drew or painted her directly she appears in many of his pictures as the words *"Ma Jolie"* (they come from a song they must often have heard together, either at the Médrano or at the Ermitage or indeed anywhere else in Paris, it having been very popular—*O Manon, ma jolie, mon coeur te dit bonjour*) or *"Pablo-Eva"* or *"Jolie Eva"* or *"J'aime Eva"*; and perhaps to his private eye she was there in the forms he used. They are often as light and graceful as any young woman could wish, and Eva was the antithesis of Fernande, small, tender, and gentle rather than tall, Junoesque, and confident.

From Avignon they went to Céret; but in spite of the marvelous spring this was not a success. For one thing Frika had to be killed: she was replaced by a large kind of Alsatian, as far as a dog who has shared eight years of one's youth can ever be replaced. Then the Pichots arrived, and with them Fernande. Ramon Pichot took Fernande's side: there were scenes between the women: life was impossible. Before the end of May Picasso and Eva fled, going back to Avignon and beyond Avignon to the small unattractive town of Sorgues-sur-l'Ouvèze, where his spirits revived. He took a grim comfortless little box like a railway station called Villa les Clochettes and settled down to work.

Picasso had always been a prodigious worker, but now, stimulated by his new happiness he painted harder still, and with a fresh approach. In July Braque joined him, a Braque in much the same situation, for he had just married Marcelle Lapré. Picasso had nothing against marriage, and there was probably some unsatisfactory Humbert in the background to prevent his official union with Eva: her maiden name was Gouel.

Braque took another villa close at hand; and although he was so unlike Picasso in so many ways, he chose an equally hideous house. In this instance it may have been Hobson's choice, but the fact remains that very good painters often resemble one another in a strange indifference to their immediate surroundings. Even when Picasso could afford anything he wanted, he picked upon La Californie, one of the ugliest houses on the Côte d'Azur, a country rich in horrors; and Braque went on returning to the unlovely Sorgues for the next fourteen years.

It is clear that there are regions into which the literary man cannot follow the painter, and I should be happy to think that housing was the most important; but this much is certain, both were happy in their villas, both were in complete agreement as to how they should work, both painted some of their finest pictures during this long summer of 1912, and between them they began to give the course of modern painting a new direction.

To say they deliberately brought analytic Cubism to an end and moved on to the synthetic phase would be absurd: the process was infinitely more complex than that, and it was spread over the following years. But the change is obvious, partly in the greater legibility of the pictures and partly in the gradual reintroduction of color, but of color as a form of construction, not as a statement about light, and even more in the use of collage, of sand, sawdust, and metal filings mixed into the paint, of papier collé, wood-graining, false marble, pieces of genuine or imitated "reality"; and in the fact that the process of putting together rather than taking apart gives these later pictures a greater inventiveness and an autonomous reality of their own. Then again these pictures are happier, less austere: many are light-hearted, and there can be no doubt that Picasso and Braque had great fun painting them.

The process had begun earlier, with imitated or mechanically-reproduced capitals: at Céret the year before Picasso had painted a large "Nature morte sur un piano" with the first four letters of Cortot's name carefully stenciled in the top left-hand corner; and of course *"Ma Jolie"* had already appeared on a number of canvases. And the introduction of a piece of printed oilcloth, not broken down in any way, was a decisive step towards synthesis; yet curiously enough at Sorgues he did not pursue the technique of collage that he invented for the "Chaise cannée," but turned back to these letters and indeed whole words. They inhabit the summer pictures of 1912 in great numbers: one of the best-known canvases, "L'Aficionado," which is connected with bull-fighting in the great Roman arena at Nîmes, has the name of that city neatly written, then on shifting planes *"Le Torero,"* and then the half-swallowed capitals *TOR*. Other pictures show his delight in imitating the grain of wood, a technique that Braque, trained as a decorator, possessed in all its ludicrous perfection; and there are examples of the new textures and surfaces that the two of them produced by adding dust and grit.

At the same time both Picasso and Braque were fascinated by three-dimensional constructions: sculpture is scarcely the word for these frail assemblies cut out of colored paper or cardboard or thin metal and then glued together; the few that have survived, dusty, more or less crumpled, rusted away, suggest that at this time Picasso's approach was essentially that of a painter, and of a painter whose mind was still grappling with the possibilities raised by his first collage with its ready-made facsimile of a cane seat.

It is odd that neither of them hit upon the idea of sticking paper to their canvases that summer: not until late September, after Picasso and Eva had gone back to Paris, did Braque suddenly produce the first papier collé. In a shop in Avignon he chanced upon some wallpaper that imitated oak paneling, and an answer to their problems came to him: he bought it, cut it carefully into shapes, and combined them with a charcoal drawing to make a picture of a glass and a fruit-dish standing against a paneled wall and upon a wooden drawer. The technique, as he said later, enabled him to dissociate form from color and to see that they were independent of one another. "That was the great revelation. Color and form make their effect simultaneously, though they have nothing to do with one another."

A few weeks later he showed it to Picasso, who was delighted and who at once saw that these anonymous, ready-made, submissive pieces of the phenomenal world not only did away with all personal virtuosity, but— much more important—that in their new context they could set up a won-derful series of reverberations in the beholder's mind and eye, the various realities echoing to and fro in his perception, heightening one another and disturbing all his preconceived notions of the truth. They would also pro-vide a new wealth of texture and surface: there was obviously a great deal to be done with papier collé, and he began his experiments at once.

He began them not in Montmartre but in Montparnasse. He had written to Kahnweiler from Sorgues, asking him to find a new studio and move his belongings: Kahnweiler had done his best, choosing a place in the boulevard Raspail right over on the other side of Paris, and supervising the removal-men. It must have been an appalling task. Even when he was poor Picasso accumulated papers, books, old ties, catalogs; now that he had been comfortably solvent for several years the quantity of objects in decaying cardboard boxes, old trunks and cupboards, the tottering, dust-covered pyramids had reached unnatural proportions; and by this time the merchant was well enough acquainted with his prize painter to be sure that Picasso knew every one of those heaps, boxes, and containers inti-mately and would demand an account of any valuable old postcard lost or thrown away. Poor Kahnweiler: he loved Picasso, but like most people who loved Picasso he paid for it heavily at times. The studio did not suit, of course; in the whole history of painting no studio found by a friend ever has suited; and Picasso was out of it in a few months. And then quite apart from finding the new home in Montparnasse and seeing to the move, Kahnweiler had another disagreeable, anxious, time-consuming job: Picasso had painted a Picasso on a wall at Les Clochettes: the wall had to be demolished, the picture recovered, backed with wood, brought to Paris; and the endless negotiations with the old lady who owned the villa, with her relations, with the artisans and experts, fell to Kahnweiler.

Yet even if his real esteem and affection for Picasso are left out of the account it is not surprising that Kahnweiler should have taken so much trouble. Picasso's fame was growing fast: fame in small but influential circles in Paris, Germany, and Russia, notoriety elsewhere. The 1912 Salon des Indépendants had an unprecedented display of Cubist pictures, including Juan Gris' "Hommage à Picasso" and the works of three important newcomers to the movement, the Russian Leopold Survage, the Dutch Piet Mondrian, and the Mexican Rivera. Diego Rivera, by the way, brought a very remarkable Tlatilolco head to Paris, a dual head some two thousand years old with three eyes and two mouths so that a full face could be seen at the same time as a profile with no discontinuity of the whole; he showed this symbol of duality to Picasso, and in time it bore strange fruit.

Then the Salon d'Automne showed many more, while under the title of the Section d'Or several of the Puteaux group had an important exhibition at the Galérie La Boëtie, an exhibition that included Marcel Duchamp's famous "Nu descendant un escalier."

The outcry was immense, far greater than before. The senior member of the city council wrote to the minister of fine arts, begging him to go to the Salon d'Automne, from which he would emerge "as sickened as many people I know; indeed, I hope you will murmur to yourself, 'Have I the right to lend a public building to a gang of malefactors who in the world of art behave themselves just as apaches do in everyday life?' When you come out, Monseiur le Ministre, you will wonder whether nature and the human form have ever been subjected to such an outrage . . . and whether the dignity of the government of which you are a member is not seriously affected when it seems to countenance the scandal by sheltering these horrors in a building belonging to the nation." And in parliament a deputy rose to say that it was intolerable that public property should be made use of for "manifestations of such a markedly anti-artistic and anti-national character."

On the other side the poor Cubists were abused for their prim conventionality. "Although we will have nothing whatsover to do with Impressionism," said the Futurists, "we very strongly disapprove of the present reaction which, in order to kill Impressionism, is bringing painting back to the old academic formulas. . . . There is no possible doubt that many of the aesthetic statements of our French colleagues display a kind of veiled academicism. We declare ourselves totally opposed to their art. They stubbornly persist in painting the motionless, the frozen, the static aspects of nature; they worship the traditionalism of Poussin, Ingres, and Corot; they are turning their art into something old-fashioned and fossilized."

Picasso did not exhibit at the salons, but he was known, a little unfairly, to be the chief of the Cubists, and it was as the leader of what was dimly to be seen to be a significant new movement that he was asked to contribute to the second Post-Impressionist exhibition at the Grafton Gallery in London this year. Two of his pictures had been seen at the first show in 1910, "La Fillette à la corbeille fleurie" and the modest "Clovis Sagot"; mild though it was in comparison with the "Demoiselles d'Avignon," the portrait gave offense and it was at once caricatured, together with some Cézannes and others less clearly identifiable, in a derisive counter-show put on by the Chelsea Arts Club. And the exhibition as a whole had been badly received. "The walls are hung with works . . . like the crude efforts of children, garishly discordant in colour, formless, and destitute of tone," said the *Connoisseur,* which regretted that men of talent "should waste their lives in spoiling acres of good canvas when they might be better employed in stone-breaking for the roads," while some time later G. K. Chesterton told his readers that if there were something comprehensible in Picasso's art, that something could be described in a comprehensible manner in writing: a statement that seems to me to sum up the difference between the nineteenth and the twentieth centuries.

This time there were thirteen Picasso paintings and three drawings, all, except for one Blue portrait and the Gósol "Composition," between 1908 and 1912; and apart from the splendid section devoted to Matisse the exhibition was largely Cubist. In 1912 by no means all the English were bogged down in Georgian good taste: Impressionism had been fairly well digested; Cézanne had his devotees; and both Gauguin and van Gogh had reached the middlebrows. But even the most percipient were still too firmly held by tradition to make anything of Cubism. Roger Fry thought the new painting was essentially Expressionist; and he saw Cubism, carried to its logical extremity, as "an attempt to give up all resemblance to natural form—a visual music; and the later works of Picasso show this clearly enough . . . with the exception of Braque none of them push their attempts at abstraction of form so far." Since Fry had helped to write the catalog he was obliged to be civil: *The Times* was not. Having dealt with Matisse, the paper said,

> the art of M. Picasso is a very different matter. He, too, is not a charlatan, but we do not believe that he is an artist of narrow and intense originality like M. Matisse. Rather he seems to us to be by nature extremely imitative, and to have endeavoured to preserve himself from imitation by the pursuit of a theory scientific rather than artistic in its origin. We see him in an early portrait an imitator of Goya, but without Goya's wit or spontaneity. In his large composition we see him produce a work as cleverly eclectic and as sophisticated as some Italian pictures of the seventeenth century. And lastly we have his purely theoretic experiments which are unintelligible to the eye and the mind. Forgetting that these are meant to represent anything, we see very little abstract beauty of colour or design in most of them, although the still life is an exception. They depress us as if they were diagrams of a science about which we know nothing; and whereas in "La Femme au Pot de Moutarde" a human form is obscurely discernible, it seems, but for the obscurity, to be commonplace. He has every right to make his experiments, and they may perhaps prove useful to other artists in the future. He is, in fact, such a scientific experimentor as Paolo Uccello might have been if he had had no original talent of his own, or if in him a slight original talent had been overlaid by intellectual curiosity.

(Sixty years later the same paper called Picasso "the most famous, the most controversial, in many ways the most influential and undoubtedly the richest artist of his age. He was a draughtsman of genius, and there is probably no single artist except Giotto or Michelangelo who can justly compare with him in being responsible for so radically altering the course of art in his time.")

Of course the popular press was ribald; and it continued to be ribald, in all countries, until at length it was crushed into a servile respect by the sheer weight of money paid for Picasso's works. In 1912 however the sums were modest enough: that year the Stafford Gallery showed drawings, mostly of the Blue and Pink Periods, and while the most important cost £22 a small one might be had for £2.50.

None of this depressed Picasso, nor yet Kahnweiler: there is a kind of abuse that is a guarantee of excellence and almost of success, for surely people do not utter such shrill and vehement protests unless some Freudian resistance is at work—unless at some level they are aware of the validity of what they see. Deeply untruthful painting is deeply boring; it meets with a flaccid rather than a passionate response, and no one has ever suggested burning the limp canvases, the hanging ropes, and the solemn array of boots that now crowd provincial galleries. Besides, the Cubist exhibitions this year in Berlin, Munich, Cologne (where Picasso showed sixteen works of between 1903 and 1911, having a whole room to himself), Moscow, and Barcelona evoked a more directly encouraging response, and in Paris the more intelligent journalists were beginning to support the movement, as Apollinaire had done from the first.

The young merchant was full of confidence; and he and the painter signed a contract, a most unusual contract, since it was drawn up by the painter and since it contained a clause laying down that Picasso alone should decide whether a painting was finished or not; but once it was signed Kahnweiler had achieved his ambition—he was now Picasso's exclusive dealer. Now, as far as money was concerned, the future seemed assured: Picasso returned with more than usual zeal to the new world opened up by papier collé.

Apart from a brief visit to Le Havre with Braque in the autumn of 1912, Picasso spent all the rest of that year and the first part of 1913 in Paris, his work interrupted only by another removal, this time to a dismal modern house in the nearby rue Schoelcher, a cold street that runs along the side of the Montparnasse cemetery. He had known Montparnasse ever since he came to Paris, and he had friends there, but it was quite unlike his old village on the Butte, where he knew everybody, every street, and every café; yet at least it had this advantage, that fewer people disturbed him: and the flat was comfortable, the studio well-lit.

Although he did not confine himself to papiers collés, nor anything like it, he turned out a surprising number, many of them concerned with bottles, bottles of rum, marc, maraschino, Dubonnet, Pernod, Suze, and Bass. He had great fun with them, sometimes sticking the real label on, sometimes imitating it: he had fun with visiting-cards too, particularly with those that were dog-eared to show that the person named had been there in the flesh; he used them as signatures and as allusions to his friends—André Level's is built into one picture, and the joint card of Gertrude Stein and Alice Toklas into another—thus obtaining a pleasant to-and-fro of identities.

At this stage Braque used papier collé only in combination with drawing: Picasso took it much farther—his paper forms part of his paintings, and generally speaking he handled the new technique more freely and more wittily than his friend. Newspaper titles, or fragments of them, had appeared in his pictures well before this, but now they multiplied to a remarkable degree, and now they were accompanied by pieces of the printed text, sometimes cut into strips, sometimes into shapes more obviously pictorial. It has been suggested that the words they contain should be examined for hidden meanings that may have a bearing on the picture itself. Countless hours of research have hunted down the puns in *Ulysses* and - *Finnegans Wake*; the same talents have been turned to the Cubist papiers collés, but with disappointingly meager results in Picasso's case. (Gris is more rewarding.)

Perhaps it is just as well. In one of the 1913 pictures, "La Bouteille de Suze," the paper almost entirely covers the canvas; the legible columns of print, many of them upside down, contain something like two thousand words, and it would be a strange, time-laden painting that required the spectator to stand on his head with a magnifying-glass. Patient ingenuity can strain something out of the newspaper-cuttings, and in this case the left-hand columns deal with a huge Socialist, pacifist, trade-union, Communist, and anarchist meeting at Pré-Saint-Gervais, with red flags, black flags, and the Internationale, while on the right hand, inverted, there is an account of the Turco-Bulgarian war and a cholera epidemic. But the elaborate splicing of the literary and the plastic does not seem to match with what one knows of Picasso's mind: his wit was lively enough in all conscience, but it was never laborious. On the other hand, words and phrases that the eye takes in at once belong to a different category; and it is difficult to believe that the headline LA BATAILLE S'EST ENGAGEE in the "Guitare et verre," for example, is the effect of hazard.

Where the pasted paper is the predominant element these are not his most considerable paintings, but they are never facile and they are rarely flippant; again and again they achieve a rare, strange beauty of their own; and the "Bouteille de vieux marc," which uses a cut-out print of patterned cloth, would be a continually-renewed delight upon one's wall, in spite of Picasso's strong words about the function of painting.

It was not these collages, however, that traveled across the Atlantic to represent Picasso in the United States, but six paintings, a drawing, and a bronze. Leo Stein lent two undated still-lives; Kahnweiler the 1903 "Madame Soler," a 1907 gouache called "Les Arbres" (it was sold for $243 and now belongs to the Philadelphia Museum of Art), the famous "Femme au pot de moutarde" of 1910 (offered in vain at $675), and a 1912 "Tête d'homme"; Alfred Stieglitz the 1910 charcoal drawing of a nude that is now in the New York Museum of Modern Art and the bronze head of a woman that is to be seen in Chicago. They were to form part of the huge, epoch-making Armory Show that opened in New York on February 17, 1913, and then moved on to Chicago and Boston, giving many Americans their first view of what had happened and of what was now happening in the European studios: and as far as the Cubists and near-Cubists were concerned the exhibition also included works by Braque, Delaunay, Duchamp, Gleizes, Marie Laurencin, Léger, and Picabia.

To return to the "Bouteille de vieux marc": the cloth imitated in the papier collé is of the traditional Catalan kind, woven at Arles-sur-Tech, not far from Céret; and it was at Céret that Picasso painted the picture.

He had come down with Eva and Max Jacob in the spring of 1913, the year in which Vollard brought out a large edition of the Saltimbanques suite and in which Apollinaire, the unfortunate lover, published *Les peintres cubistes, méditations esthétiques*, a muddled, enthusiastic appreciation of the leaders and some others, including Marie Laurencin, and *Alcools*, his finest collection of poems. Then came the Braques, and Juan Gris.

Gris is generally named with Picasso and Braque as one of the chief figures of Cubism, but he was a late comer to the movement and it was not until 1912 that he abandoned direct representation. Once he did become a Cubist, however, he remained a Cubist, the purest of them all; and to the end of his short life he carried on along that severe path, traveling longer if not farther than any of his companions. He has been represented as an intellectual rather than an intuitive painter, a theoretician; and it has been said that his pictures leave a feeling of cold calculation. On the other hand Kahnweiler, no mean judge, loved him and his work, while many respectable critics rank him very high. It is not his merits that are my concern, however, but his relation with Picasso. Fernande disliked him: she accuses him of being an opportunist who copied the tricks of Cubism, and although Picasso cannot have taken this seriously, her attitude may well have increased his initial reserve. Picasso liked flattery, but Gris set about it the wrong way: he called Picasso maître, which, with its implications of age, established respectability, and academies, irritated him; and in spite of the "Hommage à Picasso" which Gris had exhibited at the Indépendants in the spring of 1912 this irritation increased, eventually turning into an odd mixture of affection and antipathy, with the antipathy sometimes predominating.

Jealousy entered into it too: although Gris never wavered in his devotion to Cubism he became very much attached to Matisse; and more than that, Gertrude Stein became very much attached to Gris. "Tell me why you stand up for his work, you know you do not like it," said Picasso to Gertrude Stein, and she says he said it "violently." She also observes, "Gris was the only person Picasso wished away. The relationship between them was just that." And to Kahnweiler he said, "You know very well that Gris never painted any important pictures."

But this was later. In 1913 Picasso's natural kindness still far out-weighed his irritation, and Juan Gris was one of the group at Céret.

Picasso was installed in some splendor on the ground floor of a big eighteenth-century house, once a monastery, belonging to Frank Havilland, a china-manufacturer from Limoges with artistic tastes, who also frequented the Steins and the Bateau-Lavoir. The house had a large garden with a stream in it and a great many trees: the stream was filled with frogs, the trees with nightingales; and between them they made Max Jacob wretched. But it would have taken more than a choir of nightingales to disturb Picasso; he was working extremely hard and he went on working, although while he was at Céret he received the news of Don José's death. Céret is less than a hundred miles from Barcelona; Picasso was no longer poor; he did not go. Although he feared and hated death he buried Eva, he buried Juan Gris, Vollard, and other friends; but he did not bury his father. It was not that he was unable to go to Spain, since his friends had hardly arrived before he took them over the border to see a bull-fight at Figueras. There is no hint of an explanation in anything that Picasso said in later years; none in the letters that Jacob wrote to Apollinaire at the time. All that can be gathered from Jacob's correspondence is that they were deeply concerned about the news; that Picasso was very kind to him; that the weather was indifferent; that he found Eva charming; and that she was far from well.

Few things are easier than clapping labels on to Picasso's more usual subjects and saying, "The bull symbolizes evil," or, "The bull stands for the Spanish people," or, "The café tables symbolize Bohemia, the refusal of ordinary bourgeois life," and so on: it made him extremely impatient—"One simply paints," he said, "one does not paste one's ideas on a picture." Yet is it entirely fortuitous that at the time of Don José's death the harlequin found his way back into Picasso's painting? The harlequin, not as a symbol but as the evidence of a certain state of mind in which loneliness was an important factor?

He did not entirely vanish with the ending of the Rose Period; there is for example a sad Cubist harlequin of 1909, leaning his head on his hand; but it was not until this holiday at Céret in 1913 that Picasso painted another important member of the long series. It is not an easily legible picture: high Cubism, rigidly disciplined and as impersonal as anything of Picasso's can be impersonal, pale buff and gray, more analytic than synthetic. But it is the old harlequin, Picasso's companion, to whom he had sometimes given his own face.

A point of departure for this picture is obvious, perhaps too obvious to be altogether convincing: not only does Max Jacob record their journey across the frontier in "the charming company of cooks, engineers, and courteous draper's assistants" to Spain, "a land of squares and angles" where "the houses have no roofs and the aloes are as bitter as the people," but he also speaks of their meeting with a small traveling circus and making friends with the girls and the clowns "whose make-up might have been a Cubist joke."

The summer was wet, cold, and disappointing; a southern town, made for the sun, is even more dismal than the north when rain falls steadily; and nothing is more uncomfortable than walking about in wet rope-soled shoes. Eva's cough grew worse, and she was thought to have bronchitis.

In spite of the weather Picasso worked steadily: he and Braque carried the technique of papier collé much farther—it had greater potentialities than they had supposed, and Braque painted his splended "Clarinette," one of the finest papiers collés yet produced—and between them they established Cubism firmly on its synthetic basis.

They were back in Paris as usual for the Salon d'Automne, and it was in Paris that Picasso painted two large pictures of particular significance, the one as it were summing up the recent past and the other looking towards the future. The first is the "Joueurs de cartes," in which restrained color builds the broad unrelieved planes into a whole that possesses a relief of its own, a relief helped not by a cut-out paper imitation of a printed pattern but by a painted imitation of that imitation. It is true that the "Joueurs" also foreshadows a technique that he was to use far more extensively next summer, a kind of pointillism here confined to a small area in the middle, but it is the second painting that shows the full returning tide of color and gives a hint of the strange worlds beyond the limit of Cubism. He knew that it would be an important work, and he made several preliminary sketches, one at least in color: the resulting picture is called "Femme en chemise, assise dans un fauteuil," and it is as rounded as an egg.

As it is shown in his painting, Picasso's feeling for women oscillated between extreme tenderness and appreciation on the one hand and violent hatred on the other, the mid-point being nearer dislike if not contempt. The "Demoiselles d'Avignon" is often held up as an example of the second, and although because of the particular nature of that picture I think this is a mistake, there are plenty of other, and unquestionable, examples of his savagery; but while he was with Eva there was nothing to exacerbate his misogyny, and the "Femme en chemise" is quite benign. Superficially the picture is not at all difficult: the beautifully sunburned woman sits there in a fringed, upholstered easy chair, her columnar body bare to the navel, her shift in her lap (it looks like a crumpled papier collé), one arm behind her head, a newspaper in her other hand. The general color of the figure and the background is golden-tawny; the padded, enveloping chair is a varying magenta; and the whole picture is warm. It is also an immediately striking piece of work, especially when it is compared with the austere pictures that preceded it; it astonishes the beholder and haunts his memory.

"I am thinking about that famous picture of Picasso's, 'La Femme en chemise,'" said Paul Eluard, "a picture that I have known for close on twenty years and that has always seemed to me both so perfectly simple and so extraordinary. The vast and sculptural mass of the woman in her armchair, that head as big as the sphinx's, those breasts nailed to her chest, form a marvelous contrast—and is something that neither the Egyptians nor the Greeks nor any artist before Picasso could bring into existence—with her small-featured face, the waving hair, the delectable armpit, the jutting ribs, the filmy slip, the soft easy chair, the daily paper."

In Picasso's work a theme is often announced, apparently forgotten, and then much later taken up again for full development: the promise of the "Femme en chemise" was not fulfilled for many years. Having painted her, Picasso returned to the main current of his Cubist pictures and to his constructions. These objects now took on a more sculptural aspect, as though his view of their nature changed, as though they were no longer collages raised to a higher power but rather creations in their own right. And indeed the series runs from the almost flat "Violon" of 1912 or 1913, which is essentially a collage, to the free-standing "Verre d'Absinthe" of 1914, which is true sculpture by any definition.

Most of them are concerned with stringed instruments, though there are also a few still-lives; and in making them he used some of the resources of African and Romanesque art in which positive and negative are interchangeable, a hollow standing for a bulge or a protruding cylinder for a hole. In some, color or drawing plays an important part; in others the materials are bare; and these materials include paper, string, sheet-metal, cardboard, and wood.

An eminent authority says that if Picasso "had done nothing else, his place as a master in the history of sculpture would have been ensured," and no doubt for an art-historian that is true. Yet why are so many people disappointed by his constructions? Partly because they are clumsily botched together, which offends the general respect for craftsmanship: arts and crafts, or rather the craft through which art finds its expression, are not easily separated, and evident manual dexterity is often taken as a sign that the artist was capable of saying what he meant to say. And partly because many of the constructions are now bent, faded, limp, dirty, and falling to pieces. In the first place they were gay, as the drawings prove: and in the first place Manolo's carved butter was no doubt as satisfying as his later stone or terra-cotta; but no one will pretend that the melting butter was worth more than its dairy price. Many materials grow sad with age, as sad as the "real" skirts on Degas' dancers, once so white and crisp; and that is where the comparative failure of the construction lies, for they came fresh and happy from Picasso's hand—an uncharacteristic happiness was the mark of 1913 and early 1914—and apart from a few examples such as the cheerful, and permanent, polychrome bronze absinthe-glass neither the happiness nor the freshness has survived. We are not looking at what Picasso saw. Permanence may have nothing to do with artistic expression in the first place, but it certainly has to do with subsequent appreciation.

Why did Picasso choose to botch these things together? It has been suggested that he loved the rough surfaces. Maybe so: but it looks more like one of those many contradictions that made up his difficult character, for at other times he could be a most finished craftsman. His painting, etching, and engraving are professional to the highest degree; even his imitation wood-graining, the house-painter's technique that he learned from Braque and that they used in so many Cubist pictures, is the work of a conscientious artisan; in 1905 he worked an accomplished low relief in copper, and in the fifties he made a gold necklace for a friend to wear at bull-fights. I had it heavy in my hands a little while ago and I looked at it very carefully: first there is a great solid round, two or three inches across, with a bull's head in very high relief in the middle of it; then on either side roughly triangular lumps of gold, each having another bull's head, but in profile and either incised or in low relief; then at the ends, well before the clasp, two gold leaves; and throughout the necklace the links are bull's bones. Quite apart from its artistic excellence the craftsmanship is of the highest order: no working goldsmith could have done better. Yet the only technical guidance he had was from the dentist at Vallauris: his innate dexterity and feeling for materials did the rest.

The year 1914 opened as a happy year for Picasso, and this happiness bubbled out in color. All at once the sobriety of Cubism was overwhelmed with a copious shower of brilliant dots: soft curves came back, the remaining rectilinear forms were brightly colored, and a joyful green, a rare color for Picasso, made its appearance. The severely-disciplined compositions gave way to less ambitious merriment; the austere planes to a profusion of these dots. They were not the intellectual, scientific dots of pure color that Seurat used, but rather an expression of gaiety and a means of making the variegated surface dance. And so strong was the influence of Picasso's mood on his friends that even the sober Braque began to paint in this rococo form of Cubism, although it seemed foreign to his nature.

Friendship was of the first importance to Picasso, young and old. In 1914 Kahnweiler brought out another of Max Jacob's books, *Le Siège de Jérusalem*, illustrated once again with Picasso etchings, and its kind reception brought still more pleasure to them both. Apollinaire was also doing well: *Alcools* was a success, and apart from that he was now running the influential *Soirées de Paris*, a review that supported the avant-garde in spite of its readers' resistance—when he published five pictures of Picasso's constructions thirty-nine canceled their subscriptions. And then when La Peau de l'Ours, a collectors' club founded by André Level and his friends in 1904 with the idea of buying pictures, enjoying them for a while, and then parting with them, held their sale in March, 1914, Picasso's ''Famille de Saltimbanques'' came up for auction: they had given Picasso a thousand francs for it, a sum that terrified collectors in 1908. All his friends were there, and in an atmosphere of intense excitement the bidding rose steadily from the respectable to the surprising and then to the spectacular, closing amidst wild cheers from one and all at the figure of 11,500 francs. Neither in Montmartre nor in Montparnasse does there appear to have been any jealousy, any envious repining, though almost all the painters were poor and few of them were saints. It is true that Picasso did not touch a single sou of this sum; but even so it was a commercial consecration, not without its importance or its joy. It was prophetic too: when that Picasso came up for sale again in the States it fetched over a million dollars.

Then again the ''Gioconda'' was back in the Louvre: Italy had restored her to France, the name of the real culprit was known—Peruggia, an Italian—and Picasso could take a cab without looking behind him, or a train.

This summer of 1914 he spent in Avignon with Eva, and the Braques and Derains joined them there. Braque and Picasso still formed a most united team, although their painting was now more distinct than it had been a year or so before, since the grave Braque did not follow Picasso in all his gambolings; but Derain had moved right away from Cubism to a somber manner of his own, called by some his Gothic period, a divergence that neither altered Picasso's liking for Derain nor affected his ebullient cheerfulness.

All the survivors agree that it was a golden summer, and figures prove that this was not mere nostalgia for an exciting, adventurous, forward-looking, comparatively simple and happy world. The paintings accumulated in Picasso's studio, among them another "Ma Jolie," with the words, sworn evidence of his happiness, stenciled large and plain across the top, the brilliant "Portrait d'une jeune fille," and several kaleidoscopic still-lives.

But even so apolitical an animal as Picasso must have heard the rumbling of guns as the summer wore on. He began to paint the picture that is generally called "Vive la France," a colorful still-life of a bottle of rum, some café objects—playing cards, a packet of tobacco, jars, a spotted glass—against a background of flowered wallpaper, another imitation papier collé: one of the vessels, perhaps an opaline jar, has the words "*vive la*" above crossed tricolors, and it is said that there is a relation of cause and effect between the coming war and the picture. The painting is as cheerful as can be; but the story may be true. Picasso may have been expressing his support for France, or he may have been conjuring fate.

If the picture was intended as an exorcism, it failed. In any case it was too late. Before he had finished it the whole wretched mindless process of destruction had begun, and his friends left to joint their regiments. "I took Braque and Derain to the station at Avignon," he said. "I never found them again": perhaps the saddest words he ever spoke.

Chapter X

In the enormous all-pervading excitement, the sense of ultimate crisis, the patriotic enthusiasm, the regiments marching with flowers in their rifles, the beating of the drum, personal unhappiness was difficult to realize at first; but soon it became clear that this total disruption applied not only to daily life but to the entire pattern underlying that life.

War had been declared amid a tidal-wave of national feeling in which the longing for revenge played an important part; and in the moment of extreme danger, when the German drive through neutral Belgium brought the enemy to the Marne in the first days of September, not twenty miles from the heart of Paris, the nation's spirit rose to the highest pitch, in spite of the government's flight to Bordeaux. The Germans were halted, though at a terrible cost in lives; the peril brought the French together as a single body; and in the exalting, unifying hatred for the enemy the old divisions vanished. The Socialist, Communist, and anarchist doctrine that workers would not fire upon their comrades did not apply to German workers. Foreigners, unless they were the allies of France, were of no importance whatsoever; they did not count.

Picasso was an outsider once again. The world that had grown up around him and in which he belonged evaporated in the first few weeks of the war. His French contemporaries disappeared, and he was left with a sparse remnant of his wide acquaintance—other foreigners, old men, and invalids—the remote spectator of a quarrel that was not his own.

His temperament was that of an outsider: but no temperament is all of a piece—Picasso's less than most—and just as celibates often dream of the marriage state, imagining strange joys, so some part of the outsider longs at times for integration. The rootless Polish-Italian Apollinaire, a weaker but perhaps a happier man, solved his problem by joining the French army: there was some difficulty at first, possibly because of the statues, but by the end of the year he was a gunner, an integral part of the 38th regiment of field artillery. Picasso did no such thing. Although his general

sympathies were plain, he was not viscerally concerned by the battle between France and Germany; for him the 1914 war, as opposed to the wars
against fascism, was not a conflict between light and darkness in which he
was necessarily committed. Yet he was deeply affected, and not merely
by the inconveniences of life for a foreigner, the papers, the necessity for
a passport, the bureaucratic fuss, and the inevitable shortages; no civilian
is entirely at ease among fighting-men in time of war; his self-esteem is
diminished, and women no longer have the same regard for him. In his
case it also brought loneliness; the darkened streets of Paris were empty
of young men, apart from a few in uniform; and although the Montparnasse cafés such as the Dôme and the Rotonde still had their customers,
not many of them were people he liked. Most of his friends had been
called up or had volunteered: others were abroad, Picabia in the United
States, where he was soon joined by Duchamp; Delaunay in Spain, which
also sheltered Marie Laurencin and the German she had so absurdly married just before the war: even Gertrude Stein was pinned in England,
there being no transport for neutrals in the early days.

He could not finish "Vive la France," and that winter saw the end of
rococo Cubism. It also saw a striking decrease in his production: the pictures that he did paint were far more severe, and among them was a tall
gaunt harlequin. This harlequin was signed: he had also put his name to
some of the recent, cheerful, personal, rococo pictures, but here the identification may have a significance of its own.

Materially he was affected, too. Kahnweiler had not attended to Picasso's advice about adopting French nationality: he was still a German, and
his belongings, his shop, and his stock in trade were seized as enemy
property. He himself would have been interned if he had not happened to
be on holiday in Italy: he succeeded in reaching the safety of neutral
Switzerland, but there was nothing that he could do for his painters, and
some of them were reduced to near starvation. Juan Gris, for example,
who as a deserter from the Spanish army had no passport, was caught in
Collioure, where he had been seeing Matisse, and he kept alive only by
eating raw sardines on the shore; while Herbin, rejected by the army as
being too small, did not have even that resource, and he nearly died in the
Bateau-Lavoir from mere want of food. Picasso, however, like many
people who have been wildly extravagant when poor, had grown if not
penurious then at least careful with wealth; he had taken his precautions,
and he did not suffer to anything like the same extent. Still, his merchant
was gone; Uhde and his fellow-countrymen were the other side of the
firing-line; the Russian millionaires might as well have been in the moon;
and with the Germans deep in France—their guns could be heard in Pa-

ris—few French collectors were in the mood to buy. Vollard did not even trouble to open his shop.

Matisse was in Paris part of the time, trying to get the army to accept him in spite of his forty-five years, and Picasso saw something of him. And among the diminished band there remained Max Jacob, too sickly and purblind for service; González and Gargallo, Spaniards and therefore neutral too; some other foreigners, and farther off Serge Férat and his sister, Modigliani (when he was not dead drunk), Giorgio de Chirico, Marc Chagall for a while, Moise Kisling, Chaim Soutine, Jacques Lipchitz, and Pinchus Kremegne.

Just before the war Gargallo had carved a portrait-head of Picasso for a keystone that is still to be seen on the façade of the Cinema del Bosque in Barcelona, together with the likenesses of Nonell, Ramon Reventós, and the sculptor himself; and it was Gargallo who carved the equally cheerful and better-known head of 1917 that is so often reproduced. He had known Picasso since the days of the Quatre Gats, and unlike many of these old friends he had a delicacy about selling the drawings and pictures that Picasso scattered right and left so long as there was no attempt at forcing his natural but capricious generosity. But in the first winter of the war Gargallo found that he could no longer make a living in Paris; furthermore he was passionately eager to marry a young Provençale called Magalí. He came to the rue Schoelcher and asked whether he might in decency part with a drawing that Pablo had given him. Certainly he might, said Picasso, and at once helped him to find a purchaser; when all was settled he accompanied the now-solvent Gargallo and his bride to the station, and as the train moved off he thrust a tube through the window into their hands—a Cubist drawing to replace the first.

Autumn brought Gertrude Stein and Alice Toklas back to Paris, to the rue de Fleurus and the diminished collection. It was diminished not by any act of war but by Leo Stein's decision, taken late in 1913, to go and live in Italy. Since many of the pictures had been bought out of their common fund there had to be a sharing: but although it was agreed that Leo should have the Matisses and Gertrude the Picassos there were a great many other pictures and the division could not be made without some heartburning, particularly as Leo insisted upon having a Cézanne still-life with apples to which Gertrude was deeply attached. "The Cézanne apples have a unique importance to me that nothing can replace," he said. " . . . I'm afraid you'll have to look upon the loss . . . as an act of God."

But he was reckoning without another creator; for Picasso, observing

Gertrude Stein's distress, painted her an apple, a single apple, not indeed a Cézanne, but a picture in its way as deeply satisfying, one that almost fulfilled his promise, "I will paint you an apple and it will be as fine as all of Cézanne's apples"; and he produced it, inscribed *Souvenir pour Gertrude et Alice* for Christmas, 1914.

From time to time he and Eva dined at the rue de Fleurus, although she was far from well; and on one of these occasions there was an air-raid alarm. They put out the lights and took shelter with the concierge for a while, then returned to the studio and sat there with a single candle, shaded by the table. Gertrude Stein and Picasso talked until the all clear sounded at two in the morning: they talked then and upon hundreds of other occasions, but how much did they communicate? Neither of them understood the language well: she "rarely read french newspapers, she never read anything in french," and Picasso's resistance to the finer points can be seen from his letters. When one considers the infinite possibilities of mistaken expression in the first place and of mistaken comprehension of that error in the second, it may be thought that Gertrude Stein is not the most reliable authority on Picasso's views, at least where delicate shade of meaning is concerned.

Yet there was one point, not without its delicacy, where there was no misunderstanding whatsoever. Among the people Picasso saw at the rue de Fleurus there was Juan Gris, who had managed to get back to Paris and who was now living in abject poverty at the Bateau-Lavoir. In spite of his being, as she puts it, "a tormented and not particularly sympathetic character . . . very melancholy and effusive and as always clear sighted and intellectual" Gris and Gertrude Stein grew very friendly; she used often to go to the Bateau-Lavoir. Picasso did not like it. He had always had strong reservations about Gris; and now it may be that he did not altogether trust his clear-sighted intellect. The she-bear is often held up as the type of possessive affection; but neither the she-bear nor yet the tigress can compare with the average artist protecting his patron. This deeply-rooted sense of property readily merges with a more commonplace emotion; and Picasso was somewhat given to jealousy. He was not at all sorry, for example, to have supplanted Matisse in Gertrude Stein's esteem.

Matisse and Picasso were in agreement on the sacred importance of painting; on almost every other point they were far, far apart. Matisse's way of life was the antithesis of Picasso's; so was his attitude towards patrons, as he had proved by his magnanimous introduction of Shchoukine; and so, in this particular case, was his attitude towards Juan Gris. He was much concerned about the young man's desperate state. In a letter to the remote Kahnweiler Gris said that Matisse was *d'un dévouement extrême,* and certainly he did his very best to provide some kind of a living, some kind of a pension, to tide Gris over this difficult period. What he could not do himself he hoped to induce Gris' friends and admirers to do: among those who were in Paris he called on Gertrude Stein. He represented to her, with all the force of a man who has known bitter hardship, that if Gris were not fed he must die; she was convinced, but she deferred the arrangement of the details to another day. As Matisse reached her door at the appointed time he met Picasso coming out: inside Gertrude Stein was waiting for him with the news that taking all things into consideration she had decided that she could not see her way to granting his request. The implication is obvious: I do not know whether it is sound, but Matisse believed it was.

Shortly after, in the spring of 1915, Gertrude Stein decided to go to Majorca "and forget the war a little." Among other consequences, this left Picasso with scarcely any "respectable" dinner-giving acquaintance apart from Serge Gastrebzoff and his sister Madame d'Oettingen, who lived nearby in the boulevard Raspail. Both painted (he had been a Cubist since 1910), both wrote, both had difficulty with their names: Gastrebzoff signed his pictures Serge Férat, and she signed her writings Roch Grey or Jean Cérusse or Léonard Pieux. They were well-to-do and appreciative—they bought everything that Henri Rousseau left in his studio when he died—and it was they who had provided the backing for Apollinaire's *Soirées de Paris.* It is said that Picasso learned the Cyrillic letters that appear in some of his paintings from them: for Kahnweiler their origin was the paper that wrapped his pictures when they returned from Moscow in 1910. No doubt both accounts are true.

Apollinaire was seen from time to time when he came on leave; so were Braque, Léger, Derain, La Fresnaye, Jacques Villon, and many more; and letters arrived, sometimes bringing souvenirs—an engraved piece of shell-case from Léger—but they were letters and objects from another planet, and mercurial though he was, Max Jacob was almost the only unchanging figure remaining from the world Picasso knew.

Although to the superficial view his life seemed chaotic, it was informed by a certain order, and Picasso was a creature of habit, profoundly conservative in his ways. His deep affection for the emotional and sometimes trying Jacob increased, in spite of his friend's even greater preoccupation with religion, a subject that Picasso did not care to touch.

Jacob had recently had another vision, that of Our Lady this time: he had also found the more sympathetic Fathers of Notre Dame de Sion, who were particularly concerned with the conversion of the Jews, and early in

1915 he was baptized, Picasso being his godfather and Sylvette Filassier, of the Théâtre des Variétés, his godmother.

Picasso had wanted to call him Fiacre, after the seventh-century Irish saint who lived in a forest in the Brie, near Meaux; he would have nothing whatsoever to do with women, and he is much invoked by gardeners and those who suffer from hemorrhoids—as good a saint as could well be imagined, and of an excellent Milesian family; but unhappily the first person in Paris to let out hackney coaches in 1620 did so from a house named after the saint in the rue Saint-Martin, and by extension all French cabs came to be called fiacres. This distressed Jacob, so Picasso chose from his own array of names, and in the *Imitation de Jésus-Christ* that was his christening-present he wrote: *A mon frère/Cyprien Max Jacob/souvenir de son/Bapteme/jeudi 18 Febrier 1915/Pablo.*

Somewhat later Picasso paused in his work, set his Cubist pictures to one side, and made a pencil drawing of his godson sitting in a chair, wearing a high-necked pullover, a double-breasted waistcoat and a jacket, bald as an egg and looking deeply thoughtful and benign—a wholly realistic drawing that Don José would have loved and whose virtuosity made his friends cry "Ingres!" If the war had not been raging perhaps they might have cried "Holbein!" or any of the other names that are synonymous with total mastery of the flowing line: however Ingres was what they said, apart from Level who said Picasso, and the rank and file of the Cubists who said Traitor, seeing this realism as a betrayal of their movement.

Unperturbed, Picasso moved on to an even more precise drawing of Vollard and then to another of Léonce Rosenberg. Rosenberg was the dealer who eventually stepped in to take over Kahnweiler's painters, succoring the unhappy Cubists and saving Juan Gris. He also managed Picasso's affairs, though even at the worst of times that represented no great difficulty: at no stage did wealthy collectors, such as the Chilean Madame Errazuriz, entirely neglect his work. Léonce Rosenberg was a generous, good-hearted man, and even when he was called up he went on looking after the Cubists' interests as well as he could, buying their pictures every time he came on leave.

This abrupt and almost entirely unheralded reversion to a style reminiscent of his wonderfully accomplished student drawings or of his drypoint circus horse of 1905 was incomprehensible to his friends. It is true that he had a great admiration for Ingres; and it is true that Henri Mahaut says, "In 1915 Picasso told me he wanted to see if he could draw like everybody else"; but surely his return to a world immediately accessible to others, to a traditional manner reaching back to the time when the artist's dialogue was between himself and the whole community—a community of which he was a full, accepted member—has at least some relationship with Apollinaire's voluntary plunge into the French army?

Braque had been wounded seriously in the head, fighting near Arras in May, 1915, although the news did not reach Paris for some time. Men were being killed by the thousand in the great offensives; the field-hospitals and those in the rear were crowded with shockingly mutilated figures; his friends despaired of his life.

There are times when even the highest human activities—peace-time activities—must seem futile: Picasso's work did not come to a halt, but 1915 was his least fruitful year since he came to Paris. During some relatively happy interval he finished "Vive la France"; in his other Cubist paintings he still used these dots a little, but for variegation of texture, not for gaiety, and although he never retreated from color the pictures of 1915 and 1916, often very large, are angular and severe: not perhaps as ascetic as those of the high analytic phase, but painted with at least an equal gravity. The harlequin I have already mentioned is a canvas six feet high, and although the mass of brilliant color—vermilion and ultramarine lozenges and planes—is very great, it stands against an even more important area of black. The little pin-like head is somber: the one round eye expressionless. Collages almost died away, and the constructions were seen no more. But there were these new wonderful cool realistic drawings of his friends: why did Eva never appear in them?

Answer comes there none. Her frail slim little figure, her doe-like eyes, are known to us only from two unskilled photographs; and apart from Max Jacob's "charming woman" and Gertrude Stein's "I could perfectly understand Fernande's liking for Eve. As I said Fernande's great heroine was Evelyn Thaw, small and negative. Here was a little french Evelyn Thaw, small and perfect" and a few other passing references, Picasso's friends tell nothing. She drifts in and out of his history like a gentle ghost.

In the autumn she became very ill. By November, as he told the distant Gertrude Stein, Picasso was spending half his time in the Métro, going to and from the clinic where she lay. Nevertheless he said that his days were full, that as usual he was working hard—"*enfin ma vie est bien remplie et come toutjours je ne me arrete pas*"—and that he had painted a harlequin, perhaps his best. Yet, as well as the harlequins of 1915, he also made one of his very rare religious drawings, a Christ crucified. Neither its exact date in the year nor of course its significance to Picasso can be stated; yet there it is, an enigmatic testimony open to many interpretations, worked upon with the utmost care.

Tuberculosis was an almost certain killer then, particularly when both food and fuel were hard to find; and in the winter Eva died. A few friends went to the graveyard with Picasso—pitifully few, when one thinks of his immense acquaintance—among them Jacob and Juan Gris. Gris wrote to Maurce Raynal, far away in the trenches, to tell him about the day: "There were seven or eight friends at the funeral, which was a very sad affair except, naturally, for Max's witticisms, which merely emphasized the horror. . . . Picasso is rather upset by it."

In January, 1916, Picasso wrote to Gertrude Stein, "My poor Eva is dead . . . a great sorrow . . . she was always so kind to me," and he said he should be happy to see Gertrude and talk to her again after their long separation. That spring he did see her, but he can have derived little comfort from her presence; she seems to have been quite unmoved by Eva's death and she draws a strange picture of a cheerful Picasso in a cheerful Paris—of an equally unmoved Picasso who brought not only Blaise Cendrars and Erik Satie to the rue de Fleurus, but also "Paquerette a girl who was very nice or Irène a very lovely woman from the mountains who wanted to be free."

This picture is entirely contradicted by everything that is known of Picasso's nature and by the written evidence. For example, Crespelle says, "Picasso felt completely isolated, and although he sought the company of other artists, he kept himself apart from them. He used to arrive in the evening at the Rotonde, wearing an old brown raincoat and a black-and-white checked cloth cap. Silent and unsmiling he would go and sit down in the back room reserved for regular customers and watch people coming and going with his dark eyes. He might not have been there, he showed so little interest in the conversation going on around him, but as at Els Quatre Gats, he sometimes spoke up suddenly when something caught his attention.

"Gabriel Fournier, who met him about this time, has left us a record of one of these occasions: 'One evening I saw him emerge from his usual silence and suddenly come to life. His eyes lit up as he fixed his dilated pupils on the ribbon of the Médaille militaire pinned on a comrade's dark jacket. Pointing at it, he cried: "That yellow between those green stripes looks red to me; it *is* red!"—after which he returned to his gloomy thoughts.' "

In Gertrude Stein's account it is not Paquerette or Irène who ring false but Picasso's gaiety: of course he sought out women as well as artists, and one he found was a fine black girl from Martinique. They lived together for a little while, but in a matter of weeks she left him, unable to bear his unhappiness. *"Il était sinistre,"* she said. The contradiction between the two versions may be accounted for by Gertrude Stein's real indifference to Eva, by her impercipience, and by her imperfect memory: at this time she was much excited by the idea of "getting into the war" (she delivered American comfort-bags in the south of France) and by learning to drive a car; and she confuses her dates.

There would have been far more consolation in the company of Apollinaire. He was now an infantry-officer and a French citizen: he passed through Paris on January 11, 1916, after a leave in Oran; a little later his regiment moved up into the front line and on March 17 he was very badly wounded, also in the head. They brought him back to Paris, to the Italian hospital on the quai d'Orsay, where Serge Férat, now a male nurse, helped to look after him. After a trepanning operation he slowly improved, and Picasso drew him, still in this perfectly realistic manner, sitting in the chair that had served for Vollard, wearing a forage-cap over his bandage and the Croix de guerre on his bosom—a thinner, somewhat Hebraic Apollinaire. He had suffered a great deal, both from his wound, which troubled him for the short remainder of his life, and from his many love-affairs: this is not the place for an account of Apollinaire's wounded heart—Marie, Lou, Madeleine—but it hurt him so much that he could sympathize with a friend in great emotional stress.

Gertrude Stein describes the Paris to which she returned as gay, and in this she is borne out by other writers. By 1916 and even earlier the first great wave of solidarity and altruism had receded; the patriotic fervor was still intense but many civilians had settled down to making the best of the new life and some were doing remarkably well out of the war: Paris was full; the restaurants and theaters crowded; a very great deal of money was in circulation. From the point of view of the picture-dealers and some of the painters this was excellent: the dark days were past.

The soldiers returning from their unimaginable hell, the inhuman landscape of the western front, saw it with different eyes. They relished the lights and the gaiety, but they were staggered by the "business as usual" attitude of the civilians. That two such infinitely remote worlds could exist within a short day's journey of one another passed their understanding: Apollinaire spoke with bewilderment of the "feverish activity in painting and sculpture—Cubism of course . . . they can sell anything, at ridiculous prices."

Yet like so many others he too was reabsorbed by the common world in time—within a few months in fact—just as Picasso took to women again. Both were thirty-six in mid-1916; both artistically mature; both emotionally adolescent—"undeadened" is the better word—as perhaps creative artists must necessarily be.

Not all the painters were doing well, however. Soutine hanged himself from despair in the Ruche, the left-bank equivalent of the Bateau-Lavoir, filled with Slavs, and was cut down by Kremegne; and Severini, the best-known of the Futurists, was near to dying of tuberculosis and want of food, although he had excellent contacts in Paris, having married Paul Fort's daughter, with Apollinaire as his best man. Max Jacob helped him, as he invariably helped all his friends; and it was probably in relation to this fund-raising that Picasso wrote:

MY DEAR GODSON MAX,

I am sending you the money you ask for and I shall be very happy to see you again soon. I am deep in house-moving and you will arrive just right to give me a hand such as you have always offered as a friend. You know how little I ask on these occasions: only your moral support, encouragement, in short the friendly hand of Max Jacob. Meanwhile, here is mine,

Your old friend,
PICASSO

The letter is undated, but it must have been written in October, 1916, since we know that Picasso moved house in that month. His reluctance to stay in the rue Schoelcher is understandable; his decision to leave the heart of Paris less so. He chose a suburban house, grim, square, and prim, out at Montrouge, beyond the Porte d'Italie and the limits of Paris.

He was not the only artist to bury himself by any means—Matisse had lived at Clamart, Vlaminck at Chatou, and at this very time Erik Satie was living even farther out in the same direction, at Arcueil—but the suburbs do not seem to match with Picasso's nature, and in fact this was his only experiment in living there. It was almost his only experiment in living alone, too: he was no good at it, although someone, perhaps the wealthy Madame Errazuriz who supplied his pink silk counterpane, eventually found him a reliable servant. Nor was he good at moving alone: many of his constructions were broken in the process, and then thieves came and took away not his pictures but his linen. Yet they might easily have had the "Demoiselles d'Avignon," for the great canvas that had dominated the rue Schoelcher, where it had astonished Cocteau, among so many others in the last ten years or so, was now lying there, taken off its stretcher and rolled up, ready for them.

He may have chanced upon the house in Montrouge when he was seeing Erik Satie home. Satie was an assiduous frequenter of the Dôme and the Rotonde, and late at night his friends would often see him back to Arcueil, a two hours' walk. At this time Satie was fifty, though he looked older, and he was perhaps the most advanced composer of his day, or rather of his tomorrow. His music was appreciated only by a few, and Picasso was not one of those few: "I am no musician," said Picasso to Stravinsky, "I know nothing whatever about music": and he said it as though he did not mind at all. Neither Picasso nor Satie took much notice of the other's work, though in time Satie came to love Cubism; their acquaintance was of long standing, and although each had a difficult character, quick to take offense (Satie quarreled with Debussy after a friendship of half a lifetime, and with Georges Auric and many more), they had never fallen out.

At first sight there was nothing striking about Satie: with his pince-nez, his little beard, and his formal clothes he looked like a minor civil-servant. But the gleam of his extraordinarily knowing, young, intelligent eye changed all that; and when he began to talk it became evident that a most uncommon and entirely modern spirit inhabited the dusty, old-fashioned shell. For dusty it was: Satie felt that a composer should dress respectably, and he put on clothes that were no doubt respectable at first. That was the limit of his concession to the world, however. He never brushed them afterwards; he rarely changed—his high stiff collar was usually gray; nor did he feel the need to wash. And although he was exceedingly poor for most of his life he did not open letters either; when at last he died, his den-like room in a working-class tenement was found to be full of still-sealed envelopes, some of them containing checks.

Jean Cocteau, on the other hand, made an immediate impression on the beholder: it was his intention so to do, and he had been suceeding in his aim for some years now. When he was introduced to Picasso in 1916 he was twenty-seven and he had a considerable reputation as a poet. He had been launched not as an infant but as a stripling prodigy in the salons so familiar to Proust, and he was very well with Madame de Noailles, Etienne de Beaumont, and their friends: industry, wit, and somewhat equivocal good looks rather than a steady flow of verse maintained his reputation, but youthfulness and modernity were essential ingredients and sometimes he seemed rather to labor to acquire or to retain them. The war might have broken his career, but it did not. After a brief and irregular though not inglorious campaign in more or less official ambulances, some run by his friend Misia Sert, he was allowed to put aside his Poiret uniform and return to equally well-cut civilian clothes.

His appearance recommended him among the leaders of a certain society, but not in the Montparnasse which he began to haunt in 1915. Many of the painters disliked his air of fashionable wealth, his restless avidity for notice, and his incessant flow of words, witty though they sometimes were.

Picasso did not mind him, however: rather the reverse. Although there were only some eight years between them, young Cocteau was particularly deferential, as to a much older man; he could be far more diverting in talk than he was in verse or prose, and Picasso always liked being flattered and amused. In any case he did not object to a touch of the charlatan or adventurer in his friends: Apollinaire had something of it; so had Max Jacob, who described himself with poetic rather than literal truth as a translator from the Old Breton, as an aged seadog, a great voyager, and as a quartermaster from Macao; and "Baron" Mollet, who lived solely by his wits, was dear to Picasso for fifty years and more. Besides, Cocteau possessed flair to the pitch of genius: nothing less could have decided him upon the extraordinarily improbable course of persuading Picasso and Satie to collaborate with him in a ballet.

Cocteau knew about ballets. He had been in contact with Diaghilev ever since the first astonishing Paris season of the Ballets Russes, and with Frédéric de Madrozo he had written the scenario for *Le Dieu bleu,* a ballet with music by Proust's particular friend Reynaldo Hahn and choreography by Michel Fokine that was danced by Tamara Karsavina and Nijinsky at the Châtelet in 1912. It had not been successful; but now he had the powerful backing of Etienne de Beaumont and many of the salons, and although his suggestion sounded outrageous there was good sense in it.

Picasso could not see it at first, and the avant-garde painters of Montparnasse, particularly the Cubists, could not see it at any time: for them, the obstinate followers of a man who declined to lead, the idea of Picasso's painting scenery and designing costumes for a ballet was sacrilegious, far worse than realistic drawing. Nor could Max Jacob: while Cocteau employed all his arguments and all his charm to convince Picasso, Max forgot his Christian charity and wrote to Jacques Maritain, "God *hates* Cocteau."

Whether or not Max Jacob was right on this point, Cocteau succeeded, and Gertrude Stein records, "One day [in the winter of 1916/17] Picasso came in and with him leaning on his shoulder was a slim elegant youth. It is Jean, announced Pablo, Jean Cocteau and we are leaving for Italy."

Italy, because the Ballets Russes were to reach Rome in February, 1917, coming from America, where they had spent much of the war. But before leaving France Picasso made models of the stage and his settings for the ballet, which was to be called *Parade, ballet réaliste,* and which, in Cocteau's original idea, was to be based upon a music-hall performance with a Chinese conjurer, some acrobats, and an American girl. Picasso had never seen a ballet, but he had seen music-halls and circuses by the hundred, and he set about his models with confidence and enthusiasm, much helped by his long practice with constructions.

Even in peace-time Paris to Rome is a weary run; with both France and now Italy at war it was tedious beyond measure. But Picasso, with his experience of the Spanish railway, was hardened to such things, and he instantly revived upon getting out of the train. They found Diaghilev installed in the great Palazzo Theodori with his company around him, including Massine, who was to provide the choreography for *Parade*. Stravinsky was there too, working on the music for *Feu d'Artifice,* and Bakst: Picasso drew their portraits—only quick sketches, however, because the ballet took up almost all his waking hours at first.

It is scarcely believable that so complex a performance, with its split-second timing, should ever get organized among such hopelessly impractical people as those that inhabit the ballet world, many of them Russians with little sense of time. Diffident and peace-loving souls have been destroyed by the total disorder, the extreme nervous tension, the indecision, the hurry, and the fits of temperament; and Gris' days were shortened by his contact with the ballet. But on Picasso it acted as a powerful stimulant. His chaos suited their chaos; his demoniac energy redoubled; he flung himself into the task. It might have been less arduous if he had started with a classical ballet; but *Parade* was not classical. Far from it: indeed, its main aim was to knock classical ballet sideways, much as Picasso's painting had done with academic art. It called for frenzied toil, and as they worked upon the shifting mass of ideas, sketches, and suggestions so it changed and grew. There were to have been only four characters, the conjurer, the acrobats, and the girl, with voices off; but Picasso insisted upon three more, the managers of the troupe, a Frenchman, an American, and a horse. These characters were essential to his view of the ballet: the two human managers were to be huge architectural figures ten feet high, something in the nature of his constructions, who would lurch about the stage bawling through megaphones, more real than common reality, dwarfing the ordinary performers, and imposing an essentially Cubist conception on his otherwise fairly traditional sets, costumes, and curtain.

It may be doubted whether, with all his volcanic energy, conviction, and strength of personality, Picasso could have persuaded Diaghilev to accept these revolutionary ideas but for the fact that in March, 1917, while the ballet was in gestation, the Tsar and the imperial government of Russia were swept away. It was clear to the more intelligent Russians that the revolution would not stop half way to the left, and that in all probability they could never go home again. If they were to stay in the West, then

Western modernity was required; and Picasso was the pace-setter of the Western avant-garde.

The background against which these tremendous figures were to appear was conventional enough: monochrome houses with a gap in the middle for depth. As for the dancers' costumes, the two acrobats, blue and white with stars and curving stripes, were reminiscent of Picasso's earlier circus people; and only the conjurer was really startling in his brilliant orange and yellow, black and white, with asymmetric curves and spirals. And the curtain was a gentle mockery of such compositions, with an added charm of its own. It was an enormous expanse of cloth, over fifteen hundred square feet; and it is difficult to imagine how Picasso ever painted it, even with the help of a team of Italians: there is a photograph of them sitting about on it as it lies on the floor of some vast building, and three men fit easily into the harlequin's lap. Yet no branch of his trade was out of Picasso's reach, and when it was done the curtain was as professional as if he had painted dozens.

It has survived, and it was to be seen, rather dusty and battered, at the Tate Gallery's retrospective exhibition in 1960. One either side of the background there are conventional great curtains, looped back to show a pillar and far away an arch, perhaps a ruin; in front of these and on the right a group of strolling players including this harlequin, sit on boxes and trestles drawn up to a table, while one of them, a traditional Spaniard, plays his guitar. Over on the left a gentle winged mare suckles her foal, while standing on her back a winged girl reaches up to a monkey on a striped ladder. In the foreground, an acrobat's ball, a sleeping dog, a drum, circus impedimenta. Red and green predominate, and a mild happiness.

The amount of hard labor on the curtain alone was prodigious; and then there were the costumes, particularly the ambitious great constructions for the managers, to say nothing of the frequent and shattering conferences, arguments, defeats, and victories, mostly victories; and the rehearsals. Yet still Picasso found the time to visit Naples and Pompeii with Massine, to catch a glimpse of Florence, to see his Futurist friends, and to paint at least one Cubist picture, "l'Italienne." Although the greater part of it is black and gray the picture is eminently cheerful, decorative, and superficially legible: an elegant black woman with a long neck carrying a blue basket and wearing a papery coif of three planes—green, white, and blue—holds a blue mask in profile up to the full-face pink mask that already covers her face. Behind her is a small St. Peter's and part of the lower background is strangely disrupted by amorphous rents that contrast with the many straight-edged planes. When he chose to show the power of his hand Picasso could paint a wonderfully clean, spontaneous, incisive picture, and this is a good example of his effortless technique. It is perhaps the first in which masks appear, those masks that were later to assume such a great and even sinister importance in his work; but in "l'Italienne" they seem to be there for the fun. At any rate he was enjoying himself in Rome, and he also found time to walk in the moonlight with the dancers.

In the green-room the white bosoms and the silk stockings of the actresses did not arouse Cocteau's amorous propensities, nor yet Diaghilev's; they were not gifted in that way; but Picasso was, and of those with whom he walked in moonlit Rome he chiefly prized Olga Koklova.

It is very useless to inquire why a man should like a particular woman; the spectator can only wonder and exclaim. Those who offer to account for this connection say that Picasso was attracted to Olga Koklova by her beauty, her virtue, and her birth. The beauty of her face, as he depicted it during the early days of their courtship and their union, barely achieves prettiness, in spite of a good complexion; and it is sadly marred by an habitual expression, still more evident in photographs, of stupid determination, dissatisfaction, and sullenness, an expression, emphasized by a somewhat undershot jaw, that was to grow far, far stronger with the years. The beauty of her person may have been more alluring: the rigid discipline of the ballet gives the dancers firm, supple bodies and an elegant carriage; but there were many lithe young women in the company, far better dancers than Olga Koklova, who had taken to the ballet late and who never rose above mediocrity. Her virtue, surprising in such a world, certainly resisted Picasso's first advances; and it certainly raised her in his esteem, accustomed as he was to a brisk and willing submission. As for birth, Olga is said to have been the daughter of a colonel of artillery, of a distinguished officer, of a general; in any case of a noble family. It would be naïve indeed to expect noble conduct as the necessary consequence, the evidence of noble birth; and in the event of Picasso's ever having entertained such hopes he was soon to be disappointed. All observers agree that Olga, though socially eager, was bourgeois to the core. But what is more to the point as far as technical nobility is concerned, a diligent search in the Russian equivalent of Debrett or Burke has failed to discover a Koklov, Khoklov, or any variant of that name. Yet if she had been an authentic daughter of Rurik, would that have made any difference to Picasso? In those days perhaps it might: at the age of thirty-six he knew little or nothing of the great world; he was still absurdly young in many ways and the unknown is often much the same as the wonderful.

At all events he became much attached to her; and there is one small factor that may have added to her charms. Hitherto Picasso's companions had been Frenchwomen, who naturally spoke their language without fault, or at least without hesitation: a foreigner with an imperfect command of the tongue is at a disadvantage, for although he may be kindly treated, his words, ill-pronounced and stumbling, count for little more than the prattling of a child, and in time this weighs upon his spirits; he is oppressed by a sense of inferiority. Olga Koklova spoke French—it was the only language in which they could communicate—but she spoke it no better than Picasso. The Russian accent in French, though less hideous than the Spanish, is even more indelible: I know a member of the Académie française who came from Russia as a little boy, who was brought up and naturalized in France, who did his military service there, fighting in both wars, and who nevertheless governs the French language with the accent of Odessa.

In about a month's time Picasso went back to Paris. There was still a great deal of work to be done, particularly on the music. The conferences about the settings, costumes, and choreography in Rome had been wearing; those in Paris about the score were far worse. Cocteau wanted to add a great many noises to the music: typewriters, trains, dynamos, sirens, planes; noises on Cubist principles. Satie wanted to abandon the whole enterprise.

Towards May the company came to Paris. The ballet was to be presented at the Châtelet on the seventeenth of the month, and it seemed unlikely that anything but Apollinaire's program notes would be ready in time. This cannot have surprised Diaghilev, since it appears to be the invariable prelude to any ballet; nor can it have perturbed Olga Koklova, whom Picasso welcomed with renewed affection. There is a drawing of his dining-room at Montrouge made in this year, and although its details are not quite clear, it seems to show Picasso feasting Olga at a round table while his servant passes a dish and two large dogs sit on either side of his chair, silently yearning.

If this interpretation is correct, and if the meal took place just before May 17th, then it is likely that she ate with far greater appetite than Picasso. The ballet was explosive stuff: if it were not a great success it would be an even greater failure, and all their work would vanish in a derisive hiss.

On the opening night Picasso was there in Diaghilev's box with Misia Sert: Diaghilev in tails, Misia Sert in diamonds, Picasso in a red roll-neck sweater. The house was crowded. Diaghilev had given a large number of tickets to soldiers from the Russian divisions in France, perhaps out of kindness to his fellow-countrymen, perhaps to ensure a certain volume of applause.

Everything began well. The audience was pleased with the curtain, pleased with Satie's overture. But the appearance of the gigantic managers was greeted with shocked surprise: first came the French manager, beating the ground with an enormous stick and announcing the Chinese conjurer; at the same time the music changed, and although many of the superimposed noises, the sirens, dynamos, and trains, could not be produced because of a failure in the compressed-air system, the typewriters—rods struck together—came in with redoubled zeal. They were disagreeably like machine-guns, and in spite of Massine's brilliant dancing as the conjurer, the audience grew hostile. Then came the American, an even more striking, even more Cubist figure that combined cowboy boots, skyscrapers, metallic tubes, and a top-hat: he danced a stamping dance that made all his metal clank again and through his megaphone he bawled praises of his American girl. Although the United States had just come into the war and although the American girl was an important figure in French mythology he was received with even greater hostility; and in spite of the Russian applause the anger of the bourgeois who had paid to see a ballet and who were being shown Cubism in motion to the sound of typewriters grew louder and louder. Had they read Apollinaire's introduction they would have known that their fare was to be transcendent reality, "a kind of sur-realism in which I see the beginning of a series of manifestations of the Esprit Nouveau, of that new state of mind which . . . cannot fail to enchant the élite and which, amidst universal gaiety, intends to change our arts and customs from top to bottom, since common sense requires that they should at least keep pace with scientific and industrial advance." But it was too late for reading now; and in any case the élite or the universal gaiety or both were lacking.

The American girl went through the motions of riding a bicycle, imitating Charlie Chaplin, boxing, dancing ragtime, and so on, but they were not to be appeased. The acrobats did nothing to help, either; nor did the activities of the managers, who roared to one another over the even greater roar of the audience. There never had been much of a story to *Parade;* it was just these performers parading before an imaginary crowd of bystanders to persuade them to come into their imaginary theater: vain efforts, the imaginary crowd supposing the parade to be the show itself and going away, but so vehement that the managers collapsed from exhaustion. Yet simple though it was, few of the audience could have followed the argument through, because towards the end the whole theater was filled with shrieks and catcalls, howls of disapprobation, malevolent hissing and boos, while some people cried *"Sales Boches"* from a notion that anything they disliked must be German.

A Parisian audience can always be guaranteed to rise to anything regarded as an affront to their dignity; now they were furiously angry, and the evening might have come to an ugly end for Picasso, Cocteau, and Satie had it not been for the presence of Apollinaire, bandaged, in uniform, with his Croix de guerre, who rose splendidly to the occasion and who, passionately haranguing the mob, at least persuaded them that *Parade* was not the work of Huns.

The ballet was not a success, but it was not a real failure either. It had not been received with tepid, deadly boredom; the brighter members of the audience, including Proust and his friends, had been entranced; and when it was produced again in Paris after the war it was in fact recognized as a brilliant manifestation of the new spirit that had come into the world.

In the meantime no one was particularly upset. Picasso was hardened to abuse; Diaghilev's confidence was unshaken; Cocteau's friends took pains to comfort him. The only one to suffer was Satie, who was sent to prison.

The sentence was not pronounced at the request of the outraged public, but at that of one Poueigh, a critic. His employment was mean; he rendered it infamous: at the theater he came up to Satie to compliment him on his music and then went straight home to his bed of slime to write a base and cruel review. Up until this time Satie had kept his temper wonderfully, but on reading the criticism he seized a postcard, wrote:

Monsieur et cher ami

Vous n'êtes qu'un cul, mais un cul sans musique.

[My dear sir, you are a mere arse; but you are an arse devoid of music] signed it, addressed it to Poueigh, and sent it off.

The vile Poueigh sued him on a charge of criminal defamation. The trial became a trial of modern art—Apollinaire, Dunoyer de Segonzac, La Fresnaye, Derain, and others were described as Boches (modern art being of course anti-national)—Satie's friends were turned out for protesting—Cocteau, pale beneath his make-up, slapped Poueigh's lawyer—the police beat him—and Satie was condemned to a week's imprisonment.

But by this time, Picasso was far away in Spain. The Ballets Russes were performing in Madrid and Barcelona before they left for South America, and Picasso had gone with them. During their short stay in Madrid he met with Santiago Rusiñol, who brought back something of his younger days; and in Barcelona his youth came back with a rush. He may possibly have come down from Paris for Christmas and the New Year of 1917, but if he did so then it was very privately, just to see his mother and his sister, now married to Juan Vilato y Gómez, a physician. In June his coming was known beforehand—echoes from the Châtelet had reached Barcelona—and he appeared, if not quite as a conquering hero then at least as a figure of wide and international renown; and in July his friends and admirers gave a banquet for him. Among the fifty and more who attended there were many from the old days of the Guayaba, the Quatre Gats and even from the Llotja—Pallarès, the Junyer and Soto brothers, Gargallo and his Magalí, Brossa the anarchist, Reventós, Jaume Andreu—and when the inevitable speeches came Iturrino, who had sh·red his first Vollard show, rose to state that Picasso was the only painter he admired, the only painter he envied.

It was on this occasion that Picasso made an indiscreet but no doubt sincere remark to a journalist who asked him about *Parade:* the libretto, he said, was merely a pretext for the music, the dances, and above all, above all for the settings and the costumes—words that could not but cause anguish when they reached Cocteau.

During his stay in Barcelona Picasso lived with his mother in their old home in the Calle Merced, while Olga went to the Pension Ranzini in the Paseo Colón, at the bottom of the Ramblas, quite near Picasso and the Liceo, where the company was performing. At the end of June they gave *Las Meninas*—how prophetic—and Olga danced the part of one of them, perhaps the highest point of her career.

After a pause for the dog-days the performances started again in the autumn; and at the end of the season, in November, Diaghilev put on *Parade*. The reaction of the Catalan audience was far less extreme than that of the French; there was at least some enthusiasm, since many of Picasso's friends and admirers, including the young Joan Miró, were in the house; but although the *Anuari de Catalunya* spoke of the ballet season as having been "a complete success, particularly *Parade*, with settings by En Pau Ruiz Picasso," the other papers, though respectful, were more reserved.

"It is harder to speak about Picasso than about anyone else at all," said Aragon. "He instantly gives the lie to whatever one puts forward." One of the reasons for this may be that Picasso's spirit had the power, denied to all elements except quicksilver, of being in several places at once. In Barcelona he combined the duties of a son, a lover, a friend, a public figure, and a zealous follower of the bull-fight with painting in at least three styles that would, in another man, have been contradictory if not mutually exclusive.

One of the first of these pictures was an elaborate virtuoso portrait of Olga in a white mantilla for his mother. It is a careful, almost photographic resemblance, and compared with some of the later portraits it is curiously unidealized: the undying shrew shows clear, and the old lady's heart must have sunk when she saw it. Was he aware of what he was doing, did he know what that face said so clearly, or did he suppose that love would take away that hard look of profound dissatisfaction?

Señora de Ruiz had always preserved every scrap of her son's work with religious care, but in later years she let this portrait go. She is said to have told Olga, "I don't think any woman could be happy with him," perhaps in an attempt to avert the hopeless marriage.

Another, in something of the same manner, is a portrait of an unnamed young woman, the companion of his friend and fellow-townsman Padilla, in whose studio Picasso worked. Large areas of the canvas are bare; the arms, lap, and part of the mantilla are only drawn in; and although it is a bold man who says that a picture by Picasso is unfinished, I doubt that he meant to leave one eye in that pretty face lightless and dead—it is not that kind of picture at all. Finished or not, it is a most arresting work, and it has been much admired for the great skill of its pointillist technique and for its purity of line. My own opinion, for what it is worth (and I do not believe it is widely shared) is that these two portraits are proof that like most great men Picasso had a streak of rather comforting vulgarity, and that the early French critic Gustave Coquiot was right in saying that because of Picasso's astonishing command of his means the greatest danger for him was facility.

Far removed from these are the strong red and black Cubist pictures, including the "Blanquita Suarez," where flat green joins the black; and the pensive harlequin, based on Massine, who looks back to the days before Cubism and forward to the classicism of the coming years. Quite different again is the view, presumably from Olga's room, of the Paseo Colón: an open window with a balcony again; beyond it trees, the tall Columbus statue, the sea, a pointillist sky; dun buildings to the right, and blazing against them, red-gold-red, the Spanish flag.

And even more remote is the agonizing horse, disemboweled, collapsing, alone in the unseen bull-ring, its head wrenched high in a last spasm while the blood pours in a hard jet from its chest. This is a big charcoal drawing on canvas, allied in time to his pencil drawings of the bull-fight; but its nature is entirely different, and the only true parallel to this silent shriek is the horse in "Guernica," painted nearly twenty years later.

Picasso was strongly affected by his surroundings; he picked up an atmosphere at once. Yet the influence of place, or of things that he had seen, often took a great while before they appeared, transformed, in his work: in 1917, for instance, there is scarcely the least hint that he had ever been to Italy, that he had been enormously impressed by some of the sculptures in Pompeii, by Raphael, and so much more. But he had an unequaled visual memory, a power of draining the essence of what he saw and storing it up; and Leo Stein, speaking of his extraordinary eyes, observed that when Picasso looked at a print or a drawing, so absorbent was his gaze that it was surprising to find anything left on the paper.

These surroundings were soon to change: the warm autumnal Barcelona, its markets overflowing with all the later fruit and every kind of fish and flesh, the neutral Barcelona where peace, the unaltered pattern, were taken as the natural order, was to give way to winter in the cold, dark, austere, and wartime Paris, threatened by an enemy far more powerful now that the Bolshevik government was taking Russia out of the war and setting free scores of German divisions for the western front, shattered by the monstrous, heartbreaking losses of Nivelle's disastrous offensive on the Aisne, and the subsequent mutinies.

There was trouble of course with Olga's Imperial Russian passport. A friend of Picasso's, Manuel Humbert, was on his way to Paris, so Picasso took him aside, explained the difficulty, and asked him to call on Cocteau. A young poet might not seem the most suitable man for such a purpose, but in the France of those days well-placed friends could work miracles, and some of Cocteau's were very well placed indeed. Magnanimity is a quality rare in the jealous, competitive, back-biting world of the arts; but Cocteau overlooked Picasso's injurious words about his libretto, pulled the right strings, resolved the difficulty, and Olga was free to go wherever she pleased.

Two choices were open to her, South America or Paris. France meant marriage, protection, a nationality, probable security, perhaps even wealth: South America meant statelessness, the continuation of a career that was unlikely to see any success greater than that she had already enjoyed, and that in an unmarrying milieu. She chose France, and once again Picasso climbed into the Paris express at the Estación de Francia with a companion at his side.

Chapter XI

In Barcelona he had had his first experience of being a wonder-figure, of that pleasing flattering veil which, if it grows too thick, can cut a man off from the refreshment of contact with ordinary life and which can cruelly distort his relationship with others, even with those nearest to him in blood. Few people speak to a wonder as if he were a man, which is disagreeable no doubt and impoverishing; but how much more painful when he finds that he is a wonder even in his own home, worse still when he is living on the other side of an invisible barrier—a wonder that can be exploited, and therefore by definition an outsider. If that were to happen to a suspicious mind every word, gesture, or kindness would come to have an ulterior motive. At some point, unspecified in time but certainly after Barcelona, he said to Gertrude Stein, "You know, your family, everybody, if you are a genius and unsuccessful, everybody treats you as a genius, but when you come to be successful, when you commence to earn money, when you are really successful, then your family and everybody no longer treats you as a genius, they treat you like a man who has become successful."

But this first experience was neither intense nor long-lasting, and it was tempered by the presence of very old friends: one can hardly imagine Pallarès being deferential to En Pau. If it did affect him, if Picasso did have a bitter foretaste of what success might mean, there was a great deal to overlay the painful impression: his present attachment, of course; his future work; plans for more ballets. And back in France he was one among many, a respectable but not a unique figure: Matisse probably stood higher, to say nothing of the older men; at Sorgues Braque was beginning to paint again; while presently Modigliani, Utrillo, and Gris were to achieve reputations that brought them if not to the front rank then very near it. In Paris there were no banquets for Picasso.

Circumstances also helped to restore the common realities: torrential rains had flooded the studio at Montrouge; coal was very hard to find; and

229]

although the German air-raids seem trifling to later generations, the anti-aircraft guns made a shattering din night after night and all the shells they sent up necessarily came down again in fragments, an iron hail rattling on the city.

The house was a dull little box from the outside, and neither its position nor its style suited Olga: yet the inside had a special quality of its own. The poet Ramón Gómez de la Serna first saw Picasso there, and he describes his visit: he was greeted by what he calls a Labrador; Picasso quietened the dog and led Gómez into "the most perfect example of bourgeois dining-room, with a few pictures from his earlier periods on the walls . . . the most important detail, the one that came to him from his Spanish past, was one of those alabaster fruit-dishes . . . a centre-piece dating from his childhood." He observes that Picasso was aware of alabaster's great longing to be woman's flesh, and goes on to speak of the rest of the house. He was surprised to see a huge polychrome figure of Christ on the Cross in the well of the staircase, and on the upper floor a whole infant-school of Negro figures—he calls them *ídolos*—quite covering the lower walls. Higher up were pinned bits and pieces, children's toys, guitars and the like made of cardboard boxes, string, lengths of wood, "the pure exoskeleton of pure stringed instruments." And there were the pictures, of course.

In his *Completa y verídica historia de Picasso y el cubismo* and elsewhere Gómez de la Serna dwells upon Picasso's essential Spanishness. "In the great nation of the Gypsies of art, Picasso is the most Gypsy of them all. You have to understand Spain to know how rugged, blasphemous, and ungovernable is the background from which he springs," he says, though it must be admitted that his words sound nobler and more convincing in Spanish. And in another place he speaks of "the Spanish Moor crossed with the Moorish Christian yet never losing what he inherits from the Roman citizen or the unfathomable Iberian: four genes in the foundation of his being, fighting and stimulating one another."

But Olga had no notion of being a Gypsy's mort nor of sleeping in damp grassy lanes; she had had enough of the ballet's version of Bohemia and she meant to lead an entirely different life from this time on.

She suited well enough with Picasso's newer acquaintance such as Eugenia Errazuriz and those from Cocteau's world; or at least they were willing to accept her as Picasso's necessary accompaniment. But she dismayed some of his older friends and angered others. When Alice Derain said, "The first time I saw her I took her for a maid-servant; she was a plain little woman with freckles all over her face," she may not have been wholly candid, for others speak of Olga's beautiful skin, but she was certainly expressing a sincere and probably mutual dislike. The men were naturally more tolerant or more discreet, and although both Apollinaire and Max Jacob had long practiced the cutting remark, they did not leave any harsh judgment of Olga upon record.

In any case, Apollinaire was too busy and it is to be hoped too happy to demolish his friends. Although 1918 began with an attack of pneumonia, it had all the appearance of being a most auspicious year for him. Not only was he in love again, this time with the red-headed nurse who had looked after him both at the time of his wound and of his illness and for whom he wrote his poem "La Jolie Rousse," but he also brought out his *Mamelles de Tirésias,* damned as a play, praised as a book, and his second important collection of poems, *Calligrammes,* which was received with great applause. And then on May 2, with Picasso and Vollard as his witnesses, he married his *jolie rousse:* Jacqueline Kolb was her name. It is true that he was engaged at the time to Madeleine Pagès; but she was in another country and he had made his offer long ago; and it did not seem to affect his happiness. With death so near, and in these days of the great Ludendorff offensive when every morning had a casualty-list with thousands of names in it, men married easily.

Three months later Apollinaire, Cocteau, and Max Jacob took turns in the arm-breaking duty of holding crowns over the heads of the servant of God Pablo and the servant of God Olga as they stood before the altar of the cathedral of St. Alexander Nevsky in Paris amid a cloud of incense while the deep-basses of the choir intoned the Old Slavonic liturgy and the bearded priest married them. In the Orthodox service the couple walk round the altar three times, returning to the carpet in front; and among the Russians it is believed that the first to set foot on this carpet will have the upper hand throughout the marriage. It does not seem that Picasso was ever warned that he should mind his step.

But the sorrow and woe that is in marriage did not affect the Picassos immediately. They spent their honeymoon at Madame Errazuriz' splendid villa in Biarritz, and if one may judge by his work Picasso was thoroughly happy. He was only some twenty miles from Spain, almost as far from the war as he could possibly be in France, and in those days of unlimited servants his patron's wealth had full scope to show him just how comfortable a certain kind of life could be.

Happiness in Picasso released his natural generosity, which was sometimes repressed by the more unfortunate sides of his often tormented and always complex temperament—by extreme susceptibility, secretiveness, odd fits of parsimony, and possessiveness—as well as by sadness imposed from without, and when he wrote to Gertrude Stein to announce his marriage he sent *her* a wedding-present, a watercolor of a guitar, as well as a photograph of the new portrait of Olga that he had painted at Montrouge, a large, naturalistic picture of her holding a fan and sitting in an armchair whose bold flower pattern is worked out with all the painstaking care of a Rousseau: a puzzling "fashionable" portrait, in which the sitter looks so like a stubborn doll that one wonders whether Picasso was making game of her, of himself, of that kind of painting, or whether connubial bliss had blinded him for the moment. In his letter he used the expression *une vraie jeune fille,* which in French usage means a virgin; even now the Mediterranean way of life sets what might be considered an exaggerated and even an unhealthy value on this state, and if Picasso's *vraie jeune fille* is to be taken at its face value it would account for part of his esteem for his wife. The esteem was real and lasting; and another part of it derived from his opinion of her talents in society and as a hostess: some observers thought her pushing, too obviously ambitious, and even histrionic, as though she were over-acting a part that did not naturally belong to her; but Picasso, who in any case possessed little social discrimination, having had no training in it during his youth and having no use for it in his later days, was impressed. Very late in his life, after all the horrors of separation and long-drawn-out wrangling, he could still say to an old Catalan friend who had known Olga during their marriage, "She really was a lady, wasn't she?"

At Biarritz, apart from decorating Madame Errazuriz' walls with cheerful scenes calculated to give her pleasure, he made some astonishing drawings, astonishing not only for their virtuosity but even more because they show him breaking out into yet another form of expression: one of these is a composition of at least a dozen figures—young women on a beach—a linear drawing, all contours, far more like Ingres than the realistic drawings of the year before: Ingres in the subtle disproportion, more than Ingres in the pure delicacy of line. At the same time he painted another group of women by the sea, these in bathing costumes, employing a completely different manner; and here the beach is strewn with those isolated, strangely significant stones that the Surrealists were soon to use so very often. Then again in this same year he finished a Cubist "Femme en corset" that he had begun in 1914 and he painted still another strictly Cubist guitar, close cousin to the one he gave to Gertrude Stein, but much larger and painted in oils with a good deal of sand mixed in. Looking back still farther he remembered the peasant of his Gósol composition and used him again for a half-naked fisherman carrying his catch in a broad flat basket on his head: and these are only a few examples of the work he did in each of these different idioms.

Biarritz is not the Mediterranean, but it can be warm there, and the Atlantic sweeps the beach clean twice a day, leaving wonderful shapes lying on the low-tide sand. He enjoyed himself: there were quantities of Madame Errazuriz' friends and acquaintances, many of whom he drew, and they were far more cheerful than holidaymakers had been in France these last three years, for the war was going well. It seemed that there might be some end to the bloody nightmare at last: in July Mangin's great tank offensive drove the Germans back, capturing thirty thousand of them; in August the British stormed the Siegfried Line; and in September Pershing took the field with six hundred thousand Americans. Picasso was not directly concerned—his country lay to the south—but their happiness added greatly to his.

Among the summer visitors was Paul Rosenberg, Léonce's brother, with his family. At this time Picasso was not tied to any one dealer: Paul Guillaume, for example, had shown both him and Matisse earlier in the year, with a preface to the catalog by Apollinaire. Paul Rosenberg had been brought up to the trade by his father, an important dealer, and he was in a large way of business: a thoroughly able merchant with a harder head and perhaps a harder heart than his brother, who had kept Gris and the minor Cubists alive. He came to an arrangement with Picasso, and for many years he handled much of the painter's work.

In Picasso's view, a dealer owed many duties to a painter apart from selling his pictures; and just as in 1912 he had called upon Kahnweiler to move him from the boulevard de Clichy so he now desired Rosenberg to find him a more suitable dwelling than the house in Montrouge. Rosenberg saw the relationship in the same light, and when he returned to Paris in the autumn Picasso was the tenant of a flat in the rue de la Boëtie, quite a grand street that runs into the Champs-Elysées.

It was a fine spacious flat on the sixth floor with a splendid view over the roofs of Paris to the distant Eiffel Tower; but it was not spacious enough for two such strong and divergent temperaments—they disagreed almost from the start. Happily the flat above was vacant, the top floor, Picasso's natural habitat, and he took that too, turning its five rooms into a desolation of his own: not so much a studio as it is ordinarily understood as an interconnecting series of little echoing deserts, their death as rooms made even more emphatic by the remaining marble fireplaces with their pier-glasses above. This was quite a good arrangement for a semi-detached couple, and it worked for a long time. Picasso had been there for fifteen years when Brassaï first went to see him:

> I had expected an artist's studio, and this was a flat turned into a glory-hole . . . four or five rooms emptied of their ordinary furniture and filled with stacks of pictures, heaps of cardboard boxes, parcels, bundles (mostly containing moulds of his sculpture), piles of books, packets of paper, miscellaneous objects higgledy-piggledy on the floor along the walls, covered with a deep layer of dust. The doors of these rooms were open, or perhaps they had even been taken off their hinges; and this turned the whole great flat into a single workshop, broken up into a number of separate compartments for the painter's many activities. You walked on a dull, stained parquet, long starved of wax and covered with a carpet of cigarette-ends. . . . . Picasso had set up his easel in the largest, best-lit room, which was the only one that had a few scraps of furniture in it—no doubt it had once been the drawing-room. Madame Picasso never came up into this flat. Picasso admitted no one at any time, apart from a few friends. And the dust could fall and gather as it pleased, never dreading the servant's feather brush. . . .

Long before Brassaï saw the studio, Picasso had drawn it, or at least a corner of one of the rooms; and although this is a somewhat idealized study, showing three of the palettes that he never used except as symbols, it is clear that as early as 1920 the tide had reached something near high-water-mark: the pictures leaning against the wall, against one another, on easels or on a Spanish chair, already made it impossible for anyone but the nimble Picasso to thread his way among them without knocking something down.

But in November, 1918, these rooms were gaunt and bare: the flat, particularly Olga's white salon and the other deeply respectable parts of her domain, were not yet ready. The Picassos waited for the workmen's inevitable delays in the grand, new, and expensive Hôtel Lutetia. In spite of the victory and the imminent armistice, joy flooding through the streets of Paris, Picasso was sad and worried, for Guillaume Apollinaire was seriously ill with the Spanish influenza that swept Europe at the end of the war like a plague. Picasso hated illness; he was terrified of it, and this influenza was extremely infectious. Yet he and Olga spent the evening of November 9th by Apollinaire's bedside.

Perhaps he did not expect Apollinaire to die: a man of thirty-nine, even one so badly wounded and brought so low, might very well survive a bout of flu. In any case he was shocked when the news was telephoned to him; terribly shocked and terribly grieved. He was standing in front of the bathroom mirror at the time, and he was either shaving or drawing a self-portrait—the accounts differ. But in either event he saw mortality reflected in his own features. He had drawn or painted them ever since he was a child; and whether the pictures were self-exploration or another kind of exercise altogether, they form a fascinating series, and anyone who values Picasso's work must regret that from that moment on there were none or very, very few.

"Picasso has painted no self-portrait for many years," wrote Antonina Vallentin in 1957. "When I asked him the reason he said, 'If mirrors did not exist I should not know my age,' and gestured towards his deeply-lined face in explanation. . . . I asked him the date of his last. Without hesitating he answered, 'The day Guillaume Apollinaire died.' "

It was not only Picasso who was so deeply affected: a great many people had admired Apollinaire as a poet and had loved him as a man: on November 12 Max Jacob wrote to René Fauchois:

> Within a few hours of each other I received the news of your wife's concert and of my poor friend's death. You will have seen in the papers that we have lost Guillaume Apollinaire from pneumonia and perhaps a heart-attack. I watch night after night by all that remains of him. We spent hours enough laughing together for me to pass some hours now weeping by his side.
>
> I tell you all this—and it is a poor description of my heart—so that you will not be surprised if I do not come on Thursday. I tell you truly, neither my friends' successes nor the victorious triumph of France can revive what this death has withered in me forever. I had not known he was my life to that degree.
>
> I feel that somewhere there is something broken. If I were a little less numbed it would seem to me that it was I who was the corpse.

Picasso had expressed his grief when Casagemas died; he expressed it again in the anguished "La Danse" when he lost Ramon Pichot (though long estranged) in 1925. But no specific picture marks the death of Eva nor that of Apollinaire. Did he feel them too deeply? It may be that of all the languages he had at his command none was adequate.

Certainly the poet's death marked him as few things had done: it may also be described as a turning-point in his career. Not indeed as an obvious crisis that set off the past very sharply from the future but rather as a date that most decisively marked the gradual change in his pattern of life. The loss of Apollinaire was the loss of one of Picasso's few strong links with a time of the most intense and exalting struggle. Max Jacob was still there, but like so many close, long-standing relationships their friendship was a complex matter and hidden resentments, odd rancors, and unresolved tensions formed part of it, the more so because of Jacob's somewhat exclusive and jealous temper and his comparative lack of success: at this time it was badly strained. Braque and Derain were gone almost as far as Apollinaire. They had lived in a dimension that no neutral civilian could possibly understand to the full, and although this was not the direct cause of the coldness between Braque and Picasso it had a strong and undoubted influence. The direct cause seems to have been their long-masked incompatibility and some plain jealousy, and the immediate pretext talebearing by common friends; but five years earlier not even such a wounding remark as "Braque is only Madame Picasso" would have set them apart. There was no open, lasting break; they were civil when they met; but after so very close an intimacy, so unparalleled a collaboration, politeness must have been painful indeed. And of course their work diverged, so that presently not even the most uninformed spectator could wonder whether he were looking at a Picasso or a Braque.

Fernande and Eva were gone; they were replaced by a woman from a completely different world. And although minor figures from the heroic days of Cubism survived by the score, even by the hundred, not many of them came to the rue La Boëtie. Far more important, the heroic days themselves were gone. The victory had been won.

By the time of Guillaume Apollinaire's death Picasso was just over thirty-seven, the age of Raphael, van Gogh, and Toulouse-Lautrec at theirs. If he too had died his reputation as a revolutionary would have been as high as it is now: perhaps more than any man he had overthrown the academy, and by 1918 everything that flowed from that revolution was well in train. The new vision, the new freedom, the benign anarchy, or what Apollinaire called *l'esprit nouveau*, had spread far beyond the few studios in Montmartre and Montparnasse where it was conceived; the Cubists' name was Legion, Dada had already made its appearance, Surrealism was not far away. The twin worlds of art and anti-art were now in permanent revolution; there was no longer any need for heroic figures and in fact no man to be compared with Picasso, Matisse, and Braque has emerged since those days.

It has been said that Picasso has few followers among the young, that he is not an influential figure; and in a narrow sense it is true: a painter who destroys all rules, all requirements except for that of genius, integrity, and vision cannot have many followers; but all those who have come after him walk in a post-Picasso world, as he did himself from at least 1918.

From this time onwards he repeatedly revolutionized his own painting, drawing, and sculpture; but these were personal revolutions, since by definition he could not throw down what was already laid in ruins.

For the moment his private revolution consisted of an approach to a new colossal style, a mannerism in which the figures swell to gigantic proportions and which was soon to merge with some aspects of his neo-classical period: but at the same time he carried on with his Cubist pictures, some as taut and severe as any yet painted in this synthetic phase, though never as impersonal and ascetic as the pale canvases of the high days of analysis; others so relaxed that their Cubism seems one element among many others rather than the full expression of his mind. Many are variations on that continually-recurring theme of a window giving on to a balcony with the sea and sky beyond: he painted such pictures at intervals throughout his life, and it is surely significant that in the early days of his attachment to Françoise Gilot he likened their relationship to "a window that is opening." Then, as if he and Henri Rousseau had left something unsaid that haunted his mind, he turned to some curious little landscapes and interiors that might be called wholly representational if it were not for their dream-like quality. He also made more of those extraordinarily accomplished drawings that had so shocked Montparnasse in 1915. One is of Olga receiving guests at the rue La Boëtie: Cocteau, Erik Satie, and Clive Bell, all wearing spats and sitting prim, polite, and uneasy in chairs poised on the edge of a curious deep step in the drawing-room; there is no sign whatever of Picasso's presence except for a fiddle on the wall reflected in the looking-glass, not a single heap of filth anywhere in that neat, comfortless apartment. Another shows a most elegant Diaghilev in a top-hat standing by the fat, wary, cynical lawyer who looked after the interests of a wealthy American backer. The Ballets Russes were back in Europe: they reached London just before the end of the war, and Diaghilev was preparing new works for the particularly brilliant season of 1919; one of these was *Le Tricorne*, and as Martínez Sierra's libretto was set in his native Spain, while the music was written by the Andalusian Manuel de Falla, Picasso was the obvious choice for the scenery and costumes.

This meant an interruption of his work just when he was feeling out in new directions; but Picasso agreed, and he flung himself into the task with his usual zeal and perhaps with more practical sense of the theater than he had brought to *Parade:* in any case this ballet was far less revolutionary than his first and it called for no prodigious innovation. The simple text dealt with an aged hidalgo's unsuccessful attempt at seducing a village maiden engaged to a young miller, and to deal with it Picasso had only to look over his shoulder at his youth, for his youth contained not only the "Spanish" pictures that he had shown at Vollard's and Berthe Weill's but also his Pink Period; and a combination of these produced a charming if somewhat facile setting for the tale. His curtain was a view into a bull-ring, with women in mantillas and men in cloaks watching from the shade of an arched box, while in the brilliant sun beyond, a dead bull is being dragged out of the arena. The back-cloth showed a great arch among houses—perhaps the gateway of a fortified village—with a bridge in the distance: all pink and pale ocher under a blue starry sky. And his costumes were fairly straightforward versions of Spanish tradition. If it was not particularly significant, it was remarkably effective; and although the puritanical Cubists of Montmartre might call it whoredom, surely a man may have fun from time to time.

This was a period at which Picasso was determined to have fun as it is generally understood; he was extremely curious by nature, and he wanted to see whether fashionable life was all that it was represented to be—whether the efforts of Cocteau, Olga, and some of his more recent acquaintances bore any reasonable proportion to the resulting pleasure.

In this case, when he came to London in the early summer of 1919 to supervise his work on *Le Tricorne* and to see how the English public would react to *Parade*, he and Olga stayed at the Savoy, and he bought himself the clothes he considered suitable. Although in the last fifteen years or so his attention to dress had not gone much beyond the critical choice of ties, the dandy who haunted Soler's shop at the turn of the century, who paraded the Ramblas sharing a pair of gloves with Soto, and who impressed Vollard as being *"vêtu avec recherche"* had not perished in the cold of the Bateau-Lavoir; now Picasso could afford a whole pair of gloves for himself; to these he added several good wool suits and even a dinner-jacket, and it was in this garment that he attended the first London performance of *Parade* at the Alhambra.

A few days later, on July 22, 1919, *Le Tricorne* was presented. The settings and costumes had been begun from his maquettes well before he left France, but in spite of frenzied work they were not quite ready even at the very last moment, and Picasso hovered in the wings, dabbing paint on to the dancers before they took to the stage.

Yet his natural anxiety must already have been relieved by the applause that greeted the curtain. This was a promising start, and in fact the ballet, beginning well, ended triumphantly, with the audience clapping and even cheering, the dancers delighted. *Le Tricorne* was a complete success, and one of the results of this success was to bring Picasso into contact not only with Bloomsbury but with a large number of rich and party-giving people. Perhaps they entertained the Picassos very well, or perhaps Pablo's total ignorance of the language veiled the tedium: in any case his appetite for party-going increased, and he was now ready to plunge into the nearest vortex of dissipation.

Derain was not. He too was in London, having been invited to design the setting and costumes for the equally successful *Boutique Fantasque.* Although the old intimacy was gone, he and Picasso were on terms friendly enough for Picasso to draw his portrait and to invite him to the rue La Boëtie: but Derain, like Braque and many other painters, disapproved of a way of life dangerously like that of a fashionable artist. It was not that Derain or Braque or Montparnasse in general took a high moral stand; they could be as dissipated as sailors ashore on occasion, and apart from Max Jacob few seemed oppressed by a sense of guilt. But they felt that a serious painter's vocation required him to remain aloof from the Establishment; and mixed with this attitude there was in some cases an uninformed, doctrinaire, and almost racist scorn for the "upper" classes. For his part Picasso never seems to have felt inferior to any man, much less to any woman who stepped; and his curiosity, his great vitality, and his interest in other people made him unwilling to leave any region or any potential pleasure unexplored.

When the Picassos returned to France, somewhat spent and worn, they went down to the Côte d'Azur, to Saint-Raphaël; although the place was not very well chosen, being somewhat dreary and poor in beaches, and although Picasso's mind was largely taken up with two other ballets, the peace, the sun, and the Mediterranean so stimulated him that he began a long series of brilliantly-lit paintings. They were nearly all in gouache, probably because of the hotel's reluctance to have its floors, carpets, and furniture daubed with oil-paint: Picasso was not yet so famous that he could do exactly what he liked anywhere at all.

It is strange now to think of the Côte d'Azur as a peaceful place in high summer, but until well on into the twenties people believed that the heat was mortal, that exposure to such a sun would be certain death, and they went there only in winter and spring: in fact, it was not until about 1925, when Coco Chanel appeared with a fine bronzed back, that women thought of sun-bathing at all, and the clean, empty August beaches were left to such salamanders as Picasso.

These Saint-Raphaël pictures returned again and again to the open window, often with a table in front of it piled with a variety of objects, including of course a guitar, since they were all essentially Cubist. Several are so small that they can almost be called miniatures, and they have something of the miniaturist's technique that he learned in his childhood; but large or small, the whole series glows with happy color.

Picasso was very pleased with them; so was Paul Rosenberg, and that autumn the dealer arranged an important exhibition, including drawings but no oils, at his gallery in the rue La Boëtie, next door to Picasso's flat.

This was the first one-man show that Picasso had had in Paris for a great while, and to honor the occasion he took to the lithographic stone and designed his own invitation, using the Saint-Raphaël window with the table and guitar; but here the table, instead of being seen simultaneously from the top and sideways in the full Cubist manner, was shown in more or less conventional perspective, almost as though it were meant to reassure the visitors. Lithography was one of the few mediums that Picasso had not yet employed, and although this invitation-card and the portrait of Olga for the outside of the catalog were not the happiest examples of his work, he was inevitably to become a master of the process and one of the most outstanding innovators.

During the last few years Picasso had neglected neither etching nor engraving, and he had often used his talent for his friends. After the illustrations for Max Jacob's *Saint Matorel*, Picasso made three etchings for his *Siège de Jérusalem*, an engraving for special copies of *Le Cornet à dés* in 1917, and the next year another etching for *Le Phanérogame*, two books which Jacob published himself with great pains and little reward in very small editions; though in 1919 the Société littéraire de France brought out his *Défense de Tartufe*, with a Picasso engraving in twenty-five of the copies. For Apollinaire's *Calligrammes* he produced a portrait drawing, and another for Cocteau's *Le Coq et l'arlequin*, while he also designed the cover for Stravinsky's *Ragtime* and supplied the illustrations for Salmon's *Manuscrit trouvé dans un chapeau*—a handsome return for Salmon's preface to the Rosenberg catalog. This brings us to 1919, and if the list were carried on into the twenties it would contain many other poets, Aragon, Valéry, Reverdy, and Breton among them; for Picasso felt more kindness for poets than any other set of men; they lived on the same plane as himself, yet there was no rivalry, no poisonous competition. He was not alone in this, nor in illustrating their books; Matisse did the same for Reverdy, Dufy for Apollinaire, Derain for Dalize and Breton, Léger for Cendrars, Gris for Paul Dermée.

The exhibition was successful, not only commercially but in showing a very large number of people several aspects of Picasso's work. Gertrude Stein's reaction is not recorded: she and Picasso had fallen out, Gris being one of the underlying subjects of discord, and they were not on speaking-terms for a year or two. But Gris himself and the minor hardline Cubists were indignant at what they considered a betrayal of the movement and what was in fact a refusal on Picasso's part either to be bound to them or to any one language. The critics and the gallery-going public were, on the whole, pleased and impressed; and those who did not already know it were given the proof that the hand which could produce the barely legible metaphors of Cubism could also make an instantly entrancing, instantly recognizable drawing. Joan Miró was there, yet another young Catalan from the Llotja seeking his fortune or rather his way in Paris; and both his acquaintance with Picasso, who received him very kindly, and this exhibition had a decisive influence on his development. For although by this time Cubism and the esprit nouveau had so permeated the general consciousness that the Salon d'Automne and the Indépendants were now filled with works imitating the gestures of Picasso and Braque, just as for some time past the official salons had shown countless examples of diluted Impressionism, there was still enough startling freshness of vision in it to influence a young and uncommonly gifted painter and to decide him to become not a follower but a fellow traveler.

The ballet in the forefront of Picasso's mind during the winter of 1919/20 was *Pulcinella*, and it was probably a far less harmful absorber of his energy, far less of an interruption of his true vocation than *Le Tricorne*: it was based on pure eighteenth-century commedia dell' arte and it was therefore right up Picasso's street. Not only had his work long been filled with the slightly watered-down characters from the commedia who still overspread the popular entertainment of Western Europe in his youth, but he had early identified himself with Harlequin. Furthermore, when he and Stravinsky were in Naples together in 1917 they had been deeply impressed by the full, traditional commedia, which they saw "in a crowded little room reeking of garlic" and where the Pulcinella, the remote ancestor of our Punch, was a "great drunken lout whose every gesture and probably every word . . . was obscene."

The ballet was ideally suited to Picasso, but even so it gave him a very great deal of trouble. His first sketches for the costumes were in a mid-nineteenth-century style, with sidewhiskers instead of masks; but Diaghilev hated the whole idea, and their disagreement mounted to such a pitch that he flung the drawings down, stamped on them, and left the room slamming the door behind him. It is difficult to imagine how even so insinuating a character as Diaghilev ever induced Picasso to carry on with the project, but he did; and what is more he even persuaded him to give up his sidewhiskers in favor of the traditional black masks.

Then again, all Picasso's maquettes, the result of a great deal of hard work, had been sent to Rome well before May 15, 1920, the date the ballet was to open in Paris, there to be transformed by the Roman scene-painters and sent back to France in the form of a most ambitious full-sized stage-set, an eighteenth-century Italian theater within the theater and a view through this play-house to arcades leading down to the harbor, the general baroque effect being tempered with that degree of the esprit nouveau which brought it into harmony with Stravinsky's version of Pergolesi's score, a score that Diaghilev disliked almost as much as he disliked Picasso's costumes. On May 13th it was found that all the scenery was still in Italy. That at least is one account; but the accounts are as various and confused as the muddles they purport to describe, and the only certainty is that Picasso was obliged to run up a new setting at breakneck speed with hysteria bursting out all round him. His plans had to be drastically reduced, and the red, white, and gold baroque theater dwindled to a severe, somewhat Cubist, gray, blue, and white street going down to the Bay of Naples under the stars and the moon, with Vesuvius in the distance. Yet in spite of everything the ballet was a great success. Stravinsky, no mean judge, said that it was one of the very few in which all the elements fused into an entirely satisfying whole; and he spoke of "Picasso's miracle."

The praise was divided, but a great deal necessarily fell to Picasso; and this, together with the triumphant Paris production of *Le Tricorne* and the successful representation of *Parade*, made him one of the most talked-about and sought-after men in Paris: he was to be seen, looking elegant, at every cocktail-party and first night, and he dined out continually, accompanied by Olga in dresses from Chanel. If he had wanted to see "high life" his wishes were fulfilled; this was a time of great social activity, enormous parties—Scott Fitzgerald was there—and although many of his new friends were rich Levantines, Rumanians, South Americans, and their hangers-on, others belonged to great French families, for in Europe, as opposed to England or the United States, the glories of the Renaissance still hang about a successful artist, and although he may privately be considered as an *amuseur*, an entertainer (as Proust and others before him discovered), this is usually concealed from him, and he has the impression of being received as an equal.

With all his gadding about and with all the spiritual wear and tear of the ballet, Picasso did not age. By the calendar he was thirty-nine in 1920, but the photographs of that time show a man so young that adolescence can still be traced in his rounded features and gleaming eye; he still had energy for ten, and although the main stream of his development may have been slowed down or confused or even, as the Cubists of the strict observance said, perverted, he was not to be separated from his brush or pencil.

Among other activities he made several more drawings of his friends, including the well-known portrait of Stravinsky; and in some of these, particularly the Stravinsky, the curious magnification and foreshortening of the hands is reminiscent of the ballet-dancer drawings of Rome: it appears to be part of the same line of thought that led to the bulky sleeping peasants and the still more bulky giantesses of the years to come.

Some of these drawings were based on photographs or postcards. Why not? Picasso never made any secret of it, nor of the fact that he would use any element that caught his eye: "When things are concerned there are no class-distinctions. We must pick out what is good for us where we can find it—except in our own work," he said to Zervos. "I have a horror of copying myself. But when I am shown a portfolio of old drawings for instance I have no qualms about taking anything I want from them." It seems fair enough: all chemists use the same elements, all writers the same few dozen basic plots. Yet there were some things about Picasso, above all his success, that irritated many people, so much so that as his success grew even more and more prodigious the sport of puncturing him reached international dimensions. These photographs and postcards were fished up as something profoundly discreditable, and all kinds of sources were discovered for his paintings: if he arranged three figures in a triangle there were critics ready to say, "But this is copied from Raphael." Yet three figures must either be in a line or a triangle. Even now this search is carried on with surprising vehemence and sometimes with evident bad faith; often it looks like the rationalization of a general dislike, and when the sources are not absurd they are usually about as relevant as Shakespeare's knowledge of Holinshed or Chaucer's of Dante, which are rarely the subject of malignant triumph.

One of these drawings is of Renoir, who died in 1919 at the age of seventy-eight, and it too was probably done from a photograph, since Renoir disliked Picasso's work (he advised Paul Rosenberg to have nothing to do with him) and they do not seem to have met. Harsh words travel fast in the world of the arts; nevertheless Picasso admired Renoir's painting to the point of buying one of his more important pictures, and the portrait is a most intelligent, piercing, and respectful study of the old man with his poor crippled hands and his lively authoritative eye.

Renoir, as it happens, is another of those originals so often brought forward to confound Picasso, on the grounds that his later work was also concerned with massive female bodies; and to be sure, if one earnestly wishes to beat Picasso, Renoir will serve as a stick.

Stravinsky, Satie, Manuel de Falla, and many more: the brilliant portraits came in quick succession, all with the same pure line he had used in his more recent drawings of Max Jacob. Yet in this series Max himself is not to be seen; he and Picasso were somewhat out of touch for the moment, and a little later Max withdrew for many years on end, retiring to a religious life in the shade of the great Benedictine monastery at Saint-

Benoît-sur-Loire, far from the noise and the temptations of Paris, and living somehow on the sale of his gouaches and the meager royalties from his books.

By the time the summer of 1920 came round and the Picassos began to think of their holiday, his own work, the turmoil of the ballet, the cocktail-parties, dinners, feasts, had worn even Picasso's powerful frame; and although social activity continued with tireless zeal in the fashionable watering-places on the Channel, particularly at Deauville and Dinard, he longed for the Mediterranean, so much so that he painted an imaginary landscape: rocks, umbrella-pines, a beach and pure sea, all brilliant in the sun. There was Olga's reluctance to be overcome—the Midi was not fashionable in summer—but in time he managed this and they went south together, to Juan-les-Pins in the Var, a small place then, quite unspoiled, and one that Picasso had never seen.

When they arrived they walked straight into Picasso's landscape. "I'm not trying to make anyone believe I have the second sight," he said, almost uneasily, when he was telling Antonina Valentin about it. "But everything was there, just as it was in the picture I had painted in Paris: I was absolutely amazed. And it was then that I grasped that this landscape was my own."

It was indeed: the same sea that bathed Cadaqués, the same sun that blazed on Málaga. And here, sitting in a restaurant that smelt of hot olive-oil and looking at the evening sea, sometimes as dark as his wine, he was as much at home as he could be anywhere.

Some years later, when the Surrealists thought it their duty to demolish the existing order by outraging the bourgeoisie, Miró walked about Paris saying, "Down with the Mediterranean," and in explanation he pointed out that the Mediterranean was the cradle of our whole Greco-Roman culture. Few would deny it, least of all Picasso: and here on its shore he turned back to the classical world whose air he had breathed in, though with a Moorish tinge, with the first gasp of his uncle's cigar, and which he had seen fresh and lively in the ruins of Pompeii.

The various aspects of his classicism took two main forms: the one a long-continued series of exquisite line-drawings of mythological subjects, often as realistic as those portraits of his friends; the other paintings of colossal women, great sculptural nudes whose volumes are studied with loving care. A splendid example of the first is a centaur carrying off a young woman: she is struggling and pulling his hair, but he looks quite pleased. Most of Picasso's centaurs do, and so, quite often, does his early Minotaur, a far more important character who was presently to make his appearance. Horses and bulls were naturally of great symbolic significance to Picasso; there were subtle degrees of identification, sometimes for fun, sometimes in deadly earnest; and in later years the Minotaur was to assume the most tragic appearance. But those times were still far away, and in the early twenties the classical figures wrestled, conversed, and raped with a wonderful serenity, bathed in their own clear day; for, as Picasso said to Kahnweiler, when they were talking about painting and the imitation of light, ''the line-drawing has its own innate light, and does not imitate it.''

The colossal women are calm too, but theirs is a calmness that arises not only from their remote, almost expressionless faces, but even more from their noble mass, their generally immobile volumes. They are more nearly related to Picasso's earlier excursion into the ancient world, to those great brick-colored nudes he painted just before bursting out of all Western tradition with the ''Demoiselles,'' than the mythological drawings are to the horse-riding boys and ephebes of 1905: and it appears that in those days he was thinking more in terms of archaic Greece, whereas in 1920 Hellenistic sculptures, bas-reliefs, and even frescoes and mosaics were present, and far more clearly present, to his mind.

Picasso would not have been Picasso if this new departure alone had satisfied him. During these months at Juan-les-Pins he also painted an unusual number of landscapes and many beach-scenes, often with his giantesses in the sea; but he had not yet said nearly all he had to say in the Cubist idiom, and a quantity of still-lives, some as rigorous as anything since 1914, flowed from his pencil, pen, and brush.

He also perpetuated if not his race (for there could scarcely be a flock of Picassos any more than a flock of phoenixes) then at least his name: he begot a child in June; and as Olga's condition became more evident so his interest in the subject of maternity revived.

In his circus days and before he had drawn and painted many poignant studies of mother and child. Often they were young, fragile women, pretty and wonderfully graceful, and in most of the pictures there was some degree of social comment. Overt comment had vanished long since, perhaps with the ''Demoiselles''; and now he was thinking on another plane. These women are great massive figures, not particularly young, with huge stubby hands and feet: milky, even lymphatic, godlike, often detached. They have no resemblance to Olga whatsoever.

The full time for his maternities had not yet come, however: in autumn he took the pregnant Olga back to the rue La Boëtie and plunged into the ballet once again. Diaghilev had asked him to provide the setting and costumes for *Cuadro Flamenco*, a suite of Andalusian songs and dances with traditional music arranged by Manuel de Falla, himself a Grenadine. Gris said that Picasso took the commission away from him and Diaghilev's un-businesslike ways may have given some color to the suspicion; but in any case it was Picasso who did the work. He returned to his idea of a theater within a theater, and this time it was a nineteenth-century Spanish theater that appeared on the stage of the Gaîeté-Lyrique—rows of red-plush boxes against a black and gold background, with rich nineteenth-century Spaniards in them: the costumes, since they were to be worn not by ballet-dancers but by real Gypsies from Sevilla, were as traditional as Falla's version of the music. The setting was perfectly adequate; it was amusing; it neither aimed at nor attained any higher level.

There was a certain amount of adverse criticism, and not only from the purists of Montparnasse; but Picasso was untouched, because only a few weeks before the opening-night Olga had given him a son.

Curiously enough Picasso had never been a father before, and now he was absolutely delighted. He was filled with good will towards all men (except Braque and Juan Gris) and even to all women: he went up to Gertrude Stein in a gallery and said, as she puts it, oh hell, let's be friends, thus taking the first step in a reconciliation that lasted, though tepidly, the rest of her days.

But there was nothing tepid about Picasso's reaction to young Paulo, nor to motherhood: within a few days of the baby's birth, his father drew him avidly feeding, and these sketches continued at very frequent intervals—a fluent and most loving line—while at the same time the great series of vast, hieratic maternities began.

Chapter XII

Money has always been banished from civilized conversation; yet it has a profound though unclean interest of its own and in the privacy of his closet a writer may, for example, calculate Jane Austin's 24.8% on an edition of seven hundred and fifty and compare it with modern publishing practice. And a biography that aims at showing Picasso in the round cannot be squeamish in this respect, because money meant a great deal to him.

Just what it meant cannot be summed up in a neat single phrase, since the meanings varied from the plain equivalent of food, shelter, and materials in the early days, to a complex symbol later on, and to power later still, with an infinity of shifting nuances between these on the one hand and freedom, success, self-esteem, and the pleasure of giving on the other. His attitudes varied too: he could be mean with it, particularly in small and daily things; and he could be open-handed—in 1958, when Alice Derain and Marcelle Braque told him that Fernande, now a deaf, arthritic old woman, was not only sick but needy, he stuffed a million francs (about £1,000 in those days: a good year's living) into an envelope and sent it off, although she had vexed him to the heart in 1933 by publishing *Picasso et ses amis*, reminiscences of their years together, which, though far more restrained than Françoise Gilot's, nevertheless violated his sacred privacy. But one of its meanings, from the time of his recognition onwards, was that of a yardstick by which he could gauge his standing within the group of painters who might be thought of as his peers. Even late in life it made him uneasy to hear of a picture of Braque's being sold for a swingeing price, and now, in 1921, he followed the Uhde and Kahnweiler sales with the closest interest.

Since both Uhde and Kahnweiler were Germans, their pictures had been seized in the first days of the war, and this year they were to come up for auction. They formed the most important body of Cubist paintings ever put on the market at one time, and probably the largest collection of

Picassos ever brought together in Paris up until that date. And like almost everything to do with Picasso the published accounts are confused if not contradictory.

Without naming him, Gertrude Stein states that the expert in charge of the sale, in diabolical league with the older merchants, meant to kill Cubism by discouraging the public and keeping the prices as low as possible; that on being reproached at the sale by Braque he called him a Norman pig; that Braque stuck him to the ground; and that the buyers being frightened off, the pictures went for very little.

Yet the expert in question was Léonce Rosenberg, and it seems strange that the nursing mother of so many Cubists should have wanted to ruin them. On the other hand, the danger of flooding the market with hundreds of pictures was apparent even to the most unbusinesslike. But we do have the list of prices, and these prices, though low, show a triumph for Picasso over the other Cubists. A triumph too, now that he had been in his grave eleven years, for Henri Rousseau, whose works did very well indeed, one of them, "Femme en rouge dans la forêt," fetching 30,500 francs (£ 587), the highest price in the first day's sale.

The Uhde sale began on May 30, 1921; and in 1921 the exchange rates were approximately fifty-two francs to the pound sterling and thirteen to the dollar.

During this first day seventeen Braque paintings fetched 10,904 francs, the highest price being 1,703 francs for "La Guitare." Thirteen Picassos fetched 65,094 francs 25: "La Joueuse de mandoline" reaching 21,150 francs, while the portrait of Uhde went for 1,938 francs. The more important Kahnweiler sale began a fortnight later, when twenty-two Braques were sold for 25,114 francs and twenty-six Picassos for 36,403 francs. These figures give the sale-room scale of values thus: Picasso averaged 3,203 francs, Braque 891, and Gris 537 francs.

Before this, at the very beginning of 1921, the Leicester Galleries in London had put on a show of seventy-two Picassos, representative of his oils (including the "Femme en chemise"), gouaches, watercolors, papiers collés, drawings, etchings and dry-points from 1902 or 1903 to 1919: the preface was by Clive Bell, and since 1912, when he wrote, ". . . the latest works of Picasso . . . leave me cold. I suspect them of being descriptive, of using form as the Royal Academicians use it, to convey information and ideas. I suspect Picasso of having come for the moment under the spell of the Futurists," his views had so changed that he could now explain why Picasso rather than Matisse was the enormously influential leader of the modern movement, a point that he made with great force not only in the catalog but also in *The Athenaeum*, his essay appearing in both. The graver critics were respectful, if not laudatory. The *Telegraph* said, ". . . were Picasso not Picasso we would look and pass on. But we have before us sufficient proof of what he could accomplish if he would not to give expression to our profound sadness in facing him in his cubistic developments." And the *Burlington*'s article corrects the impression that England was then very, very far behind the times; to its readers at least Picasso was obviously a familiar figure: "Picasso is the object of more worship and more abuse than any contemporary painter . . . this alone gives special interest and importance to the exhibition of his works at the Leicester Galleries. Almost every phase of his development is to some extent illustrated . . . the familiar Blue phase, with form more emphasized, but overlaid with sentiment. . . . Difficult to believe the exhibition is really representative of the artist's best work: it shows his versatility and technical skill . . . it is another question what rank Picasso will take as a creative artist . . . Picasso's present Ingres phase must be singularly disquieting for those who believe that in cubism truth was at last found."

The right-wing and gutter press hooted away just as it might be expected to hoot: the Conservative *Morning Post*, wrote, "It has been said that Pablo Picasso's art has a logic of its own like that of music. What sort of music? The caterwauling love songs of cats in the night? That is the only kind of music suggested by Picasso's cubistic diagrams at the Leicester Galleries." The lower-middle-class but equally Conservative *Daily Mail* had the stock piece dating from Turner about a picture's being upside-down: "A Cubist conception of a packet of tobacco by Pablo Picasso, arch-apostle of this extraordinary art. We are not sure, however, if this is the right way up." And the *Sketch*, having observed that it was "a cheap business to sneer at what one does not understand" went on, "But to draw a few triangles and a segment of a circle, colour them crudely, stick on some patches of cement with sand in it and call the whole 'Nature Morte' smacks of idiocy," while the headlines in the *Graphic* and the *Evening News* read FREAKS AT £700, KING OF CUBISTS IN LONDON, and CHAMBER OF HORRORS FOR THE WEST END.

The only familiar phrase that seems to be lacking is "a child of seven could do as well": otherwise everything is in order.

Harsh newspaper articles never had much effect on Picasso, although being insatiably curious he always read them attentively; on the other hand he did like praise, particularly intelligent praise, and Clive Bell's piece must have been honey to his heart. At this time he was more obviously pitted against Braque, but it was Matisse who really worried him, then and for the rest of his life, Matisse at whom he looked with a mixture of uneasiness, respect, and emulation.

Picasso read no English, not a word; but Kahnweiler, who had spent some time in the London money-market before becoming a picture-dealer, was fluent in the language, and he could have translated Bell's article for his friend. Kahnweiler came back to Paris as soon as he could after the war and he tried to prevent the sale of his pictures. In spite of his valuable contacts he was unsuccessful; and in spite of his long association with Picasso he was unable to dislodge Paul Rosenberg. Picasso's memory of the sordid hours of haggling when the merchant used to wear down his resistance at the Bateau-Lavoir may have had something to do with this; for although it is clear from his writings that Kahnweiler was an unusually perceptive and intelligent dealer, the mercantile side with its love of buying cheap and selling dear often prevailed, and his deeply-rooted passion for bargaining was as strong as ever in Françoise Gilot's time, forty years after he first began to harass the young Picasso.

In the early twenties things looked bad for the dealer; but with the help of his sister-in-law, the wife of Michel Leiris, he did manage to open a gallery again: many of his former painters, including Juan Gris, came back to him, and after many years his tenacity, Picasso's friendship for him, and Rosenberg's departure for New York eventually resulted in his becoming Picasso's chief dealer once again. Picasso liked what he was used to, and the deeply conservative side of his nature meant that custom might outweigh though not wipe out resentment.

Since Olga was still feeling the effects of having her baby, she and Pablo did not go far away for the summer of 1921. He found a house at Fontainebleau, under forty miles from Paris, and there they stayed for the modest joys of a northern holiday. The place was large enough for Picasso to be isolated from the roar and squalor of a baby; and at this time he was about as domesticated as it was in his nature ever to be. He drew the stuccoed villa and its interior repeatedly, using a particularly fine pencil line and piling up the niggling detail in a kind of gentle, touching mockery.

He did express a certain impatience at times, but for once Picasso was sharing the common lot, and this was a period of singular happiness, of great creative energy. The baby, cleaned and produced at stated intervals, was a fascinating new object, earthy, genuine, timeless, peculiarly his own, and one that he drew again and again. Yet even more important was its action as a catalyst; for without the presence of the baby Picasso would scarcely have carried out his sequence of maternities, which, although they are intimately related to his monumental neo-classic women, have a special quality of their own. Until babies reach the human stage they are so alike that they can hardly be told apart, and it is impossible to say whether these sucklings are in any way portraits of the infant Paulo, but in all probability they are not, since the mothers have nothing whatever to do with Olga. Olga was about five foot four, a little shorter than her husband, and these are vast mild women, with simplified classical features; they exist very calmly, on another plane, unaffected by earthly contingencies; often they recline in an absolute landscape of unrelieved, almost undifferentiated, strand, sea, and sky; and they wear a simple, vaguely classical garment from which their high, unsensual bosoms escape. When they do sit in an armchair, it looks strangely irrelevant, an intruder from our ordinary world rather than an anachronism.

At the same time—how often Picasso's biographer must begin his paragraphs with these words—and in the same place, he painted the two large, very closely related pictures which are generally held to be the high mark and the summation of synthetic Cubism: both are called "Trois musiciens aux masques" and both are just that—three masked musicians sitting tightly side by side in a line behind a table. In the one, the darker picture, they are a pierrot playing a wind-instrument, a harlequin playing a guitar, and a monk holding the score, while a dog lies under the table. In the other the harlequin has changed places with the pierrot and he is now playing a fiddle; the pierrot has the wind-instrument; the indeterminate monk has become a friar, a Cordelier, and he has an accordion: the dog has vanished. In both the figures are huge: physically they would be about ten feet tall if they were to stand up, but they are really huge because of their significance, and, on another scale, because of their tiny hands.

Having made several preliminary studies he set to work on both pictures at once in what must have been a most enviable fever of creation: except in the "dog" picture, where a passage of traditional perspective gives depth, they both obey the strict Cubist canon, and space is the result of flat, generally rectilinear planes alone; the colors are often vivid, and in spite of a good deal of somber blue they should be cheerful. Yet the word is altogether wrong for the "Musicians," and the wrongness lies not only in the scale and obvious importance of the pictures: these masked figures of traditional amusement possess a menacing quality, particularly in the case of the "dog" version, and I believe that the reason for it is that the "Musicians" are essentially magic, that the pictures give certain unnamed spirits a form and thereby exorcise them. They are part of that African revelation which Picasso had so many years before.

One apparently trivial point about these pictures is that the fiddle-playing harlequin holds his bow in his left hand: he may of course have been a left-handed harlequin, but as I have said before Picasso was never good at telling the difference between the sides, and in many of his self-portraits between 1902 and 1918 his forelock falls over his right eye, whereas all the photographs show it drooping over the other, just as it does in Max Jacob's and Modigliani's portraits of him: far be it from a layman to say what effect this uncertainty may have had on Picasso, but it seems that the sense of handedness is an important factor in perception, helpful but at the same time limiting, and that freedom from it may perhaps enlarge one's powers.

The two versions of the "Musicians" were the most important Cubist pictures of 1921, although the brilliant "Chien et coq" ran them close. For some people they are the most important pictures of that year without qualification and indeed of many years on either side of 1921; yet on the other hand it can be argued that the "Musicians" look back to earlier achievements, whereas the neo-classical figures, though less striking and to certain appetites less satisfying, look towards the Picasso yet to come.

Of these no doubt the finest is the "Trois Femmes à la fontaine," a monumental canvas that looks much larger than its six and a half by five and a half feet; it was the outcome of a great deal of thought and of many preliminary drawings and sketches in pastel and oils, a surprising number even for Picasso, who never spared himself when he knew that a great composition was forming in his head or heart. In these studies he arranged his three women in different positions and different relationships to one another; and when finally they fell into what now seems their necessary, inevitable, and effortless sequence, he took great pains with the smaller parts that were to make up the whole. At intervals during the last year or so, and at Fontainebleau itself, his interest in hands had received a fresh impulse, and he had made precise, realistic drawings of his own: now he turned to those for his three women.

Some of the larger studies are complex and highly-detailed, particularly those which show reminiscences of Pompeii: but Picasso said himself, "in my case a picture is a sum of destructions," and as the definitive version of the "Trois Femmes" took shape all the pleasant but unessential inventions disappeared, together with most of the Hellenistic echoes. The hands took on massive dimensions, devoid of apparent grace—fat hands with sausage-like fingers, three hands at the heart of the picture, around which all the rest is organized. The three women sit, stand, or lean about a source of water, a little piped jet coming from a rock: with her open palm one idly guides the stream into a pitcher that another holds with one finger hooked through its ear, while a third stands by with hers. Their arms and their short, columnar necks match their hands; so do their massive, pale terra-cotta bodies. The women do not look at one another; they do not converse. Their large bovine eyes gaze far away, but it is doubtful whether they see anything. Although the water flows they do not even seem to be waiting, but rather to be content with existing, motionless and outside time.

These however were not the women who were expecting the Picassos when they returned to Paris: hostesses who wish to cultivate the latest values are necessarily poised on the utmost limit of advancing time as they perceive it. Far from damaging his reputation, the large number of Cubist Picassos thrown onto the market had increased it: most of them had stayed in France—there were few foreign buyers at the Uhde and Kahnweiler sales—and because of the low prices men like Breton, Tristan Tzara, Eluard, and others very much in the foreground had been able to buy them. Incidentally, the low prices did not last as far as Picasso was concerned: Paul Rosenberg saw to it that his current work sold at such rates that there was not the least difficulty in keeping up the establishment at the rue La Boëtie.

People who buy a painter's work often wish to know him, and they often feel that their purchase gives them a right to do so: Picasso was therefore in even greater demand. Furthermore, in the course of 1922 he began work on the settings for Cocteau's version of the *Antigone*, and this brought him into contact with the theatrical world and with even more of Cocteau's innumerable grand friends. If he had chosen to do so he could have dined out every night of the week, and with his prodigious energy he often did choose.

Some artists have been killed or sterilized by activity of this kind: others, like Picasso (a born night-bird) and Proust, have survived it very well—have survived it that is to say as artists—for physically poor Proust was a wreck by 1922, although he was only ten years older than the painter, whom he was invited to meet that spring. The occasion was a supper party given by Mr. and Mrs. Schiff, a wealthy English pair, after the first night of Stravinsky's *Renard*: Diaghilev and his dancers were there as well as a host of other people, but the splendor of the evening was to be the appearance of the four men of genius the Schiffs most admired, Picasso, Stravinsky, Proust, and James Joyce. The party and the unfortunate encounters between Proust and Stravinsky on the one hand and Proust and James Joyce on the other (Joyce "could not see any special talent" in Proust and Proust said, "I regret I do not know Monsieur Joyce's work") are described in George Painter's definitive Life; here I am concerned with giving an example of Picasso's social experience and with Proust's earlier reactions to him, which I quote from the same valuable book. "In a letter to Walter Berry in 1917 Proust pointed out the affinity between prehistoric cave-painting and the art of Picasso. 'Picasso is an artist whose work and person are by no means unknown to me,' he declared to Blanche in 1919; and in his preface to Jacques-Emile Blanche's *De David à Degas* he wrote of 'the great and admirable Picasso, who had concentrated all Cocteau's features into a portrait of such noble rigidity that, when I contemplate it, even the most enchanting Carpaccios in Venice tend to take a second place in my memory.'" Picasso's views on Joyce, by the way, are contained in a remark to Gertrude Stein. "Yes, Braque and James Joyce, they were the incomprehensibles whom anyone can understand." But the words were uttered at a time when he was vexed with Braque, and they probably did not represent his considered opinion of Joyce if indeed he had one, which is unlikely.

At this time Picasso was a kind if not an uxorious husband, and in the summer of 1922 he gave up the Midi and agreed to take Olga and Paulo to the fashionable resort of Dinard. It is just in Brittany, on the Channel coast opposite St. Malo, a pleasant little place with a fine beach, charming when the sky is clear; but unfortunately Brittany is the cloudiest, wettest province in the whole of France, and even when the sun does pierce through it cannot blaze with the ardor of the south. Still, at that time Dinard did possess two casinos and quantities of grand hotels with palm courts, orchestras, and dance-bands for the rainy days; and these and the company satisfied most of the people who went there.

Picasso's good nature or good humor or happiness (an artist in full flow is often kind) bore up against the rain; his powers of concentration enabled him to work in spite of all the inconveniences of a summer villa, a child cutting its teeth and bawling, a socially-active wife, and a number of acquaintances in the little town. Besides, it did not rain every day: he painted at least one sunny little view of Dinard, looking out over the sparkling water to the steepled church on the other side, and others of St. Malo; and there were many drawings that show the place both clear and dry. He also painted some women and children, including one particularly gentle maternity, in which the mother, though still massive, is no longer carved from ponderous stone, and in which the kind pink and gray has the warmth of the Rose Period, a tendency that spread to many other pictures of this time. But most of his work that summer was Cubist still-lives, sometimes in the direct tradition, sometimes in what has been called the zebra manner, with stripes lying across and across a plane of color, not so much to variegate the texture as to affect the light that emanates from it. There were twenty or thirty of these, nearly all of the conventional Cubist glasses, bottles, tobacco, or cigarette packets, and many restrained in color, almost monochromatic. Others are as brilliant as can be, and one of the most cheerful shows the familiar open window, so wide that it cannot be seen at all, and the inevitable balcony and table; and on the table there are some fishes, lying on a piece of paper: painted paper, not papier collé. Why did the collages dwindle away? They certainly had not reached the end of their road. Picasso himself wondered, and some appeared in 1924.

If one may judge by his painting, the holiday at Dinard was happy right up to the end: but the end was both premature and sudden. Olga fell ill. Had she eaten the fish? Probably not, since it was the surgeon's knife rather than the physician's draught that cured her; and in any case Picasso's family no longer sat yearning, as once the little Matisses had sat, until an edible subject, sometimes showing desperate signs of age, was at last committed to paint.

Sir Roland Penrose, my only authority for this episode, states that Picasso "was obliged to rush her to Paris, nursing her with ice-packs on the journey, while little Paulo was violently car-sick all the way." I am sure Sir Roland's account is exact: I am equally sure that if Picasso had time for reflection it would have occurred to him that the common lot was more attractive from a distance; that it was not at all suitable for a painter; that the entrance-fee to the community was far too high, the price for being an insider excessive. Yet if these thoughts did in fact come to him, they remained deep in his consciousness for the time, finding no outward expression for some years.

Back in his studio, which was filled with things that might come in useful, he took a wooden panel, only about seventeen inches wide, and on it he made a tempera painting of two of his tremendous women, wildly distorted as they race across a beach, hair and bosoms flying, hands clasped high. They can scarcely have been a memory of Dinard, but as he painted them he may already have had some notion of using these giantesses, gigantically enlarged, for the theater curtain that they were eventually to become—the curtain for Diaghilev's 1924 production of Cocteau's old *Train bleu*.

Even on the little panel the women are enormous: without being in the least obese they would tip an earthly scale at fifteen stone, and although they advance at this breakneck pace they do not seem to get much farther: in spite of the outstretched arms, the streaming locks, they share much of their sisters' immobility. This may have something to do with the fact that their faces are directed to the beholder's right. There is a theory, supported by much research, that our perception assumes figures facing leftwards to be in actual or potential motion and those facing right to be static. Perhaps Picasso, aware of this, meant his two women to run forever, never gaining an inch; or perhaps his own confusion of left and right was at the bottom of it all. In any case he had a particular affection for the little panel, and it joined the collection of his own Picassos, those that he would never part with.

Cocteau and Cocteau's version of the classical world and its pieties were much in his mind during the later part of 1922. Like Picasso and a great many other people after the war, the poet looked back to the ancient values, not so much abandoning modernity as giving it a classical ballast; and his *Antigone*, which brought the great Sophoclean tragedy down to a single act, was now in brisk preparation. The formidable, and fashionable, Coco Chanel was providing the costumes, Honegger the incidental music, and Picasso the stark décor. He was helped or hindered by the author, whose demoniac energy was almost equal to his own and who was now in a state of more than usual excitement, having met the young, death-bent Raymond Radiguet sometime before at Max Jacob's flat. This excitement may account for the fact that within hours of the first night Picasso was confronted with a stage on which nothing was ready except the masks that he had prepared: they hung on either side of a hole high in a blue back-drop with a white wooden panel beneath them. What he was required to do, as Cocteau records, was to make use of this surface "to bring to mind a hot sunny day," anything else, authentic or not, being too costly, above all in time. He walked to and fro upon the stage, then began to rub the rough white boards with a stick of sanguine: they assumed the appearance of marble. Then, holding a bottle of ink, he swept out some masterly lines: and then "all at once he blackened a few blank places and three columns started into sight. Their appearance was so sudden, so astonishing, that we all burst out clapping."

In its way this was a "Picasso miracle," but it was scarcely on the scale of the one that had so surprised Stravinsky.

When the play was presented at the Théâtre de l'Atelier just before Christmas it had the success guaranteed by the names of those concerned and the great number of friends they could bring to their support; but no more than that. Yet it was by no means a failure, and it did not disgust Picasso with the stage: indeed, not long after he undertook the scenery and costumes for *Mercure*, an enterprise of his and Cocteau's wealthy, sociable, ballet-loving friend Count Etienne de Beaumont, one of the leaders of the "artistic" social world of the twenties.

In tracing Picasso's progress, it is often convenient to concentrate on his summer holidays, for it was more often in the south than in Paris that he could find the solitude he needed, to say nothing of the sun; and often it was in the south that he took his new departures, working them out in more detail when he went back to Paris.

When one knows Picasso's views on the want of evolution in his painting, the word progress seems out of place; but here it is used in the sense of sequence in time rather than any advance towards a goal—of a king's rather than a pilgrim's progress. And at first glance solitude seems equally inappropriate when it is used in connection with Picasso, to whom company was often the breath of life—almost any company at times—and who was so often to be seen in a crowd. Yet solitude was necessary to him, not only because he was an essentially lonely man, requiring the two extremes and often disliking both, but because of his work. Some men can work in a noise with people all around them: many French authors do their writing in cafés; Satie composed the music for *Parade* in the café-tabac of the place Denfert-Rochereau; and it was in a series of Italian cafés that Scott-Moncrieff translated Proust. But Picasso was not one of them. "Nothing can be done without solitude," he said to A. Tériade; and to Salles, "I have to live my work, and that is impossible without solitude." Admittedly he said these things later—the conversation with Tériade probably took place in 1931—and perhaps the need grew more apparent as his enormous energy diminished a little, but it was always there; and in 1923 he set out to find his solitude at Antibes.

Before he left he had many things to do, and one of them was to give an interview to Marius de Zayas for the New York review *The Arts*. America had not yet seen much of Picasso's work, but what had been shown had excited a great deal of interest, and everybody concerned with modern art knew that he was one of the most important figures in Europe. The interview was long; it covered Picasso's opinions on research in art (invalid); on art as a lie that reveals truth; on nature and art (mutually exclusive); Cubism; and evolution; and it was carried out in Spanish. Zayas condensed the dialogue into a series of direct statements, showed them to Picasso for his approval, and then translated them into painstaking, rather formal English. The whole, amounting to some two thousand words, is to be found in Alfred Barr's *Picasso: Fifty Years of his Art*, a most scholarly analysis of his work up until 1945. In an earlier chapter I quoted some passages to show what Cubism meant to Picasso: here I draw upon the same source for his views on progress, or rather on evolution.

I also often hear the word evolution. Repeatedly I am asked to explain how my painting evolved. To me there is no past or future in art. If a work of art cannot live always in the present it must not be considered at all. The art of the Greeks, of the Egyptians, of the great painters who lived in other times, is not an art of the past; perhaps it is more alive today than ever it was. Art does not evolve by itself, the ideas of people change and with them their mode of expression. When I hear people speak of the evolution of an artist, it seems to me that they are considering him standing between two mirrors that face each other and reproduce his image an infinite number of times, and that they contemplate the successive images of one mirror as his past, and the images of the other mirror as his future, while his real image is taken as his present. They do not consider that they are all images in different planes.

Variation does not mean evolution. If an artist varies his mode of expression this only means that he has changed his manner of thinking, and in changing, it might be for the better or it might be for the worse.

The several manners I have used in my art must not be considered as an evolution, or as steps towards an unknown ideal of painting. All I have ever made was made for the present and with the hope that it will always remain in the present. I have never taken into consideration the spirit of research. When I have found something to express, I have done it without thinking of the past or of the future. I do not believe I have used radically different elements in the different manners I have used in painting. If the subjects I have wanted to express have suggested different ways of expression I have never hesitated to adopt them. I have never made trials nor experiments. Whenever I had something to say, I have said it in the manner in which I have felt it ought to be said. Different motives inevitably require different methods of expression. This does not imply either evolution or progress, but an adaptation of the idea one wants to express and the means to express that idea.

Some of Picasso's words in this interview, particularly those on research, are flatly contradicted by other remarks of his; but upon the whole this seems to be a most considered statement of his views, and it is one that he made to a friend of many years standing who neither irritated him nor tempted him to be paradoxical.

While he was still in Paris it is probable that he etched "La Source," and possible that he made the lithographs called "La Coiffure" and "La Couronne de fleurs," in all of which the slender forms, the graceful and indeed pretty lines of a more conventional neo-classicism make a strong contrast with the sculptural women of his painting. His drawing, his painting, and his social activities had left him little time for engraving or lithography, but he had abandoned neither, and in these last few years he had produced a score of plates, some of them portraits of Olga, Radiguet, and Paul Valéry; others, like the four lithographs published by Marius de Zayas in 1921, of fairly slender classical figures by the sea, with some beautiful horses. Although he began exact dating at least as early as the studies of his hands at Fontainebleau, he was not yet consistent, and much of this work cannot certainly be assigned to any one season nor even to any one year. Yet the general picture remains: that of a less ponderous neo-classicism making its appearance in drawing, lithography, and etching well before it does so in paint.

Cap d'Antibes, the peninsula that runs out into the Mediterranean between Juan-les-Pins and Antibes, was then almost deserted: a few hotels and villas had sprung up, and the vogue for the Riviera in summer was just beginning, but Antibes itself was still essentially a fishing-village, and what industry it had was based on scent from the cultivated fields of flowers and from the aromatic herbs and bushes that grew all over the rocky headland and the wild country farther from the sea. It is difficult to imagine now, when one is faced with the flood of concrete, the aspiring urban towers, and the hordes of campers bathing cheek by jowl in a polluted soup to the sound of a million transistors while coaches deliver fresh swarms of pale Teutonic flesh to join the tight-packed sweating mass; but it must once have been a paradise. Picasso was happy there, much of the time: the sun poured its energy into him, and at intervals of bathing, eating, and talking with friends, he drew and painted a large number of serene and comely women, many harlequins and saltimbanques, and both Pan and people playing pan-pipes. The women are well-covered (he hated them skinny) but they are no longer massive and their faces are often pretty: most are still more or less classical, at least in their drapery, though the nudes might belong to any age. The saltimbanques never really belonged to our time, and although some of them now take on an eighteenth-century air, particularly the deliberately sentimental "Saltimbanque assis avec canne," often known as "The Sigh," others retain their timelessness and come close to merging with the equally timeless pipe-players in what can be called a classical world: though there is a good case for calling it a world that has always existed and that is still to be seen by the seeing eye around the Mediterranean.

One of these pan-pipe pictures, too outstanding to be really typical, is a big oil of two plump boys on a rampart, seen in conventional perspective, high over the sea: something of the archaic bulk remains in their thick, powerfully modeled bodies, something of the immobility, particularly in the listening figure on the left, but it is no longer stony, and it is tempered with a certain unsentimental grace. They are wearing bathing-trunks and one sits on a block of stone, playing, while the other stands motionless, gazing at nothing with the protuberant eyes that Picasso so often painted in those years. He was very pleased with the picture, which he added to his collection; and it is generally held to be the climax of his classical period.

It was in connection with these boys that Reverdy wrote, "His characters are splendidly immobile; they are solely plastic; and these are the higher qualities of the entirety of his art. Not a single pose, not a single gesture, is anything but the plastic outcome of the means brought into play. Never a head, body, or hand whose position and shape is anything other than an element whose unique purpose is to add to the expressive whole, having no function whatsoever outside the plastic building-up of the picture." I do not quote this to mock Reverdy, whose words seem to me to be profoundly true in the case of Picasso, but partly to give an example of the flood of hurrah-words, unspecific and meaningless except to those who both know the pictures and agree, and applicable to virtually any painting one admires, that constitute a great deal of the literature on Picasso, especially that part of it written by his poetical friends. Yet the real significance of the quotation is that Picasso liked that kind of writing: and it is, after all, a sign of friendship, that quality he valued so highly.

At the same time Cubist still-lives accumulated in his studio; and here too in this immensely productive year there was a most important change. The old rigor of the straight edge and the angular plane gives way to soft curves and flat free-form shapes and to flowing lines that sometimes define a given form but that more often envelop it like an irregular cartouche. This change, as it is so often the case, had been heralded by a few minor works as early as 1922, quite apart from the rococo phase; and now it appeared in full force. Some people, either fascinated by the ascetic analytic period, which to many still seems the true high Cubism, or perhaps so conditioned by association that the image of the eponymous cube with its hard angles seems inseparable from the underlying state of mind that produced the pictures, refused to consider these as part of the tradition at all. However, they were comforted from time to time by the reappearance of the rectilinear compositions, often brilliantly colored, that they were used to.

On another plane, one perhaps less important in the history of art but equally significant in the history of the man, are the many pictures of his family. Señora de Ruiz came to stay with them at Cap d'Antibes, and he painted a portrait of which any mother would be proud and of which no painter would be ashamed, although it was obviously meant to give pleasure to one formed in another age. It is the picture of a dignified middle-aged woman with a fine carriage of her head; her face is set in kindness, but her large black eyes state that she is not to be trifled with. Her son's eyes, by the way, though they are usually described as black, and although they certainly gave that impression, were in fact dark brown: their strange compelling quality and their apparent blackness may have come from their curiously dilated pupils, which even in strong sunlight were as wide as a cat's by night.

And he often drew and painted little Paulo: the boy was now two, walking about and talking better French than either of his parents—his grandmother spoke not a word. Earlier in the year Picasso had made a pastel of him, wearing woolen drawers and clasping a wooden horse: now, copying from a photograph, he painted him sitting nervously on a donkey, still thickly dressed, with a white bonnet: the hairy donkey and the child with the pure lines of his infant face belong to different worlds, both agreeable. Picasso also painted his son in vermilion slippers, drawing at a low table; and the child's apparently non-figurative drawings bear a strong resemblance to those his father was to make next year. There are some pictures of Olga as well: one, a pastel, shows her looking particularly sullen; and in this case the likeness can scarcely have been meant to please.

Perhaps it is no more than coincidence, but 1923 also produced another departure, a picture of three women by the sea, three nudes; and looking at them no one could think of Tanagra nor of Attic grace. One lies on her back, her vast body filling the foreground and her tiny head resting on her hand; another stands with one leg high on a rock and the other, immensely long and ending in a great flat foot, planted on the sand; the third is rushing into the sea. She is so wildly foreshortened that her massive legs are still on the shore while her pinlike head is already a great way off.

For some this picture is four-dimensional, the running figure's elongation being an elongation in time as well as in space; for others it is a skit on the bathers of Cézanne, Renoir, and Matisse. But may it not be the forerunner of the monstrous distortions of the female body that were to appear (or to reappear, when one thinks of the ''Demoiselles'' and some other pictures) in his work a few years later—a savage twisting of forms for which at other times he could show such tender love? As well as the ordinary *intermittences du coeur*, there are periods when most men hate women, seeing them as eaters of their life, as the enemy. Certainly most creative men, who require, and sometimes receive, an exceptional degree of freedom, kindness, and abnegation. The toothed vulva is an image to be found in all ages and all countries; and what adolescent boy has not heard tales of lovers being broken, mutilated, or swallowed up entirely? No simple cause can explain the strength of this emotion, the dark side of the sexual drive; but some part of it may have to do with the resentful acknowledgment of the enemy's indispensability, a resentment all the more furious the greater the male's vitality: and who was more masculine and vital than Picasso? Latent homosexuality is often put forward as a deeplying factor, as well as a host of others, including the fact that in a man's civilization many women are bores out of bed and often in it; and it is surely unnecessary to mention domestic disagreement as an immediate cause, the obvious and apparently rational catalyst that sets the whole complex series of reactions in motion.

Even without this deep revulsion the war between the sexes can be bitter enough, and from daily conflict of interest alone many a loving relationship has ended in hatred: but when the two are combined the results can be spectacular indeed, especially if they are expressed by a man with a perfect command of his medium. Friendship is a somewhat different matter, though it would be a bold writer who presumed to trace the dividing-line; and as it is usually far less intense, so in case of shipwreck it ends in indifference rather than in flaming disaster.

The particular new friendship of this summer did in fact come to an unhappy end some twenty years later, when Breton found that he could not approve of Picasso's attitude during the war; but on the whole Picasso kept his friends. Although he had a very difficult character this was a relationship for which he was peculiarly gifted, so much so that he had many true and deeply affectionate friendships with women, which is more than most men can say.

In 1923 Breton was twenty-seven, a striking, leonine young man with a considerable reputation as a poet. He and Picasso liked one another at once, and very soon Breton's portrait joined that remarkable gallery which, if it were collected together, would show so many of the really interesting men of the first part of the century: the fifteen years between them made no difference, for until physical age forced itself upon his notice Picasso paid little attention to the passing of the calendar years; and even then it did not prevent him from making immediate, direct, and wholly human contact with people of other generations: he was a perpetual contemporary.

It is odd that they should not have known one another earlier, since they had many friends in common, some of whom Breton had met as far back as 1917, when Reverdy founded the review *Nord-Sud*, which Apollinaire, Max Jacob, Aragon, and Breton helped to run; somewhat later he was to be seen in Max Ernst's picture "Au rendez-vous des amis," together with Chirico, Eluard, Desnos, Arp, and others; and naturally he knew Tristan Tzara.

I say naturally because Tzara was not only another of Picasso's friends but also a leading figure among the Dadaists—in fact he was the author of their 1918 Manifesto, no less; and at that time Breton was a Dadaist too. As the sequence of years has been disturbed in these last pages, a backward glance at Dada may restore the order: it might be called an avant-garde artistic movement if garde did not imply some notion of preservation or defense; for the Dadaists did not wish to preserve anything, least of all art as it was generally understood. They were disgusted with the established order; they wished to subvert it; and as far as art was concerned they meant to do away with all existing ideas, replacing the rational by the irrational and divorcing thought from expression. The true parent of Dada was probably Marcel Duchamp with his ready-mades in New York, but it was a group of poets and painters in Zurich, all somewhat anarchistical and most of them refugees from the war, who gave the movement its name (they opened a *Petit Larousse* and settled for the first word they chanced upon), worked out its manifesto, published a review, and opened a gallery. The review reproduced works by Picasso and Modigliani; the gallery showed Kandinsky, Klee, Chirico, and Max Ernst.

As soon as the war was over many Dadaists came to Paris, and they at once began to organize exhibitions and performances, extremely noisy performances that were often broken up by the police. Picasso, perpetually curious, was interested in the movement—he was at one of the meetings at the Théâtre Saint-Michel, where the Dadaists were putting on a kind of anti-play, when the dissident Breton and his followers invaded the stage, and the police arrived to quell the riot—but he was far more interested in the men, several of whom he esteemed.

In time, however, the Dadaists preceived that the weapon with which they were trying to destroy all forms of morality, political government, memory, logic, literature, the plastic arts, including their most recent forms, and the products of the mind in general was in fact the mind itself: this put them out of countenance—they quarreled, excommunicated one another as heretics, and launched passionate anathemas at their former colleagues. The movement died of its inherent contradictions in 1922, and from its ashes arose the more significant, more positive Surrealism, whose manifesto Breton was to write in 1924.

Surrealism interested Picasso infinitely more than Dada; more than any of the movements that had preceded it. The Surrealists proclaimed Picasso as their prophet; they reproduced the "Demoiselles d'Avignon" in *La Révolution surréaliste;* and they pointed to "La Femme en chemise" as an evident precursor of their philosophy. And when the avowed Surrealist painters Chirico, Klee, Ernst, Arp, Miró, and Masson held their first exhibition in Paris they borrowed some Picassos to hang beside their own. Although as a painter Picasso was not a committed Surrealist in the strict sense of the term, nor perhaps in any other, there is no doubt that the Surrealists' work came very close to his own at times; that he watched the movement with the utmost attention; and that it had an important effect upon his work.

For the time being, however, he could not turn his full attention to Surrealism. Not only had he a great number of summer ideas to commit to paint on his return to Paris and a show of his works at Paul Rosenberg's gallery to prepare, but he also had to design the costumes and scenery for another ballet, or rather for a performance that in many ways resembled a ballet.

This was *Mercure, poses plastiques,* and it was to be staged by Etienne de Beaumont, with music by Satie and choreography by Massine. The Surrealists, as puritanical as most revolutionaries, disapproved of the ballet as decadent and bourgeois; but even if Picasso could have been prevented from doing what he chose by what other people said, their words would have amounted to nothing compared with the fact that Derain, Braque, and Gris had all entered the same field and that they had done remarkably well. And far more important, Matisse agreed to do the curtain, sets, and costumes for Stravinsky's *Chant du Rossignol.* When Picasso heard the news he cried out angrily, "Matisse! What is a Matisse? A balcony with a big red flowerpot falling all over it."

Conscious, perhaps, of the Surrealists' severe and respectable gaze, and certainly aware of his friends' achievements, he turned to *Mercure* - with more zeal than to any ballet since *Parade*; and when in June, 1924, the audience gathered in the theater they beheld neither Naturalism on the curtain nor angular Cubism on the stage, but a new Picasso devoted to the flowing line.

On the subdued, twilight curtain they saw two familiar figures, a tall white harlequin playing a guitar and a red pierrot playing a fiddle; but they were enveloped rather than defined by undulating continuous curves, and this dynamic line set the key for everything that appeared when the curtain rose to show a totally unfamiliar world. Much of the scenery also flowed, not only figuratively, not only in its line, but in fact: it was made of great free-form shapes that vaguely hinted at the form of the more precise signs inscribed within them or overflowing the borders and drawn with curved, black-painted wire or supple rods. Since the argument of the ballet had to do with the capers of Mercury some of the figures were those of horses, a chariot and so on; they moved not only as entities but also within themselves. The Managers in *Parade* had walked about and even danced, but this was entirely different—this was more the presence of mobiles, forming not only the setting for the ballet but an integral part of its motion. Night, for example, a woman on a starry bed, swung to and fro.

It is a pity that so much creative power should have been spent on a libretto that was by all accounts devoid of inspiration if not downright offensive, but *Mercure* was Picasso's farewell and it was fitting that he should end his association with the ballet in a blaze of glory before going back to his real and solitary vocation.

Of relative glory: the public, even the restricted public of the Soirées de Paris (that was the name of Beaumont's entertainments, and they were charity performances, under the patronage of the President of the Republic, for the benefit of war-widows and the Russian refugees), did not like the ballet as a whole, nor was it a success in later performances; but the setting was admired, and what is more, Picasso's contribution to *Mercure* converted the Surrealists. They had begun by disliking the whole idea: during the earlier scenes Breton, Aragon, Soupault, and their friends booed, hissed, and hooted; but they stayed to applaud and the next day they wrote to *Paris-Journal* to apologize, saying, "We wish to express our profound and total admiration for Picasso, who, despising all sacrosanct convention, has never paused in his perpetual creation of the disquiet, the searching anxiety of our modern days nor in giving it the highest form of expression . . . Picasso, *far beyond his colleagues*, is now to be seen as the everlasting incarnation of youth and the unquestionable master of the situation."

Chapter XIII

MODERNISMO had had a powerful effect on the adolescent Picasso; but Modernismo was an indefinable atmosphere made up of countless different and often contradictory elements rather than a coherent movement. Fauvism too had had its influence, yet here the effect was to bring about a violent reaction; and a lover of paradox could maintain that the true father of Cubism was therefore Matisse. All the other movements of his twenties and thirties had left Picasso untouched; but now Surrealism attracted him as no other had ever done.

Yet before deciding how much Surrealism influenced Picasso and to what extent he was himself a Surrealist, it might be as well to ask whether the question is rightly posed, whether in its plastic aspect Surrealism did not originate with him—whether the Surrealists were not in fact Picassoites rather than the other way about.

They certainly thought that their aesthetic was exemplified in some of his works. André Breton said, "If Surrealism is to adopt a line of conduct, it has only to pass where Picasso has already passed and where he will pass again." But what Breton and his friends saw in the "Femme en chemise" for example and what Picasso felt when he was painting it may have been as widely different as their views on what constituted Surrealism.

For Picasso the meaning of the word was much nearer Apollinaire's: speaking to André Warnod in 1945 he said, "I attempt to observe nature, always. I am intent on resemblance, and resemblance more real than the real, attaining the surreal. It was in this way that I thought of Surrealism," and André Warnod was a very old friend—he had been one of the guests at the banquet to Rousseau. Brassaï was another friend to whom Picasso was likely to open his true mind, and to Brassaï he said, "For my part I always aim at likeness. . . . For me surreality is nothing else, never has been anything else, than that deep likeness far beyond the shapes and colors of immediate appearance."

For the Surrealists themselves their movement was at once simpler and far more complex. The simplicity lay in the notion that transcendence could be achieved by deliberately and "scientifically" bringing the subconscious into play and making this the dominant factor rather than the host of infinitely delicate interacting forces set in motion by aesthetic sense, cerebration, keen intelligence, and innumerable other motors including no doubt the subconscious as well, to say nothing of genius; the complexity in the immense apparatus of symbols, things-in-themselves, references, associations, programs, and eroticism that they used according to their abilities in trying to achieve their stated aim of facing the material world with closed eyes, of letting "a certain psychic automatism" take over the controls in order "to set free what lies, unknown to him, in the depths of a man's mind," and of consciously trying with all their might to be unconscious.

Obviously the Surrealists were very much in debt to Freud, whose teachings were widely and sometimes accurately diffused by the early twenties; but although these doctrines were of great value to what was primarily an intellectual and literary movement they were of less relevance to the Surrealist painters, for whom in any case the oneiric vision cannot have been so startlingly fresh, since they had before them the example of Bosch, not to mention Signorelli, Arcimboldo, Fuseli, and so many others. And for painters even the explicit theory had nothing particularly new about it, seeing that long before this Redon had said, "Everything is done by a quiet submission to the coming of the unconscious mind," and Matisse, "You begin painting well when your hand escapes from your head." Besides, although it is possible to speak, write, and even draw "automatically" with one's eyes shut, and the more earnest Surrealists really did so, it is much harder to paint, and the painters were at a disadvantage. These handicaps, less evident in the days of Chirico, became obvious in the decline of the movement, when the puerilities of the second generation of Surrealists were little more than illustrations of fabricated, unconvincing dreams, of essentially literary anecdotes as old-fashioned as Art Nouveau.

Not surprisingly in a man who so valued his privacy, Picasso loathed Freud and all his works, maintaining that Freudian psychology was unscientific; nor, although no man was less of a prude, did he care for Freud's great emphasis on the sexual drive, which also filled the Surrealist pictures with so many symbols.

On the face of it there was a great deal to set Picasso and the Surrealists apart, the most important being a radical difference of vision, and, if the hypothesis of exorcism is correct, a radically different purpose; for whereas in some of his most important pictures Picasso's aim was surely to cast out a spirit, the Surrealists' was to call it up; and this they did consciously, to the utmost extent of their powers. "Surrealism's dearest aim now and in the future must be the artificial reproduction of the ideal moment in which a man is prey to a particular emotion," said Breton.

Yet Surrealism was also a state of mind, an anarchistic, turbulent, youthful, sanguine, iconoclastic state of mind that matched Picasso's. He was far too much of an individualist to like the Surrealists' rigid sectarianism or to put up with the papal role assumed by Breton; but no bull presumed to gore Picasso; the Surrealists treated him with great respect, and he was much attached to the poets, the flower of the movement, Leiris, Eluard, Aragon, Desnos, Soupault. There were times when he was so close to the Surrealists that they could claim him as one of themselves without provoking a denial on his part or incredulity on that of the public.

Even so, their ideas did not yet impinge upon him in their full force, partly because they had not at this time been fully formulated, much less carried into practice, and partly because he was still at the height of his dinner-jacket period.

The dandy had revived, and he wore his dinner-jacket with a difference; for while in those times ordinary men put on a black waistcoat, Picasso girt his evening loins with the old Catalan *faixa* of his Barcelona days. It is a long strip of cloth, black or red and fringed at the ends, that goes three or four times round one's waist, giving grateful warmth and support but making it impossible to take one's trousers off quickly. It is considered a very healthy garment all round the Mediterranean, and on settling in Paris Picasso long retained his, wearing it under his overalls as a protection against the falling damps of Montmartre; but now it shone, a pure ornament, in the dry, well-warmed drawing-rooms of his grander friends. There is a photograph of him wearing his *faixa* in conjunction with a boiled shirt and black tie under a bullfighter's embroidered jacket at a great ball given by the Beaumonts in 1924. He stands, straight and proud, between Madame Errazuriz and Olga, who glare rigidly at one another like a pair of angry cats: he seems quite detached.

If he was detached from these two ladies, he was even more so from his former life. Montmartre saw him no more; nor did Saint-Germain-des-Prés, then the great resort of all those who counted in the arts and of far greater numbers who did not but who nevertheless had known Picasso well.

The summer of 1924 found the Picassos at Juan-les-Pins again, but apart from some tall, slim, pretty Graces and some draped standing or sitting figures, poor relations of his water-carriers, the ancient world, Pan, fauns, satyrs, did not make their way into his studio. Indeed, this year was the end, the rather disappointing end, of his neo-classic period as it is ordinarily understood and perhaps of his specifically Italian memories and associations; yet his minotaurs, nymphs, and demi-gods were not far away, and they were to reappear in his work, particularly in his drawings and engravings, every time he came back to the south.

His great achievements during 1924 and the years that followed were big still-lives, full of color: they could be called Cubist, and they retain many of the traditional objects such as guitars, bottles, sheets of music, often set on a table, although synthesis and simultaneity have receded almost as far as the straight line. These most decorative pictures are all curves, a far cry from those he painted twelve years before in a different world: and they are informed by a different spirit, as though Picasso were drawing on a private source of joy, less esoteric and more generally available, though not necessarily of a lower order.

This source may have been the presence of his son. Paulo seems to have been an entrancing little boy, and Picasso was not the only father to see his first-born as a continuation of himself, a promise of physical immortality, a *non omnis moriar* with pretty ways: something of great consequence to a man who hates the idea of death.

He painted and drew him; most significantly a large oil of this year shows Paulo dressed as a harlequin; and what is more, from this point on the harlequin, as an important symbol, vanishes from Picasso's work. The child sits as good as can be, sideways on an upholstered chair, his feet dangling, and he gazes out at his father a little anxiously, his head held up and his hands clasped on his knee. He has evidently wriggled at some time, because two ghostly feet can still be seen to the left of his present position. Another, painted some months later, when Paulo was just four, shows him as a torero in the traditional *traje de luz,* with the arcades of a huge bull-ring in the distance. In these pictures the little boy's pure lines, eyes, and complexion have the same infinite tenderness that are to be seen in Renoir's portraits of his own son; the similarity is increased by both children's having auburn hair and the delicate skin that goes with it; and perhaps at that time the feelings of the two painters were much the same.

There were some landscapes too, views of the village with its lovely umbrella-pines and the sea beyond, and of course a great many drawings, watercolors and gouaches: among them is a small papier collé, a still-life in front of a window whose lace curtain must surely have been taken from some catalog. And this little picture, rather severe apart from the absurd lace, seems almost archaic in 1924; it contrasts so strongly with the curvilinear Cubism of the middle twenties that one wonders whether a term so all-embracing serves much purpose.

The statement that *Mercure* was Picasso's farewell to the ballet is not quite accurate, since a few days after *Mercure*'s first night Diaghilev put on Cocteau's *Train bleu* at the Théâtre des Champs-Elysées, with music by Milhaud and Picasso's enormous women, enormously enlarged, as the curtain—the ballet was about people playing on the beach, so they were appropriate, in a way. But Picasso did nothing about the scenery, which was designed by the sculptor Laurens, nor about the costumes, which were the work of Chanel. Yet this does not mean the Picassos had lost interest in the ballet; they were both often to be seen at performances, and Olga took particular pleasure in the company of the dancers; apart from anything else, they spoke her language. And she would scarcely have been human if she had not relished the contrast between her precarious maiden days and her present security as the wife of a successful, and financially successful, man, and if she had not been happy to show her expensive clothes, her elegant flat, to her former colleagues, now in a most uneasy situation. She was living well, and whatever her origins may have been, she behaved in a way she thought suitable for nobles: the nursemaid who took Paulo walking was required to keep three paces behind her charge, a spectacle that amazed her neighbors, of whom Matisse was one.

From the financial point of view Picasso was doing well: he bought a motor-car, which at that time was a prodigious status-symbol; and since neither then nor at any later period could he ever learn to drive, he employed a chauffeur, a more impressive symbol still. Even now among painters a large car retains a certain mystic aura, and Saint-Germain-des-Prés will not soon forget the universal howl of indignation, envy, and disapprobation that greeted Bernard Buffet's appearance in a white Rolls-Royce.

Towards Christmas his year's work culminated in the great still-life called "Nature morte à la tranche de melon." A table, of course, a guitar, some music, a slice of melon, all on a splendid red patterned cloth or rug: and on the left a newcomer, the classical bust or portrait-head that in various forms was to inhabit so many pictures in the years to come. Here it is black, with its Roman features briefly sketched—a nose and eye in Cubist profile—a calm figure in a picture so full of life that the French term *nature morte* seems even more than usually inappropriate.

The year 1925 began with the same rich tranquillity: more glowing still-lives, those charming domestic portraits, a pleasant girl with a mandolin, all denials of his statement that painting had nothing to do with decoration. Then in the spring the Picassos went to Monte Carlo, where

Diaghilev was rehearsing his company. Picasso came not as a collaborator but as a friend; nevertheless he spent hours and hours at the rehearsals, making beautiful flowing classical line-drawings of the dancers at work or resting.

The smooth flow of his days came to an abrupt, even a violent, end with the news of Pichot's death. Ramon Pichot and Picasso had not seen much of one another since Fernande's unfortunate visit to Céret in 1912, but before that they had been very close friends. Picasso reacted furiously to criticism, but, despising weakness and want of courage more than anything, he respected those few who stood up to him: and in addition to strength, Pichot possessed a mass of qualities that commanded respect and affection, a high sense of honor being one of them, and independence another. He was neither a very good nor a successful painter, but being a far more cultured man that most of his colleagues he managed to live reasonably well by finding rare books for an American bibliophile, seeking them out not only at auctions and among the antiquarian dealers but in the second-hand shops and the stalls along the banks of the Seine: this was a calling that Apollinaire and many another well-read penniless literary man had followed, sometimes with great profit, and if he had not been so scrupulous Pichot might have made a large amount of money—his employer was a millionaire, his search often fortunate. But the millionaire had proposed a monthly sum; Pichot had accepted; and his principles did not allow him to profit from his bargains in any way. The profit went to Dives.

Picasso often quarreled with his friends, sometimes with extreme violence; but he hated to let them go entirely and he rarely or never dismissed them from his mind—that was not in his concept of the relationship. His liking would survive the quarrel, often for many years, and often the friendship would revive, sometimes diminished, as in the case of Braque, sometimes stronger, as in that of Matisse. He had loved Pichot; his affection had lived on through the intervening years; and it survived Pichot's death, for in spite of all his reasons for resenting Germaine Pichot he helped her when she was old.

The irremediable loss of a friend was enough to distress him; but in Pichot he also lost an important part of his youth, going back to the Quatre Gats and his earliest days in Paris. There were not many others he had known so long or loved so much: Manolo was far away, so was Max Jacob, and Apollinaire was dead. Then again there was Pichot's intimate connection with Casagemas, whose death had affected Picasso so profoundly and for so long.

In addition to all this the news reached him at a time when a deep dissatisfaction seems to have been taking shape in his mind: a dissatisfaction with his way of life and more specifically with Olga; an awareness that his painting of the last few years, although it was enough to make any other man's reputation and although it was widely recognized and applauded, lacked the explosive force it had once possessed, as though by the age of forty-four he had already made all his most important discoveries and as though a well-fed man in a well-cut suit with a handkerchief in his breast-pocket and a neat bow-tie had necessarily sold his private sun.

The result was the violent, convulsive picture called "La Danse," or "The Three Dancers." He may have begun painting it before he heard of Pichot, but if so by the time he had finished the original intention was entirely overlaid. He worked on it for months, just as he had worked on the "Demoiselles d'Avignon"; and the pictures are comparable in their importance and their shocking impact.

They are also comparable in size: the canvas is seven feet in length and the grotesque, barbaric figures stretch to more than human height as they dance, their hands linked, against a tall french window, partly closed, that provides two great rectangles of blue framed in black and that shows a black balcony beyond. The body of the central figure, naked and flesh-colored, is a long taut line from foot to head against the dark-blue gap between the windows: her arms reach high and wide. The savage figure on the left, more wildly distorted by far and in frenzied movement, wrenches her head back at right-angles to her trunk; her breasts fly high and her left hand joins the other's right; she has a diagonally-striped kilt, and on her left side an unexplained saw-edged shape, perhaps part of her, points towards the middle of the picture. Her small round head, mad, ecstatic, or agonized, with its mouth like a toothed vulva, is more extreme than anything in the "Demoiselles d'Avignon." Over on the other side a calmer, comparatively sexless, brown and white figure also dances (they each have one foot raised) with its right hand straight and high, holding the first woman's upstretched left, while its other reaches behind her pink waist to link with the second's brutish paw, thus completing the chain. And behind this third figure, his head defined by the raised arms, looms the somber form of Ramon Pichot, as black as the window-frames and as massive as an Easter Island statue—a silhouette. But it is the young Pichot, the Ramonet whom Picasso knew long before Pichot grew his striking beard. We know it is he, or rather his presence, because Picasso told Penrose so, saying that "La Danse" should really be called "The Death of Pichot."

The picture is shocking, beautiful, and terrible; and if "La Danse" is not a proof of Picasso's faith in the power of exorcism then the whole theory falls to the ground and he was not telling Malraux the truth. It was a turning-point in Picasso's painting almost as important for him though not for the course of Western art as the "Demoiselles," although its effects were far less immediately obvious. The "Demoiselles" had been the most violent possible break with tradition; but a virginity cannot be lost more than once and a man cannot destroy a tradition that he has already shattered. Then Picasso never felt that he had really finished the "Demoiselles," and for months after putting it to one side he kept making different versions of various parts—postscripts to the main picture. Nothing of the kind happened with "La Danse"; and what is more, instead of moving straight on into a new country once he had painted it, Picasso returned to his still-lives, as though the exorcism had worked entirely.

Most authorities say that after Monte Carlo the Picassos went to Juan-les-Pins for the summer of 1925; and either there or in some unnamed but certainly Mediterranean retreat he certainly painted, and dated, several more of these pictures, as if his flow had never been interrupted. One of them has a fish-net, carefully brought into existence by a point scraping away the dark surface to show the light priming underneath: another has a splendid ram's head, lying among sea-shells: and another is dominated by the bust of a bearded classical person, with a couple of arms broken from a statue on the table beneath him. They are quite large for this kind of painting, about four foot by three; they are all highly colored; they are all in the general Cubist idiom, particularly the last, in which a set-square and some fine hard angles recall the severity of former years; and, so long as the definition of the term is wide enough, they and most of the painting of these years can be said to represent late Cubism, a Cubism diluted from the point of view of discipline, cerebral rigor, and clarity, but sumptuously enriched from that of curve, color, and sensuous relish.

If he had not seen the entirely exceptional "Dancers," a critic writing in the middle twenties might have supposed that the different currents of Picasso's thought were now converging to form the mainstream of his art, a stream that would carry with it all he had learned in the various regions he had explored but that would run its course with no new important tributary.

The critic, with his hypothesis of a unified vision, would find it difficult to account for the curious drawings made about this time, unlike anything Picasso had done before or was ever to do again. The easiest solution would be to dismiss them as unimportant exceptions; and striking though they are, no one would claim that they are epoch-making. They consist of dots joined by lines. The dots vary from the size of a pea to that of a pin-head: the lines are sometimes straight, more often curved. Sometimes the drawings have to do with violins or guitars, but those which are perhaps the most confident and most successful seem to be abstract calligraphies; and it may be that when he made them he had the Surrealists' sessions of automatism in mind. But their great significance is that they prove his readiness and his ability to break out in new directions.

The form that his new directions would take could be foretold by no one: the time of their beginning was less unpredictable. Picasso was the very type of the creative man, and since upon the whole creative men have more sensibility than they have sense it is rare to find them happy; in a world that has so much to distress even a common mind they pay a high price for their keener perceptions. And often their sexual drive is very strong, which may procure them vehement joys but which is quite certain to lead to unhappiness, equally piercing and far more durable. Picasso's own emotions were passionate, complex, and extreme; he had been brought up in a culture that had little to say to self-control in personal relationships; and early in his life both Señora de Ruiz and Fernande observed that his nature was not of a kind to make him happy.

Whether this was inevitable or not, whether or not fate, the planets, or his humors necessarily put steady mild contentment, domestic felicity, out of his reach, he now had external reasons for unhappiness: his marriage was deteriorating, and some years later it fell to pieces entirely. That it should have lasted so long is puzzling until one recollects Picasso's strange want of decision in ordinary life, the extreme difficulty he experienced whenever he had to make up his mind, a characteristic noticed by all his friends from Sabartés to Françoise Gilot. When it was all over Gertrude Stein wrote: "when I saw him again I said how did you ever make the decision and keep it of leaving your wife. Yes he said you and I we have weak characters and no initiative and if I had died before I did it you would never have thought that I had a strong enough character to do this thing. No I said I did not think you ever could really do a thing like that, hitherto when you changed anything somebody always took you away and this time nobody did and how did it happen. I suppose he said when a thing is where there is no life left then you either die or go on living, well he said that is what happened to me."

It may be that a man has only a given power of decision, and if he uses it all up, making vital choices every day in his studio, he has none left for everyday life. Certainly Picasso came to none as far as his marriage was concerned during these years that led to the great depression, nor about his way of life. His show at Paul Rosenberg's gallery was one of the fashionable events of 1926; the same year found him at a fancy-dress party given by the Beaumonts at Antibes, for he spent that summer at Juan-les-

Pins once more, just along the coast; and when he went down to Barcelona in the autumn for a big show at the Galerias Dalmau (which also included Dalí, Jaume Sunyer, Manolo, Robert Delaunay, Raoul Dufy, and Marie Laurencin) he stayed at the Ritz. When he was interviewed on this occasion he begged them not to ask him to talk about painting: his trade was simply to paint and to draw. Making up his mind was a long process with Picasso: the seed of an aesthetic idea, for example, often took several years to germinate. But the process, with its hesitations, reversals, and changes of attitude can be followed in his work: most clearly, of course, where his thoughts on expression—on what was to be expressed and how it was to be accomplished—are concerned, but also in connection with the whole man, the source of the expression itself. It is absurd to make a distinction between even a mediocre artist and the man—no disembodied spirit ever held a pen or brush—and even more absurd in the case of painters like Picasso, whose lives, including of course their sexual lives, and painting were so inseparably linked. Renoir, asked whether painting came from the heart or the head, said, "From the balls"; and Cézanne's words, though coarser, mean much the same. This conjunction, so clear in so many great men, is even more obvious in Picasso: the tide of his work obeyed the pull of Venus and each new love was marked by a flood, each new disappointment by an ebb that left strange wreckage on the shore. For a great many years common circumstances, wealth and poverty, success or the want of it, squalor or comfort, had no effect upon him; but women always did, and so did family.

Olga was both woman and family: and she was cursed with a jealous, possessive nature, and with as little training in self-control as her husband. She had nothing to do—servants were plentiful then—and her decisions were at once simpler and more easily reached. "After a while," says Crespelle, "she had only one aim left in life—to make her husband's existence unbearable—and she even gave up her social activities to devote herself entirely to this exhilarating task." Crespelle is not a wholly reliable witness, but even a far less extreme attitude on Olga's part, to say nothing of the dark, impersonal revolt against women in general, would be quite enough to account for the monsters that began to appear in her husband's painting.

She had no obvious causes for dissatisfaction: Picasso, though a difficult and exigent companion at times, had a great deal of kindness to make up for it; he had given her a nationality, a handsome income, and a baby; he was at least an adequate husband. But want of obvious causes has never prevented anyone from being dissatisfied and it does not appear that she ever had much liking for Picasso or his work. Then again the gap be-

tween her social pretentions and her real acceptability would set up conflicts that could only result in gloom, a gloom increased by the fact that
an active ballerina's liver, kept as trim as an egg by daily exercise, is apt
to grow flabby and sullen when she leaves the stage. And as for the baby,
it does not seem to have been markedly less disappointing, troublesome,
noisy, selfish, and unamiable than most as it grew to be a child and then a
hairy adolescent.

Picasso himself said that his work was his diary, and although it is easy
to read this diary in too literal or too literary a fashion, the presence of
these monsters is deeply significant: so is the absence of the child: there is
no important reference to Paulo between the brush-drawing of a child
with a rocking-horse in 1926 and the painting of the boy dressed as a pierrot in 1929. And after that, nothing at all.

One of the earliest of the monsters is the "Femme endormie dans un
fauteuil" of January, 1927, a grotesquely distorted figure with her snout-
like face thrown back, her toothed and probably snoring mouth wide
open: the metamorphosis of a woman's body into an amoeba with a cruel
and deadly trap, the whole defined by a flowing line as firm and solid as
those which surround stained glass. But before the "Femme endormie"
he had made a collage: he took a floor-cloth, made a hole in the middle,
stuck it to a canvas beside a long piece of newspaper, stretched two vertical strings to turn it into a guitar, and then drove sharp nails right through
from behind so that their points stood out a couple of inches. Although
this sounds innocuous or even trifling, the effect of the rough texture of
the cloth, of the menacing nails, and of the whole spare composition is
very striking indeed: the savagery of the collage is surely allied to that
which produced the painting, and here the symbolism is clear enough; in
Spain a guitar, with its curves, its hole, and its responsive cords often
figures a woman's body, and Picasso had used the metaphor quite explic-
itly, though more kindly, in former years.

Yet these were early days: they were not all trouble and strife, and his
painting was not filled with these toothed, predatory women. An artist in
his studio, sometimes a painter, sometimes a sculptor, often with a
model, made his appearance as a member of Picasso's cast: this figure,
who was to stay until the end of Picasso's life, takes a great many forms,
none of them to begin with self-regarding.

He is often a burly man, bearded, rather classical apart from his drawers, apparently bemused or stupid, as a bull seems bemused at times or
stupid; and in one of the first etchings he is sitting right up to his easel,
gazing intently at or through his model while his right hand sweeps out a
magnificent series of curves and rectilinear planes that on the face of it

seem to have little relation to her, for she is a pleasant middle-aged woman in a pinafore, knitting, and like the artist himself she is drawn with that perfection of descriptive realism which Picasso could produce whenever he chose.

It would be extremely interesting to know whether the etching was made before Vollard began talking to Picasso about his intention of bringing out an illustrated edition of Balzac's *Chef d'oeuvre inconnu* or not, since the book is about a painter whose masterpiece can be understood by no one but himself, but unfortunately scholars differ and Vollard's own memoirs are vague. It would also be interesting to know whether Picasso read the book through: from his description of it to Geneviève Laporte many years later it would seem that he did not, yet few works could have pleased him more. Very briefly the tale, set in 1612, is this: the youthful Nicolas Poussin goes to see the well-known painter Pourbus in the rue des Grands-Augustins, and after some hesitation he walks in at the same time as a rich aged man called Frenhofer. Frenhofer criticizes Pourbus' work with great freedom, saying some remarkable things about painting: Poussin, unknown to either, breaks in and is acknowledged by both as a true artist. Pourbus is kind to the young man; urges him to work; tells him that Frenhofer was a pupil of Mabuse, is now a painter, amateur in the sense that he has never had to sell, being rich, but so brilliant that Pourbus has taken his work for Giorgione's. The acquaintance grows, helped by the fact that Poussin has a lovely young mistress ("one of those generous, noble souls who come to suffer with a great man, sharing his anguish and his difficulties and doing their utmost to understand his whims, resistant to poverty and strong for love") whom Frenhofer would like as a model. Presently they are all in Frenhofer's studio, where Poussin sees some astonishing pictures that Frenhofer dismisses as of no great worth, nothing to compare with his masterpiece: he is unwilling to show this masterpiece, but eventually does so. Poussin can make out nothing in the chaos of colors, "the uncertain graduations, the kind of formless haze" except for "one exquisite, living foot." He says he can see no woman there at all. Frenhofer weeps, comforts himself for the moment by imagining that they are thieves, but burns his picture that same night and dies.

At all events, when at last it was printed in 1931, the book contained etchings, together with many of Picasso's dot-designs and some Cubist drawings that certainly preceded Vollard's idea, in addition to some etchings certainly made for the purpose—eighty illustrations in all.

And then apart from his work, Picasso also led a more varied, less fashionable life, seeing something of his older friends and still more of the Surrealists, whose ideas on neolithic, Eskimo, Oceanic, and particularly Easter Island art interested him. There was also death to be reckoned with: death, which always surprised and distressed Picasso, although it was so much part of his culture. Modigliani had died in poverty, alcoholic and consumptive, some years before, at the age of thirty-six. (His dealer, giving him forty francs and a bottle of brandy for each picture, had scarcely prolonged his life.) And now it was the forty-year-old Gris, undermined by earlier privations, whom Picasso followed to the grave.

That summer, the summer of 1927, he spent at Cannes, and although there are some monstrous women, including the frighteningly malevolent "Femme assise," it is tempting to see a memory of happier days and of Gris in the quite unexpected and almost pure synthetic Cubism of "L'Atelier," a big picture, some five feet by eight, of a painter with his brush poised, looking at a fruit-bowl and a white bust on a red-covered table. Formally almost pure: but the spirit is quite different; so is the nature of the legibility, and the whole statement is of another order, as though Picasso were not looking back at all but rather forward to a world dominated by human relationships.

Sculpture was also in his mind again: his friends' proposals for a monument to Apollinaire would have brought it back if it had ever been absent, which, when one considers the sculptural nature of much of his work in the twenties, is most unlikely. And now he made several strongly modeled drawings that were in fact studies for figures in the round, one of which he carried out when he returned to Paris.

The resulting bronze had nothing to do with Apollinaire, however: his monument, the real Picasso monument to Apollinaire, never left the stage of drawings, and the half-hidden object that was eventually set up by the municipality near the abbey-church of Saint-Germain-des-Prés after years and years of wrangling is nothing more than a rather unsatisfactory head of Dora Maar, who had not the least connection with the poet apart from the fact that both she and Apollinaire, at a distance of a generation, were deeply attached to Picasso. The 1927/28 figure was another example of Picasso's metamorphoses of the female body, in which breasts, limbs, heads, and features are not only distorted but redistributed: a passionate metamorphosis with a strong sexual element, often very cruel, as retaliation for cruelty is apt to be.

Conceivably in an attempt to please, even to placate, his wife, Picasso returned to Dinard for the summer holidays of 1928 and 1929; and naturally enough the sexual element traveled with him. Whoever speaks of sex speaks of symbolism and plunges straight into the deepest, darkest water known to man. I have no intention of floundering where the wisest heads can scarcely keep afloat, and I shall do no more than point out that the women in the many beach-scenes he painted here, like those he drew at Cannes, are preoccupied with keys, with fitting keys into the key-holes of their bathing-cabins. Keys were of a great though perhaps undefined importance to Picasso: he carried a heavy bunch of them and when they wore through his pockets (he never had the good fortune to find a woman who could sew) he attached them to his person with string. "I am very fond of keys," he said to Antonina Valentin. "It seems to me very important to have one. It is true that keys have often haunted me. In the series of bathing men and women there is always a door which they try to open with a big key." Clearly, those who are outside and who want to get in will use a key, perhaps the wrong one, just as those who wish to communicate will use a language, sometimes misunderstood, even incomprehensible.

These little beach-scenes of brightly striped figures playing with a ball strike many people as cheerful, and indeed the colors are gay enough: others find the distorted triangular bodies with their tiny heads, flat, oar-like limbs, and emphatic sexual organs obscurely menacing and oppressive. Yet Picasso was not more than usually oppressed at Dinard: for one thing his friend the Surrealist poet George Hugnet was staying close at hand, which provided him if not with rational then at least with agreeable company. There is something oddly touching about Picasso's love for poets and about his way of lumping them all together: so long as they wrote verse it does not appear that he made much distinction between them— Breton, Reverdy, Desnos, Cocteau, Leiris, Eluard, Aragon, Hugnet, Salmon, Apollinaire, Jacob, and many others were all seen and often drawn with the same kindly eye, and for several of them he provided illustrations to help sell their books. Max Jacob, it is true, sometimes tried Picasso's friendship very hard, not so much by selling Picasso's presents and not so much by his prolonged retreat to Saint-Benoît as by his convert's zeal, which made him at times more Catholic than the Pope while at others his obscure loves caused him to labor under a sense of sin—an unrestful companion. Now, in 1928, he was in Paris once more, living in high style at the Hôtel Nollet, with a car-borne friend, selling his gouaches well and dining out continually, and once more Picasso drew his portrait, a bald, plump Max Jacob, crowned with a laurel-wreath that might to a necromancer have signified the Légion d'honneur he was to be given or even the fortune that he was presently to acquire. This fortune was not the reward of his widely-known, little read, and rarely reprinted books, but the result of an accident in his friend's motor-car: it was pitifully small, but at least it allowed him to buy an annuity of 9,400 francs (then about £100 or $420)—just enough for him to flee temptation, to return to his village and lead a monastic life with his food assured for the first time since he left home.

The essence of their friendship was unchanged, but they now lived in worlds that rarely overlapped. Picasso's was not the happiest he had known: far from it. He was probably the best-known painter in Europe; he was working hard; yet already he looked back to the Bateau-Lavoir with longing. Art is often said to be the result of conflict—no call for art in Eden—and on the simple-minded basis of equating conflict and output it could be asserted that Picasso's life, and particularly these years of it, was spectacularly unhappy, for his production was enormous. On the other hand no man connected with the arts will deny that there are immense compensations—that when the tension is not too great and that when his work runs well he finds a peace entirely of his own.

Work was not only a necessity for Picasso: it was also his surest refuge; and his mind turning more and more to sculpture, for which his flat in the rue La Boëtie was not suitable, he went to Juli González' workshop when he came back from Dinard in the autumn of 1928.

Picasso had known the González brothers since the time of the Quatre Gats and his earliest days in Paris, for in spite of their name they were Barcelona Catalans and they had migrated to France in 1899. Their father had had a forge, working mostly in wrought iron, and the brothers were accustomed to metal from their childhood. Juli had first to be a painter, but his gift did not lie that way, and by the time Picasso came to work at his place he had not yet discovered that his true vocation was that of a sculptor, although he was now in his fifties. He was a modest, retiring man, somewhat lost since the death of his elder brother, and he looked upon himself as a craftsman, no more: and a fine craftsman he was, the kind that Picasso loved, with a deep understanding of the nature of his material and a complete mastery of his techniques: among others he was perfectly familiar with that of oxyacetylene welding, which he had learned at the Renault factory during the war.

It was in González's workshop that Picasso said, "I feel as happy again as I was in 1908"—when Cubism was in its first flood and before Fernande plagued him with her "little ways"—and with Juli's help he made a fascinating sculpture or openwork construction of slim iron rods. The welded points of junction give it something of the appearance of his dot drawings; the severity is allied to the Cubist "Atelier" of early 1928, and the triangles to the Dinard women on the beach; but this cage full of light is something quite new, new in Picasso and almost entirely new in sculpture, although in another spirit Lipchitz was already using strips of metal and wire to make his figures transparent. Most of the lines are straight, but towards one end there is a large oval traversed by a long rod with a small disk on top of it, and this oval is connected to a pair of upright curves by two double triangles. The composition is certainly not abstract, but it is not clearly legible either and it has been read in many ways, one being that the oval form with a pin head is a woman and that the curves are a fleeing man, held back by the triangular arms.

He probably made several of his other constructions with González in 1928 and early 1929, though the dating is obscure; but he did not carry out the plans he had made at Dinard for some monumental figures. It is difficult to say how big they were meant to be from the drawings, but they would surely have been immense: he had had the notion of setting them along the Croisette, and if the municipality had not been so appalled by the news from America—in October, 1929, the New York stock-market crashed, and it was obvious that the great depression must reach Europe very soon—Cannes might conceivably now possess the most striking sea-front in the world. The great figures seem to be made of smooth bone, and some people speak of a "bone period" starting at about this time in both his painting and his sculpture. The two were indeed more closely related now than at any other time, partly because the huge figures could not be realized by a private man, not even by one so well-to-do as Picasso, and the sculpture therefore overflowed into the other medium. One monument, for example, is a terrible woman's head thirty feet high: two fixed, stupid eyes surmount it; there is a hint of nostrils to the left, while sparse strands of hair appear to the right and a toothed sideways mouth in the middle, the whole poised on or against what must be a great block of masonry, if not a house.

But most of the projected "bone" sculptures are as calm as the word monument, and so are the earlier paintings into which the sculptural feeling moved: there is one of a woman in an armchair, one of the several works of this period called "Métamorphose," that is as smooth and serene as the moon. Yet at the same time, in the vast and even bewildering quantity of work that Picasso poured out, we also see the return of the minotaur, once in the shape of an immense papier collé; the last picture of his son; the seven-foot iron sculpture called "La Femme au jardin"; a number of metamorphic heads; and still another "Femme dans un fauteuil," a savage one this time, like the 1927 picture but even more extreme.

Then as the summer of 1929 approached, the monsters and the bone figures came together in one of the most horrifying and the most moving of his paintings, the "Femme assise au bord de la mer." The pale wood of which she is made is as smooth as bone, and the articulations of her spine are clearly to be seen. She sits sideways in the sand with her back to the sea and the paler sky, her hands linked on her upraised knee, one taut arm parallel with the horizon, the wrinkled elbow being the only hint of flesh; her other leg is tucked under her: she has no trunk properly speaking, and her bosom, a single slanting plane, stands out against the sea with no belly to interrupt the blue. From her collarbone rises a process that joins her head to her dissected but coherent body, and this head, a little sharp triangle of nose with two colorless insect eyes in it, is almost entirely jaws, jaws with a backward mane of hair. But these jaws move sideways, as an insect's do; and one is reminded of the mantis, that deadly carnivore.

Picasso knew the praying mantis well, and he knew what was said about her ways. The females are powerful creatures some three inches long, and they are to be found, green or straw-colored, all round the Mediterranean in late summer: although they can both walk and fly they usually stand motionless on four legs, with the other two, like long toothed arms, hanging in front of them, waiting for some grasshopper or cricket to come within their reach. When this happens the pendant arms fly out and seize their prey, gripping it in a serrated trap; then the little triangular head comes down, the jaws open sideways and deliberately tear a piece off the jerking body. From time to time the mantis pauses to look about— hers is one of the few insect heads that can turn—and in the evening light her eyes glow purple. But this is in the common course of nature, and what has struck men from remote antiquity is the report that she also serves her mate in the same way. Whether she ordinarily does so is another matter, but in captivity she certainly will, and the fact has been observed again and again. The smaller male approaches cautiously, for she is sexually phlegmatic and until he is on her back, stimulating her, he is in danger; he mounts safely; the long copulation begins; then without warning her head pivots sharply and she decapitates him. He goes on copulating, and with greater energy, his inhibitions having been removed with his head. She eats his thorax: still he persists, his lower legs gripping tight. Eventually he is spent, and she finishes her meal.

That is the report, held to be universally true by those who live in mantis-country, and by the Surrealists; and that, I am convinced, is the significance of the monster's head.

And the picture is far more than this head, however significant: it is not only a picture of a monster nor even principally a picture of a monster any more than Rembrandt's side of beef is primarily the representation of a large piece of raw meat; it is a great deal more besides, including a statement about an almost lunar stillness and silence, a certain kind of transcendence, heightened by the imminent danger and arising from the great sheets of color and the subtle interplay of the planes that form the sitting figure. But no attempt to account for the moving quality of this Picasso, or of the Rembrandt, could succeed unless one were capable of identifying and unraveling the countless strands that go to make up the aesthetic emotion. I cannot do so: it seems to me that the essence escapes all rationalization and that Braque was right in saying, "The only thing that matters about a painting is what cannot be explained." Assertions that the picture *is* moving accomplish nothing, and the only hope of conveying some ghost of the feeling lies in description.

There the monster sits with a strange awkward grace against the pure sea and the sky; the facets of her anatomized body are delicately shaded with their blue and with the colors from the sand and their smooth relaxed surfaces have a calmness of their own that is in no way disturbed by the menace of the jaws above. She is not wicked; she is only insatiably voracious by nature. The picture is both tranquil and extremely intense: tranquil in its sunlit planes of color, tense with the crossing arm and the implicit threat.

As a painter Picasso must have been deeply satisfied with his work: as a man he must have seen that the jaws were opening wide and that it was time to flee.

Chapter XIV

I<small>F</small> man's oppressor is wicked, there is some hope that she may be reclaimed by kindness, submission, brute force, or another pregnancy; but if she is a cannibal by nature then there is none at all, and the man must run away. But where to flee, and how? For one as incapable of making up his mind as Picasso this was a grave question, and its solution was made no easier by his natural indolence and endless procrastination in common affairs, by his love for what he was used to, however unpleasant, by the fatal results of disturbance on his work, by a lingering respect for his wife, the former *vraie jeune fille*, whose social status he never seems to have questioned, by a desire to keep his son, and even perhaps by a sense of duty, or at least of tradition: in his Spain men "deceived" their wives; they did not leave them.

Just when he eventually found his refuge cannot be told. Picasso was intensely secretive about his private life, and some of his closest friends knew nothing about Marie-Thérèse Walter for years; while her discretion and her sense of what was due to herself and her friend were such that to the best of my knowledge she never, even at the times of greatest publicity, yielded to the importunities of the gutter-press. One sees no photographs of Mademoiselle Walter looking soulful, understanding, winsome, bereft, intelligent, motherly, artistic: one reads no interviews, no ghosted articles on how to preserve or destroy an old master.

She seems to have been a most admirable young woman; but in speaking of her I must observe that I do not do so from any personal knowledge: with Picasso's other companions I have either some acquaintance through common friends or I have read their works, for no less than three burst into print. Marie-Thérèse I have seen only through Picasso's eyes or in published reminiscences: these nearly all agree in stating that she was tall, Swiss, young, fair-haired, fine-skinned, healthy, devoted to sport, good company, calm and gay. One of the rare dissentient voices is that of Penrose, who calls her coarse, aloof, and inconsequential, "as though controlled by the influence of the moon or by some even less calculable force." It is also apparent, from the writings of others, that she was totally disinterested, undemanding, and affectionate, and that she naturally and genuinely despised convention; while from Picasso's paintings of her it is even more apparent that she was beautiful.

It was probably in 1931, when she was twenty or less and he in his fiftieth year, though boyish still, that coincidence brought them, each from a different part of Paris, to a given point in the neighborhood of the Galéries Lafayette, where they fell into conversation. The season and even the year of their meeting is uncertain, but at all events, and whatever the progress of their friendship, it took place after the "Femme au bord de la mer" and before the "Fauteuil rouge" of late 1931, where she certainly appears in his work though perhaps not for the first time.

Yet between these dates what a mass of pictures, drawings, sculpture, constructions, engravings, and works without a name! One of these was the glove he stuffed and glued to the back of a canvas next to a head made of felt with coarse teased-out cloth for hair, the whole covered with more glue to hold a sprinkling of sand, its parts overflowing the frame formed by the wooden stretcher. The hand, perfectly realistic or indeed real at one remove, combined with the almost abstract sign for a head, has a marked Surrealist flavor—a flavor that was growing stronger in his work and that is most obvious in his use of objects picked up, carried home, and made part of his reliefs or paintings.

Among the etchings of 1930 is the suite he produced for Skira's edition of the *Metamorphoses* of Ovid. From Françoise Gilot's account it seems that Albert Skira, then a young moneyed Swiss with vague ambitions in the publishing line, asked Picasso to illustrate a book about someone— about Napoleon, for instance. Picasso had nothing whatsoever to say to Napoleon. During the summer Skira's mother waylaid Picasso on the beach at Juan-les-Pins, pleaded her young man's cause with gentle persistence, and gradually wore down Picasso's resistance: he hated to see a disappointed face. To give pleasure he would make an amiable but insincere reply; and well-conducted importunity could then extort marvels from his unwilling hand. This time he said that her son should think of "a classical author—perhaps something mythological."

By great good luck Skira chanced upon Ovid, and the *Metamorphoses*: Picasso had come by a nodding acquaintance with the poet in the remote La Coruña; he had recently designed a number of works actually called "Metamorphoses"; and at that moment he was living on the shore of the classical sea, in a landscape inhabited for him by fauns, satyrs, minotaurs, and even nymphs. He agreed.

Back in Paris Picasso withdrew into this ageless retreat and turned out plate after plate with great zeal; and after each plate was done he would reach for a trumpet that he happened to possess, open the window, and blow a blast. Skira, who had taken an office next door, so that now Picasso had his dealer on one side and his publisher on the other, would come running.

All these plates were neo-classical outline-drawings that kept closer to Ovid than ever his earlier work did to Balzac, both in the letter and the spirit; and they illustrated the death of Orpheus, the fall of Phaeton, and many other powerful myths with compositions that from a lesser hand would have been a welter of tight-packed limbs but that he imbued with a fine flowing harmony. They are exquisite, and when they were published the next year they were received with great applause. Yet as he said himself, "You can't be a witch-doctor all day long," and the feeling remains that Ovid was little more than a refuge for Picasso, that these illustrations, delightful though they are, were of no essential importance to him.

This cannot be said for his painting. The year 1930 saw one of his most significant pictures, a Crucifixion. For many observers it marks the most desperate point of his extreme unhappiness in what might be called the period between Olga and Marie-Thérèse, and I agree with them entirely; yet at the same time some can find no religious content whatever, which seems to me astonishing. Obviously there is no right or wrong about these subjective judgments, and obviously a great deal depends on the concept of religion, which is no doubt different for Protestants or Communists on the one hand and Catholics, however lapsed, on the other. And if to the traditional Catholic's earliest notions of mysticism and intercession, so close to magic for a child, one adds Picasso's own ideas of mediation and exorcism, then the difference becomes greater by far. Picasso, after all, was brought up in a country where mysticism, ethics, and morality are rarely confounded, where the Mother of God is often seen as a fierce, squat black figure, devoid of apparent tenderness, and where Catholicism, with all that it had absorbed from ancient days, was part of the daily air. Then again, much also depends on one's definition of religious painting: for one who is continually surrounded by another world, good or evil, the distinction between sacred and profane hardly exists. Picasso himself said in Penrose's hearing, "What do they mean by religious art? It's an absurdity. How can you make religious art one day and another kind the next?"

The picture has been explained by critics and art-historians and its symbolism analysed, often with great learning: I shall attempt no such thing, and apart from saying that for me Picasso's Crucifixion is a passionate, savage outcry of an essentially religious nature and a statement about death, agony, and sacrifice, I shall offer no more than a brief description.

It is quite a small picture, twenty inches high, twenty-six across, and it is painted on a wooden panel. The colors are brilliant, a strong yellow predominating, with a great deal of red on the right-hand side and more blue and blue-green on the left; but in the middle, lit by another light entirely, the small Christ, the Cross and the draped "bone" figure standing open-jawed against His bosom, are a deathly, insubstantial white, more deathly still from their black outline and black background. On the right two huge arms, their hands clasped in anguish, rise from a confusion of forms, green, blue, and parti-colored, and far away against the red stands the empty tau cross of one of the thieves, while with their customary indifference the soldiers throw dice on a drum for the seamless robe. In the foreground on the left hand lie the two thieves, naked and dead: from one stiff and livid body a ladder runs up to the arm of the cross, where a little red figure is driving home a nail. An even smaller horseman, almost overwhelmed by a shrieking head, thrusts his lance into Christ's side: and high on the left, turquoise-blue, ringed and mottled with blood-red, there is the sponge of the Passion, enormously enlarged. All the figures in this composition have been subjected to various kinds of distortion, often extreme and often related to different periods of Picasso's work, so that they can be seen as a summary of his metaphors; but in spite of the different idioms that are present, the picture is very much a whole, and this wholeness arises, I believe, from its passionate intensity.

The Crucifixion was a most important picture to Picasso, and he never parted with it. From sketches made as far back as 1927 it is clear that the idea had been in his mind long before it reached paint, and in the years that followed he made several further drawings, particularly in relation to Grünewald's masterpiece. The preliminary studies include some naked Magdalens allied to the frenzied left-hand figure in "La Danse" but arched back in an even stronger convulsion and with their sexual characteristics, literal and symbolic, more pronounced by far. There are people to whom any association of sexuality and religion (and there are other examples in these drawings) is directly blasphemous, and that may account for some of the reactions to the picture.

The Crucifixion marked the trough of his unhappiness, but Picasso painted many other pictures in 1930 and 1931 that also show a mind in much the same condition: tormented and almost desperate, but never beaten, always savagely protesting. His better days were recorded by still-lives full of curving forms enclosed by broad black lines in his stained-glass manner; and these big pictures could be described as the latest manifestation of curvilinear Cubism. They have a certain resemblance to the work of Matisse, particularly in their fine free coloring, as though Picasso, by going through some of the same motions, hoped to capture the serenity he so much envied in his friend.

However that may be, full happiness does not reappear in Picasso's painting until well after his meeting with Marie-Thérèse. Forerunners are to be seen towards the end of 1931, when, in something of the same curvilinear style as his recent still-lives, he painted a sculptor sitting and contemplating a bust that because of the characteristic nose and forehead can only be Marie-Thérèse, while a little picture on the wall behind may conceivably be Picasso himself: he was now dating his work exactly, and on the back of this is written *7 Décembre M. CM. XXXI.* Some weeks later there she is again, quite unmistakable, asleep in a red armchair, wearing a dress with a fine blue sash; her heart-shaped head is divided to show full-face and profile; and the stretcher has the words *fait dans l'après-midi de Dimanche 24 janvier M. CM. XXXII.* Then during the spring of 1932 happiness came flooding in: with even more than his usual demonic energy he suddenly produced a series of large canvases, mostly nudes, and all of the same woman, often distorted but always kindly so—a big, firm body, flowing in great sensuous curves, often fast asleep. And these, as one can see from the dates, followed one another at intervals of a couple of days or so. Their style, which has been labeled curved graphism, is quite new, and so is the nature of their relaxed happiness, itself no usual quality in Picasso's work.

A wife with more understanding of her husband's work, or one who took more interest in it, would at once have known what was afoot; and she might have tried to be less disagreeable. Judging by the monsters that continued to appear from time to time, Olga Picasso did no such thing.

To begin with Picasso made a typically indecisive attempt at living a double life, and for a while it seemed to answer tolerably well, possibly because theirs was less a full-throated passion than an *amitié amoureuse.*

A curious thing about Marie-Thérèse is that Picasso had already imagined her: he had already drawn girls with bodies and faces like hers. Now he painted her tirelessly; but it was above all as sculpture that he saw Marie-Thérèse—he was fascinated by her head, particularly by the way her classical forehead ran into her well-marked nose.

But this was not yet a time for sculpture. Quite apart from Marie-Thérèse, 1932 was one of the busiest years away from his studio that Picasso had ever known, for apart from having to see to a great deal of business he also became a landed proprietor.

It was a cruelly hard year for many painters, since the depression, which had taken its time to reach Paris, was now so firmly installed that for most people it was already a way of life; and naturally the artists suffered first. Soup-kitchens were opened in Montmartre and Montparnasse, and Kahnweiler worked out a system of allowances to keep his painters alive. No publishers seem to have followed his example: Robert Desnos and Alejo Carpentier for example were reduced to a single pair of shoes between them, and those they lined with cardboard; and even Gertrude Stein was obliged to sell many of her pictures. None of this affected Picasso: in his frugal way he had put by a great deal of money; people still bought a certain amount of his work; and he and his dealers so carefully dosed the market that there was never a glut of Picassos.

On this whole question of money, Picasso's attitude had evolved: he had long since lost his pauper's wondering, delighted avidity, and by the thirties he had already reached something like his final state of mind, which was not one of indifference—far from it—because where selling his work was concerned he was a ferocious bargainer, full of deep-laid stratagems, while in daily life he could be parsimonious, if not mean: yet in the first case money was part of a game he was determined to win, and in the second his native frugality came into play. Perhaps absence is the better word, for although when the subject of money came up he was intensely interested, there were long periods when it never crossed his mind: it never, never affected his painting in the least degree, not even when money was still wholly real and of vital relevance to the next day's living; and he did, after all, spend most of his life in his studio. It is as though once the days of his pressing need were past he no longer believed whole-heartedly in the stuff, any more than he believed in the enormous sums his pictures fetched in later years; as though he used it as a toy or a weapon, as a not particularly convincing symbol of his domination and success, and as a standard of comparison in which he did not really believe either but which flattered him. His attitude was complex and often contradictory: yet this notion of absence is supported by the fact that he did not trouble with investment. A man to whose life the subject is deeply relevant will make his money breed: but Picasso, in some passing fit of financial concern, would buy gold coins and then forget them; Françoise Gilot saw a boxful, covered with dust, in the rue La Boëtie, and after his death bundles of bank-notes, some no longer current, were found stuffed into drawers and cupboards.

In 1932, however, he used some of this weaith to buy the seventeenth or eighteenth-century Château de Boisgeloup, some forty miles from Paris, on the edge of a hamlet in the Vexin. Compared with some châteaux it was nothing very extraordinary, and what the French so touchingly call its park amounted to no more than half a dozen acres; but it was a fair-sized country house with perhaps twenty rooms, a much earlier chapel, and a great round dovecot. At the depth of the depression it would have been a bargain, and far more important than that, it possessed a great range of out-buildings, stables, loose-boxes, a coach-house, capable of being transformed into sculptor's studios, to be inhabited by splendid figures still in Picasso's mind; or, from a different point of view, into a slum unparalleled even in the experience of Picasso's victims, filled with objects that accumulated dust.

And in addition to this important purchase, which was not only to provide the vast ground-space needed for ambitious sculpture but also to do away with the need for carrying easels, canvases, luggage, women, children, dogs (a St. Bernard now, and a smelly Airedale) far away for the summer holidays and then back again, a task for which even the stately Hispano-Suiza was inadequate—in addition to this Picasso had to make the arrangements for his first great retrospective exhibitions, which were to take place during this summer of 1932 at the Galérie Georges Petit in Paris and at the Kunsthaus in Zurich; and his zeal was stimulated by the fact that the year before Matisse had had a most successful retrospective in both these places and at the New York Museum of Modern Art as well. He was also much engaged with Christian Zervos, the editor of *Les Cahiers d'Art,* who was beginning his monumental catalog of Picasso's works, an undertaking worthy of a conventful of Benedictines that has now passed its twenty-fifth volume. And he had to see to the preparations for installing his family at Boisgeloup. This, however, he did in a summary fashion: two small upper rooms were fitted up, the huge inconvenient kitchen, and little else. Picasso was no longer the neat and biddable husband of the early twenties; he was rapidly returning to the Gypsy state natural to him, and the good wool suits were now the prey of moths; the bow tie, the handkerchief in his breast-pocket were rarely to be seen, and soon they were to vanish altogether. Picasso's dandyism was of a kind peculiar to himself: he had seen the great world, and on reflection he did not think much of it, nor of its taste in clothes. His considered opinion was that he had never seen any man better dressed than Modigliani; and Modigliani wore a corduroy jacket, none too clean, corduroy trousers, and checked workman's shirts.

In spite of all these pressing occupations, Picasso found the time and the energy to paint some of his most famous Marie-Thérèse pictures and to begin peopling the stables at Boisgeloup. In his paintings he made what amounts to a total statement about her, using all the techniques of Cubism and of symbol to show not only her golden superficies, but her serene, uncomplicated sexuality and even her inward composition—her anatomy. But in sculpture he was primarily concerned with her head. One of the first inhabitants of the converted stable was a more-than-life-size plaster bust, classical in its simplicity and restraint, like the 1905 terra-cotta of Fernande. This head was soon joined by others, and almost at once Picasso began to vary the part that fascinated him most, the junction or rather the continuity of her forehead and her nose, which he turned into a protuberance not unlike that which is to be seen on a high-bred merino sheep. He carried this and other distortions very far indeed, molding her head into disturbing archaic forms and redistributing her features: he could do so without disturbing her tranquillity or affecting her cheerful good nature in any way at all. She was not interested in painting or sculpture, nor did she pretend to be: she just liked Picasso, and she liked being with him.

Picasso took a very great deal of trouble over the retrospective exhibition: he had had other shows these recent years, including half a dozen in America, while London had seen, and praised, thirty-seven of his pictures at Reid and Lefevre's in 1931. But this was to be far more important, a true and representative view of his achievement that would fix his standing for the better or for the worse. Hitherto Paris had seen Picasso in bits and pieces; and although he was now fifty his reputation, unlike Matisse's, was founded more on talk, partial information, and general notoriety than on a firm, widely-based appreciation. From a variety of sources and particularly from his own collection he assembled over two hundred pictures ranging from Casagemas in his coffin to Marie-Thérèse in her looking-glass and embracing the Blue, Rose, Negro, proto-Cubist, high Cubist, synthetic Cubist, rococo Cubist, classical, and later Cubist periods, together with some monsters, the Crucifixion, and these latest canvases—a singular diary for those who could read it. He saw to the hanging of them himself; he set the sculptures in the proper light. He stated the case for his children to the best of his ability; he could do no more; and the verdict was to be given by others.

The vernissage on June 15, 1932, the day before the common herd was allowed in, was the high point of the Paris season: Picasso was there, neat and brushed, with his bow tie making one of its last appearances; he rarely attended his own shows, but this was no ordinary exhibition, and this time he received everybody who counted in the town. He had, as it were, put his cards on the table; and he won. The public, the social success was immense; the intellectual success greater still. *Les Cahiers d'Art* devoted a special number to Picasso, with a list of contributors including André Salmon, Stravinsky, Cocteau, Reverdy, Maurice Raynal, Breton, Paul Eluard, Vicente Huidobro, Georges Hugnet, and many of his early admirers.

The retrospective, which continued until July 30, confirmed his reputation as one of the moşt important painters of the century, if not the most important. Some might say that Matisse, whose fame was perhaps more widely spread, particularly in America, led by a neck; but Braque, though going well, had fallen behind; and Derain was scarcely in the running.

Braque and Picasso were friends again by now. It could not be the old intimacy, amounting to something near identity of mind, but there could be strong liking short of that; and apart from anything else Picasso's great respect for his friend was increased by the way Braque had survived and was surviving the depression; for Picasso despised weakness, failure, and want of fortitude or courage, sometimes to the point of brutality. The Braques therefore came to Boisgeloup, and they saw the stables, with more heads now and many other pieces, more beautiful perhaps in their original plaster than in their later bronze, with a whiteness into which the light can sink, so that it is not so much a surface as a dreamlike presence.

Later in the year Brassaï made the same journey, to photograph the sculptures. They had increased in number by the winter, and in his *Conversations avec Picasso* he describes how Picasso opened the door of one of the stalls "and in all their brilliant whiteness we beheld a nation of sculptured figures." And he goes on to speak of one of the consequences of his visit, which by its implications says more about the state of Picasso's marriage than any day-by-day account of domestic misery. In spite of the painter's reputation for unapproachability, at this first meeting Brassaï found that he was "direct, unaffected, devoid of arrogance or pose . . . kind and natural." Picasso was equally pleased with Brassaï, and suggested that they should all go to the circus together, to his old love the Médrano, which he had not seen for years. So they did, and it had not changed: still the same clowns, fat horses, lean acrobats, wild beasts, the same smells. It was not an outstanding performance, but Picasso enjoyed himself immensely, laughing at the clowns and having a splendid time; while all the evening his son, aged eleven, sat bootfaced, determined to show no sign of pleasure, and his wife said not a word but sat equally glum, taking no notice of the common people's fun at all.

The purpose of Brassaï's labors was to provide the newly-founded *Minotaure* with illustrations for its first number. *Minotaure* was a luxurious review, financed by Skira, edited by Tériade, and largely devoted to what might be called Surrealism in the wider sense: by now the Surrealists of the strict obedience were a meager body; Artaud and Soupault had long since been expelled for heresy, and the excommunications had multiplied with the years, striking Desnos, Jacques Prévert, André Masson, Picabia, Marcel Duchamp, Georges Bataille, and Queneau among others, and in 1931 even Aragon himself, guilty of deliberate Communism. A magazine confined to the true believers would scarcely have sold a hundred copies. But Picasso remained on good terms with most of the outcasts as well as with Breton and Eluard, which says a great deal about their reverence for him; and *Minotaure* had some contributors, such as Picasso's old friend Raynal, who were not Surrealist at all, others who were unorthodox, and still others who never belonged formally to the group. The first number contained some thirty pages of Brassaï's photographs; and apart from the few pieces included in the Georges Petit retrospective this was the first the public had ever seen of Picasso's recent sculpture, which was made without much idea of show and even less of sale. It also had an essay by Breton called "Picasso dans son élément." And Picasso himself provided the cover. It was a collage: one of his etchings of the minotaur stuck onto corrugated cardboard fastened with drawing-pins and the whole adorned with ribbon, lace, and some rather worn flowers from one of Olga's discarded hats; and when one sees what an extraordinarily successful jacket it made on being reproduced one wonders less at Picasso's lifelong refusal to throw anything away.

Minotaure came out in May, 1933, and subsequent numbers had covers by Derain and Matisse as well as by the Surrealists Miró, Magritte, and Dalí, the new star of the movement. Dalí had taken part in an important exhibition at the Dalmau gallery in Barcelona at the time of Picasso's visit in 1926 and the two were introduced. Picasso liked some of the young man's work (Dalí was then twenty-two); and with his usual generosity he told Paul Rosenberg and Pierre Loeb of his merits. Although it led to no agreement, the dealers traveled south to see him. Then three years later Picasso received Dalí very kindly when he came to Paris at Miró's invitation. First and last Picasso must have been called upon by some hundreds of young Catalan painters, and there is no recorded instance that I know of his ever having turned a single one away; but this was an exceptional visit, for Dalí possessed not only great technical ability but also a most dynamic companion who until recently had been married to Paul Eluard. (A band of Surrealists, including the Eluards, Buñuel and Magritte, had gone to see Dalí at Cadaqués; and there Madame Eluard remained.) This time Picasso was more than usually kind: he introduced Dalí to people who might be useful to him, such as Gertrude Stein, and some time later he lent him the money he needed to go to America. The outcome was banal in the extreme, for as Brassaï says—and these are the only harsh words in the whole of his good-natured book—"after this Dalí continually spoke evil of him, running him down and even, once the Spanish civil war had begun, insulting him."

Picasso also provided *Minotaure* with nourishment in the form of little drawings of an almost entirely Surrealist nature, sculptural drawings of basically female forms closely allied to the "bone" compositions of 1928 and called "Anatomie": yet these assemblies of chairs, bowls, balls, cogs, and arbitrary shapes are much more cheerful than their bony cousins; and their sexuality, though quite as evident, has not the same brooding, obsessive quality.

These he drew in February 1933, and as spring came on he turned his mind in a completely different direction, settling down to a series of classical etchings of the sculptor in his studio that were to form part of the great suite commissioned by Vollard some years earlier. The bearded sculptor is much the same man as before, but now the model is unmistakably Marie-Thérèse. Sometimes they lie naked and relaxed in one another's arms, gazing at some piece that he has made, often another Marie-Thérèse, exaggerated; sometimes at plump horses playing, or bulls; his gaze is mild and thoughtful, the somewhat absent look of a man gently revolving some problem of surface and volume, solved or to be solved. The general feeling in most of these forty-odd plates is one of calm, light-filled happiness, even when the sculptor is present only as a gigantic bust and a minotaur is having a quiet orgy with one model while two more look on, amused. The minotaur is a companionable monster: at times he lies on a couch drinking champagne with a wreathed classical beauty; at others he carouses with the sculptor, somewhat the worse for drink, amidst the voluptuous curves of two women, sex-objects from head to toe. But one of the last plates in the series, drawn at the end of May, shows him in a bull-ring, diminished, down on his knees, about to receive the puntilla, the final dagger-stroke, from a beautiful youth, while crowded along the barrier, leaning low over it like the spectators in some of his very earliest works, several women and a hairy man watch closely, interested but unmoved. The strangely quiet, immobile, poignant scene has received many different explanations, most based on the simple equation minotaur equals Picasso, with further speculation on Mithras, sacrifice, and so on; but Picasso's own mythology and symbolism were highly personal; they followed a logic peculiar to himself; and I will only venture to observe that he was now past fifty, a time when most men become aware of the looming tragedy of old age with all its mutilations; and that the minotaur, the only member of his race, is the very type of the outsider; but this does not necessarily mean a total identification by any means.

These etchings coincide with what was probably Picasso's happiest time, precariously poised between Olga and Marie-Thérèse; and curiously enough although they show some very lovely statues they mark the end of Picasso as a sculptor himself until 1941.

The quiet and productive beginning of the year soon came to an end. After June at Boisgeloup, where he drew a standing minotaur making love to an ecstatic young woman, the summer of 1933 found the Picassos at Cannes; and in a photograph Olga is to be seen, looking glum, on what appears to be the terrace of an expensive restaurant. Picasso's painting fell off both in quality and quantity, and almost the only memorable things he produced during this holiday were some directly Surrealist drawings of furniture with limbs. He was now closer to the Surrealists than he had ever been before, partly because of his growing friendship with Eluard; and apart from the "Anatomie" there is, among the spring-time etchings, a perfectly classical girl looking at a Surrealist hermaphrodite made of a chair with arms, a variety of sexual attributes, and a fetish head.

It is scarcely surprising that his work suffered, for in addition to his obvious difficulties, a totally unexpected voice from the past came to destroy what peace he had left. This was Fernande Olivier's: she now made her living by teaching French to foreigners, and either some one of them or the Devil himself had prompted her to write her memoirs. Parts began to appear in Le Soir and Mercure, and they ripped his jealously-guarded privacy wide open. Then the memoirs came out in book-form. Fernande Olivier's Picasso et ses amis is not a grossly offensive book: it is indeed an exceedingly interesting and fairly accurate picture of the Montmartre of a quarter of a century before; but it does present him in an unheroic light at times, particularly in connection with Guillaume Apollinaire and the Iberian figures, and there is a certain hint of physical as well as moral cowardice on his part; while Fernande is of course pure white and blameless throughout. He was exceedingly distressed; he tried in vain to stop the publication of the extracts and it is said that he negotiated more successfully to prevent the appearance of even more wounding incidents in the book. But even if it was toned down, the book was a cruel blow to him: he had not looked into a mirror nor drawn more than a faint shadow of himself for ten years and more; and it was more painful for him than for most men to have this reflection forced upon him.

Olga's reactions are not recorded, but they can scarcely have added to his tranquillity: she was and always had been violently jealous, especially of Fernande, and only a few months before she had given proof of it. Gertrude Stein was reading to the Picassos out of her *Autobiography of Alice B. Toklas,* translating as she went: "So I began at the beginning with the description of the room and the description of our servant Helen. You made one mistake said Pablo you left out something there were three swords that hung on that wall one underneath the other and he said it was very exciting. Then I went on and Fernande came in.

"I was reading he was listening and his eyes were wide open and then his wife Olga Picasso got up and said she would not listen she would go away she said. What's the matter, we said, I do not know that woman she said and left. Pablo said go on reading. I said no you must go after your wife, he said oh, I said oh, and he left . . . " She did not see him again for another two years.

Half way through August, 1933, Picasso could not bear Cannes any longer: he got into the Hispano-Suiza, picked up Marie-Thérèse somewhere on the road, and driven by the discreet Marcel Boudin went to Barcelona. This was his first visit to the Peninsula since the Republic had been proclaimed in 1931, yet strangely enough there is no evidence of his having been particularly moved either by the fall of the king or the advent of a president, although the upheaval meant that Catalonia now had some measure of independence at last, including the official use of its own language. Politics, except in the broadest lines, never meant much to him once he was grown up; and at this juncture he had plenty to occupy his mind.

Some of this plenty was very agreeable. He cannot have failed to be affected, however indirectly, by the feeling of hope and joy in the new Republic—it must have been reflected from his friends. He saw Manolo again, amnestied and allowed back into his own country; and many other old companions, such as the Soto and Junyer-Vidal brothers, and his own nephews and nieces, Lola's children. He went to Sitges, and of course he went to the bull-fight. But in spite of his discretion the journalists found him out: he refused to give an interview, muttering that "he had only come to see his mother," and a few days later he left.

Back in Paris and Boisgeloup he painted a number of pictures based on the bull-fight, savage pictures in which the bull, the horses, and sometimes a woman bullfighter suffer and die horribly, often in a wild confusion of distorted limbs, horns, swords, and bodies; and these carried well on into 1934, that unhappy year for him.

The unhappiness is to be seen in his drawing and engraving as well as in his pictures; and there was no sculpture worth speaking of. At Boisgeloup that summer he made the drawing sometimes called "The Death of Marat," from David's picture of Charlotte Corday killing him, and sometimes just "Le Meurtre"; it shows an utterly hideous toothed female monster rushing upon the fainting Marie-Thérèse to stab her again with a huge kitchen knife, and as she stabs so she sticks out her great pointed tongue. And a day or two later there is Marie-Thérèse once more, mingled with a bullring horse and ripped up by the bull, itself already pierced with a sword.

As warnings, moral examples, these and many others like them could not be improved: nevertheless in the high summer of 1934 Picasso set off again with Marie-Thérèse, and he showed her a great deal of northern Spain, from Irún to San Sebastián, Burgos, Madrid, el Escorial, Toledo, and Zaragoza, and then through Aragón home to Barcelona. Again he almost entirely evaded the journalists, and the only article that appeared was one about his visit, accompanied by the curator and several friends, to the museum of Catalan art, where he saw more pure Romanesque than he had ever seen in his life before, since in the boundless enthusiasm of those early Republican days the new authorities had gathered the imperiled frescoes from the remote, sometimes deserted and half-ruined Pyrenean churches, making apses to fit them and forming a splendid collection that is still unrivaled in the world.

Another man—Gauguin comes to mind—might have stayed in Barcelona or indeed anywhere else where he was at peace. But Picasso was a creature of habit; a fixed routine, however unpleasant, was necessary to his work; and although Paris meant scenes, bitter wrangling, unhappiness—all the more so now that concealment was no longer possible—to Paris he returned.

Spain and Barcelona, obviously, were breaks in this steady unhappiness: and there were others—the illustrations for Gilbert Seldes' translation of the *Lysistrata* are in Picasso's most cheerful neo-classic tradition; and far more important, far more apparently serene, are the pictures of girls reading or writing or drawing. Yet there is a strange tension too in many of these, and on one of them, the deceptively casual "Jeune fille dessinant dans un intérieur," Picasso worked for months, piling up the preliminary studies and then painting out the whole composition before he fixed the one girl drawing and the other sleeping with her arms on the table just as he wanted them. These particular girls are nubile, but some of the others are children, and towards the end of the year the little girl, the girl child, became his particular concern: the fact that Marie-Thérèse was pregnant may conceivably have had something to do with this.

The child—she is about the age of Alice when she passed through the looking-glass—makes her appearance in the autumn of 1934 in some terrible yet comforting engravings in which she is leading a gigantic minotaur, a blind minotaur, with his lamentable great head pointing up into the sky and a blind man's stick in his hand.

These prints carry on naturally, perhaps inevitably, to Picasso's most important work of 1935, the "Minotauromachie." It is an uncommonly large etching, more than two feet across, and the vertical line of a house divides it down the middle: in the right half, filling almost all of it with his bulk, the huge minotaur advances from the sea, no longer the sculptor's cheerful friend, nor the pitiful blind monster, but a different minotaur entirely, far more savage brute than man; his powerful arm stretches out over a disemboweled horse across whose back lies a dead or unconscious woman bullfighter, her bosom bare, her hand still holding a sword. She and the horse fill the lower middle of the plate. On the left there is the darker house, and at its high window two young women stand; but they are concerned only with the doves upon their windowsill. Still farther to the left, on the edge of the picture, a ladder rears up with an almost naked bearded man climbing it; and he is looking fixedly at the monster. In the foreground at the ladder's foot stands the little girl, wearing a hat, an old-fashioned frock, holding a bunch of flowers in one hand and a lighted candle in the other. She holds it high, and the flame almost touches the horse's agonizing head and the minotaur's outstretched hand, lighting up its half-seen palm. She is quite fearless.

The general impression is one of darkness, appalling menace, suffering, and hope. Here again there are analyses and explanations by the score: the ladder is connected with the Crucifixion, the candle with truth and light, the doves with innocence. Picasso had been intimately familiar with doves and pigeons from his earliest childhood; he liked to have the libidinous, promiscuous birds around; but his own opinion of them was that they were among the cruelest creatures living; and although he could sometimes use them as a conventional sign it seems to me that pinning down his symbols in so personal a work as this, attaching the usual labels to them and explaining the whole upon that basis is a rash if not a presumptuous undertaking.

The "Minotauromachie" is immensely impressive, and even in a prolific year it would stand out as a most striking achievement; but 1935 was not a prolific year; in fact by Picasso's standards it was almost barren.

Just when in late 1934 or early 1935 his relations with Olga reached the breaking-point cannot be told, but presently he was talking of divorce.

Any man who talks of divorce, meaning what he says, steps straight into a squalor that far exceeds anything that has gone before. Picasso found this to be the case, and it very nearly destroyed him. He had had no experience of divorce; it did not exist in Spain until the Republic, and in Montmartre and Montparnasse people troubled even less with legal dissolution than with legal marriage. It was generally known to be difficult, slow, and expensive, but possible on adequate grounds. For reasons that do not appear it seems that Picasso supposed that he had these grounds (his knowledge of the law was negligible) and that he attempted to begin a suit. That at least is the common report; though how even he could imagine that any court would regard him as the innocent party is difficult to conceive, and perhaps in fact he tried to induce Olga to initiate proceedings.

However, after he had been taking legal advice for some time it became clear to him that his position was hopelessly complicated. Since he could not have been divorced in his own country until very recently it appeared that he could not be divorced in France either, at least not until the new situation in Spain had been digested by the French courts—a very slow process—and that it would be useless to attempt it even if Olga were willing, which she was not: she was bitterly opposed to the whole thing, although divorces were common enough in Russia and were fully recognized by her church. So when at last he came to understand that full divorce was impossible at this point, there arose the question of a legal separation: but this, the lawyers told him, involved the separation not only of their persons but also of their goods; and now the contest reached a new pitch of bitterness. Olga does not seem to have been a money-grubber; in that respect she was comparatively disinterested, her chief aims being revenge and the retention of a hold rather than spoliation; but translated into legal terms it came to much the same thing.

Roughly speaking, marriages in France are of two kinds, those in which there is a contract specifying the degree of separate ownership and those in which there is none. In the second case, the *communauté légale*, the spouses share all they possessed before the ceremony and all they acquire after it; this is the regime preferred by women with no dowry or private fortune, and this was the regime under which the Picassos married.

In the event of a separation, a breaking of the *communauté légale*, the acquisitions as well as the original property have to be divided according to the directions of the court; and in the course of the last seventeen years Picasso had acquired a great deal—a very great deal indeed, if the pictures he painted were to be regarded as acquisitions. Olga or her lawyers certainly looked upon them in that light, or at least as valid security, and in their eagerness they had official seals put on the door of his studio so that he could not get at them while they were being wrangled over.

Quite early in the proceedings it became apparent to him that getting rid of Olga would be expensive, and it was: but he cannot have foreseen the full expense of spirit that it cost him—the tireless shrieking scenes until she broke off direct negotiations and left him in July, 1935, and both before that and for long after the busy prying of the lawyers into his possessions and his private life.

In the end the pictures were not seized; but the action bit deep. Picasso had to pay very heavily to retain them: Olga obtained a thumping allowance, Boisgeloup (which she hated) and the custody of Paulo, while Picasso was left with the flat in the rue La Boëtie and his pictures. Although he had a strong personality, although he was much attached to his possessions and furiously opposed to parting with them on compulsion, he was no match for Olga and her lawyers. For one thing, he had not a legal leg to stand on: and for another, he could not devote his entire being to the battle: she could: and in a way she won.

In all this wretched period of prolonged and distracting unhappiness there were a few events that comforted him. One was the birth of his daughter María Concepción, whom he called Maya and whom he loved dearly—she was the prettiest little girl—and the other was the coming of his old friend Jaime Sabartés.

After a quarter of a century and more as a journalist in Latin America Sabartés had returned to Spain: he was there when Picasso wrote to him on July 13, 1935, "I am alone in the house. You can imagine what has happened and what is still in store for me," and he was still there in the autumn when Picasso, having gone through some part of what had been in store, wrote again, asking him and his wife to come and live with him in the desolate rue La Boëtie.

In his *Picasso, retratos y recuerdos*, which describes their long friendship, Sabartés jumps straight from the Barcelona of 1904, when they parted, to the Paris of 1935, when they met again, as though the intervening years did not count: and perhaps for Sabartés they scarcely did; Picasso was by far the most important factor in his life.

"November 12, 1935," he wrote, "I came back to Paris, this time at Picasso's request, meaning to live at his flat in the rue La Boëtie.

"He was waiting for me behind the barrier at the Gare d'Orsay. This was the fifth time that I had arrived from a great way off and that he had come to fetch me. The other two I had not told him I was coming.

"From that day on my life has followed in the track of his without my ever wondering how long this dream would last, since we intended that it should be forever.''

Señora Sabartés supervised the household, though from her husband's book one would never know that she existed. What she made of it there is no telling, but her task cannot have been very restful: Picasso was at no time an easy man to live with, and now he was more than usually difficult. He had his own ideas about how a house should be run; he liked some things to be cleaned, but as he could never bring himself to give a direct order, those who did not make out his wishes by intuition were liable to be frowned at for days or even savagely rebuked when it was all too late. Furthermore, now that Olga was gone, her trim bourgeois order was rapidly overwhelmed by Picasso's slum, which flowed downstairs and all over her domain. He had respected her frightful strength; he respected it still, although it no longer restrained him; and absurdly enough he missed her. He turned to Sabartés for human contact, talking incessantly of their old days together and keeping him up until very late at night: this suited Sabartés perfectly, and he became Picasso's companion, secretary and, most fortunately, his historian, idiosyncratic, snipe-like in his flight, but invaluable.

That was well before the final settlement with Olga, and Boisgeloup still belonged to Picasso. A great deal more squalor was still to come, but at least for the time Picasso could still retire into the country: Sabartés says that at this period he could still sculpt and paint, but if he did so, little trace remains. On the other hand he did draw, and there was his baby daughter, in whom he took such delight that he would wash her dirty linen, partly to express his affection and partly to change the horrible current of his mind.

Yet still the writs, the lawyers' letters came pouring in; the endless arguments and the odious interviews multiplied, growing even more insistent and unbearable. As a creative man he was nearly at his end, and by 1936 he could not paint at all. ''He no longer went upstairs to his studio,'' says Sabartés, ''and the mere sight of his pictures and drawings infuriated him.''

He could not paint. It was his opium or hashish nightmare come true, and but for poetry it might have been the end of Picasso altogether: even so, Barr reckons that the crisis struck twenty months out of his life as a painter, while Gertrude Stein says two years. (Neither is right according to the letter; but that is the general spirit.)

The poetry, like so many things to do with Picasso, was a secret; and the equally secretive Sabartés was probably the first person ever to be told about the new, strangely diffident departure—told confidentially, as something not to be repeated. This was in the summer of 1935, when Sabartés was still in Spain; and presently Picasso was sending him pieces such as:

> Today is the fifth of the month of September XXXV the hastened thrust of the sword in the quince's flesh opens the hand and like a cache-sexe lets out its secret prime the emerald so that it will let itself be eaten dressed up as a watercress salad with pieces of gross good eating whispering in your ear behind the lane damn beforehand happy to go to the stake try to be clever and make a bag of nuts and a shopping-basket of sorrows for every sailor who is irked by the unravelling cotton that scratches his mask length of his yard-stick the tan whose wheat adorns the head of the wounded man gnawed by hope to which . . . catapun chin chin gori gori gori . . .

In November, when Sabartés reached the rue La Boëtie, the poetry was still a most private refuge, and Picasso would write it in a little easily-hidden notebook, sometimes sitting in the privy but more often behind closed doors in the dining-room. Yet the dining-room was not ideal, since the table had to be cleared for meals and there was no more room on the other pieces of furniture for the various heaps: the Renoir on the sideboard was already vanishing behind papers and objects such as a marble piece of gruyère cheese.

With a falsity that did not deceive Sabartés for a moment, Picasso said it would save a great deal of trouble if they were to eat in the kitchen, where everything was within reach: now he had a free hand in the dining-room, and the heaps grew, covering everything except the small area upon which he wrote. But Picasso had his standards, and in the kitchen he would receive only some particular friends, such as Madame Errazuriz, Braque, and the Leirises; it was not ideal from many points of view, and they tried eating in the Sabartés' bedroom and then the place where the linen was kept before returning at last, much against Picasso's will, to the dining-room.

Picasso had already made four portraits of his friend, the first as long ago as 1899: in December, 1935, he made a fifth. At this period they were still eating in the kitchen: Sabartés was waiting for him to come to lunch, and to pass the time he straightened the cloth on the marble table and fiddled with the crockery, the mineral water, the rusks, making sure that everything was in its invariable place, just as Picasso liked it: at last he heard him coming, preceded by the dog Elft. Picasso stopped in the doorway, waving a piece of paper, and said, "Here's your portrait."

Living coals of friendship
Clock that always tells the time
Happy flag flying
Wafted by the breath of a kiss on one's hand
Stroke the heart's wings
Which mounting flies from the very top
Of the tree in the garden heavy with fruit

it began; and although they often talked Catalan together it was written in Spanish. (Picasso's Catalan was, I believe, almost entirely a spoken language, though he would lard his letters to Sabartés with Catalan phrases.)

Encouraged by Sabartés' praise, Picasso soon began to read other pieces to a few friends, sometimes in French, sometimes in Spanish. Then he let Zervos have some for *Les Cahiers d'Art*, and the secret was out. The Surrealists were delighted; Breton introduced the poems, while Hugnet, Eluard, and others wrote laudatory pieces welcoming their new colleague.

Towards the end of February, 1936, Vollard and the Braques came to eat a paella with Picasso: Vollard, in aging, had become a bore, and having told his invariable anecdote about Meissonier once again, he went to sleep. Picasso was very easily vexed at this time and he could only just contain himself: he managed it, however, and when Vollard woke up and went away the party grew more cheerful. Picasso and Braque began to talk about poetry, and Picasso read some of his in French, observing that he did not think highly of what he wrote. The discussion grew animated: Picasso stated that punctuation merely served to hide the private parts of literature—he had begun by using dashes, but even they were improper— and furthermore that for his part he would like to run all the words together. They talked on and on: it must have been something like their early days, with perspective and shattered academic standards flying right and left, and revolution—aesthetic revolution—in the air.

But here the revolution had already been carried out. For once in his life Picasso was no longer an innovator. Apollinaire had suppressed punctuation more than twenty years before and Mallarmé even earlier: the Surrealists had made it an article of faith: and without Max Jacob and then Breton, Leiris and Eluard, above all Eluard, Picasso would never have written this essentially Surrealist verse with its free association and its background of automatic writing.

In the portrait of Sabartés these qualities are not particularly evident, perhaps because like many of his visual portraits it was intended to give a certain specific pleasure; but in other pieces the scorn for all conventional form, the wild fantasy of a liberated subconscious, and the obscurity inherent in what is sometimes a private and incommunicable sematology (obscurer still where a foreign language, with its unshared associations, is concerned) is as apparent as it is in many of his predecessors.

Curiously enough, just as Picasso was entering this phase Eluard was moving on to another. This did not harm their increasing friendship, and early in 1936 Picasso drew Eluard's portrait, while some months later he illustrated two of Eluard's books, *La Barre d'appui* and *Les Yeux fertiles*, with etchings, one of which is a portrait of Eluard's frail, exquisite Nusch, his second wife. There were to be three pictures for this book, and Picasso used a single large plate divided into four; at the top there is Nusch; next to her a strange calligraphic drawing of a woman looking at the sun; below Marie-Thérèse asleep on her arms; and in the fourth space Picasso set the imprint of his broad, capable, short-fingered hand. And Eluard, in spite of his comparative poverty and uncertain health, went down to Barcelona to speak at the opening of a traveling exhibition of Picasso's works organized by the Amics de l'Art nou, Friends of Modern Art, an occasion upon which Dalí uttered the curious statement, "Picasso is a first-class express that has reached Barcelona forty years late."

Some, like Eluard and many readers extremely sensitive to poetry, liked Picasso's verse: others, like Gertrude Stein, did not. She said, "He commenced to write poems but this writing was never his writing. After all the egoism of a poet is not at all the egoism of a writer, there is nothing to say about it, it is not. No. . . . Picasso, he did not work, it was not for him to decide every moment what he saw, no, poetry for him was something to be made during rather bitter meditations, but agreeably enough, in a café.

"This was his life for two years, of course he who could write, write so well with drawings and with colours, knew very well that to write with words was, for him, not to write at all. Of course he understood that but he did not wish to allow himself to be awakened, there are moments in life when one is neither dead nor alive and for two years Picasso was neither dead nor alive, it was not an agreeable period for him, but a period of rest, he, who all his life needed to empty himself and to empty himself, during two years he did not empty himself, that is to say not actively, actually he really emptied himself completely, emptied himself of many things and above all of being subjugated by a vision which was not his own vision."

Still others, though in tune with much of Picasso's visual work, feel uneasy when they are confronted with his verse: insofar as it is Picasso, they say, it cannot fail to have a true poetic content; but the Surrealist process is rather hit-or-miss, rather private, not to say hermetic, and probably, since it is an open invitation to self-indulgence, facility, and enthusiasm, much more fun to write than it is to read. They do not deny that Picasso's concatenation of earthy, concrete signs, filled with color, can take on a certain magnificence, above all in its original Spanish, but they say that like most poetry it goes on too long and that it lacks the taut discipline of his plastic expression; and sometimes they are embarrassed. Yet how fair is it to judge poetry, above all this kind of poetry, in anything but its original language? Picasso's portrait of Sabartés, for example, begins *Ascua de amistad,* and a Spanish ear will instantly, unconsciously, catch the echo of *pascua,* with its associations with the warmth and happiness of Christmas and Easter, all of which are completely lost in translation.

Good, bad, or a mixture of the two, poetry was a sheet-anchor for Picasso in late 1935 and early 1936. Sabartés was another; and so was going out at night: Picasso took to haunting Saint-Germain-des-Prés—Lipp, the Deux Magots, the Café de Flore, meeting friends almost lost to sight during Olga's social reign. But the hold was frail enough, and the storm increased; not only were there all the preparations for the ADLAN show, but two more exhibitions in Paris called for all his attention just at a time when, after a temporary lull, the legal proceedings reached a fresh crisis.

One was a show of drawings at the Galéries Renou et Colle, the other an important exhibition of paintings at Paul Rosenberg's. People were in and out of the rue La Boëtie all day long, dealers, friends, unknown well-wishers, lawyers' clerks and process-servers; and although Sabartés was a great help to him, both as a watch-dog and a secretary, Picasso became entirely overwrought. "I can't bear it any longer," he said to Sabartés, day after day. "You can see for yourself that this is no sort of a life."

He was not present at the Rosenberg vernissage, which, with Picasso's new notoriety as a poet as well as with all the gossip about his private life, was one of the events of the Paris year; but he went eventually. He was received with ecstatic applause, congratulations on the many pictures sold (dealers could never understand that he hated selling his pictures, parting with them), and with flatulent praise of a kind harder to bear than any blame.

This, together with the incessant importunities of friends and strangers, the inveterate malice of the law, and his sterility as a painter, was more than he could stand: harassed by the past, harassed by the present, and appalled by the future, he made his decision: to forget everything he left Paris, determined never to come back. On March 25 Sabartés saw him off at the Gare de Lyon: and he went to Juan-les-Pins, where one would have thought he must meet the memory of Olga at every step. Perhaps that was what he intended. Sabartés explains it by the analogy of the bullfighter who does not run away from the bull. However that may be, in order to avoid meeting her in the flesh he went there under a name very well known to him and to Sabartés but not to many others; and his letters, writs, and processes were forwarded to Pablo Ruiz.

Chapter XV

F<small>ROM</small> Juan-les-Pins Pablo Ruiz wrote to Sabartés quite often: he was sleeping eleven and twelve hours a day; he was working; he was giving up painting, sculpture, drawing, engraving, and poetry to devote himself entirely to singing; the rags Sabartés had sent him to clean his brushes had made him very happy. The letters had a tone of deliberate facetiousness, as though Picasso were withdrawing some part of his unreserved confidence and retreating into his privacy: Sabartés found it difficult to make out what was really going on in his friend's mind.

According to Sabartés Picasso was alone at Juan-les-Pins; but Sabartés' literary discretion is such that he and Picasso appear to move in an entirely male society, where women are mentioned no more than they are in the traditional Moslem world. Other writers say that he had Marie-Thérèse with him. It may be so: no one can possibly tell what rules either or both laid down for their friendship, and although Picasso did not install her in the deserted rue La Boëtie he may well have taken her to the south—he hated to be alone.

Whether Marie-Thérèse was there or not, the block between Picasso and his canvas was moving at last. Not very much—a great new stimulus would be required for that—but just enough to allow him to paint a little. "Femme à la montre" is dated April 30, 1936: it is a small oil of a woman with a wrist-watch sitting on the ground in a curiously confined space; a comb lies next to her and she is looking into a glass. The reflection is only a blur, and on the wall behind her there is a shadow, something scarcely to be seen in Picasso's painting since his neo-classical period and not often then. Her forehead is Marie-Thérèse's, but her curves are not; yet this may be due to her dress, whose pattern of squares with a dot in the middle of each was particularly suitable to the angular planes of long ago. No one would describe the "Femme à la montre" as an outstanding picture; but on the other hand no one but Picasso could have painted it.

The block against graphic work had never been so strong: when Picasso returned to Paris in the middle of May, and when he could at last be induced to show Sabartés what he had done, he produced a number of drawings, some colored. The minotaur (or rather *a* minotaur, for they were many), looking pleased, drags a little hand-cart loaded with a dead or dying mare and her new-born foal, carefully roped in, with a lantern hanging from her upright leg. Sabartés says he is moving house, a pretty thought that he probably had straight from Picasso. Another minotaur is doing much the same, a huge grim minotaur with that outstretched arm, carrying a gaunt white horse from a dark cavern with pale hands reaching out of it to a sunlit cavern inhabited by a blond girl with flowers in her hair. Then there are scenes of a faun sitting quietly at a table; something very like a Holy Family; and two horrible old men laughing at themselves in a mirror. Sabartés' language, symbolic and otherwise, was close to Picasso's; and reading these drawings as a record far more legible than the letters he had received and taking the absences into account, he saw that the whole sea itself was not enough to wash away all the bitterness in his friend's spirit.

Still, work had begun again: and for Picasso work was a sovereign remedy. Long before, he had committed himself to illustrating Buffon's - *Histoire naturelle* for Vollard: according to his invariable custom he had put it off until tomorrow; but now tomorrow had come at last, and he turned to his animals with the greatest zeal, producing at least one a day. Here there was no constraint, no question of following the text: Buffon named the creature, Picasso drew it. Few techniques were unknown to him, and for this series of thirty-one plates he used that of sugar-aquatint which, though more laborious in its stopping-out and burnishing, can give a wonderful variety and delicacy of tone, like that of a brush-drawing. Forty years before, in Pallarès' village, he had come by an intimate knowledge of sheep, goats, cattle, the farmyard in general, and long before that he had been drawing bulls, horses, and dogs. Now all this came to the surface again, fresh and clear, in a delightful sequence of naturalistic prints: he worked on them high up near the Sacré-Coeur, without the slightest need for a model to produce the fluffed-out broody hen, ready to step from the page in indignation; and his ram, a half-bred merino, might have come straight from the Horta sketchbook that had lain unopened all this time at his mother's house in Barcelona. He spent his days in Lacourière's ramshackle workshop, and when the craftsman, the best in Paris, was treating the plates or printing them off on his archaic press, Picasso and Sabartés walked about Montmartre: there had been important changes, but the village of those early years was still essentially the same; the Bateau-Lavoir had neither yet collapsed nor burned, and Frédé was still sitting there outside the Lapin Agile, a little way down the hill from one of the remaining vineyards.

These were better days. The legal settlement was moving towards its costly end; and if Picasso's work was not of the very first importance it was still work in which he took great pleasure. The Eluards were in Paris, and their friendship increased; Paul was writing exquisite lines about Picasso in his *Les Yeux fertiles,* and Nusch enchanted him with her fragile beauty and her full jolly laugh. Except that she had more style, and of course more merriment, she might have come straight from some family of his saltimbanques. She had a small round head on a long graceful neck; she was lithe and willowy, as well she might be, since like her father before her she had been a tumbler. It is said that Eluard saw her performing in the street, fell deep in love with her, and married her directly.

Picasso, the Eluards, and many other friends often met at the Deux Magots, and one evening Picasso was there with Sabartés—the Eluards were elsewhere that day—when he saw a young woman take off her elegant embroidered gloves, lay her hand on the table with its fingers spread, and stab between them with a pointed knife: her aim was imperfect, and every miss was marked with blood.

Highly individual behavior was common enough at the Deux Magots; but in combination with beauty and obvious intelligence it was very rare, in Saint-Germain-des-Prés or anywhere else. Picasso was fascinated and he said something to that effect in Spanish to Sabartés. The young woman looked up: she had lived in the Argentine and she understood the language. In spite of her answering look, and in spite of his enterprising temperament, Picasso did not presume to risk the perhaps inevitable rebuff; but Dora Maar was a friend of the Eluards, of Man Ray, and of many of the Surrealist group close to Picasso—it was odd that they had not met before—and presently the proper introductions were made.

Dora Maar was far and away the most intelligent woman Picasso had ever met: the only intellectual with whom he ever shared part of his life. She was the daughter of a Yugoslav architect married to a Frenchwoman and now settled in Paris after some years in South America: in 1936 she was a professional photographer—Brassaï speaks highly of her talent— but earlier she had been deeply concerned with painting, only to find that her work did not come up to her own exacting standards. By any count, and even more so by Picasso's, she was a strikingly good-looking woman: black hair, pale blue-green eyes, a pure oval face with rather high cheekbones, a splendid, distinctive carriage, beautiful hands. What relation there may be between merit and the possession or loss of beauty has yet to be determined, but there is no doubt that once beauty is present it is enormously enhanced, brought to full life, by intelligence; and there is no doubt either that Dora Maar possessed intelligence as well—so much so that we find virtually none of those kind, instantly legible portraits that were usual in the early stages of Picasso's friendships. ·

Dora Maar was still living with her parents and she and Picasso had not seen very much of one another before high summer came, July, the time for Paris to empty southwards; and with it the appalling news from Spain, the outbreak of the civil war.

The Spaniards in Paris reacted violently: overnight even those who had lived in France so long that they thought in French became passionately Spanish once again; and there were few who could see any middle way. Picasso's friends among them belonged to all shades of opinion from Catholic royalist to atheist anarchist, passing by every kind of anticlerical liberal, Marxist-Leninist, and Trotskyist; for most the answer was clear-cut black and white. Hardly any were indifferent: but for a moment it looked as though Picasso might be one of these. Although some of his closest friends were Communists he had not shown much concern over the battle between the Right and the Left in France, the Stavisky riots of 1934, or the triumph of the Front populaire, with the enormous changes it brought in the pattern of working-class life; he had taken little notice of the extreme tensions, the shifting balance of power in Spain and Catalonia, nor indeed of the mortal danger to the Republic and to Catalan autonomy. It was as though he were above or below or in any case outside politics. Yet this was only an appearance: where matters of primordial importance and his own country were concerned his decision was loud, determined, and unequivocal. He declared for the Republic.

His support was of great value, and the Spanish government appointed him director of the Prado. But by this time half Spain was in Franco's hands; his troops were on the Guadarrama, some twenty miles from Madrid; in August his planes bombed the city, and the treasures of the Prado were hurried away to Valencia. Whether Picasso ever performed any of the duties of his charge is doubtful: a statement that he made when he was painting "Guernica" contains the words, "In Valencia I investigated the state of the pictures saved from the Prado," but the translation may be at fault, since neither Sabartés nor any of his friends speak of this journey, while Antonina Valentin says, "Bergamín told him that when he was in Valencia supervising the arrival of the pictures from Madrid he unrolled a canvas and found that he had 'Las Meninas' in his hands. Picasso sighed and said, 'How I should have loved that!' "

However, he did do all he could: his weapons were paint, his fame, his credit with the world to back his repeated, unhesitating condemnation of the Fascists, and his money; and with these he fought as long as there was a cause to fight for.

In August, 1936, there was no way in which he could be immediately useful: the Prado pictures were safe for the time being, and Catalonia was still unaffected, the rising in Barcelona having been put down. He too went south to join the Eluards at Mougins, then an almost undiscovered little town perched on a hill five miles inland from Cannes. Several other friends were there, with more scattered along the coast; among them was Dora Maar, holidaying with Lise Deharme at Saint-Tropez.

He fetched her back to Mougins, where they stayed at the Vaste Horizon, a pleasant little hotel with some remarkably pretty girls to look after the guests; but their happiness was untimely damped. He wrote to Sabartés, "Between ourselves . . . the other day, as I was coming back in a car from Cannes with an Englishman [it was Roland Penrose], I had an accident that has left me shattered, almost unable to move, shattered, pulverized."

He was convinced of course that bones were broken: in fact they were not, but even two or three weeks later he could still write, "up until now I have been a pitiful sight, thumped black and blue by the motor-car."

I hope it is not unkind to Sir Roland, who was totally blameless, to suggest that this accident was one of the factors that reduced Picasso's painting in 1936 to such a low ebb. It came at a bad moment; without it the new and powerful stimulus of Dora Maar might have started the flow again. In the event almost all he did, apart from drawings, was to start a large, somewhat monstrous nude lying under a starlit, moonlit sky—started, presumably, before he found Dora Maar at Saint-Tropez—and then lay it aside until October; while the first portrait he painted of her is no earlier than November 19.

In the autumn they drove northwards, taking with them two of the Vaste Horizon girls, Inès and her sister, to cook for Picasso and to do the housework at the rue La Boëtie. In Paris Dora Maar showed him some of the mysteries of photography, and as he had done with Brassaï he at once took some of her plates away and began to experiment with them, producing something in the nature of Man Ray's rayograms.

About this time the legal settlement that gave Boisgeloup to Olga and shut Picasso out of it was reaching its final stage: he had nowhere to work in the silence of the country, and the studio in the rue La Boëtie was still poisoned by the memory of Olga's seals. But it so happened that Vollard had found himself an old house in a large garden with a barn deep in the country near Versailles, at Le Tremblay-sur-Mauldre. He converted the barn into a studio and in the later part of 1936 he offered it to Picasso, who was very pleased. He liked the quiet, he liked the comparative secrecy (few friends were ever invited), and he drove down three or four times a week, starting a series of quite remarkable still-lives.

When eventually Sabartés saw them he was "overwhelmed, paralysed, dazzled"; but he did not see them until November, 1938, and one of the reasons for his paralysis was that in the interval he had not been following his friend's daily progress, so that once again "it was very different from the work I knew, and I felt that I had no base-line, no starting-point from which I could measure the admiration that so entranced me."

He had not been following his friend's progress because he and Picasso had parted; and so he had no notion of this new departure until he beheld close on two years' work all assembled in a private exhibition as it were for himself alone at Le Tremblay: "a huge number of canvases . . . what a feast of color! As well as the pictures there were countless drawings and objects made out of pieces of wood and string."

With his usual discretion Sabartés leaves this break in his "dream that was to last forever" largely unexplained, merely observing that at the end of 1936, "it was now about a year that I had been living with Picasso. I had tried to help him when he would let me; and now I felt that I was in his way."

With his mute, invisible wife, Sabartés left the rue La Boëtie in January, 1937, just as Picasso was getting down to work at Le Tremblay: they did not see one another again until April in the following year. Apart from reciting pieces of his word-portrait, Sabartés says no more; but it is clear that the parting very nearly broke his heart. What it did to his finances there is no telling: he was extremely poor.

The most probable immediate cause of their separation was the plain fact of Sabartés' physical presence in the rue la Boëtie, and even more of his wife's presence. Although Picasso had to some degree taken against Marie-Thérèse (a man under great emotional stress will often transfer part of the blame for his suffering from his wife to his mistress) he had not the least intention of losing her and his little daughter. Nor had he the least intention of giving up Dora Maar. But whereas in Picasso's circumstances one avowed mistress would have caused little or no embarrassment, the production of two concurrently was quite a different matter: between men it might have passed without remark, although it would have meant sharing his secrecy, but with a respectable married woman in the house the case was altered. Where servants were concerned it was not at all the same: Picasso did not give a damn what servants thought, and he treated them with an archaic familiarity; but Señora Sabartés was not a servant, nor anything like one. The presence of the Sabartés would either have meant restraint on his part, which he could never bear at any time, or it would have meant opening himself to adverse criticism, which he could never bear either, however silent.

But a much more important underlying cause it seems to me was a change in Picasso's character, or rather a strengthening of certain strands in that most complex skein. He was born and bred in Spain: and although it is mere determinism, silly and facile, to say that because of his blood he was bound to do this or that, the fact remains that he was brought up in a pattern of behavior unlike that of the other Western countries. Every child has heard of Spanish pride and anyone who has crossed the border into that undeferential country, meeting its police and officials, will have seen this pride in operation. It takes the form of an extreme unwillingness to be trampled upon and an even greater willingness to do the trampling; of a different social contract in which the assertion of independence if not of superiority is an essential element. On the other hand anyone who has spoken to a Spanish peasant for any length of time, as equal to equal, will have found that this contract can also include the utmost sensitivity to another's feelings. In short the scales of rudeness and consideration are unlike those of Europe: as in other countries there is disrespect at times and gentleness at others; but these times and the occasions differ entirely from those the foreigner is used to, and he is confused.

Yet generally the desire for conquest seems to predominate, at least among the less polished Spaniards and even Catalans: this was the aggressive atmosphere in which Picasso's earliest companions had swum from birth; yet even so they noticed—they could not fail to notice—his restless urge to subjugate.

He carried his Spanish pattern with him to France, whose milder influence scarcely had any effect at all, and there he applied it with an unfortunate degree of success; for in addition to his background he also possessed this dominant personality. His dominance could be held in check by respect and affection, as in the case of Apollinaire and Eluard; but there were few painters apart from Matisse and perhaps Braque to whom he did not feel superior, and most of his friends and acquaintances, if they competed at all, were reduced either to subordination or, if like Sabartés they were equally proud, to retreat in the face of increasing roughness. This roughness could reach a surprising pitch on occasion: after another decade or so of notoriety and silly adulation (yet still not the height of his fame) he could savage importunate fools most barbarously. When he and Geneviève Laporte were wandering about Saint-Tropez one summer morning in the fifties they were accosted by a young Austrian painter, unknown to either of them, who asked Picasso to come and look at his work. He was carrying a bunch of gladioli. "Why the flowers?" said Picasso mildly. To paint them, said the Austrian: and asked why he painted flowers he said "because they smelt pleasant."

"Are you married?" went on Picasso.

"Yes."

"Then bring me your wife and I will —— her: after that you can smell my —— and see if it is not better than your flowers."

In English the assault sounds gross beyond belief, but the French are accustomed to a warmer language, and Geneviève Laporte, a well-brought-up young lady, laughed heartily. What is more, the Austrian did not find it intolerably offensive: he returned to the attack that same evening, sitting down uninvited at their restaurant table and asking Picasso for advice.

"You are Austrian . . . " said Picasso, busy with his crayfish. "You have a father?" The Austrian nodded. "And where does he live, *monsieur votre père?*"

"In Vienna."

Picasso looked up from his plate, gazed at the Austrian, and said, "Then go to Vienna, b—— *monsieur votre père,* and after that you will paint well." And holding out his hand, *"Au revoir, monsieur."*

Dominance and aggression was one strand: it was very, very often obscured by affection and kindness (for one Austrian who failed there were scores of Catalans who succeeded), but in any close relationship it always showed sooner or later, and the sooner the less force there was to oppose it. Olga, though devoid of parts, had possessed a concentrated destructive strength that compelled his respect; but she was gone. He never found such another Tartar, and after his release the trait, unchecked, grew more pronounced.

Another was the effect of success. In Barcelona, when he was there in 1917, he had already had a hint of the price to be paid, chiefly in the distortion and even the destruction of ordinary intercourse. By 1937 his notoriety had not reached the monstrous proportions it was to attain after the war, he could still walk about without being recognized and pestered, and by the world in general he was still treated as an ordinary human being rather than a *monstre sacré*; but since his great retrospective of 1932 he was very well known to everybody who was in any way concerned with the arts and to a great many besides, some of them tolerably self-seeking and sycophantic already. He was quite wealthy; he was the director of the Prado; and in the nature of things he was surrounded by his inferiors. He was powerful, as a character, as a painter, and as a public figure, and the corruption inseparable from authority was beginning to make itself felt;

very agreeably at this point, no doubt, like the early, euphoric stage of consumption.

Maillol was better known for the suavity of his sculpture than for that of his reflections on his fellow-artists, but with all allowance for sourness of temper and the rancor of old age (he was twenty years older than Picasso and eighty-two at the time of these remarks) this testimony from Henri Frère's *Conversations avec Maillol* is valuable.

> What finished Picasso was people's adulation. They told him that God was nothing in comparison with Picasso. So he wanted there to be no other painter at all, apart from himself. There's arrogance for you! . . .
>
> Picasso was twenty when he arrived from Spain. He was slim, with an intelligent face; he looked just like a girl. He came out to Ville-neuve-Saint-Georges on purpose to see me. He sang me a Catalan song [Maillol was a Catalan, a French Catalan from the Roussillon]. He was very agreeable. Now he's grown thick, with a face like a toad. I should never have believed it. I made him very welcome. Well, the last time I saw him, in 1937 I think it was, he would hardly speak to me. For my part I was very pleasant; I reminded him of his visit to Ville-neuve—indeed, I sang the song he had sung to me. He never even answered. He had come to see van Dongen in the studio where I was busy on "La Montagne"—he wanted van Dongen to work for him. Van Dongen was fine. He said he was bound to me. My statue was standing just there. I said to him, 'Have a look at it and tell me what you think.' Would you believe it? He turned his back on me and walked off without so much as a glance. Do you call that an artist? Do you think Michael Angelo would have turned his back if I had asked him for advice? He would have given it to me. And kindly, too. I dare say he would have shown me with the tool.

Success, release from oppression, and a greater degree of self-assertion also had their effect upon Picasso's sexual life. He now had two adoring women, and there were plenty of others in the near background, pretty, available, and none too shy. Almost any generalization about Picasso is apt to fall to pieces at once under the weight of exceptions; but although he was capable of completely disinterested candid friendship with women, and beautiful ones too—I say this with authority, since I have had the happiness of sharing some of these friendships—his attitude to those with whom he had a closer connection tended to be extremely primitive, and now it grew more so. He looked upon few as completely human: those who were unwilling to accept this view were compelled to do so; and some part of his life might be called the tragedy of a successful phallocrat. His often-repeated remark to Françoise Gilot about women being either doormats or goddesses was intended to annoy, yet unhappily it contained a good deal of truth—most unhappily, indeed, for what pleasure can there be in the company of either? Common sense might have told him that; but, as Einstein observed, common sense is the sum of the prejudices one has absorbed by the age of eighteen; and those that Picasso had absorbed by then were calculated for a different longitude, almost a different age.

No one will deny that it is often the duty of the creative man to be selfish: yet it may be that Picasso carried selfishness beyond the call of duty, and that he paid an exorbitant price for doing so. Heaven forbid that I should write a moral tract or cry up abnegation on anything but hedonistic grounds. But some degree of happiness is necessary for work; and work was necessary to Picasso: yet, although companionship, and female companionship, was even more valuable to such a lonely man than to most, he did his best to destroy the possibility of it. It is a matter of record that once he was no longer young he was a difficult if not an impossible creature to live with for any length of time; after years of cohabitation even the fanatically loyal Sabartés could speak of a *"solitude à deux."* And to one who has never thought like a man and acted like a child it is no doubt a matter of wonder that so intelligent a person as Picasso should not have seen that his vehement desire to have his cake and eat it was self-defeating; that by entirely subjugating Marie-Thérèse and Dora Maar for example he could no longer enjoy their company as full, free human beings; and that in a human relationship of any continuance there was no victory but only universal defeat.

In Dora Maar's case the defeat was, at least apparently, more spectacular than in Picasso's. Hers was a better mind in some respects; her education and her general culture far superior. But quite apart from the fact that he was a creator rather than a consumer of culture, and quite apart from his elemental strength, he had at least twenty years more of experience and far less scruple in dispute. It is also said, though by a hostile witness, that he was incapable of love—certainly a steady course of conquest and egoism must diminish that capacity—and if that was so in his case but not in hers, then in any conflict she would have been totally disarmed. Hypotheses aside, her relationship with Picasso eventually brought her to what may be termed a nervous breakdown, and to the brink of something worse; while the effect on his happiness, though less evident, was perhaps deeper and longer-lasting still.

But all that was years away. In 1937 everything seemed well enough: Olga, though always present on the edge of his field of vision—she wrote to him continually, and she had the custody of Paulo—belonged chiefly to the past; he was pleased with Marie-Thérèse and Maya, and delighted with Dora Maar.

She did not live with him, but she found him a magnificent studio so that he could work in Paris, and presently she moved into a flat of her own, just round the corner in the rue de Savoie.

The studio, or rather the set of studios and other rooms, consisted of the top floors and the attics of a noble though now decrepit town-house that had been built for the Savoie-Carignan family in the seventeenth century: absurdly enough it stood in the rue des Grands-Augustins, where Balzac had situated the beginning of the *Chef-d'oeuvre inconnu;* and from the description of the winding staircase Picasso's number seven may have been the very house. It lies back from the narrow ancient street, with a walled courtyard in front of it, and until a little while ago it looked as though Poussin or Watteau or Balzac himself might have walked out of the door at any moment. Now it has been done up: white, trim, severe, uninviting, and somehow false, the very opposite of what it was in Picasso's time when, to his delight, he found that his part of it strongly resembled the Bateau-Lavoir.

Even before moving in he had done a great deal of work. Under the stimulus of Dora Maar and the Spanish war the flow had begun again: yet a little disconcertingly the earliest picture of 1937 is a curved, brightly-colored Marie-Thérèse sitting in a small armchair, set in that same confined space with barely head-room for her cheerful hat. She is wearing a garment whose many colors are traversed by close-set black lines, so that the different surfaces resemble the corrugated cardboard he liked to use for his cast-plaster figures: she is perfectly serene, with her mild eyes both on the same side of her face—an economical device which allowed Picasso to retain the profile-line and which created an uproar at the time, though it is now so easily accepted.

But the war in Spain was not going well: although the direct assault on Madrid had been thrust back after terrible hand-to-hand fighting in the streets and the university, it was becoming even more clear that non-intervention by the great powers was an ugly farce; France and England may have acted in a muddled good faith, but they lost themselves in a cloud of words while Hitler and Mussolini poured in their forces on the Fascist side. By this stage there were some ten thousand Germans and four times as many Italians with Franco's armies, to say nothing of the Moors, while Hugh Thomas puts the number of Russians at any given time at about five hundred, though of course they also sent planes, guns, and tanks, some of which were used by the International Brigade of foreign volunteers. The

German and Italian troops, moreover, were highly trained regulars; and among the Germans there were many Luftwaffe commanders and pilots, eager to improve their skill and to try out their methods and their weapons on living targets in preparation for the coming even greater war.

With passionate energy Picasso wrote a poem, "The Dream and Lie of Franco," a Surrealist poem with the furious words tumbling upon one another in something near the delirium that Eluard once thought the expression of reason at its purest: *"fandango de lechuzas escabeche de espadas de pulpos de mal agüero estropajo de pelos de coronillas de pié en medio de la sartén en pelotas—puesto sobre el cucurucho del sorbete de bacalao frito en la sarna de su corazón de cabestro—la boca llena de la jalea de chinches de sus palabras.* A literal translation of this fragment— "mad dance of screech-owls sharp pricking sauce of swords of ill-omened squids swab of tonsure-hair standing stark-naked in the middle of the frying-pan—set on the cornet of fried stockfish in the itch of his bell-ox heart—his mouth crammed with the bed-bug jelly of his words"— gives little of the sonorous violence of the Spanish and nothing of its associations: but it was meant for a Spanish audience, and it was illustrated in the traditional Spanish and Catalan way, as an *aleluya* or an *auca,* with a series of little pictures, each self-contained but all connected. They are etchings, some showing the horrors of war—women killed, houses burning, innocence destroyed—others describing Franco, who is represented as a loathsome amorphous thing, a kind of sea-squirt, with short, sparsely bristled protuberances, yet sufficiently man-shaped to be recognized as human: he destroys a classical bust with a mattock; he is a jackbooted phallus walking a tight-rope with a holy banner; encircled by barbed wire he prays before a monstrance labeled *1 duro* (five pesetas—the word for money in general); he kills Pegasus; he is a kind of vile centaur ripped up by a bull: the bull appears three times, twice attacking the Caudillo and once merely terrifying him. At first there were fourteen of these scenes; then in June Picasso added four more of shrieking women, slaughtered babies, a murdered girl.

The sequence is not clear, but sequence is not necessary: the whole set of prints and their integrated poem express the hideous chaos, unreason, and meaningless cruelty of the war, and Picasso's utter rejection and loathing not only of war but of the right-wing values. It is perhaps significant that the Cross does not appear.

The "Sueño y mentira de Franco" was the clearest statement of Picasso's attitude at a time when there were rumors of his being not entirely in favor of the Republic: it deliberately committed him to a position from which there was no possibility of retreat. And since 1937 was to be the year of another great international exhibition in Paris, the Spanish government asked him to contribute, to undertake a whole wall in their pavilion.

Picasso said yes, certainly; but in Spain yes, certainly very often means no, and even if the officials who made the request did not already know that Picasso hated anything like an order or a commission that would bind him, they must have gone away in a state of gloomy doubt.

In fact he turned straight to another calm Marie-Thérèse with a garland of flowers on her pretty head; to some more still-lives; to Marie-Thérèse sitting with her legs tucked under her on the floor, her back turned to a partly-opened window with a balcony beyond it, a partly-opened mirror by her side, and she facing a plant in a pot. The slashing portrait of Dora Maar probably belongs to the same period, though its month is not known for sure: here the color is more violent by far and the feeling is wholly different; yet here again there are the double eyes (one white, one orange) of the full-face and the profile, and here again she is sitting in a small arm-chair in the same confined and carefully described space or cell.

Some more still-lives, for now, after his long unnatural rest, he was working with enormous speed; and then he turned to a very curious group of pictures. The most frequently reproduced of the four or five is the "Baignade," and at first glance it looks as though it might have been painted at the same time as the terrible mantis-headed bather of 1929. The vast space of sea and sky is the same, and the great figures made of smooth wood or even bone have an obvious kinship with the monster; but the whole spirit has changed, and the figures, in this case two architectural girls with minute faces, egg-like bellies, and pointed oval breasts, playing with a boat on the edge of the water, are mild, no more poisonous than milk; and even the prodigious head that rears up over the horizon towards them has only a look of pleased curiosity on its face. The calmness is in no way menacing: there is no nightmare at all.

Yet at this very time Picasso's own Málaga was undergoing the worst nightmare in its long history of siege, storming, fire, and massacre. Since the early days of the war Málaga and the country round it had been a Republican peninsula in Fascist territory, connected with the rest of Republican Spain by the coast road and little more. In mid-January, 1937, the attack began: by early February the Fascists, including nine battalions of Italians with armored cars and tanks, entered the shelled, bombed, and ruined city. A most savage proscription began at once, and death reached out along the Almería road, where the armor and the planes caught up with the countless refugees.

The fall of Málaga almost exactly coincides with one of the calmest new "bone" pictures, a woman sitting on a beach, taking a sea-urchin prickle out of her foot, and with the Marie-Thérèse by her looking-glass. There is no doubt that the news reached Paris slowly, incomplete and unreliable; but even so it came in time. At one point it seemed to me that the absence of an immediate reaction on Picasso's part was significant of his detachment from his native town and of his greater identification with Catalonia: on reflection I think the fury was there, mounting steadily as the reports came in but not finding its expression for some weeks, when another hideous tragedy acted as a catalyst, releasing all his pent-up emotion in an outburst that embraced not only its immediate cause but the whole of the Spanish war.

About March or April Picasso moved into the rue des Grands-Augustins. Although he did not mean to live there—he retained the flat in the rue La Boëtie—moving his easels, canvases, tools, and all the objects he needed about him was a serious upheaval. Yet his output scarcely faltered: almost at once the big studios took on the familiar smell of paint and turpentine, and the pictures began to line up along the walls.

Now at last he had almost as much space as he could want, at least for several years. The house does not look very large from the street, but inside the scale is altered and Picasso's two top floors had studios like low cathedrals, all the more impressive since they were approached by a dark winding staircase. In the course of centuries the building had been cut up in a haphazard sort of way, so that there were also quantities of little additional rooms, together with more and unexpected stairs, but it was the studios that remained in the visitor's memory—vast dusty spaces with huge beams and bare rafters, old red hexagonal tiles on the floor, tall windows giving on to the courtyard. They opened to the west, but Picasso never worried much about the light: as a boy he had used a candle or a lamp when the day would not serve, and now he turned on the electricity when the Paris sky was dark or when, as it often happened, he chose to work through the night.

On the second floor of the house a great room opened off the little antechamber, and it was here that Picasso received his less familiar visitors; another, lying beyond it, which had been a weaver's workshop, came to be known as the sculpture-studio, and that on the floor above, where once Jean-Louis Barrault had rehearsed, as the painting-studio: its walls sloped inwards, and through the boards of the low ceiling a thin rain of dust floated down from the loft above. A little booth opened off it, with running water, for his engraving, and all this gave him room and to spare: but to begin with he worked entirely in the lower studio.

It was here, in May, 1937, that he painted one of his most important pictures, perhaps the greatest of his life.

On April 26 German planes under Franco's orders attacked the open town of Guernica: wave after wave of Heinkels and Junkers dropped incendiary and high-explosive bombs and machine-gunned the streets from half-past four until nightfall. Of the 7,000 inhabitants they killed 1,654 and wounded 889: and the town was virtually destroyed.

After the second world-war, after Hiroshima and Nagasaki, to say nothing of London, Dresden, and the Ruhr, 2,000 casualties in an evening does not sound remarkable: in 1937 it shocked the whole world as the first cold-blooded, systematic destruction of civilians, as a new pitch of inhuman savagery and as a victory of darkness over light. Independent war-correspondents and photographers were there, and in spite of Nationalist claims that the people of Guernica had themselves blown up their town with dynamite in the sewers nobody had the least doubt of what had happened: the news came almost at once, authentic and utterly convincing. It reached Paris on April 28.

Picasso now reacted instantly, with his whole being; and his response was of course in terms of paint. On May 1 he made five sketches, three of separate figures and two of the whole composition as he then conceived it; and from the very first the three essential forms were present: the dying horse, the bull, and the woman holding a lamp from a window. From then until mid-June he worked feverishly: indeed, Zervos says that, "the first stage of the picture was conceived in a state of extreme emotional stress." Yet he also found time to write a considered statement, which began, "The Spanish conflict is reaction's fight against the people, against freedom. My whole life as an artist has been nothing but one unceasing war against reaction and against the death of art. How could it be thought, even for a moment, that I was in agreement with reaction and evil? . . . In the picture I am now working on and which I shall call 'Guernica' and in all my recent work I clearly express my loathing for the military caste that has plunged Spain into a sea of suffering and death."

In spite of his boiling fury and distress he worked with the utmost care. "Guernica" was not thrown on to its huge canvas in the excitement of a day: it was the result of weeks of sustained tension, and like his other very great works it was preceded by scores of preliminary studies that brought all his emotion, all his power of original thought, all his vast experience to a focus. This was to be his indictment of evil, and if it was to succeed he must use his weapons perfectly: there was no room for hasty improvisation.

The studies have been preserved—many are to be seen in the New York Museum of Modern Art, together with the great mural itself—and thanks to them, to their careful dating, and to the presence of Dora Maar, who took brilliant photographs of Picasso at work, the development of "Guernica" can be followed from the first pencil sketch to the finished canvas: they give a fascinating, unparallelled view of the processes of Picasso's mind brought to its highest pitch of creativity.

Before touching on these successive stages, one should perhaps attempt some description of the picture itself, of the final version as we now see it. It is immense, twenty feet across and nearly twelve high; yet it is not the size that strikes one first but rather the shock of being in the presence of a world in which the emotion itself is vast. Nor does one notice the total lack of color: black, gray, and white are natural to this silent world, silent in spite of the screams—the stunned silence of extreme grief, of disaster, and of the moments after the explosion of a bomb.

High in the middle of the picture an electric-light bulb blazes from the darkness in a shade that is like an eye, the all-seeing eye of many an early fresco; beneath it staggers a gaunt shrieking horse with the stump of a lance through its back, the point emerging from its side; under the hoofs lies the body of a man, shattered as a statue is shattered, with clean breaks, one arm stretching to the left-hand edge of the picture, the other grasping a broken sword: it touches a little growing flower. To the right of the horse a woman's horrified head stretches from a window and her long arm holds out an oil-lamp, reaching almost to the horse's head and lighting up not the house from which she leans but a single sharply-defined area, the horse's chest and the upper part of another woman, partly naked and moving painfully, as it were dazed, towards the center: her trailing leg with its huge knee and foot reaches the right-hand lower edge of the picture. From the darkness to the left of the horse, but on another plane, the dangerous head, shoulders, and one leg of a great bull emerge into the light, while below the bull and to the left a screaming woman squats, holding a dead child between her feet. Far to the right her shriek is answered by another, by a woman trapped in burning wreckage with her white arms stretched up and her white head flung back in the same atrocious agony. The small lit square window above her, with pale flames over it, corresponds to the white tail of the bull, which rises from the brute's hindquarters against a gray rectangular plane, the connection between its lit head and its dark body being obscure. And dimly, behind that menacing head, a bird—dove, chicken, goose: certainly domestic—shrieks upwards in the darkness from its ledge.

All these figures are treated with a high degree of distortion—in every case except for that of the dead baby (whose nose most shockingly hangs over the forehead of its inverted face, like some of those in his Crucifixion studies) their eyes, for example, are both on the same side of their heads—and their surfaces are flat, without the least modeling. There are hints of depth in the perspective of the little window and the lines of the dimly-seen houses, in the foreshortening of the horse's mouth, and of the broken sword, but otherwise the space about the figures is organized in superimposed angular planes.

After the first shock one sees that order underlies the apparent chaos and that although at a casual glance the picture might seem to be a polyptych made up of panels containing the bull, then the horse, then the woman with the lamp, and lastly the woman trapped, the whole is in fact bound together not only by the interpenetrating planes and the almost continuous sequence of limbs at the bottom but also and even more powerfully by a broad-based triangle formed by drawn lines and the superimposition of planes and reaching its apex just above the central lamp, with less obvious answering diagonals rising from near the base to the outer edges.

This final stage, so apparently spontaneous, was not reached without a great deal of labor: although from the beginning the three main figures were there, and although they nearly always ran bull, horse, lamp-holding woman, they and their attendant forms had to be shifted again and again to give each its utmost value and to realize the full potentiality of the whole. Some fifty studies, drawings, and paintings came before the main picture was firmly settled, with perhaps another fifty during and after the painting of it.

On May 2 the dead man appeared, a classical warrior: in this drawing the bull's head and its whole body face away from the woman with the lamp and the horse's head rears up against the bull's hindquarters, while from the wound in its belly comes a little Pegasus: in another made the same day the bull is in motion, going away from the woman and looking back at the lamp, the horse has collapsed, and the warrior is turned with his head to the left. Still on May 2 Picasso painted a large version of the horse's head, almost a mirror-image of the one he eventually used, but stretched even higher—the head of an old worn-out hack, with the outthrust pointed tongue familiar from his earlier work.

Gradually other figures appeared, some to be retained, others discarded; and by May 9 the composition had reached something near to its definitive shape. At this stage the essential figures are the lamp-holding woman (she had disappeared for a moment) and the bull looking at her: the horse has completely collapsed by a cart-wheel; there are more dead or wildly mourning figures; and the fire on the right blazes higher than it does in later versions, while from the ruins an arm reaches up, its fist clenched in the Republican salute.

The next day he gave the bull a pleasant, rather stupid human face: but this he did not keep, any more than he kept the ladder that he at one time intended to set against the burning house with a woman carrying her baby down it.

Then on May 11 Picasso squared up his enormous canvas. There was just room for it between the walls at the end of the great studio, but although it stood right down on the floor it would not quite fit under the beams without being tilted; so for the lower parts he had to squat on the floor while for the higher he climbed on a pair of steps; and in either case he had to paint on a slanting surface. None of these things worried him in the least. Dora Maar's photographs of the work in progress show the awkwardness of the canvas, the little heaps of newspaper that he used as a palette, the pots, the crushed tubes, and innumerable cigarette-ends—he always smoked heavily, and now under this almost continual strain he must have gone far beyond his usual number. Almost continual: for where painting was concerned Picasso was capable of extraordinary self-discipline, and in spite of the pressure to carry straight on he still drove out to Le Tremblay to paint his still-lives in that totally different atmosphere: without this rest it might have been impossible for him to keep his cool, incisive judgment throughout a month and more of most intensive creative effort.

The first of Dora Maar's photographs of the full canvas shows the bull turned resolutely from the woman, the horse crumpled on the ground with its head arched convulsively downwards, and the warrior, an almost neoclassical figure compared with the rest, lying on his back with his right arm, enclosed in a narrow rectangle, raised in the Republican salute: and this vertical arm, seven feet long and reaching to the lamp, is one of the most important elements in the picture, while the lamp itself has a second vertical, like a distaff, running straight down to the horse's leg. From the top of the lamp a diagonal slants down towards the bottom right-hand side of the picture, where it rises again in the burning house. On the left, though less distinctly, can be made out the answering side of the triangle and the corresponding rise. These remained constant, the firm underlying structure of the composition: but the next photograph shows a petaled sun behind the clenched fist, which now holds some ears of corn. In the third the sun has given way to a white pointed oval; the arm (already diminished in the last) has vanished, for the soldier, turned with his head to the left again, is now lying on his face.

The abolition of this vertical made an enormous difference to the picture—to its possibilities—and after some important but less vital changes Picasso all at once seized upon the opportunity offered him by the central gap, to which he had no doubt been feeling his way from the outset. The exact date of his final decision is not known, but it may well have been after a pause at Le Tremblay or when he had taken some hours off to add four etchings in the spirit of the painting to the "Sueño y mentira." With this free space at his disposal he was at last able to return to his earlier idea for the horse, rearing its head right up so that it stood as we now see it, one of the most significant figures in the picture once more: but this obscured the rear of the bull, whose tail was towards the woman. Picasso at once reversed the creature's body, leaving its head as it was; so that now while the body faced the woman the horned head was sharply averted.

Then turning to the horse again he gave it a ridged, collage-like texture with light, regular strokes of paint: he took the soldier, dismembered and broke him as though he were in fact a statue, set his open-mouthed face to the sky, and strengthened the flower (all that remained of a woman in an earlier stage) so that it came to his sword-holding hand: lastly he gave the great eye which had been the sun an electric-light bulb for its pupil, and apart from some minor changes the painting was done.

This was well on in June. Shortly afterwards it was in its place in the Spanish pavilion. From the moment it was first seen "Guernica" excited admiration, dislike, astonishment, controversy, and explanation. And in fact it is one of the few of Picasso's works where words do not necessarily leave the heart of the matter untouched, since it is one of the rare pictures of his maturity with an overt literary content, so that some part of its statement can, however roughly, be transcribed.

Admittedly, a great deal can also be said, and has been said, about its purely aesthetic aspect, about its possible sources in the mass of tradition upon which Picasso could draw, about its place in the history of art in general and of Picasso's in particular; and much of this is uncommonly interesting, for in "Guernica" one sees something of the Picasso of the Blue Period, more of Picasso the strict Cubist, the extraordinarily accomplished draughtsman, the friend of the Surrealists, the painter of the Crucifixion and the metamorphic pictures, and the author of the "Minotauromachie": a kind of epitome of the Picassos of the last thirty years and more, since all his experience and all his discoveries went into the making of it. And although we are still so near the event that few but the very young can dissociate the picture from its emotionally-charged historical context, a very great deal has been written about its merit as a painting: I shall add no more than the observation that I agree with the majority in thinking "Guernica" a noble great picture, and that as far as I am concerned it purges with pity and terror.

But "Guernica" is also an allegory, making an entirely conscious use of symbol, and it is reasonable to ask how successfully and at what level this part of the "message" is conveyed. Here we are on slightly less subjective ground; for whereas if a man is asked, "Does this picture move you?" he can usefully answer only yes or no, he can make a far more meaningful reply if he is asked, "What does this picture say?"

Everybody is agreed that the essential statement is a denunciation of the crime of war, of mindless cruelty, hatred, the massacre of innocents; but beyond that opinions differ, many seeing "Guernica" as a specific indictment of the Spanish Nationalists and some of these decrying it as a mere piece of propaganda. Yet surely this is a mistaken view: Picasso *did* condemn Franco, and he made it perfectly clear in the "Sueño y mentira"; but in "Guernica" he lifted his protest to a far higher plane, making it a passionate and universal outcry against all war, all oppression. It would have been simple for him to multiply the fists clenched in the Republican salute: he abolished them. He avoided all specific mention of either side; and although the horse and the bull had their origins in Spain, as signs they transcend the local reference.

They and the woman with the lamp were his chief symbols, and the apparent success of the allegory would seem to depend upon their interpretation by the world. They have been variously interpreted, generally in direct relationship to the Spanish war: for some the bull is Fascism, dreading the woman with the light, another version of the girl with the candle in the "Minotauromachie," who is supposed to repel the monster, and the horse is the Republic; while for others the roles are reversed and the horse, surprisingly enough, is Spanish Nationalism. Others again have looked back to Picasso's earlier work to elucidate his signs, particularly to his many bull-ring scenes; and they have been sadly puzzled by his ambivalent attitude towards both the bull and the minotaur, either of which can be now villain now hero—as recently as the "Sueño y mentira" it is the bull which confronts Franco, eventually goring him to death.

As far as the "Guernica" bull is concerned, however, we know exactly what Picasso had in mind. After the Liberation of Paris an American soldier, Jerome Seckler, called upon him and asked him, in effect, to explain his painting. The young man must have been as appealing as he was naïve, for although Picasso had been bored and distressed by this perpetually-recurring question for more than thirty years he took him upstairs, listened patiently to his voluble analyses of various pictures, including "Guernica," and talked to him for a long while, very kindly and I believe without any of the perversity he often displayed when badgered. "I talked about the symbol of the bull, the horse, the hands with the lifelines, etc., and the origin of the symbols in the Spanish mythology. Picasso kept nodding his head as I spoke. 'Yes,' he said, 'the bull there represents brutality, the horse the people. Yes, there I used symbolism, but not in the others.' "

During the same interview he observed, apropos of his political consciousness, "There is no deliberate sense of propaganda in my painting."

"Except in the 'Guernica,' " said Seckler.

"Yes," he replied, "except in the 'Guernica.' In that there is a deliberate appeal to people, a deliberate sense of propaganda."

Picasso's own attitude towards symbols varied: at one time he said that it was the duty of the viewer to create them out of the material the painter provided and to interpret them. But if in the case of "Guernica" we take him at his word, accepting the bull as mere brutality and the horse as the people, then the allegory takes on a universal aspect. The crime is no longer committed by Fascists in a given incident in the Spanish war but by all brutal, evil stupidity in power, and the painting is a huge protest against the universal suffering that it causes. It can also be read not as a moral exhortation but as a despairing assertion that there is no victory, that both sides inevitably lose, leaving only a brute in a desolate, apocalyptic battlefield full of hate, devoid of decency, art, and humanity. And this reading is supported by the fact that when Picasso was painting "Guernica" he made some experiments with papier-collé: one of the collages was a tear of blood which he moved from one face to another, lingering longest on the bull as though it were a creature to be pitied equally with the rest. In the end he discarded the tear but he said to the poet José Bergamín, "We'll put it in a box and we'll go at least every Friday and stick it on the bull."

It has been said that the symbolism of "Guernica" is private, obscure, even hermetic; that the message therefore does not and cannot come across, and that the widely-differing interpretations prove it. This would be a damaging criticism of an advertisement that extolled some product or some given course of action; but does it really apply to "Guernica"? Outside the exact sciences scarcely anything worth saying can be said except by indirection; by its very being a valid symbol acquires an almost sacred power, and even though it may be but dimly apprehended in a literal sense (who "understands" the Easter Island statues or the older African carvings, yet who is unmoved by them?) it is apprehended at some very sensitive level, unconcerned with common logic, that reacts with a primitive strength. The half-heard old Latin of the Mass, its literal meaning perhaps scarcely grasped at all, may well have had a more profound effect than the audible everyday vernacular words of the present ritual, with their sadly commonplace associations. And it may be said that as the truth and life of Picasso's high Cubist pictures stem from their basis in observed reality, so the value of his symbols arise from their initial validity for him.

Another criticism is that propaganda enters into the picture; and that just as remarks are not literature so propaganda is not art, which has nothing to do with politics nor with morals. In view of Picasso's own words it is impossible to deny that propaganda was intended: in his first fury he may well have meant as direct an attack on the Fascists as he had already made on Franco, but in the course of his painting he sublimated all particularity and all reference to immediate events.

As to the universality of "Guernica," only the future years, the objective centuries, can judge; but those who believe in it, and the present writer is one, already have somewhat disconcerting allies in the Spanish government itself, which, far from feeling condemned, is doing its utmost to get the picture to Madrid.

Perhaps art has nothing to do with politics nor with morals: but it quite certainly has to do with the distinction between true and false. At a certain level the difference between aesthetic truth and falsity merges with that between light and darkness; and when those issues were presented to him, there was no doubt where Picasso stood.

Chapter XVI

WHEN Picasso traveled south in the late summer of 1937 he did not leave "Guernica" behind him. The theme remained, working in his mind, and in the next few months he painted, drew, or engraved a number of postscripts, either directly related to the main picture or in the same spirit. He had done this after the "Demoiselles d'Avignon"; but whereas in 1907 he had been concerned solely with aesthetic problems, thirty years later the whole framework within which painting or any other spiritual activity had any meaning was in question: the Spanish war was the obvious prelude to an even more appalling conflict: as Michel Leiris wrote with terrible prescience, "in a black and white oblong . . . Picasso sends us our mourning-letter: everything we love is about to die."

Many of the postscripts were the heads of women, weeping: and here again there was an essential difference between them and the pictures that followed the "Demoiselles d'Avignon," for not only were they directly connected with outside events but many of these distraught, pain-racked faces also referred to Dora Maar. She was very deeply attached to him, and he in his own way to her no doubt, although he denied it later; but she was a keenly intelligent woman, better informed about the state of the world than her lover and perhaps even more alive to the hideous consequences of the coming war. She had as great a capacity for elation and suffering as Picasso, though without his power of surmounting them, and like all intellectuals in those years she was unhappy when she looked beyond her own immediate boundaries: but in that particular couple there was room for only one tormented mind.

Yet this gives a picture of unrelieved distress, which is completely untrue. Anguish there was, with the Spanish war going from bad to worse, quite apart from the less tangible causes for unhappiness built into Picasso's temperament: which perhaps made it inevitable that in speaking of his loves he should refer to "two bodies wrapped in barbed wire, each tearing the other to pieces.'' But at the same time one has to reckon with Picasso's astonishingly rapid change of mood, with his vivid pleasure in Dora Maar's company—he could talk to her as he could talk to a man, and she was strikingly beautiful as well, a woman of his own world entirely, completely disinterested, wholly devoted to painting, above all to Picasso's painting—and with the effect of the Mediterranean sun.

They drove down in the big Hispano-Suiza, together with Kazbek, an Afghan hound, the most recent in Picasso's line: he had not been fortunate in his dogs these last few years, and Elft, Kazbek's predecessor, had been retired to the country for incompatability of temperament; but Kazbek, though neither particularly brave nor intelligent, gave Picasso great pleasure. Picasso's relationship with his dogs was of a particular kind: in some ways he was extraordinarily close to them (as he was to cats, owls, and doves), in others strangely remote; while at no time was there any question of whose convenience came first. After the early mongrels they were nearly always animals of a given race, or thought to be so, of little use apart from their looks, the intelligence of their forms, their presence, and a certain fidelity, while for his part he would often leave them for long periods or abandon them entirely. Yet when they were together there appeared to be the closest bond, the painter and the dog communing on the same level. It was a contract unlike other contracts and perhaps it satisfied most of his creatures.

Their destination was Mougins again, where Eluard and Nusch were already installed; and either on the way or during an early excursion Picasso stopped at Juan-les-Pins, where he painted a very happy picture of boats on the shore with the French flag flying bravely in the middle.

Happiness glows in much of the remaining work of 1937—in the splendid sunflowers at Mougins, in the charming portraits of Dora Maar, of the infinitely stylish Nusch and other friends—and there is tranquillity at least in the portrait-etchings of his old friend Vollard and some smaller pieces: perhaps also in the strange December drawing of a distorted minotaur sitting on the strand, his breast pierced through and through by an arrow, while a calm sea-maiden, not unlike Marie-Thérèse with flowers in her hair, holds a glass up to his amazed and dying face. The drawing has been interpreted as the death of Picasso's sexual drive, and although the evidence of at least three more acknowledged mistresses and two children makes the suggestion seem a little strange, the drawing may still be the expression of a release of some kind, for this was the end of the minotaur: he never appeared again. It was a cheerful holiday in many ways, with quantities of friends at Mougins and along the coast. Matisse was at Nice: Picasso often went to see him, and their relationship took on a new cordiality. They were made to be friends, and in later years they did in fact come much closer to one another. Had their friendship matured when Picasso was in his twenties or thirties life might have been happier for him—certainly less lonely—and he might have absorbed something of Matisse's serenity, to say nothing of his good manners, which (though bourgeois no doubt) are thought by many to ease the strain of daily contact, leaving more energy for work: but from the first they had been pitted against one another and the tension had been much increased by friends who carried unconsidered remarks to and fro, sharpening them on the way. It is true that there were plenty of cracks such as "In comparison with me, Matisse is a young lady" on Picasso's part; and the discipline he observed in drawing would sometimes abandon him in the heat of argument, so that Matisse, an extremely sensitive and naturally very well-bred man, came positively to dread the wounds that Picasso could inflict, and to avoid the possibility of conflict. Yet their mutual respect never wavered for a moment; and while Picasso would not allow anyone else to attack Matisse, Matisse never attacked Picasso at all.

Yet upon the whole, in spite of the sea, the sun, the gaiety, and a kind of extra holiday in the form of an autumn journey to Switzerland, where he saw Paul Klee, stress and anxiety predominate in these later pictures of 1937. It could hardly have been otherwise, insofar as Picasso was a Spaniard through and through, a Republican and, though not committed to any party, one who swam in the left-wing atmosphere of his time: for in Spain the whole of the north was gone, and although Madrid still held out, two-thirds of the country, together with the Basque industrial towns and the Asturian mines, was in Franco's hands. And Klee, one of the few painters Picasso liked and respected, was a living example of what Fascism had in store for the rest of the world—living only because he had escaped from Germany, where the Bauhaus had been liquidated, where much of Klee's work had been confiscated, and where some particularly fine examples were now being shown in the official Nazi exhibition of Degenerate Art at Munich.

On the same basis 1938 might have been expected to be a barren year: it was nothing of the kind. In January he made some portraits of Maya, now between two and three years old, a squat child at this time, though later, when her legs grew, she became far prettier. These have little in common with the early portraits of her half-brother, though there is the same childish delicacy of color: in one the lumpish little girl in a check pinafore sits grasping a wooden horse and a brutish doll; both Maya and the doll are double-faced, in that they each have both a profile and a three-quarter-face nose, and their eyes are on what would conventionally be the same side of their head; her ash-fair hair, inherited from her mother or perhaps from her paternal grandfather, Don José, is green, and green also invades her complexion. But in both this and the companion portrait where the doll is a more comely object in a sailor hat, she is entirely Maya. Sometimes Picasso's women tend to merge in a general moon-faced type, but his friends and children never, however much he might redistribute their features for simultaneity or other reasons: nor do his dogs.

Then early in the year he rediscovered cocks. He had already modeled one at Boisgeloup and he had etched another for Buffon and of course he had drawn them at Horta, but these were even prouder birds, spurred, crowing, full of male aggression. It is all the more shocking therefore to find one upside-down and helpless on a woman's lap, its legs tied, its bosom already half-plucked, its furious head straining up: the woman is horrible, almost bald and entirely indifferent; one hand grasps a wing as she gazes into the distance; and there is a kitchen knife on the floor beside her. The bright colors, the silence, the woman's lunatic composure, are indescribably shocking. In a way she is allied to another woman painted the summer before, a strange figure with mad eyes and a mad knowing smile (said by Penrose to be Paul Eluard) suckling a cat: or rather a stiff-legged tiger-striped kitten that is also upside-down on her lap. The identification seems curious, but Penrose was at Mougins when the picture was painted; he was intimately acquainted with the people concerned; and he can scarcely be wrong. He speaks of Picasso's "diabolical playfulness" that summer, and it is not impossible that this Tiresias Eluard is connected with a circumstance that Penrose, his hands tied by decency and respect for his friends, could hardly have mentioned, but what Picasso did not mind relating—it was in fact fairly common knowledge. "Nusch was wonderful," he said to Geneviève Laporte. "Exactly what Paul needed. You know Paul would have liked me to go to bed with her, and I didn't want to. I was very fond of Nusch, but not in that way. Paul was furious. He said that if I refused I was not a real friend. Sometimes he used to take a whore to an hotel. Nusch and I would wait for him, gossiping in the café downstairs." Picasso had a great tenderness for Madame Eluard, and he was very much her friend: one of his portraits of her is inscribed *Poor Nusch, poor Nusch,* for he knew, in reverse, something of the trials of being married to a creative man—Eluard was as temperamental as Picasso, though in another way.

The picture may therefore contain a private reference to Eluard's notion of friendship, a reference important only in that it would show Picasso's cheerful acceptance in those he loved of ways so very unlike his own; but on the other hand the woman with a cat, which was preceded by a likeness of Eluard dressed as an Arlésienne, may simply be part of Picasso's delight in dressing up, wearing masks and false noses, a taste that grew on him with the years and that may in its turn give some support to the suggestion that the woman with the cock is in fact a self-portrait. Her lock of hair certainly resembles Picasso's; and had one no fear of wandering in the jungle of hypotheses the cock, the knife, and the transvestite man might be made to take on a startling symbolic significance.

This spring also saw the beginning of a new manner, and whenever it is mentioned the name of Arcimboldo comes up, since Picasso took to painting figures with the texture and the appearance of more or less natural substances, such as matting or woven straw, while some four hundred years before the sixteenth-century Lombard Arcimboldo had used exquisitely painted fruit, vegetables, wheatsheaves, and so on, according to the character and the season, to build up his ingenious, amusing, somewhat uneasy people—pieces of virtuoso, slightly Surrealist decoration. There the likeness ends; and citing Arcimboldo as Picasso's predecessor, inspiration, and model is as valid as pointing out that two poets, belonging to widely different civilizations and saying entirely different things, both used something like the same meter.

A little while after Hitler swallowed Austria, which he did in March, 1938, Picasso met Sabartés in Saint-Germain-des-Prés and took him back to the studio in the rue des Grands-Augustins. Picasso was obviously at his most agreeable, and he could be wonderfully charming on occasion: Sabartés was completely reconquered, and they saw one another several times before July, when Picasso and Dora Maar went down to Mougins again, suddenly darting off by night with the Eluards at an hour's notice.

Here he carried on with his basket-work pictures, with portraits of Dora Maar, sometimes combined with the matting texture and carried to the extremity of distortion, and of Nusch Eluard, in much the same cheerful company as the year before. There are photographs of him sitting by the sea, as brown as an Indian and gleaming with health: he is fifty-six, but there is no sign of age in his trim, well-made body, very little in his still boyish face, and only a streak or two of gray in his thick black hair.

Yet presently the sun was overcast. In September the dispute between Germany and Czechoslovakia suddenly rose to a horrifying crisis, and after some days of feverish, fruitless negotiation by the Western politicians everybody thought that a general war was inevitable and imminent—Armageddon in a few days time. All Europe was in arms: the French began to mobilize their enormous armies; men vanished from the beaches, and the endless columns of troops moved into position, while in England the air-raid sirens howled by way of trial and eager volunteers dug shelters from the bombs. Picasso was very deeply disturbed: as the news grew even worse he packed everything into the car and drove north through the night to the seclusion of Le Tremblay. Then on the very last day of the month, against all hope, the Munich agreement was signed: it betrayed ten million Czechs and Slovaks, gave the Nazis another highly efficient armament industry, and made the war inevitable. Daladier flew back to cheering crowds in Paris, Chamberlain to cheering crowds in London. He told them that he had brought back peace with honor, peace for our time.

Did Picasso share in the general sigh of ignoble relief? Perhaps not: war would have withdrawn the Axis forces from Spain, and once they had gone the Republicans might well have beaten Franco. It is true that by this time the position was very grave, the Nationalists' drive having reached the Mediterranean coast between Valencia and Tortosa, so that they occupied a belt a hundred miles in depth, cutting off Madrid from Barcelona; but they had been held and counter-attacked on the Ebro. The war was still in the balance, and the removal of foreign troops, above all of foreign aircraft, would probably have been decisive, while a French invasion would have made victory certain.

In the precarious, guilty euphoria that followed the betrayal of Czechoslovakia Picasso returned to Paris; and there he met Sabartés again. They talked about Munich, about the friends they shared, about Picasso's poems, old and new; Picasso took him to Le Tremblay, where he saw the recent works that moved him so; and presently they came to a discreet agreement that bound Sabartés to Picasso's service (but not to the same house) for the rest of his life.

It was at this time that Picasso painted the menacing still-lives with bulls' heads, heavy with reference to "Guernica," and probably the curious picture, related to the Mayas of January, in which an equally dwarvish child in a sailor-suit, the ribbon of the hat reading PICASSO, holds a butterfly-net while a red butterfly flies between the net and his nose. As well as "Guernica," one of these still-lives and the child caught the ingenuous American soldier's eye at the Liberation Salon, and he explained them to Picasso. The child: "I said I thought it to be a self-portrait—the sailor's suit, the net, the red butterfly showing Picasso as a person seeking a solution to the problem of the times, trying to find a better world. He listened intently and finally said, 'Yes, it's me, but I did not mean it to have any political significance at all.' I asked why he painted himself as a sailor. 'Because,' he answered, 'I always wear a sailor shirt. See?' He opened up his shirt and pulled at his underwear—it was white with blue stripes! 'But what of the red butterfly?' I asked. 'Didn't you deliberately make it red because of its political significance?' 'Not particularly,' he replied. 'If it was, it was in my subconscious!' 'But,' I insisted, 'it must have a definite meaning for you whether you say so or not. What's in your subconscious is a result of your conscious thinking. There is no escape from reality.' "

Whatever the state of his subconscious mind may have been, at this stage Picasso was certainly not a Communist, in spite of the passionate commitment of many of his friends. In Spain the Communists, under the direct control of Moscow, were fighting the Trotskyists and the anarchists with almost as much ferocity as they fought the Fascists, thus weakening the already divided Left to a catastrophic degree; and many of Picasso's friends were anarchists. Furthermore, the Communists had made a partly successful attempt at importing Stalin's great Russian purges into Spain. It took an even more obvious, even more immediate tyranny, together with the Communist share in the French resistance, the influence of his friends, and the enormous exaltation of the Liberation to make him a card-carrying member of the Party, perhaps the most apolitical Communist in France.

The young man then turned to the still-life with the bull. There were two of these pictures, both with a candle on the left, a palette and brushes on an open book in the middle, and the bull's head on a little plinth, lowering away on the right: in one the candle has a green shade and the bull is red; in the other a candle burns unshaded and it is accompanied by another source of light, perhaps the sun, while the bull is black. It was the black bull that was shown in the Liberation Salon, and it was the black bull that the American soldier explained. "The bull, I said, must represent Fascism, the lamp, by its powerful glow, the palette and the book all represented culture and freedom—the things we're fighting for—the painting showing the fierce struggle going on between the two. 'No,' said Picasso, 'the bull is not Fascism, but it is brutality and darkness.' "

Then at a later interview, when Seckler told him that the political significance of those things was there whether he consciously thought of it or not, "Yes," he answered, "what you say is very true, but I don't know why I used those particular objects. They don't represent anything in particular. The bull is a bull, the palette a palette, amd the lamp is a lamp. That's all. But there is definitely no political connection there for me. Darkness and brutality, yes, but not Fascism."

Whether the train of thought that is evident in these bulls' heads would have continued through the rest of 1938 cannot be told, for in that cruel winter he was struck down with sciatica. It is one of the most painful maladies known to man; in no position can the suffering body find lasting rest, and the nights stretch out for centuries; and it is made even worse, if possible, by being somewhat ridiculous. Like many hypochondriacs Picasso was more alarmed by the prospect of illness than by disease itself: he was not the best of patients, but he did put up with the excruciating pain surprisingly well.

Fortunately, since the doctor had said the sciatica would lay him up for at least three months, Sabartés was back, and every day Sabartés came through the vile weather to keep him company in the evenings and late into the night, Picasso keeping him as long as ever he could, sitting there by the fire in the crowded, inconvenient main bedroom of the rue La Boëtie. It had been the heart of Picasso's one sad attempt at an orderly life, and the two brass beds were still there; Picasso lay in one, amid a heap of papers; Olga's, of course, was empty. But since her time the room had gradually taken on the appearance of a doss-house: the closely-packed chairs were covered with further heaps that had to be removed for the stream of visitors; some fair-sized tables had been brought in to take up what little space was left, and all but one were hidden under papers, books, portfolios, and a confusion of objects such as dead electric bulbs, empty match-boxes, and packets that had once held cigarettes. Upon the one exception stood the boot of some defunct motor-car, probably salvaged from a rubbish-dump. Between Picasso's groans they had long, desultory conversations about painting, truth in painting, portraiture: to fill a gap Sabartés observed that he would like to see himself as a Spanish gentleman of the sixteenth century, with a plumed bonnet to cover his bald pate. In an offhand tone Picasso said he would do it, but at this point he was interrupted by another bout of agony, and his voice changed to a howl, a howl mingled with a description of the picture—a life-sized Sabartés accompanied by a naked woman and a very lean dog, like Kazbek.

The next day was Christmas: the sciatica had been going on for a week. Sabartés had virtually dismissed the idea of the portrait, not only because of the pain but even more because Picasso had already thought the picture out, and once that was done, its freshness gone, he lost interest. While they talked about painting that day Picasso said as much as he explained the process of his thought: he also said a number of other things—that he had never had a guitar in his hands before he took to painting them, that he bought one with the first money he received, and had never painted a guitar since (this was not literally true nor anything like it; but Picasso often spoke somewhat at random); that it was a mistake to suppose that when young he went to the bull-fight and then painted what he had seen— not at all, he did the painting first to earn the entrance money; and that a picture was *never* finished. At midday Sabartés went home in compliment to his wife's Christmas dinner, but in the afternoon he noticed that Picasso was somewhat absent, gazing at him fixedly from time to time: he was in fact drawing, and among the drawings he had made was one of Sabartés in a ruff, wearing a velvet hat with a feather in it.

The next day Picasso's present was an immensely accomplished portrait of his friend as a monk, together with all the designs for the costumes and settings of the *Tricorne*, done up in a perfect imitation of a Barcelona schoolboy's satchel; and the day after that Sabartés in a ruff again, but without a hat.

Each of the many visitors had prescribed remedies for sciatica, and by this time the most active and convincing of them all, a picture-dealer, had persuaded Picasso to see his uncle, a medical man with a way of treating the disease by remote cautery. The first day the doctor blew all the fuses in the rue La Boëtie, but the next he brought a transformer, assembled his apparatus with the help of the chauffeur, peered at Picasso's nose, thrust an instrument into it, and immediately cauterized a nerve. There was a smell of roasting meat. "There," said the doctor. "That's all." With disarming candor he added, "If the pain goes within twenty-four hours, it's my treatment. If it only goes later, then I have nothing to do with it."

In fact the pain had gone already. Picasso moved in his bed, stirred more and more briskly, got up, stood on one leg and then the other: he was cured. To call the treatment quackery would not only be unkind but absurd, if only because the legitimate bounds of psychosomatic medicine are so very wide: but perhaps they were even wider than usual for Picasso, since Picasso, more than any painter in Europe since neolithic times, was susceptible to magic in every form.

Although the patient was cured, the hypochondriac reasserted his rights, and Picasso went straight back to bed, explaining that it would be imprudent to expose himself to the weather at this stage, and staying there for much of the time until his show at Rosenberg's gallery in January, 1939, an important exhibition that included many of the still-lives painted at Le Tremblay.

By this time the long agony of the Spanish civil war was nearing its end. After furious battles in the wild Maestrazgo country, where Picasso and Pallarès had painted in their cave, the Republicans were driven back across the Ebro with the loss of seventy thousand men. The road into Catalonia was open, and by Christmas, 1938, the main attack was under way. The Republicans, outnumbered, short of weapons and ammunition, almost devoid of armor and aircraft, were thrust north with ever-increasing speed; the retreat became a rout; and just before the fall of Barcelona on January 26, 1939, the government fled to Gerona, then to Figueras.

The Prado pictures were there, in lorries, and they crossed into France a few days before Franco's armies reached the frontier to thrust half a million refugees, soldiers and civilians, into neutral territory, where they were interned in desolate naked camps. And at the end of the war Picasso's mother died, still in Barcelona: she was eighty-three.

Although none of this is directly apparent in Picasso's work of the time, a great deal of his mind was taken up with the tragedy. From the very beginning of the war he had supported the Republic with his painting, his public statements, and his money: early in 1939 a government publication stated that he had given three hundred thousand francs, while Juan Larrea, an official engaged in distributing relief, put the figure at four hundred thousand. Exchange rates do not mean a great deal, because life was still unbelievably cheap in Europe in those days, and one could live quite well in Paris and run a car on three thousand francs a month: Picasso, it is true, lived better than most, but he was an abstemious man, and this sum probably represented at least three years of his expenditure. But the three or four hundred thousand francs was only the amount given to official agencies. In December, 1938, he set up two centers for feeding children (food was terribly short in the Republic), the one in Barcelona, the other in Madrid, and he started them off with two hundred thousand francs. Although he had been prosperous for the last twenty years and although his work sold well when he could bring himself to part with it, the sums he then received were small in comparison with those paid in the fifties and minute compared with those of today; he also had to provide Olga's handsome allowance, and to look after his son and daughter and some discreet pensioners. He did not find this money easy to raise, and he forced himself to sell some pictures, such as the "Jeune fille avec un coq," that he had always intended to keep. Then as the refugees poured into France many of them turned to him, and I have not heard of a single case where they wrote or called in vain. A typical example is to be found in Palau i Fabre's *Picasso i els seus amics catalans*: in February, 1939, the time of the exodus, a group of Catalan writers escaped from their concentration camp at Le Boulou, just on the French side of the border, and reached Perpignan, some thirteen miles further on, but still in Catalan-speaking country. There they found a restaurant that gave them credit for a few days: they slept in the station waiting-room. After these few days the restaurant-keeper presented his bill: Republican money was so much waste-paper and they had not been able to find any other; they could not tell what to do. None of them knew Picasso, but one had written some articles on him: the restaurant-keeper advanced enough to pay for a telegram asking for help—a message with little hope, there being no acquaintance whatever, no proof of identity, and none of good faith. The next day, also by telegram, the help arrived, enough to pay the bill, to buy shoes and clothes for all six men, and to take them to Toulouse with some money to spare. Then there was Joan Rebull, the sculptor: Picasso bought two of his pieces and arranged an exhibition for him in his own house. And there were many, many more, some, like Rebull and Enric Casanovas, known, but others, the greater number, total strangers.

During these harrowing months Picasso was also preoccupied with his own mundane daily problems, one of which was moving house, always a matter of grave concern, endless indecision, and great nervous expenditure; he abominated the upheaval as an interruption to his work and his set habits; he disliked leaving what he had once possessed; and there was always the possibility that some removal-man or some person charged with receiving or giving at either end might disturb a heap or throw something away. Eventually he worked out a compromise: he would live at the rue des Grands-Augustins, taking everything he needed, but he would also keep on the flat in the rue La Boëtie, leaving some of his accumulations there, and using it if he chose. The move was complicated by the fact that the flat in the rue des Grands-Augustins had to be transformed; it had to have central-heating and many alterations and an engraver's press had to be installed; and the workmen neither came when they were expected nor finished by the time they had agreed.

Then there was the business side of a successful painter's life: quite apart from the Rosenberg show in January, which could be dealt with by word of mouth or by the hated telephone, Picasso had no less than twelve exhibitions in the United States during 1939, including the very important retrospective, Picasso: Forty Years of his Art, at the New York Museum of Modern Art (where "Guernica" came to rest, for the time being on the typically noncommittal Picasso terms of "extended loan" which meant that he did not relinquish possession of it), and two in London; and at least until the return of Sabartés he had no filing-system but his heaps.

But now Sabartés was back, and although his business methods were those of the middle ages they were more efficient than Picasso's, and it is no doubt thanks to his presence that we have a surprising amount of work dating from this year.

In January, 1939, Picasso painted a "Femme couchée lisant," a particularly engaging, quiet, rounded picture related to Marie-Thérèse: she is lying sideways on a divan, dressed, her head on a cushion and her feet tucked up, and beneath her clasped hands lies a book; but she is nearly asleep. The same day he painted another, of exactly the same size, "Femme couchée sur un canapé," and here there is no quietness at all:

the figure is made up of strong, mostly triangular, planes, and the distortion of her features is rendered the more extreme by the comparatively naturalistic treatment of the trees seen through the window, the same window that is in the other picture. An obvious but not necessarily mistaken explanation of the violent difference between the two is that it is the result of a mind deeply disturbed finding peace for a few hours and then shattering it immediately afterwards.

During these early months of 1939 he also went regularly to Lacourière's workshop in Montmartre, where he made a number of colored etchings, experimenting with the various techniques and inventing new ones. A little earlier he had produced an ambitious, unusually large aquatint of a woman with a tambourine: she is dancing and both the front and the back of her body as well as the two sides of her face are visible, the simultaneity of the early Cubist pictures and of much later work here serving a double purpose, for she is clearly in the frenzied motion of the Charleston or the black-bottom. But now he had an idea of working on his own poems, perhaps as he and Eluard had collaborated on the *Grand Air* in 1936, or at least of printing them on pages adorned by himself. Vollard was very eager to bring out the book, and had Picasso's interest lasted it might have been one of his most remarkable publications; but Picasso grew bored as the newness faded, as the problems were solved one by one, and as the details of production dragged on in tedious length. Besides, there were other things upon his mind: his painting among them. At the end of March, almost on the very day that Madrid fell at last, he painted still another portrait of Dora Maar.

There is no connection with the end of the war—all hope had gone even before Barcelona fell—and there is no kind of protest: for although in some ways Picasso was extraordinarily open, discussing his mistresses' problems with his chauffeur, for example, and doing so in their presence, in others he was as secret as the tomb. What he considered his private affairs (and this included bereavement) remained completely hidden; and although "Guernica" is of course a furious protest, it is essentially impersonal, the outcry of light against darkness rather than the direct attack of one man against another body of men who have injured him. Yet the portrait of Dora Maar is one of the few pictures to which the term Expressionist, for what it is worth, can be usefully applied; and even when all allowances for hindsight are made it can still be said that the portrait is the expression of a mind that has acquired a greater intensity of perception through suffering: although it is not an unhappy picture it has a gravity of a kind scarcely to be seen before, an even fuller maturity. The face is indeed distorted in what was by now his usual manner and the features redistributed, with a hint of a double-faced nose on one side and the mouth on the other; but the two huge full-face eyes staring out and beyond the spectator and the wealth of color give the picture a singularly commanding power.

In the quietness of Le Tremblay a month later, after some more heads of Dora Maar, he painted a shocking cat with a bird in its mouth: this has been interpreted as a statement about cruelty, as a prevision of the coming war and its senseless destruction, and even as a reference to Mussolini's attack upon Albania of the Good Friday of 1939. Picasso himself said that the theme had been in his mind for a long while, but he did not go farther: if he had been pressed he might well have said that the cat was a cat and the bird was a bird. The nature of cats is after all to catch birds, and Picasso, though kind, had no more sentimentality than can survive a childhood familiar with the bull-ring.

Even builders go at last, and in June, 1939, Picasso's momentous move took place. By July it was over: both places were now more or less habitable, and one was at least for the moment spick and span. Although his dwellings have often been called slums, and although they looked very like vague depositories, they were not really dirty, as Picasso understood the term. He did not mind dust in his working quarters, nor cigarette-ends, crushed paint-tubes or the mess of birds, but he was very particular about cleanliness elsewhere; he would never, for example, allow Inès to scour the bath with an abrasive powder that might make its surface dirt-absorbent in the course of time: she was always to use old-fashioned household soap, and nothing else. It may not be impertinent to add that ever since he had been able to afford a place with a bathroom he also used a great deal of it on himself. It is true that in the twenties he said to Cocteau, who wanted to bring a miracle on the stage, "A miracle? There's nothing surprising about a miracle. Why, it's a miracle every morning that I don't melt in my bath," and that Derain, hearing of this, observed, "A few years ago it would have been a greater miracle if Picasso had taken a bath at any hour of the day." But Derain was voicing the general dissatisfaction at Picasso's prosperity rather than stating an acknowledged truth, for a tin hip-bath had been one of Picasso's very earliest acquisitions when he came to live in Paris.

Early in July he and Dora Maar set off for Antibes, where Sabartés was to join them in a few weeks time; they went by train, with Marcel Boudin following by road; and this was, I believe, because Dora Maar tended to be car-sick. There would be no difficulty about finding a lodging, even at the height of this glorious, menacing summer, since Man Ray was about to leave a flat with a room big enough for a studio; they could walk straight into it, and in all likelihood Picasso would be at work within a few days.

But before the month was out there was Picasso knocking on Sabartés' door at dawn: Vollard had died suddenly, and in spite of Picasso's dread and hatred of everything to do with death he had driven all night to be present at his old friend's funeral. He lingered a few days in the discomfort of the empty rue La Boëtie and then traveled south again with Sabartés, lured by the prospect of a bull-fight at Saint-Raphaël. Sabartés was an idolater, but not a blind idolater, and it is fascinating to read his account of Picasso suggesting the bull-fight, imposing his wishes, morally obliging Sabartés to agree, and then by a subtle, totally unscrupulous twist reversing the roles, so that it was the importunate Sabartés who longed to go, Picasso who kindly acquiesced, and Sabartés who would bear all the responsibility if the performance were disappointing—fascinating because it is a circumstantial, detailed, kindly, and entirely convincing account of a pattern of behavior, very closely allied to Picasso's strong inclination to transfer the blame for a disagreeable situation to any shoulders weak enough to accept it, that repeats itself throughout the course of his recorded life. There are many instances in Françoise Gilot's book, for example, described with a rancor absent from Sabartés; and they sadden those admirers who like a great man to be great for twenty-four hours a day. It is as though Picasso paid for retaining the creative genius of a child by being obliged to keep some of the less amiable qualities of a little Spanish boy as well, combining them with the oppressive strength of a most formidable adult personality.

Back in Antibes, where he had not yet been able to settle down to work, he spent several days showing Sabartés the country; for Picasso very often made up for his fits of bad temper or domineering by acts of an instinctive, almost feminine kindness. He was also distracted from work by the presence of his nephews, Fin and Javier Vilato, Lola's sons, who had crossed into France after the fall of Catalonia and who had escaped internment: they brought him real pleasure, a certain sense of family, and news of Barcelona; their home at least had not been destroyed in the month-long bombing of the city, and their parents were well. But eventually, growing desperate at the thought of continued idleness, he went to Nice and bought a whole bolt of canvas: he and Sabartés pinned the cloth to the walls of the studio; Picasso primed it, and there he was ready to paint whatever came into his head without having to trouble about fitting his subject to any given size.

Almost at once he began working with concentrated energy on the largest panel. His first notion of painting what he chose and then cutting the pictures out and mounting them separately went to the winds, because this new theme was of such importance that it called for all the space he had. The idea had come to him as he and Dora Maar and another young woman were strolling about Antibes one warm night after dinner: they went down to the harbor and ate ices as they watched the fishermen floating over the dark surface in boats with brilliant acetylene lamps and peering down into the luminous water with their four-pronged fizgigs poised to spear the dazzled fish.

This, in the baldest terms, is what he painted during these last weeks of peace—the fishermen, the dark town behind, two girls on a jetty, one with a bicycle and an ice-cream cornet, the moon, and the flares lighting the men and the bright fish, making darkness visible. But of course a literal description takes no account of Picasso's own language, nor of his transpositions—the girl licking her ice, for example, has a blue tongue, as pointed as a sting, and the green-flecked moon, with its orange spiral, blazes from a square of light—nor even of the night-blue sky, the unnatural lamp-lit mauve and green, nor of the way the moon presses down on this confined piece of night, making it almost claustrophobic in spite of the great spread of canvas—seventy-five square feet, no less.

In spite of the mounting tension, the strident, bellicose Fascist voices in Germany and Italy, he fell into something like his good summer working rhythm, bathing in the morning, working in the afternoon until the light faded, and then after dinner meeting his friends in a café. But even in his studio he could not entirely escape from the world; he worked fitfully, sometimes without satisfaction; and as August wore on the news grew steadily worse. Once Hitler had devoured Czechoslovakia it was clear that he would turn on Poland next: appeasement had been meaningless and war was now as inevitable as death; but just as most people hope that they may still live for some indefinite number of years, so many hoped that Hitler would be deterred for a while by his fear of Russia, if not by the formidable armies that France had already mobilized. Then, on August 23, to the horror and amazement of the West, the Germans and Russians signed their non-aggression pact and all restraint was gone.

The group of Picasso's friends who met every evening at the café had been dwindling as further mobilization notices appeared: now the few who remained were convinced that the invasion of Poland was only a few days away, that those who stayed on the coast would be cut off—the trains were already crowded—and that Paris was likely to suffer from appalling air-raids in the first hours of the war.

Picasso was deeply disturbed: he was also very angry. "Just as I was beginning to work!" he cried, going back to his great picture.

Then all the lights went out: the black-out had come. Troops filled the roads, moving into positions on the Italian frontier just at hand. There was a strong likelihood that Mussolini would attack, and the atmosphere grew even more intolerably tense. Roland Penrose came to say goodbye—farewell for the duration of the war. Most of Picasso's friends had already gone: the concierge of his building was called up at a few hours' notice and the house, like the beaches and the cafés, was empty and dead.

But the picture was finished, that is to say as finished as Picasso would ever allow it to be, and he could go. Leaving Marcel to roll it up and follow in the car, Picasso and Dora Maar and Sabartés and Kazbek took the packed train for Paris. Four days later the Germans attacked the Poles, and on September 3 France and England declared war.

Even before the inevitable declaration a very great many Parisians determined to leave the city as quickly as they could: Brassaï puts the number at two-thirds of the population, and although this is certainly too high there is no doubt that thousands and thousands of people lost their heads entirely. He met a distracted Picasso in Saint-German-des-Prés hurrying about in search of packing-cases, trying to assemble his scattered possessions at Boisgeloup, Le Tremblay, and his Paris studios so as to leave them in some kind of order and in safety. But it was a task beyond human strength, and after a period of feverish activity, of listening to contradictory rumors and of wretched indecision, Picasso suddenly decided to abandon everything and to follow the general example. As usual he imposed his will upon those around him, and at about midnight on September 1 he and Dora Maar, the Sabartés, Kazbek, and Marcel got into the car and drove south, Picasso not having had time for dinner. By dawn they were at Saintes, where the waiters in the café where they breakfasted were all in uniform; and at seven in the morning they reached Royan, where they stopped.

Why Royan does not appear. Picasso had no friends there and the place had nothing much to recommend it apart from its bathing-beaches. It was a small, fairly modern town on the right bank of the Gironde, where the broad river meets the sea, and possessing a harbor it had a certain naval and military significance—not the best place for a foreigner; and Picasso was very conscious of being one. Perhaps they were just too tired to go any farther in the crowded car. In any event they found rooms in an hotel, and Picasso at once began to draw the horses they had seen on the road and that continually passed through the town: strings of horses requisitioned by the army.

But soon Picasso found that foreigners who had arrived in Royan after August 25 were not allowed to stay. This worried him extremely, for although nobody could have been more contemptuous of authority in the realm of the spirit, he hated the slightest prospect of trouble with the law, hated it so much that now he drove straight back to Paris, which he reached in time to hear the first air-raid sirens and the thump of anti-aircraft guns firing at a false alarm, spent a few hours getting the necessary permits, ate his lunch at Lipp's, took his coffee at the Flore, and then drove straight back again. But he had not had time to buy canvases, and they were not to be had at Royan, so some days later he ventured north again, this time with Sabartés. Brassaï, who had been commissioned by *Life* to take a series of photographs for an article on the forthcoming Picasso exhibition in New York, found him in the rue des Grands-Augustins. Brassaï had not been there before; in fact he had seen little of Picasso these last few years, because Dora Maar was Picasso's photographer as well as his companion, and she was liable to explode at anything she considered an intrusion into her territory. Picasso was welcoming and he cheerfully submitted to being posed at Lipp's, talking to Pierre Matisse, at the Flore, signing some prints, and in his studio. He was cheerful, even gay; but in these photographs one sees signs of age, almost for the first time. He wears spectacles to sign his prints, and although he wore them for etching at least as early as 1912 they now look habitual; his famous forelock is much diminished and the remaining hair behind it is carefully spread over the bare dome in sparse strands. Fifty-eight years and three wars had taken their toll, and there was every likelihood that far worse was at hand. This uneasy lull could not last; and Picasso, having collected and packed at least some of his pictures, hurried back to Royan.

They had prepared themselves for a cataclysm, for an overwhelming German attack, and for the virtual destruction of Paris. Nothing happened. Far away the Germans and the Russians devoured Poland, but scarcely a murmur reached the West. France and England settled down into the phony war, and in Royan Picasso began to build himself a daily routine.

A morning walk, exploring the market and rummaging among the objects in the junk-shops and the auction-rooms; then after lunch work until nightfall in a room he had hired as a studio. In his headlong flight he had either forgotten to pack an easel or there had not been room for one in the car, so in the Royan auction-room he bought a villainous little thing— Sabartés says it was meant to stand on a piano, holding a photograph— which he was obliged to lash to the back of a chair; but even then he had to work squatting on the floor, as he had done in his youth. And in spite of all protests and of two visits to Paris, where he had easels in profusion, he went on painting like this until the end of the year.

It was on this spindly affair, in a small room that he had crammed with purchases from the junk-shops, such as a valuable steelyard, and with a chair-seat for his palette, that he painted a number of portraits of Dora Maar, including one called "Le Chandail jaune" in which he returned to his matting texture of the year before, some still-lives of course, and a head of Sabartés. Although there is a great deal of systematic distortion in most, they are not violent pictures; the general atmosphere is one of deep but contained torment, even in the portrait of Sabartés, which was a carefully-contrived surprise, meant to give pleasure. Here again Sabartés is a seventeenth-century hidalgo in a ruff and a plumed bonnet, but now his face is pulled out in length and twisted about its vertical axis, and his spectacles, upside-down, cross beneath his bald, domed forehead in a melancholy droop. It makes a sad contrast with the blue portrait of thirty-eight years before, sad for both the friends; but Sabartés received it with his usual composure.

This gravity continued into 1940: if anything it became even more apparent, since in January Picasso found a better studio, and with more space and light, and with the real easel that he had at last brought back from Paris, he could paint larger pictures, such as the monumental and indeed monstrous "Femme nue se coiffant," whose hard-edged, massive, powerfully-modeled volumes have some relation to the bone figures of ten years before, although her vast belly and buttocks and even larger, curiously naturalistic feet, all crammed into a small bare low-ceilinged cell combine with the somber color (dark green walls and a moonlit purple floor reflecting into the pallid flesh) to remove her to another plane—to a plane in some ways resembling that of the "Demoiselles d'Avignon," for there is the same shocking brutality. But whereas the "Demoiselles" are almost flat, the "Femme nue" is vividly three-dimensional: the rough beast starts from her background with the ponderous majesty of a great block of stone.

Yet the period was not without its moments of relief. Already, in the autumn of 1939, there had been the gratifying reception of "Picasso: Forty Years of his Art" in New York, the most important exhibition of his life so far, with no less than three hundred and forty-four paintings, drawings, prints, collages, constructions, and sculptures carefully chosen to show every stage of his career. The lavishly-illustrated, percipient, appreciative catalog was a masterpiece of its kind, and it gave Picasso great pleasure; so in general did the reaction of the public and the critics, for although there were some piercing cries of dissent, the exhibition (which traveled on to Chicago and other cities) finally established his reputation in the United States. And then, a little while after the big nude, Picasso and Dora Maar went up to Paris again for a few weeks—there was a show of his gouaches, watercolors, and drawings in April—and there he painted a gay picture of eels on a table with a garfish and a sole. Soles, more obviously than most creatures, have anticipated Picasso in the redistribution of features, and a day or so later, perhaps feeling that he had been outdone, he returned to the subject with a particularly enchanting version of them, all superimposed roundnesses upon a pattern of colored planes, with their eyes and mouths set in a new arrangement and their forms echoed by the round pans and the chains of a pair of scales. He spoke of them when he wrote to Sabartés, adding that he missed the market at Royan: and this note, which was written on the back of an invitation to attend a requiem Mass for all Catalans who had died for their country, ended in that language *embolca-te amb la flassada del abraçada que t'envia el teu amic de sempre*—wrap yourself in the rug of the hug sent by your past present and future friend.

But the Paris of April was filled with anxiety. The Germans had dealt with the Poles long since; they had had plenty of time to regroup their forces, build up their armor, and increase their air strength, and once the winter was over they had made use of it to invade Denmark and Norway: the phony war was almost over. The Maginot Line, prolonged by the Belgian defenses, was thought to be impregnable, but even so Paris was extremely nervous; Picasso caught the mood and returned to his earlier task of making his possessions as safe as possible. In the first place there were his own works, and then an important collection of pictures by painters he admired; these he entrusted to his bank, which pleasantly enough was called the Banque du Commerce et de l'Industrie, where he had two strong-rooms next to the one used by Matisse, who had also left Paris on the declaration of war. (In Picasso's vault there were Matisses, and in Matisse's Picassos.) And although Sabartés does not mention them, just as he does not mention Dora Maar's presence at Royan, so that she has no more than a ghostly being in his narrative and her many portraits are unexplained, there can be no doubt that Picasso also attended to the well-being if not to the equal safety of Marie-Thérèse, Maya, Olga, Paulo, and his nephews, for however intermittent it may have been where his art was not concerned, his sense of responsibility was active and whole-hearted when it was aroused.

Matisse had also spent much of the spring in Paris, and both painters were still there in May when the long-dreaded blow was struck, when the unbelievably violent and successful German blitzkrieg shattered the defenses of neutral Holland, Belgium, and Luxembourg, drove the British into the sea, outflanked the Maginot Line, and hurled the French armies southward in total confusion.

On May 16 Picasso met Matisse in the street and gave him the news that the front was irreparably broken, adding that the French generals were the equivalent of the professors of the Beaux-Arts. When he wrote to his son Pierre some months later, Matisse spoke of "the shame of a disaster for which one is not responsible. As Picasso said to me, 'It's the École des Beaux-Arts.' If everyone did his job as Picasso and I do ours, this would not have happened." For the moment he set out for Bordeaux, while Picasso took the first train back to Royan, leaving Paris a little ahead of the main flood of refugees.

In June the Germans were in Paris, an open city from which the government had fled: in another week Pétain had signed an armistice, handing over the northern half of France and the entire Atlantic coast. In a few days time, following fast upon the disorganized host of soldiers and civilians, the occupying forces appeared at Royan: they marched through the streets and set up their *Kommandantur* a few yards from Picasso's studio.

Picasso feared the potentialities of an unknown future, the inimical forces that surrounded him on every hand, but when what had been an undefined menace crystallized into present reality it found him unmoved. The present was now a country under German occupation, a country where Jews were hunted openly, where the Gestapo took people away in the night, where he himself was not only suspected of being partly Jewish but was known to be the most notorious leader of the *Kunstbolschewismus* so abhorred by Hitler; his work, like that of the other degenerate artists, was proscribed in all territory ruled by the Nazis; he had taken an unmistakable and very public stand against Fascism, and Hitler's friend Franco hated him; he knew and liked a great many Communists, and he was thought to be one of them. The present was field-gray, and it contained a whole new nation of those authorities he disliked and dreaded—a superstitious dread. It was open to him to leave for the United States or for Mexico; or he could, like Matisse, have had a visa for Brazil; and of course there was the unoccupied zone in the south.

But after a period in which he made sheet after sheet of macabre drawings, filled with pain—his earlier Royan still-lives had sometimes contained skulls, but while those were the skulls of sheep, these were human, or nearly so—a curious gaiety came over Picasso. On August 15, the day of Our Lady's assumption and a great feast in Spain, he painted an entrancing, brilliantly-colored "Café à Royan," with bright awnings in the sun, the lighthouse and the sea beyond, filling the picture with cheerful blue. Then he began to pack, and on August 24 he deliberately drove back to Paris.

Miles away Matisse had had much the same reaction: he was at the frontier with his passport in his pocket and the boat was waiting at Genoa to take him to Rio de Janeiro; but, as he wrote to his son, "When I saw the endless line of people leaving I had not the least desire to go . . . I should have felt like a deserter. If everything of any worth runs away, what will remain of France?"

France meant different things to Matisse and Picasso: but although Picasso remained a Spaniard through and through, France and above all Paris nevertheless for him meant light, freedom, and the living arts, and that intemporal country, beyond all national or geographic boundaries, was where his patriotism lay.

Chapter XVII

THE Paris to which he returned was a strange, dark city, its lights reduced to a sinister pale-blue glow: the curfew, rationing, endless queues for food and for permits of every kind. And although at first it was sparsely inhabited by Parisians, since the Germans had taken huge numbers of prisoners and multitudes had fled, the streets were filled with hateful uniforms, gray, green, and black; and the swastika flew over countless buildings, while the Louvre stood dark and empty.

As winter approached it was also a cold and hungry city; for although the Germans had received orders to be "correct" and although many of them were outwardly civil for a while, their politeness at no time concealed their greed, and from the very beginning a steady stream of fuel, food, and valuables flowed northwards to the Reich. In the earliest days of the occupation they systematically opened all strong-rooms, confiscating all Jewish and a great deal of Gentile property and making lists of the rest: Picasso spent some time at his bank with two of these inspectors, more familiar perhaps with gold teeth from the corpses at Auschwitz than with modern painting; and as Matisse's vault was also open he hurried them from one set of pictures to another, worrying them with exact sizes and dates, darting to and fro, asserting that they had already seen these, and then all those, and assuring them, when they came to the end of their meager, garbled inventory, that all the paintings in all the vaults, Picassos and Matisses together, were worth sixteen thousand francs, rather less than £1,000 or $4,000 at the time. It was a perilous game, but it succeeded.

Then as winter came on, German correctness wore thin and Paris became more dangerous by far. Official Teutonic charm, the call for collaboration, had worked on comparatively few Frenchmen and those few were scarcely of the kind that even Nazis could respect: furthermore, although the nation as a whole was still behind Pétain, a nascent Resistance began to make its presence known, and this made the German attitude more savage still.

In time the Resistance took innumerable forms: highly-specialized intelligence-work and armed attack, often combined with the Resistance of the spirit—writing, publishing, painting in defiance of the authorities—was one; and another was sabotaging the German and Vichy machines of government, supply, and oppression. This included helping, comforting, and hiding Jews, *résistants*, and suspects; and the black market could also be considered a useful kind of subversion.

Picasso did not attempt armed resistance, nor, as far as I know, was he in immediate touch with any intelligence network; but he practiced all the other sometimes equally dangerous forms, and it is significant that he was regarded as absolutely reliable by the most active leaders of the movement, men whose lives depended on their perspicacity.

Ever since the first introduction of taxes and regulations, the French have devoted much time and energy to evading them: it is so much a part of the French way of life that even now there is an official consolation of 10 percent for those who have no possibility of concealing their exact incomes. They would naturally have plunged straight into the black market in any case, but now that it might be represented as a protest against the Germans and Vichy, almost as a patriotic duty, they took to it with such universal zeal that the official systems of rationing were turned upsidedown. Picasso followed their example with all his might; he found a black-market restaurant right away, and an illegal source of bronze for his sculpture; but in Paris no amount of effort could obtain black-market electricity or gas. A very little fuel was all that could be hoped for.

Nearly all Parisians were cold, but since few lived in vast seventeenth-century barn-like rooms, few were quite as cold as Picasso. At one time he had meant to live in the rue La Boëtie and work in the rue des Grands-Augustins; but it would not do. The smaller flat may have been easier to heat, although it was at the top of a tall building, exposed to the icy winds and with no warmth coming up from the lower floors any longer; but it was two miles from the studio, and with few buses, few underground trains, no taxis, and no petrol for his own car that meant a great deal of time spent walking—walking made unpleasant by the weather and odious by the presence of the Germans. Work had to come first, so after a while Picasso shut up the flat, leaving some remarkable treasures—Corots, Matisses, a box of gold—and settled in the comfortless rue des Grands-Augustins for good.

His newly-installed central heating did not work; nor did the gas and electric fires he bought; and the monstrous iron stove he had acquired because he loved its barbaric lines burned all his fuel in a trice, emitting a sullen roar but little heat. Presently friends lent him a kitchen range, which did give some heat when he had any coal to put into it but which also filled the place with smoke.

With all its frigid inconveniencies the studio was an excellent place for work, particularly since Picasso, as a Spaniard, could withstand almost any degree of discomfort and cold; and although the remaining months of 1940 did not produce any painting or sculpture of the first or even the second importance, this was due less to the want of fuel than to the general upheaval, to the time-consuming domestic arrangements, and to the fact that until the illegal lines of supply reached their steady flow it took a great deal of energy to keep oneself in food and tobacco. And it had other advantages: his black-market restaurant, where he could eat without giving up his ration-tickets, was in the rue des Grands-Augustins itself (the place was called Le Catalan, and it was run by a Catalan, and Catalan could be heard there every day) and, far more important, Saint-Germain-des-Prés was now the center of what intellectual life Paris still possessed, whereas the rue La Boëtie, so hard to reach, had grown peripheral. Even more than a stove that worked, Picasso needed the blaze of friendship or at least of congenial company from time to time, as a relief from the profound and necessary solitude of his work and as a means of tying himself into ordinary life again after his lonely exploration of unknown regions. This, together with plain bodily warmth, he found to some extent at the Flore, and he was to be seen there, generally with Dora Maar and Kazbek, every evening.

Saint-Germain was a center, a rallying-point; but it was far from crowded. Although demobilization brought Eluard and others back, and although some prisoners of war such as Jean-Paul Sartre returned in time, the war had scattered many of Picasso's friends: Breton, Ernst, Kisling, Lipchitz, Chagall, Léger, Mondrian, and many more were in America, Matisse was at Vence, Marquet in Algiers, Miró had gone back to Spain. It is true that both Derain and Vlaminck remained, but it would have been far, far better for their reputation if they had fled from the temptations of German flattery, preferential treatment, and journeys to the Reich. Kahnweiler, as a Jew, was hidden somewhere in the South Zone, and Picasso's other Jewish friends, condemned to wear the yellow Star of David, rarely left their houses: and later, as the war grew darker, colder, and more deeply sad, he too tended to stay at home, shut up alone with his work: the cafés saw little of Picasso after 1942. It was, as he said later, one of the loneliest periods of his life, and all the more so as some people he knew took to avoiding him as a dangerous contact. Others went further, and it is painful to record that Vlaminck, for one, saw fit to attack him in a review published under German authorization. In general there seems to be little or no connection between moral and artistic worth—Goya would have been called a collaborator—yet it is a striking fact that none of the three great names of painting left France during the war, and that none of them, however apolitical, would have the least truck with the Germans, nor with Vichy.

His loneliness was of course much diminished by the presence of Dora Maar and Sabartés as well as by that of Marie-Thérèse and Maya in their little flat on the Ile Saint-Louis, which he regularly visited at least every Thursday, Maya's holiday from school, and generally on Sundays. But none of these was an ideal companion for Picasso: indeed, his requirements were so great and grew so much greater with the years, that the ideal companion, had she existed at all, would have been as rare a being as Picasso himself. She would have had to possess a strength equal to his own, a devotion just short of worship, for worship would not do at all, and those who prostrated themselves were trampled upon and destroyed, and a commensurable talent: given his great respect for verse, a beautiful poetess might have answered, and some years later one very nearly did in the person of Geneviève Laporte. But neither then nor at any other time did Picasso have the good fortune to secure this nonpareil; and on occasion he would speak wistfully of a harem.

In the winter of 1940 to 1941, however, his mind was turned less to women than to literature. He had written a good deal of verse before the war and at Royan, and the book he and Vollard had planned would have had a considerable bulk: now he set himself to a play, *Le Désir attrapé par la queue,* and on the first page he drew himself seen from above, spectacled and rather bald and wispy, in the act of writing about the desires that his characters catch, or attempt to catch, by the tail. Where Picasso's writing is concerned the distinction between poetry and prose has not much meaning, and although few but his unconditional admirers would say that he was a poet in the same sense that he was a draughtsman, painter, and sculptor, he was incapable of writing a piece without brilliant poetic flashes in it. His dramatis personae have an undeniable splendor: Big-Foot, a writer, in love with the Tart (the edible kind); Onion, friend to Big-Foot; the Round Tip; Silence; the Tart (in love with Big-Foot); the Tart's cousin; Fat Anxiety (friend to the Tart and in love with Big-Foot); Thin Anxiety (friend to the Tart, also in love with Big-Foot); two dogs; the Curtains. And any poet would be proud of Sordids' Hotel, where one of the scenes is set. The desires these people pursue are to do with food, warmth (they suffer much from the cold, and when they leave their feet in the corridor of the hotel, the feet cry out, "Oh my chilblains, my chilblains"), money, and coarse love-making: it would be difficult to summarize the argument of the play, for there is none, but the violence, the pace, and the brutal Ubuesque hilarity carry the action along very well, and at a private reading at the Leiris' flat some years later it gave the utmost delight.

But that was a private reading, packed with Picasso's friends—Braque was there—and the parts were taken by such people as Simone de Beauvoir, Sartre, Michel and Louise Leiris, Reverdy, Raymond Queneau and Dora Maar, she being Thin Anxiety: they were all thoroughly accustomed to Surrealist tropes, and for them the wild play of associations was far less private than it would be for outsiders, who may see little more than a dazzling but mysterious and perhaps rather labored play of fireworks from which there emerges an occasional splendid piece or some wonderfully funny dialogue. And even among those who so thoroughly enjoyed the reading there were some who regretted that Picasso should spend creative energy on his pen when he could have spent it on his brush. For his own part he had no exaggerated opinion of his writing; he was diffident about his abilities and taking his cue from his friend, even Sabartés emphasizes that Picasso wrote the play "solely for his own amusement." This was an open, acknowledged diffidence, as about something that was by no means vital to him: it was quite unlike that deep anxiety as to the validity of his own art that pervaded his mind on occasion, particularly when he was away from his easel or when work would not come—a paradoxical anxiety, since at the same time he knew there was no other painter living except Matisse and possibly Braque who had as much to say and as great a power of saying it, and one that only his most intimate friends were aware of.

Underlying humility is perhaps an essential component of greatness; but the paralysing doubt that may accompany it never or very rarely affected Picasso when he was confronted with a virgin canvas or a sheet of drawing-paper. The Zervos catalog shows a surprising number of paintings for 1941, several of them having a bearing on food: the particularly affectionate treatment of the black pudding in the still-life called "Le Buffet du Savoyard" for example, makes it clear that Picasso loved the simple dish for itself as well as for its aesthetic properties. Others are to do with Dora Maar. They can still be called portraits, for although in some the twisting of the head about its vertical axis is carried even farther than in the Royan "Sabartés," while in others the hatchet-faced woman in a chair has little human about her at all, the sitter can be no one else: yet it has been said that they are more pictures of a state of mind, or rather of their tense relationship, than of Dora Maar. On the other hand, at this point Picasso was preoccupied with a simultaneity of vision achieved by means somewhat different from those of Cubism: in May, for instance, he made one of his beautifully fluent drawings of a woman lying both on her back and on her front. At first glance she seems to be split like a kipper, with her two classical profiles sharing the same pillow and the same head of hair, but following down one sees the belly and up-flexed knee on the right and on the left the buttocks and the downward knee: it knocks common logical perception sideways, and the result is both convincing and deeply satisfactory.

The pictures that are either directly of Dora Maar or that are based upon her are open to question and to various interpretations: the sculpture is not. Since his peopling of the stables at Boisgeloup in 1932 and 1933 Picasso had done little apart from some grim dolls for Maya and a few constructions, but if one may judge by the increasingly sculptural nature of some of his recent painting, such as the "Nu se coiffant" of 1940, his mind had been tending in that direction, and now, with fewer distractions than he had known for years, he modeled a more than life-size head of his companion, a great smooth serene head, finer in plaster than in its indifferent bronze. (It is the one that was set up as a monument to Apollinaire.)

His return to sculpture was certainly the result of inward necessity, but his decision may have been precipitated by the arctic winter of 1941–1942. Once even in the coldest months some warmth emanated from the houses of Paris and rose in wafts from the gratings of the Métro—the city was not unbearable even for those who slept out, wrapped in newspaper—but this was no longer the case, and in the vast painting-studio Picasso's hands, stoical though they were, grew too numb to hold a brush, although he wore all the clothes he had. The bathroom was the only place that he could heat; the water for damping clay and mixing plaster was conveniently near at hand; the mess did not signify; and in this narrow but at least tepid space he worked with his usual fierce intensity.

The sequence of his sudden spate of sculpture is uncertain: for one thing Kahnweiler, the authority on the subject, was far away; and for another there is a tendency to date a piece by the year of its casting, in spite of the fact that Picasso loved to keep his figures by him in their first fragile purity. And at this period the connection is more than usually tenuous, because his supplies of illicit metal were not be be relied on: the Ger-

mans were commandeering every scrap of bronze they could lay their
hands on, including all the public statues, for the benefit of one Breker,
Hitler's favorite maker of colossal images—a person visited by more
French artists than I like to name. Yet it is probable that apart from this
head of Dora Maar, 1941 also saw the two disreputable alley cats to
which he was so much attached, the one pissing with its tail held stiff, the
other pregnant, as well as one of the most moving sculptures he ever
made, the "Tête de mort."

It is no more than a foot high, though one remembers it as far larger: a
dark bronze that is neither quite a skull nor yet a living head. The eye-
sockets are empty and the flesh of the nose is gone, but the bare jawbones
and the grinning teeth of the traditional memento mori are not to be seen,
being covered with as it were a tight shrunken leathery skin—a skin that
does not obscure the gleaming dome above the eyes, however.

Everyone who has ever written about Picasso refers again and again to
his loathing of death: yet the skulls of animals and men were a usual part
of his vocabulary, and this piece of mortality made tangible is an object
modeled with love, a work that one gazes upon with grave satisfaction,
longing to touch it. If the apparent contradiction needs resolving, there is
an answer at hand, as simple as the bronze itself and perhaps as true. If I
am not mistaken, the "Tête de mort" is Picasso's most consummate
piece of exorcism: he gave the spirit a shape and so, at least for the time,
he broke free from it.

In 1941 death was near at hand, even nearer than before: in June Hitler
attacked Russia and the French Communists instantly faced about, throwing all their weight on the side of the growing Resistance. They had been
outlawed in the earliest days of the war and then savagely persecuted by
Vichy; by now they therefore had the advantage of a well-tried clandestine organization and a disciplined, wholly committed membership, already purged of the faint-hearted. It is none of my business to enquire into
the motives or the patriotism of the leaders, a question so passionately argued in France ever since 1941, but I do know that many of the rank and
file were men and women who would die under torture for their convic-
tions, that some joined the Party when membership, if discovered, meant
a concentration-camp or summary execution, and that Picasso had a number of friends among them. The Communists' change of front had a deep
effect upon him, but it did not become immediately apparent in his work;
nor indeed can it be said to be unquestionably evident at any time. Attempts have been made to link various pictures with particular outside
happenings, but with a few exceptions they are unconvincing: Picasso's

painting may have been his diary, but it was a private diary, one in which a man is not likely to record public events such as the attack on Pearl Harbor, the American declaration of war which brought hope to Europe at the end of 1941, or the advent of the infamous Pierre Laval early in the year, the hunting of the Jews, the massive deportations.

Although in fact, with the American intervention, the tide had turned, 1942 began badly for the civilized world, with the Germans deep in the heart of Russia and the Japanese carrying everything before them in southeast Asia: yet the daily life of even the greatest men is conditioned by circumstances that it seems ludicrous to record on the same page as such pregnant events, and Picasso's own corner of this world was brightened by the return of Inès. At the beginning of the war he had left her in safety at Mougins, and there she had married a young man called Sassier, who now brought her back to Paris. Picasso, who had been making do as well as he could with the help of Marcel Boudin, the nominal chauffeur, took a small flat for the couple in the warren-like house that contained his studios, and Inès looked after him. There was not much for her to cook in Paris, apart from Jerusalem artichokes, swedes, and rhubarb, but there had been even less on the Mediterranean coast, where the people lived on tomatoes, sunlight, and a little fish: and even the fish disappeared later in 1942, when the Germans occupied the south zone and forbade the boats to put to sea. However, Inès did a great deal with a very little; she was thoroughly used to Picasso; she fed him as well as she could, and she kept the house neat where he wanted it to be neat. Theirs was a pleasant southern relationship, tyrannical at times, with loud expostulations on either side, but entirely human, and the place was far less austere with Inès in it. She was also a very pretty young woman—Eluard admired her much—as one may see from the charming portrait that Picasso made of her in April, one of a series of presents that carried on year after year until she had a collection that any millionaire might envy.

Throughout 1942—indeed throughout the war—most of Picasso's pictures show a somber, muted range of colors; and there is often the same insistence upon food—a hat made of a large fish, with crossed knife and fork, still-lives with eggs, with fruit, with a pigeon (many people tried to eat the Paris pigeons during the war, luring them with crumbs; but they were found to have a vile blackish flesh, as inedible as crow). An apparent exception is the powerful still-life with a guitar and a torero's sword, which he painted in April: here the color, especially the startling red of the sword-grip, is more brilliant, but even so the strong blue, the green, and violet drain the gaiety away. It is an unhappy picture in spite of its fine yellow and scarlet, and for Pierre Daix it is a reflection of the death of Picasso's very old friend Juli González: the news of it reached him a few days before he painted the picture.

In the same month he painted a couple of still-lives of horned ox-skulls, the one seen by day, the other by night; these too are somber, brooding pictures; and in their spare, angular stylization they mark a mid-point between two of the manners he was using at this time, on the one hand a faceted series of often straight-edged planes (one recumbent nude might almost come from the early days of Cubism), and on the other strongly rounded and sometimes modeled volumes that emphasize his distortions, particularly of Dora Maar's face, to an almost unbearable degree. The many portraits of Nusch Eluard, by the way, show no such tension.

Most of these were fairly small pictures, three to four feet high at the most, but in May he set to work on a far larger canvas, six and a half feet tall and nearly nine feet broad. "A picture is not thought out and settled beforehand," he once told Zervos, and what he had in mind when he started "L'Aubade" there is no telling: the result is one of the most enigmatic of his pictures—enigmatic, that is to say, if one is not content with its direct statement, with the hallucinating play of triangles and quadrilaterals of quiet color, the monstrous multiply-simultaneous nude made of some firm grainless substance that can be carved with a perfect definition, thus allowing the distortions and the planes of simultaneous vision to be carried out with no solution of continuity: she lies stiffly on or just above a divan whose stripes give it the appearance of a fakir's bed or perhaps a rack; and at her feet, in a rigid Spanish chair, sits another woman holding a mandolin, wearing some clothes and a pair of felt slippers. Her head is made of three more triangles, and their common apex strikes against the angle of three of the facets of the complex prism in which they live. Why does she sit there so quietly? Why does she not play her mandolin? What is the reason for the empty mirror-frame? I do not know: nor do I know what place the "Aubade" has in Picasso's long sequence of pictures in which two women appear, sometimes friends, sometimes enemies, sometimes in an ambiguous relationship. But at least the "Aubade" and the sequence to which it belongs do emphasize, if emphasis were necessary, both the vast importance of women to Picasso and the price he had to pay for having them in his life. Each singly brought him great joy, and no one could have been happier than Picasso painting in the first flush of his emotion; but when they began to eat him—and he really seems to have believed that the process was not reciprocal—he resented it, and some part of his savage distortion of the female form and face may be put down to this resentment as well as to purely aesthetic considerations. And when they amounted to two or more at a time, seriously interfering with his work, his resentment grew greater still: for they did interfere with it, and not only by worrying him, bringing his mind down to mundane jangling, but sometimes by their physical intrusion. When he was actually painting "Guernica," for instance, his creative powers at their utmost stretch, Marie-Thérèse came in and found Dora Maar there: after screeching at one another for some time they had a brutish, squalid battle, pushing one another about in the very studio itself; and although Picasso affected a cynical amusement when he told the story some years later, the man then engaged on one of the most important works of his life cannot have found it so very droll.

It was in the summer that followed the "Aubade" that the Germans and the French police carried out their vast sweeps in Paris, rounding up thousands of Jews in July and August, 1942. And it was now that the great deportations began, trainloads of *résistants,* Communists, Jews, and suspects from all over the country, many of them victims of denunciation, traveled up through France to Buchenwald, Auschwitz, Dachau, Mauthausen. The shooting of hostages had started long before, but now the Nazis killed two hundred just outside Paris in August and September alone. These were the days of the delator, when an anonymous telephone-call or an unsigned note could bring the Gestapo thundering on the door in the dead hour of the night; and these were the days when Germans kept coming to the rue des Grands-Augustins to ask whether Lipchitz were there (of course he was not: he was in America, as they knew very well), and whether Picasso were not also a Jew; and then they would search the place. Whether there was anything for them to find, apart from the illicit bronze, I do not know, but if there was they never succeeded; the hopeless confusion of Picasso's mounds may well have discouraged the most eager. They were "correct" with Picasso, who for his part took great care to have his papers in order so that they should have no hold on him; and in his case, either from ignorance or from some uneasiness about his fame, the Gestapo did not attempt the private blackmail that they practiced with so much profit elsewhere. Not all the Germans came to search, however: there were some who appeared as semi-official intermediaries, hinting at privileges, coal, extra rations; and others who professed to love the arts. Their charm had no effect upon Picasso's unbending severity: they got nothing out of him at all, nothing but postcards of "Guernica," which he pressed into their hands, saying, *"Souvenir, souvenir."* There is the story that Abetz, the German ambassador, came one day with the intention of making himself agreeable: looking at a reproduction of the great picture he said, with a civil leer, "So you did that, Monsieur Picasso?" "No," said Picasso, "you did." The tale is not literally true, but it was told everywhere, and it is highly significant of the esteem in which Picasso was held. No one, not even the most poisonous tongues of a milieu notorious for slander, ever accused him of the slightest concession to the Germans or to Vichy.

And it was in this dismal summer—he did not go away, of course—that Picasso began the drawings that were to culminate in his statue "L'Homme au mouton." The work can be seen as a counterpart to his "Tête de mort," since it is an equally powerful statement about life. At first he was not sure what form it should take, but he inclined to the idea of an engraving, a lithograph, or a picture; then as he sank deeper into the subject, and as the drawings accumulated—there were more than a hundred of them—he saw that the figure had to stand free in space: it had to be a sculpture. This was one of the projects upon which he spent a very great deal of time and thought, letting it ripen thoroughly in his mind, a rare process with him and one that his friends could have wished more usual, if the outcome had always been as successful as "L'Homme au mouton," or "à l'agneau" as those call it who either have an elastic notion of a lamb or who wish to emphasize the religious connotations. It was not until the end of this year or the beginning of the next that he ordered the armature or set about looking for the large quantity of clay that would be needed: for sculptor's clay, like everything else, was hard to find in the war; and even when it was found it was often of poor quality.

In the meantime he carried on with smaller pieces of sculpture, often ephemeral constructions or collages, and with painting, some of it of capital importance. From a distance the portrait of Dora Maar painted in October, 1942, looks simple, a straightforward picture of a young woman in a red and green striped dress, looking straight in front of her and sitting rather stiffly, much as Henri Rousseau's models sat: in fact it has something of the air of a Rousseau. Then as one walks closer the Rousseau innocence vanishes, and with it the apparent simplicity. The stiffness is not the ordinary embarrassment of a young woman having her likeness taken but the extreme tension of one who can only just maintain her tight-lipped self-control: her nostrils quiver with the effort; her great eyes are filled with tears. Antonina Valentin, who speaks with authority, states that while the picture was being painted Dora Maar's mother died; Dora Maar nevertheless went on sitting; and that Picasso, although he did not alter the now incongruous dress that he had invented for his color-scheme (he often painted Dora Maar in clothes that did not exist or that he had seen on other women), changed the background, painting out the bars that marked her as his prisoner, and the symbolic crust of bread and water-jug.

There was hope in the world in 1943, but for Paris it seemed very remote and theoretical indeed: certainly the Allies had landed in North Africa at the end of 1942, but two days later the Germans had invaded the South Zone, occupying the whole of France; and as the Resistance grew, so did the repression. Food was even shorter; the electricity was cut off for long periods at a time, so that Picasso worked by candle-light as he had in his youth; gas-fires burned with a weak, uncertain flame or went out altogether. For a month and more Picasso gazed at the armature, the metal skeleton to support the weight of clay for his statue. He had already fixed the more than life-size scale and all but the last details of the figure; he had already laid in his clay; but still he let the iron rods stand there while his idea grew to its full maturity.

Then one day in that cold, dark February, and at a time when there seemed to be no end to the war in human sight, he set to work. He knew exactly what he meant to do; he had no need of models; everything, even to the arch of the sheep's nose, was in his head; and with incredible speed a great statue unlike anything in Picasso's past or future work took shape: a tall, powerful, lean, bald, bearded middle-aged man with long straight legs, his big feet firmly planted on the ground, advances carrying a large shorn sheep; he is perfectly direct, perfectly simple, as he poises himself against the weight: so is the sheep, which strains its head away from him, as sheep will when they are in a man's arms. His right hand is under its rump, supporting it; his left grasps its feet in that antique gesture familiar to Hesiod, Virgil, the peasants of Horta, and to Picasso himself; his face is grave, set, matter-of-fact, unaware of his own nobility.

At one point the feeble war-time armature and the indifferent clay began to yield, but Paul Eluard was there, sharing Picasso's warmth and writing in the studio, and between them they stayed it with ropes: then the sheep fell to the ground and had to be wired back. But by the end of Picasso's working day the whole statue was finished, though by now the clay was in such a state that he dared not model the legs as he had wished, and to this day they are rather stick-like.

Almost at once he encased the wavering figure and cast it in plaster. Even with all Picasso's ingenuity and his innumerable contacts there was not the least possibility of bronze for so large a work while the Germans were still in France, so "L'Homme au mouton" stood, fragile but splendidly white, in his studio until after the Liberation. A very great many people saw it there, and although there were differences of opinion about its direct meaning and its underlying symbolism, there was a general agreement that the statue represented an assertion of hope, of faith in fundamental decency, and that at a time when both were rare it gave those who saw it courage. Some critics have connected the directness of communication, the immediate "comprehensibility" of the figure with Picasso's move towards the Communists, a theory that would be more persuasive if Picasso had ever modeled or painted anything of a comparable nature, in tune with the workers' allegedly simple tastes and power of understanding, after he became a member of the Party in October, 1944.

Of the move itself, however, there is no kind of doubt. The influence of Eluard and Aragon was already great and that of events perhaps even greater, but it appears that the decisive factor was his prolonged contact with Laurent Casanova. Casanova was one of the leading men in the Party and in the Communist Resistance, a most impressive figure as an intellectual and above all as a man of action: his wife had been killed by the Germans and he had been captured and recaptured three times; on his fourth escape he eventually reached Eluard, who passed him on as an anonymous Communist to the safer hiding of the Leirises' big flat. This was at the end of Picasso's little street, on the quai des Grands-Augustins: it was here that Picasso met him, and during the weeks of his concealment they saw a great deal of one another.

"L'Homme au mouton" was not the end of Picasso's burst of sculpture. In the same year he produced his most surprising piece, the "Tête de taureau": poking about in a rubbish-heap he came upon an old bicycle saddle, and next to it a pair of rusty handlebars. In a flash, without any mental effort on his part, their potentialities were revealed to him. All he had to do was to fix them together in a given position and there was a fine bull's head of the same spare race as his recent still-lives. He did so and had the result cast in bronze, which, as he observed, has the power of giving a wonderful unity to disparate elements. For Picasso there was no such thing as an ignoble substance or a contemptible object; the color and the texture of a packet of tobacco was as valuable as that of a sapphire. By casting this head in bronze he passed his more lively, totally unprejudiced perception on to those who could not surmount the barrier without help; though at the same time he was aware that they might not make the transformation in reverse, and that if they did not see the saddle and handlebars in the bull, then much of the point was lost.

He was very pleased with the head; so were many other people, but by no means all. Some looked respectfully at the bronze, then detected the saddle and the handlebars and no longer loved the sculpture; they felt obscurely that they had been made game of. Then there was the fact that the head had taken Picasso five minutes whereas "L'Homme au mouton" had called for the best part of a year: could both be valid? And even some of those who admit that once beauty is present the time, skill, and material required to bring it into being are irrelevant still remain anxious and dissatisfied.

Picasso went out rarely these days, and much of his painting has an inward quality: there is one view from his studio window, with the useless radiator under the sill, that is particularly moving, not so much because of the lack of heat (in fact the window is open) as because it looks out from a sad room over an even sadder town. Those who went through the war will remember how at intervals between boredom and alarm one became aware of the shift in one's perception of time; it seemed that the slaughter and destruction had been going on forever and that they must necessarily continue; one was a prisoner in this endless nightmare, and only more darkness, more battles, crueller repression, and heavier air-raids could be ahead: that is the feeling of this picture. Yet there are others: early in 1943 he painted Inès' child learning to walk. With an idiot determination the little boy raises one huge foot, his bald, unformed, pliable face staring straight ahead, while on either side his clumsy hands hold those of his mother, bent over him from behind in a maternal curve and filling the canvas to its utmost limits. It may not be a picture that gave Inès much pleasure, although its composition, the juxtaposition of the heads, the planes of the child's coat, and the archaic use of the painter's space are unusually interesting; but it is not a desperately sad one. Nor are the many still-lives of this period, unless one takes the skull and jug literally, which would probably be a mistake since it was painted on Assumption Day, when Picasso's mind was apt to fly back to Spain: and what more Spanish than a skull and jug? On the whole they are grave, reflective pictures with much the same range of subjects as those of his full Cubist days; they have a remarkable strength, made more emphatic by the firm black lines that define each jug or candlestick or chair. Some of them, however, like the "Nature morte aux cerises" with its pretty coffee-pot and its dish of cherries, are positively gay; but that was painted in November, 1943, and even by the middle of the year the whole world had changed. The Germans had been thrust out of North Africa; in Russia they were in full retreat; the Allies were deep in Italy and Mussolini's army was on the verge of collapse. In France the Resistance had grown enormously, harassing the Germans, sending out military and political intelligence, preparing for the invasion, and keeping the country's spirit alive by every possible means, including of course clandestine publication. And in Paris overt intellectual life was recovering: at the end of 1942 Fabiani had been able to bring out the edition of Buffon that Vollard had commissioned, while in 1943 Picasso illustrated *Le Chèvrefeuille* for Georges Hugnet and *Contrée* for Robert Desnos, his friend from the early days of Surrealism. Desnos lived near at hand, in the rue Mazarine; and Picasso, who saw him often, had noticed that his round, plump face had grown haggard these last few months, taking on the expression often to be seen in those committed to the more dangerous forms of resistance. There were more shows in the picture-galleries, with some new talents emerging; and the Salon d'Automne began its series of retrospectives, starting with Braque, who for some reason was officially less degenerate than Picasso—he too had returned to Paris in the autumn of 1940 and he stayed there throughout the war, painting interiors and still-lives.

And then there was a chance encounter that added some brightness to Picasso's private world. He was having dinner with Dora Maar, Marie-Laure de Noailles, and some other friends at the Catalan one evening in May when he noticed two good-looking young women at another table with an actor he knew. Picking up a bowl of cherries, he went over and obliged the actor to introduce him: the girls having said they were painters he invited them to his studio. Presently they came, first the two together and then one of them alone: this was Françoise Gilot, then aged twenty-one. She was studying law and literature in a desultory fashion at the Sorbonne and at the same time she was learning to paint. Her father was a wealthy businessman who made scent and eau-de-Cologne among other things: she had received a thorough-going middle-class education and she was a typical product of the richer bourgeoisie. "That, of course, was a great incentive," said an old lady who had known Picasso for more than sixty years, when we were talking about Françoise Gilot. "It would naturally have given him the utmost pleasure to undress a girl belonging to that world." She was a very intelligent Frenchwoman, and she was probably right; for although Picasso knew Bohemia in all its forms as well as certain aspects of the grander world, the closed French bourgeoisie, with its smooth surface, its materialism, and its incredible hardness, was quite foreign to him, and this no doubt gave Françoise Gilot a certain exotic charm; but with her dark-red hair, her fine complexion, the pure oval of her face, and above all her youth, she also had qualities of her own.

However, in June, before their acquaintance had reached any very advanced state of intimacy, she went away for the summer and she did not come back to the studio for several months. At this point she was an agreeable interlude, but one of no great importance.

Early in that fine September of 1943 Brassaï came to the rue des Grands-Augustins again, this time to photograph the sculpture; although since he refused to ask the Germans for a permit he had no more right to publish his work than Picasso had to exhibit his. He found Picasso wearing shorts and a striped singlet: he was in great form, but as soon as he had seized Brassaï and had kissed him on both cheeks he cried, "Tell me the truth—we haven't seen one another for some time—I've changed a great deal, haven't I? Look at what has happened to my hair! When I come across one of my old portraits, it quite frightens me." Picasso was going bald: the top of his head was bare, its sides were gray, and his forelock was no more than a spectral wisp. It seemed absurd: his face and that brilliant eye, the window to his mind, were as full of ebullient life as ever they had been; yet in fact his body had now served him for sixty-one years and for at least forty of them it had been driven very hard indeed. The signs of wear were clearly visible, and when he thought of it, it either depressed him extremely or he flew out in passionate revolt. Fortunately there were a thousand other things that he felt with equal vehemence and passion, and on this occasion he branched straight off to his sculpture. The studio was now crowded with earlier figures from Boisgeloup and with new works, so crowded that they overflowed into another place that he had taken just down the street: like Brassaï, he had preferred most of them in plaster; but that wretched Sabartés had so worried and badgered him about the permanence of bronze that in the end he had been forced to yield to his importunities.

Picasso was in excellent spirits: his cheerful bad faith, his delight in his sculpture, particularly the "Tête de taureau," and his affectionate kindness to Brassaï were all in tune with the glorious weather and with the feeling of hope that filled the town—Italy had surrendered, the Russians were on the Dnieper, the Allies might be in France at any moment: they were dropping greater quantities of arms to the Resistance, and now they were bombing factories, railways, marshaling-yards, military installations by day as well as by night.

Yet it nearly always took a considerable lapse of time before any general feeling showed itself in his work, and often it did not do so at all. While Brassaï was photographing his sculpture that September Picasso was painting such pictures as "Le Corsage rayé" and "Le Buste de femme." The first is the head and shoulders of a woman wearing a kind of geometrical hat and a blouse striped vertically from neck to bosom and then horizontally; her face is made of three curved planes in which signs for her features are incised, and these sharply-defined surfaces, lit by a light of their own, swirl about a central point that may be the tip of her nose. The second is a woman with a triple head—two interpenetrating profiles that also make a full face—sitting in a wicker armchair and wearing garments of that "matting" texture which he had used in 1938. They are fascinating pictures, but they have not the slightest connection with the state of the war in 1942. Nor do his illustrations for Desnos' book, etchings that look straight back to the "Sueño y mentira de Franco," with the same hatched polyp-like forms and the same concentration on the squid's siphon. And the list could be carried on to a tedious length.

As I have said, Picasso went out little once he had settled firmly in the rue des Grands-Augustins. He rose late, and he usually gave up his mornings to the friends who came to see him in ever-increasing numbers; he worked in the afternoon and evening, sometimes walking a few yards up the dark street to dine at the Catalan, often in company with the Leirises, Paul and Nusch Eluard, Dora Maar of course, and Robert Desnos, who came less to eat than to collect scraps for his cats. Then he would work again late into the night by powerful electric lamps when the current was not cut off, otherwise by candle. It was disagreeable walking about Paris, although the streets were almost empty of cars; there was always the sight of Germans to give offense and of the even more offensive collaborationist organizations such as the LVF, the Milice, or the PPF, the louts who beat up Jean Cocteau in the Champs-Elysées for not saluting them; then there was always the probability of being stopped for one's papers, and the possibility of grave unpleasantness. As for traveling farther, that was even more disagreeable, especially for a foreigner. Nevertheless, as winter came on Picasso made the journey down to Saint-Benoît-sur-Loire to see Max Jacob.

Max had been living there in the village by his monastery ever since 1936; they had corresponded, particularly on Max Jacob's side, and messages had passed to and fro; but Picasso was a poor correspondent, and in 1942 Max complained to his friend Michel Béalu that he was forgotten—that André Salmon wrote rarely and Picasso not at all. That was an exaggeration, as he knew very well; and only a little while later he observed with satisfaction, "What explains my forty-one years of friendship with Picasso is the fact that we made this agreement: 'Nothing people ever tell you about me is to count, and that is to work in both directions.'"

Picasso found his friend old and very sad: his brother and sister had been arrested for being Jews and deported to Auschwitz. He was not afraid for himself, being sustained by a faith that took unusual and sometimes disconcerting forms but that nevertheless gave him an extraordinary inner strength; and presently his spirits rose as he showed Picasso his gouaches and as they talked over the innumerable days that had passed since they shared the same bed in a world now infinitely remote.

Max had always laid claim to occult powers that allowed him to foretell the future; he read his friends' palms, told their fortunes with tarot cards, and gave them talismans. No doubt he made fun of them to a certain extent—Max could never resist a laugh, whatever it cost him—but now, shortly after Picasso's visit, he deliberately wrote the year of his own death in the visitors' book at the basilica: Max Jacob, 1944.

Back in Paris Picasso painted more of his gravely beautiful still-lives. In November, 1943, Françoise Gilot came to see him again. She had run away from home because her father would not let her give up the university for painting and she had taken refuge with her grandmother: she appeared at the studio two or three mornings a week, but although she became attached to him their relationship did not yet reach its obvious climax. Once indeed he took her from the usual group of friends in the lower studio and led her upstairs; but it was to show her André Malraux, who had come secretly to Paris from his maquis in the Corrèze, a maquis that now had at least some weapons to use against the Nazis.

Everywhere the Resistance was making ready to play its vital part in the decisive stroke; every night when the moon served arms were being dropped; messengers plied to and fro, by air, by submarine, and across the Alps and Pyrenees; and the whole country was alive with rumors of the coming Allied invasion somewhere on the Channel coast. On all fronts the Germans were in retreat; in the east their losses were appalling; and at last it appeared that the war might really come to an end. But they clung to their hold on France with unparalleled fury: for the French it was like being penned up in an ever more constricted space with a mad bear, a very dangerous brute determined to do all the harm it could before it was brought under control. The deportations and the executions multiplied; the dreadful trains crept north and east to the overflowing camps.

On February 24, 1944, Max Jacob was arrested and taken to Drancy, the usual first stage in the long journey to Auschwitz or Dachau. As soon as the news reached Paris Cocteau set about organizing a petition, while other friends used all the influence, all the contacts they possessed to set him free.

Some twenty years later Pierre Andreu stated that Picasso, on being applied to, refused to intervene, saying, "It is not worth doing anything at all. Max is a will-o'-the-wisp. He has no need of our help to take to the air and fly out of his prison." In *L'Irregulière* (1974) Edmonde Charles-Roux repeats these words. I do not believe that they are true: not only are they in direct contradiction with the rest of Picasso's behavior at the time, but the emissary is stated to have been Pierre Colle, the picture-dealer and Max Jacob's literary executor; and Pierre Colle, like Cocteau, remained on good terms with Picasso after the war.

But even if any intervention could have moved the pitiless Germans, it was too late. In the cold, damp, filthy hole where they had imprisoned him, Max Jacob caught pneumonia, and on March 5 he died. He was sixty-seven, an entirely harmless and very gentle old man, a poet as distinguished as any of his generation.

His body was buried provisionally in a Jewish cemetery and those of his friends who had courage and devotion enough attended his funeral: Picasso was among them. (After the war Max was taken back to Saint-Benoît.)

Next month the Gestapo came for Robert Desnos. He had some hours' warning, but if he had escaped they would have arrested his companion Youki, once Foujita's wife: he waited for them, and died in a concentration-camp, like so many of the finest men and women in France. No one was safe: no fame was a safeguard—Matisse's wife was in prison and a little later the Germans seized his daughter, the Marguerite whose portrait was one of Picasso's most valued possessions.

In addition to all this the air-raids increased: some Parisians cheered the planes, but that did not always save them from being killed by the bombs.

Life was uncertain from one day to the next, and in this atmosphere tense with violent and conflicting emotions many people determined to enjoy it while they could. The seduction of Françoise Gilot, if such a word can be applied to a young woman so very willing and to a process in which there was no deceit on Picasso's part, no promises of any kind, advanced more rapidly. They agreed that she should come to the studio in the afternoons, thus avoiding Sabartés, who had disapproved of her from the start and who foretold nothing but unhappiness; and Picasso said that he would "teach her engraving" upstairs. Young as she was, she did not take engraving literally, and she arrived, dressed with great care for the sacrifice: a sacrifice that was not accepted on this occasion, however. Later she collaborated on a book about her life with Picasso, and if I understand the veiled terms rightly, she was at this time still a virgin.

Before the year was out she did of course become Picasso's mistress; but it does not seem that she was of any considerable importance to him in these early days. There was no explosion of portraits or of pictures based upon her, no sudden fresh burst of creation, as there had been in almost every other case. On the contrary, he went on painting his wonderfully satisfying, quiet still-lives, some of them showing the tomato-plants that he grew in pots on his window-sill among the cactuses and calceolarias; and these were diversified by small views of Paris.

In June, 1944, the Allies landed. The Resistance instantly attacked the German lines of communication, pinning down essential divisions, and as the Germans retreated from the south they killed without mercy: in Oradour, for example, they massacred every living soul, 634 men, women, and children burned in the village church. In August the Allies broke through, and the massive slaughter began in the concentration-camps. The fighting neared Paris, and there was every likelihood that the Germans would lay the city in ruins, decimating the population, before they were driven out.

Picasso painted steadily. His tomatoes were ripening now, and as General Leclerc's French armored division raced up for the honor of liberating Paris he painted four pictures of the growing plants. The Germans were ready for Leclerc, but not for the people of Paris. Before the tanks reached the outskirts the whole city rose against the oppressors; barricades went up overnight and thousands upon thousands of men and women joined in the fighting, police, railwaymen, secretaries, officials, all the members of the Resistance groups, and an enormous battle broke out. Hidden stores of arms appeared, far more than the Germans had expected: in spite of their heavy weapons they could scarcely move except in tanks, and even those were often burned in the streets. But there were a great many Germans; they were reinforced by the now desperate armed collaborationists; and they had hundreds of strong-points all over Paris. The fighting grew in intensity. It was extremely dangerous to go out: merely watching from his window, Picasso was within an inch of being killed—the bullet passed right by his head. Nevertheless, with the strange, unorganized battle going on all round him, and with the likelihood of a German tank in any street or a *milicien* with a rifle on any rooftop, killing for the sake of killing now that all hope was gone, he made his way to Marie-Thérèse's flat on the Ile Saint-Louis, the best part of a mile away, where there was very heavy fighting.

Here he painted two careful portraits of his daughter, a sweet child now, the best kind of little girl, and the head of a young woman—of what young woman I do not know. Then, as the days went by and the battle grew still more furious, he took a reproduction of Poussin's "Triumph of Pan" that happened to be in the flat and set himself to transposing the picture in his own terms, using what materials he had to hand, watercolor and gouache. He painted with the utmost brilliancy of tone; and as he

369]

painted, says Penrose, he sang at the top of his voice, partly drowning the thunder of heavy guns (the French armor was in the city now), the crash of falling glass, the rifle and machine-gun fire, the rumble of the tanks.

His love for Poussin did not bind him to any servile fidelity: he took over the general scheme, the landscape almost tree for tree, the person with a trumpet on the left and the lunging figure on the right, the vase and the masks in the foreground; but whereas Poussin's Pan triumphed with at least some sense of measure, Picasso's splendid party is in wilder movement by far, a swirling maze of pin-headed nymphs, fauns, happy bare limbs and bodies, liberating themselves with love and music and great quantities of food, fruit, and wine.

Chapter XVIII

THE Liberation filled the whole of France with joy, and Picasso was as happy as any of his friends; yet for him it was the beginning of imprisonment within his own myth and of banishment from ordinary society, a sentence that he was to serve for the rest of his life.

Before the war he had been a very well-known painter, famous at least by name among all Europeans who knew anything about art, vaguely notorious among the general public. He was no more exempt from vanity than the ordinary run of men and for many years he had enjoyed this limited fame; while at the same time he was clearly aware of its disadvantages, its isolating effect, and its corrosive action on some human relationships. But it did not spread far beyond his own world; his reputation, though great, was largely a matter of hearsay for those out of reach of the galleries in the capital cities; the time of the sumptuous books of colored reproductions was not yet come; the French museums possessed little of his work, those of most other countries even less; and in spite of his enormous output few people had had the opportunity of seeing any considerable body of his pictures except at the two retrospective exhibitions, the one in Paris in 1932 and the other in the United States at the beginning of the war. Until this time his personal appearance was not widely known; few who had not met him knew who he was, and he could walk about like an ordinary mortal. Self-awareness was not forced upon him: he was not a public figure.

Now everything was changed. Of the three great and irreproachable names upon which the love of art could focus only Picasso had the robust, outgoing temperament that could stand the glare: the invalid Matisse, now in his seventies, lived in retirement far away at Vence; the reticent Braque abhorred publicity. Furthermore, throughout the Occupation great numbers of *résistants* had met in Picasso's studio, and the place itself, dominated by "L'Homme au mouton," together with its uncompromising occupant, became a symbol of the Resistance, of light, freedom, and all they were fighting for. Then again, in the confusion of the battle Picasso's absence from the rue des Grands-Augustins had been misinterpreted; it was widely supposed that the Germans had taken him at last, that in their retreat they had seized upon him as a hostage or as still another victim; and when he was found to be safe the whole world rang with the news.

From that moment on his name was continually in the papers; and when on October 5 of this Liberation year it was announced that he had joined the Communist Party the publicity increased to an extraordinary degree. He now possessed a world-wide notoriety; as well as this he was a combination of the highest art, of what might be called constructive Resistance, and of the left-wing outlook, and in order to set the unmistakable mark of the Liberation on their show, the Salon d'Automne, backed by his Communist friend Jean Cassou, the new curator of the Musée national d'art moderne, invited him to take part, offering him an entire gallery to himself. For the first time in his life he accepted, and the visitors to the Salon de la Libération, which opened on October 6, were astonished to see no less than seventy-four paintings and five sculptures, mostly of the recent years and mostly quite unknown: they were even more astonished when groups of hooligans tried to destroy the paintings, bawling insults as they did so. What these people represented is hard to say: perhaps reaction in its final gasp: perhaps French bourgeois anti-Communism and xenophobia—their cry of "Money back" is surely significant of a certain set of values. They were easily overcome, but the repeated scenes added to the already enormous publicity, which now grew to such a pitch that Picasso's studio was filled day and night with journalists and with American soldiers (they slept on the floor in heaps, says Françoise Gilot).

I do not believe for a moment that Picasso organized this publicity in any way: but in the wild excitement of freedom recovered he did enjoy it. He loved new contacts, he loved fun and clowning, and he had the immense vitality that enabled him to withstand these incessant assaults. And then of course with the frightful strain removed and with his friends coming out of hiding or set free from their prisons (Marguerite Matisse-Duthuit was just saved from deportation as her train neared the frontier) he overflowed with kindness, as may be seen from his unexampled patience with Pfc. Seckler.

Yet at some point in all the happy turmoil Picasso changed, or was changed, from a capital painter, known as such a painter should be known, into a *monstre sacré*, a holy cow surrounded with an enormous, self-perpetuating, inescapable, and generally irrelevant notoriety. And whereas a capital painter may be a man among other men, of finer essence no doubt but still capable of bleeding when pricked, a sacred monster may not; and when he is pricked he must ooze gold rather than blood, or at least a kind of contagious fame. To the natural inequality between him and most men is added a factitious and often somewhat tawdry rank: he is never allowed to forget his status and he must live almost as lonely as the phoenix, surrounded by courtiers rather than friends—a hard fate for one who loved company as much as Picasso.

The change did not come about at once, and its accompaniment of vast wealth, with all the possibility of corrupting power, authority, and freedom from restraint that wealth implies, was still some few years away, together with his full realization that fame was "the castigation by God of the artist," and of the fact that a certain kind of fame means solitude.

In those early, ecstatic months his association with the Communists, quite apart from his union with his other friends, gave him a perhaps illusory and transient feeling of belonging to a larger body, of escaping from his role as a permanent outsider. Many people were astonished at his joining them—the gesture was entirely against his best interests as they were seen by the dealers, since it was obvious that some American collectors at least would stop buying works by a Communist—and very soon he was asked why he had become a member. He replied in an interview conducted by Pol Gaillard for *New Masses* of New York that was also published in *L'Humanité*, the French Communist paper.

I should much rather answer with a picture for I am not a writer; but since sending my colors by wire is far from easy, I shall try to tell you in words.

My joining the Communist Party is the logical outcome of my whole life and of the whole body of my work. For I am proud to say that I have never looked upon painting as an art intended for mere pleasure or amusement: since line and color are my weapons, I have used them in my attempt at gaining a continually greater understanding of the world and of mankind, so that this understanding might give us all a continually greater freedom. In my own way I have tried to recount what seems to me the truest, the most exact, the best; and naturally, as the greatest artists know very well, that is invariably the most beautiful too.

Yes, I do feel that by my painting I always fought as a true revolutionary. But now I have come to see that even that is not enough: these years of terrible oppression have showed me that I have to fight not only with my art but with my whole being.

So I joined the Communists without the slightest hesitation, because

373]

fundamentally I had been with the Party from the very start. Aragon, Eluard, Cassou, Fougeron and all my friends know that perfectly well; and the reason why I had not joined officially before was a kind of simple-mindedness on my part, since I used to think that my work and the fact that my heart belonged were enough; but it was already my own party. Is it not the Communist Party that works hardest at understanding and molding the world, at helping the people of today and of tomorrow to become clearer-minded, freer, happier? Was it not the Communists who were the bravest in France, just as they were in the USSR or my own Spain? What could possibly have made me hesitate? Fear of finding myself committed? But I have never felt more free nor more wholly myself! And then again I was so impatient to have a country of my own once more: I had always been an exile and now I am not an exile any longer. Until the day I can at last return to Spain, the French Communist Party has opened its arms to me, and in the Party I have found all those I most respect, the greatest scientists, the greatest poets, and all the glorious, beautiful insurgent faces I saw in those August days when Paris rose: I am among my brothers once again!

Since French Communism, as it is ordinarily practiced, is a great way from Moscow's version (in the last elections there was a poster in Provence that read "Vote Communist, the party of the small proprietors"), and since many French members are not doctrinaire Communists, no great readers of Marx or Lenin, but join out of a generosity of heart and a hatred for the injustices and inequalities of the capitalist system, in a sense Picasso was among his brothers, particularly in those exalting days of the Liberation and then the victory, before party politics and party dogmatism resumed their sour old grind, destroying the unity and joy. But even then there were very few among them with whom he could possibly talk about painting and even fewer of the leaders who had any notion of what his work was all about. The Communist views on art, on Socialist-Realism, and on the necessity for educating the masses by direct propaganda were of course the antithesis of Picasso's, and in their disagreement neither side ever yielded an inch at any time.

Picasso's declaration was pronounced at a moment of the utmost enthusiasm (at no other time could he possibly have bracketed himself with the Socialist-Realist Fougeron), and his strong sense of occasion may have led him to say more than he meant. Some weeks later, when he was talking to Geneviève Laporte, he gave a simpler, more private, and perhaps more convincing explanation. "You see, I am not French but Spanish," he said. "I am against Franco. The only way I could make it known was by joining the Communist Party, thus proving that I belonged to the other side.''

Geneviève Laporte was then at the Lycée Fénelon, not far from the rue des Grands-Augustins, an entrancing girl of seventeen, all long graceful lines in his drawings of her; and her Resistance group at school had a majority of Communists. In an attempt at becoming a Marxist she had read Politzer and Stalin, but it would not do; she could not honestly join the Party. "Have you read Marx?" she asked.

"No," said Picasso. Nor, it appeared, had he read anything else on the subject.

She was not a Communist, but she was a *résistante;* and it was as a *résistante* and as a reporter for her school newspaper that she called at Picasso's studio, almost blind with shyness, shortly after the ugly scenes at the Salon de la Libération. Sabartés opened the door on his way out; she took him for Picasso and poured forth her prepared speech, glowing crimson as she did so. With a distant expression on his face, Sabartés listened until she had quite finished, observed, "I am not Monsieur Picasso," closed the door, and began to walk downstairs. But after a moment he added, smiling for the first time, "Come again tomorrow at noon: then vou will see him."

Although he disapproved of women in Picasso's life and would willingly have kept them out of the studio at least, he was as good as his word. She was admitted, taken into the lower studio full of visitors, and introduced; Picasso received her very kindly, led her into another room, sat her on a park bench, and talked to her about her lycée. She showed him her school paper; he showed her some of his drawings, recent pictures, and reproductions of earlier work. Presently she gathered courage enough to come to the point: the purpose of the interview was to elicit a general explanation of Picasso's art, which her schoolfellows did not quite understand, an explanation that would provide them with ammunition against the vile Fascist reactionaries who decried him and who said that he mocked the public; and she began with the familiar words "I don't understand . . ."

"Understand!" cried Picasso. "What the Devil has it to do with understanding? Since when has a picture been a mathematical proof? It's not there to explain—explain what, for God's sake?—but to awaken feeling in the heart of the person looking at it. A work of art must not be something that leaves a man unmoved, something he passes by with a casual glance. It has to make him react, feel strongly, start creating too, if only in his imagination. He must be jerked out of his torpor, seized by the throat and shaken up; he has to be made aware of the world he's living in, and for that he must first be jolted out of it." Growing calmer, he told her a great deal about aesthetics that she had not known, about beauty, its relative nature, the beauty of ugliness, the prime value of imagination; then he guided her, blushing again, to the door, asked Sabartés (in the midst of a dead silence among the visitors) to give her his telephone number, and invited her to come again when her article was written.

This was the beginning of such a pleasant relationship. She came every Wednesday, in the afternoon, when he should have been working; they sat on the park bench and she prattled away while he fed her chocolate, a treasure scarcely to be found in France, brought him by the American soldiers.

In spite of these stolen afternoons and of the time he spent with Françoise Gilot, with his innumerable visitors and with his work for the Spanish refugees, he painted steadily, often far into the night: still-lives, his tomato-plants, views of Paris. And in spite of the happy upheaval of his public and his private worlds, there was little change in his painting. The still-lives, often with candles, sometimes with skulls, are perhaps even more powerful than before, and one neo-Cubist view of Paris which brings the Sacré-Coeur into the same landscape as Notre-Dame is more brilliant and considerably larger than the rest of the series; but in general his pictures of 1944 and 1945 are those of a man neither more nor less Communist, neither more nor less committed than ever he was, nor overwhelmed either by the Liberation or by his more intimate emotions.

Indeed so little did any particular engagement appear that some people doubted or affected to doubt the sincerity of his Party membership, especially as he was reported to have denied any connection between art and politics. Françoise Téry of *Les Lettres françaises*, the intelligent Communist weekly, told him of what was being said; he reacted violently, darted out of the room, and came back some minutes later with a hastily penciled statement that ran: "What do you think an artist is? A half-wit with nothing but eyes if he is a painter, ears if he is a musician, lyres installed on every floor of his head if he is a poet, or just muscles and nothing else if he happens to be a boxer? Far, far from it: at the same time he is also a political being, keenly and perpetually aware of the heartbreaking or passionate or delightful things that happen in the world, and he molds himself entirely in their likeness. How could you conceivably cut yourself off from other men and from the life they bring you in such abundance? In the name of what uncaring, ivory-tower kind of attitude? No: painting is not there merely to decorate the walls of flats. It is a means of waging offensive and defensive war against the enemy."

As a political credo it is about as specific as Voltaire's *écrasez l'infâme*, and it can scarcely have given much satisfaction to the Party theorists; but as a picture of what Picasso meant by politics it could not be improved.

As his friendship with Geneviève Laporte increased so his relations with Françoise Gilot became more difficult. There was no necessary connection. For him Geneviève Laporte was still a delightful child: all through the autumn and the harsh winter of 1944 to 1945 her visits continued. She was promoted to a seat on the hairy bull-skin that covered his bed, and there she sat, while Picasso made her tea and fetched her his week's drawings and engravings. Once, indeed, he did suggest that she should stay with the skin she so much admired, but she understood it as a joke; and it is a fact that even then he said *vous* rather than the familiar *tu* that was to come in later years. Françoise Gilot, on the other hand, was now his mistress; familiarity had done its usual work; and she, unlike Geneviève Laporte, was now acquainted with the choleric, irascible side of his character, expressed in such warm terms as, "I don't know why I told you to come. It would be more fun to go to a brothel."

This aspect of Picasso was well known to his friends, his household, and himself; they dreaded his pale silent fury even more than the black rages during which, as Brassaï puts it, "flame burst from the nostrils of the Minotaur." I have not spoken of them hitherto for fear of giving the impression that Picasso spent a considerable proportion of his life in a state of fulminating discontent, which is untrue. Long before he was an old man, habitual kindness had set its mark upon his face, and although on occasion he could erupt like a volcano, kindness always comes into any description by those who knew him well, and often it is the first trait they mention. Brassaï, who frequently uses the word, was one of those men to whom accidents occur: he was alone in the studio one day in November, 1943, photographing the plaster "Homme au mouton," and as he turned it so that the light should strike at a fresh angle one of the sheep's legs fell off, shattering to pieces as it hit the plinth. After a long and very unhappy pause—like most people he had heard of the Minotaur's rages; and this was perhaps Picasso's most highly-valued figure—he went to tell his news. On hearing it, Picasso said nothing; he walked into the studio, examined the damage with a knowing eye, and quietly observed that it was not very serious—the slot had not been deep enough—he would repair it one of these days. And when Brassaï left him some time later Picasso said, "I was not cross, was I?"

But the potentiality for rage was there, and sometimes the rage itself; and few people could withstand either of them or the full force of Picasso's personality. Certainly Dora Maar could not, and Françoise Gilot found it difficult. In 1945 she took to seeing less of him, staying away for a week or a fortnight or sometimes as long as two months. Dora Maar's reaction was quite different. She scarcely came to the studio at all but waited in her flat just round the corner for him to telephone her, and then they would go out together: she was permanently at his disposition. But she was reaching the limit of her endurance, although she still did her best to join in Picasso's very active and often very gay social life, Brassaï gives an account of her appearance at a luncheon-party at the Catalan, where Picasso and his many guests were in the greatest form, laughing, talking, telling stories (Picasso was a splendid mime and a perfect host). She came late, alone, unsmiling, mute, and sat down; two minutes later she stood up and left. Picasso hurried after her. An hour later he came back, looking utterly horrified, and called Eluard out of the room. Neither returned.

At this juncture, Françoise Gilot, coming back to the rue des Grands-Augustins after one of her absences, found her lover in a frame of mind that she could not understand at first. He told her that Dora Maar had had a nervous breakdown, with hallucinations, and that his friend Dr. Lacan had taken her away to his nursing-home. This had happened not in one bout, but over several days, in the course of which (I quote Gilot) Dora Maar had said, "As an artist you may be extraordinary, but morally speaking you're worthless," while Eluard had blamed him for her condition, thumping a chair on the floor so passionately that it broke to pieces.

Picasso expected others to be as strong as he was himself—it seemed normal—and Dora Maar's collapse not only distressed but puzzled and disconcerted him. He had a great respect for Eluard, and Eluard's denunciation, coming on top of Dora Maar's, shook him badly. Even at the time, of course, he had found an argument that satisfied some level of his mind: Dora Maar frequented the Surrealists; the Surrealists advocated irrationality (Eluard himself had said that delirium was the purest expression of reason); it was therefore their fault. But the question of his moral worth remained with him, never entirely resolved.

By the time summer came the war in Europe was over. The concentration-camps, having shown the world the unimaginable baseness of the totalitarian mind, gave up their survivors: many who came back to France were walking skeletons, often tubercular. Some of them had been with Robert Desnos when he died from starvation and ill-treatment after the journey from Buchenwald to Terezine; and what he heard from them, and the photographs, moved Picasso very deeply.

Although the road to the south was now open at last he did not go away until long after the victory. During these months he was preoccupied with a picture on a scale comparable to that of "Guernica." Like "Guernica," "Le Charnier"—the charnel-house—has no color: everything is gray, shading to black on the one hand and to white on the other. Although it is not a quarter of the size of "Guernica," which was designed for a given wall, it is still a big canvas, about six feet by eight and a half, and it seems larger because of its grayness. High on the left stands a white table with a crumpled cloth, a jug, a saucepan, perhaps a piece of bread; they are seen only in line, but otherwise they are in the same spirit as his recent still-lives. The table exists on one plane: on another, physically below it and extending in a diagonal from the lower left-hand corner towards the upper right, lies a tumbled heap of bodies, a man, a woman, and a baby, thrown together pell-mell. Almost in the middle of the picture the starved man's stick-like legs, rigid in death, with their huge feet tied at the ankles, rise as once the soldier's arm with its clenched fist had risen in "Guernica." The painting makes no concession to popular taste; it is entirely Picasso in its use of the Cubist idiom, its distortion, and its sculptural planes. Yet it is a direct, not a symbolic statement: a silent, massive condemnation of the stated facts.

"Guernica," with all its scores of drawings and composition-studies, was painted at great speed, perhaps in little more than a month, one stage following the other with bewildering rapidity. "Le Charnier" would not come. All the essentials were there by July, yet the picture was not finished for the Salon d'Automne of 1945. Nor was it finished by February, 1947, when it was shown in the exhibition of Art and the Resistance, nor even some years later when he sold it to an American collector.

It is a picture that possesses great force and clarity; it is a proof, if proof were needed, that he did not live in any ivory tower; but it has nothing like the emotional impact of "Guernica." The everlasting wrong of the concentration-camps, the cold, deliberate slaughter of millions upon millions of people, was evil of an order of magnitude new to the world, horrible beyond the powers of Picasso or of any other man.

And while he was working on "Le Charnier" Picasso's mind could not be as wholly fixed upon his subject as it had been in the days of "Guernica." There was his renewed grief for Desnos and Jacob and many other friends; there were the contrary, insistent claims of his living friends, who in spite of Sabartés devoured his time, bringing about wild fluctuations of mood; there was Dora Maar's illness; and there was his consciousness of growing old. More than most men he felt the mutilation of

379]

advancing age: most feel it cruelly enough, the hopeless struggle against castration and declining powers, the battle that can only end in defeat; but few are so wholly committed to life as Picasso was; few have ever had his powers to lose. His grand climacteric had come and gone, a time when age often presses on one's mind more than it does later; and his awareness of it, and perhaps his resentment of their youth, may account for some of his occasionally savage treatment of his mistresses.

A ludicrous but significant instance is his deep concern over his fore-lock. Time out of mind, well before Samson, hair has been a symbol of virility; it has always had a great magic power and the loss of it has been a disaster. Picasso's hair was primarily the lock drooping over his eyes, and now in his sixty-fourth year the lock was leaving him; that spring, at the risk of turning himself from a fiery bull to a dull-eyed steer, he cut off the sparse remains, recording the event on the title-page of a book by Poe: "No more forelock! Paris, May 12, 1945."

Then there was the showing of his pictures in London. It was an unusually important exhibition, and Picasso was sensitive to newspaper criticism—that is to say, although he never took the slightest notice of any man's strictures, never changed his approach for praise or blame, he read the papers with the utmost attention, just as he watched his visitors' faces as he showed them what he had done. Once again he was exhibiting with Matisse, as he had first done forty-three years ago, but this time it was at the Victoria and Albert Museum rather than in Berthe Weill's little gallery, and it was organized by the British Council, no less. But while the Matisses were more in the nature of a general view or retrospective, all but one of Picasso's paintings belonged to the war years: the contrast between the serene detachment of the one and the violence and often savage introspection of the other was startling, but even without that the British public would have been amazed. It was long since they had seen anything of Picasso, and this concentration of his recent experience, much of it expressed in manners they were not used to, shocked them extremely, the more so for being in that staid, official building, with its smell of established death. But at least they did not pass the pictures by with a casual glance: many of them reacted by writing to the papers, and day after day the middle page of *The Times* was filled with attacks and counter-attacks of a rare virulence.

Finally, late in the summer, leaving the unfinished picture behind him, he took Dora Maar to the south. They drove down, for at last there was petrol for civilian cars and now the elderly Hispano-Suiza could take to the road again. There they stayed part of the time at Golfe-Juan and part of the time at Cap d'Antibes, with Madame Cuttoli, a collector whose wealth allowed her to indulge her real passion for the arts—she was a leading figure in the revival of French tapestry—and one in whose villa he was free from the cries of *Give, give* that had worn his spirit ever since he became well-known and that now increased even faster than his notoriety, from the sprats artfully designed to catch a whale, and from the impression that he was an inexhaustible source of free (and marketable) pictures, drawings, and engravings for the first fool with flattery to spare or a handsome wife to prostitute.

It was perhaps an anxious holiday in some ways, for although fauns appeared as soon as Picasso stepped on classic ground (he etched some, piping to ecstatic maenads) and although he stayed well into the autumn, it does not seem from most of his work that the Mediterranean or the recovered sun had anything like their full effect. Apart from other causes, the great picture was waiting for him in Paris. But he did enjoy himself some of the time, and he did travel inland, to the remoter Provence behind the Lubéron, to the village of Ménerbes in the Vaucluse, across the valley from Gordes and not far from the Sorgues of his days with Eva. Here, right in the village, stood a house that a man in Paris had offered him for one of his still-lives: Brassaï speaks of a color-merchant in a blue suit who haunted the studio during the war, urging Picasso to make just such an exchange, and although there are some differences of detail—Brassaï mentions a park—it was probably the same man. In any case Picasso accepted the house at Ménerbes: it is said that he did so without having seen it; it is certain that having seen it he liked it and that he at once gave it to Dora Maar.

Returning north in late October he made the acquaintance of Fernand Mourlot, who had the finest lithographic workshop in Paris, and he plunged straight back into the medium he had used with such success in the twenties.

He had made a number of prints by the end of November, when Françoise Gilot, finding that she could not do without him and having persuaded herself that her continuing absence "probably would not restore his deteriorating relationship with Dora Maar," came to the studio again, and there she noticed that some of these lithographs had direct reference to her.

As portraits they were not flattering, but in fact he had missed her; and although he delighted in lithography, the warm workshop full of busy, skilful artisans, a refuge from his cold studio (fuel and many other things were still rationed) with its crowds of visitors, most of them idle, he was nevertheless lonely, particularly as there was no more Geneviève Laporte to come and drink tea with him on his bull's hide. She had done with school, and some months earlier Picasso had helped her to realize her ambition of going to the United States, where she went to Swarthmore College, in Pennsylvania.

He was therefore all the more pleased to see Françoise, who at this time certainly had the most fetching air of youth and freshness. Their relationship assumed a new quality, and when in February, 1946, she broke an arm and decided to recuperate in the south he took rooms for her in a house at Golfe-Juan belonging to a friend of his, the aged master-engraver Louis Fort, who had printed many of Picasso's illustrations for Vollard.

Françoise traveled down with her grandmother, with whom she was living; but when they reached the coast she left the old lady at Antibes and with a former school-friend she went to Golfe-Juan, where Louis Fort taught her something about engraving. Picasso soon arrived to stay for a while; he got rid of the school-friend by offering to rape her; and before he drove Françoise back to Paris he took her to see Matisse at Vence. Although he was very poorly, Matisse could now paint for a few hours a day, but when they came he was in bed, cutting out shapes in colored paper for his immense, joy-filled collages. The two men talked about painting, colors, and their interaction, and at one point Matisse said, "Well, in any case, if I made a portrait of Françoise, I should make her hair green."

Before the return journey and during the course of the drive Picasso said that he wanted Françoise to come and live with him. She demurred on the grounds that it would mean leaving her grandmother, and in this she was supported by Marcel, the chauffeur (they all sat on the front seat) whose view was that she should be given time to think it over, and that at this stage Picasso should let her go home.

Another reason for not living with him that Gilot brought forward was his continuing connection with Dora Maar. Picasso assured her that it was over, that Dora Maar understood it to be over, and that she would say so herself. He pressed Françoise to go with him to her flat: she was unwilling, but eventually did so, and she was present at a scene as ugly and cruel as can be imagined, in the course of which Dora Maar, having been compelled to state that the liaison was finished, said to Picasso, "You've never loved anyone in your life. You don't know how to love." Françoise describes it in loving detail, asserts that she was very much upset, and gives the date of her going to live with Picasso as towards the end of May, 1946.

From this time until their final parting seven years later Picasso's life is fully documented: the vagueness about his movements, the contradictory evidence about pictures that he did not date himself, the confusion that hangs over much of his earlier life and work, now appears to vanish; here is Picasso living day by day, working and talking about his work, and the biographer seems to be in possession of the most precious material he could hope for. But what is the value of the document?

The French translation of *Life with Picasso* by Françoise Gilot and Carlton Lake was published in 1965: it had been known that she was busy with her memoirs and those who disliked Picasso eagerly bought the book; they were disappointed—it was not an obviously vicious attempt at destruction, there were few scandalous revelations, and the general impression, after a superficial reading, was that although the book handled the man with some severity it treated the artist with respect. His friends, however, and those who read deeply in the hope of some closer understanding of the painter, were startled to find that the book was not about the Picasso they had known either in life or through his work but about a small man, ill-tempered, unkind, self-indulgent, and essentially weak, nothing like the Picasso who had painted the "Demoiselles d'Avignon" or "Guernica," nothing like the man of whom Clive Bell said, "Two people I have known from whom there emanated simply and unmistakably a sense of genius: one is Picasso. . . . It has been my fortune to be friends with a number of very clever people: Maynard Keynes, the cleverest man I ever met, Roger Fry, Lytton Strachey, Raymond Mortimer, Jean Cocteau. None of them cast the peculiar spell I am trying to characterise. The difference between these very clever people and the less clever, between Roger Fry and me for instance, was it seemed one of degree rather than kind. . . . But Virginia [Woolf] and Picasso belonged to another order of beings; they were of a species distinct from the common; their mental processes were different from ours; they arrived at conclusions by ways to us unknown."

The most disappointing parts are those many long passages which purport to give Picasso's views on art in his own words; for the wearisome, didactic voice that drones on and on is that of a stranger. The Picasso the world knew had many faults, but he was never, never dull: Gilot and Lake's Picasso is a bore.

The form of the book may be partly responsible for this. *Life with Picasso* was written down by a journalist in the cosy, folksy style usual in lives "as told to," and the presentation of Picasso as a tedious, theorizing man is less the result of malice than of incomprehension, self-complacency, and want of respect for a mind far beyond the reach of a commonplace understanding.

Ill-will there was, however, particularly towards the end of the book, but it serves rather to give a picture of the woman Françoise Gilot had become by middle age than to discredit Picasso: as *The Times* said, this "inflated, waspish, tritely-written narrative. . . . turns out to be much more of a 'revelation' of the character and mentality of its author than of the great man whose name is involved. It would not have seemed surprising had it been entitled *Life with Françoise.*"

Distasteful though the book may be, it contains factual material that can be safely used, while some of the opinions, remarks on painting, and aesthetic judgments do no doubt contain a certain amount of Picasso; but I shall not quote Gilot and Lake for any of these, nor for Picasso's character, unless there is corroborative evidence from other sources.

But in 1946 Françoise Gilot was not yet sour: few people would have called her a particularly affectionate, warm-hearted, or sensitive young woman, but she had a splendid blaze of youth, and in those days she could be cheerful, even gay. No one who has seen that well-known photograph of her walking up the beach in a long dress and a fringed straw hat with Picasso behind, holding a huge umbrella over her, is likely to forget the triumphant grace of her movement or her radiant young happiness.

Her unusual looks, much helped by her asymmetric eyes and what Matisse had called her circumflex eyebrows pleased Picasso now more than they had before; and his new delight in her company showed itself in a fresh outburst of work. Until this time he had painted only two unimportant pictures of her, but soon after she came to live with him he made a number of drawings and lithographs, far kinder than those of the previous November, and then he began the portrait known as "La Femme fleur": a delicate blue stem for her slim-waisted body, long pods for her arms, two round ripe fruit for her breasts, a sideways oval for her face, and dark green leaf-like processes for her hair; and on the oval heart of the flower there are her features, little more than the formal marks a child might make, but perfectly unmistakable. It is an exquisite thing, in fresh, delicate colors, and it says a great deal about his notion of her then. And in the fruitful month of June he painted, among many other pictures, a big "Enlèvement d'Europe," with a massive, highly-simplified, and sculptural woman, upright and slim-waisted, riding the red-eyed bull, guiding it with a firm hold on one of its horns: it was not his most successful picture, but it was his first important classical reference for a great many years.

In July, still enchanted with her and with his flowing work, he drove down with Françoise to Provence. It scarcely seems credible that the place he chose to take her to should be the house he had given Dora Maar at Ménerbes, but the fact is attested not only by Gilot but by some cheerful landscapes of the village. Quite apart from this the holiday began badly, since the town-bred Françoise had an exaggerated fear of the scorpions that swarmed in the house, and she resented the letters he received from Marie-Thérèse, giving news of the little household on the Ile Saint-Louis. Presently she ran away: that is to say she walked along the highroad until Picasso's car came up behind her. According to her account they prosed away to one another by the side of the road for a considerable space of time, with Picasso uttering such remarks as, "It's up to us to build something together." However that may be he induced her, perhaps without much difficulty, to come back to Ménerbes, and (says she) to have a baby.

At this point there is a conflict of testimonies: Gilot says that Picasso wanted her to have both this child and its successor in order "to bring you back to nature and put you in touch with the rest of the world." Picasso told Geneviève Laporte that it was Gilot who wanted the children for reasons of her own; he did not. Whichever is right, the baby was soon on its way: but by this time they were on the coast again, at Golfe-Juan and then at Antibes; and at last Picasso's holiday, his first true holiday since 1939, began in a splendid burst of joy.

The last painting he had made on the eve of war in 1939, the "Pêche de nuit à Antibes," showed the looming towers of the Grimaldi palace, or rather castle. Having suffered from long neglect and even more from the presence of troops, the great building had for many years been the local museum, housing a few Greek potsherds (Antibes was once Antipolis), the usual sad Roman remains in dusty cases, and some objects to do with Bonaparte—meager collections that did not nearly fill the rooms. But some time before this holiday a new curator had been appointed, Romuald Dor de La Souchère, a highly-cultivated man, a hellenist, who had fresh ideas about the function of a museum. Under his direction the castle had already housed the British Council's exhibition of children's drawings, and Picasso had come to see them when he was in Antibes in 1945. Between that time and September 8, 1946, when La Souchère was on the beach at Golfe-Juan with Picasso and a group of friends, he had been urged to ask the great man to give the museum a picture. He felt all the awkwardness of making such a request, but nevertheless he brought it out. "Of course," said Picasso, to whom these solicitations were unpleasantly familiar, "I'll find a little drawing." A chill fell on the conversation but presently Picasso, who for some time past had been complaining of his want of space in Louis Fort's house, observed, "I've always wanted to paint really large surfaces, and I've never been given any."

"Surfaces!" cried La Souchère. "You want surfaces? I can give you some." He could indeed. The museum had a whole upper floor of vast rooms completely empty.

Picasso took him at his word, moved into this warm, sunlit, self-contained world, closed the door behind him, and began to paint. He was short of colors and materials—he had to use sheets of plywood and even fibro-cement instead of canvas, boat-paint and coarse brushes instead of the finest Paris could afford—but he had never had such a store of energy, and in these months until the winter cold, shut up from noon till nightfall, he poured out a great number of happy pictures. He had the sea at hand whenever he chose to emerge, good food at last—the Mediterranean was crammed with fish after these years of restrictions—and many friends. The Eluards came to see him; there was the sculptor Sima; the Cuttolis were close by; and once he was taken to Vallauris, a little pottery town a mile or so inland, to visit the kilns belonging to the Ramiés, a couple who were trying to revive the ancient industry, where he made a few small objects from the clay, leaving them to be fired.

He had plenty of company, plenty of amusement, and he could have had much more, but his mind was turned to his pictures entirely. "La Joie de vivre"—and that for once was Picasso's own title—is perhaps the gayest of them all: among blue hills, with black to enhance them, goats with smiling human faces dance on a golden ground to the piping of a centaur and an ambiguous blue creature that has climbed on to a purple eminence, while a sort of *femme-fleur* capers in the middle with the sun caught in her hair and a boat sails by on the high blue sea. And there were many more, most of them great big pictures with horned demi-gods, satyrs, nymphs, and goats in profusion. This latest flowering of the ancient Mediterranean tradition has often been called Theocritan: but Theocritus never had Picasso's sense of fun, and since he wrote in the crabbed Doric his verse is necessarily Greek to most people of today, whereas Picasso's language is direct and timeless, legible to one and all; and as he said later, speaking of Antibes, "I did what I could there, and I did it with pleasure, for then at least I felt that I was working for the people as a whole."

By no means all the pictures were idyllic pastorals, although it is they that give the general tone to the museum; there are also grave still-lives, some of them very much larger than any he had painted hitherto, but all filled with a sanguine harmony—here there is none of the brooding introspection or latent threat of the war years, no edge of madness. Several have to do with sea-urchins, and in one picture the urchins are combined with a figure, that of an owl perched on the back of a chair.

It is a scops owl, the kind to be seen on Athena's shoulder: it comes to the south of France every spring, a familiar little bird, often living in the village trees; this one had got into the castle, had hurt itself, and had been brought to Picasso, who, having dressed its wounds, tamed it. That is to say, it lost all fear of him and would bite his finger. He was much attached to the bird, however, and in time it grew more amiable, perching on his shoulder with every appearance of affection. He drew the fierce, proud little creature, painted and modeled it; and now, though it was buried long ago, it is at least as immortal as bronze.

There were still other pictures—fishermen, the woman who sold sea-urchins, some highly geometrical yet curiously light nudes, one of which, like the owl and urchins, shows what looks like the wood-graining technique that he had learned so long ago from Braque but which is in fact the true grain of the ply either covered by a transparent coat, like a stain, or left bare. And there were many, many drawings, as pure in their line as anything he had ever done. All these he left at the museum when at last the winter drove him back to Paris. He did not exactly give them—he hated parting with his work, and he grew very testy indeed whenever it was suggested that he should make a formal donation—but there they remained in a kind of vacuum of ownership, and there they still remain in their perfect setting, an unexampled expression of what may well have been the happiest months of his life.

For Picasso Paris now meant lithography and Mourlot's workshop; but after so long an absence he had first to attend to many things and to see his friends—Braque, for one. He took Françoise with him to Braque's house, where his attempt at forcing an invitation to lunch was defeated by his friend's determination not to yield to pressure: a humiliating incident that she relates in detail. Then there were the Eluards, Joan Rebull and many other Catalans, Dora Maar. With few exceptions he never lost touch with his former mistresses, in spite of the frightful scenes that often marked their parting. Even Olga remained in a kind of contact, at least by letter, and he never dismissed her from his mind. Françoise Gilot, a great imputer of motives, interprets this as an insatiable desire for possession, an unwillingness to allow any victim to escape: another explanation is that Picasso had a great capacity for friendship, that he was a friend as well as a lover, and that when the lover evaporated the friend remained. He and Dora Maar were most companionable after their break, abidingly fond of one another; and he was with her that November when they learned of the sudden death of Nusch—a shattering brain-hemorrhage that struck her when she was alone, Eluard being in Switzerland, and that killed her in a few hours.

The effect of her death, so young and fine, was catastrophic for El-uard—few of his friends expected him to survive—and it shocked and distressed Picasso extremely. This, as well as the ideas that were boiling in him and his love for the work, may account for his extraordinary as-siduity at the lithographic studio. In his usual course of life he would breakfast in bed, look at his post and the newspapers, and sometimes it would be close on noon before he was up and about; but now he appeared at the workshop in the rue de Chabrol, over on the other side of Paris, at nine o'clock, and, says Fernand Mourlot, he would often stay until late in the evening.

The warm, dim, rambling place with its cubicles and presses was a ref-uge for him in many ways—apart from anything else he was having trou-ble with his unoccupied flat in the rue La Boëtie, which the authorities wanted to requisition—and he had a horror of anything to do with the law. He worked there with such steadiness that his late morning recep-tions, his levees, were given up for months on end. Although his dark tan faded in Mourlot's shop (it is difficult to imagine Picasso unsunburned), the piping fauns, the nymphs, the spring of the world, were still with him, and they poured out in a stream of lithographs that showed every known technique together with some some new discoveries of his own that the craftsmen said would never print but that nevertheless produced wonder-ful results: his famous dove was one, though that came somewhat later.

The owl appeared, too: it had come to Paris to join the pigeons, turtle-doves, and canaries, and it was fed from the studio's abundant supply of mice. And the classical world also overflowed into his illustration for *Dos Contes.* He had often been obliged, by friendship or importunity, to illus-trate books, sometimes against his will; but *Dos Contes,* by his very old friend Ramon Reventós, was one that he suggested himself and that he worked upon with great affection. The two stories, written long before and now to be collected into a volume, were *El Centaure picador* and *El capvespre d'un faune* (*capvespre* being twilight), and they were to be published in Catalan and in a French translation. Picasso not only made four plates for the one and four different plates for the other (some friends had to be content with a single, often irrelevant etching) but he also im-pregnated himself with the text, copying it out by hand, and he designed the initial letters and both jackets. The books themselves, limited edi-tions, quickly vanished, bought by collectors, but they revived and confirmed Reventós' reputation in Catalonia, and the illustrations have often been reproduced. One shows the birth of the last centaur: in a maternity-ward that has something of a stable—a manger and a sort of horse in the foreground—one midwife shows another the baby with little horns, hoofs, and a tail, while a figure on a bench, perhaps the woman's husband, bows his head in his hands. And in one of the others the centaur, grown up, has attached himself to one of those small covered carts that used to be seen all over Spain—a reminiscence of the minotaur.

Spain and childbirth were much in his mind at this time: the first indeed was never far away, and now it was brought even closer by Reventós and by the Catalan friends who came up to Paris in increasing numbers; while the second arose from the prospect of Françoise's baby.

In May, 1947, Françoise had this child, a boy whom she named Claude, and presently Picasso took them, together with a nurse, down to Golfe-Juan again. It was perhaps just as well, for by this time Françoise Gilot had thoroughly antagonized the other members of the household. She represents Inès as a sly, disagreeable minx, Sabartés as a bear, intellectually null, and both of them as jealous. Geneviève Laporte saw them in quite a different light: for her Inès was charming, beautiful, and welcoming, entirely on her side, while Sabartés, though harsh to exploiters, was as kind as could be. He was also a considerable writer, as she knew very well; for although she traveled much during these early Gilot years she was in Paris from time to time, and when she was there she translated some of Sabartés' pieces, including a novel, from Spanish into French, a most elegant French, since she was herself a poet.

At Golfe-Juan they lived in Louis Fort's small house again, and now, with two more people in it, the house was smaller still. There was another disadvantage: Olga Picasso appeared and she began to haunt them, sitting close by on the bench and calling out to her son, now a young man of twenty-six who had grown up without the benefit of any particular education, trade, or profession and who was often with his father; and she followed them in the street. Picasso was irritated: once he slapped her. No doubt the crowded rooms displeased him too. But after a short while he spent little time either on the beach or in the house. Gilot says that he went to Antibes to paint the huge "Ulysse et les sirènes" at the castle, which was now beginning to function as a Picasso museum, and certainly the catalog dates it 1947; yet on the other hand he spoke of it as a finished picture when he was telling Brassaï about Antibes in November, 1946, and he showed him a photograph. There are innumerable contradictions of this kind in the record, but one quite undisputed, fully documented fact is that in the summer of 1947 Picasso went back to Vallauris.

He went merely to see what had happened to the little objects he had made the year before: then he returned to make more, with no strong in-clination at first, but presently with a mounting enthusiasm as he began to get the feel of this new medium, plastic above all others, and to realize its potentialities, coming back day after day until the days lengthened into months, the summer waned, winter came on, and the tale of his pots mounted to close on two thousand; and still he twirled, kneaded, shaped, incised, glazed, and painted his now docile clay.

Chapter XIX

IT has been said that pottery is not a medium that can express any very significant concept; that the technical processes which necessarily follow the artist's work blur his line and color, destroying fine differences and taking away from the immediacy of his touch; that it is at its best when it is anonymous form and color; that in "personal" ceramics gaiety, decorativeness, and fantasy can survive but not much else; and that quite apart from the limitations of size and surface the ceramic equivalent of a "Guernica" is unthinkable. And in this particular case it has also been said that in the course of years the dispersion of Picasso's energy over some thousands of minor objects encouraged his facility and, by sapping his concentration, did lasting damage to his creative power.

This seems to me to overstate the case: but although I love many of the Picasso vases, figurines, and dishes I have seen I think few people would place his ceramics on the same level as his drawing, painting, or sculpture. It may be that he did not intend to express more than in fact he did express: or it may be that Picasso was no more able to perform the impossible than another man—that neither he nor anyone else could do away with the inherent nature of baked clay.

Yet even if one were to admit that pottery cannot rise much above gaiety, fantasy, and decoration (and there are Sung bottles by the thousand as evidence to the contrary, to say nothing of the Greek vases), what a range is there! Picasso certainly thought it wide enough, and he worked on and on, learning and innovating among the wheels, the various kilns, and the damp mounds of clay in the Ramiés' Madoura pottery, taking little time off for anything except some studies of young Claude, a certain number of lithographs and illustrations, particularly for Reverdy's *Le Chant des Morts*, and for Góngora. He had always valued Góngora and this selection of twenty poems was another book that he set himself to do with great good will: he carefully wrote them out (his hand was to be reproduced) and then embellished nineteen with etchings—the twentieth, Góngora's sonnet on El Greco, he left untouched, out of respect for the painter.

Paris saw scarcely anything of him apart from a short visit about the turn of the year, and in February, 1948, he was back in the south, living at Golfe-Juan and working at Vallauris. Still the pots came from his hands by the hundred: doves and owls; figurines allied to those of archaic Greece or at least born under the same sun; plates with his Antibes fauns, others with Mediterranean fishes, with bulls, bull-fights, and with the sun itself; every combination of the creature and the hollow vessel, nearly all for use. His square, stubby hands had always been quick to learn the use of any implement, and here they were the living tool: by now he had a mastery of the craft, and some of his new, hazardous techniques were surprisingly successful. At times he came near to achieving a wholly satisfactory synthesis of painting, sculpture, and collage, of color and the third dimension, and that on a scale comparable to what he had accomplished in each of them separately. Although in general his aim was not nearly so high, he may in fact have done so; and if he did then it was when he molded and shaped his great vases, turning them into smooth, perfectly rounded women, sometimes without heads and on occasion transmuted into bronze, with its more living surface.

He loved women's bodies as much as ever Maillol did or Renoir, and his pleasure can be seen in every flowing curve. But those he had not shaped himself left him little peace: Françoise, idle and discontented in the small rented house, now had real cause for complaint. Olga had come back again and she renewed her persecution with greater zeal. Taking advantage of the fact that Madame Fort knew her, she even got into the house, and there she would slap her rival when they met in the hall, while at the front door she would both pinch and scratch.

According to Gilot's account Picasso was not particularly moved when she told him, so she "drummed into him, day after day, my dissatisfaction" until the month of May, when, badgered beyond endurance, he found and bought a house above Vallauris itself, a horrid little villa called La Galloise, half a mile or so out of the town and up a steep hill.

The removal came at a bad time, and Picasso refused to have anything to do with it: the powerful, healthy young woman had only the chauffeur and Paulo and the nurse to help her take the baggage and some papers from Golfe-Juan to the villa, and her sense of grievance stayed with her for fifteen years. As she says herself, "the new house didn't improve my disposition all at once, however. In one of the photographs taken of us sitting on the beach at that period, I have a long face—brooding, if not actually sulky."

A less tender witness might have said "positively sulky, discontented, and deeply selfish"; and Picasso, who loved to laugh, remembered her as a kind of permanent tragedy-queen. At no time does she seem to have had the least idea of the tension under which a creative man must work; her convenience was to come first, or there would be the steady domestic hostility that Picasso knew only too well—a sadly familiar pattern. Even before this he had learned so much of the young woman's developing nature that a tactless suggestion of marriage caused him to react violently. The suggestion, to be sure, was accompanied by other ill-timed and perhaps even more provocative words, but even so the outburst is significant.

Françoise Gilot speaks of the incident—it is fairly well known from other sources—and the passage in which she does so is one of the few in her book that show an entirely recognizable Picasso. They had invited Madame Cuttoli and her husband the senator, a typical southern politician and a man of great local importance, to dinner at a restaurant on the shore. The senator blundered into the delicate subject of the pictures in the Antibes museum. He urged Picasso to make a formal donation—to relinquish his right to his own creation—and he went on to say that Picasso should also become a French citizen. This would allow him to get his divorce and to marry Françoise: after all, they had a child now.

Picasso was not half the size of the politician, but his instant explosion of rage completely dominated the big man. He spoke intemperately, it must be admitted: among other things he cried out that to the quotation "I do not seek: I find" should be added "I do not give: I take" (a palpable falsehood, by the way: he spent his life giving, and at about this time he handed over ten capital pictures, of enormous value even then, to Cassou's Musée d'Art moderne which could not afford to buy them), adding some furious remarks about the relative importance to him of the Spanish Republic on the one hand and Françoise Gilot and her son on the other, and asserting that he had no intention of submitting his life "to the laws that govern the miserable little lives of you *petits bourgeois.*"

This took away their appetite. Gilot continues: " 'Well, why don't you eat?' he shouted. 'This food isn't good enough for you? My God, the stuff I get at your house sometimes! But I eat it anyway, for friendship's sake. You'll have to do the same. You're my guest.' Pablo was out of all control now, beating his feet up and down on the floor and rolling his eyes like a hysterical woman. [This simile is pure Gilot.] No one answered him. He stood up, picked up his plate, and hurled it into the sea."

The little scene is valuable not only for showing Picasso's hatred of being manipulated, his love for Spain, and his aversion to marrying Françoise, and all this in a short space, but also as an example of his remarkably forgiving nature. Few people can overlook having given or received an affront, but Picasso was one of those few, and presently he and Madame Cuttoli, and even the senator, were as well together as ever they had been: he looked upon such things as part of the normal give and take between friends, and his personality was such—he was so pleasant at other times—that many of them agreed with him.

For a long while he even forgave Françoise her glumness, her martyrdom, and her nagging about the house; he had a remaining fondness for her and he was very much attached to the little boy; and she says that this summer he suggested she should have another child, to cure her discontent. Her statement is difficult to reconcile with his words "I did not want any children. It was she who wanted them," though perhaps not with his "for me, getting a woman with child means possession and it helps me destroy the feeling that was there. You can't imagine what an everlasting need I have to break free!"

In any case, by the time Picasso went off to Poland in August, 1948, Françoise was pregnant again. The journey was no sudden whim—he did not break the routine of his days without great reluctance—but the result of much negociation and pressure on the part of the Communists. The cold war between Russia and the West had begun, a war in which moral and intellectual standing played an important part; and among the intricate maneuvers was the calling of a Congress of Intellectuals for Peace at Wroclav, or, as it used to be called, Breslau, a heterogeneous assembly that included some men of great eminence and passionate sincerity. Although in spite of his conversion Picasso's painting showed no signs of Socialist-Realism, and although it was still as degenerate for the Russians as it had been for the Germans, his reputation and his known integrity would add such weight to the manifestation that the Polish embassy sent a woman down to Vallauris to deal with his procrastination; he had said he would attend, but he showed not the least sign of moving. She went to work with the energy of one well acquainted with Stalin's short way with saboteurs: Picasso's obsolete Republican passport did not signify—the Poles would fly him there in one of their own planes without formalities—there was nothing to be frightened of: the plane would certainly not fall down: there were aerodynamic laws to keep it up—he would like the congress when he got there. After three days or so she got him into a flying-machine for the first time in his life: he was despondent and anxious, but at least he had Eluard and Marcel Boudin with him—they would all fly in the face of nature together, three Icaruses sharing, and thus dividing, the impiety.

The woman was right about the plane; it stayed in the air all the way to

Poland. But she was mistaken about his liking the Party when he got there. Picasso had always bored easily, and there were innumerable speeches: a photograph shows him wearing earphones and listening to the simultaneous translation with an air of dismal resignation. His round bald head looks younger than it had some years before, as though he now reached an age that really suited him, an age that he wore as naturally as he had worn his long-lasting youth. His dark eye is more lustrous still now that no forelock competes with it; no surrounding wrinkles are to be seen, and the fold of the eyelid, the most expressive part of a face, shows a purity of line often found in Orientals or very young children. He has a respectable suit on for once (though a button is missing) and in his lapel there is the chain attached to the schoolboy watch in his breast-pocket: it was many, many years before his conservative mind could be brought to accept the modern fashion of wearing it on his wrist.

There were some brighter moments, however. At one point a Russian delegate saw fit to make a speech reproaching the Impressionist-Surrealist Picasso for his decadence, representative of the worst in Western bourgeois culture, and Picasso replied with all his wonted fire, drawing the obvious parallel between this attack and those of the Nazis. On another occasion he read out a speech of his own, in which he denounced the imprisonment of his friend Pablo Neruda, in Chile. And then he and Eluard had time to visit Warsaw and buy embroidered Polish clothes for Claude and to see the Leonardo at Cracow. It is probable that the Poles also meant to give him pleasure by awarding him a decoration, the cross of one of their orders: the French government, perhaps in an attempt at forestalling the Communists and diminishing the value of their gesture, perhaps out of real gratitude for his gift to the Musée d'Art moderne, had already given him the silver medal of the Reconnaissance française just before he left. What Picasso thought of these honors does not appear, but it is a fact that unlike many of his eminent contemporaries he never put in for the Légion d'Honneur—a formal solicitation is required, and Cézanne had begged for it in vain.

Françoise Gilot had expected him to be away for three days: he stayed for three weeks. This was a very grave offense, particularly as her interesting state entitled her to every consideration. It is true that he sent her a telegram every day, but as they all ended with the proletarian formula *bons baisers* she suspected them of having been written by Marcel, and when Picasso returned, bearing gifts, she greeted him with a blow in the face and then locked herself into the little boy's room. She relates the incident with a self-applause undiminished by fifteen years of reflection.

In October they went back to Paris, partly for an exhibition of 1946

Antibes drawings at the Leiris gallery, partly for a larger if not more important show of Picasso's pots at the Maison de la Pensée française, the Party's window on to its intellectual activities, and partly because his first enthusiasm for ceramics had waned. It was in Paris that he painted his charming picture of Claude in his Polish clothes—one of many portraits of the child—as well as two versions of "La Cuisine," large canvases based on the kitchen in the rue des Grands-Augustins with its birdcages for the turtle-doves and the owl, but so far removed in its extreme, almost monochrome simplification and its use of rectilinear signs that it is as nearly abstract as anything he ever did. The same tendency, in some degree allied to his dot compositions of 1926, is to be seen in other pictures of this time, and one possible explanation is that it represents a reaction from his pots, with their physical continuity and flowing line, a return to a more rigorous organization of an ideal rather than an actual space.

The exhibition of Picasso's ceramics, a hundred and forty-nine of his best pieces, excited no great outcry, which rather disappointed him; but on the other hand it sent all the other painters, sculptors, and handymen hurrying to the nearest pottery, so that for the next twenty years France was flooded with misshapen jugs and ashtrays, while at the same time tourists flocked to Vallauris, bringing a material prosperity hitherto unknown and destroying what was left of the ancient craft: old kilns revived, producing near-Picassos by the gross, and new chimneys poured more smoke into the already polluted air.

The year 1948 moved into 1949: Françoise's pregnancy grew more evident, and Picasso painted some pictures of her in which the schematic face, sometimes black and white, is strangely divorced from the fine color of the rest. Then in April her daughter was born. The birth coincided with a great Communist peace congress in Paris for which Picasso had been asked to provide a poster. It is certain that he agreed: it is equally certain that he had nothing ready by the appointed time, although he spent many of his days in Mourlot's workshop. With only a short while to go Aragon looked through the portfolios at the rue des Grands-Augustins and found an exquisite print of a pigeon, a white pigeon of the breed that has a frilly neck and long feathers covering its feet: Matisse, who had even more birds in his house than Picasso, had given him the pigeon some time before, a present that filled Picasso with uneasiness: was Matisse making fun of him? Would it not be better to eat the bird rather than to draw it? Finally he made this lithograph, white upon black, one of his most successful prints, and of course without the remotest hint of propaganda. Aragon, immeasurably brighter than his Party colleagues as far as indirection was concerned, at once saw its possibilities as a poster and carried it off. The bird, the symbol of the peace congress, now became a dove, with all the connotations that implies; it appeared overnight on every wall and hoarding in Paris, applauded even by violent anti-Communists; and Picasso, very pleased (he loved applause) christened the baby Paloma.

Paloma was a fine child, and in his own way Picasso was delighted with her. He esteemed intellectual power of the kind possessed by Matisse, Giacometti, Braque, Eluard, and some of his scientific friends such as Lacan and Langevin, but the ordinary range did not interest him much; he looked rather for an intelligence of another order, that of the heart in some cases and of the body in others, a quality often to be found in the young, an almost impersonal and perhaps undeserved attribute that so very often fades entirely, like the ability to produce pictures with no effort of any kind.

For a while he found it in these children, and he painted them often, sometimes singly, sometimes together, and sometimes with their mother : they are admirable pictures, but they are worlds apart from the intensely personal earlier studies of Paulo as a little boy—finer paintings, maybe, yet far more detached, the work of a man who was primarily an artist rather than a doting father.

This was a rich year, with his lithographic versions of the Cranach Venus, with paintings by the score and a renewed outpouring of ceramics; rich for the public too, with his big exhibition of recent work at the Maison de la Pensée française from July until December, 1949; but the next was richer still, for it produced not only many of his finest pots and some remarkably interesting pictures, including his restatement of Courbet's "Demoiselles des bords de la Seine" and of El Greco's portrait of a painter, but also "La Chèvre," one of the high points of his sculpture, and several other pieces.

Picasso had been thinking of a return to sculpture as early as 1949. By that time, with still another child in the house and with an even greater accumulation of pots and canvases, he was short of room at Vallauris, and in the summer he bought a disused scent-factory down the hill from La Galloise, a ramshackle building that provided him with two painting-studios and the barn-like space he needed for his modeling, carving, and fitting together of improbable junk—a kind of three-dimensional collage taken far beyond the limits of the Surrealists' *objets trouvés aidés*. What is more, quite near the new studio were rubbish-heaps, full of possibilities, and in 1950 he began to make the most of them.

Sculpture had been in his mind, but some particular circumstance was required to bring it into action on a large scale, and it may be that the presence of a bronze cast of "L'Homme au mouton," fresh from the foundry, worked as a catalyst. Early in the year Vallauris, grateful for the prosperity he had brought, for the *"publicité énorme,"* made him an honorary citizen of the ugly and now very smoky little place, and in return—for it was impossible to outdo Picasso in generosity on such occasions—he presented the statue to the town.

For a while he was still busy with his ceramics, his painting, and his lithographs. Although there are signs of strain many of them are agreeably domestic, showing the children and Françoise: but it is significant that at least one of the heads related to her is broken up in the savage way reminiscent of his days with Olga, and that these children are not seen with Maya, although the little girl and Marie-Thérèse were spending their holidays close at hand. But presently the new inhabitants of the sculpture-studio began to appear: a pregnant woman, her distended belly being part of a round pot and her breasts two more, all from the rubbish-heap: a little girl skipping, her body and arms a flat basket with two handles, her face incised plaster cast in a box, her wooden legs wearing two huge old shoes, the whole held up in the air by an iron tube that rises from the ground to make the skipping-rope: and above all the goat.

When one has been told about the materials Picasso used, materials that were by definition rubbish, they can be seen there in the unifying bronze, with all their potentialities realized: a worn-out basket, two imperfect jugs, a palm-frond thrown up by the sea, a tin, some bits of wood and metal strip, cardboard, plaster. From these he formed the essence of all goats, a disgraceful, aggressively female creature, as pregnant as can be and rather larger than life-size. The differing textures of the materials, reproduced by the bronze, explain some small part of its value; its stance, form, volumes, and inspired distortions explain much more; but the whole goat far exceeds the sum of its parts, and in its way it is the most satisfying sculpture Picasso ever made—surely something very near the Platonic idea of that powerful, somewhat diabolic, salacious, unshapely, ill-smelling yet companionable beast.

The "Tête de mort" is no doubt a more important statement, but on its own level "La Chèvre" stands alone. As well as all its other virtues, the creature conveys that pagan sense of fun proper to goats and to Picasso: indeed, a friend who was at Vallauris while it was being made, a painter, told me that originally there was a rubber squeaker in its belly, directed towards the protruding tube that forms the anus and that Picasso could make make it sound at will. This vanished in the process of casting, but the simple merriment remains.

Picasso was happy when he was in his studio working on the goat and the other sculptures. Yet the circumstances did not seem favorable for happiness, for although the children gave him the liveliest pleasure, their mother was not an easy companion at all. She often felt aggrieved, and one task that she resented even more than the others was lighting the stoves in the factory-studios early in the morning so that they should be warm by the time Picasso got out of bed, much later in the day. By her account he worked her very hard, although at this time she was going back to her own painting; but a woman who is inclined to play the martyr is likely to become one in earnest whether she chooses to or not, and there is a curious contrast between the beautiful slattern Fernande, lying in bed at the Bateau-Lavoir, sleepily watching Picasso sweep the lane that led from the divan "along a narrow valley among the empty sardine-tins and the respectable depth of oyster-shells" to his easel, and the indignant Françoise shoveling her ashes some forty years later. Martyrdom in a marriage or its equivalent is rarely left unshared, however, and perhaps this was but one more example of two people wrapped together with barbed wire and tearing one another to pieces: certainly Picasso, who could be more agreeable than most men to a woman who pleased him, could also be exceptionally unpleasant to one who did not—he justified the comparative absence of servants by saying that since Françoise Gilot had wanted the children it was but right that she should look after them herself—yet upon the whole he seems to have come off worst in these dreary, long-drawn-out and destructive battles.

The one thing that he felt more than all the rest was gloom in the house. The summer mornings were very well, with quantities of friends on the beach at Golfe-Juan, and the working part of the day was even better; but glumness, wry looks, and resentment were but too often his lot for the rest of the time. One should never underestimate the power of a woman, they say, nor her capacity for eating a man alive; and after some time of this, Picasso, as he told Eluard, was near to killing himself.

The fact that he did not do so in spite of the steadily increasing gloom he put down to the presence of Geneviève Laporte, who "made him laugh again" and thus saved his life: and although the exact dates are uncertain it is likely that the happiness of his sculpture was also due to her.

Since 1945 she had grown up into a very elegant slim young woman, much given to country life, the writing of verse, and the company of dogs and horses: at intervals of traveling she had flitted through the life of Picasso and Sabartés and the Eluards, retaining all their affection and her own cat-like charm. By 1950 she had settled in France again, and she was seeing a good deal of Picasso, in and about Paris: and by 1951 they were lovers. Those are almost the only firm dates that can be advanced: but Geneviève Laporte was a poet rather than an annalist and when in 1972 she came to write *Si tard le soir* . . . her purpose was less to set down a chronology of their loves than a portrait of the man. This she did with a success comparable to that of Sabartés and Brassaï, and the Picasso she described was essentially the same man they knew, though of course seen in an entirely different light—a very, very much kinder and a far bigger man than the character of the same name in Lake and Gilot, a great artist rather than an art-master. There is almost no bitterness in the book, although in time they parted: only a certain disillusion and a few strokes, mostly directed at people other than Picasso, that one could wish away: yet it must be admitted that some of his less attractive sides, such as his jealousy of Braque and Cocteau, are to be seen both in Laporte and Gilot. (Geneviève Laporte took her title from a dedication that Picasso wrote on one of his presents to her: *Si tard le soir le soleil brille* . . . the lateness of the day being no doubt his age and the blazing sun his love.)

It must also be admitted that Sabartés' dictum "Picasso is never to be taken literally" is exemplified in *Si tard le soir* . . . . Sometimes he is obviously just having fun—the monkey of his Céret days, for example, swells to a chimpanzee the size of a twelve-year-old child—but there are places where his words are more disturbing, as when he is reported to have said that the Rousseau banquet was really a joke—nobody believed in his talent—and to have reproached the Cubist Braque with copying him.

Yet although he uttered some curious statements and although one sometimes has the impression that Picasso liked making game of a young, very pretty, and rather credulous friend—that he did not think himself on oath when they were talking and laughing together—he almost always did so in the pleasantest way, and apart from those ungenerous flings at Cocteau and Braque (whose work was fetching remarkably high prices at this time, higher even than Picasso's) and an unfortunate incident towards the end of the book, the general picture is one of a tender, generous, kind, and most affectionate Picasso.

While it lasted theirs was an idyllic relationship. In many ways they were admirably suited: she loved the man for himself and she had the deepest admiration for his work, while he respected her poetry, her lovely person, and her rare attitude, uninvading, unpossessive, gay, and above all entirely friendly, wholly with him and on his side. When she says, "I believe I was Picasso's only deep love and in all likelihood his last" she may well be right. The years between them did not signify: Picasso's spirit was as young as hers, and in his seventieth year he climbed the Provençal hills with the same elastic step, talking to her as to a contemporary, telling her about Max Jacob and Guillaume Apollinaire, who were so living in his mind. He had now outgrown that fear of age which had haunted him some years before—"You know, if I never looked in a glass I should not know I had grown old," he said—and now he rarely thought of it except when some unlucky word forced it into his mind: once Geneviève Laporte observed that in fifty years' time she would be able to tell her grandchildren about him, and his eyes filled with tears. And of course the word death was never to be spoken.

It was a singular as well as a beautiful relationship, and one of its singularities lay in its uncalculated discretion. Geneviève Laporte was quite at home in the rue des Grands-Augustins once more, and the whole household welcomed her heartily when she came to stay: Picasso and she traveled about the countryside, and since he could not drive they were necessarily in the company of Marcel: the Eluards hired them a little house at Saint-Tropez: Cocteau and Jean Marais knew them well: yet none of these people talked. From the summer of 1950 onwards the Korean crisis and then the war filled the headlines, but Picasso was still front-page news in a certain kind of paper, yet no word leaked out. None of the serious books on him speak of Geneviève Laporte as anything but the author of a collection of poems that he illustrated in 1954, and even Crespelle's curious *Picasso and his Women* of 1967 does not mention her name. Perhaps she engendered a protective affection in many of those who knew her: she certainly did at the rue des Grands-Augustins, where she had nothing but allies.

But the world was too much with Picasso for him to be allowed to swim indefinitely at Saint-Tropez with Geneviève Laporte, to climb the scented hills, or even to continue with his series of happy landscapes. Among other things there was the unlucky flat in the rue La Boëtie: he had not lived there for years, but he valued it as a storehouse, as something belonging to him, and he furiously resisted attempts at requisition, particularly as he believed that on the pretext of dealing with the shortage of houses the authorities were in fact persecuting him as a Communist. He stirred up all his influential friends—he had an enormous acquaintance—but the comradeship of the Liberation was long past now, the tide was running strongly against the. Communists, and presently the seals were back on his doors again. Picasso and all his belongings were put out: seventy crates full, says Gilot. But this did not happen until the end of the protracted, hard-fought legal proceedings, that is to say in August, 1951, and before that, in November, 1950, he went to England to attend another peace congress.

The British government was strongly opposed to this Sheffield meeting, held in the middle of the Korean war; so was a wide section of public opinion, not all of it merely anti-Communist. The delegates, including the Nobel prize winner Frédéric Joliot-Curie, were turned back at Dover: all of them except Picasso, who, having been allowed through the barriers, suddenly found himself alone. He was furious: he could not understand why he should be considered harmless. Perhaps, as Penrose suggests, it was because the British Arts Council was holding an exhibition of his recent work in London at that very moment.

So many appalling things have happened since 1950 that it is difficult to remember that Korea seemed to be the certain death of peace, the signal for an atomic war between the great powers, perhaps for total destruction. Whatever Picasso may have thought of Russian policy there is no doubt that he was passionately concerned about peace. Without any hesitation at all he risked popularity, influence, wealth, and personal comfort to support it, and shortly after his return from England he set to work on a picture that he entitled "Massacre en Corée" and that he deliberately based on Goya's "Third of May."

On the right a group of anonymous, modern, visored, armored figures under the command of an officer with a sword are about to shoot a captive group of naked women over on the left, some of them pregnant, some of them with small children. The picture is almost as monochromatic as "Guernica": the comparison is inevitable, and it is more than the "Massacre en Corée" can bear. Even on the physical side it is not a tenth the size, and in other respects the disproportion is possibly even greater. Perhaps, as some have said, it was no more than a sketch that he finished in time for the Salon de Mai and that he did not pursue. In any case it pleased nobody. The simpler-minded Communists complained that the killers were not identified—the picture was not politically correct; those who understood it to be a protest against all killing rather than an indictment of the Americans complained that it did not have the emotional impact of its great predecessors—that it was painted with the head rather than with the heart; and of course the anti-Communists decried it as a piece of propaganda, while those who were committed by friendship or other motives to unconditional admiration of all Picasso's work spoke in embarrassed tones of his humanity and other valuable qualities.

Picasso was grieved at the reception of the "Massacre," the cold silence of the Party, and the comparative indifference of the Right; he was puzzled too, since his statement was as clear as he could make it; but he was not discouraged, nor prevented from going straight on with his work, although in addition to this life with Françoise was growing still more difficult.

As for work, it may have been the armor that he used to give his firing-squad their dreadful, modern, science-fiction impersonality which moved him to carry on with a number of drawings, pictures, and lithographs to do with medieval characters—knights, pages, and armored horses, the last closely allied to the gaunt padded creatures of the bull-ring, still his delight and joy, even in the indifferent French performances. These knights and pages, apparently so anodyne (and influenced, in Kahnweiler's opinion, by the kind of comic-strip *Ivanhoe* that was coming out in *L'Humanité*), were related to the most ambitious of his works, "La Guerre et la Paix"; but that was still a year away, as yet unformed in its creator's mind.

As for the difficulties in his own home—as far as Picasso can ever be said to have had a home—it can only be said that war was more evident than peace, and that Picasso was growing very restive. Yet it is clear from his work that there were tolerable moments: it is even clearer that he was very deeply attached to Claude and Paloma, particularly to the little girl. And then Picasso was not only very much averse to losing what he possessed and to changing his habits, but he also hated giving pain. At all events he and Françoise were together in June, 1951, when they acted as witnesses at Paul Eluard's marriage at Saint-Tropez to Dominique Laure, whom he had met in a Vallauris pottery-shop.

But almost immediately afterwards Picasso was back in Paris, and he and Geneviève Laporte drove slowly down through France. When they were within easy reach of Saint-Tropez he telephoned the Eluards, asking them to lunch: they came, but they were dismal guests, cold, almost silent, severe, and even moral. It was only after some time that they came to understand that the presence of Geneviève Laporte, the obvious relationship, was not a mere whim, a gross insult to Françoise. Eluard was Picasso's closest friend, an exceedingly percipient, intuitive man, but it took him twenty-four hours to grasp what Inès had understood in five minutes. However, once he had been brought to see into Picasso's mind after lunch at Saint-Tropez the next day, he spoke as wisely and as kindly as he could. To Geneviève Laporte he said, "We've been talking a great deal about you. There's no answer to this problem of Françoise that is worrying Picasso, because the problem does not exist. *Carpe diem.*" And to Picasso he said, "Even if you were entirely free to choose, there is no answer that would make you entirely happy." Then later, in reply to Picasso's "I was ready to kill myself. She made me laugh. Laugh, you understand me? Laugh . . ." he said, "And even if she had made you weep, she would still have saved you."

To help Picasso *carpere diem* the Eluards found him the little house I have mentioned, and there at least for a while he was entirely happy. So happy that when Paul asked him to illustrate *Le Rendez-vous allemand* he would not: as he explained to Geneviève Laporte, "The *Rendez-vouz*, don't you see, is a book that was written at a time of the deepest misery. Now for the first time in my life I'm entirely happy. How can I possibly draw wretchedness?" They nagged gently and persistently, the only way to make him move; but although he cherished them so, all he could be brought to draw on the block that Dominique Eluard put before him was a series of portraits to do with love: and those which show his own face are, according to one eminent authority, the first to do so since the death of Apollinaire.

August saw the end of these happy days ; Picasso wanted to buy the house in which he had spent them as a present for Geneviève Laporte, but she would not allow it. From the earliest days of their friendship he had always found it difficult to make her take anything; even as a schoolgirl she refused a print of a lamp until he said, "You bring me the sun. It's only fair that I too should give you light."

She went back to Paris, and the next month he was there as well, partly to attend to the distribution and housing of his treasures from the rue La Boëtie and partly "to see what could be done about Françoise." One of the things he did was to buy two floors of a house in the rue Gay-Lussac, near the Sorbonne. And although this was nothing to do with Françoise, who could not drive, he also bought a new car to replace the white Oldsmobile that the American dealer Kootz had given him just after the war: Marcel Boudin had taken it on a private jaunt to Deauville, had utterly destroyed it in an accident, and had been dismissed. Geneviève Laporte tried to intercede for him, but Picasso was in one of his cold, implacable rages and it was no use, and from that time onward Paulo, Olga's son, who had no other occupation, acted as his father's chauffeur, sometimes driving the new Hotchkiss, sometimes the huge old Hispano-Suiza. Boudin had been a well-known character at the rue des Grands-Augustins, where he acted in many capacities, and Picasso's friends discussed his dismissal after some twenty-five years of service, as friends will: some said that the destruction of the car justified it, others that the chauffeur had overplayed his role of confidential servant and had talked far too much, others that this was one more mark of Picasso's hardness.

That he was capable of hardness, and of extreme hardness, cannot be denied; but whether hardness was an important, often-seen part of his character is another question. As far as Geneviève Laporte was concerned, of course it was not. Although he went back to Vallauris for his seventieth birthday, which fell in October of this year—a widely-celebrated occasion, with *Les Lettres françaises* devoting the best part of an issue to him—he found time on that very busy day to send her too a present, so that she should not be left out, with a pretty note in his strangely unformed hand. The feast at Vallauris itself was a strenuous, long-lasting event, with the municipality and the Party joining in, to say nothing of innumerable friends.

His iron constitution and his tireless conviviality withstood it very well, just as his power of work had withstood the distractions of this year, which also included another peace congress, this time in Rome. Some of his pleasantest landscapes, such as that of Vallauris with its smoking kilns at work, belong to 1951; and there are pictures of his children, lithographs, ceramics and sculpture, with owls in both, and a particularly interesting goat's skull and bottle cast in bronze, which he painted—a technique unseen for centuries.

Feasts, sociability, late nights, bull-fights whenever they were within reach, and traveling, to say nothing of emotional stress, left him comparatively untouched as far as work was concerned. But depression was always lying in wait under his gaiety, and since he was extremely sensitive to atmosphere the one thing he could not cope with was domestic gloom.

He spent the whole dark winter of 1951/1952 with Françoise in the rue Gay-Lussac, for scarcely had he bought the flats before the authorities tried to requisition them on the grounds that they were not occupied and he had to hurry back from Vallauris to retain possession. There he and the children caught colds; the children carried on with measles; Françoise Gilot was deeply concerned with her own painting, getting enough pictures ready for her forthcoming show with Kahnweiler; and for the first time since his parting with Olga sadness so overcame Picasso that his production dwindled, almost ceased entirely.

Nineteen fifty-two began more happily, with an early return to Vallauris and the sun. Picasso's spirit revived: he went back to his ceramics, his painting—some enchanting pictures of the children, enigmatic variations on the theme of a goat's skull and bottle, landscapes—and his sculpture. This was the year of his disconcerting, highly successful "Guenon et son petit," a she-monkey whose face is made of a model car taken from young Claude, while jug-handles form her ears. She stands up on her bent hind-legs, and her child clings to her bosom with all its limbs: although they belong to no particular species, the two are as simian as they can possibly be; and here again the difference of texture between the clay and the metal toy gives the resulting bronze an extraordinarily satisfying quality.

But the great work of 1952 was "La Guerre et la Paix"; and although its beginning lies farther back in time, its execution may well be due in some degree to the presence of another factor in Picasso's daily life, Edouard and Hélène Pignon. I do not mean that they had anything whatever to do with the painting, even to the extent of holding a brush at a distance—indeed they never saw the panels until they were finished—but Pignon's company was a joy to him at a time when joy was rare. Circumstances separated him from Geneviève Laporte at this point, and there was little delight in the lachrymose Françoise.

Pignon was quite a young man then, a painter more appreciated by other painters than by the general public. He was a Communist, a big tough man from the coal-mining northern parts of France—he had been down the pit as a boy. Picasso had known and liked him for several years, and before this he had invited him and his wife, Hélène Parmelin, also a Communist, to share the old scent-factory, where there was a painting-studio free. Now, early in 1952, the invitation was accepted, to the dismay of both sides: both Pignon and Picasso, outwardly so strong, had a secret fund of shyness, and both were afraid that this proximity would not answer. In the event mutual respect and affection did away with all difficulties: the Pignons lived happily in their stark factory room (two primitive beds, a minute chest of drawers, one stool, a piece of string to hang their clothes on, a thin table, a music-stand) and in the spare studio Pignon painted with steady zeal, remarkably uninfluenced by his formidable colleague immediately below, while at regular intervals Picasso, always a creature of habit, brought out the pictures he was working on and the two painters discussed them. Among the pictures were two portraits of Hélène Parmelin, who observed Picasso as attentively as he observed her, though with less penetration: she was—she is—a writer, and her record of these years show still another Picasso in many ways as youthful as Fernande's. She did not know him as Geneviève Laporte knew him, and she saw him with the eyes of a grateful, respectful guest for whom the sun shines all the time, of a happy young woman with an admired husband who was working hard, enjoying the south and the close contact with his friend: Parmelin's Picasso is gay, wildly gay at times, a very sociable, more public Picasso; but in his way he is as authentic as Laporte's or Brassaï's, and here again one sees his quite outstanding spontaneous kindness, his total lack of pomp, his rejection of the role of Grand Old Man, his natural fellowship with people of other generations, and his enormous industry. Her books are written in an intimate, highly personal, somewhat ecstatic style that does not translate very happily, but she has a gift for dialogue and it is generally admitted by his friends that she catches the tone of Picasso's voice better than most.

Pignon worked hard, but Picasso worked harder still. He had promised to embellish the deconsecrated castle chapel of Vallauris, in which "L'Homme au mouton" had been kept before being set up in the square—a medieval building with a perfectly simple barrel-vaulted nave and a somewhat later chancel. The summer before, Matisse had finished his Chapel of the Rosary for the Dominican nuns at Vence, an entirely Christian building, of course, in spite of his unorthodoxy ; Picasso's idea, however, was not to restore the Vallauris chapel to its original purpose, but to turn it into a Temple of Peace, and he had been accumulating drawings for the purpose ever since the time of his promise. By summer there were close on two hundred and fifty of them; yet curiously enough not one was a compositional study in any way comparable to those for "Guernica," and in fact when he came to the actual painting he worked with such spontaneity that he might almost have made no notes at all.

He began in August, 1952, and he worked in the strictest privacy, deeply settled in his steady and valuable routine. He would get up quite late, come down to the studio at about eleven or twelve, go off to swim at Golfe-Juan, return at two or three in the afternoon, and then work for nine or ten hours at a stretch by strong electric light in a silence broken only by the owls. Nobody, and that included Françoise Gilot, was allowed into the studio: whether she was in any way affected by her exclusion is doubtful; by this time her interest in Picasso's painting was so slight that she scarcely mentions the Antibes pictures, while she passes over "La Guerre et la Paix" in complete silence. The only exception was Paulo, who came to drive his father back to La Galloise. Nor did Picasso ever speak about his work, even to the Pignons. This went on week after week until October, when the two panels were finished. Two panels, each measuring thirty-three and a half by fifteen and a half feet so as to cover the side walls and the vault of the chapel entirely, and each made up of several rectangles of flexible hardboard: there was to be a third to fill the west end of the nave when the door should be walled up, but that was not yet begun.

They were designed to follow the rise and the steady curve of the chapel walls and vault, meeting in the middle, and except in their proper place they were difficult to see as a whole: the friends who were allowed in were pleased, excited, and somewhat at a loss. A powerful effort of the imagination was required to see the plane surfaces as curves meeting overhead and entirely filling a given vaulted space; an infinitely more powerful effort to supply the missing third piece that was to bind the far ends together. These friends, particularly Pignon, were better qualified than most to make the effort, better qualified in any event than the critics who looked at the panels when they were first shown to the public at the Picasso retrospective in Milan and Rome next year and who pronounced them to be failures, poor in line and garish in color, bad Picassos that attempted a fatal compromise between the Party's aesthetics and his own form of expression. A great many ordinary people were disappointed too, and as this came at a time when Picasso's heart was cruelly wounded he felt both the criticism and the disappointment far more keenly than usual—so much so that even when the two main panels were installed early in 1954 he did not carry on with the third; and as a result of his vexation of spirit and of a quarrel with the authorities he shut the pictures away for years on end.

There would have been far less adverse criticism if others had possessed Picasso's eye, enabling them to see "La Guerre et la Paix" as it can now be seen, completed, in its own place, and lit by one uniform light from below. The visitor walks into the chapel by the south door and finds himself in a rather large square chancel with a lovely apse on his right hand and a counter with postcards and reproductions on his left. Beyond the counter the westward chancel wall is pierced by an arch some six feet wide leading into the primitive little nave: walking through this arch he finds himself inside a long low narrow space, a tunnel or cave filled with a diffused light of its own coming from behind two low brick walls. He is also inside a picture that fuses over his head in a cloud of brown at the farther end. Yet although he is inside the picture he can scarcely take in more than one aspect of it at once, since he has to back away the full width of the nave to see either War on his left hand or Peace on his right; though to be sure the brilliant third panel at the west end that links the two and closes the tunnel, making it a world of its own, is visible all the time.

War is a naked figure with small curved horns standing in a clumsy black chariot (Picasso had a provincial hearse in mind) drawn over the blood-red ground by three lean black horses that are now trampling a blazing book and that are about to trample green standing corn. He has a bloody sword in one hand, a basket scattering evil things—germs or the like—in the other, and on his back a net or basket full of skulls. In the background dark silhouettes of men hack and thrust with axes, swords, and spears. The chariot is almost over a black hole from which two green hands reach up, but it seems that the horses have balked at the sight of a statuesque figure in front of them, standing against a fine blue on the extreme left of the picture. He is holding a spear and the scales of justice in his right hand, a shield in his left; and on the shield, overlying a dim head, perhaps that of Athena, is the blue outline of a dove with upraised wings, very like that which stands for the Holy Ghost.

Peace, on the other long wall, lies in several planes: on deep blue a faun plays his double pipe, two girls dance ecstatically, a boy with an owl on his head balances a cage of fish and a bowl of birds, a heavy horse with iridescent wings draws a plough guided by a child: on a green field under a vine and a glowing orange-tree a man sets a dish on a hearth of stones; close by another is writing, while a woman lies with her head on her hand, suckling a baby and reading a book over it: and the whole is dominated by a many-colored faceted sun with rays like palm-fronds.

The third panel, at the far end, which fixes one's attention from the moment one steps into the chapel, is strikingly simple, with purer color than the rest. In the horseshoe arch four men, black, yellow, red, and white, hold up a large pale round with a white dove outlined upon it: here again the bird's wings are raised, and this time its beak holds up an olive-branch. The figures, symmetrically arranged against pale blue and a lower green, hold the disk with their upstretched left arms, and their right arms join at waist-height in the middle: they are as simplified as can be, and although they are entirely Picasso they have something of the look of Matisse's late collages. They are not in fact pasted paper, but when one moves close one sees why them seem to be: Picasso has very carefully taken the paint away from their outlines, scraping right down to the bare board, isolating each of the forms. They are called, upon what authority I do not know, "Les quatre parties du monde." And the dove they hold up in the high point of the arch gives the key to the whole picture; it is even more important than the sun or the blazing tree and without it "La Guerre et la Paix" would lose a great deal of its significance.

It was not there at the time of the Italian retrospective. But even if it had been, and even if the whole triptych had been seen in ideal conditions, there would still have been some hostile criticism, for even now opinions are divided. At present few people deny that "Guernica" is a very great painting, but there is nothing like the same near-unanimity about "La Guerre et la Paix," even though it has now been discussed for more than twenty years.

The first time I saw the picture it did not seem to me to have anything at all of the very great urgency and emotional charge of "Guernica"; Picasso's deliberate survey of the two extreme states of the human condition appeared to me to have some of the weaknesses usually to be seen in Last Judgments; but whereas in most Last Judgments the blessed seem condemned to an eternity of boredom while the damned and their attendant fiends are filled with passionate life, here it was Peace that was convincing, while War, apart from those hands and the trampled book, struck me as literary and remote. Even the round-faced figure of War himself looked quite good company. I was tempted to say that Picasso, in spite of his longing for vast surfaces, could not deal with them when they were provided—that with the exception of "Guernica" his genius flowered best when it was confined. But that was a first sight, after a long day's drive in beating rain; and it is notorious that a traveler, harassed by his voyage, by hunger, by other sightseers, tends to be captious and unreceptive—in an Italian journey Picasso himself saw Giotto unmoved—and presently, rested and fed, with the chapel to myself, I found the whole painting grow enormously in power, above all the arched picture at the end. Although some passages in War still seemed rhetorical, the grimness of others increased beyond measure; and the pagan joys of Peace, with their more personal, less obvious symbolism, filled me with satisfaction. The picture still does not move me as "Guernica" did in New York, but the comparison has little meaning, since the two statements are of a different order: even so, upon reflection "La Guerre et la Paix," in spite of those parts to which I am insensitive, now seems to me a picture of such a size that if I had to cross the Atlantic again to see it I should do so.

Almost immediately after he had finished the two panels, Picasso set off for Paris. Geneviève Laporte had been there most of the year, seeing much of the Eluards: the friends met with great pleasure, but within a few days Paul Eluard fell sick. He was only fifty-seven, and although his health had always been frail nobody thought he was in any danger. A week later, calling in at the rue Gay-Lussac on her way to lunch with the Eluards, Geneviève Laporte heard from Inès that he was dead: Picasso was already with his widow.

They buried him at the Père-Lachaise with an immense crowd of friends and admirers—few men have been more loved than Eluard. Picasso was very deeply moved: death always shattered him, and this death perhaps more than any. Some days after the funeral he too fell ill, while at the same time still another death so affected Geneviève Laporte that she left Paris for the remote Auvergne, where she lived in complete solitude for several months.

Before Picasso left Vallauris Françoise Gilot had proposed that she should go with him: she had, it seems, been plied by Madame Ramié with reports of another woman; she said that from now onwards she and Picasso "should be together all the time," and her words were accompanied by a threat that she would "do something about it" if he did not comply.

He did not comply, of course, and on his return, ill and very sad, she told him that she saw no reason for staying. This was a solution, but it was not the solution that Picasso wanted: it would mean the loss of his children. He asked whether there were anyone else in her life; she said there was not; but on going to Paris by herself in the spring of 1953 she formed a connection with a Greek.

In her book she denies ever having said that she was leaving him because she was tired of living with a historical monument (a crack that was widely repeated at the time, the decay of their relationship being common knowledge): the words to which she does own were less lapidary and perhaps even more unkind, since they were entirely humorless—"So I began to tell Pablo that if I was leaving him, it was in order to live with my own generation and the problems of my time." And now on her return she told him about her Greek.

In spite of all this he begged her to stay, swallowing his pride in a manner inconceivable to his friends: it was, they have told me, a very painful sight indeed. His words, or her uncertainty, had some effect, and 1953 dragged on in a state of unstable equilibrium, broken by frequent scenes and the repeated intrusion of journalists, for these were the years when the price of Picassos was beginning to soar and the combination of money, notoriety, and sex brought reporters to La Galloise by the score.

It was a wretched period: through some failure of communication he was cut off from Geneviève Laporte, buried in her far retreat, and since by temperament and by his natural size he had long since dominated most of the people he knew, he had nobody, now that Eluard was dead, with whom he could talk on an equal footing. Matisse, one of the very few who might in happier circumstances have advised or at least comforted him, was now very ill; the intimacy with Braque had suffered irreparable damage from rivalry and time. Picasso had friends by the hundred, some of them distinterested, but none of the right stature, and he lived in a crowded solitude.

There were a few intervals of peace, however, as when he made the acquaintance of Sylvette David, the wife or fiancée of a young English chairmaker in Vallauris, who became his model—her pony-tail is to be seen in many a charming picture—or when he conversed (sometimes in Spanish) with Jacqueline Hutin, a young woman Madame Ramié had brought to Vallauris some months before to help in the pottery-shop. Madame Hutin—her maiden name was Roque—had been married to a man sometimes described as an engineer, sometimes as a minor civil servant; at this point the divorce proceedings may or may not have begun, but in any event she was living alone with her daughter Kathy. Jacqueline Hutin, or Roque as she was known after the divorce, was very small, shorter than Picasso, neat and trim; and if her modest origins and her lack of any very advanced education worried him at all, which is unlikely, it was outweighed by her total and evident admiration—in spite of all his experience, Picasso still liked worship from young women: at this time Jacqueline Hutin was twenty-seven. But apart from these intervals his reactions to the present situation, though often contradictory, were violent: the most obvious was a sudden and extreme sociability. Far from avoiding people other than his closer friends or those who might interest his perennial curiosity, he now flung himself into almost any company and scoured the country with a changing band of hangers-on, going right over to Nîmes for bull-fights and haunting the night-clubs all along the Côte d'Azur, particularly at Saint-Tropez. He did so in the hope of finding Geneviève Laporte, who in her even younger days had enjoyed such places: the journalists were unaware of his quest however, and his sad capers, presented literally, filled many a page in the cheaper illustrated weeklies. And this was the time when his comic disguises (once the occasional expression of merriment) began to increase; when visitors, embarrassed or amused according to their nature, might be received by a Picasso with a red cardboard nose, a false mustache, and a paper hat. He racketed about continually, expending an immense amount of time and energy, but in spite of the weariness and boredom he still worked.

Among his pictures were two of a woman savaging a dog: in both she has got it down on its back; she grasps a fore and a hind leg in each of her powerful hands and she stares down into its helpless face. The woman is Françoise Gilot, the dog Kazbek's successor, a boxer called Yan, stupid, demonstrative, and wanting in judgment, but affectionate. Another is of a lean she-cat stalking towards a cock on a kitchen table: the bird's wings flap, but its legs are tied and it cannot move. And at about the time of the second "Femme au chien" he produced a drawing that caused more fuss than a dozen pictures: in March, 1953, Stalin went to his long account and Aragon, as editor of *Les Lettres françaises*, asked Picasso for a portrait. Picasso was unwilling—he had never seen Stalin—but since it was for Aragon he turned out a workmanlike and recognizable, if uninspired, head of a youngish Stalin and sent it off to Paris. Aragon liked it; so did Pierre Daix, who did most of the work at *Les Lettres françaises;* and they were amazed at the storm that burst over their heads. They had underestimated both the passionate idolatry of the father-figure among the rank and file of the Party and the spirit of intrigue among their rivals in the Communist press. *L'Humanité* and the Party leaders censured the drawing and publicly humiliated Aragon: Picasso was roughly handled too, but before things went to extreme lengths, before these authoritarian methods disgusted the Party's most spectacular if most unorthodox member, Casanova came to see him and smoothed the matter over.

Picasso's violent sociability at this time was tiring and wasteful, but it did lead to one of his pleasantest friendships and very nearly a complete change in his way of life. His old friend Totote Hugué, Manolo's widow, and Rosita, their adopted daughter, a great favorite of Picasso's and now an elegant young woman, came to see him, bringing the Comte and Comtesse de Lazerme, both French Catalans from the Roussillon. Monsieur de Lazerme had known Totote ever since his boyhood, when his father, also a lover of the arts, had taken him over to Céret to see the Manolos, and they had been friends from that time on; and he had met Picasso in 1951, when he drove Pierre Brune, the painter, all along the Côte d'Azur to visit other artists on behalf of the museum he had founded at Céret.

Picasso received them with his usual splendid hospitality, and in return the Lazermes invited him and Françoise Gilot to Perpignan, where they had a house of the kind that would be called a palace in Spain and which in fact dated from the time when Perpignan belonged to the Spanish crown. On this occasion Françoise did not choose to accept—she had other plans in view—but Picasso did, and on August 12, 1953, he arrived with Paulo and Maya.

Picasso had never lost touch with his Catalan friends nor even with their children—among others, Pierrette, Gargallo's daughter, and Jacint, the son of Doctor Cinto Reventós, had come to see him not long before, and Pallarès was a regular summer visitor—but this was the first time he had been in the Rousillon for forty years. As I have said, the social contract is not the same in Catalonia as it is in France; superficially it is rougher in some ways, but beneath the surface it is often far more friendly, direct, and indeed more sensitive. It was the contract that had formed Picasso's social mind, and here in the narrow streets of Perpignan, with Catalan spoken all around him, he was very much at home.

A little while later his hosts took him to Collioure to see the bull-fights and the extraordinary firework display given every year in honor of Our Lady's assumption. Picasso left directly afterwards, but at the beginning of September he was back for the Perpignan bull-fight, bringing his elder children, his nephew Javier, Totote, and Rosita, all in the old Hispano-Suiza. They left for Vallauris the next day; then about a week later Picasso was in Perpignan again for a longer stay, this time accompanied by the Pignons. There would be no point in giving a detailed list of his movements during this short period were it not for the fact that two hundred and eighty-two miles lie between Vallauris and Perpignan. No east-west motor-ways existed then; much of the narrow road was bad, and in August and September all of it was crowded, so that each journey took at least nine hours. The heat, the noise, the smell, and the weariness can be imagined, and the fact that he freely accepted them when he was well over seventy gives some idea of how desperately he needed to escape through company and perpetual motion.

Many friends, including the Aurics and the Leirises, joined him in Perpignan: he liked most of them individually, but in the mass they tended to be overwhelming. Once some critical number had been passed, group-psychology started to operate, and the members of the court, as he called it himself, began to display the stock symptoms of jealousy, competing for status and attention, showing-off and emphasizing their intimacy with the great man. It was flattering no doubt, and Picasso liked flattery, but the tension was wearing, and presently he went off to spend a few days in the more relaxing air of Collioure.

It was absurd that he had not known the village earlier, for it was only twenty miles from Céret; and just as Céret was closely connected with Cubism, so Collioure was the first haunt of the Fauves. Matisse had worked there for years, bringing Derain as early as 1905 and Marquet not long after, while countless other painters, including Juan Gris, had followed them.

However, Picasso knew it now, and his liking for the place grew with his acquaintance. Here at last he had a little peace: he stayed at René Pous' Café des Sports, eating Pauline Pous' wonderful soupe de poissons, her Catalan bouillabaisse, or fresh crayfish fished up by various Pous cousins, and he lay in the sun or bathed most of the day.

This real rest, this swimming in the sea, the language and atmosphere of his youth, restored his spirits and his strength: he needed both, for immediately after his return to Vallauris on September 29 Françoise Gilot walked out, taking the children with her. At some time, it appears, she had told him that she was leaving on September 30, but after so many unfulfilled threats of this kind he can scarcely have believed that she would really go.

In her book she justifies herself by saying that he would not let her have an operation for some female complaint; but when she reached Paris she seems to have been more concerned with seeing her Greek than with going into any hospital.

In a way it was a relief. Within a few days Picasso was in Paris too: some time before this Geneviève Laporte had emerged from her desolate silence, though by letter alone, to discuss her poems and to tell him that she had found a farmhouse at Arbonne, on the edge of the forest of Fontainebleau, and now he sent her a telegram begging her to ring him up. Picasso was no letter-writer, nor was he much of a hand with the telephone, which he loathed, and Geneviève Laporte reached the rue des Grands-Augustins with no more than a general sense of emergency.

Inès opened the door to her with a welcoming smile and whispered, "Françoise has gone at last. Monsieur was too shy to telephone—I was the one who told him . . ." At this point Sabartés came to welcome her, and then Picasso. There were several people in the studio, including Totote Hugué and Rosita; presently they all had lunch, and in time everybody went away. Geneviève Laporte told him about her farmhouse, and he asked if he might see it. He might indeed, she said, and she would drive him there: her car was outside the door. He told Paulo to join them with the Hugués later, and they set off. Picasso and Geneviève Laporte had not seen one another for nearly a year; both had been through a great deal and now there was something tentative in their relationship. The journey began in comparative silence: Picasso wanted to ask her to share his life but he could not find a way of bringing it out; the shyness that was usually an inconspicuous though important part of his character now became evident, partly because of their long separation, partly because he was far better at granting favors than asking them, and partly because what he wished to ask was of the very first importance to him. Furthermore, Françoise Gilot's steady insistence upon his age had left him with no illusions: people of her generation saw him as an old, old man, somebody who had been heard of forever, like Julius Caesar or Joan of Arc. Shyness is the most catching of all the emotions, and Geneviève Laporte had not only that to contend with but also her private knowledge of the situation: in addition to this she was an inexperienced driver taking a new car out of Paris through heavy traffic. She had little or nothing to say, and they were well south of the city before Picasso spoke of Françoise Gilot's disappearance.

By the time the car reached Arbonne they were almost on their old footing of complete confidence: but not entirely—Picasso, though happy, was not wholly at ease; he misunderstood an innocent remark, detecting an unfavorable inner meaning, a kind of fling at his past, that it did not possess; and above all he had not made his clear request by the time Paulo appeared in the other car. They dined at a restaurant, just the two of them together, but still he did not speak out directly: not that night, nor yet the next morning, when he told her he was going back to Vallauris.

Geneviève was surprised and deeply wounded: apart from anything else she had expected him to stay a while. The groping for communication, the shyness, and the tension must have been very great, for when

Paulo and the Hugués were there, the car about to leave, and Picasso, gathering his courage at last, turned to her and said, "You're coming?" she was so upset, so confused and overcome that all she could reply was, "Change the sheets first."

What she meant by this she could hardly tell, except that it referred to her dislike for La Galloise and that period of Picasso's life; and the words were scarcely out before she blushed for them. But they had been said; there was no calling them back; and the car drove away.

Chapter XX

PICASSO, believing himself to be rejected, and acquiescing in the rejection, returned to Vallauris, to a house now silent, empty of its children.

At the level of immediate companionship he was not alone, nor anything like it: Totote and Rosita looked after him at La Galloise for a while, the Pignons were still in the studio down the hill, the Ramiès and Jacqueline Hutin in Vallauris, and the children came for a few days at Christmas, while of course there were the inevitable interviewers and journalists. But Geneviève Laporte was five hundred miles away and apparently farther still in the distance that signified; and the only work he did was a certain amount of pottery, including some rather mechanical black plates, each with a white house traced upon it.

Winter can be very cruel in the south of France, with the mistral shaking the orange-trees and the cold forcing its way into houses built to keep out the sun; but it is an invigorating cold, and this winter suddenly brought Picasso such a furious burst of creativity that in December and January he produced almost all the hundred and eighty drawings of the - *Verve* suite, so called because they first appeared in that magazine, with a preface by Michel Leiris.

They have a certain resemblance to the collection published by Vollard many years before, sometimes sharing the same pure line and always the same breath-taking virtuosity, while here too the artist and his model are of the first importance. But whereas the Sculptor of the thirties was a calm, heroic figure, gazing mildly at somnolent young women, the Painter of 1953/1954 is often an old, ludicrous man or woman or even a baboon, and many of the models are full of eager sexuality. They are young, for the most part, with all the insolence of their age; and the suite can be seen as a hymn to youth and beauty, or, from another point of view, as an obsession with the female body; yet Michel Leiris called it the record of a sojourn in Hell, and that is what it amounted to for those who could read Picasso's private report about old age and its power of making one ugly, even repulsive, often stupid, positive, and absolute, and of abolishing the future—about the inevitable reduction and defeat, the horror of the last.

Many of the plates are full of delight—a lovely girl plays with a cat; a second with cupids who fly about holding old-man masks to their faces; a third offers an apple to an ape—and others, taken separately, are droll—the artist dwindles to a pedantic, myopic little creature surrounded by admirers wondering with a foolish face of praise, as stupid and humorless as Brueghel's amateur. But the whole series, with its insistence upon the aging painter, sometimes declining from a fine Sculptor-like demigod to a monkey, with each stage drawn, makes one steadily more uneasy. The diminished, impotent, childish old men in hideous contrast with the models may be ridiculous, but they do not raise a smile. Nor does fat aged lechery; nor the withered bawd who had already appeared in many early works as well as in the recent "Ivanhoe" drawings and who was presently to become an important character in Picasso's cast. And then there are the circus-people from his youth, sometimes as sad and poor as they were fifty years ago; and models who, like the painters, have grown old—drooping female flesh, alas; and again and again those who wear masks, sometimes obviously in play but sometimes with ambiguous motives, men's masks on women, women's on men, at times both partners masked—who is deceiving whom?

But the drawings did not take up all those lonely winter days and nights, when work was his only refuge. He also painted what could almost be called self-portraits, pictures in which his shadow at least appears as he stands with his back to the sun, painting a woman on his deserted bed: there were other nudes as well, and more interesting still, several drawings of "La Guerre et la Paix." Two of the largest are full compositional studies, as though Picasso had intended a new version of the whole: and if he had done so he would perhaps have left a more sanguine as well as a more generally accessible "War and Peace," for in these the war looks as though it might be won, and peace is full of undistorted neoclassical grace.

Many years before this dismal winter there was a time when Picasso noticed that Sabartés was discouraged, spiritless, and impatient, and he recommended his panacea, work—in Sabartés' case the writing of a book, no matter what kind of book. The remedy answered, to some degree, for Sabartés, though he never did become a cheerful man; and to some degree it now answered for Picasso too, and although it could scarcely heal his wound, by the spring of 1954 it did lead him to another kind of painting.

This was a series of portraits and studies of Sylvette, some positively academic, others using hard-edged planes, distortion, simultaneity, and many another resource to interpret her fresh young face and form, but all of them remarkably objective and direct. He was pleased with them, and he showed the whole set in a special exhibition in Paris later that year; most people shared his pleasure, but some observed that so little was Picasso himself involved in the pictures that they might almost have been exercises. The same could not be said of two pictures painted early in June, one that Picasso entitled "Portrait de Madame Z" and another of the same woman sitting on the ground with her hands clasped round her drawn-up knees, usually catalogued "Portrait de Jacqueline aux mains croisées." The model was of course Jacqueline Hutin, whom Picasso used to call Madame Z because of the name of her house, Le Ziquet. They are splendid pictures, full of fine powerful color, and they both show a young woman with a feline head superbly poised on a very long neck, square in section, which by some private miracle Picasso endowed with an extraordinary grace. In both Jacqueline wears a modern dress, and in both her elaborate, vaguely Egyptian coiffure is of great importance. Generally speaking Picasso made as little use of cast shadow as Henri Rousseau, which is no doubt one of the reasons why their people belong to a purer world; but in the case of this seated figure he laid a strong, illogical shade behind her, and its effect, combined with the simple, massive planes and the remote, severe gaze of her enormous eyes, is to give her the monumental quality of a sphinx.

The likeness to a young, proud, high-bred, dangerously beautiful sphinx has often been commented upon, far more often than the likeness to Jacqueline Hutin, which is less evident. But Picasso's pictured women often ran into one another, for as he ingenuously observed, his hand grew so used to drawing a given set of features that of its own volition it mingled them with those of the successor: there is something of Sylvette in Madame Z, but very much more of Geneviève Laporte, with her fine bone-formation, her cat-like head, her long neck, and her thoroughbred air, none of them qualities for which Jacqueline was remarkable.

Qualities she had, however, including youth and the promise of unlimited devotion, and from these pictures alone it is clear that Picasso was very much aware of them. Yet even so it does not appear that at this time he wanted any deep commitment, perhaps because, as he told Laporte, "I could not possibly go to bed with a woman who had had a child by another man'' and Jacqueline had had a child by another man, a visible child, the little Kathy.

Françoise Gilot had brought the children down for the Easter holidays; she now brought them to spend the summer with their father. Her affair with the Greek had lasted for no more than three months, and at present she and Picasso were on perfectly civil terms—so civil indeed that he asked her to open the bull-fight that was to be held in his honor at Vallauris. This she did, riding a horse into the improvised arena. She says that the compliment caused Jacqueline Hutin great distress: she also says that Picasso asked her to stay and that when she refused he fell into a very deep depression.

It may be so. But when I saw him in the Roussillon a few days later he looked as cheerful as his best friends could have wished, brown, plump, contented. In recent months he had seen much of the Lazermes, in Paris, at Vallauris just after his return from Arbonne, when they found him sadly reduced, at Vallauris again to see the New Year in, and several times in the summer; now he and Maya were staying with them again in Perpignan—Picasso begged that she might be given a bed in his room, for his loneliness had bitten deep and he hated to be alone, especially at night.

They arrived early in August, and very soon the Lazermes brought Picasso back to Collioure. This second visit strengthened all his earlier ideas, and he came back every day, accompanied by various followers, except when the bull-fight or some other occasion called him away to Céret.

He liked the place extremely, and well he might, for even in 1954 the little town was still almost as Matisse had first known it, infinitely less spoiled than the Côte d'Azur: it still had no more than two or three thousand people, and although the streets were crowded at the time of the bull-fights, massive tourism had not set in; no concrete blocks of flats reared up, dwarfing the ancient pink-tiled houses; the people still lived chiefly by fishing and making wine; and even in high summer there was room on the small beach for everybody who chose to bathe. Here Picasso swam almost every day, looking like a benevolent, round-headed turtle; and as he swam out into the sheltered bay he could contemplate first the medieval lighthouse, now domed and serving as a bell-tower for the parish church—a tower often painted by Matisse—then the fishermen's beach, crowded with brightly-colored boats with high archaic prows, then the vast mass of the castle, built on a rock jutting out into the sea, its walls rising sheer from the water and dividing the bay into two pure curves: a farther strand beyond, with still more fishing-boats, beyond them a line of houses, washed with faded pink and blue, and the Dominican church, then steep vineyards rising to hills crowned by an El Greco kind of castle, and farther still the Spanish frontier itself, the wild mountains with their remote watch-towers against the Saracens, high up on the edge of virgin forest; and all this in the purest light of the sun, for the summer of 1954 was perfect.

He could also reflect upon the difference between the attitude of the Colliourenques and that of the mongrel inhabitants of the Côte d'Azur, where he could scarcely move a yard without being stared at by a gathering crowd or directly importuned. Here he could walk about the streets, sit in a café, or take his ease by the sea without exciting the least comment; and here, if Paloma, presuming on her status, tried to tyrannize over the other children on the beach, strong Catalan voices would instantly bring her to a better way of thinking.

Only once, as far as I know, was he ever disturbed by anything more serious than a mild wrangle with other parents about the ownership of a rubber ball or a pair of water-wings. The disturber was a literary man then living in Collioure, Jean-Marc Sabatier-Lévêque: he came from the austere, Protestant Cévennes where, as a love-child, he had had an exceedingly hard life, and he had written an ambitious, difficult, talented book about it, modeling the form and progress of his narrative upon Bach's Christmas Oratorio. No publisher would entertain his manuscript, though one did suggest, by way of a joke, that if it were illustrated by Picasso it might have a chance of being printed. He walked up to Picasso and explained his case: Picasso looked at him with that curiously piercing eye, saw that he was young, poor, and obviously gifted, and that alcohol and distress had already done him no good: he smiled and said, "Come to Perpignan tomorrow." There in two days he drew fourteen portraits of the young man and gave them to him. The book was indeed published, and by the respectable firm of Gallimard; it made Sabatier very happy for a while; but in spite of Picasso's kindness it had no success—it attracted so little attention that I have never seen it mentioned in any of the catalogs of Picasso's graphic work nor in the lists of the books he illustrated—and presently the author, like so many French writers, was obliged to take to journalism to keep himself alive; and journalism soon killed him.

One of the most marked Catalan qualities is independence, a refusal to be impressed by wealth, rank, fame, or anything else: this un-deference is carried to a point that might seem uncivil to other nations, but Picasso was perfectly used to it, and here at least, when he escaped from his court he also escaped from his role of sacred monster. The people of Collioure liked him for his total lack of airs and for his knowledge of their language and their ways, while he liked them for their proper pride and the directness of their contact with him—a frequent contact, since he frequented the Café des Sports, hung with the mixed offerings of all the painters who had been there from the time of Matisse onwards, and there he often kept it up until very late at night, adding quantities of local people to his already considerable band of friends.

They invited him to preside at the bull-fight, which he did with spectacular success, insisting on the rigid protocol of Spain and reproving one ill-behaved torero with a flood of Catalan invective that is remembered to this day. But his summer in the Roussillon was not all swimming, lying in the sun, and attending every bull-fight in the region: he also had a set of cool bare rooms in a remote part of the house in Perpignan where he could put up his easel and withdraw into total solitude; and here, among other pictures, he painted a portrait of Madame de Lazerme wearing the traditional Catalan white lace cap.

The atmosphere in Perpignan was very favorable for work, and Picasso began to look for a place like the Lazermes', a vast cool secret house built round a central court with trees. He was happy with them and at peace; and for all his want of domestic qualities he thoroughly enjoyed the quiet civility of a well-run household, the un-restaurant meals, the absence of fuss. Admittedly, he almost destroyed the civilization he admired: the cook never knew whether she was to prepare dinner for ten or for twenty, nor when it would be eaten; and at the height of the invasion by his followers mattresses had to be spread in most of the fifty rooms of the house. But this was later: in the early days there was little in the way of court, and at intervals between looking at houses in Perpignan Picasso sat quietly in a café with his friends, watching the *sardana*, the dance he loved, returning to dine at a Christian hour.

There were few houses in Perpignan to compare with the Hôtel de Lazerme, however, and in any case the more he saw of Collioure the more he thought he would like to live there rather than in a city. The village had no houses of any considerable size, but high above, where the last of the Pyrenees runs into the sea, stood the Fort Saint-Elme, a splendid piece of Spanish military architecture built by Charles V in the early sixteenth century, dominating the ancient fortifications and the bay. Picasso climbed up with Madame de Lazerme, gazed longingly at the moat, the drawbridge, the great salle d'armes, the vaulted chambers, the enormous cisterns cut into the rock, the windswept round tower: but he gazed in vain; the place was not to be bought.

When his disappointment was known in the village, it was suggested that he should be given the castle, much as he had been given the Grimaldi palace at Antibes but on a more permanent basis, and Picasso was filled with enthusiasm. It was more magnificent than Antibes by far and very much larger, covering several acres. The towering rock had been a stronghold in the days of classical antiquity, and the present fortress contained Visigothic work, the remains of a commandery of the Knights Templars, a splendid hall where Peter the Catholic, Count of Barcelona and King of Aragon, did his utmost to strangle his wife, and the massive constructions of the kings of Majorca, Spain, and France, all given a strange unity by the passage of time and by the unmistakable hand of Vauban, whose disciples did their best to make it impregnable. The castle had suffered from various sieges and even more from the peace-time presence of the French army, which had only recently abandoned it; but it had been spared the hand of the nineteenth-century restorer and it was still a noble pile, a village in itself and one in which Picasso might have been very happy.

Unfortunately many authorities had to have their say, and before the various councils and ministries even began their slow deliberations the situation had changed in Perpignan.

Whenever he visited the Roussillon it was natural that Totote and Rosita should come to see him, all the more natural since they too often stayed with the Lazermes, sometimes for months on end: though there were also occasions on which they did not have to come, since he brought them with him from Vallauris. Picasso had always been very fond of Rosita, but now his fondness had developed into another emotion; it may not have been a passionate love, but it was certainly so ardent a desire for her uninterrupted company that it was apparent to his friends at the rue de l'Ange that Rosita, by giving him the slightest encouragement, could become Madame Picasso. She did not choose to encourage him: in fact, she withdrew. This led to no violent scenes, no kind of break, and from his portraits it is clear that his affection for her, and for Totote, remained unaltered: yet it was a heavy disappointment to a man in his lonely, bereft condition. Rosita spoke his languages, and she was, in a way, part of his youth. She was also beautiful in an unusual, archaic fashion; and she was young.

At the beginning of his holiday Picasso had arrived with no followers. At about the time when he saw that for the moment at least there was no moving Rosita, some began to appear, among them Jacqueline Hutin and her little daughter Kathy. Madame de Lazerme asked if Madame Hutin should be invited to stay; Picasso said no. Jacqueline went to an hotel, but she came to the house every day and ate her meals with the rapidly-growing company, and presently she put her child out to board at Font Romeu, in the mountains.

As the weeks went by and Picasso's enthusiasm for Collioure grew greater still, it became clear to those about him that there was a strong likelihood of his leaving the Côte d'Azur entirely—a likelihood that would be all the stronger if he were to overcome Rosita's reluctance, since a marriage with her would attach him to Catalonia for good—and some of them looked upon this as a danger to their friendship and their interests. The news spread; other friends and associates came to Perpignan to dissuade him, and presently the house in the rue de l'Ange was full. Picasso had the greatest esteem and affection for Madame de Lazerme, and as he saw still more tables carrying into the big dining-room it came to him that he might perhaps be giving her trouble—that he was not quite the easiest man for a young hostess to entertain—and it distressed him. He apologized again and again: but still they came, and although he had put Paulo and his wife into an hotel there were some he could not turn away.

Up until this time Jacqueline Hutin had been a minor member of the band, attracting little notice; but now a striking change occurred. Maya left toward the end of August and that same night Jacqueline moved into her empty bed. Two days later, after what had obviously been a violent disagreement, she came down to breakfast much upset, wondering whether she should go or stay. Nobody gave any decisive opinion, and after a long hesitation she drove off homewards at about noon. Shortly afterward Picasso appeared, expressed his satisfaction, and joined the throng for luncheon. During the meal the telephone rang: it was Jacqueline calling from Narbonne. Picasso was reluctant to speak to her, but eventually he did so, very briefly, returning to the table with a harsh remark. An hour later another telephone-call, this time from Béziers; and having answered it Picasso told the company "She threatened to kill herself if she could not come back to Perpignan. She can do whatever she likes, so long as she leaves me in peace." He was particularly gay that afternoon, but in the evening there was a ring at the front door: it was Jacqueline, who said, "You told me to do whatever I liked; so here I am." They went upstairs, and not a sound was heard until dinner, when they came down. Picasso was furious and perfectly mute: he would not even eat his pudding. During the next weeks his attitude towards her was embarrassingly disagreeable, while hers was as embarrassingly submissive—she referred to him as her god, spoke to him in the third person, and frequently kissed his hands.

Some small part of his coldness might be attributed to a telegram that came from Edmonde Charles-Roux, announcing Derain's death. It did not affect him to anything remotely like the same extent as Matisse's some weeks later, but it did remind him of his age. Another reminder appeared shortly after in the person of Françoise Gilot, who brought Claude and Paloma for the rest of the holiday: she went off the next day, but the dinner-party on the evening of her arrival, with Jacqueline sitting on Picasso's right, separated from Françoise only by young Dr. Delcos of Collioure, was quite exceptionally tense.

After another week or so of bathing at Collioure, the band now swollen by the smaller children and their nurse, the holiday came to an end. There were times when Picasso was extraordinarily open and unreserved; others when he was so closed in upon himself that even those nearest to him had no notion of what was going on in his mind; and now, to the general astonishment, Picasso went back to Vallauris with Jacqueline; and from that point on, for the better or for the worse, his fate was sealed.

It is easier to state these facts than to explain them, but one may hazard the guess that quite apart from the discouragement and weariness of his disappointment with Rosita, the steady dissuasion of his interested friends had done its work; that the contrast between Françoise Gilot's strongly-emphasized independence, coldness, and detachment and Jacqueline Hutin's even more evident total devotion had a powerful effect; and that lassitude, consciousness of age, and a longing for peace in which to work induced Picasso to give in. There may well be other factors of which one knows nothing, but that was the only explanation those who knew him well at the time could give. To them it seemed that he just gave up the struggle—that he abandoned his castles in Collioure and the renewal of his Catalan life for the sake of quietness.

Yet there is a good deal of comfort in defeat, and back in Vallauris the portraits of Jacqueline began again. They are quite unlike those fierce, striking women of the June pictures: the sphinx has gone; so have the memories of Sylvette; and there is nothing whatsoever of Geneviève Laporte: the tall neck, the high fine cheekbones have vanished, and the "Jacqueline dans un fauteuil à bascule" of October is a plump and above all a comfortable little figure.

In the autumn, at the time of the exhibition of the Sylvette pictures, Picasso and Jacqueline were in Paris: it was too late for the much larger retrospective at the Maison de la Pensée française, which the Russians had made even more interesting by sending thirty-seven of the pictures bought so long ago by Shchukine. That admirable collector had survived the revolution, and for many years he lived in Paris, still attending the sales and the galleries, though no longer as a purchaser; he was dead now, and his daughter felt she had a right to her inheritance—she began legal proceedings, and the Russians hurried the pictures back to Leningrad and Moscow only a few days after the exhibition opened. Picasso did not see them: but he would not have gone to the show even if they had been there for months. His sense of embarrassment was as particular as his sense of privacy, and as strong; for while he did not at all mind displaying his works to friends and even casual acquaintances, the idea of attending an exhibition of them among an anonymous crowd filled him with distress.

He did see Geneviève Laporte, however, and although it was now too late for their misunderstanding to be done away with they met most affectionately: he was delighted at the success of her collection of poems, *Les Cavaliers d'ombre*, which had come out in June with seven of his drawings by way of illustration; and there was a generosity in his friendship for her that would be inconceivable in the Picasso depicted by Françoise Gilot, whom he also saw that autumn.

They quarreled at once, and when she went to see him a few months later to tell him that she meant to marry a man called Simon they quarreled again. She gives a description of Picasso "feigning illness" and behaving discreditably, but she does not mention one of the causes of their disagreement, which was La Galloise. The villa, like one of the flats in the rue Gay-Lussac, had been bought in her name; by law it was hers, and she meant to hold on to it. I do not say that the place was not morally as well as legally hers: I have no knowledge of the facts. All that is certain is that Picasso had to find new quarters, giving up a house that suited him in spite of all its drawbacks, with the rambling studios near at hand, his pottery and the kilns close by—a house, above all, to which he was thoroughly accustomed.

Between these two quarrels (and after the second Picasso and Françoise Gilot never met again) there was a period in which he did little work. Friends were one reason for this: they flocked to see him after his long absence; so did strangers; so did journalists, eager to hear about his private life. And these last exhibitions, as well as all those I have not even mentioned, had so increased his fame that Paris was now almost as bad as the Côte d'Azur, and he could not even walk about Saint-Germain-des-Prés in peace. If he joined a crowd to stare at a gushing broken drain (great quantities of rain fell that winter) they turned from the spectacle and he himself became the flood, an inhuman phenomenon. There were other factors too: early in November, 1954, Matisse died after his long illness and the news affected Picasso deeply; when he was asked for a statement he said, "Since Matisse is gone, there is nothing whatsoever to be said," and his tone was more eloquent than many of the eulogies that appeared. Then in the same month the war in Algeria broke out.

In December, 1954, Picasso began his versions of Delacroix' "Les Femmes d'Alger": but although the Communist Party was opposed to the

North African war there is little likelihood that the horrible conflict had anything to do with his decision. His admiration for Delacroix went back to his earliest visits to the Louvre in 1900, and in this particular picture, Picasso's and Cézanne's favorite Delacroix, one woman is absurdly like Jacqueline.

It is clear that some important change had come about in their relationship, a change far greater than can be accounted for by gratitude for her good looks and her youth, but that may be connected with his realization that this was not an adventure on her side but the devotion of a lifetime, and in the next two months he painted no less than fifteen variations in which she figures, many of them highly colored, some as representational as Delacroix, and all of them far more openly erotic; and in the last, the most brilliant of them all, he accomplished the feat of combining a relatively naturalistic Jacqueline-odalisque, full of curves, with three others cut into often rectilinear planes and disposed upon firmly-ruled striped backgrounds, set at angles to one another; the transition is carried out by means of a mirror that belongs to the perfectly legible figure but that nevertheless reflects a woman whose geometry comes from another world; and the whole is triumphantly bound together by a color-scheme strongly and without any doubt purposely reminiscent of the later Matisse.

There was nothing in the least slavish about Picasso's admiration for Delacroix, whom he treated with even less ceremony than El Greco, Poussin, or Courbet, moving his figures from place to place just as he saw fit, switching the erotic charge from negative to positive and preferring his own strong light to Delacroix' mysterious shadow; though in nearly all he did retain the horseshoe arch of the original. As he worked, says Hélène Parmelin, he wondered what Delacroix would say if he walked in: she also affirms that Picasso would not look at Delacroix' "Les Femmes d'Alger" nor even at a reproduction during this period; and no doubt a man with Picasso's astonishing visual memory could easily carry both the Louvre and the Montpellier versions (for he used both) in his head, perhaps already so transmuted that direct contact would have been harmful.

The series came to an end in February, 1955, and at about the same time Olga Picasso died in a hospital at Cannes, where for a long time she had been suffering from cancer and partial paralysis. Picasso and she had never been entirely out of contact—her photograph was to be seen in the rue des Grands-Augustins, and he wore her ring all his life—and now, returning to the south, he saw to her burial.

He did not settle in Vallauris again. It had been made plain that La Galloise was no longer his home, and although he so disliked change he now made a great effort, soon finding a far larger and even uglier house like a vast wedding-cake that had belonged to the Moëts on the outskirts of Cannes, in the wealthy, villa-studded district called La Californie; the house was also called La Californie, and its ugliness was that of wealth as expressed in the uninhibited days of 1900; still, it had a great deal of space, it was bathed in light, and it was surrounded by a fair-sized garden. It is true that the garden looked like a municipal park, but at least it was heavily protected against intruders.

At the same time he virtually abandoned both his remaining flat in the rue Gay-Lussac (Valentin says he gave it to Inès) and the rue des Grands-Augustins. If this was an attempt at a clean break with his past, it was not at all successful; for although Picasso was wonderfully indifferent to houses and to their comfort, nothing could overcome his passion for objects, for portable possessions, and within a very short time almost everything he had ever owned, including the knife he had used when camping with Pallarès in 1898 and the English chairs from his childhood home in Málaga that his father had sent him in 1909, began to converge upon La Californie, filling the vast, high-ceilinged rooms and making them look like something between an ill-run pawnshop and a remover's warehouse. Pieces of sculpture also arrived, gathering round their maker in troops, the bronzes, headed by ''L'Homme au mouton'' and ''La Chèvre,'' living outside, where Picasso's dogs and eventually his pigeons gave them a patina they would never have acquired in a museum: but well before they were all unpacked the big house was permeated with a smell that was never to leave it until Picasso himself went away—oil-paint and turpentine, the smell of creativity rather than that of wealth: though as it happened creativity also meant wealth in Picasso's case. Money rolled in upon him from all sides, and presently it was to reach full flood, making him the richest painter who had ever lived.

He at once took over the greater part of the ground floor, including the best drawing-rooms, and turned them into studios, quickly gathering his familiar slum around him; and here he painted a large number of portraits of Jacqueline and what he called interior landscapes—the studios themselves with her in them and the trees and sky showing through the open Art Nouveau windows—fine free pictures full of happiness.

But pleased though he was with La Californie, his heart did not forget the Roussillon, and at Whitsun he was back at the rue de l'Ange with Jacqueline, Maya, Cocteau, the Leirises, and many others. They went to the bull-fight at Céret, and Picasso thoroughly enjoyed himself: during this visit he had much more time to look about him and he found that the little town had scarcely changed since he was there with Eva; water still gushed up from hidden springs and flowed along the gutters, the huge planes still shaded his favorite café, the scops owl uttered its unvaried note, and many of his old friends were still to be seen, including Frank Havilland, now the curator of Brune's museum, to which Matisse had given some lovely drawings just before his death. Quite apart from his kindness for the town, Picasso did not choose to be outdone, and he behaved even more handsomely than usual, giving the museum a large number of presents. And his generosity did not stop there; in 1957 he designed the poster for the museum's Manolo exhibition, and for many years after that crates would arrive, bringing his more remarkable ceramics. But Picasso never brought them himself, nor did he ever see Perpignan again: this was his last visit to a Catalan country, and when it was over he settled down to painting at La Californie.

Yet a culture pays little attention to political boundaries, and Picasso did not become French for having lived seventy years in France. The influences that had formed him (as far as any outside force could form so exceptional a being) were largely Catalan, and a demi-Catalan or more he remained to the end of his life. One of the last friends to sit by his death-bed came from Barcelona, and between 1955 and then he saw scores and scores of people from his youth—the thread was never broken. This uninterrupted contact owed much to Sabartés, who was not only a far better correspondent, but who could travel to and fro without any opposition from either the Spanish government or from Picasso, who never required his friends to share his views (he was much attached to some leading Carlists). In 1955, for example, Sabartés was in Barcelona, and returning to France he brought Joan Vidal Ventosa, once of the Quatre Gats, and Antoní Clavé, together with the Gaspars; and one of the results of this meeting was a Picasso show at the Sala Gaspar in Barcelona in October, 1956, an exhibition that excited immense interest and that was followed by many more.

Picasso worked well in the tall, light-filled rooms of La Californie, but 1955 was not his most productive year, although with his great "official" retrospective of paintings, including "Guernica," at the Pavillon de Marsan (the Musée des Arts décoratifs, part of the Louvre itself) and of graphic work at the Bibliothèque nationale, it was the richest year hitherto for the public, and the reason for this was that he spent much time and even more energy making a film with Georges Clouzot, *Le Mystère Picasso*. It was not the first film about him—there had been three or four documentaries in earlier years—but it developed into the most ambitious by far, a full-length film in color. Clouzot saw fit to make it at Nice and in the summer months, when the heat of the powerful electric lights, added to that of the sun, was enough to make a salamander quail; but Picasso loved a new technique, he loved people who really knew their trade, and he was seized with an enthusiasm at least as great as Clouzot's. Although the film was based on the notion that laying on the colors constitutes the act of creation, as though no more of a love-story were to be filmed than its consummation, a fallacy that cannot have deceived Picasso for a moment, he lent himself wholeheartedly to the scheme and laid on the colors with a zeal that is a delight to watch.

Sometimes he did so in the oven-like film-studio, using a newly-invented and disagreeably "chemical" pigment that would soak straight through an absorbent surface, thus allowing the camera to follow his work from behind, sometimes ordinary paint in the open, on a beach just by Antibes, sitting at his easel and getting up every few seconds to let the last brush-stroke be filmed; and perhaps the most astonishing thing about the whole undertaking was the way he carried on his solitary pursuit amid the host of directors, cameramen, technicians, and idle spectators, perpetually interrupted yet never for a moment losing his concentration, sitting there with his brown person shining with sweat, clothed in a pair of canvas drawers, his luminous eye fixed upon his picture and his hand sweeping out the perfect curves. Even a trivial film calls for an immense amount of time and of coordinated work by a large number of people, and this film was by no means trivial: Clouzot and the technicians worked on and on, and Picasso worked with them, sometimes twelve and even fourteen hours a day, producing bull-fights, still-lives, nudes, collages and drawings, some of them memories of the *Verve* suite. Hélène Parmelin reproduces about thirty in the third volume of her *Secrets d'alcôve d'un atelier*, but it is said that there were many more, some given to the people in the film-studio, some "mislaid." No masterpiece was born before the eye of the camera; but what is far more surprising is that in these appalling circumstances Picasso did not fall far below himself and that when he was on the beach of La Garoupe he even painted pictures that would have pleased him at any time.

It is many years since I saw the film and I cannot speak of it with any accuracy; but, mixed with the pleasure of seeing him at work, I do remember an uneasy impression that he was being put through his paces, that the fruit of immense thought and experience was presented as something like a most accomplished trick, almost a music-hall turn, carried out in minutes, as though celerity were of real significance; and this impression was strengthened by the music, the drum-roll for the vital stroke that gave apparently random lines their meaning, and indeed by the nature of some of the things that Picasso drew when he was amusing himself. The incredible virtuosity was there, but so it was when Picasso was amusing himself in a restaurant after dinner, when he drew on the napkins or made creatures out of crumbs; and Picasso is so very much more than that.

Yet for all its probably inevitable shortcomings the film was a most fascinating spectacle, since apart from showing many pictures in the act of birth, though not of conception, and Picasso's technical approach, it also conveyed his immense vitality with more success than one would have believed possible. And if Clouzot left the mystery of Picasso's creative process even more impenetrable than it was before, that was perhaps because he used a camera rather than a double gas metaphysical microscope of extra power working outside the limits of time and space imposed by his medium.

Nearly forty years earlier Picasso had flung himself into the mad, gregarious world of the ballet; this summer he flung himself into the even madder, more gregarious world of the cinema. But whereas in the ballet the dancers at least have to keep trim and neat by abstinence, film-people tend to carry on after working-hours, drifting from bar to bar with hordes of companions. Picasso could no more resist their strenuous conviviality than their strenuous work: at the age of seventy-four he painted by day, surrounded by a crowd, and he played by night, surrounded by an even greater number of new acquaintances and people more or less connected with the cinema, among whom such truly valued friends as Pallarès, Geneviève Laporte, and the Lazermes seemed rather lost, although he welcomed them with all his heart. In addition to the film-people and the holidaymakers there were also the men and women who got into La Californie on the grounds that they were fellow-Communists, Spaniards, or painters, or simply because they wanted to see Picasso. Some asked him for friendship, some for money, all for time; and once they were in, Picasso's code forbade him to put them out. He must often have longed for the drawbridges of Collioure: but still, squandering his strength and spirit like a twenty-year-old, he went on and on, late nights, comic hats and all, until the triumphant end of the film, the scattering of the crowds at the time of the mass return to Paris, and the comparative calm of autumn.

He paid heavily for all this, although he still had energy enough to go to Paris himself in October. Here he saw Geneviève Laporte again, and she showed him Cocteau's illustrations for her second book of poems. Cocteau was a recent friend of hers, and his charm had so subjugated her that she really does not seem to have seen the difference in size between the two men. Picasso was fully aware of it, however, and in the summer he had already displayed some irritation when she spoke enthusiastically of her new acquaintance. Cocteau was a person with whom Picasso had a curious relationship in which irritation and resentment, not to say jeal-

431]

ousy and even a certain amount of disdain, mingled with habit and affection: this was just at the moment when Cocteau was elected to the Académie française, and Picasso was openly displeased. "There, you see!" he cried on being shown the proofs, "What did I tell you? He's always copied me." He handed them back, quite out of temper. Their meeting ended pleasantly, however: she showed him some other poems, which he read attentively and praised. He commended her for working so hard (work was a cardinal virtue with him) and said that presently he would illustrate another of her books. And in time he overcame his ill-humor about Cocteau, designing a hilt for the new academician's sword; but for the moment he was quite wretched. Some part of this must be put down to his reduced condition, for he was not in form at all. That autumn he did manage to paint a gray and white Jacqueline in Turkish clothes, looking very like the submissive inmate of a harem, and some more interiors, all vaguely Moorish, with the Californie palm-trees outside, but the winter found him exhausted, emptied, anxious about his health; and some observers thought that this, his seventy-fifth year, might be his last. Van Gogh and Modigliani between them had not lived so long, nor Raphael half that time; but in general painting is a healthy trade, perhaps because painters work out their conflicts in a perpetual self-analysis, and when Cinto Reventós came to La Californie with his family in February, 1956, he found Picasso in better spirits. They had not met for the best part of a generation, but Picasso took up their conversation just where it had left off. "What about the Salome?" he asked. "I'll buy it."

"That you will not," said Dr. Reventós hotly: he had cherished the etching since Picasso had given it to him in 1905 and he had no intention of parting with it. This pleased Picasso, who secretly loathed seeing his presents sold: he was pleased too with the favorable opinion of the two doctors (for Cinto's son was also a medical man), and although he was much pestered by tourists when he went out with them, the visit was a great and tonic success. It was followed by another, this time from Gustau Gili, the son and successor of the Barcelona publisher who had commissioned Picasso to illustrate a book as long ago as 1927. The book was *La Tauromaquia o arte de torear,* and it was written by the famous eighteenth-century bullfighter José Delgado, otherwise Pepe Illo or Hillo, whose portrait Picasso had copied when he was a boy in Madrid. The title-page stated that the work was of the greatest value to every kind of person who loved bulls: Picasso was the obvious choice as illustrator, and when he was approached—Gili senior went to Paris for the purpose—he agreed with enthusiasm. But what with procrastination and two wars he did nothing, and now Gustau Gili II had come to bring the affair to life again. Again Picasso agreed, and with equal enthusiasm: he liked the Gilis (it was they, I believe, who brought him the fan-tailed pigeons that soon came to occupy so much of the upper floor of La Californie), he liked the idea; and the pleasure of these visits, these renewed contacts with Barcelona helped to set him up, while the coming Provençal spring confirmed their good effect.

He did nothing about Pepe Illo; but under the influence of the spring he turned to a large canvas of a shepherd sleeping under a tree while a goat grazes on its leaves, all pleasant planes, as cheerful a picture as those at Antibes. Earlier in that year he had worked on some nudes, one pair reminiscent of his heavy great women of Royan, with the massive columns of their bellies and buttocks seen simultaneously, and another of his bathers of twenty years before, as though he were flexing his muscles before returning to a more important series of "interior landscapes," most of them including Jacqueline, to his sculpture and his pots.

His sculpture had taken a new form at about the time of Sylvette or a little earlier: it was now a sculpture of painted planes, cut out of boards or ply-wood or sheets of metal. A typical example was a head of Sylvette herself, made of tinplate painted light gray with black strokes for her features and her pony-tail, the whole bent along four straight lines to form a free-standing figure about two feet high. Others were taller, raised on broomsticks or thin columns, and from a distance their flat surfaces looked rather like finger-posts, while the more constructed, brilliantly-colored sort were akin to totem-poles.

In 1956 these figures grew larger and often flatter: the well-known group of bronzes called "Les Baigneurs"—six pieces ranging from four foot six to eight foot eight—give the impression of having no more than two surfaces each. About the time he made them Picasso said to Hélène Parmelin, "A dreadful thing about these days is that no one says anything unpleasant about anybody else. . . . There is something good in every show. And in any case everything is sound and worthwhile or pretty nearly so." His remark encourages me to observe that I do not like "Les Baigneurs" at all: they say nothing to me. But this opinion, or this confession of insensibility, is less widely shared than that of Georges Salles, then the head of all the French museums, including the Louvre, who spoke of "Les Baigneurs" as "a most delightful success in which Picasso lets the prime mover of his genius work without the least restraint: and for his genius artistic creation is above all a magic act. Each Bather culminates in a minute bird-like head, so light that it cannot but be gay. All this would be merely clever, fantastic, startling, and droll if it were not for the fact that a mystery inhabits the strangeness of these beings, the darkest, most impenetrable mystery, that of life itself.''

Nineteen fifty-six was a year in which the Algerian war grew even more savage and the French left-wing opposition to it more articulate: it was also the year of the Twentieth Congress in Moscow and Khrushchev's denunciation of Stalin. His revelation of the tyranny that had filled Gulag and so many other graves and concentration-camps struck many French Communists with horror and dismay. Neither of these events has any obvious echo in Picasso's work.

Although Hélène Parmelin's *Picasso sur place* is resolutely and even compulsively euphoric, from what little she says it is clear that Picasso was deeply concerned about what had happened in Russia, and that he was downcast and worried; but unlike some of his friends he did not find it impossible to go on with the Party. He retained his card at this point, and although with Pignon and some others he signed a letter protesting against the French Communist Party's official attitude to the Soviet intervention in Hungary later that year, he retained it to the end of his life in spite of Poland, Czechoslovakia, the reversal of Khrushchev's policy, and the persecution of the Jews. Loyalty to the underlying cause? Political unconsciousness? The lapsed Catholic's need for a dogmatic basis? Pasternak and Solzhenitsyn were extremely unwilling to leave their fatherland in spite of all they suffered; and to a certain extent the Party was Picasso's fatherland.

In any event he painted few pictures of much consequence apart from some cheerful garden-pieces in which Claude and Paloma are to be seen, they being at La Californie for the holidays, and political distress may have had something to do with this: though a more obvious immediate cause is the summer invasion of the south by friends and tourists.

Among the visitors was Geneviève Laporte, bringing the book that Cocteau had illustrated, as she had promised. He asked her eagerly whether she was alone, and he was pleased when she said yes; but after that their conversation dwindled. Their direct communication, even their real knowledge of one another, vanished in the silences.

The relationship, perhaps the sweetest in Picasso's life, was almost dead. It just survived an autumn meeting in Paris, when Picasso went back on his promise to illustrate another collection of poems—it was also to have two gouaches by Cocteau—on the grounds that the publisher had put out a book illustrated by Jean-Gabriel Domergue, a fashionable painter of pretty pictures, and that he would not allow his name to appear in the same catalog; but it perished entirely the next summer. She had come to see him at La Californie: they talked in one of the vast bare rooms and again the silences stretched out between them. Picasso's boxer, the foolish Yan, brought her a piece of wood from the garden and she tossed it for him. "This is not a suitable place for playing with dogs in," said Picasso, and for Geneviève Laporte he was no longer there—her Picasso had died.

A man can change surprisingly even in his seventies; but a young woman of under thirty is likely to change even more, and in their movement away from one another it may have been Geneviève Laporte who had traveled the farther. Certainly the Picasso who turned at last to Pepe Illo was recognizable as the same man who had drawn and painted bull-fights twenty and forty and even sixty years before, whereas there is little in common between the schoolgirl who wrote her piece on Picasso in 1944 and the author of *Les Cavaliers d'ombre*.

He did so, says Douglas Duncan, immediately after a disappointing bull-fight at Arles. He came home, shut himself up, and did not emerge until he had finished the twenty-six aquatints that were used for the book as well as several more that were not. Into these few hours of intense activity he poured seventy years of experience as an aficionado, and the suite is a delight even to those who do not take much pleasure in seeing bulls tormented. Apart from the virtues of its separate plates, the whole has an unrivaled unity, arising no doubt from the speed of execution and the technical mastery which allowed that speed.

Bulls had long been present in his ceramics, but now they increased in number, and he made some very fine oval dishes which are the arena itself, with the ritual going on in the middle and the crowd spotted all round the edge, much as he had painted them when he was a child in Málaga. There were owls too, for another had entered his household, joining the pigeons, the goat Esmeralda that wandered upstairs and downstairs, almost wherever it chose (there had been a goat at La Galloise, but Gilot got rid of it: Jacqueline Roque put up with Esmeralda) and the dogs—a dachshund called Lump was now Yan's companion. The pigeons had multiplied to an extraordinary extent, and Picasso fed the squabs himself; but one of the original hen-fantails must have been a flighty bird, for now there were signs of common blood in the dovecote, vulgar mottled gray and brown creatures whose looks could not have recommended them to anyone except Picasso, who gave them the run of the top story.

The sculptures, now even more two-dimensional, had multiplied too, and they stood all about the garden: there were also some modeled bronzes, particularly a noble bull's head with designs covering its smooth surface in something of the Easter Island manner. And of course there were more paintings, including another "Plage de la Garoupe," the result of a large number of experiments with cut-out forms.

But for all this the summer of 1957 was a trying season: many other bull-fights as well as that of Arles were disappointing; the invasion was as bad or even worse; Jacqueline had an operation, Picasso's old sciatic leg was giving trouble, and even without that he was often ill-tempered—so ill-tempered that from Hélène Parmelin's account (and she was well placed to know, since she was more or less a fixture at La Californie) few people apart from those who liked being trampled by a famous man or who earned their foothold by toad-eating could have put up with it: as she says herself, "one could never move on his plane with a sense of equality," and those who did not care for a state of permanent subordination kept away except for brief visits. Picasso loved pride and independence in others: but he could not always refrain from destroying both, just as he would so often exercise his Midas-touch, although he deplored its effects. Jacqueline addressed him as Monseigneur, a title usually reserved for royal dukes and bishops, Kahnweiler trembled at his frown, and the mood of the whole household was strictly regulated upon that of the master. At this point the mood was far from agreeable; yet among his intimates there were surely a few who saw in this nervous tension and increasing irritability the signs of an approaching work of great importance. And it would be strange if Jacqueline were not among those few, for although a great many unpleasant things have been said about her, mostly by excluded friends, nobody has ever questioned her devotion.

In August there was a great turmoil at La Californie. Picasso deserted the lower part of the house, where he was too often interrupted, and moved up to the top story among the pigeons. Some time before this he had been asked to paint a big mural for the UNESCO building in Paris, but up there, in a solitude shared only by the birds and Velásquez and occasionally Jacqueline, the commission was the least of his concerns. He worked steadily day after day and often far into the night; he showed nothing to any of his friends other than Jacqueline, nor did he leave off except for bull-fights until October, when he took Pignon upstairs and showed him his great series of variations on Velásquez' "Las Meninas."

He had not yet finished all he meant to do, but even so there were "twenty or thirty" canvases up there, and all of them, apart from a few balconies with pigeons and views of the light-filled sea and land embraced by his window, were Meninas. The first was a large statement of his theme, a picture comparable in size with Velásquez' but proportionately broader, which assembled all the characters of the original in much the same relative positions, the whole painted in a pinkish gray. The little infanta is there with her two maids of honor (or perhaps children-in-waiting would be a better translation of meninas), her dwarf and her fool, a dog, two tutors in the background, and a cloaked figure in an open·door still farther off, all watching Velásquez painting the king and queen, who, since they inhabit the emptiness in front of the picture, the emptiness shared by the spectator, are only to be seen in the looking-glass behind the artist.

In this first version the painter is a gigantic figure with a double profile, his head reaching the ceiling; and in this ceiling there are two great hooks, filled with a significance of their own: in a later picture, almost at the end of the series, a dark, highly schematic picture, he appears again, a pied triangle with a huge cross of Santiago (the order of knighthood to which Velásquez belonged) painted on it, standing well back from his easel, farther from the curiously insistent hooks. But between these two Picasso was less concerned with Velásquez and the other men than with the infanta and her little court: she and they are taken out of the main picture and they are to be seen in a score of transpositions, some of them wonderfully gay and full of color, others filled with sadness, and still others with the indefinable anxiety of dreams.

When the pictures were shown publicly they excited a great deal of comment, most of it favorable, and once again they were interpreted in countless different ways. Some people saw political comment in ''Las Meninas,'' a symbolic refutation of the social order; some really thought that Picasso had spent weeks and months of his time making a parody of Velásquez. The various interpretations were no doubt valid for each of the interpreters, as Picasso said himself on another occasion; but when one has read several of them the question arises: are such essentially subjective views worth communicating? There was also a good deal of more informed discussion of Picasso's treatment of space and its relation to analytic Cubism: in ''Las Meninas,'' of course, he took no account of Velásquez' traditional perspective, and this adds even more to the quality that can be called dream-like, since in dreams the traditional sequences of space and time so often vanish, together with the common operation of cause and effect, yet without affecting one's profound sense of reality—of another, almost always stronger reality. To be sure, some dreams make sense according to one's waking mode of thought, and they can be put into words without losing too much of their essence: but those that cannot do not therefore lose their night-time significance nor their reality; they retain both in some non-verbal region of one's mind, and, I believe, in painting. And if some part of ''Las Meninas'' can be described as a dream-like though very active meditation on Velásquez then that would go far towards explaining why so many of the reasonable interpretations are unconvincing. Clearly this also applies to much of Picasso's other work as well as to that of most worth-while painters, particularly Uccello, but it seems to me most strongly exemplified in "Las Meninas."

They were finished at the end of the year, and early in 1958 Picasso turned straight to the UNESCO commission, a mural about thirty-three feet broad and twenty-six high for the conference-hall. The technical difficulties were considerable; he dealt with them by using a large number of separate panels that could be fitted together, but this meant that he could never see the full-scale picture as a whole.

It was first seen in a school at Vallauris, when Georges Salles came down to unveil what was to some degree the offspring of his zeal, since it was he who had urged the unenthusiastic Picasso to undertake the task. The curtains were drawn aside and the local people saw an enormous picture quite filling the far end of the playground: to the right a man standing on a beach, another lying in front of him with his head raised, and a third sunbathing figure whose Matisse-like curves contrast strongly with the harsh line of the other two; to the left a woman with a minute head, a vast undivided bosom, and feet like an inverted heart stands looking away from the men; and into the sea between them falls a white and apparently calcined form, all little round head and attenuated limbs enveloped in a sharply defined shade. The fall, coupled with the indifference of the bystanders, has led most people to call him Icarus, though others, including UNESCO, speak of "Le Combat du Bien et du Mal." The inhabitants of Vallauris applauded respectfully, and at the parties given for the occasion Picasso's friends were lavish with their praise; but when the picture was seen in Paris—or partially seen, since it is impossible to stand back and view it as a whole—it was received with almost universal condemnation.

Almost universal. UNESCO gave a dinner for those who had adorned the building: Picasso did not attend, but Brassaï, who had also contributed a panel, did, and here I quote him. "During dessert Evans, the director of UNESCO, stood up to propose a toast. Much heated by whiskey and good wine, he thumped the table and cried, 'There we are! The place exists! And it's we who brought it into being!' Then with a sly look he went on, 'And now our friend Georges Salles will give us his candid, unvarnished opinion of Picasso's mural.' Rather startled, Salles was getting up, but Le Corbusier cut in before him. 'All I can say—and you can rely on my judgment and experience—is that this mural of Picasso's is a masterpiece. . . . Never mind what people think of it now. In ten or say twenty years its beauty will be obvious.' "

The twenty years have nearly passed, and soon perhaps the voice of authority, speaking through Le Corbusier, will be heard: but so far the UNESCO picture is not looked upon as one of Picasso's successes.

That summer at Cannes was very wearing at times. Every highly-publicized exhibition increased the number of people who wanted to see Picasso and who were not always very delicate about the way they did so; and recently there had been several, including another great retrospective at the Museum of Modern Art in New York. Jacqueline protected him as well as she could, sometimes perhaps without much discernment; but lion-hunting is a trait combined with extraordinary pertinacity, and the prey, Picasso reduced to the status of an object, was sometimes hunted down; although, on the other hand, he was often separated from friends he would have liked to see.

It was not only lion-hunters. Scores and even hundreds of people from all over the world wanted help, advice, introductions, encouragement; many of them were interesting or pathetic creatures, and Picasso's kindness was assailed on every side. There were also those who wanted him to collaborate on an article that would explain his painting, to write a preface, to illustrate a book, or to support a movement against poverty, war, and injustice, to say nothing of those whose eager search would be satisfied with a free picture, a comfortable sum of money, or even an autograph. Even after all these years of paying for his notoriety Picasso still often tried to see each member of the horde as an individual; but the numbers made it impossible; and the distraction of his mind, the waste of time and energy, the unpleasantness of refusing, the even worse consequences of feigned compliance (his frequent line of retreat), and the insistent servile graspingness with which he was surrounded tended to sour his temper. Above all he hated the incessant attempts at manipulation by those who looked upon him as a milch-cow.

Then again 1958 was the year that very nearly saw the subversion of the Republic. In May some of the generals in Algeria, displeased with the conduct of the elected government of France, took authority into their own hands, and for some days it seemed that there might be open war between part of the army, particularly the parachute-troops, on the one hand, and the supporters of the Republic, particularly the Communists, on the other. General de Gaulle, called out of his retirement, dealt with the situation; but while he was doing so French democracy hung in the balance. During this tense period Picasso painted one of the few pictures that is a direct reflection of his political ideas. It is a large still-life of a table in front of an open window and a balcony: on the table stands a bunch of lilies-of-the-valley and a black, desiccated bull's head. The bloody sun is reflected in the panes, and the red, strengthened by the black window-bars, is full of menace. The political or ethical content is by no means obvious, but it was clear enough to Picasso, and later he told Pierre Daix that he "painted the picture with curses."

Apart from this he painted some enchanting pictures such as "La Baie de Cannes" as it was seen from the villa, and "La Californie la nuit," and he made some pots and sheet-metal sculptures; but his output diminished; there are almost no studies of the children; and it is noticeable that he spent far more time than usual over his paintings and drawings—there is one of a woman from Arles with the dates of no less than twenty sittings written down the left-hand side like an inscription in Chinese.

When this tiring, crowded, and not very fruitful summer was over, the Picassos and the Pignons went to Arles for a bull-fight. They dined with Douglas Cooper, who then lived at the Château de Castille, not far away. Picasso, tired of the noise and fuss of the Côte d'Azur, asked if he might buy the house: Cooper said that he might not, but observed that the Château de Vauvenargues was for sale, adding that it was a splendid place, the very thing for Picasso.

The next day they found it, a great square seventeenth-century house with two round towers in a lonely valley under the Montagne Sainte-Victoire: it came suddenly into sight as the road turned to the village, a few hundred yards from the château and slightly above it. In that severe, silent, and largely uninhabited landscape the pink and ocher building, all of a piece, was extraordinarily beautiful. It also made the strongest contrast with the villa-crowded hills of Cannes: what is more, the mountain could not be built upon (there were threats of development in front of La Californie) since it all belonged to the house. The house in its turn had belonged to the Clapiers, a great Provençal family which took the title of Marquis de Vauvenargues from this estate; and their arms were still to be seen over the noble doorway. Indeed, it is said that the famous Vauvenargues wrote his *Maximes* there, which might possibly have added to Picasso's mounting enthusiasm, though it is difficult to imagine him feeling much sympathy for that prim young moralist's writings apart from some odd remarks such as "Prosperity makes few friends," "Subjects pay their court with more pleasure than princes receive it," and "Genius cannot be feigned."

Picasso gazed eagerly down on the château from the village, looking right into its court, and his enthusiasm blinded him to the fact that from the same vantage-point others could stare just as well and even better if they were equipped with binoculars and telephoto lenses. Then although it was Cézanne's Montagne Sainte-Victoire that reared up behind the house, Vauvenargues lay on the northern, the far less sunlit side. The stark landscape was very fine, and most congenial to a Spaniard; but in fact the place was awkwardly situated even as a refuge from the crowds, since although it had all the disadvantages of remoteness it lay within the easy range of cars from Aix. These drawbacks did not appear at first sight, nor even when he had explored the enormous rooms, so capital for working in: he did see that the house lacked running water, drains, and central-heating, but he did not see that it possessed a strong, antagonistic personality of its own. Vauvenargues had been lived in for generations by people whose civilization was quite unlike Picasso's and even inimical to his; it was not a mere shelter, not a more or less derelict rue des Grands-Augustins nor the costly bower of a champagne-merchant but a still-living entity, one that summed up many values for which he had little use but which nevertheless impressed him: it was a house that could not be ignored.

Chapter XXI

It was months and even years before Vauvenargues overcame Picasso, and in the first spring of his enthusiasm he spent some very happy days there. He had bought the house within forty-eight hours of first seeing it, and with equal (and characteristic) precipitation he had radiators and the necessary pipes installed, piercing the splendid plaster-work in every direction. All this cost a great deal of money; but money in itself no longer meant anything to him. He had lost track of the changing currency somewhere in the thirties, and by now he had no idea of what things cost: when he reckoned at all he did so obscurely, in the archaic sous of his youth or even in reales. In restaurants Jacqueline always dealt with the bill, and when by some unusual chance he had to pay for any-thing himself he would take a large note from the wad he carried in his pocket, still fastened with a safety-pin, after all these years, and sweep up the change.

He also sent for his pictures stored in Paris—Matisse, Derain, Rous-seau, Le Nain, Cézanne, Corot, van Dongen, Degas, Chardin, Braque, Miró, Modigliani, Renoir, and many more, together with early works of his own that he had bought back—and he brought much of his sculpture from La Californie, as though he meant to settle at the château for good.

With these familiar objects round him he at once began to paint. He was influenced and even impressed by his surroundings, the great hall, the chapel in one of the towers, the sinful magnificence of the chimney-pieces, and one of his earliest pictures was the "Buffet de Vauve-nargues," in which the lowering mass of the ancient sideboard is made as cheerful as can be by a green light on its carving, a stroke of singing blue, and the presence of a green-pinafored child and a fine plum-pudding dog, a recent addition to Picasso's menagerie. He had already made one ver-sion of this at Cannes while he was waiting for the central heating to be put in, and now without finishing it he turned to a series of still-lives, the jugs and bottles of so many years ago and even a mandolin, painted with as much grave sobriety as ever, though without the same rigid discipline. Then, after a number of other Jacquelines, a portrait of her in a medieval kind of hat, lettered large and clear across the top JACQUELINE DE VAUVENARGUES: and there were several more, including Jacqueline as a queen, as though he were trying to make her fit into the house—a form of magic that did not work. She remained ill at ease; for her Vauvenargues was lonely, sinister, even perhaps haunted. For his part Picasso looked more out of doors than in during these early days, and he found himself very much at home in this stark, arid, melancholy limestone country, so like that of Horta, while the village was almost as Cubist as Gósol. He painted it, though in an eager, dashing manner far removed from the pure, ascetic Cubism of the early days; and at about the same time, his mind never being far from Spain, he also drew bull-fights: bull-fights in which the figure of Christ appears. None of the memoirs I have read accounts for the resurgence of this uncommon theme. Parmelin was a far more thorough-paced Communist than Picasso, and although she never despised the capitalist fleshpots she had little use for immaterialist superstition; and no other literate person was in constant attendance at the time. But it may be that Picasso, with something very like Spain outside his window, wished to add the Spanish dimension to the ordinary bull-fights he could see in France—the element of ritual sacrifice, the omnipresent background of Catholicism.

The drawings—wash for the most part—appear in a book upon which he and the bull-fighter Luis Miguel Domínguin collaborated, if collaboration is quite the word to describe the strange haphazard way they set about producing *Toros y toreros* for Gili of Barcelona. Long before, Picasso had spoken about a book on an unspecified subject that he was going to publish some time and he had said that he would like his friend to contribute to it. Then he suddenly telephoned from Cannes. During their conversation Domínguin still could not find out the nature of the book nor what he was expected to do. Should he write a preface, a text, a commentary? Should he speak about painting or bulls or the pole star? Any of these would answer, said Picasso; or if Domínguin merely chose to write until he was tired Picasso knew that the work would be well done. And Domínguin would write it that very night, would he not? The book was ready and Domínguin's piece was all it was waiting for.

Domínguin made a last effort. "Pablo," he said, "I don't understand painting and I don't know how to write: I should at least like to see the book so as to have some notion . . . ." "There's no connection at all," replied Picasso. "The book is about the kind of thing I do: all you have to do is write." Dominguín abandoned the hopeless attempt and took up his pen. He wrote about the nature of the Spanish bull-fight, the Spanish bullfighter's deeper motives, and the affinities between him and the artist; again and again he stressed how totally a Spaniard Picasso was, and spoke also of his great capacity for friendship, his simplicity, and his age-less character—the painter and the bullfighter were generations apart in years, but they treated one another as contemporaries without any loss of respect on either side. And he too dwelt on that inexplicable radiation that emanated from Picasso, that quality which made people realize that he possessed a power unlike that of other men, unlike not in degree but kind; and Dominguín did so with such directness that his words have no hint of silly adulation. Directness was at the heart of their relationship: once he said to Picasso, "Why don't you tell me something about painting, some explanation that would help me to find out which way round I am?" Pi-casso said, "Some day, without anybody having told you anything at all, you will realize that it has come to you. In the meantime nothing I can say would be of the least use to you."

Picasso's part of *Toros y toreros* turned out to be the reproduction of three of his sketchbooks, together with sixteen additional sepia drawings; and all the plates apart from some Jacquelines on horseback and some heads drawn upside-down, are to do with bullfighting. The Christ figures are in the second book, filled between March 2 and 12, 1959; in the very first of these drawings a bullfighter, his arms held out horizontally, is wafting his cape to draw the bull away from a fallen picador: and on the same day one of the outstretched hands is pierced, while the torso is bare. Still on March 2 Picasso drew Our Lady, crowned and weeping, her heart pierced with the seven sorrows, figured by what I take to be bullfighter's swords. The thought develops through fifteen more drawings in which Christ is present without the least ambiguity, nailed to the Cross but with one hand free so that with His loincloth He can lure the bull from the man and the gored, dying horse. That day ends with Christ's head, young, bearded, and crowned with thorns. The next begins with studies of the arm: then comes another head, slighter than the last, still crowned but now turned to the right, the mouth open as though following the success of the pass; then the whole scene in shorthand, very small, with the addi-tion of a man falling to his knees in the arena; and lastly, with the fallen picador, the horse, the bull moving away from them beneath the crucified feet, the theme vanishes, never to reappear.

These grave drawings have excited a great deal of comment and a great many interpretations: almost anything can be read into them except blasphemy or, as Geneviève Laporte put it in a poem about the dying Harlequin, "the kitchen-knife of ridicule."

It is tempting to attribute much of the difference between the pictures painted at Vauvenargues and those painted at Cannes to the Spanish landscape and the darker sky, and indeed the far more sober colors, deep red and ocher, point in that direction. He also took to using a dark green, quite unusual in his palette and allied to the evergreen forest and the maquis of the Montagne Sainte-Victoire and to that of Horta, and it overflowed from his occasional landscapes into his still-lives and his Jacquelines just as the northern green had invaded much of his painting at La Rue-des-Bois.

Yet on the other hand it was at Vauvenargues that he began his variations on Manet's "Déjeuner sur l'herbe"; and although much of the classical world appears in some of his versions and of the archaic in others, it is probably true to say that in all the hundred and fifty-odd drawings and the twenty-seven paintings of the full suite there is little that is specifically Spanish. He did not work on them continuously but in sudden bursts of intense activity separated by intervals, sometimes of several months; yet it is clear that they filled part of his mind for the rest of 1959, all though 1960 and 1961 and even into the beginning of 1962: he never dwelt so long upon any other undertaking. The visible evidence for his preoccupation is all dated, and it provides not only a fascinating though of course incomplete view of the process of creation but also an exact account of Picasso's use of his time as he reached the age of eighty. It is for this rather than for analysis or detailed comment that I think it useful to speak of the "Déjeuners" at some length.

The first drawings were made on August 10, 1959, a fairly straightforward, simplified version of the original composition, which was itself a restatement of Giorgione's "Concert Champêtre" in the Louvre. (Art historians say that it also owed much to an engraving of Raphael's lost "Judgment of Paris.") Manet had set four figures in a woodland clearing with a stream winding through it: in the foreground on the left of the picture is the remains of their picnic, rolls and cherries scattered around a green-lined basket; then comes a fine lively plump girl, sitting on her discarded blue dress, her elbow on her knee and her chin on her hand. She is Victorine Maurend, who posed for the lovely "Olympia" that caused such a scandal in 1863 and for the soldier-boy in red trousers playing a fife, and who finished her days as a little dim old woman selling violets in the streets of Paris. She sits there with nothing on, perfectly unconcerned and looking straight out of the picture as though at the eye of a camera.

Close to her and in the same diagonal is Manet's younger brother Eugène, bearded and wearing a snuff-colored coat. Some way beyond him but in the same line, another young woman, holding up her shift, paddles in the stream, which carries the diagonal up and away through the trees. Opposite Eugène reclines the painter's brother-in-law, the sculptor Ferdinand Leenhoff, in a black coat, gray trousers, black boots, black beard, and a strange voluminous kind of black smoking-cap with a tassel whose rabbinical appearance is increased by a hint of side-locks at his ear. His pale left hand holds a walking-stick and his right is held out towards his two companions in the gesture of one who is making a point in argument or exposition. But he makes it in vain: although his companions in the foreground cannot have failed to hear him—they are so close together that their legs overlap—they are quite unmoved. Eugène gazes dreamily out into the void; Victorine looks brightly at the spectator; while the young woman in the water is too busy and perhaps too far away to pay attention. A bullfinch flies overhead, and a small boat lies against the bank a little way up the stream. The boat, the bullfinch, the trees, and perhaps the girl paddling belong to one reality, that of a landscape observed: the three central figures belong to another, that of an immediate contact, a strong Spanish realism reminiscent of Zurbarán. (Manet loved the Spaniards.) They are strangers in this clearing, far more so than Giorgione's idealized classical nymphs in their Trentine vale; and it was this contrast, this particular truthfulness of flesh, that caused the violent outcry when the picture was first exhibited.

It may also have been one of the reasons why Picasso chose it as his starting-point. Another is that almost any restatement of Manet's "Déjeuner" would require Picasso to paint a landscape with figures, to deal with an unenclosed space and with the relationships of his people within that space, something he had rarely done. Certainly he had painted dozens of landscapes in the last few years, and his beach-scenes are unenclosed space filled with people; but the uninhabited countryside seen from the window of his studios, even when it is as lively as his recent "Baie de Cannes," is a subject presented rather than chosen and might more properly be called a view, while his beach can be looked upon as a vast flat stage: in any case neither presents anything like the problems of a woodland setting with the light filtering through the trees and all the spatial autonomies which that implies. Then again here was the relation between the artist and his model once more, and Picasso had by no means exhausted all he had to say upon the subject. And lastly, although Picasso spoke disparagingly of the "Execution of Maximilian," he had a great admiration for Manet, particularly for his "Lola de Valence."

Picasso's first drawings, therefore, placed the figures more or less as Manet had set them, though in one Picasso already dismissed the younger brother. The next day he made five more sketches, three of the woman at the back and two, in color, of the whole composition; and from these it was quite evident that Picasso had not the least notion of following Manet's light, nor his color.

At this point he left Vauvenargues for Cannes, and he seemed to have abandoned Manet as well; but although he spent much of his time at La Californie on a splendid series of bull-fight drawings (nearly a hundred of them, in wash) and on linocuts, he also made a number of studies of a woman bending forwards, often washing her feet. At Vauvenargues she had appeared in the place of Manet's paddler, and now she was certainly connected with the "Déjeuners"; but her origin was far earlier. She was an important member of Picasso's personal and obscure mythology and many examples of her are to be seen: sometimes she is old, as in the drawing of May, 1944, sometimes young, as she is in these; sometimes naked, sometimes wearing a smock; but she is always leaning forward, generally with her breasts strangely high, and nearly always the open cleft of her sex is sharply defined.

In February, 1960, Picasso was back at Vauvenargues, and here he worked with an energy surprising even in him, committing to paint the ideas that had been maturing through the winter. In these compositional sketches, some of which are very large (51 × 76 inches), Eugène Manet comes and goes, so do the trees and the boat; but the paddler is always of great significance, almost as great as that of the man with the walking-stick, the mild but tenacious prophet who continually harangues his audience, now attentive, now indifferent. Then in March he began his first definitive variation, the most famous of the sequence, a big green picture, almost flat except for a blue hole in the middle where the atomized paddler wades at a certain distance: the brother has dwindled to a faint hint, but Victorine has become a fine pyramidal Picasso nude raised high upon the base of her massive thighs and terminating in a two-eyed profile turned towards the prophet, who talks on and on as they sit there under a dense, formally-patterned canopy of trees.

He broke off half-way through to start another study, far lighter, in which the brother returns with a mauve robe and a tobacco-pipe, and the nude is almost oval; the paddler still washes, however, and the sculptor still prophesies, his tireless didactic right hand raised high. Picasso set both of these aside until the end of July; but in the interval, which he spent at La Californie, he painted some variations on Manet's "Le Vieux Musicien," and as soon as he returned to Vauvenargues he finished the pictures. But that was by no means the end of his project, and very shortly after he made several drawings of a woman attending to her foot; she is one of the paddler's sisters, if not the paddler herself.

Now came the longest pause, while Picasso devoted himself to folded metal sculpture and other pursuits, and it was not until April, 1961, that more evidence appeared to prove how the "Déjeuners" had been evolving in his mind. Without any preliminary sketches he suddenly painted two clean, cheerful little pictures in which the characters form a loose wreath in the middle of the picture and the surrounding wood is reduced to a few signs for trees. The paddler stands in a bright blue pool; in one case the pink Victorine is as curved as a serpent, while Eugène is no more than a shadowy form, and in both the prophet, dressed in cherry or a darker red, talks away with the same calm persistence.

In early June Picasso made twenty-two drawings of a pair of nudes, most of them in his purest line: Douglas Cooper associates these closely with the "Déjeuners," and apart from several of the attitudes he also points to a curious straw hat, which certainly reappears in some of the later paintings. Picasso included this hat in one of his many drawings of a lovely young woman tying the ribbon of a Catalan sandal on her raised foot—drawings that he made just before he moved from La Californie to Notre-Dame-de-Vie—and on June 16, 1961, after the move, he repeated it, with adornments and the inscription "For Jacqueline, first drawing made at the Mas Notre Dame de Vie."

Meanwhile he had sent for everything he had done at Vauvenargues, and from now on, all through the summer of 1961, he worked steadily at his "Déjeuners," in spite of visitors, children, bull-fights, and intruders. First came two somber, night-lit pictures, in one of which the prophet has turned green and Victorine dull blue, then thirty drawings, some of all the characters, others of the women alone or in pairs, others of the paddler and the prophet together. On July 8 he made up his mind that the men too would be better without clothes, and another score or so of drawings followed his decision: at first the effect on the prophet was lamentable; he sits as bald and naked as a worm, deprived of his hat, which had grown even more hieratic, and sometimes even of his stick; but still he talks, his right hand in the air. Eugène does better, however: having been absent for some time he reappears, lying on his belly in the grass and reading a book while Victorine listens to the prophet and the paddler paddles, sometimes picking a flower.

As July wore on the figures became smaller; they moved farther apart and the trees grew enormously, so that now the "Déjeuner" was taking place in a deep forest clearing. But Picasso's mind had also been moving along another, surprisingly different path, and within a few days of the later drawings he painted a large green picture that quite contradicts their tendency: here the people might be in an underwater cave with green stalactites, opening on to blue; the prophet talks, Victorine listens, the brother lies on his stomach (an attitude he was rarely to abandon), and the paddler picks her flower; and they are all palely naked. The boat has come back, but on the left of the picture: its hull and the crossed oars catch the pallid light, and its presence, apart from altering and broadening the whole composition, has a strange portentous significance: one might say that Charon was just at hand but for the fact that the picture has no literature in it at all; it exists, splendidly and entirely, in terms of paint.

This was quickly followed by three other pictures, all smaller but of much the same general tone. In the first place Picasso suppressed the boat and strengthened the trees and the prophet; in the second, bluer, he brought the pool into the middle and set his people round it, the brother receding even farther than the paddler; and in the third, where Eugène is no longer to be seen, Victorine's head soars to the top of the canvas, bending a double profile not unlike Dora Maar's towards the shrunken prophet, while far from their green shade the paddler wades in a blue pool of her own, wholly divorced from the rest.

Then after a short pause in which he made several quick compositional sketches in crayon, Picasso plunged into a perfect debauch of painting. On July 27, dismissing Eugène, who appears in none of these pictures, he placed his three figures in their green cave again, the prophet now wearing a yellow robe with a green stripe. The tree-trunks or stalactite pillars are violently modeled, and this or the strong brush-strokes of the bearded prophet's dark hair and body or the striking play of the light gives the picture a particular oneiric tension. On July 30, without any warning, he abandoned his broad, horizontal canvas and with it all the earlier forms of composition; in the following pictures the figures are generally arranged in a pyramid, the paddler at the apex. In all of them (and there were two on the thirtieth, three on the thirty-first) the menacing, dream-like quality grows. They are all predominantly green, and in all of them the talker increases in intensity, so that he is no longer a prating bore but a major prophet; at one point indeed he is a terrible figure with a black head and what I take to be a brown, bearded mask—the colors of archaic Greece—a living magic idol very, very far removed from Manet.

In August Picasso returned to his horizontal pictures with two afterthoughts in which the nightmare tension falls: the second is dated August 19, and one might have supposed that it was the end of the series. But not at all. Three days later he burst out in a completely new direction: seven drawings transport the "Déjeuners" to the Golden Age, and they are a joy to see, for Picasso was the draughtsman of the world, and the first is as lovely as anything in his long career. The picnic (grapes and peaches now, and a jug of wine) and the paddler and the clearing are still there, but the trees are wide apart, there is no claustrophobia in the light-filled air, and the talker, wearing only a wreath of flowers, is a handsome youth who holds out his eternal hand not to predict any kind of woe but to say a poem to the exquisite long nude lying over against him while the brother, bearded, classical, sits listening with pleased attention, his chin on his hand. In the other drawings (which did not, alas, produce a picture) the talker changes, sometimes classically beautiful, sometimes older, snub-nosed and unshaved; but he always has his stick, and everybody, including the usually unconcerned paddler, listens to him with approval.

Seven more drawings followed on August 28. They are still idyllic, and here the brother, lying on his belly with his head held up, seems to have strayed from Antipolis; but now the talker has talked too much; the girl has gone to sleep, the paddler has returned to picking flowers, and the brother's smile is quite derisive. In the end the talker's hand sinks, never to rise again until the very end of the year, when Picasso made another set of drawings of the clothed, hatted, early prophet haranguing the nude, while occasionally the paddler appears far away, between them. And so the "Déjeuners," carrying on into 1962 in the form of brilliant linocuts, come to their end at last.

In following them through from beginning to end I have necessarily thrown my narrative out of line, and now I must bring it back to 1959, all the more so since I may have given the impression that this was all Picasso did. That would be absurdly incorrect: he also made a great many ceramics—pots and painted tiles—and he spent much of his time on sculpture. The period was rich in metal cut-outs, constructions, flat and folded forms, some of which were reproduced, perhaps unfortunately, on a gigantic scale in sand-blasted concrete. And as well as his great suite of bull-fight drawings he also painted still more pictures of Jacqueline and still more pigeon-filled views from the open windows of La Californie. Furthermore, apart from his still active social life, he had to undergo the turmoil and the trials of moving house once more.

As it will have been seen from the account of the "Déjeuners," he did not settle at Vauvenargues. The place was a disappointment to him. As his enthusiasm waned he often came back to Cannes, and it was here, rather than to the château, that Pallarès came for his regular summer visit.

His presence was good for Picasso: in the first place there was the pleasure of his company, and in the second Picasso could always be not only himself but his best and easiest self with Pallarès. The early prestige of the gifted Horta countryman who had helped Picasso "learn everything he knew" still held; the extra five or six years still counted; and Picasso would never presume to let himself go in front of Pallarès. Then again, while many of the members of Picasso's court looked indignantly upon the rest as intruders who devoured the master's time, hangers-on and parasites, so that there was often a wearisome current of animosity as well as a servile vying for favor that stimulated the tyrant in Picasso, Pallarès had not the least notion of competing. Nor had he the least notion of worshiping his old friend, young Pau, and he beheld their extreme complaisance, not to say their cringing, with a detached curiosity. The seniority of his friendship gave him a standing that no living man could rival, and he and Picasso exchanged their minds with the ease and freedom of sixty years before.

It was a respite, and one with a delightful flavor of nineteenth-century Catalonia; but it could not last, and soon Picasso was back in the present again, moving between La Californie, from whose doomed windows he painted the builders' cranes, and Vauvenargues, disagreeable to himself and oppressive to his wife. He was busy not only with his "Déjeuners" but also with almost every other form of plastic expression known to man, including linocuts. This was one of the few techniques he had not mastered long ago: his first posters are no earlier than 1948, and they can scarcely be called masterpieces, but now, having proved by his brilliant version of the younger Cranach's "Bust of a Woman" that neither the process nor the material necessarily produced the heavy, slab-sided things that are usually to be seen and that the current practice of cutting into a separate piece of linoleum for every color was nonsense, he went on to make a number of remarkable prints, some of the "Déjeuners" and oth-.ers having an obvious connection with his sequence.

The "Déjeuners" themselves might have proceeded at a brisker rate if he had been shut up in a lighthouse or even if he had been at Gósol: as it was there were countless interruptions, arising not only from those who broke through his defenses but also from his need for company, even second-rate company, and from the necessary business of his life. The general run of exhibitions could be left to Sabartés, who still attended daily at the rue des Grands-Augustins, coming down to Cannes or Vauvenargues from time to time although he was now far, far older than his friend; but the great retrospectives, such as that in New York in 1957, in London in 1960 or in Tokyo some years later, required Picasso's own attention. Arranging such a show with him was a harrrowing experience; he regarded letters as something to be received, read with intense curiosity, and then put silently away in some heap, rarely or never to be answered; cables had little more effect; and he was difficult to reach by telephone. Yet when the patient organizer did surmount all the barriers he usually found Picasso helpful, kind, prodigal of his time, and solicitous for the success of the exhibition. He did not paint in an ivory tower: communication was of great importance to him, and now with his fame reaching almost as far as his silly notoriety the potential range of communication was immense. Four hundred and fifty thousand people, for example, saw the London show at the Tate gallery, which included the Russian pictures.

He had a liking for London, but Barcelona was infinitely nearer to his heart, and in 1960 the city's incomparable Museo Picasso took shape. Some years before he had asked Sabartés what he meant to do with his collection: the words "after his death" were understood, but it is a moral certainty that they were never uttered. Sabartés said that he intended to found a Picasso museum and that in compliment to his friend's birthplace it was to be at Málaga. Picasso said, "Why not Barcelona? I have so few ties with Málaga," and Sabartés fell in with the idea directly. Since Picasso was a Communist, a Republican, a supporter of Catalan autonomy, and a most determined and public opponent of the regime, the negotiations took some time; but by 1960 they bore fruit, the city responding nobly with the offer of either of two fourteenth-century palaces. Picasso chose the Palacio Aguilar in the narrow, ancient Calle Montcada, familiar to his boyhood and only a few minutes from the Calle de la Merced: here Sabartés' gift was to be housed, together with everything Picasso had already given to the town, everything that the Barcelona museum of modern art had acquired, and many capital pictures given by friends and collectors.

Sabartés was a poor man all his life, and when one considers that by 1960 an early Picasso drawing was worth a great deal of money, while a portrait represented a fortune (that of Lola fetched £32,000 a little later), and when one considers that nearly all Picasso's friends sold his presents, although many of them had possibilities of making money that Sabartés did not possess, then the extent of his donation will give some measure of his magnanimity, and incidentally of Picasso's generosity to his friend. Sabartés presented the museum with no less than five hundred and seventy-four items, ranging from his portraits to unique canceled proofs of engravings, often inscribed in the most affectionate terms.

The project interested Picasso to the highest degree, but the final decision had not been taken in May, 1960, when Brassaï brought his wife to see him in Cannes; and although he spoke of the huge sand-blasted concrete panels that he had designed for the College of Architects in Barcelona and mentioned the possibility of the museum, he did not elaborate, perhaps to avert ill-luck, perhaps out of his deeply-rooted sense of secrecy. Otherwise he was as open as the day. Brassaï was one of the many friends who would not join the competing band of courtiers and he had not seen Picasso for thirteen years. He found him unchanged, as full of youthful vitality and physical alertness as ever; and during the afternoon they spent together there was a curious proof of this. Brassaï dropped his cigarette-holder and Picasso caught it before it touched the ground, with the same instant reaction that he had shown in 1944, when the unlucky Brassaï, photographing a group in the studio, plunged into Kazbek's water-bowl just as the shutter clicked: the developed film showed that of the whole group Picasso and the dog were the only ones to react in that split second.

Picasso was unchanged, welcoming, affectionate, and attentive; but he would not have been the same Picasso if he had not denounced his fate. And now it was no longer a matter of people wilfully moving his electric torch, attempting to steal his drawing-pins, hiding his valuable rubber, malignantly dusting his mounds: now it was with a far deeper conviction, indeed with real distress, that he could say, "I should not wish my fame on to anyone, not even my worst enemy . . . it makes me physically ill . . . I protect myself as well as I can . . . I am barricaded behind double-locked doors day and night." And Vauvenargues was even worse; people came in droves to stare; they peered at him through binoculars; he could never go out. As for Cannes, a huge block of flats was about to rise in the next-door garden: it would hide the sea and its inhabitants would look straight down on to him. And what was the good of money, once one had enough? Being rich did not mean that he could eat four luncheons or four dinners; and rich or poor he would never smoke anything but Gauloises, the only cigarettes he liked.

Nor would he have been the Picasso Brassaï knew if his mood had not suddenly changed. Learning that Madame Brassaï was partly Catalan, he observed, "One always belongs to one's own country" and spoke to her in that language. The poor lady could remember little apart from the word for black-pudding, but Picasso was not deterred: he whistled a *sardana*, raised his arms, and stepped the hieratic paces of the dance with a look of enchantment on his face.

Brassaï spoke of the first time he had ever seen it—the grave expressions of the dancers, the absence of laughter: he might have been at a religious service. "But the *sardana* is a very serious matter," said Picasso,

". . . a communion of hearts and minds. It does away with all class-distinctions. Rich or poor, young and old, all dance it together: the postman and the banker, and the servants hand in hand with their masters.''

Picasso was not exaggerating when he told Brassaï of the persecution at Vauvenargues: but it was not only the starers nor even Jacqueline's aversion that destroyed his pleasure in the place—there was some fatal incompatibility between the man and the house, an incompatibility expressed on his side more by uneasiness and ill-humor than by any direct admission. Often, when they were driving there, they would reach Aix or even the gateway of the château itself, and then he would abruptly give the order to turn about and drive right back to Cannes. After the spring of 1961 he never worked there, never stayed more than a night or two: henceforward it was only a store-house and a useful stopping-place when he went to the bull-fights at Arles or Nîmes.

It would surprise no one at all acquainted with his mind to learn that he never sold Vauvenargues: on the other hand, his closest friends were astonished when they heard that he was to be buried there, in the garden by the house, and to lie forever in a place he had come to hate.

He did not hate Cannes, far from it, although as Paulo told Brassaï he would have been much happier in the Roussillon, particularly at Collioure; and in his son's opinion it was indolence alone that kept him on the Côte d'Azur. Yet La Californie was no longer a lasting refuge, for the developers had carried out their threat, and the grim concrete was mounting just at hand.

Behind Cannes stands Mougins on its hill, and Vallauris is no great way off: all country that Picasso knew by heart. The winding inland road from Mougins to Vallauris first drops and then turns right-handed under a wooded ridge; and upon this ridge stands a chapel dedicated to Notre-Dame-de-Vie, some way out of Mougins but still belonging to it, a place of local pilgrimage. Not quite so high as the chapel Picasso found a house. It was screened by towering cypresses, it had a fair amount of land round it, and though it was not wholly secluded it could be made more so: he bought it out of hand in early 1961 and by the summer he was installed as thoroughly as ever he was likely to be installed anywhere. La Californie was not sold, of course, any more than Vauvenargues, and many of his possessions were left in both houses, while others, particularly crates of books, still trailed here and there in Paris.

The house was called the Mas Notre-Dame-de-Vie, and it belonged to a Guiness, just as La Californie had belonged to a Moët. In the south of France a *mas* can be anything with an agricultural flavor from a peasant's hovel to a pretentious villa with some olde worlde features, usually round tiles on the roof and olive-jars on the terrace. Picasso's appears to have begun about two hundred and fifty years before as a genuine *mas* of the more prosperous kind, a substantial, stone-built house with the great rounded arches of Provence: later generations and later owners added to the building, so that when Picasso moved in he already had plenty of room for painting and sculpture studios. Presently he built more, for the fever of work was still on him, as it had been with a few short breaks these last sixty years and more; and it was at Notre-Dame-de-Vie that he finished the "Déjeuners" in the winter of 1961/1962.

No house could have had a better name: the Notre Dame is less incongruous than it might appear, for although one does not usually associate Picasso and Our Lady, there is no doubt that he had a deep religious sense, however archaic and manichaean; at this very time, for example, when he and Parmelin were wondering what it was that set certain paintings quite apart from the ordinary run, he said, "Something *holy,* that's what it is. That's the kind of word you ought to be able to use, only people would get it wrong, give it a meaning it doesn't possess. You ought to be able to say that such and such a picture is what it is, with all its latent potentialities, because it has been touched by God. But people would take your words in another sense. Yet that's what comes nearest to the truth."

The second part of the name fitted far more obviously, for at eighty Picasso abounded with life. For most men living and for all under forty he had always been there and he had always been famous. He was in fact a historical monument. Yet it never occurred to anyone to say, "Picasso? Is he still alive?" As I have said before, he now had little immediate influence on the younger painters, for the liberation had been accomplished long ago and both he and they were living in a post-Picassian world; yet while the young followed the successors of his successors (often falling into the academicism of "modern" art with all its tricks), or, like the Americans, struck out on paths of their own, Picasso carried on with his lonely, prolific investigation of reality, or as he often said, of truth, still in a state of permanent, personal revolution. He was a presence of much greater value than any school.

La Rochefoucauld says that we enter each distinct age as novices, earlier experience being irrelevant to the new situation: that is probably the case with most people, but it was certainly not with Picasso, exceptional in this as in so many other respects. Although he resented the passage of time he seems to have had no difficulty about the various stages, perhaps because he remained entirely himself throughout, untroubled by the changing roles imposed by society. His hypochondria, always pronounced, may have grown a little, but apart from that the only sign of age at this period was a disinclination to see new faces; and even that may have been no more than the effect of experience, since almost all new faces wanted something, and he was deathly tired of solicitation. The fact that he very often spoke of old friends long dead, particularly of Apollinaire and Max Jacob, is neither here nor there, for although aged men do go back to the past it was in no sense a return for Picasso: his past friendships rarely left him, and both Max and Apollinaire were fresh and living in his mind.

The extreme secrecy of his marriage to Jacqueline, which took place on March 2, 1961, at the *mairie* of Vallauris* (it was a civil marriage only) and which was attended by almost no one apart from the necessary witnesses, Maître Antébi, a lawyer from Cannes, and his wife, might be taken as a consciousness of age, as though the marriage of a man in his eightieth year to a woman of thirty-five were slightly ridiculous; but the more probable explanation is that they feared persecution by journalists, the incessant click of cameras and the blinding flash, and the congratulations of Picasso's enormous acquaintance. His reasons for marrying again remained obscure to his friends: yet if his intention was to provide for Jacqueline after his death, then he did so handsomely. French law does not allow a man to dispose of his property as he chooses, and at that time a companion, even one with a *certificat de concubinage* (to be had for the asking at any *mairie*) had no rights at all, as the lady who shared Dufy's life found to her cost; but a wife necessarily inherits a large proportion of the estate, and although Picasso's prices were still nowhere near their height, in this same year "La Mort d'Arlequin" fetched eighty thousand pounds; and when in fact Picasso died the equivalent of several million fell to his widow.

More evidence on the side of youth is the fact that Picasso took to watching television (often confusing and even incomprehensible to those who allow themselves to age) and that since he disliked going out and being mobbed he also overcame his aversion to the telephone. He had white ones put into every bedroom in the house, as he proudly told Kahnweiler, and Paris was at the end of the line. So was the Roussillon, where his heart still lingered, and he often spoke to the Lazermes.

Before finishing the "Déjeuners" at Notre-Dame-de-Vie he had also painted scores and scores of other pictures, many of them based on Jacqueline's head and closely related to his cut-out sculpture, the planes

*Different authors give widely differing dates. This I have from the Mayor of Vallauris, who was also good enough to tell me that Olga Picasso was buried at Cannes and not, as Françoise Gilot asserts, in his town.

turning, the features taken apart and reassembled. Several of them also show Kaboul, his second Afghan hound; and here again, however much the woman may be distorted, the dog is left alone. And after he finished the "Déjeuners" the steady flow increased, sometimes reaching three or more canvases a day: it is remarkable how these Notre-Dame-de-Vie pictures differ from those of La Californie even when they deal with the almost obsessive theme of Jacqueline. The difference is more easily apprehended than described, but at least one can say that they are generally graver, more inward-looking; and of course the peculiarly Californian interior landscapes, with the curly windows wide open looking out on to the pigeons, palms, luminous sea and sky are no longer to be found.

Although he was much given to dosing himself, Picasso was wonderfully fit in his early eighties, so fit that on his eightieth birthday itself he not only stayed up at a kind of variety show in Nice until two in the morning, but attended a ceremony in his honor at Vallauris the next day, before watching Dominguín and Ortega kill their bulls in the arena. He saw quantities of friends, including many Catalans who came to talk about the museum in Barcelona; and although if the children were not there he often spent the blazing summer days in the shelter of Notre-Dame-de-Vie, with innumerable cicadas shrilling in his trees, the autumn would find him swimming placidly about the quieter bays. Illness and death were not far off: Sabartés had a stroke in 1961 and two years later both Braque and Cocteau died; but Sabartés recovered, and in the peace of Notre-Dame-de-Vie the deaths lost their immediacy. Then again Pallarès was strong and well, and Picasso was much younger than Pallarès: above all he was working as steadily as he had ever done, and in fact there were few periods when his production had been so great in volume.

In this great body of work, and Parmelin counted close on a hundred and sixty Jacquelines for 1963 alone, there were naturally some pictures that did not satisfy Picasso nor please those of his friends who admitted that he might fall short of perfection. Such people were rare; for nearly all the members of his court it was treason to suppose that anything Picasso produced was less than a masterpiece; yet it is noteworthy that two or three of his friends, and not the least beloved, were unmoved by his painting. Indeed there was Marie-Thérèse Walter, who was unmoved by any painting at all, yet that did not prevent Picasso from remaining constant to her, in his own way, until the advent of Jacqueline, when she was sacrificed to domestic peace.

Of those pictures that excelled the rest the various "Rapes of the Sabines" come first to mind. They had their immediate origin in the suggestion that the exhibitors at the coming Salon de Mai, that of 1963, should think of Delacroix' bloody "Entrée des croisés à Constantinople." (The Salon de Mai was and still is an annual show of the works of resistant artists and those they invite to join them: the organizers often propose some central theme.) Picasso began painting warriors' heads by the score, but presently he moved away from Delacroix and towards Poussin and David, the "Massacre of the Innocents" of the one and the "Sabine Women" of the other.

He began in October with a big, gray "Rape": classical buildings in the background, swirling combat in the middle, swords, horses, helmets, Sabines being carried away; and beneath the turmoil, crushed figures, a baby, a woman trampled by a horse. The next day he painted another gray picture of a girl knocked off her bicycle and a sandaled foot about to tread her down. After many other studies she appears again in November under the hoofs of a galloping horse, while a woman, reminiscent of "Guernica," shrieks from a window above. This girl with the bicycle, one of the rare examples of the specifically modern world in Picasso's later work, is not to be seen in the two best-known versions, the full "Rape" of November in which women are carried off by horsemen while a towering yellow warrior attacks the enemy with a huge butcher's knife, and the February, 1963, battle between a rider and a man on foot, both trampling a woman and her child. But she is there, lying in the foreground of a more detailed lithograph of the whole brutal conflict, and she adds an even greater poignancy to the littered mass of more anonymous victims, the babies, the slaughtered women, the severed limbs, particularly as her face is that of Marie-Thérèse, once so passionate a bicyclist.

Daix, who was then still a member of the Party and who watched the political conflict with the utmost attention, relates this series to the Cuban crisis, which, threatening atomic war, rose to its height in October, 1962: he may be right, but the Delacroix, the Poussin, and the David that Picasso had been considering, all of them connected with the arrogant, sterile, subhuman face of violence, were quite enough to bring his hatred of war and his compassion for its victims into play.

He worked exceedingly hard on his "Sabines," pushing himself to the limit during his long night sessions; and, as he told Hélène Parmelin, one of them, the two warriors fighting, "very nearly did him in." Yet he moved straight on from this sequence to another, perhaps less emotionally expensive but longer in the doing. Some weeks after he had begun it he wrote on the last page of a sketch-book, "Painting is stronger than I am. It makes me do what it wants."

What painting made Picasso do in the first half of 1963 was to embark upon a long discourse on the painter and his model. The forty or fifty resulting canvases are nothing like the *Verve* suite of nearly ten years before: here the painter may not be a particularly heroic figure, but he is neither old nor ridiculous; and it seems to me that the series is much less the result of strong present emotion than of prolonged and comparatively objective thought on the subject.

He is first seen sitting gravely at his easel, holding a palette and painting a rudimentary face: no model is visible, but on a chest-of-drawers stands a bust. Presently the model appears, a green woman, nude of course, in various attitudes on a couch. She changes color, place, and size, but she is an object throughout; she has taken off her individuality with her clothes, and the dialogue is not between the painter and her as a person, still less as an object of desire, but between the painter and the piece of reality that she represents: her volumes speak, not her mind nor yet her sex. Admittedly this is no more than an assumption, since one rarely sees what the painter is at: most of the time his canvas is sideways-on, and even when it is not, only vague shapes appear, generally at variance with what is visible in his studio.

He paints on and on with the same steady concentration, wholly given over to his task: his appearance alters somewhat; beards come and go, so does hair, and later in the series furious color suffuses his face; but he remains a thin dark figure of indeterminate age, slightly absurd at times but always respectable in his dogged, unyielding struggle. And throughout he is utterly alone. Picasso liked him, called him *le pauvre,* and watched him work with a compassionate eye.

Most of the time he paints in his somewhat cramped, conventional studio (he and the place and the model are clearly signs, not particular remarks) but he can also work out of doors, even by night on occasion, with his model in a deck-chair or under a tree; and wherever he is the colors that surround him say even more than his absorbed, attentive face and his poised hand about the process of creation. The colors speak in their own terms and there is little point in trying to transpose their language; but no one can fail to understand the progression from somber blue-gray to the excitement of green and vermillion (the painter's form becomes a fine, sharply-defined black at this point, and his hand more decisive), then to the blue and pink that suffuse the picture, then the general fading of the colors, followed by the sudden brilliance of the painter's face and hair. Picasso emphasized the significance of this last phase by momentarily abandoning his own painter for Rembrandt: he revered the Dutchman, often using him as a point of departure, and the picture he now had in mind was the Dresden self-portrait of the young Rembrandt with Saskia in his lap; for the purpose of his argument Picasso turned him into a splendid double-profiled painter working in a blaze of gold and red, while the blue-haired Saskia and her green bosom are shifted to other planes to conform with the local laws of space. Then he returned to his own painter: the colors darken, lighten again, break into a frenzied corruscation, and so through gradual transitions return to their primitive sobriety. But still he paints on, even though in the last pictures his face is a white blur or an ill-looking gray, bald and beardless: he never wins; he is never beaten.

Picasso was very fond of "Le Peintre et son modèle" (so were other people: the exhibition at the Leiris Gallery next year was a great success) and in the winter he engraved a large number of the pictures, often changing them in the direction of an even greater simplicity. He had spent a pleasant summer after the hard work of the first six months of 1963, relaxing in his usual way by turning out hundreds of pots and painted tiles as well as by swimming, sun-bathing, and watching all the bull-fights he could reach. He would take off for Nîmes, Arles, or Fréjus with his traditional caravan of friends and children, a caravan now headed by a massive white Lincoln Continental: and this monster was now driven not by Paulo but by an orthodox chauffeur. Some few of the bull-fights were uncommonly spectacular and Picasso's heightened sensibilities were not disappointed; and although he, like so many aficionados, suffered from something resembling the post coitum sadness after the moments of ecstatic mass-excitement, they left him eager for the next. A more enduring pleasure was the fact that the Barcelona museum opened at last this year, after the delay caused by the appalling floods that ravaged Catalonia in the autumn of 1962. It opened quietly, with no drums or trumpets, perhaps because of Picasso's Communism, perhaps for reasons connected with internal politics; but the existence of the museum, the friendly, appreciative attitude of the city, and the evident competence and good will of those in charge of the foundation gave him a profound satisfaction.

In spite of the bull-fights this summer was quieter than most. Jacqueline, as Madame Picasso, now had rights that she had not formerly possessed, and she protected him with greater effect than before, if not necessarily with greater discrimination; and although a house with growing children in it can scarcely be an abode of peace, Picasso did not mind the din: at least it did not stop him working, although at times it was very considerable. Claude and Paloma were at the noisiest age; so were Kathy Hutin and Isabelle Leymarie, the daughter of the poet and curator Jean Leymarie, her companion at school and for two years and more an inmate of Notre-Dame-de-Vie; so were Pablito and Marina, Paulo's children; and in the holidays they were often all there together.

With the turn of the year he took to painting large nudes in some degree related to those of his "Painter" and in some to Jacqueline. Then in February of 1964 a long-legged kitten, generally black, joined the nude, who grew far more like Madame Picasso and who played with the little creature much as the very different models of ten years before had played with their young cats.

A great number of bucolic heads followed the nudes, reminiscent in feeling though not in technique of those he had painted at Mougins just before the war. Then came more nudes, still-lives, Jacquelines, and some postscripts to the "Peintre et son modèle." It was a productive year, though with no great blazing masterpieces, and one has the impression of an agreeably busy turning-over of ideas long matured and restated, often in a highly-colored shorthand, for the pleasure of it, a somewhat private rumination. This impression is strengthened by the surprising autumnal series of what might be called secondary "Painters": a German publisher who had reproduced a Picasso of an artist close up to his easel, working away on a canvas whose back is towards the spectator, sent a whole parcel of the prints to Notre-Dame-de-Vie by way of compliment, and Picasso, very pleased, spread all the identical sheets about his studio. Then he took them one by one and painted over them so that as the days went by an astonishing number of variations appeared—the man's features changed and shifted, his hat and beard came and went, but in every version he still worked with the same fixed intensity, while the untouched areas of the prints, perpetually repeated, and the unvarying spatial relationships gave the strangest feeling of eternity.

Long ago Matisse had said that the disaster of May, 1940, would not have come about "if everyone did his job as Picasso and I do ours." Yet this total devotion had its dangers, and one was that in time the painter might overcome the man; that his art might become wholly concerned with itself, sinking or rising to an inward meditation so personal that communication would be lost, as it was lost for Frenhofer in *Le Chef-d'oeuvre inconnu.*

However, there was no want of communication in the Picasso who received his guests at Notre-Dame-de-Vie in the summer of 1964, nor of communicative merriment. Most were old, approved friends, although there were still a fair number of intruders and people who had to be received out of kindness to those who sent them; and one of the particularly tiring things about these new acquaintances was that as the introduction was a great occasion for them they expected Picasso to react with greatness—they expected the great man to utter great thoughts. They had seen concentrated Picasso in his pictures and they supposed that the same concentrated Picasso would sparkle out in words at any hour of the day: he was aware of their hopes—no man more sensitive to atmosphere—and having a wonderful gift for paradox and repartee he did his best to fulfill them. Occasionally sudden gloom would keep him mute, as it had done ever since the Quatre Gats, but far more often he succeeded: yet it is wearing to be Sir Oracle and to be listened to with bated breath, and perhaps it was because of this that he continued to wear false noses and comic hats, by way of jerking the interview on to another, less reverential plane.

Others came on business, among them emissaries from Paris, making the first approaches for the celebrations that were planned for his eighty-fifth birthday. Then there were the organizers of the exhibition in Tokyo and other cities; and they showed him how to write his name in Japanese. He was delighted, and he traced the characters over and over again.

Visitors were distracting, of course, but builders in the house were infinitely more so. This year he added another studio to Notre-Dame-de-Vie, bridging a terrace with a flat roof on to which he could climb: the place was growing crowded as the household increased—a secretary as well as the chauffeur—and as more and more pictures, more and more pots and possessions accumulated; and although he liked the craftsmen and loved seeing their yellow crane at work (he wanted to keep it, says Pierre Daix), their inevitable delays and the necessity for supervising them no doubt deprived the world of many a picture.

It is pleasant to think of Picasso in the tranquillity of a house free of them at last, working steadily with fresh space around him. It was a golden autumn in 1964, unusually beautiful even for the south of France, and although the threat of war, the final cataclysm, met one every time one opened a paper, Picasso seemed to be living in another world, sheltered behind his cypress-trees. There appeared to be no reason why this should not last forever; his small, trim form, brown and unaltered apart from a sprinkling of silver where any hair was left, had already defied the common laws of mortality so long that they did not seem to apply to him. Why should not this autumn stretch out to 1965, 1966, and beyond, indefinitely?

The reasons why it should not were in the first place Françoise Gilot and in the second real illness at last. For some considerable time there had been rumors that Françoise Gilot was going to bring out a book that would demolish Picasso: early in 1965 it appeared in French, German, and Spanish translations from the original English, and it was far worse than he had expected.

I have already said that I think it a nasty piece of work, nastier the more one reads it. This opinion was widely, though not universally, shared in France: *Le Monde*, the most influential and intelligent paper in the country, spoke of "a scandal-mongering production in which she recounts her private life, often quite without shame," and a large number of the most distinguished artists, including André Beaudin, Pierre Soulages, Léon Gischia, Hans Hartung, E. F. Fenelosa, Joan Miró, Raoul Rebeyrolle, Vieira da Silva, and Léopold Survage signed a public protest in which they impugned its accuracy as well as other aspects, while many painters refused ever to exhibit with her again.

Why she published it I cannot tell; but it does occur to me that at least some of the malignancy may be due to the sacking of La Galloise in 1955. It will be remembered that Picasso was obliged to leave the house early that year, since legally it belonged to Françoise Gilot: when she returned in August or September she found much of her property gone, including the paintings and drawings that Picasso had given her and that she evidently intended to keep, together with the house.

The effect of the book on Picasso was disastrous. In 1933 Fernande Olivier's had vexed him extremely; but *Picasso et ses amis* had been about a youth long since vanished. Gilot's book was about the mature and virtually unchanging Picasso, about Picasso in what amounted to the present: it distressed, wounded, and angered him as a gross betrayal that laid his privacy open to his enemies and as a caricature that exhibited him to the world as a ridiculous, an odious figure and even worse a bore. His friends, with understandable though perhaps excessive zeal, heightened his anger; messages of indignant sympathy poured in, some of them from people whose condolence was exquisitely painful. He began to take measures, none of them successful except in one small but particularly touching case, when he telephoned Madame de Lazerme and begged her not to read the book, which she never did. His lawyers instituted proceedings, but in the widely-publicized trial they were unable to persuade the judges to halt the distribution of the book or to order changes. The court decided against Picasso, apparently on the grounds that if Gilot chose to expose her private life, which was clearly a marketable commodity, she therefore acquired a right to expose Picasso's, which was not. The only result of the case was to increase the book's sale prodigiously and to strengthen Picasso's hatred for Françoise to such a degree that it extended to everyone favorable to her.

Most unhappily this included her children, Claude and Paloma. They had not spent the summer of 1964 with their father, possibly because of the builders, possibly because of some abortive attempt at a compromise about the threatened book, and now, apart from a single embarrassed interview, they never saw him again.

It appears that they knew nothing of their parents' disagreement; and it must be supposed that they either never read their mother's book or that they found nothing offensive in it. They often came to the outer gate of Notre-Dame-de-Vie, and they were always turned away except on one occasion when Picasso himself happened to open it and Paloma was allowed in. Eventually much the same applied to Maya (now Madame Widmayer and a mother herself) and to Paulo's children, Pablito and Marina. Much of my information comes from newspaper interviews given after Picasso's death, when an unbelievably squalid battle for the inheritance broke out: the statements are always emotional, sometimes inconsistent, and never wholly to be relied upon; but even allowing for all the exaggerations of one-sided testimony it does appear that their exclusion reached monstrous proportions, and that they attributed their misfortune not to any fault of their own but solely to undue influence exercised upon their father. Journalists quoted Emilienne, Paulo's wife, as saying, "Jacqueline created a vacuum around him," Marie-Thérèse, "When that person arrived, Picasso's whole life underwent a change," and Marina, "Every time I went up to the house, Jacqueline received me for a few minutes and told me that grandfather was too tired to see me."

Another explanation, quite apart from the book, is often put forward to account for Picasso's unfortunate relationship with his children and grandchildren: according to this, once they were no longer small their presence reminded him of his age and he wished them away. It is true that Picasso resented the insults of time more than most men, but it is hard to believe that so complex and so affectionate a spirit could be moved by so simple a spring.

Yet affectionate though he was, none but his most ardent worshipers could maintain that Picasso was as effective a parent as he was a painter. He brought up his eldest son to no calling and he kept him in a state of dependence until the boy was a middle-aged man; and as far as education and professions were concerned his other children and his grandchildren fared little better. And then he cast them off, leaving no provision for them after his death.

These facts have been brought forward again and again, as though they were in some way relevant to his painting: they form part of the detractors' common stock of ammunition. I am not concerned with making a case for or against Picasso; my aim is to see him whole, as far as ever I can; and to do so one must get the evidence as straight as possible.

In the first place, Picasso had little to do with the bringing up of his children. He lost the control of Paulo when the boy was about thirteen and of Claude and Paloma when they were six and four. And as far as Paulo was concerned, he does not appear to have had the least aptitude for learning at any time nor the least desire to take up any profession. Most people who knew him agree that he was an amiable young man, full of animal spirits and little else, not particularly interested in anything but motor-cycles, cars, and bull-fights, and that he was perfectly content to hang around, living on an allowance and having as much fun as possible with the riffraff of the Côte d'Azur. After a number of adventures he married, and at one time he tried running an hotel (the Unic-Hôtel in the rue de Rennes); but neither the marriage nor the hotel answered his expectations, and presently he returned to his life of waiting, while his children, Pablo, born in 1949 and known as Pablito, and Marina, stayed with their mother. Brassaï found him at Boisgeloup in 1961, "looking after" the abandoned house. It had been occupied during the war by the French and German armies, and although it was in a fairly desolate condition, Picasso retained it still. By French law Paulo should by now have inherited his mother's claim to a large share of Picasso's fortune, but Picasso still felt that in natural justice a man might do what he liked with money he had earned himself and it is said that Paulo's filial piety or his father's overwhelming personality induced him to accept a monthly sum until such time as he should inherit the combined estate. When that time did come he surprised those who had known him as a pleasant though weak and insignificant youth by suddenly displaying an extraordinary hardness towards his own children and all other possible claimants. (It is true that the stake was huge: the estimates vary from twenty to fifty million pounds.)

Then as for Claude and Paloma, Picasso had no hold over them whatsoever: they were *enfants adultérins,* love-children of the most unprivileged kind, since they were the fruit not of fornication, which for French law results in *enfants naturels,* but, Picasso still being married to Olga, of adultery; and according to the legal fiction then in force *enfants adultérins* could not be recognized—they were necessarily the children of an unknown father, and they belonged to their mother entirely. Nevertheless he did what he could, and some time after the parting with Françoise he won a certain legal status as their guardian, while later he obtained a decree that gave them the right to bear the name Ruiz-Picasso. (Not that this overcame the legal fiction: officially they were still the children of an unknown father.) He also asked the court to give him the guardianship of Pablito and Marina, with whose upbringing he was dissatisfied; and although in their case he was unsuccessful, on the face of it he does not look like an altogether careless parent, begetting children and then leaving them to sink or swim.

In the second place, where a relationship is unsatisfactory, it is unlikely that all the faults should be on one side. On the whole Picasso was not lucky with his women, nor with his children. What he expected of the little creatures he drew and painted with such affection there is no telling, but surely it was something more than the rather common, uninteresting, and indeed unamiable young people most of them became. Admittedly they would have had to be exceptionable beings to overcome the disadvantages of having a sacred monster as a father, to withstand the unhealthy influence of his court (the flattery and the deference overflowed on to them), the notoriety in which they shared, and the prospect of enormous unearned wealth; but in spite of all the examples to the contrary it was still natural for Picasso to hope that they *would* turn out exceptional beings, as indeed they had been as babies, like everybody else.

But they did not. Paulo was a disappointment to him throughout, and the later conduct of the rest, who eventually sued their father to compel him to recognize them—an action that would give them a legal right to share in his estate—justified him in supposing that their eyes were fixed less on his heart than his pocket. As Marie-Thérèse observed, he loved to give but he hated to be asked; and asking could hardly have taken a stronger form.

By the time he was eighty Picasso had been preyed upon by several generations of parasites, and disillusionment may have gone too far, so that he discounted the affection that might exist side by side with cupidity and saw nothing but interested motives. At all events, when this general disappointment and suspicion is added to his anger at Gilot's book and perhaps to a certain amount of domestic influence as well, there are quite enough factors to account for the unhappy situation of 1965 without invoking any criminal indifference on the part of Picasso. Parents are supposed to love their children: yet surely there is the implied condition that the children should be reasonably lovable?

An unhappy situation it was, although in the early stages few people could have read the unhappiness in Picasso's journal, his daily production of drawings and pictures, unless it was in the reappearance of a thin and devilish cat approaching a lobster. But both the lobster and his companion the crab have claws; they defend themselves, and the cat is kept at arm's length.

This is mere interpretation, however, and probably mistaken: most of the other pictures are apparently as cheerful as can be—more heads, more painters, a particularly charming "Homme à l'enfant" (the Notre-Dame-de-Vie gardener and his egg-faced baby wrapped and swaddled as though in an outer egg), Jacquelines, some still-lives, including a fine blue lobster on a flat basket, landscapes from his new studio, a pair of nudes, one holding a looking-glass to the other, echoing a theme dear to him in the thirties, a guitarist who looks back to a still remoter past. And nearly all these are painted in a manner that flows naturally from the pictures of La Californie but that is nevertheless quite distinct: fierce color, strong, hard, almost brutal line slashed on to the canvas so that one sometimes has the feeling that the picture is little more than a sketch (a slapdash sketch, say his detractors) more important as part of a larger work as yet unexpressed and perhaps never to be expressed than for itself. This is particularly so in the many bucolic heads, twelve of which he fitted together and sent to the Salon de Mai under the title of "Douze toiles en une, une toile en douze."

But that was in the early part of the year. Soon the legal proceedings about the book, the eager intervention and contradictory advice of his friends, and the unfortunate decision to carry the case to appeal dragged him so far into the ordinary world that for months on end he could scarcely get back into his own, even when he was in the shelter of his studio. Then his body let him down at last. He had cared for it with an abstemious diet all his life, pills, days in bed, and catskin comforters; and, which was perhaps more to the point, he had always followed the advice of a physician who recommended "plenty of sex and red wine"; but still it let him down.

After he had been out of form for some time, he was found to be seriously ill with prostate trouble among other things, and in November he went to Paris, to the American Hospital at Neuilly. The grim operation was successful; the scars healed; there were no complications; and in a surprisingly short while he was back at Notre-Dame-de-Vie.

There he was visited by his Catalan friends the Gilis, and they, as well as the few others who were allowed through the increasingly severe defenses, found him as lively and gay as though the surgeon had removed old age together with all the rest. But the appearance of instant recovery was fallacious. Picasso had been weakened by the long, slow infection and by months of worry, exasperation, and blazing anger; and tough as he was, his body had received a terrible shock.

All through 1966 he did not paint a single picture: this had never happened to him before, even at the height of the crisis in Olga's day. He did draw, and he did etch the splendid plates for *El entierro del Conde de Orgaz*, which Gili published in 1969, but he could not paint. His eyes had given him trouble even in his youth; now they were worse; and now his hearing began to fail. There was no comfort from his family, either, for although he was on speaking terms with Paulo, the other children were firmly on the other side of the electrified fence that now surrounded his retreat.

He had all the convalescent's irritability, and it was exacerbated by the continuing publicity about Gilot's book, the extracts in the local papers and in many magazines: he had never been a good invalid, and now it called for an almost superhuman degree of devotion in those who looked after him. Early in 1966 the Soviet government awarded him the Lenin Peace Prize, and it is said that when the Russian representative (the ambassador himself, according to some accounts) came to hang it round his neck, Picasso was in such an evil mood that he would not even let him through the gate. Eventually he did receive the decoration, but from the hands of his old friend Ilya Ehrenburg, for many years *Izvestia*'s correspondent in Paris, a haunter of Montparnasse and the owner of the finest private collection of degenerate art in Moscow; and the photograph taken on that occasion shows him looking perfectly delighted. Whether the tale of the Russian ambassador is true or not, it is quite certain that a want of tact on the part of the officials concerned very nearly upset all the French government's plans for celebrating Picasso's eighty-fifth birthday, and it was only at the cost of a lavish expenditure of soothing spirit that Jean Leymarie, Isabelle's father and the curator of the Musée national d'Art moderne, whom Picasso respected as a poet and loved as a friend, managed to persuade him to withdraw his opposition. Once he had decided to cooperate, however, he did so with all his heart, opening his store of pictures, sculpture, drawings, engravings, and ceramics wide.

When the nineteen-year-old Picasso first came to Paris at the turn of the century the Exposition universelle was in full swing: a great many buildings had been put up, and of these the most important were the Grand Palais and the Petit Palais. These only had been preserved, and now, in homage to Picasso, they were filled with his works. The Grand Palais held two hundred and eighty-four pictures, including all the greatest except for "Guernica"; and since the Russians too were happy to honor their comrade, the exhibition provided one of the finest general views of Picasso's achievement in painting ever to be assembled. The Petit Palais showed two hundred and five drawings, ranging from the accomplished studies he made at La Coruña to some heads as recent as July, 1966, as well as five hundred and eight ceramics and three hundred and ninety-two pieces of sculpture, by far the most complete collection ever brought together and one that called for a total reassessment of Picasso as a sculptor. It was the most splendid exhibition that had ever been organized in the honor of a single artist, living or dead: and that was not all. The Bibliothèque nationale showed room after room of his illustrations, etchings, engravings, lithographs, and linocuts, and every commercial gallery that could possibly find the means of doing so put on its own Picasso exhibition.

The great retrospective lasted until February, 1967. The criticism ran from downright abuse to ecstatic praise, showing every shade of feeling except indifference: and the unprecedented number of eight hundred and fifty thousand people went to see the show.

Picasso was not among them. He stayed at Notre-Dame-de-Vie: and one day he telephoned Madame de Lazerme, as he often did when he was feeling lonely for his own people; but this time it was to tell her that he would not call again; he was growing deaf, he said, and he could no longer make out her voice.

Chapter XXII

THE year 1967 showed the old eager life returning: as early as February a painter-musketeer appeared, sitting at his easel in a seventeenth-century chair, his sword at his side, painting with a long delicate brush; and this time one can see what he is painting—a nude with a tiny head and a massive bosom, drawn in sure, sweeping curves. He is still only in pencil, but in March he takes on color in a fair-sized painting from which he gazes out at the spectator, more Porthos than d'Artagnan but no doubt a good companion in an equally assertive band. Picasso certainly liked him, and presently musketeers came in arrogant troops to inhabit his studio: they came in the first place from Rembrandt, as Jacqueline told Malraux, and indeed quite an early musketeer is entitled "Personnage rembranesque"; but during their journey they underwent a metamorphosis as complete as Manet's sculptor. Picasso's musketeers are formidable, swashbuckling creatures, armed with swords, guns, fierce tobacco-pipes, Louis XIII beards and mustaches, and with flaming color; derisive, violent men; for although Picasso loathed war his attitude to violence was at least ambivalent—his own life and his own painting were filled with it, and as for derision, he would not have been Picasso without a fund that nothing could exhaust, derision for every generally-received idea, for the establishment and art of course, but also for himself.

Yet he also remained faithful to his very old friends the circus-people. He had drawn them again and again during his convalescent year and now they joined the musketeers, no longer the sad, lean, blue forms of long ago, occasionally lit with a tragic patch of red, but sharing in the brilliant, aggressive color that came flooding into Picasso's later work to reach its height in 1969 and 1970. And at the same time he painted more of his bucolic characters as well as a monumental nude or so: but still this was not a rich year for painting. His mind was turning more in the direction of the engraved plate, which, in spite of all his immense experience, still had possibilities as yet unexplored. For some years now he had had two perfect collaborators just at hand, the brothers Crommelynck, whose press at Mougins itself allowed him to pass through the various states of an engraving at great speed; and when Cinto Reventós and Antoni Tapiés came to see him this year he talked mostly about the experiments he planned to make. Tapiés was one of the younger Catalan painters whom Picasso particularly valued: they had met through Dr. Reventós in the fifties, and at the time of the terrible floods in Catalonia in 1962 he and Picasso made remarkable contributions to the fund for relief—Picasso's share was said to be in the nature of four million pesetas.

The etchings that Picasso had in mind might have started earlier in 1968 but for the fact that Sabartés died on February 13. Picasso felt the blow very keenly indeed, and his sense of loss can to some degree be gauged by the prodigious extent of his gifts to the Barcelona museum, which he saw as Sabartés' creation, perhaps as a continuation of his being. He sent the blue portrait of his friend that he had painted in 1901, together with the entire sequence of the "Meninas," his most successful "Jacqueline," nine big sunlit pictures of the view from his window at La Californie, filled with doves, and some smaller landscapes. Then later, when the museum had made room for them by acquiring the next-door palace, he added the vast store of juvenilia and early work that his family had been keeping for him ever since he settled permanently in France, a hoard that amounted to about a thousand items, ranging from his decorated schoolbooks through his vast academic prize-pieces to paintings of the Blue Period, as well as some from his later visits. And from the end of Sabartés' life to the end of his own he sent the museum a copy of every one of his engravings, always with a dedication not to the memory of his friend but to the living Sabartés.

Picasso went back to work in the spring, and among the first prints the museum received in this new donation was the astonishing series of three hundred and forty-seven etchings that he carried out between March 16 and October 5, working with such concentrated energy that the turmoil of May, 1968, seems to have left him unmoved: at least it never checked the continual flow.

Much of Picasso's drawing in 1966 and 1967 had looked back to the circus, to Pierrot and Harlequin, and even farther back, to his family; and this carried on into many of these etchings. Others belong to his contemporary world, particularly those of the musketeers, who sometimes join the characters of long ago and who often assume a most Spanish air. And a great number of both, reminiscent or modern or in every combination of the two, are erotic, so much so that about twenty are rarely reproduced, being thought unsuitable for the general public. They have been called pornographic, and since some "describe the life, manners, etc. of prostitutes and their patrons" while others "express or suggest unchaste subjects" I suppose they are; but with some strange dark exceptions that I speak of later it is a gay, witty pornography as well as a most dazzling display of his command of the medium, to say nothing of his ebullient life.

Scarcely had he laid his etching tools aside before he seized his brush and returned to color; and if he had been sparing of it in his younger days, if from a sense of discipline he had approached his problems primarily in terms of line, he now made up for his restraint, indulging himself to the utmost possible degree. Picasso had always been an extraordinary man, but perhaps never so extraordinary as he was in these last years, when he blazed out in furious blue and green and above all in Spanish red and yellow, with black playing a most important part. And the color was a direct expression of the vitality within. In thirteen months alone, those running from January 5, 1969, to February 2, 1970, he painted a hundred and sixty-five pictures, many about six foot by four and few much smaller, as well as making scores of drawings. All these were shown in Avignon in 1970, but I did not see them properly at that time and I will postpone what I have to say for a few pages.

As far as numbers go, 1969 and 1970 were among the most productive years of Picasso's life as a painter; yet still he had time and energy enough to make some pots as well, to grow keenly interested in tapestry (the Gobelins factory was weaving a huge version of his collage "Femmes à leur toilette"), to see the bull-fights, and to receive a fair number of friends, including Josette Gris, the widow of Juan. There were also several Catalans of course, and one of them, a lawyer, had the unenviable task of inducing him to sign a document that would give Barcelona the full ownership of his vast donation. Picasso had always loathed even the simplest legal formality, and this was not simple at all, since he had to look at photographs of every single work before he signed them away forever. All the united forensic eloquence of Barcelona would never have brought him to it in any other circumstances, but the prolongation of Sabartés in time and in the city's esteem was another matter: running steadily through the sheaves of photographs he said, "These are not my works: this is my life itself," and then set his signature to the deed.

These were years of giving for Picasso. In 1969 he had brought himself as near to making a will as ever he could bear: this testament referred not to money or real estate but to something of much greater importance to Picasso, to "Guernica" itself. He had been importuned by General Franco's government, working through Kahnweiler and other connections, to let the picture come to Spain, where the recently completed Madrid Museum of Modern Art had a room specially designed to receive it. All sorts of honors, such as being hung in the Prado with Velásquez, were proposed; but Picasso would have nothing to do with them. He called for his lawyer and they drew up a document in which Picasso laid it down that "Guernica" and the preliminary studies should go to Spain, but only when the Republican liberties were restored; and in the event of his death (the word actually used was I believe "disappearance") then his family and Maître Dumas, the lawyer, were to decide when this condition was fulfilled.

Then when Arles gave him the freedom of the city, and he gave Arles more than fifty drawings; and when representatives of the New York Museum of Modern Art came to Mougins in 1971 Picasso sent them away with the present of one of his few surviving and highly treasured Cubist constructions, the "Guitar" of 1911; and there were many private donations.

The year 1971 was also that of his ninetieth birthday. Paris celebrated it not with the massive splendor of 1966 but with the crowning homage of an honor never yet paid to any living artist. The great gallery of the Louvre itself was rehung, and some of the most illustrious names in the history of art having been moved aside, eight magnificent Picassos took their place. It was a most delicate, triumphal stroke, worthy of the nation and the man.

But Picasso was not there to see it. He sent Paulo to represent him at the opening by the President of the Republic, while he stayed at Notre-Dame-de-Vie, painting still. Some photographs were taken of him on the day itself, and they show him looking much as he had looked for the last twenty years and more, his huge dark eyes gleaming with intelligence and life, not at all an ancient man: a perfectly human being. Yet in some way the ceremony of the Louvre resembled the shadow of death: no man had entered there alive: it was the painter's true apotheosis. For no one can become a god without first dying—"Die, Diagoras," said a Spartan to the Olympic victor, "thou hast nothing short of divinity to desire."

And although I knew from common report that he was busily at work in his retreat, still painting in the powerful color of these later years, he seemed to me to be living now in a world removed, somewhere between this and the next: an impression made the stronger by his much increased

473]

seclusion and by the reverential tone with which these last exhibitions and above all the homage of the Louvre had been received.

It was not until late in 1972 that I could get to Avignon to see his recent pictures in the Palace of the Popes. My excitement at the prospect of seeing an unknown aspect of Picasso's work was mingled with anxiety, because as I have said I was there for the first exhibition, the showing of all he did in 1969 and the first few weeks of 1970. In 1970 the hundred and sixty-seven paintings were hung in the great chapel of Clement VI, the hall of the notaries, and that of the chamberlain, but filming of some kind was going on when I arrived and it was not until much later that I was able to form any reasonable idea of them: those that I could make out through the intervening screens, cameras, technicians, and the attendant crowd bore all the marks of furious haste, coarse slashing brushstrokes, the paint flung on to the canvas or in some cases on to the bare brown paper and running down in streaks, a deliberate denial of all technique. There were some huge heads, sometimes coupled in a violent kiss and always crammed into their limits, always too large, too near for comfort, an enormously emphatic gesture right in front of one's nose. They made me feel uneasy for the painter, for although it was absurd to look for the serenity of Matisse in Picasso or his particular aged wisdom, this half-seen striving had a nightmarish quality.

"Do not go gentle into that good night,/Old age should burn and rave at close of day," says Dylan Thomas, and it seemed to me that this was just what Picasso might be doing. It would have been in accordance with his extreme character that in his old age he should defy and smash everything in reach; yet such an attitude, however natural and even awe-inspiring, could not be reconciled with any kind of happiness. But, as I say, at that time my view of the pictures was little more than a fleeting glimpse.

It was disappointing, but I was consoled by the knowledge that I should find the sacristy unencumbered: it was here that the drawings were shown, and like most people who have seen a great deal of Picasso's work I had the highest possible respect and admiration for him as a draughtsman, sharing the common opinion that he was one of the greatest the world had ever seen, certainly the greatest of this century.

Row after row they stretched away, cold black and white for the most part, colder than the stone walls of the sacristy, a continual reiteration of themes stated long ago—the whore and the ancient procuress, the goatish elder, the lewd girl sprawling with her legs wide open, many variations on loveless sex. Even in earlier years there had been a harshness in the brothel scenes of whores and bullfighters, though far more often desire was expressed with pagan gaiety and even tenderness: but now the icy brothel squalor invaded everything, and everywhere there was a continual nagging insistence upon women's hairy genitalia and even more upon their anuses. Many of the same subjects had appeared in the 1968 etchings, a series into which he introduced his father on occasion, sometimes as a voyeur, sometimes as a more active participant; but then the insistence was far less marked, the scenes less exclusively ruttish; the vitality of the drawing raised the prints to another plane entirely; and if they were bawdy, they were also cheerful. Now it seemed to me that wit and invention had flagged, though not alas the artist's perseverence: the incessant fingering depressed me; the copulation appeared joyless and brutal. Everyone knows that desire often outlives ability, but it was sad to see the fact exemplified at such length, above all in a place that retained so much of its austere reserve. The superlative technique was still there—never a tremor in the sure, perfect line—yet the formal beauty that I could not but acknowledge did nothing to lift my depression: the drawings struck me as frigid, sterile, and obsessive. I reflected upon the mutilating effect of the surgeon's knife and of physical old age on a man whose virility was so important a part of his essence: could it geld *his* spirit—such a spirit? Must it necessarily reach the core?

Writing about this same exhibition Rafael Alberti spoke of the embracing couples with rapture, and one paragraph ends "Antique kisses. Bald kisses. Ancient kisses with the spittle and slaver of centuries," while a little later he said, "to paint or draw love as it is done today by the Graeco-Latin-Malagueño Pablo Picasso is absolutely the contrary of pornography. It is health." Alberti is a noble poet, a sweet Spanish swan, and I should like to share his enthusiasm; but surely a brothel, for all its archaic charms, is hardly the place where one expects to find health, physical or metaphysical, to say nothing of love?

And one of his poems about Picasso begins (in the translation of Anthony Kerrigan),

> For you every day begins
> like a powerful erection, an ardent
> lance pointing against the rising sun.
> Priapus is still the one who swells
> the invention of your grace and your monsters.

Priapus is a potent god, there is no kind of doubt: but just what does a maimed Priapus swell? It occurred to me that Alberti might have let his friendship run away with his judgment: but on the other hand was my notion of normal sexual behavior necessarily right? In supposing that amorous busyness in the ancient was grotesque and that vicarious satisfaction was repellent, was I not merely accepting the conventional role that society allots to the aged—the role of the half-dead sage whose sun has gone out and who is to live, resigned, free from all desire, in the pale moonlight of accumulated wisdom? Did I dislike the drawings because they offended my possibly false idea of what was becoming in the old? I could not tell; but in any case I left the sacristy disturbed and sad, and I did not return to Avignon until 1972. And even then, as I stood looking up at the fortified palace, I hesitated for a while.

During the last few years the friends we had in common had heard little of Picasso, and that little was not good. Almost every contact appeared to have been broken: even Kahnweiler might be turned away from Notre-Dame-de-Vie; and when, in an attempt at seeing his grandfather, Pablito climbed the defenses, guard-dogs—creatures very different from the Lump and Yan of former days—were let loose upon him: the police took the young man away. And when the papers spoke of Picasso, which they usually did to give the news of some enormous price paid for his works (£98,000 for "Ma Jolie et bouteille de Bass," $430,000 for a "Paysage de Gósol") they referred to him as the hermit of Mougins. There were ugly rumors of sequestration, and indeed it is probably easier to confine a very famous, very wealthy, very closely guarded man than a common mortal. Some maintained that the group financially interested in Picasso's production cut him off from his friends and kept him at work, encouraging him to produce, produce and produce, even if it meant spreading his invention thin: quantity alone was what mattered, since any canvas daubed with paint and signed Picasso was worth a purse of gold. This rumor was repeated by those who could not speak too much evil of Jacqueline: certainly she had a great deal of power—the fulsome official praise made that clear enough—but the accusations did not take into account the fact that some old friends or their children were admitted. Ana Reventós, for example, the daughter of the second Dr. Cinto and the great niece of Ramon Reventós, came to see him in 1971 about a charitable foundation in memory of the first Dr. Cinto Reventós (a foundation to which Picasso gave the magnificent Blue Period "Femme morte à l'hôpital"), while Maurizio Torra-Balari was at Notre-Dame-de-Vie just before Picasso's death, and Sir Roland and Lady Penrose in 1970, not to mention several others. Kinder acquaintances said that she sacrificed her whole life to looking after Picasso, and that if she had a fault it was in taking him too literally when he fulminated against his friends for eating up his time—that perhaps she went far beyond his real wishes in isolating him to the extent that he seemed to demand.

I did not really believe the stories of sequestration, but belief is an odd cat and although it is rejected some smell remains—a depressing smell. Yet I was far more concerned with another, less melodramatic but even uglier possibility. Picasso was of course a mass of contradictions and there had always been some sides of his character that guaranteed unhappiness quite apart from that arising from his built-in melancholy and his status as a wholly exceptional man—an outsider: he could be overbearing, selfish, tyrannical, self-indulgent, and on occasion brutally hard. He was now surrounded by a small circle of his inferiors and dependents; no one could keep him in order, as once Eluard had done; those he respected most were long since dead, and he could let himself go just as he pleased. He was, as he said himself, a man "who could say shit to anyone on earth." He was enormously rich; and riches expose a man to pride and luxury, and a foolish elation of heart. As for pride, Lucifer could never have held a candle to Picasso at any time, riches or not; but it did occur to me that in his case luxury might, after so many years of discipline, emerge as facility, and the foolish elation of heart as a persuasion that anything he did was worth showing—that his briefest jotting down of a passing thought, in his private shorthand, was a valid communication of real importance. In short, that the rot of self-indulgence might have spread to his art. If that was so then neither his way of life nor even his work could be a satisfaction to him. If servile adulation, intensive coddling, guarding, shielding from every draught, had so reinforced the deep contradictions in his own character that they had turned him bad then obviously there was no question of happiness. It seemed unlikely that that fine head, with habitual kindness, gaiety, and strength carved deep into all its lines and wrinkles could go bad; but it was not impossible—there are innumerable instances of disastrous change pitiably late in life—and the prospect grieved me.

It was not a matter of his reputation: in its main lines that was fixed and nothing he might do now could destroy the past. What filled my mind was the idea that his last years were unhappy, for if in addition to sexual wretchedness he had also to bear a low opinion of himself (for it was impossible to believe that his critical faculty had died, however it might be overlaid by indulgence) then his end would be miserable indeed. That was something I found hard to contemplate: although I was by no means an unconditional admirer of Picasso—it seemed to me that less than fifteen thousand canvases could have contained even his genius as a painter—he had given me more than any other single creative man; and slight though our acquaintance was it had produced real affection on my side, an affection strengthened by most of what I heard in later years from the many friends we shared.

So now, in the autumn of 1972, it was with mixed feelings that I walked out of the sunlit square and into the Gothic darkness, along the cold stone passages and so to the vast chapel. There I met the sun again, a fierce, gay, truculent, many-colored sun coming not from the pale windows but from the crowd of pictures blazing on the walls. Arrogant musketeers with swords and broad-brimmed hats; formidable piratical characters with huge eyes at different levels; old friends such as Harlequin on a stage with half-drawn red curtains, almost overwhelmed by the furious activity of a nude racing across the scene, trailing a cupid in the air behind her; hundreds of women; and most of these people crowded into small squarish canvases so that their abounding vitality overflowed on to the next. Hundreds of pictures, brilliant color everywhere, and springing life. In a way it was not unlike standing in the transept of Chartres cathedral: yet there was an essential difference, for here there was nothing in the least anonymous—it was an intensely personal confrontation, and the immense personality that filled the whole space was that of Picasso, a Picasso sparkling with fresh invention; and invention, as Vauvenargues observes, is the sole proof of genius.

There were some magnificent single pictures that remain in my mind, particularly those isolated at the east end, but my general impression was that of a host whose members, though individually distinct and even at apparent variance, tended to merge into five or six main groups; and it came to me that this was how late Picasso should be seen, that although each picture was an entity in its own right it was also part of a whole and that the full statement of say two months' work was to be apprehended only when these relationships could be seen. It was not a question of variations on a single theme but of something far more subtle, an extension of painting in time and space, allied to what he had done in the days of Cubism and to some extent in the Meninas and the other suites, though there he was obviously more bound to a given text, whereas here he was tied to no one but Picasso, as free as the wind.

Free as the wind and happy: no one but a happy man could have painted those pictures, and no amount of verbal assurance could have been half so convincing. Certainly there were shadows—the drawings were proof of that—but Picasso was not made for total happiness and in any case they did not affect the heart of the matter: though grave enough for any ordinary man, here the shadows were comparatively insignificant. Picasso was not an ordinary man: his more than ordinary suffering and rebellion was counterbalanced, and I believe more than counterbalanced, by extraordinary satisfactions. His life outside his studio may not have been all that his friends could have wished for him, but most of his waking life, most even in the common measurement of time and far more if intensity is to be taken into account, was spent at his easel, alone in the far purer world of his own creation.

It was only hours after I had left the exhibition that with a start of added pleasure I realized that never once during the whole time I spent there had I remembered that this was the work of a man very old in years. It had never occurred to me to say that this was a wonderful performance for Picasso at ninety, nor to make the least allowance; and I was delighted to learn that his fiery spirit was already deep in the arrangements for still another show in the same surroundings and that he was painting the pictures for it.

A few months later, on April 8, 1973, he died, died suddenly with his mind full of plans for the coming year, which might have seen a full working-out of his latest concept.

In the winter he had caught influenza, a bad attack from which he slowly recovered but which left him weak and run down. Nevertheless he was working again in the early spring, getting up at about noon and sometimes staying on in his studio until six the next morning, and on April 7 he invited friends to dinner. But when he went to bed that night he had a feeling of breathlessness, and the local doctor detected a bad infection of his lungs and the strong likelihood of very serious heart-trouble. The next day an eminent cardiologist—a friend of Picasso's—was called in, flying down from Paris by the early morning plane. He saw at once that there was no hope, but he did what he could to make his patient comfortable. Picasso was fascinated by his instruments, full of the liveliest curiosity; he had got up and shaved—he wanted to show the specialist some of the pictures in his studio—but presently shortness of breath made him lie down again: he had not the least notion that he was dying. At times he drifted off, talking quietly to himself, and the doctor often heard him speak of Apollinaire. He sank gradually through the morning, but with no pain; and in a lucid moment towards the very end he spoke quite clearly to the specialist, a bachelor, saying, as he reached out his hand to Jacqueline, "You are wrong not to marry. It's useful."

Then a little before noon his heart failed at last and he died, there in his own bed, amid a jumble of his pictures and possessions, and surrounded by his household.

After a pause of several days, during which his son Paulo arrived, they buried him very privately in the garden at Vauvenargues, traveling through untimely snow to reach that remote and isolated house: he left the world with the ancient words of the Church said over him, for a priest attended his coffin, together with some local Communist councilors (but scarcely a single other friend), and between them they lowered Picasso into his solitary grave, a man almost as lonely as the sun, but one who glowed with much the same fierce burning life.

Appendixes

José Ruiz y de Fuentes
settled in Málaga circa 1790

m

Diego Ruiz
y de Almoguera
b. 1799 d. 1876

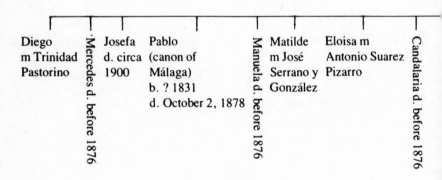

Diego
m Trinidad
Pastorino

Mercedes d. before 1876

Josefa
d. circa
1900

Pablo
(canon of
Málaga)
b. ? 1831
d. October 2, 1878

Manuela d. before 1876

Matilde
m José
Serrano y
González

Eloisa m
Antonio Suarez
Pizarro

Candalaria d. before 1876

Pablo
b. October 25, 1881
d. April 8, 1973
m (1) Olga Koklova (1918)
(2) Jacqueline Roque (1961)

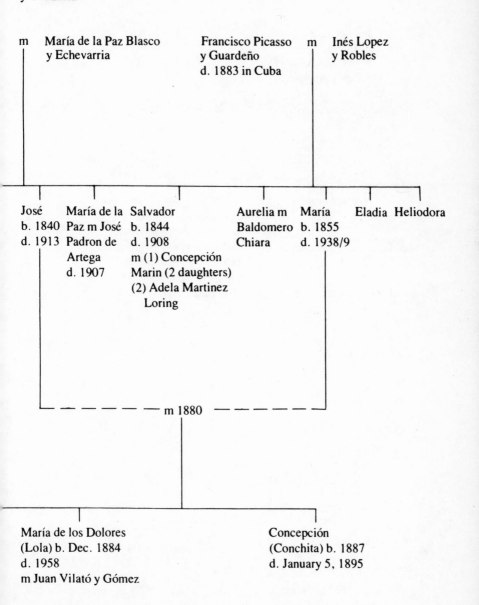

María Josefa de Almoguera
y González

m   María de la Paz Blasco   Francisco Picasso m Inés Lopez
     y Echevarria   y Guardeño   y Robles
                           d. 1883 in Cuba

José	María de la	Salvador		Aurelia m	María	Eladia	Heliodora
b. 1840	Paz m José	b. 1844		Baldomero	b. 1855		
d. 1913	Padron de	d. 1908		Chiara	d. 1938/9		
	Artega	m (1) Concepción					
	d. 1907	Marin (2 daughters)					
		(2) Adela Martinez					
		Loring					

— — — — — m 1880 — — — — —

María de los Dolores   Concepción
(Lola) b. Dec. 1884   (Conchita) b. 1887
d. 1958   d. January 5, 1895
m Juan Vilató y Gómez

2
PICASSO'S RELATIONSHIP TO
TIO PERICO THE HERMIT
(based on Sabartés)

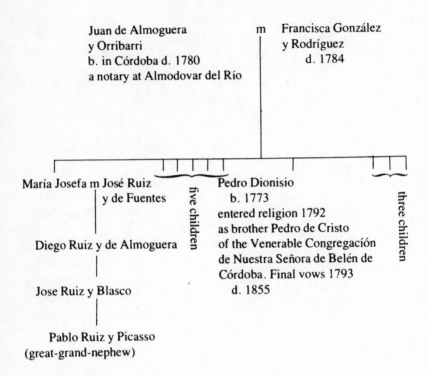

Juan de Almoguera
y Orribarri
b. in Córdoba d. 1780
a notary at Almodovar del Río

m   Francisca González
y Rodríguez
d. 1784

María Josefa m José Ruiz
y de Fuentes

five children

Pedro Dionisio
b. 1773
entered religion 1792
as brother Pedro de Cristo
of the Venerable Congregación
de Nuestra Señora de Belén de
Córdoba. Final vows 1793
d. 1855

three children

Diego Ruiz y de Almoguera

Jose Ruiz y Blasco

Pablo Ruiz y Picasso
(great-grand-nephew)

3

Picasso's Stars

MANY people have cast Picasso's horoscope, but perhaps not all of them knew that in the nineteenth century Spanish time was twenty-six minutes behind that of Greenwich: and if this difference is not taken into account the predictions cannot be quite so accurate as one might wish. Bearing this in mind, therefore, I applied to an eminent astrologer, Mr. G. C. Nixon of London, and concealing the name of my subject, desired him to tell me all he could.

He replied: "At the time [Picasso] was born the sign Cancer was rising and the Moon was in Scorpio in the 5th house conjunct the important star Antares. Saturn and Neptune were also elevated in the 10th house in Aries in opposition to the Sun in the sidereal sign Libra. Mercury was in Scorpio in opposition to Jupiter in Taurus and Venus was in Virgo in the 3rd house receiving the aspect of Mars in Gemini in the 12th house.

"The positions suggest a sensitive and artistic temperament, music, literary or painting, a stormy life and much hardship and with risk of much humiliation and downfall in the end."

4

Picasso's Palm

M<small>AX</small> Jacob's reading of Picasso's hand is not dated, but it was probably made before 1909. The ink has faded in some places and in others the writing can hardly be made out, but I think I have deciphered it correctly. Apart from its scientific value, the document gives a picture of the Picasso Max Jacob knew when they were both so young: Picasso treasured it all his life, and it formed part of his donation to the Barcelona museum.

The reading consists of two sheets, each with an elegant drawing of a hand; on one Jacob shows the geography of hands in general, with observations about their shape and the nature of their skin; on the other he turns to Picasso's hand in particular, his left hand, and after the remark *ardent tempérament* he begins:

1 line of life—weakness and illness up to the age of 68, serious at the end of his days.

2 line of luck: brilliant beginning in life—from the practical point of view cruel disappointments and a change of fortune before the age of 30 or 35, but success in the arts—brilliant (square in the line of life). Life will grow more peaceful towards the end. Wealth can be hoped for (bracelet 3). 4 - 4, the hepatic line is weak and divided, sign of indifferent health.

5 the mount of Mercury is prominent—intelligence—but the first joint of the little finger is short—näveté.

Particular observations. All the lines seem to arise at the base of this hand's line of fortune—it is like the first spark of a firework. This kind of living star is seldom seen, and then only in predestined individuals. A flight of lines stretching out towards the mount of inspiration would show us a poetic temperament even if the elongation of the hand had not already led us to form this opinion. The base of the hand is broad and square, the mark of sensuality but also of candour and integrity. A pennant-shaped hand shows a charming, sociable character.

The thumb is short, no strength of will. The line of the head forks and vanishes; perhaps the judgment is not protected from the sudden whims of the imagination nor from set, preconceived ideas.

The line of the heart is magnificent; attachments will be many and warm; on this side too the disappointments will be cruel—they frighten me.

The distance between the line of the heart and that of the head reveals a soul both broad and deep.

The line of the head bending towards the mount of the moon states that the heart will be capable of tact.

It is unfortunate that this hand should be invaded by threadlike lines which come from the mount of Venus and lead one to suppose that love will play too great a part in its possessor's life.

Notes:Aptitude for all the arts.

> Greediness—activity and indolence both at the same time. Religious spirit without austerity. Cultured mind. Sarcastic wit without malignance. Independence.

5

Jung on Picasso

HAVING seen the retrospective exhibition of his works at the Zurich Kunsthaus in 1932, Jung wrote an article on Picasso for the *Neue Zürcher Zeitung*. Almost at once Zervos' *Cahiers d'Art* translated it and printed the greater part in very, very small letters, preceded by two pages of indignant refutation in much larger type. What I offer here is a translation of this translation, but I do so with all the reservations due to a double handling of the original high-flying metaphysical German, particularly as the French text is somewhat corrupt.

An art which does not represent objects draws its subjects chiefly from the "within." This "within" cannot correspond to the conscious mind, since the conscious mind contains reproductions of seen objects in general which must necessarily have the same appearance as that which most people expect. Now Picasso's object is quite unlike the general expectation; indeed it is so unlike that we no longer seem to be concerned with objects perceived by our senses. The chronological sequence displays an increasing movement away from the empirical object and a growth of those elements which no longer correspond to outward experience but derive from an inner world lying behind the consciousness, which is as it were an organ of general perception superimposed upon the five senses and turned towards the outer world. Behind the consciousness lies not a total void but the unconscious psyche, which affects the consciousness from within and behind just as the exterior world affects it from without and before. Consequently those images that do not correspond to any exterior object must come from the "within." Since this "within," although it can have a most lasting effect upon the consciousness, can neither be seen nor represented, I ask those patients who suffer primarily from these influences to give them form as well as they can by means of drawing. The aim of this "method of expression" is to bring the unconscious elements into view so that they may be accessible to the intelligence. From the therapeutic standpoint this allows one to prevent the fatal dissociation of conscious mind and unconscious phenomena. Unlike drawings of consciously-perceived objects, these concretely-represented phenomena and influences are all *symbolic*, that is to say they possess in some degree a meaning that is in the first place unknown. This being so, it is equally impossible to make any certain statement whatsoever about an isolated case. All one has is the feeling of being confronted with a quantity of strange, varied, disparate, disturbing elements that cannot be exactly placed. One does not know the nature of the ostensible object nor what it symbolizes. The only way of understanding is to compare many series of pictures. Generally speaking, since they lack artistic imagination the patients' pictures are simpler, clearer, and therefore more intelligible than those of modern painters. Among the patients we may distinguish two groups, the neurotics and the schizophrenes. The first produce pictures of a synthetic character which display one single, uniform feeling throughout. Even when they are completely abstract and devoid of the emotional factor they are at least either clearly symmetrical or they possess an unmistakable direction. The second, on the other hand, make pictures that instantly reveal the strangeness of their emotion. In any event, they do not display any single, harmonious feeling but rather contradictory emotions or even a complete absence of sensibility. From a strictly formal point of view, their predominant characteristic is that of an intellectual laceration, rendered by what are termed broken lines, that is to say, psychic clefts or rents that traverse the image. The picture leaves one either unmoved or astonished at its paradoxical, disturbing, frightening, or grotesque flights of audacity. Picasso belongs to this second group.

In spite of the sharp distinction between the two classes, they do have one thing in common—*their symbolic content*. Both represent the outline of a meaning, but whereas the neurotic seeks out the meaning and tries to communicate both it and his emotion to the observer, the schizophrene shows scarcely anything of this tendency: on the contrary, he appears to be the victim of the signification. He seems to be overwhelmed and swallowed up by it, and one has the impression that he is being disintegrated by all these elements that the neurotic does at least endeavor to control. The schizophrene's form of expression calls for the same remark that I made with regard to Joyce—nothing comes towards the observer; everything turns away from him: even an incidental beauty seems no more than an unforgivable delay in the withdrawal. The seeking-out of the ugly, the morbid, the grotesque, the incomprehensible, the commonplace is not intended to express but to conceal; and this concealment is not directed against an investigator but is rather a pointless veil, a cold mist that stretches over an uninhabited bog: a play as it were that has no need of any audience.

In the one case it is possible to make out what he would like to express: in the other, what he is incapable of expressing. The mysterious content is to be seen in both. A series of images of this kind, whether made up of drawings or of written words, usually begins with the symbol of the Nekya, of the descent into Hades, into the unconscious, and of a farewell to the upper world. The later images still make use of the forms and shapes of the world of light, but they show a hidden meaning and they therefore possess a symbolic character. Thus Picasso too begins with paintings of objects and the paintings are blue, the blue of night, of water or of moonlight, the Touat-blue of the Egyptian underworld. He dies and his soul flies away to the beyond on a horse. Sunlit life clings to him and a woman with a child advances to exhort him. Just as day is a woman for him so too is night, and psychologically this is the same as the light and the dark aspects of the soul *(anima)*. The dark soul sits waiting, and it waits in the twilit blue, arousing pathological forebodings. As the colors change, we enter Hades. The concrete forms, expressed as they are in the dismal masterpiece of the prostituted, tubercular, syphlitic adolescent girl, are given over to death. The theme of the prostitute begins with the entry into the other world, where "he" in the form of a dead soul meets several other people who have died. I say "he" because in relation to Picasso I think of that character who undergoes the doom of the lower world, of the man who by reason of that doom turns not towards the world of light but towards the darkness, the man who follows not the acknowledged ideal of the good and the beautiful but rather the demoniac pull of the ugly and the evil, which in modern man resists and counteracts Christianity, and by veiling the sunlit world with these same mists of Hades brings into being a pessimistic, end-of-the-world atmosphere; and which in doing so begets a deadly spiritual sickness of disintegration, to end, like a country shattered by an earthquake, by falling apart in fragments—broken lines, rags, faint remnants, debris, and lifeless entities. Picasso and the exhibition of Picasso's works are, like the twenty-eight thousand people who have seen them, transitory phenomena.

Broadly speaking, when a man subjected to such a fate belongs to the neurotic group, the unconscious reveals itself to him in the form of the "darkness" of a frighteningly, grotesquely hideous Kundry or in that of a diabolic beauty. In Faust's transformation we find Margaret, Helena, Maria, and the formal idea of the "eternal feminine" answering to the four female figures of the Gnostic underworld, Eve, Helena, Mary, and Sophia. Nevertheless Picasso transforms himself and appears in the underworld shape of the tragic Harlequin, a theme that is to be seen in many later pictures: Harlequin who like Faust is implicated in a murder and who reappears in the second part in another form.

Ever since Homer the going down or back to primitive ages has been part of the Nekya. Faust looks back to the imaginary primitive world of the Blocksberg and to the fanciful illusion of ancient times. Picasso conjures up the heavy terrestrial shapes of the grotesque primitive epoch; and, endowing them with a cold, radiant light, brings back to life the soulless forms of Pompeian antiquity—a Giulio Romano could not have done worse. Rarely or never have I seen a patient who has not turned to forms of neolithic art or who has not indulged in the evocation of classical Dionysism. Harlequin, like Faust, passes through all these aspects, although at times nothing betrays his presence except his wine, his lute, or at least the lozenges of his jester's coat. And what does he learn in the course of his wild pilgrimage through mankind's long centuries? What quintessence will he distill from this accumulation of debris and wreckage, of merely potential shapes and of half-born, soon-dead colors? What symbol will be the ultimate cause and the meaning of all disintegration?

Confronted with the chaotic diversity of Picasso, one hardly dares point it out. That is why I preferred in the first place to speak of what I found in my records. The Nekya is not a titanic, pointless, purely destructive plunge but a *katabasis eis antron* with a meaning and an end; it is a going down into the cave of initiation and secret knowledge. The aim of the pilgrimage through the intellectual history of mankind is to re-establish man in his integrity by revealing the memory of his blood. Faust's descent to the Abode of the Mothers allowed him to bring back the complete man in the state of sin . . . that man who was quite forgotten because he lost himself in the maze of things of the present. It is he who caused the earthquakes in the upper world during all the periods of great upheaval and it is he who will always cause them. This man is at the antipodes of the man of the present day because he is that which was always thus, whereas the other is so only for the moment. From this it follows that my patients' stage of "katabasis and katalysis" is succeeded by an acknowledgment of the contradictions in human nature and of the necessity for the state of conflict between the opposing elements. That is why the symbols belonging to the insane visions in the period of disintegration are followed by images that show the reunion of the opposing pairs—light and dark, top and bottom, black and white, male and female, etc. In Picasso's latest pictures the union of contraries is very clearly to be seen in their immediate juxtaposition. Although admittedly it is broken by some discontinuous lines, one picture even shows the junction of the light *anima* and the dark *anima*. The brilliant, clear-cut, and even violent colors of the most recent period correspond to the unconscious mind's tendency to overcome the conflict of the emotions by force (color = emotion).

Index

Pavillon de Marsan, P's retrospective exhibition at (1955), 429
"Paysage de Gósol," 476
Peau de l'Ours, La (collector's club), 206
"Pêche de nuit à Antibes," 385
"Peintre et son modèle, 458–60, 461
Peintres cubistes, méditations esthétiques, Les, (Apollinaire), 201
Péladan, Joseph, 85
Pèl i Ploma, 67, 73, 74, 92, 96, 111, 118, 119
Penrose, Lady, 476
Penrose, Sir Roland, 100, 255, 286, 311, 332, 344, 370, 402, 476
Pepe Illo. *See* Delgado, José
Pergolesi, Giovanni, 242
Perpignan, 413–14, 420, 422 *ff.*, 429
Pershing, General John, 233
"Personnage rembranesque," 470
Peruggia, 206
Pétain, Henri, 348, 350
Peter the Catholic, 423
Petit Palais, P's retrospective exhibition at (1967), 468–69
Phanérogame, Le (Jacob), P's illustrations for, 240
Philadelphia Museum of Art, 200
Philip IV, King of Spain, 55
Picabia, Francis, 165, 183, 186, 201, 209, 293
Picaço (Moorish prince), 16
Picasso, Claude. *See* Ruiz-Picasso, Claude
Picasso, Emilienne (Paulo's wife), 464, 465
Picasso, Jacqueline Hutin, (P's second wife), 411–12, 417, 420, 423–25, 428, 435, 436, 439, 470; P's portraits of, 419, 425, 427, 428, 432, 443, 444, 445, 450, 456–57, 461, 467, 471, 479; her dislike of Vauvenargues, 443, 451, 454; marriage to P, 456; her influence, 464, 476–77
Picasso, María Concepción (later Widmayer) (P's daughter) (Maya), 300, 317, 338, 353, 398, 413, 420, 423, 428, 464; P's portraits of, 331–32, 369; P provides for during WW II, 347
Picasso, Marina (P's granddaughter), 460, 464; Jacqueline's influence on P, 464; P's suit for guardianship, 465
Picasso, Mateo, 16
Picasso, Olga Koklova (P's first wife), 226, 228, 230–33, 234, 236, 237,
239, 242, 244, 250, 254, 268, 270, 286, 292, 295, 306, 311, 314, 316, 336, 338, 387, 389, 398, 404, 465, 467; meets P, 222–23; P's portraits of, 226–27, 237, 261; marriage to P, 231–33; pregnancy, 245; birth of Paulo, 246; illness, 255; marital discord, 274, 275–76; her jealousy of Fernande Olivier, 295–96; legal separation, 298–300, 391; P provides for during WW II, 347; and Françoise Gilot, 392; her death, 427; burial at Cannes, 456 n.
Picasso, Pablito (P's grandson), 460, 464; P's suit for guardianship, 465; refused admittance to P's home, 476
Picasso, Pablo. *Under separate headings see* Collages; Cubism; Drawings; Etchings and engravings; Illustrations; Landscapes; Papier-collés; Pastels; Portraits; Sculpture; Still-lives. Birth, 11, 12, 13, 14, 17; christening, 14; ancestors, 14–17, 483–84; relationship with father, 19–20, 21, 25–26, 35–36, 38–39, 40, 49, 51, 54–55, 56; relationship with mother, 20, 39; childhood and early drawing, 20–27; education, 25; influence of Catholicism, 27–30; fear of illness and death, 28–29, 148, 234, 356; his sense of sacred, 29; move to La Coruña, 30, 31–40; art schools and artistic education, 34–36; early oil paintings, 36–38, 40; his relationship with animals, 37, 133–34, 330, 435; abbreviates name to Picasso, 39; first Prado visit, 40; move to Barcelona, 40–42, 45, 65; Málaga holidays, 40–41, 50–51, 52–53; sketchbooks, 49, 55; friendship with Pallarès, 48, 57–63, 450–51; first studio, 51; break from academic tradition, 52; his signature, 52, 53, 55, 63, 90; enters Royal Academy in Madrid, 53–55; Goya's influence on, 54, 55; his Prado copies, 54–55; early fascination with bulls, 55; first steps toward Modernismo, 55; scarlet fever and convalescence at Horta, 57–63; his difficulty with languages, 64–65; and Els Quatro Gats, 65–82, 118; El Greco's influence on, 67; estrangement from his family, 68; development of aesthetic, 69, 80,